SEVENTH EDITION

Fundamentals of Music

Rudiments, Musicianship, and Composition

Earl Henry

Jennifer Snodgrass
Appalachian State University

Susan Piagentini
Northwestern University

330 Hudson Street, NY NY 10013

To our students and mentors, who inspire us each day.
Jenny and Sue

Portfolio Manager: *Bimbabati Sen*
Content Producer: *Kani Kapoor*
Portfolio Manager Assistant: *Anna Austin*
Product Marketer: *Jessica Quazza*
Art/Designer: *Integra Software Services Pvt. Ltd.*
Full-Service Project Manager: *Integra Software Services Pvt. Ltd.*
Compositor: *Integra Software Services Pvt. Ltd.*
Printer/Binder: *LSC Communications, Inc.*
Cover Printer: *LSC Communications*
Cover Design: *Integra Software Services Pvt. Ltd.*
Cover Image: *John Dakapu/Shutterstock*

Acknowledgments of third party content appear on pages within the text.

Copyright © 2019, 2013, 2009 by Pearson Education, Inc. or its affiliates. All Rights Reserved. Printed in the United States of America. This publication is protected by copyright, and permission should be obtained from the publisher prior to any prohibited reproduction, storage in a retrieval system, or transmission in any form or by any means, electronic, mechanical, photocopying, recording, or otherwise. For information regarding permissions, request forms and the appropriate contacts within the Pearson Education Global Rights & Permissions department, please visit www.pearsoned.com/permissions/.

PEARSON and ALWAYS LEARNING are exclusive trademarks owned by Pearson Education, Inc. or its affiliates, in the U.S., and/or other countries.

Unless otherwise indicated herein, any third-party trademarks that may appear in this work are the property of their respective owners and any references to third-party trademarks, logos or other trade dress are for demonstrative or descriptive purposes only. Such references are not intended to imply any sponsorship, endorsement, authorization, or promotion of Pearson's products by the owners of such marks, or any relationship between the owner and Pearson Education, Inc. or its affiliates, authors, licensees or distributors.

Library of Congress Cataloging-in-Publication Data

Names: Henry, Earl, author. | Snodgrass, Jennifer, author. | Piagentini, Susan, author.
Title: Fundamentals of music: rudiments, musicianship, and composition / Earl Henry, Jennifer Snodgrass, Susan Piagentini.
Description: Seventh edition. | Boston: Pearson, 2019. | Includes index.
Identifiers: LCCN 2017040169 | ISBN 9780134491387 | ISBN 0134491386
Subjects: LCSH: Music theory–Elementary works. | Musical notation.
Classification: LCC MT7 .H49 2019 | DDC 781—dc23
LC record available at https://lccn.loc.gov/2017040169

7 2022

Books a la Carte
ISBN-10: 0-13-449138-6
ISBN-13: 978-0-13-449138-7

Instructor's Review Copy
ISBN-10: 0-13-449137-8
ISBN-13: 978-0-13-449137-0

Contents

KD 09.16.2022 1107

Preface

How does one begin to talk about printed music on the page? It is imperative that students, teachers, and performers understand a common language in order to convey our experiences with sound and print.

This language of music—the fundamentals—allows you to move from intuitions gained through your prior listening experiences to an informed comprehension about how music works. This enables you to communicate in terms that other musicians understand.

Today, many of us can sing, whistle, hum, or pick out a tune on the piano or guitar, but only those who read and write using the language of Western music are able to communicate in this written form. In each musical era, musical styles and vocabularies have continued to evolve. Along with each stylistic change, the language of music notation has developed, and innovative sounds have required new symbols to represent them.

Fundamentals of Music is intended to familiarize you with the notation and performance of Western music through creative composition projects, listening exercises to develop your aural skills, and the analysis of musical examples from a broad range of styles and genres. You will have the opportunity to practice your new vocabulary and performance and analytic skills in the context of complete compositions. Whether you are preparing for a career in music, or simply want to develop an appreciation for this musical language, you will learn terms, symbols, practices, and conventions that make Western music sound the way it does.

New to this Edition

The seventh edition of *Fundamentals of Music* has been thoroughly revised and expanded, yet maintains the intent of its original author Earl Henry. Virtually all topics from the sixth edition were retained, with slight reorganization of the overall format of the text. This edition includes a broader range of musical examples and styles, and revised and expanded aural skills methods and exercises. Some highlights of what you can expect of this edition are as follows:

- Select chapters conclude with two contrasting *Analysis in Context* examples. The scores are carefully paired, with one example representing the classical canon, and another from a more contemporary genre. These scores encourage students to put the skills of the current chapter in the context of complete pieces.
- The accompanying sound files for *Fundamentals of Music*, seventh edition are either available as downloadable resources on the dedicated textbook website or included in a Spotify playlist created specifically for this title.
- Significant updates in musical examples throughout the text include the addition of popular music and works for large ensemble.
- Extensive editing of lead sheet notation symbols to better represent the language of today's studio musicians.

Using the Text

Each of the 13 chapters is divided into five main areas:

Essential Terms and Symbols: An alphabetical list of key terms that appears at the beginning of each chapter. As you work through the chapter, make sure you understand the definitions of these important terms and symbols.

Review Sets: These are short drills intended for class discussion. Instructors often pause to complete the review sets as they present chapter materials in class.

Musicianship Studies: These include sight singing, ear training, and keyboard skill development activities. We have expanded these areas with more examples and guided practice examples.

Building Skills and Creative Projects: Each chapter concludes with a number of exercises and projects. The creative projects center on an aspect of analysis or composing and arranging music. Your instructors may ask you to tear out these exercises and submit them for correction. The text layout allows for this without the loss of the main content of the book.

Analysis in Context: A main focus of this edition is the inclusion of two complete scores at the end of each chapter that represent a variety of styles of music. The accompanying study questions encourage you to apply the concepts from each chapter in the context of a piece of music.

Listening To The Musical Examples

We have revised the recordings for the seventh edition to be easily accessible via streaming audio and downloadable resources on the dedicated textbook site through Pearson. A combination of original recordings from the sixth edition and new recordings created specifically for this edition are now available.

Because the best approach to understanding music notation is to correlate the sounds and the symbols, we recommend that you use these recordings while you study. We also recommend class performances of student compositions where possible.

Aural Skills Assessment

The ear training components of the text include opportunities for student practice and review. The answers for these examples are found in the Appendix D: *Answers to Ear Training Exercises*.

Acknowledgments

We are indebted to colleagues and students—both at Northwestern University and Appalachian State University—for their suggestions in the preparation of this edition and their excitement in the classroom, which inspires us as teachers every day. In particular, we would like to thank the following reviewers of the seventh edition: Berkeley Price, Barbara Murphy, Andrew Book, Steven M. Bresnen, Beverly Howard and Mariah Boucher.

New audio examples for the 7th edition were recorded at the Robert F. Gilley Recording Studio in the Hayes School of Music at Appalachian State University. We are indebted to recording engineers Cory Halterman and Michael Leckrone, as well as student performers Rebecca Willcox, Casey Wells, Caison Rogers, Suzanne Brown, Jake Urquhart, and Alexandria (Alex) Smith. Many audio files were retained from the 6th edition and were recorded at The Chill Lodge Studio, Miami, FL www.chilllodge.com, produced by Dr. Devin Marsh. Vocals were provided by Dr. Tim Brent, Andrew Dahan, Katie Kupchick, Alex Alberti, and Sierra Karr. The instrumentalists were Dr. Tim Brent, piano; Sam Hyken, trumpet; Gerardo Aguillon, violin; and Lisa Espinosa, cello. Programming was provided by Belinda Ho.

We would like to acknowledge the help of Zach Lloyd, graduate of Appalachian State University and current graduate student at Michigan State who worked tirelessly on graphics and revisions of musical examples. We want to acknowledge the Editorial and Production staff at Pearson – Bimbabati Sen (Portfolio Manager), Kani Kapoor (Content Producer), Allison Campbell (Monitor), Marla Sussman (Editorial Project Manager), and Gowthaman Sadhanandham (Production Project Manager).

We would like to thank the many mentors and teachers along the way who have instilled in us a passion for lifelong learning. These include the late Robert Turner, Meg Dornbrock, Dr. Sally Thomas, Dr. Anthony Vaglio, Dr. Thomas Delio, Laszlo Payerle, Dr. John Buccheri, Dr. Peter Webster, and many others.

Finally, we would like to thank our families, Greg and Katherine Snodgrass; Richard and Linda Sterling; Rich, Nick, and Megan Piagentini; Donald LaRue; Lois LaRue-White; and Carl White. With their support, we are both able to have careers that we love.

Jennifer Snodgrass
Susan Piagentini

Chapter 1

Notating Rhythm

Essential Terms and Symbols

|
||
·
‿ ⁀
barline (|)
beam
beat
dot (·)
dotted note
double barline (||)
flag
hook
line
measure
meter signature
music
notation
note
notehead
phrase
rest
rhythm
stem
tempo
tie (‿ ⁀)
time signature
traditional Western music

Music is sound and silence in time. If we impose further limits on what is and is not "music," some eras, cultures, or movements would inevitably be excluded. The clear, undulating tone of a Navajo flute, the tinkling of a wind chime, the massed force of a symphony orchestra, the pulse of a rock combo—all of these are pathways to musical expression.

Traditional Western Music

This text is about traditional Western music. In most cultures, music can be classified as "art" in which intellectual engagement is the aim; "folk," the documentation of life at a certain time and geographic area; or "popular," meaning music for entertainment.

These include such genres as gospel, musical theater, and top 40. When we use the term **traditional Western music** in this text, we mean both "classical" music from about 1675 to 1875 (including many great composers of the past like Bach, Mozart, and Beethoven) and *also* any music that continued those same principles in later eras—regardless of style. "Traditional composer" then includes not only European masters Joseph Haydn (1732–1809) and Johannes Brahms (1833–1897), but also ragtime composer Scott Joplin (1868–1917), Mississippi blues artist Pinetop Perkins (1913–2011), *Phantom of the Opera* composer Andrew Lloyd Webber (b. 1948), Ed Sheeran (b. 1991), and pop musician Michael Jackson (1958–2009).

Notation

Throughout the history of Western music, composers have represented sounds with symbols—a process we call **notation**. Western musical notation, in fact, is a written language. In most other cultures, memorization and improvisation are central tools of the musician, but in the West, formal musical training begins with a flexible but rather complex system of relatively precise notation. Our insistence on exact notation explains, at least in part, why Western music sounds the way it does.

The Notation of Rhythm

Rhythm is the element of time in music and is measured in *beats* or their fractional parts. A **beat** is a regular pulse like the heartbeat or the ticking of a clock. One of the duties of a modern conductor is to outline those beats so that group members can perform their parts at exactly the right time. The rhythm section of a contemporary jazz or pop group performs the same function.

Note Values

A **note** is the basic symbol for sound and can be altered in a variety of ways to indicate length (or duration). The largest single value in common use today is the **whole note** (𝅝); other notes have fractional relationships to the whole note and receive one-half its value, one-quarter its value, and so on.

The **half note** (𝅗𝅥) includes a vertical mark called a **stem** and an open notehead. It receives one-half the value of a whole note. The **quarter note** (♩), with both a stem and a solid notehead, occupies one-quarter the time of a whole note.

Examine the names, relative values, and shapes of the whole, half, and quarter notes.

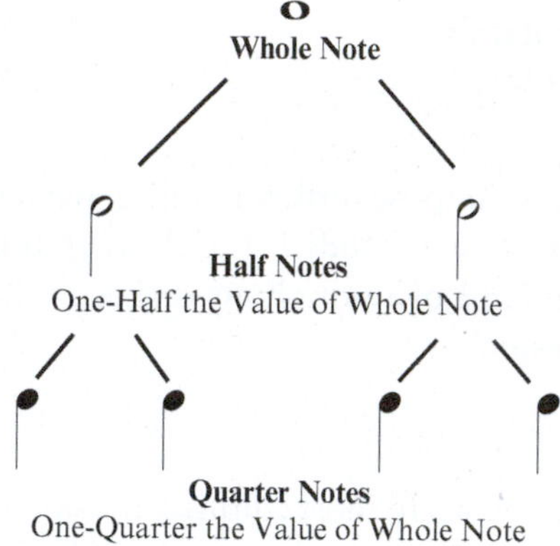

SETTING THE BEAT. We can use any rhythmic symbol to represent one beat, but once that decision is made, other symbols relate as multiples or fractions. Listen to your heart beat or a clock ticking and think of this pulse as a series of quarter or half notes. If the quarter note is the beat, for example, the pulse can be represented by a series of quarter notes.

- Practice tapping the following example while keeping a steady beat.

♩ = 1 beat

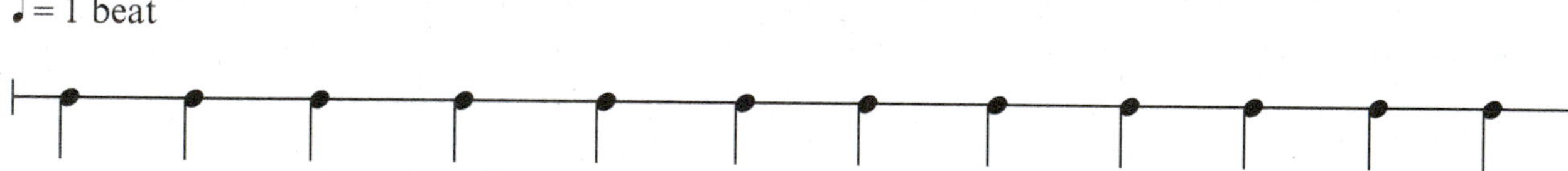

Now practice tapping a steady beat while listening to songs and compositions from various genres and performing artists.

Just as easily, we could represent our ticking clock with a half note. The music sounds the same (because each half-note symbol represents one beat), yet the notation is different.

𝅗𝅥 = 1 beat

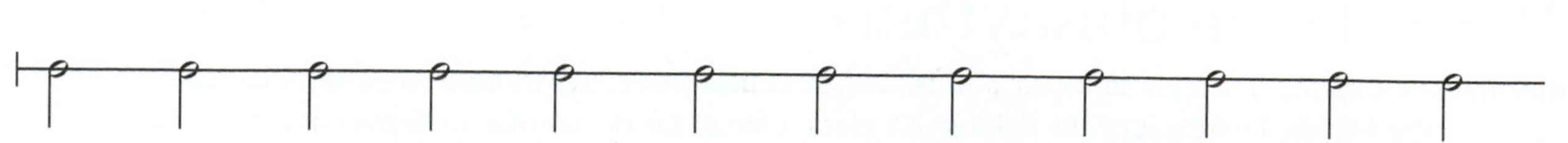

TEMPO. The speed of the beat is known as the **tempo**. In Western music, the tempo usually remains constant for a given passage, although it may change from one section to the next.[1] On the other hand, we might dramatize the ending of a section by gradually slowing down (**ritardando**). If we set a tempo, then gradually increase it, the effect is an acceleration (**accelerando**).

THE METRONOME. Since the early nineteenth century, the **metronome**, a device for measuring a certain number of beats per minute, has given performers a more exact guide to the speed of the beat. Rather than relying on the performer's interpretation of general tempo indications, composers simply write the letters *M.M.* (for Maelzel metronome) followed by a note value and the number of those notes to be played in one minute. The letters *M.M.* are often omitted.

M.M. ♩ = 132 M.M. 𝅗𝅥 = 72 ♪ = 100 ♩. = 60

Terms indicating tempi and their associated metronome markings

Italian Term	Translation	M.M.
Grave	Very slow	40 or slower
Largo	Very slow	40–60
Larghetto	A little bit slowly	60–66
Adagio	Slowly	66–76
Lento	Slow	60–80
Andante	A slightly slow walking speed	76–108
Moderato	Moderate walking speed	108–120
Allegretto	A little bit slower than *allegro*	120–126
Allegro	Pretty fast	120–168
Vivace	Lively and fast	120–140
Presto	Very fast	168–200
Prestissimo	Faster than *presto*	200–208

COMBINED NOTE VALUES. Musical phrases are constructed of longer and shorter note values. The relationships among those values never change. If the quarter note is the beat, a half note receives two beats.

- Practice tapping the quarter note beat as you listen.
- Practice tapping the rhythm of the musical line as you listen.

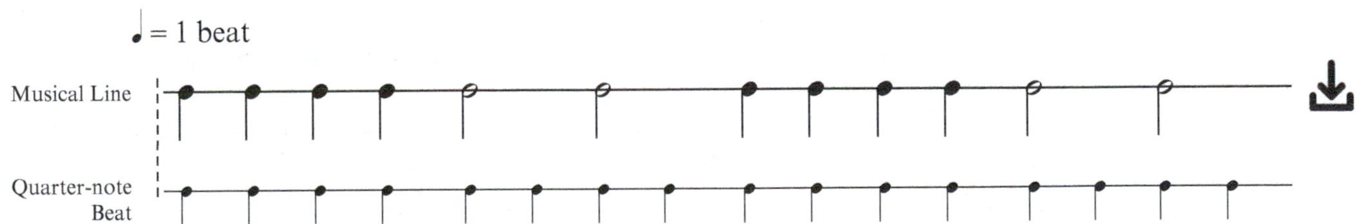

The whole note adds a value of four beats to the musical mix.

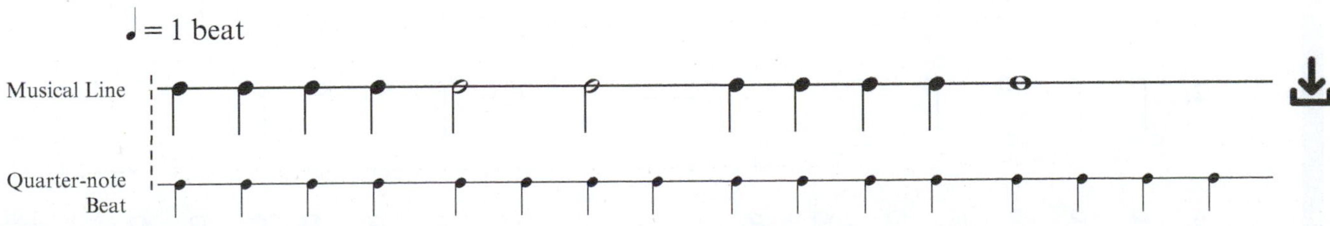

[1] See Appendix B, *Terms and Symbols of Tempo and Expression*, on pages 413–414, for more information.

Remember that we can choose any note value to represent one beat. Tap the excerpt again as you follow this notation with a half-note beat. Here, the whole note receives two beats.

𝅗𝅥 = 1 beat

Musical Line

Half-note Beat

For class discussion or assignment: please do not remove these pages

REVIEW SET

Note Values

A. Given the quarter note as the beat, provide the total value in beats for each line (2, 4, 9, and so on).

♩ = 1 beat

Sample 8

1.

2.

3.

4.

5.

6.

7.

B. The half note is the beat in these lines. As before, compute the cumulative value in beats.

𝅗𝅥 = 1 beat

1.

2.

3.

4.

5.

6.

Rest Values

Silence in music can be as important as sound. The symbols for silence are called **rests** and correspond to the values of note symbols.

- The **whole rest** hangs below a line (▬).
- The **half rest** sits on top of the line (▬).
- The **quarter rest** (𝄽) is a combination of angles and curves.

Study the relationships among whole, half, and quarter rests shown in the next example.

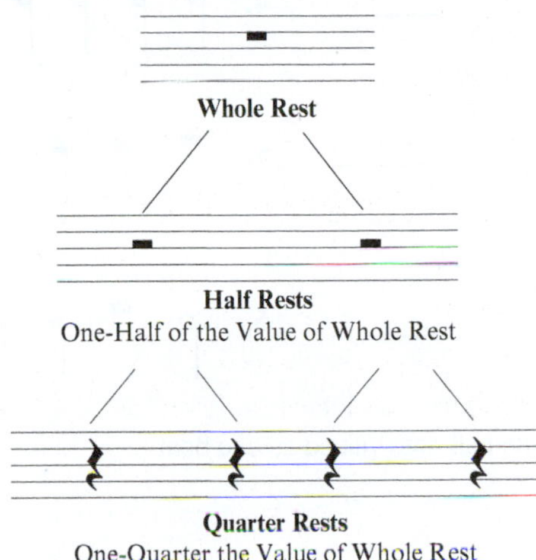

The two phrases below include whole, half, and quarter notes as well as the corresponding rests.

- Practice tapping the quarter-note beat or the rhythm of the musical line with a partner.

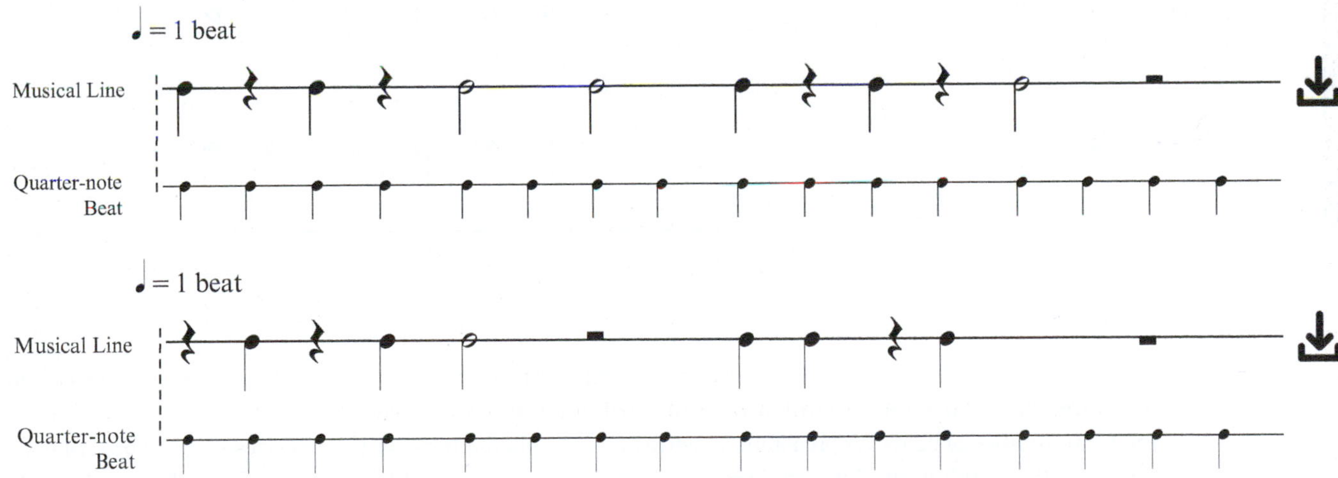

This passage has a half-note beat with the whole note and rest valued at two beats.

𝅗𝅥 = 1 beat

Musical Line

Half-note Beat

Notice that as we read music from left to right, keeping our place in a complicated line can be difficult. A division called the *barline*, discussed in the next section, helps solve this problem.

For class discussion or assignment: please do not remove these pages

REVIEW SET
Rest Values

A. Compute the total of note and rest values in each line.

♩ = 1 beat

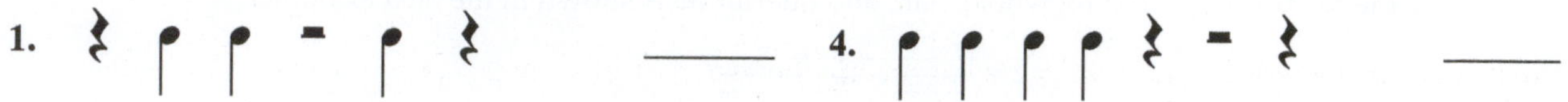

1. ______ 4. ______

2. ______ 5. ______

3. ______ 6. ______

B. Compute the total beats in these lines with the half note valued as one beat.

𝅗𝅥 = 1 beat

1. ______ 4. ______

2. ______ 5. ______

3. ______ 6. ______

Measures

Groups of notes that consist of a uniform number of beats (three beats, for example) are called **measures**. Measures may contain any number of notes and any variety of rhythmic values as long as the total number of beats is consistent. A vertical mark called a **barline (|)** precedes the first beat of each measure; this symbol divides a musical line into segments that facilitate reading. With the quarter note valued at one beat, for example, each measure in the next passage has three beats.

♩ = 1 beat

Three beats per measure

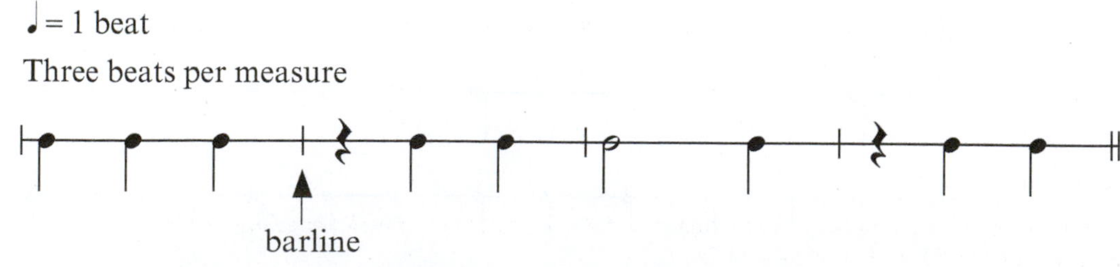

In comparison, the half note could receive the beat with two beats in each measure.

𝅗𝅥 = 1 beat Two beats per measure

DOUBLE BARLINE. A **double barline (||)** indicates the end of a passage.

Time Signatures

Instead of using words and note values to specify the beat and the number of beats in each measure (as in the previous examples), composers use a *time signature.* A **time** or **meter signature** is a pair of numbers that identifies the value set as one beat and the number of those beats in a measure.[2] The top number indicates the number of beats (in our studies, this will be 2, 3, or 4). The bottom number stands for a note value representing one beat (♩ = 4; 𝅗𝅥 = 2).

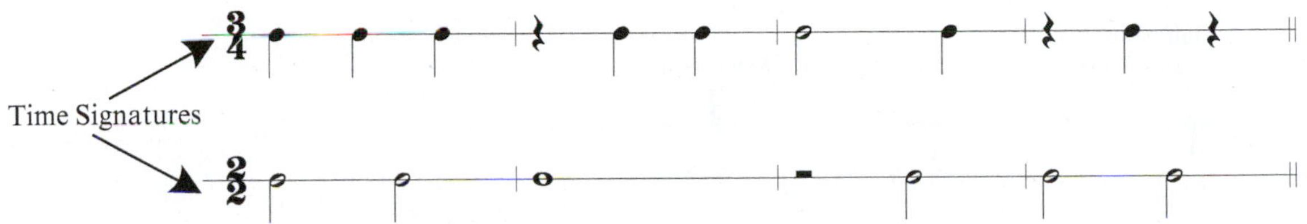

In later exercises, we will build an understanding of time signatures and measures in several different ways. For now, the next example shows complete measures in the three time signatures. The beat is a quarter note in each case.

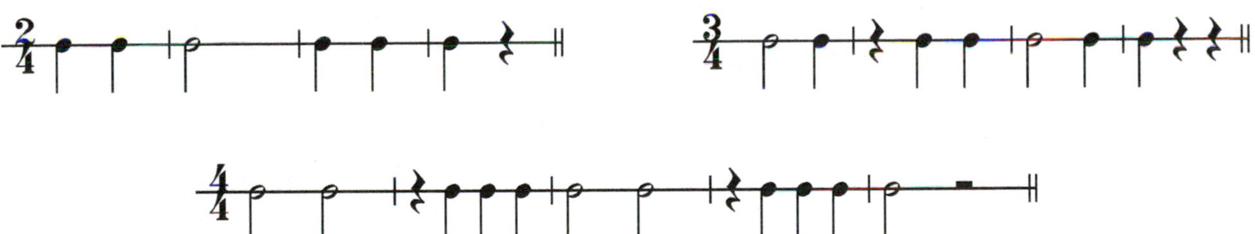

If we use a half-note beat, the principle is the same; there are two, three, and four half notes per measure in the examples that follow. These lines would sound exactly like those in the previous example.

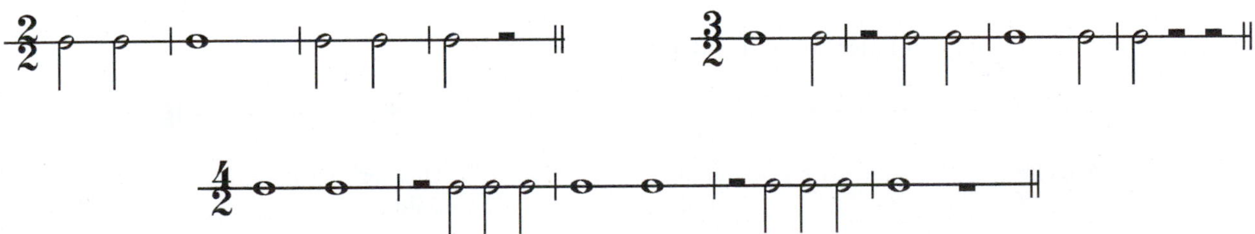

[2] Time signatures also convey crucial information about an intricate aspect of rhythmic performance called *meter*. We will cover this topic in Chapters 4 and 7.

Calligraphy

Note and Rest Values

Since the early 1990s, there has been a steady increase in the use of music notation software. Although computer notation systems are readily available, composers, performers, and arrangers must still occasionally write music by hand. We have included several sections on calligraphy in response to this need.

Note Values.

Noteheads are oval—not round. Stems extend down from the left or up from the right of the notehead. Try your hand at calligraphy in the blank spaces next to the note examples.

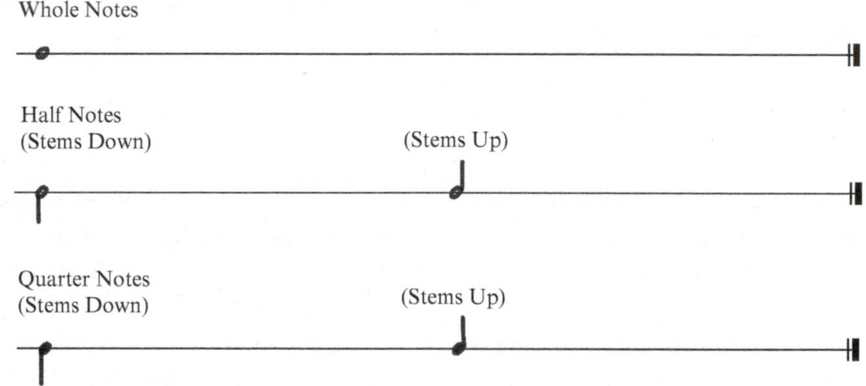

Errors in calligraphy can result in unnecessary costs for studio time and wages. Avoid the following pitfalls, for example, in notating whole, half, and quarter notes.

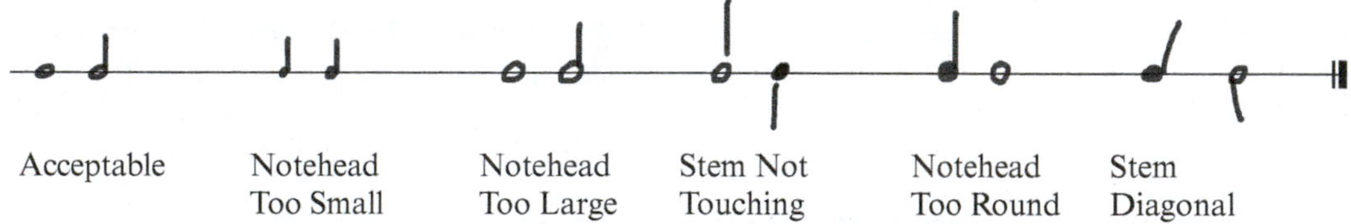

Whole rests and half rests are simply blackened rectangles—about the same width as a notehead, but only half the height. The whole rest hangs below the line; the half rest sits on top of the line.

Make a quarter rest as an angular letter "Z" and add a curved tail.

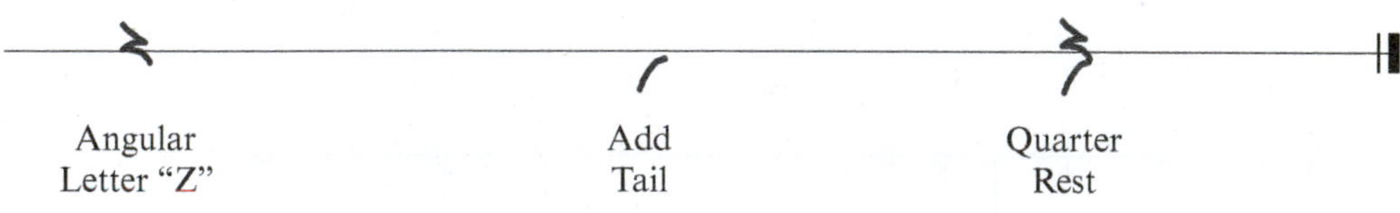

For class discussion or assignment: please do not remove these pages

REVIEW SET

Measures

Some of the measures in the following lines are complete; others are missing one or more beats. Study the time signature to determine the number of beats in each measure and the type of note receiving one beat. Next, count the beats in each measure. *If necessary*, add *one note* (whole, half, or quarter) in the blank space at the end of the measure. Each measure has space for adding a note whether it is complete or incomplete (see the sample exercise).

Sample Exercise

Smaller Rhythmic Values

In addition to quarter, half, and whole notes, composers also use notes with smaller values. A **flag** (𝅮) is a curved line added to a note stem that indicates a smaller value. An **eighth note** (♪), for example, with one-eighth the value of the whole note, has one flag; the **sixteenth note** (𝅘𝅥𝅯) has one-sixteenth the value of the whole note and includes two flags. Whether the stem direction is up or down, flags are always affixed to the right side.

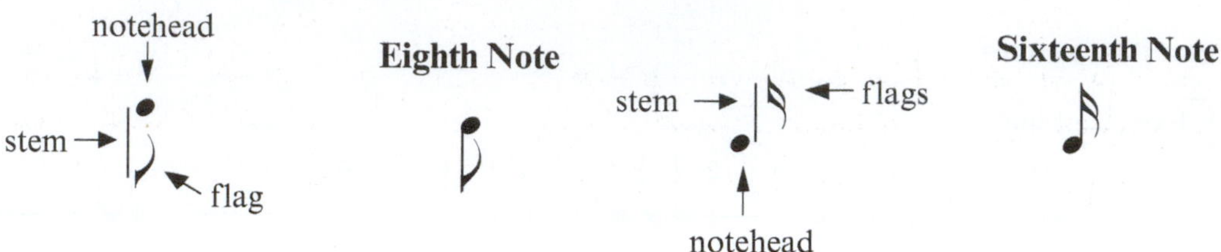

In the next example, notice the number of half, quarter, eighth, and sixteenth notes needed to equal the value of one whole note.

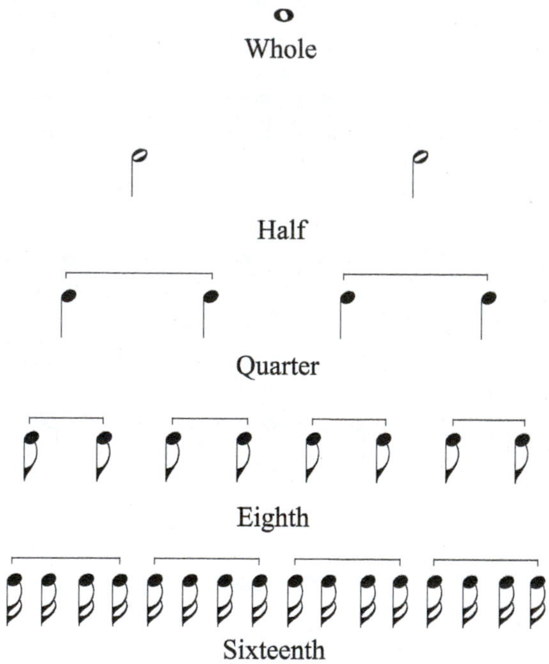

SMALLER REST VALUES. Rests with values smaller than quarter rests have **hooks** (•) that are attached to the left side of a slanted line. The **eighth rest** has one hook; the **sixteenth rest** has two.

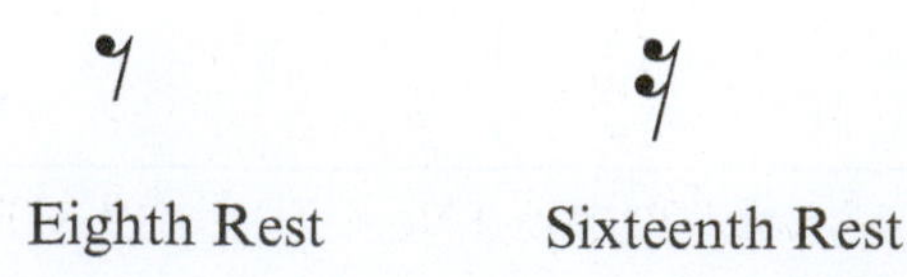

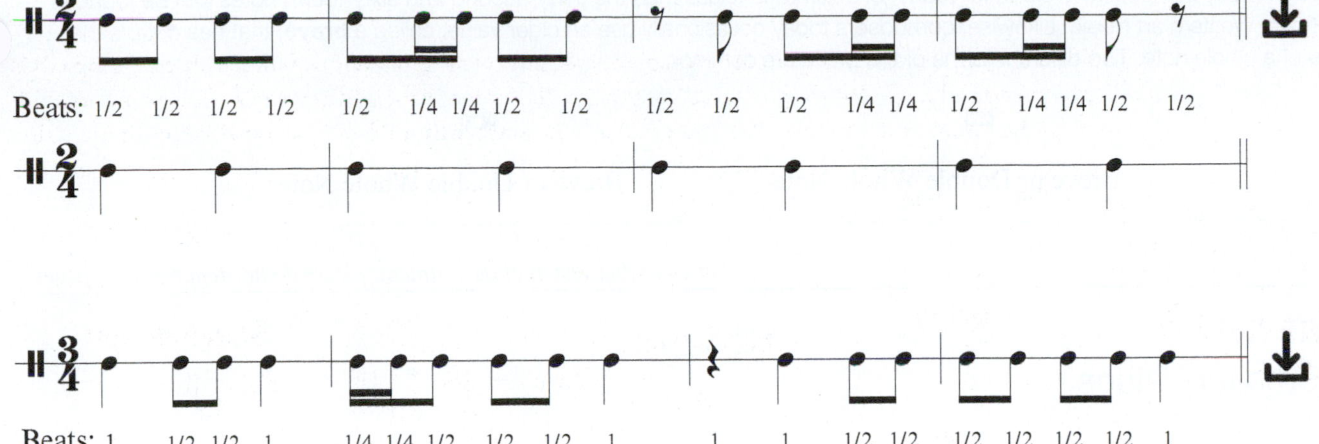

When the half note is the beat, the quarter note itself is a "smaller value" since it receives one-half beat.

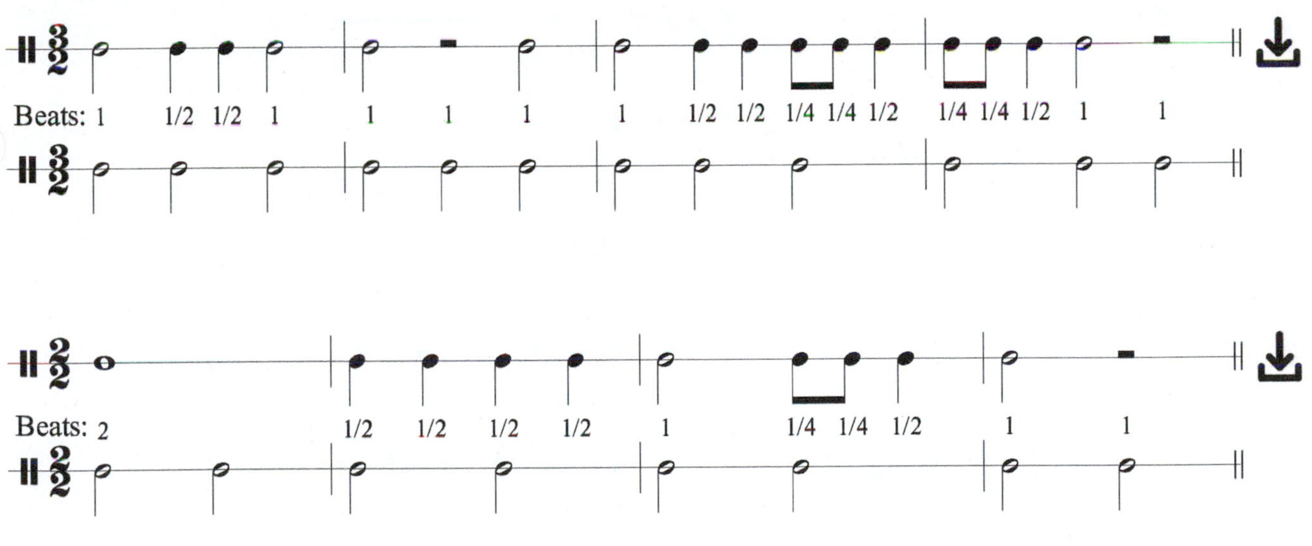

A Step Further

Larger and Smaller Note Values

While the note values we have discussed are sufficient for notating most music today, those who study more complicated music will find considerable variety. The principle of adding flags or hooks to diminish a value, for example, has few limits. If we add a third flag or hook, we have a thirty-second note or rest; a fourth flag or hook is a sixty-fourth.

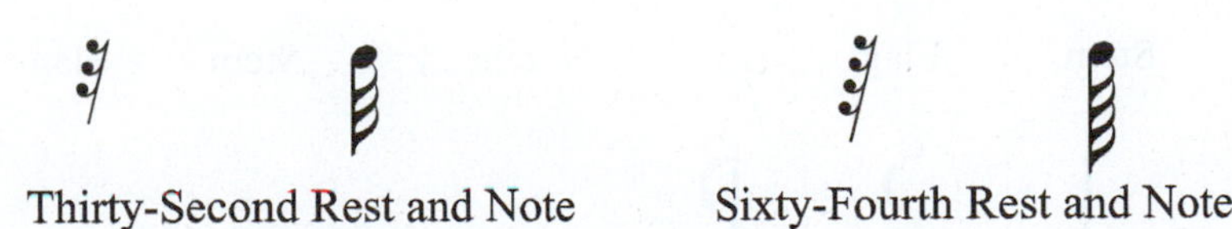

Although many composers avoid them today, *even smaller* values than the thirty-second and sixty-fourth notes can be found in traditional Western art music. Likewise, composers today occasionally use an older value, called a **breve**, that has *double* the value of a whole note. Two different forms of the breve are common.

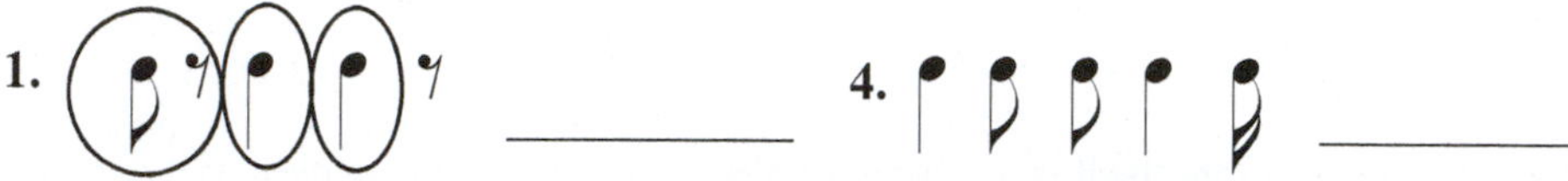

Breve or Double Whole Note | Breve or Double Whole Note

For class discussion or assignment: please do not remove these pages

REVIEW SET

Smaller Values

A. Compute the value of the notes and rests. The quarter note is the beat. Circle each complete beat unit. The first one is done for you.

1. ________
2. ________
3. ________
4. ________
5. ________
6. ________

B. In these lines, the half note is the beat. The quarter note now receives half of a beat.

𝅗𝅥 = 1 beat

1. ______
2. ______
3. ______
4. ______
5. ______
6. ______

Calligraphy

Eighths and Sixteenths

In notating flags, composers and arrangers usually use a curved stroke of uniform thickness. We suggest that you begin with the notehead, add the stem, then provide one or more flags.

Notehead Stem Flag Notehead Stem Flag

The hooks for eighth and sixteenth rests are easier. Begin with the slanted line, then add the hook.

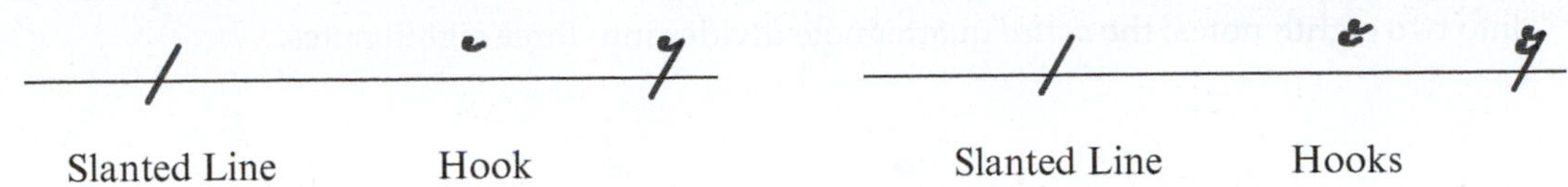

Use the space that follows to practice making eighth and sixteenth notes and rests.

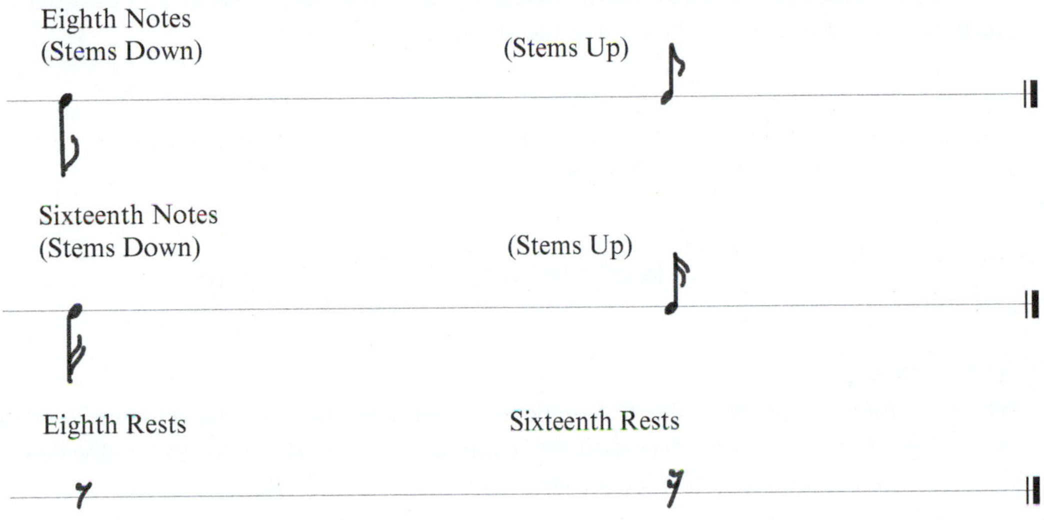

Complete Building Skills 1-1 on page 19

The Dot

The **dot** (·) is employed to extend the value of a note or rest by one-half of its original value. If the half note, for example, receives two beats, the *dotted half note* has the value of three beats.

♩ = 1 beat

2 beats + 1 beat 3 beats

When the half note is the beat, the *dotted half note* receives one and a half beats—an increase in its original value by half.

𝅗𝅥 = 1 beat

1 beat + $\frac{1}{2}$ beat $1\frac{1}{2}$ beats

A **dotted note** is one that includes a dot. As we will discuss more fully in a later chapter, dotted notes permit the composer to divide the beat into three, rather than two parts. The quarter note divides into two eighth notes; the *dotted* quarter note divides into three eighth notes.

The dot principle applies to rests as well as to notes. If the quarter note and the quarter rest receive one beat, the *dotted quarter rest* has the value of one and a half beats.

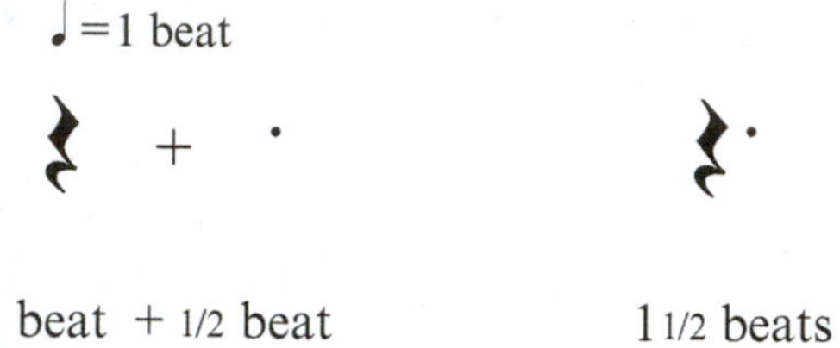

The Tie

While the dot increases the value of a single note or rest, the **tie** (⌣ or ⌢) combines the values of two or more notes of the same *pitch* (discussed in Chapter 2). If the quarter note receives the beat, for example, a half note tied to a quarter note has a combined value of three beats.

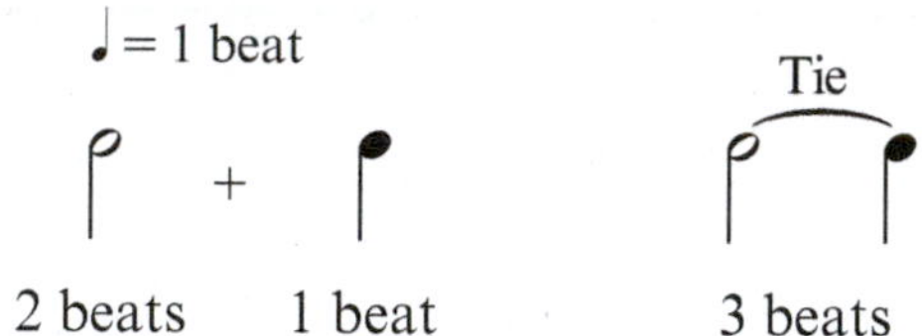

When the quarter note receives one beat, an eighth note tied to a quarter note receives one and a half beats.

Ties and dots are similar in some respects but different in others. While both symbols may extend duration, ties allow us to combine note values or continue a single note across a barline. The dotted half note in the first two examples is the same as a tie if there are three beats in a measure. With two beats in a measure, however, the dotted half is a notational error. The last example shows the correct form with a tie extending the value across the barline.

REVIEW SET

Dots and Ties

Compute the value of the notes and rests in the next lines. The quarter note is the beat.

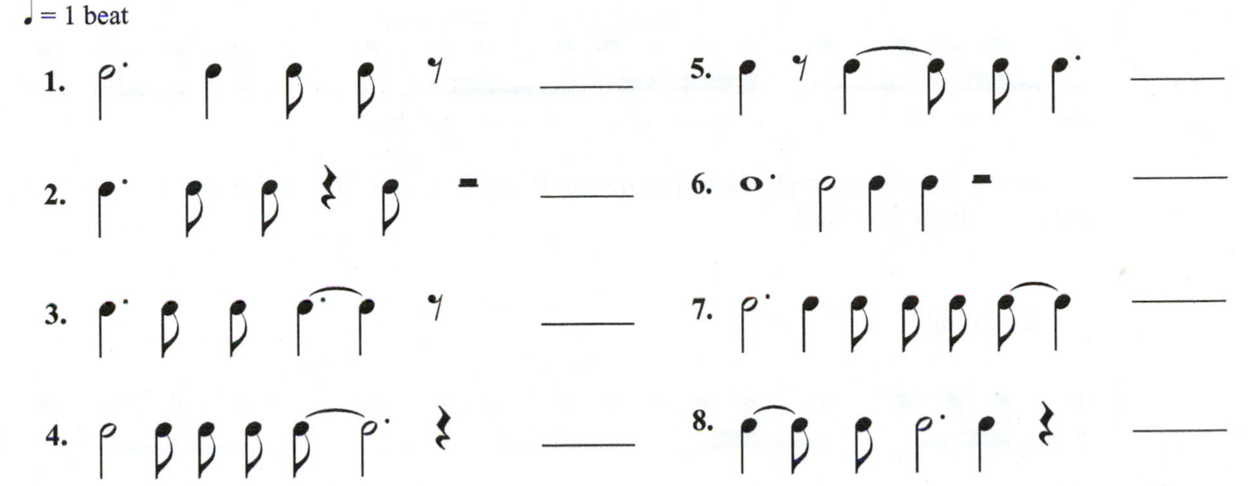

Flags and Beams

In addition to flags, composers also group shorter values into beat units with *beams*. A **beam** is a thick, horizontal or slanted bar that connects two or more note stems. Flags and beams are equivalent in value. Eighth notes, for example, have one flag or one beam; sixteenth notes have two flags or two beams.

The advantage of beaming is evident from the next example. While flags convey individual values, beams identify beat groups. Notice how the four beats in each measure are easier to identify in the beamed passage than in the flagged one.

Flags

Finally, the next example shows incorrect beaming. It is difficult to perform because the beat groups are not properly identified.

Incorrect Beaming

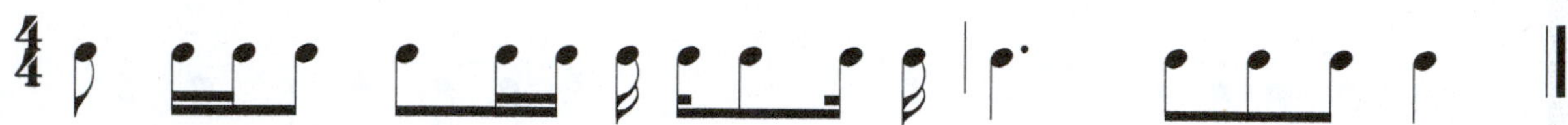

In the second measure of the previous beamed example, notice that one flagged note is retained. A beam is not correct here since it would connect notes on different beats.

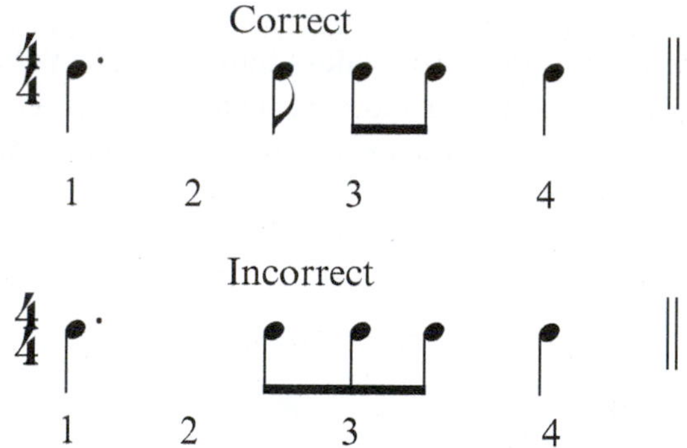

Beaming in Vocal Music

In vocal music, it is customary to use an individual flagged note for a single syllable of text. When a single syllable is sung over many notes, the notes are beamed together (or to the beat).

For class discussion or assignment: please do not remove these pages

REVIEW SET

Beams and Flags

On the lower line, rewrite the flag notation using beams to identify beat groups. Be aware that not every flagged note in the upper line should be converted to a beamed note.

Complete Building Skills 1-2 on page 21

Name ________________

Page may be removed

Building Skills 1-1

Note Values

A. **For the given unit of beat, write one note that has the specified value.**

𝅗𝅥 = 1 beat

2 ________ $\frac{1}{2}$ ________ 1 ________ $\frac{1}{4}$ ________

♩ = 1 beat

$\frac{1}{2}$ ________ 2 ________ $\frac{1}{4}$ ________ 1 ________

B. **For each time signature shown, indicate the number of beats in the measure and the note that receives one beat.**

1. $\frac{4}{4}$ Beats in measure ________ Note receiving one beat ________

2. $\frac{3}{4}$ Beats in measure ________ Note receiving one beat ________

3. $\frac{3}{2}$ Beats in measure ________ Note receiving one beat ________

4. $\frac{2}{2}$ Beats in measure ________ Note receiving one beat ________

5. $\frac{2}{4}$ Beats in measure ________ Note receiving one beat ________

6. $\frac{4}{2}$ Beats in measure ________ Note receiving one beat ________

C. **Use barlines to divide the following lines into measures.**

1. 

2. 

3. 

D. **For each rest given, provide one that has double the value and one that receives half the value.**

	Double Value	Half Value
1. 𝄽	________	________
2. 𝄼	________	________
3. 𝄾	________	________

E. **One or more measures in each of the following lines are incomplete as notated. In the blank space within the incomplete measures, add one note that provides the missing value. Practice clapping and counting the examples when you are finished.**

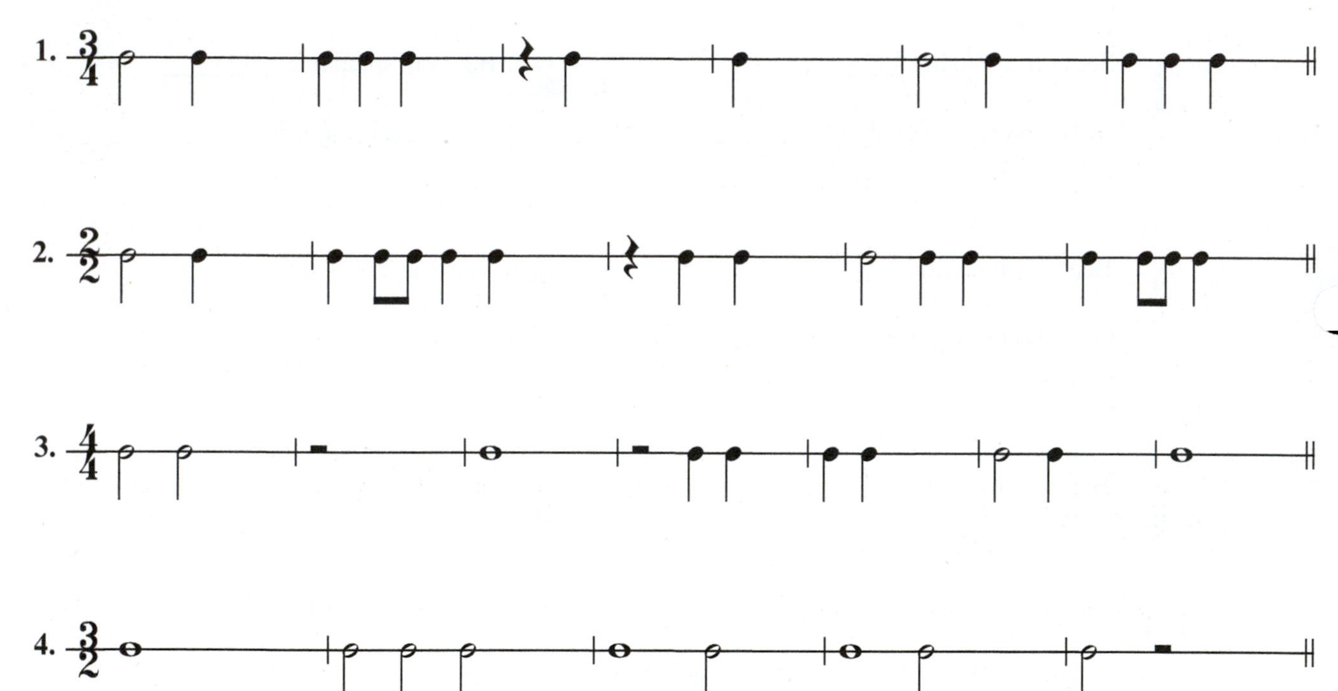

Name ______________________

Page may be removed

Building Skills 1-2

Rhythmic Notation

A. **Total the number of beats in each line of notes and rests.**

♩ = 1 beat

1.  ________

𝅗𝅥 = 1 beat

2. ________

♩ = 1 beat

3. ________

𝅗𝅥 = 1 beat

4.  ________

B. **Where appropriate, change the flagged notes to beams. Use beams for beat groups only; otherwise, leave the flagged notation.**

1\. 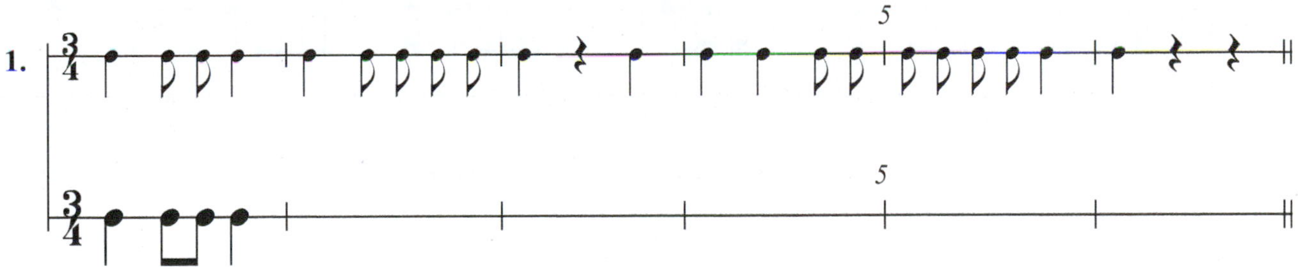

2\. 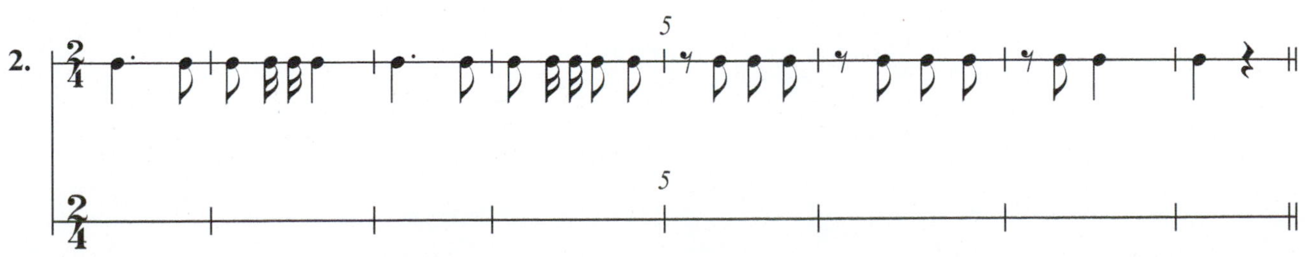

3.

4.

C. **Complete any measures that do not contain the number of beats specified by the time signature by adding one *rest*.**

1.

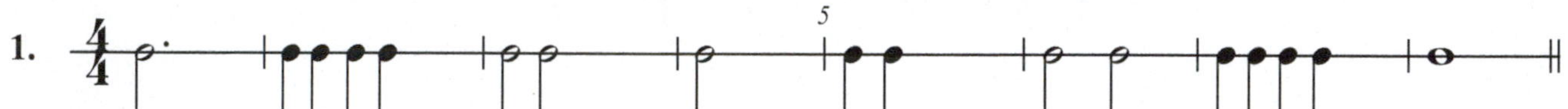

2.

3.

4.

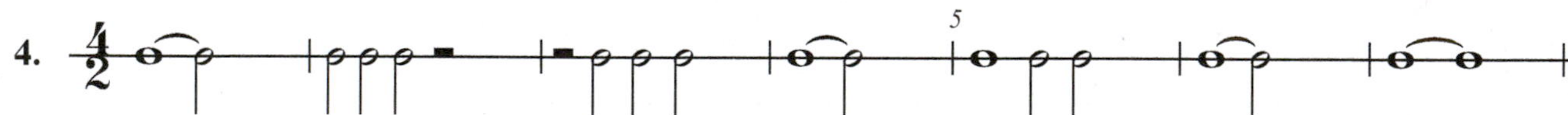

Name ____________

Page may be removed

Creative Projects • Chapter 1

A. **Complete these two clapping duets for class performance. The lower line should be only the beat (quarter or half note as appropriate). The upper line can include a mixture of beats, multiple beats, and rests. Make sure, however, that your measures contain the correct total number of beats. *Do not* use values smaller than one beat in this exercise and be sure to align beats between the two parts.**

1.

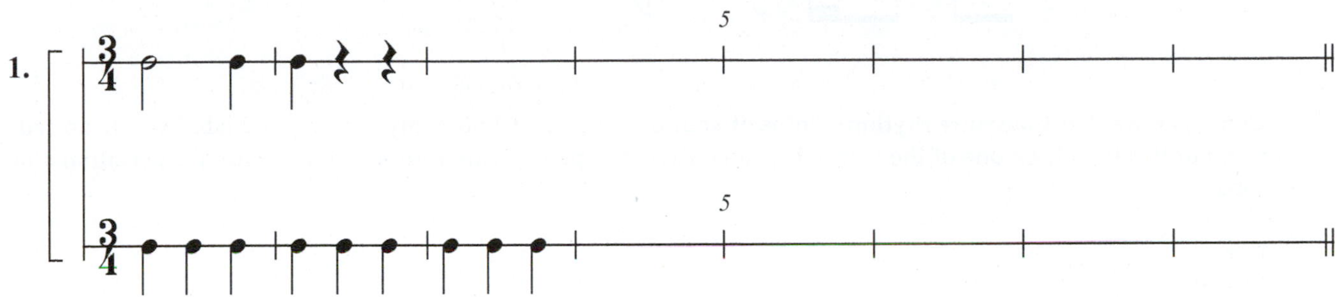

2.

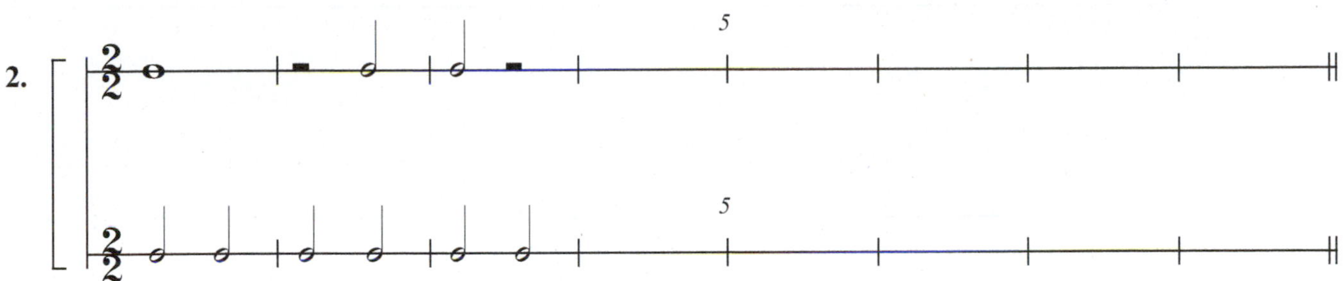

B. **Two rhythmic solos are given here as exercises in calligraphy. Several measures are provided, but others are blank. Complete all blank measures with patterns that are similar to those given. Make sure that your measures contain the correct number of beats.**

1.

2.

C. **Compose two eight-measure rhythmic solos of your own design. Choose any meter you wish. Include dotted notes or ties in at least one of the solos. Repeated rhythmic patterns are important in creating expectation and consistency.**

Time
Signature

1. ______

5

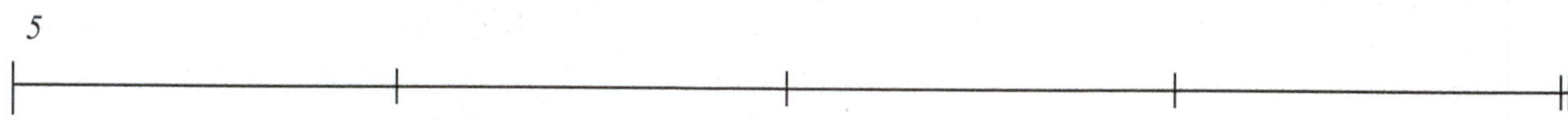

Time
Signature

2. ______

5

Name ______________________

Page may be removed

Analysis in Context 1 • Chapter 1

Rewrite the following song on the empty staves below using correct eighth-note beaming and inserting barlines at the end of each measure. Hint: The first barline is given since the song starts with a one-beat pickup. When you finish adding barlines, number the measures above the staff as shown in the first measure. Then answer the questions that follow as you study the score.

Amazing Grace

Composer, Unknown
Lyrics by John Newton

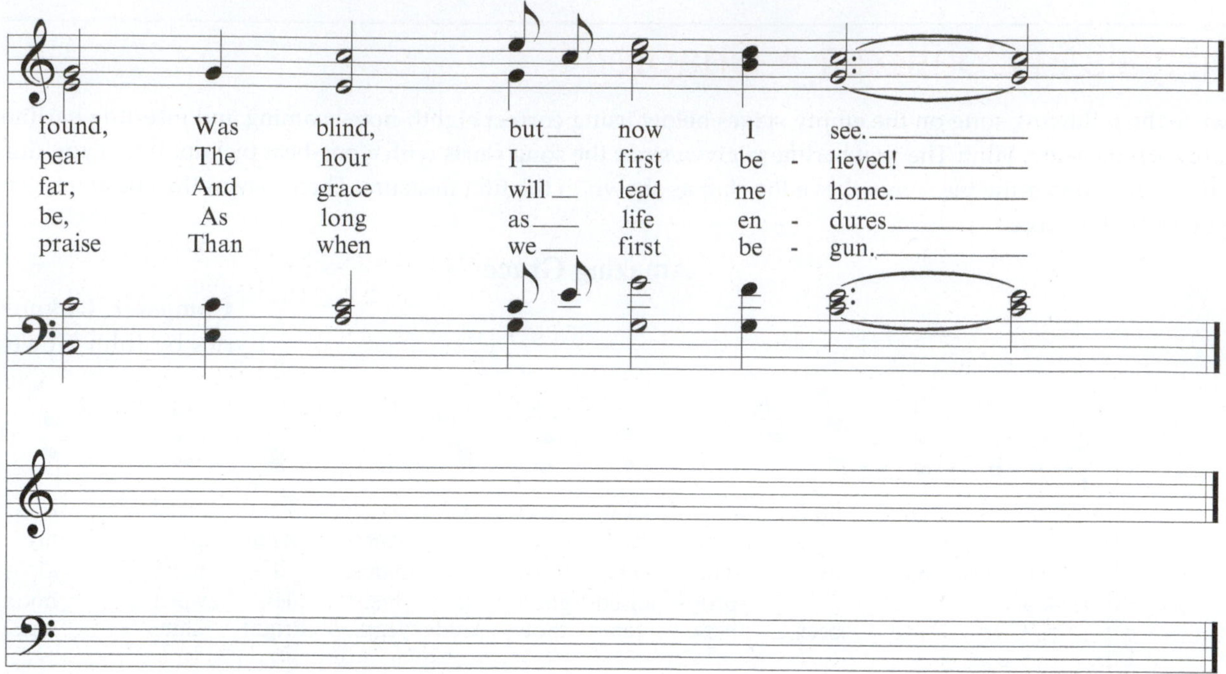

1. How many measures are in the song?
2. What is the time signature?
3. What does the 4 in the time signature indicate?
4. Circle all the half notes in the score. On which beat are most half notes placed?
5. Write check marks above all the quarter notes in the score. On which beat are most quarter notes placed?
6. In what measures do you find dotted quarter notes? Study the text in those measures. Why do you think the composer waited to use them until that point in the text?
7. Study how the composer uses eighth notes. Is the placement in the measure similar to another note value in the previous questions?
8. What rhythm patterns do you find that are repeated in the song?
9. How many times did you use eighth-note beaming to connect two eighth notes in the song?
10. What is the name of the marking that connects the final two notes of the song? What other measure includes the same marking?

Analysis in Context 2 • Chapter 1

Written and performed by members of the vocal group Pentatonix, the song "Run to You" contains a wide variety of rhythms. Answer the following questions after you listen to the performance and study the excerpt.

Run to You

Words and Music by MITCHELL GRASSI, SCOTT HOYING, AVI KAPLAN, KIRSTIE MALDONADO, KEVIN OLUSOLA and BENJAMIN BRAM.
Used courtesy of Ben Bram Music.

Run to You

13
sea.
I tried to go,
to fol - low,
to kneel down
at
your feet.
17
I'll
run,
I'll
run,
I'll
run,
run
to
you.
I'll
22
run,
I'll
run,
I'll
run,
run
to
you.

Name ______________________________

Page may be removed

1. What is the time signature of this song?

2. Based on the performance, how would you label the tempo of this song? Adagio, Andante, or Allegro?

3. The tie over the barline in measures 16 and 17 indicates that the pitch is held for ________ beats.

4. There is a time signature change in this song. Give the measure number where the time signature change occurs. How long does the time signature change last?

5. Using the vocal line only, how many ties are used in this song excerpt?

6. Would it be possible to beam all of the pitches together in measure 12? Rewrite the rhythms in measure 12 to show an alternate way of beaming.

7. Rewrite the rhythms of measures 1–4 using the half note as the main unit of beat.

8. How many beats does the dotted note receive in measure 13? In measure 14? In measure 16?

9. How many beats of rests are used in measure 4?

10. What kind of rest is used at the conclusion of this excerpt?

Chapter 2

Notating Pitch

Essential Terms and Symbols

8bassa	F clef (𝄢)	*ottava* (*8va*)
8va	G clef (𝄞)	pitch
8vb	grand staff	register
basic pitch	great staff	staff
bass clef	interval	staves
brace ({)	ledger lines	system
clef	octave	treble clef
ear training	octave sign	

For about a thousand years, traditional Western music has been based on the symbols we now call notes. In addition to duration, notes also represent **pitch**—the psychological perception that sounds are relatively high or low. Like the practices associated with rhythm, the notation of pitch in Western music evolved over many centuries. Although some early systems of pitch notation employed letters of the alphabet as note symbols, today we represent pitch simply by placing notes higher or lower on the printed page. The first three notes in the next example represent increasingly higher pitch; the last three, increasingly lower pitch.

The Staff

Although the notes in the previous example are obviously higher and lower in a relative sense, the performer needs to know *precisely* how they differ. Another part of the notational system, the *staff*, permits this exactness. The **staff** (plural **staves**) is a grid of five lines with four spaces between them. Notes can be positioned on lines, in spaces, and above or below the staff.

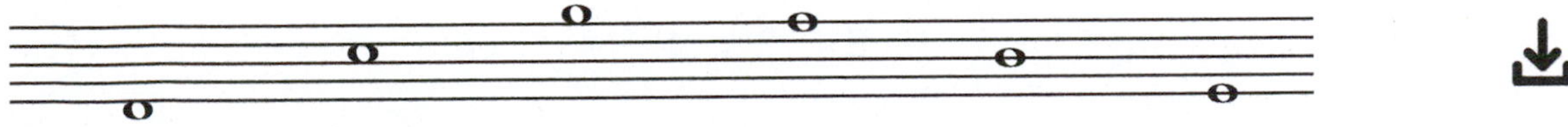

NOTE NAMES. There are seven generic notes, named according to the first seven letters of the alphabet: A B C D E F G. On the staff, these **basic pitches** always appear in order over consecutive lines and spaces. Once we identify the name of any one line or space, we know them all because the pattern is invariable.

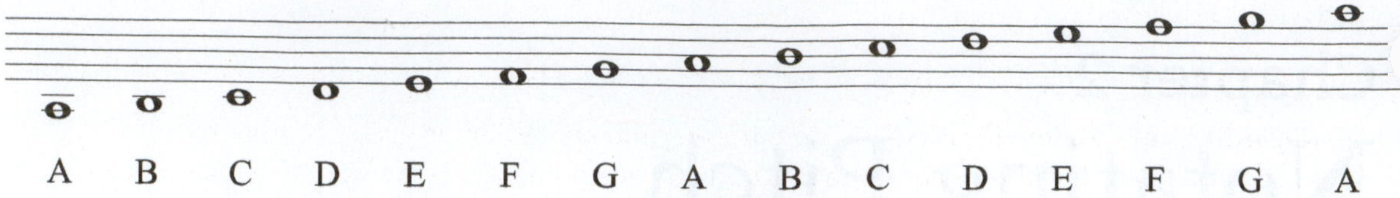

The Clef

A **clef** is a symbol that identifies the name of one line on the staff. Once we have identified the position of one pitch, of course, we know them all. Depending on the **register** (a higher or lower group of pitches) and the particular instrument, composers often use the *treble* or *bass clef*. (See Appendix C for other commonly used clefs.)

THE TREBLE CLEF. The **treble clef** (𝄞), once a florid letter "G," is used for relatively higher sounds and identifies the pitch G as being on the second line by encircling it. If G is on the second line, we know that the pitch A occupies the space above it; the pitch F, the space below. Because it identifies the pitch G, the treble clef is also known as the **G clef**.

The treble clef staff lines are E, G, B, D, and F; the spaces are F, A, C, and E.

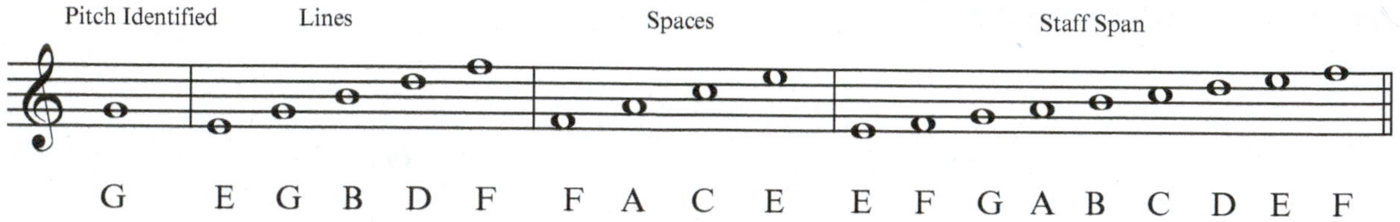

THE BASS CLEF. The **bass clef** (𝄢) is a stylized letter "F" (sometimes known as the **F clef**) and is employed for relatively lower pitches. When the bass clef is used, the fourth staff line (straddled by the two dots) represents the pitch F. If F is the fourth line, we know that the space below it is E; the space above it is G.

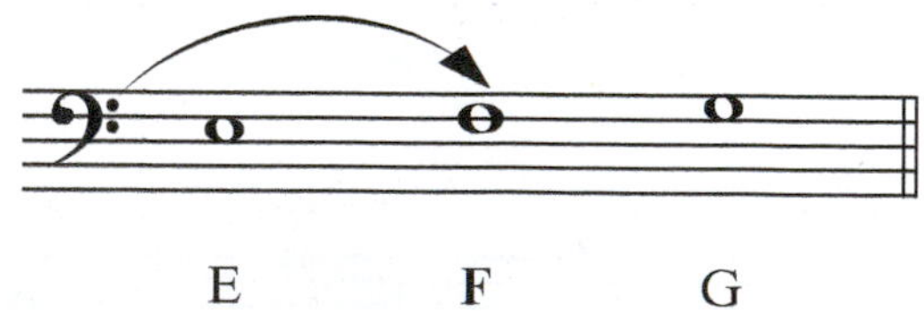

Bass clef lines are G, B, D, F, and A; the spaces are A, C, E, and G.

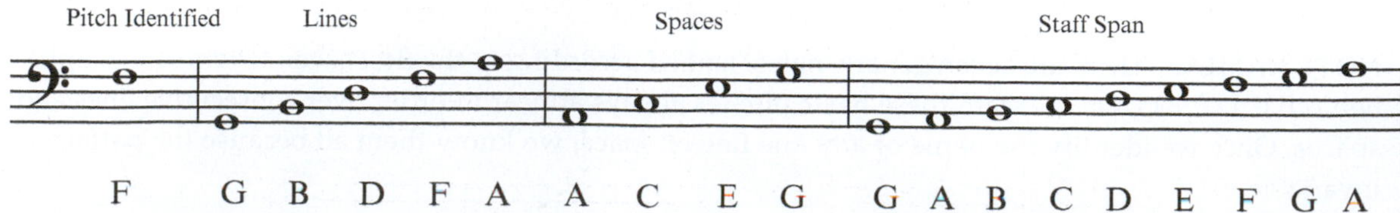

Stem Direction

When stemmed notes appear on the staff, stems are placed up or down according to the following rule:

> Regardless of duration, for notes on the third line and above, stems go down from the left side of the notehead; for notes below the third line, stems go up from the right side. Stem length should span just beyond three spaces.

Duration does not affect stem placement. Flags are always on the right side of the stem—never the left.

When several notes are beamed together, stems go up or down according to where *most* of the notes in the group lie on the staff. With the previous rule about stem placement in mind, study the next example and locate an instance where the direction of one stem in a beamed group is an exception.

Elder Joseph Brackett, "Simple Gifts"

LARGER REST VALUES ON THE STAFF. The whole and half rests are associated with a specific line on the staff. The half rest sits on the third line; the whole rest hangs from the fourth line.

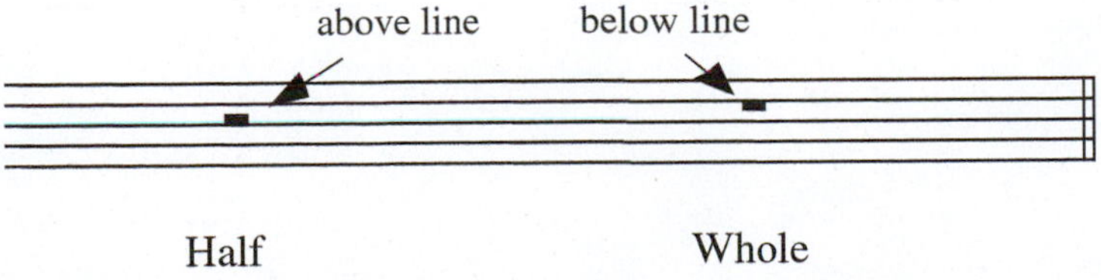

TRICKS OF THE TRADE

Learning the "ABCs"

Unless you have previous experience, your most important job at this point is learning the names of notes in both treble and bass clefs. At some time in the past, you learned the letters of the alphabet and have been using them ever since. You probably mastered the letters slowly, learning one or two at a time. Perhaps, most importantly, you received constant feedback along the way from parents and teachers.

Consider a similar process for learning the note names and their respective staff locations. A structured approach such as the one suggested here will help most students master this and other facets of music fundamentals.

Step 1. Theory. Review the principles behind the material you need to learn. For learning note names, this will mean reviewing the staff as well as treble and bass clef.

Step 2. Limit Your Work. Avoid the temptation of trying to learn too much at once. Choose a few items, learn them through repetitive drill, then move on to others. In learning note names, for example, begin with three or four pitches in the treble clef (G, A, B, and C, for example). Master the locations of these four notes, then add one or two more at each study period.

Step 3. Chapter Review Activities. Consider making flash cards with a note or other symbol on one side and the identification on the other. There are multiple webpages that include materials to review fundamental concepts such as www.musictheory.net and www.teoria.com.

Step 4. Reality Check. Based on your own self-tests and any assigned exercise material, how well do you understand the material? Are you ready to move on to new problems? If so, add a few more items to those being studied, such as using the accompaniment score from a piece you're studying in applied lessons, or one that you find on www.imslp.org. For an extra challenge, say note names in rhythm for both treble and bass clef of the piano part. If you are not ready to move on, consider asking your instructor for individual help.

For class discussion or assignment: please do not remove these pages

REVIEW SET

Note Names

A. Write half notes on the staff for each given pitch. In some cases, two different staff positions are correct. Be sure to use proper stem direction for each example.

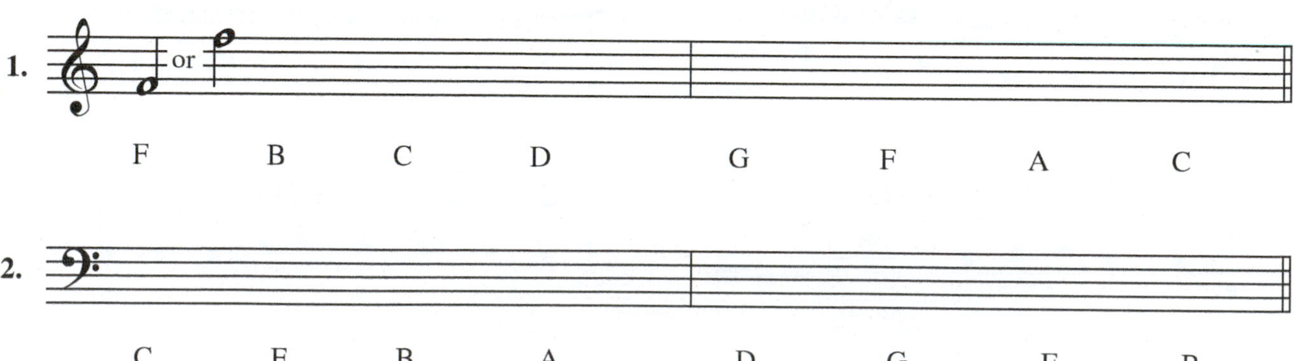

For these exercises, write eighth notes for the given note name. Be sure to use proper stem direction and length. Since many note names appear more than once, try writing them in different staff positions (if applicable).

3. 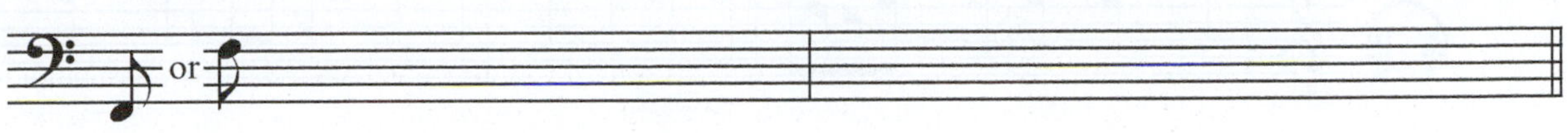 or

F G A E D E C B

4.

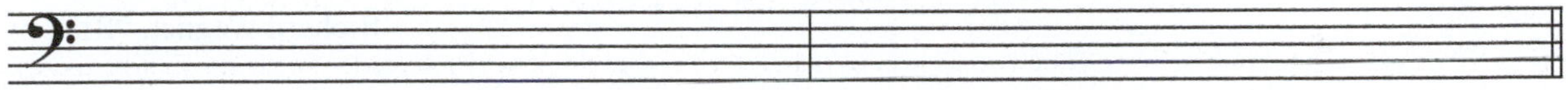

G F D E B A C G

B. Identify these sixteenth notes and quarter notes by letter name.

1.

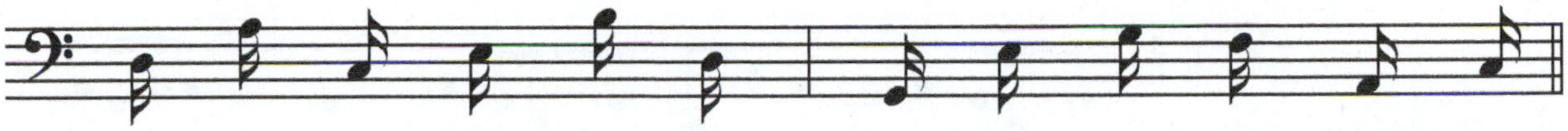

D

___ 1 ___ 2 ___ 3 ___ 4 ___ 5 ___ 6 ___ 7 ___ 8 ___ 9 ___ 10 ___ 11

2.

___ 1 ___ 2 ___ 3 ___ 4 ___ 5 ___ 6 ___ 7 ___ 8 ___ 9 ___ 10 ___ 11 ___ 12

Ledger Lines

Almost any pitch can be represented in either the treble or the bass clef. This is because we can extend the staff up or down to accommodate pitches outside the standard five lines and four spaces by adding lines, called **ledger lines**, temporarily when needed.

Numerous orchestral instruments read in the treble clef but are able to produce pitches far above the staff. Accordingly, performers must become proficient in reading ledger lines like those in the next passage.

Richard Wagner, *Die Meistersinger*

On the other hand, instruments such as the tuba read in the bass clef and use ledger lines to perform pitches below the staff.

Richard Wagner, "Ride of the Valkyries"

Calligraphy:

Clefs and Ledger Lines

Make the treble clef with either two or three strokes. Begin with a vertical stroke (long and narrow "S"). Draw a counter stroke opposite from the top to the bottom staff line; finally, let this second stroke curl around the second staff line. You may prefer to combine the second and third strokes after you have some experience.

The bass clef is basically an elongated reverse letter "C"; the two dots lie above and below the fourth staff line.

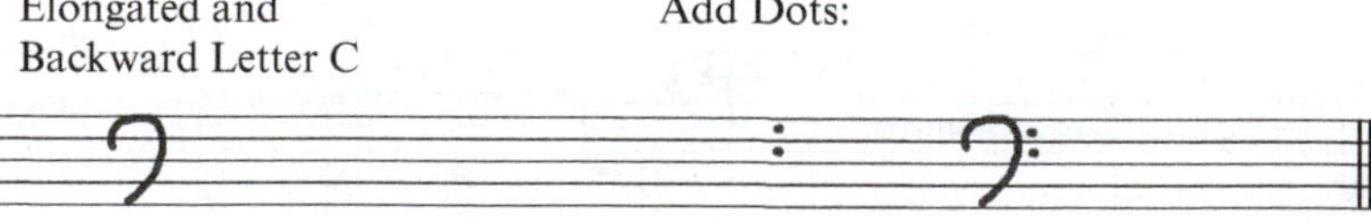

Use the staves below to practice drawing treble and bass clefs.

Remember that ledger lines are staff extensions and should be spaced in proportion to staff lines. If spacing between lines is disproportionate, it may confuse performers unnecessarily.

Each note has its own ledger line that is separate from those adjacent to it; do not connect ledger lines—even if they occur consecutively.

Notes immediately above or below the staff do not require ledger lines.

Complete Building Skills 2-1 on page 43

The Octave

Given any note on the staff, the note with the same name immediately above or below is by definition an **octave** higher or lower, respectively. When pitches are an octave apart, the sounds are so similar that they may be perceived as the *same* pitch. The distance (or difference) between two pitches is called an **interval**; the interval between each pair of pitches in the next example is an octave.

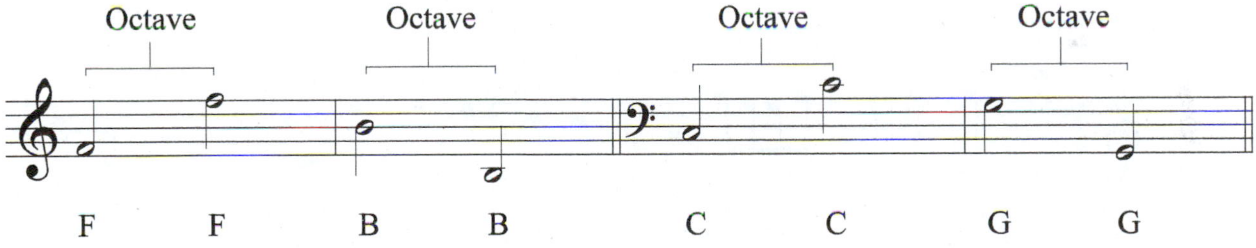

Many tunes that you know include an octave. Study the violin solo from "Winter" by Vivaldi. The opening two pitches are an octave apart. Find other instances of an octave in the excerpt.

"Winter", Vivaldi, mm.12-13 Violin I

THE OCTAVE SIGN. Because the octave is so common in traditional notation, we use a special set of symbols to indicate pitches sounding an octave higher or lower than written. The **octave sign**, 8va, is an abbreviation of the Italian word *ottava* ("eighth") and is used primarily to avoid ledger lines when parts are in an especially high register. When several pitches are included in an **ottava** passage (one employing the octave sign), they are delineated with a dotted line.

Written

8va

Sounds

If the music is to be played an octave lower, composers use the symbol *8bassa* (also abbreviated 8vb). The word *loco* (Italian, "in place") is used when music returns to the normal octave.

The following passage, by the German composer Richard Wagner (1813–1883), includes numerous ledger lines. Notice how we can use the octave sign to specify the same pitches, but within the staff. The question of whether to use ledger lines or the octave sign depends on the instrument. Violinists and flute players, for example, are accustomed to reading ledger lines; for piano, however, the octave sign is commonly used.

Richard Wagner, *Die Meistersinger*

The Grand Staff

A **system** is a set of staves. For notating keyboard music (the piano, organ, or synthesizer), we use a system of both treble and bass staves connected by a **brace ({)**. This traditional arrangement is known as the **grand** (or **great**) **staff**. The pitches in the treble clef are performed by the right hand (RH), while the pitches in the bass clef are performed by the left hand (LH).

The graphic below shows the overlap of the two staves that comprise the grand staff. The middle C shown is the same sounding pitch, whether written in treble or bass clef. Each C is an octave from its closest neighbor.

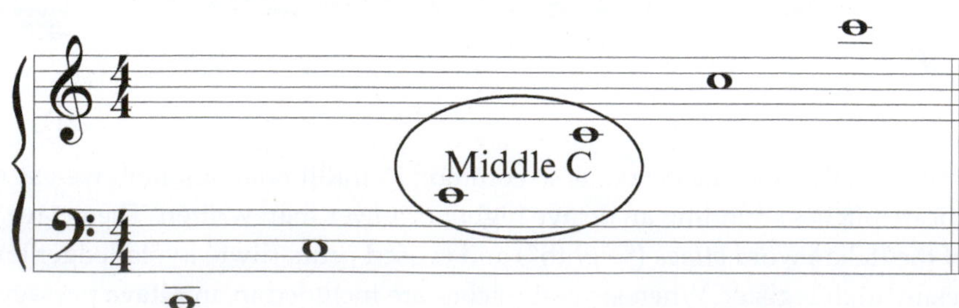

Using both the grand staff and ledger lines, we can notate pitches throughout the bass and treble registers of the piano. Further, we can change both staves to bass or to treble as the need arises. Notice in the following example that both staves begin in bass clef, but the upper staff changes to treble for the third measure; the lower staff becomes treble within measure five. This flexibility in staff notation is a regular feature of music notation and accommodates the wide range of the piano, organ, and other instruments.

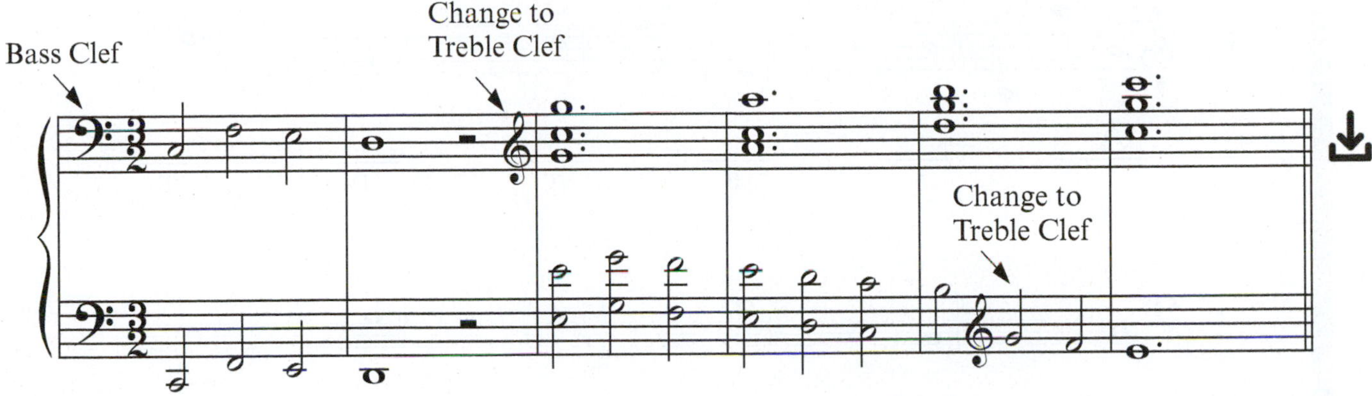

In J. S. Bach's Fugue in C Major, the melodic line is repeated at various pitch levels and as a result crosses from the treble to the bass clef staves. Notice how the stem direction is used to separate the voices. The stem direction in the treble helps us see how the melody is stated in the various voices. The first (all stems up) begins in measure 1, while the second voice enters in measure 3 (all stems down).

For class discussion or assignment: please do not remove these pages

REVIEW SET

Notating Octaves

A. For each given pitch, notate one an octave higher and another an octave lower. Use ledger lines as necessary and name the first pitch in each set. Do not use the 8va or 8vb symbols. Be sure to observe proper stem direction.

1.

2.

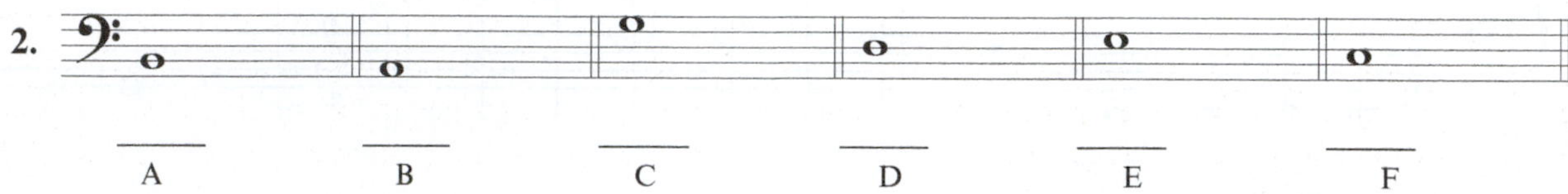

B. Rewrite the opening figure from Bach's Fugue in C major to sound an octave higher. Use ledger lines and *not* the octave sign (8va). When you are finished, play the two versions at the piano.

J.S. Bach, Fugue in C Major

C. Rewrite the same melody to sound an octave lower. Use ledger lines and *not* the octave sign (8vb). When you are finished, play the two versions at the piano.

Complete Building Skills 2-2 on page 47

MUSICIANSHIP 2-1

I. Sight Singing: Matching Pitches

Singing is central to any formal music study (whether your major instrument is voice, oboe, or saxophone). Begin by playing a midrange pitch on an instrument (preferably the piano), then sing that same pitch (called "matching pitches"). Finally, play the pitch again on the instrument. Repeat this process three or four times until you have matched pitches accurately, moving on to other pitches a little higher or lower.

If this activity is difficult for you, let your voice slide up or down until you find the correct pitch. Work with another student or record yourself if possible. When you match the pitch in your natural voice range, you actually may be singing an octave higher or lower than the instrument's pitch.

II. Ear Training: Pitch Discrimination

Ear training is the process of learning patterns that are common in traditional music so that you can recognize, imitate, and notate those patterns when necessary. Immediate reinforcement is crucial in ear training. For this reason, the ear training exercises in this text are available in two different ways. First, for some groups of exercises, the recorded material is available on the website that accompanies the text. You can work through these materials on your own or your instructor may play them in class. In each audio example, you will listen to a series of three or more pitches and indicate whether the *last* pitch is the same (S), higher than (H), or lower than (L) the first pitch. There are four different patterns in each line. After listening to your teacher play the example in class or listening to the audio, circle your answer, and proceed as before. The answers can be found in Appendix D.

Circle **S** if the last pitch is the **same** as the first.
Circle **H** if the last pitch is **higher** than the first.
Circle **L** if the last pitch is **lower** than the first.

Patterns of Three Pitches

1. S H L S H L S H L S H L
2. S H L S H L S H L S H L
3. S H L S H L S H L S H L

Patterns of Four Pitches

1. S H L S H L S H L S H L
2. S H L S H L S H L S H L
3. S H L S H L S H L S H L

Patterns of Five Pitches

1. S H L S H L S H L S H L
2. S H L S H L S H L S H L
3. S H L S H L S H L S H L

Patterns of Various Lengths (Three to Five Pitches)

a. S H L S H L S H L S H L
b. S H L S H L S H L S H L
c. S H L S H L S H L S H L
d. S H L S H L S H L S H L

Name ______________________

Page may be removed

Building Skills 2-1

Note Names

A. Write the name of each pitch on the staff in the blank below it.

B. In addition to pitches on the staff, these passages include notes with ledger lines. Name each note.

C. The next exercises are phrases from music literature. Identify pitches only where blanks appear.[1]

Joseph Bologne Saint-Georges, Six String Quartets, Op. 1, No. 1

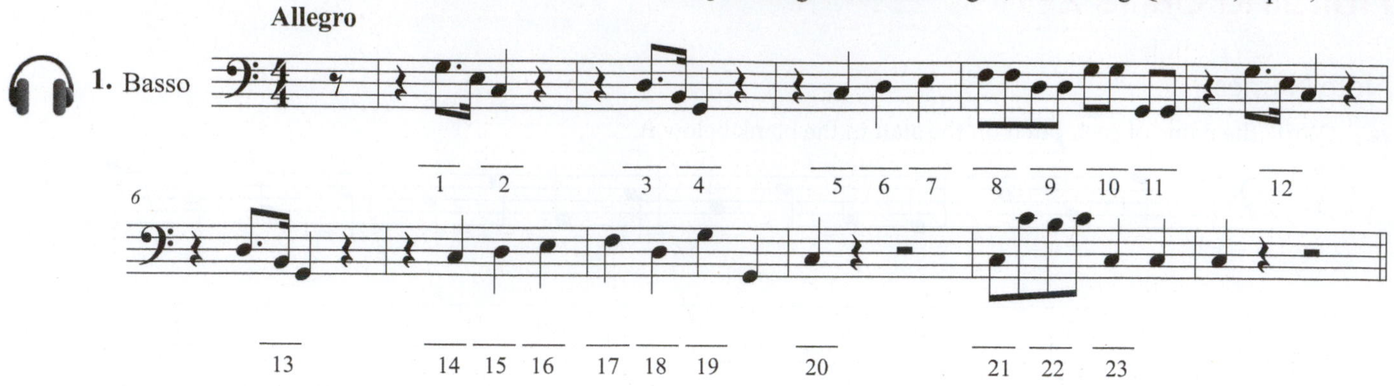

Johann Strauss, *Artist's Life*

D. Using sixteenth notes, notate each named pitch in two different staff locations. Use flags, not beams.

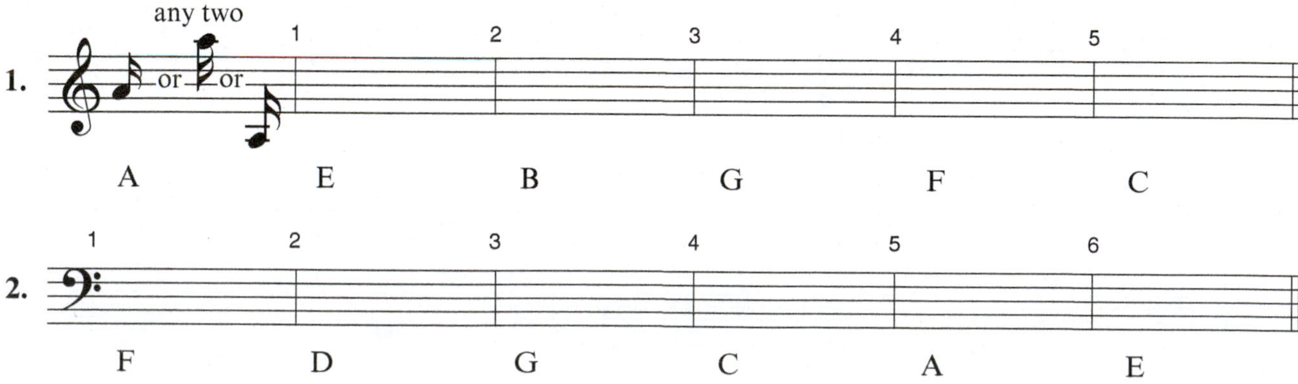

[1] Many of the musical examples in the early chapters of this book have been adapted.

Name ____________________

Page may be removed

E. Starting with the given pitch, notate four consecutive ascending or descending pitches, using ledger lines as necessary. Name the first and last pitches of each group.

F. The direction of several stems and flags in the next example are incorrect. Use the lower staff to rewrite the entire line using correct notation.

Amy Cheney Beach, *With Violets.*

Indian Folk Song, "Gananayaka"

G. For practice in calligraphy, make an exact copy of the adapted first phrase of Mozart's Theme, shown in the next example. In your copy, align notes vertically as they appear in the score.

W.A. Mozart, Piano Sonata no. 6, K. 284, III. Tema

Name ______________________

Page may be removed

Building Skills 2-2

The Octave

A. Notate the given examples to sound an octave higher or lower than written (as specified). Use ledger lines in this exercise and *not* the octave sign.

Notate Octave Higher

W. A. Mozart, String Quartet no. 16, K. 428, IV.

Symphony No. 1 in A-flat, "Afro-American" (1930) by William Grant Still. Used courtesy of William Grant Still Music.

Notate Octave Lower

Notate Octave Lower

J.S. Bach, Orchestral Suite No. 1 in C Major, "Courante"

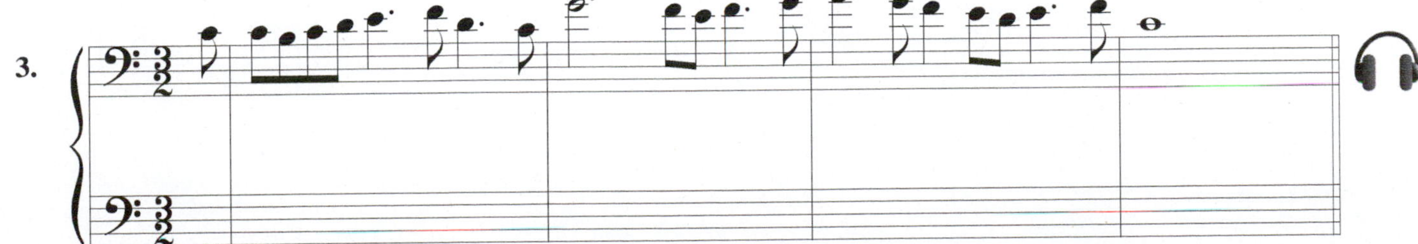

B. These melodies include the octave sign. Notate the complete line in the lower staff, writing all pitches as they will sound.

Name ____________________

Page may be removed

Creative Projects • Chapter 2

Eight different measure-long segments are given below. Using the blank staves provided, create two different solos for flute. You may use any combination of segments in any order. Plan to use a variety of octaves. You can also repeat or omit segments. When you are finished, you will have two complete 16-measure compositions (although, as we will discuss in later chapters, traditional music is far from random). The clef sign appears at the beginning of a line; unless there is a change. The time signature is given only once. Write the pitch names under each segment. Have a class member perform your composition if possible.

Second Solo for Flute

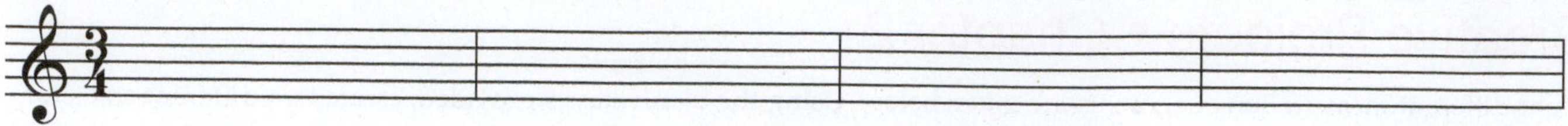

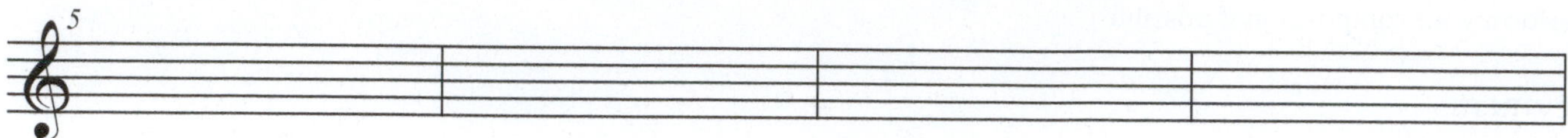

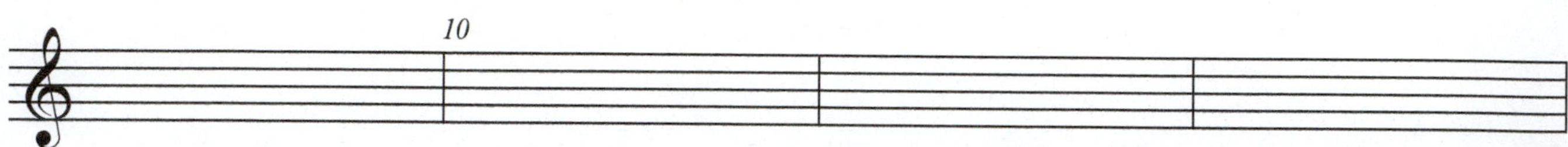

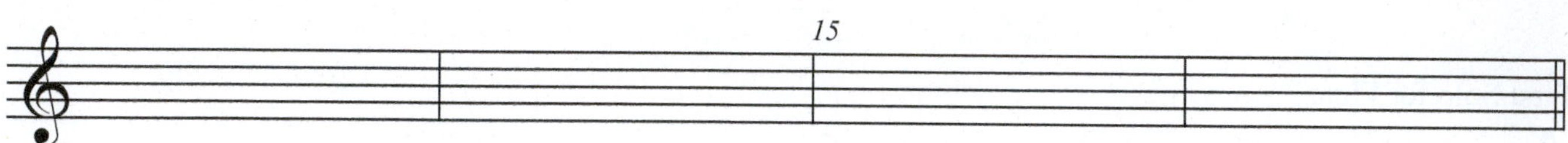

Name ______________________

Page may be removed

Analysis in Context 1 • Chapter 2

Many consider John Philip Sousa's "The Stars and Stripes Forever" march to be the official march of the United States. It's common to hear it at Fourth of July Celebrations. One well-known melody from the march is played by the flutes and piccolos. To learn more about this famous march and the composer, go to http://www.americaslibrary.gov/aa/sousa/aa_sousa_forever_1.html

Div.
ff
8va
ff
(8va)
(8va)
(8va)
(8va)
(8va)
1.
2.
fff

Name ______________________________

Page may be removed

1. Circle the treble clef(s) on the score.

2. Write in the note names above the notes in measures 1–15. Listen to a recording and practice saying them as you listen.

3. What does the term "divisi" mean?

4. In what measure(s) do you find examples of a divisi section?

5. Study the section beginning in measure 57. How does the composer use stem direction to make reading the parts easier?

6. What does the symbol 8va mean to the flute player?

7. Circle the 8va symbols you find in the score.

8. Why does the composer, John Philip Sousa, choose to use the 8va symbol in these measures?

Chapter 3

The Keyboard

Essential Terms and Symbols

accidental
chromatic half step
chromatic pitch
diatonic pitch
double flat (𝄫)
double sharp (𝄪)
enharmonic
flat (♭)
half step
keyboard
natural half step
natural sign (♮)
nondiatonic
octave designation
semitone
sharp (♯)
whole step

On a **keyboard**, an instrument like an organ or piano, the performer does not come into direct contact with the string or pipe that actually produces the sound (see Appendix A, page 409). Whereas violin, flute, and trumpet players can make minute changes in pitch, each key on a keyboard instrument produces only one invariable pitch.

Throughout the world, musical systems are based on the octave—the simplest and most natural interval. The ingenuity with which cultures divide the octave into smaller intervals, however, is a primary reason that music in one part of the world sounds different from that in another. In Western music we divide the octave into 12 equal smaller parts called *half steps*. The **half step** (also called a **semitone**) is the smallest interval in Western music. It can be understood as the distance on the keyboard from one key to the next closest key (above or below). As shown in the next example, the distance between any two adjacent keys is a half step regardless of whether we begin with a black or a white key.

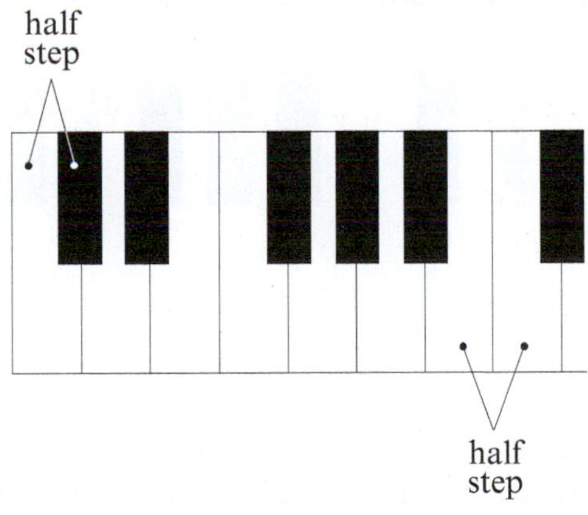

Two half steps combine to form a **whole step**—another basic interval in traditional Western music. The distance from one key to the *second* closest key above or below is a whole step.

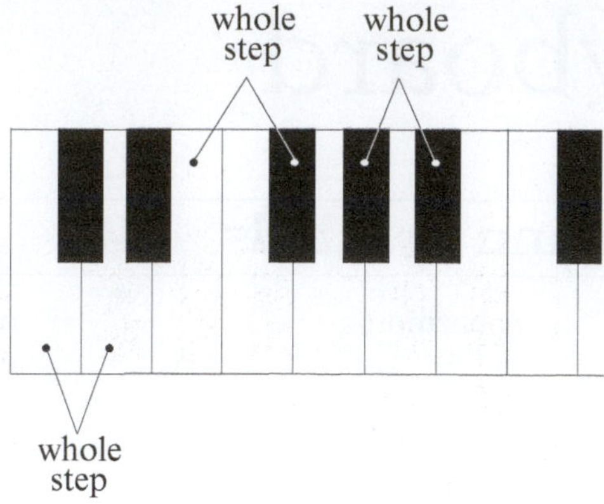

The Keyboard

Since the eighteenth century, fixed-pitch keyboard instruments, such as the harpsichord, organ, and piano, have influenced Western musical traditions. In more recent times, the electric piano and organ—as well as the digital synthesizer—have retained the same keyboard design. Starting from the center of the keyboard, pitches get lower moving to the left; moving to the right, pitches get higher.

The standard keyboard is based on the seven basic pitches discussed in Chapter 2: A, B, C, D, E, F, and G. These are the white keys; the black keys fall in between. Observe, however, that black keys do not fall between *every* pair of white keys; black keys are arranged in groups of two and three, which alternate from left to right up the keyboard.

The arrangement of black and white keys helps to identify the notes on the keyboard. In any octave, the pitch C is always the white key just below (to the left of) the first of the two black keys. The pitch F is always the white key to the left of the lowest of the three black keys.

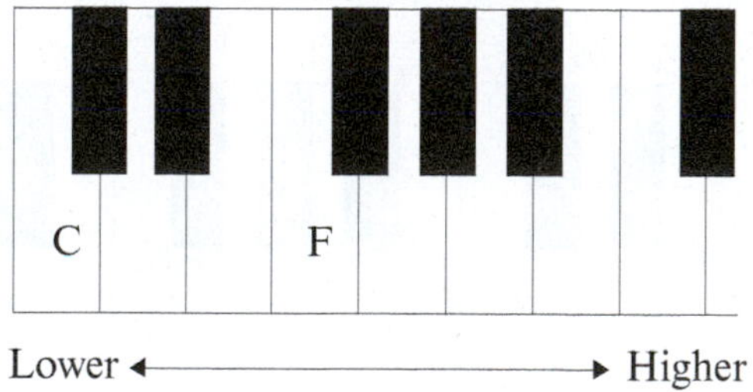

The basic pitches are arranged sequentially (A B C D E F G) over the white keys on the keyboard. As is the case with reading notes on the staff, once any pitch is located, the keys that produce the other pitches are easily determined.

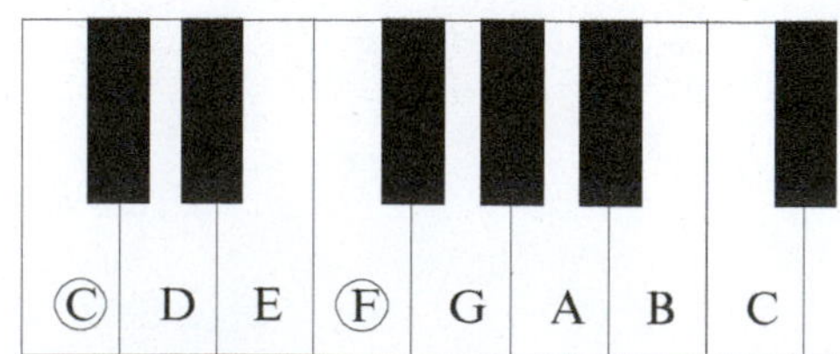

NATURAL HALF STEPS. While most intervals between adjacent basic pitches are whole steps, half steps occur between B and C and between E and F (the two points where black keys do not appear). Intervals between these pitches are termed **natural half steps**.

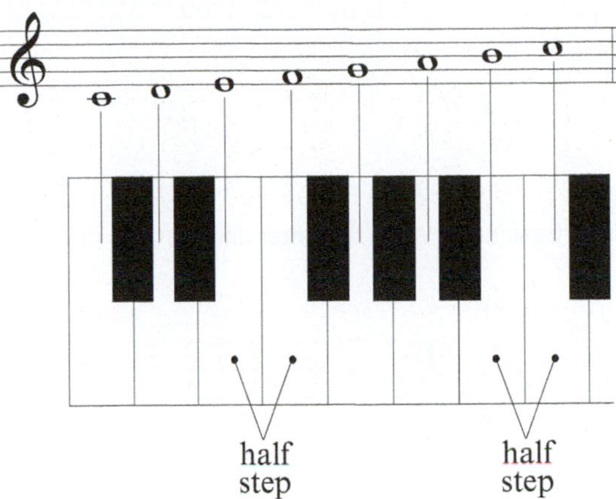

OCTAVE PLACEMENT. The standard keyboard includes more than seven octaves, allowing the performer to choose a high, middle, or low register. Although the names and relative locations of the pitches within each octave are exactly the same, the staff notation is different so that the performer knows which register the composer intends. Notice in the following example that although the pitch C is always to the left of the two black keys on the keyboard, its staff appearance is different in every octave. The example begins on middle C and ends on the pitch C three octaves higher.

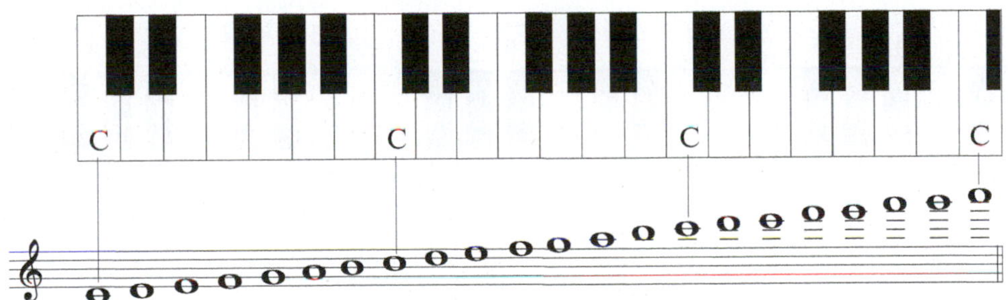

For class discussion or assignment: please do not remove these pages

REVIEW SET

Pitches on the Keyboard

A. On the two-octave keyboards given below, identify all the numbered keys that correspond to each pair of pitches named.

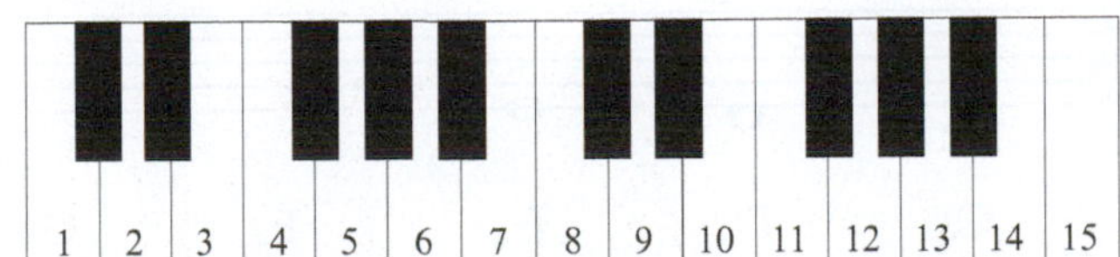

1. C and F ______________
2. G and E ______________
3. D and B ______________

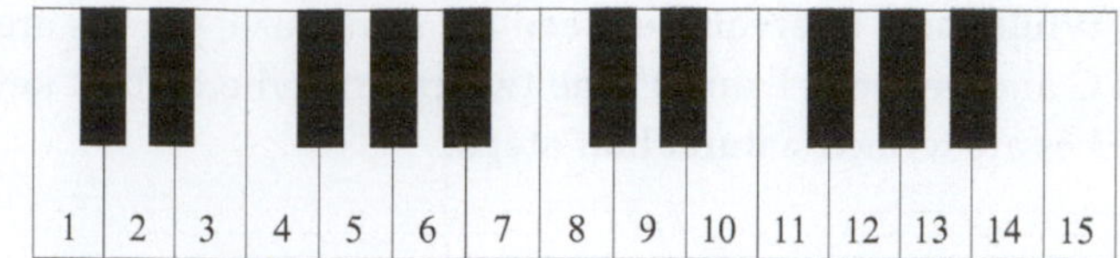

4. F and G ______________
5. C and A ______________
6. E and F ______________

B. Examine the given pitch on each treble or bass staff. Write the letter name of this pitch in the blank and draw a line to the corresponding key on the keyboard.

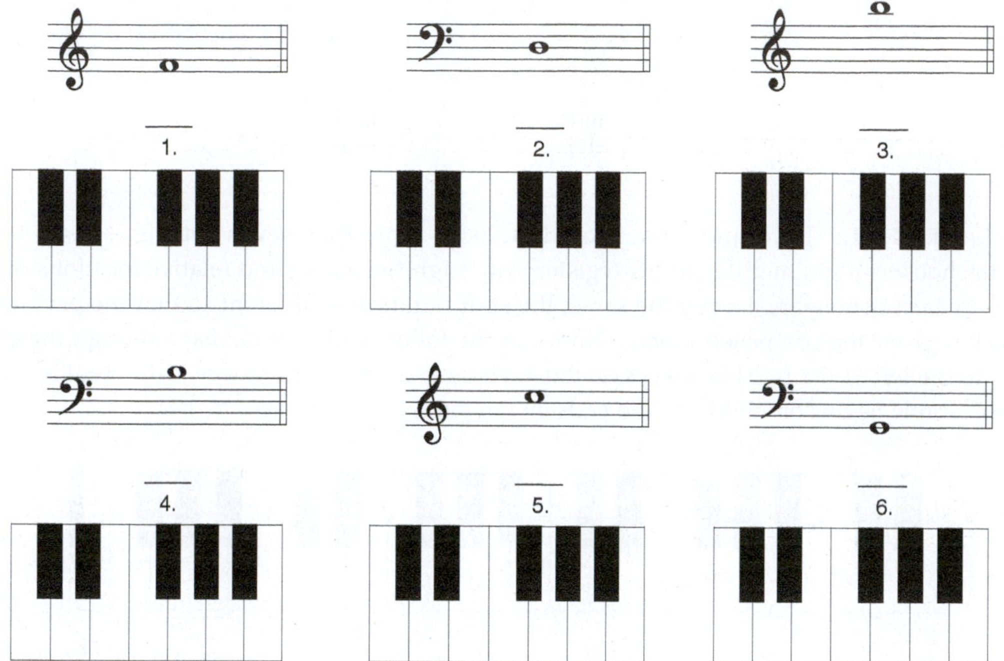

Octave Designation

As you have just seen, pitch names appear in several different places on the staff, so we use a system of **octave designation** to specify an exact register. The lowest pitch in each octave is C. The pitch we know as middle C, in the center of the piano keyboard, is more exactly identified as C4. Other pitches in the same octave also carry the subscript "4."[1]

[1]The subscript designation is most common, but the same octave range may also be identified as C_4 or C4.

The pitch immediately above B4 is C5; the pitch below C4 is B3.

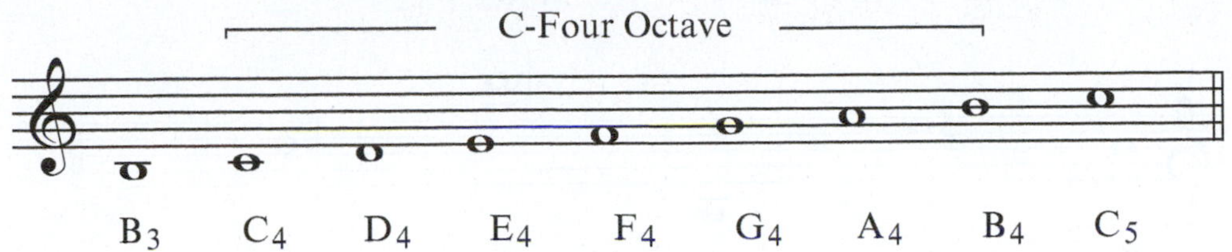

The full range of the pitch C on the piano is shown in the next example. Remember that C is the lowest pitch of each octave. The pitch C8 is the highest on the standard piano keyboard.

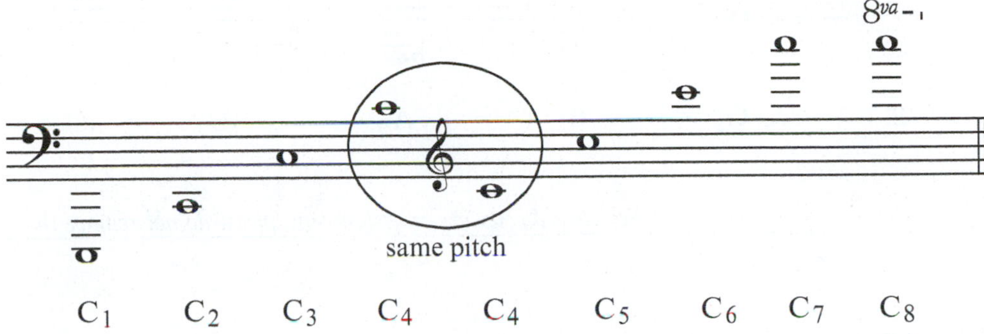

The following chart shows the entire piano keyboard along with octave designations and staff notation.

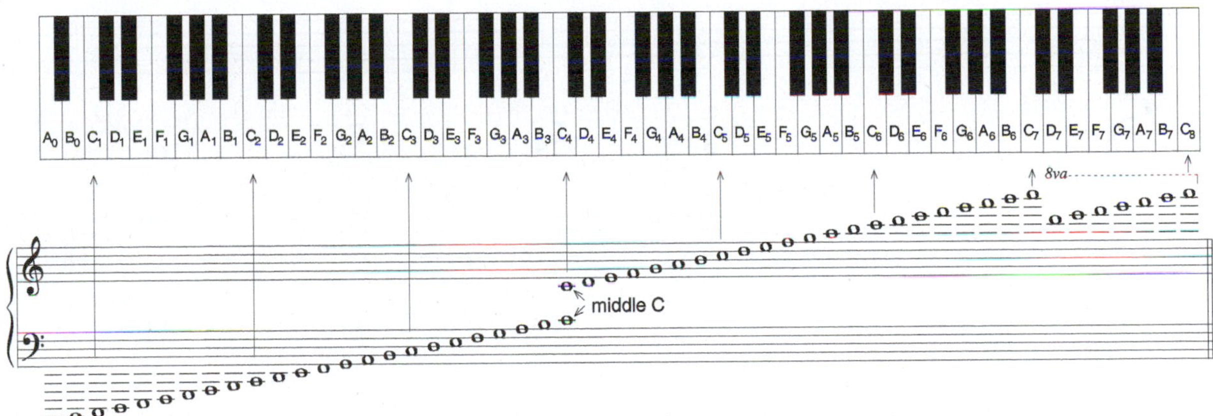

Three pitches, designated B0, B♭/A♯0, and A0, lie at the bottom of the piano keyboard and below C1.

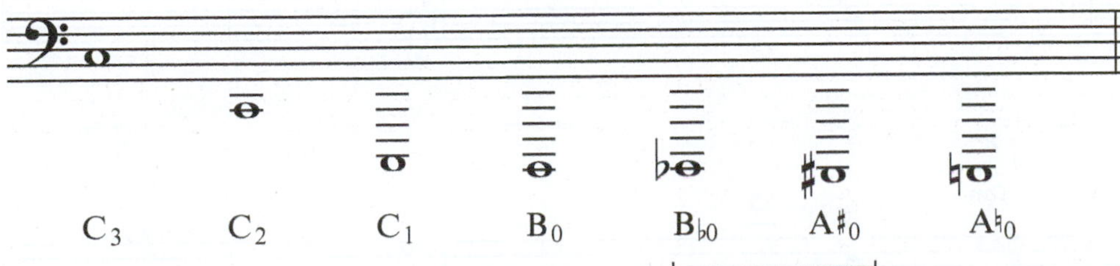

Notice the identification of several different pitches with their octave identity. While accidentals do not affect octave designation, the octave sign does (review page 37).

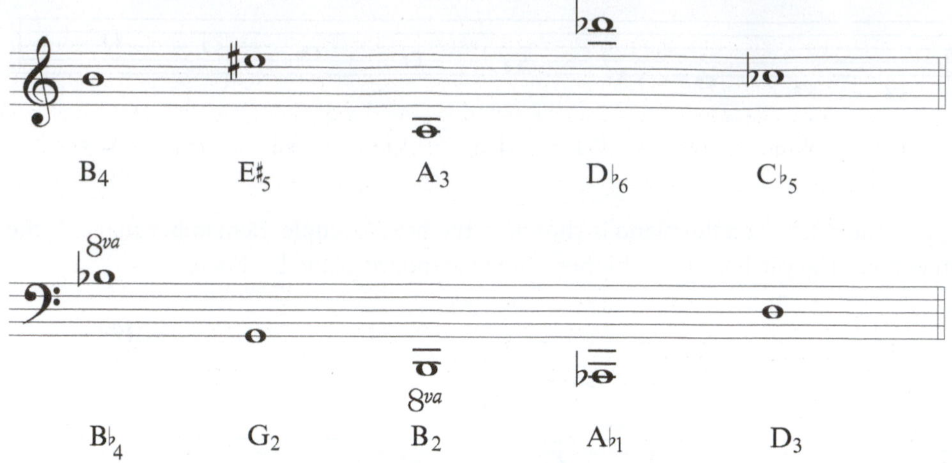

For class discussion or assignment: please do not remove these pages

REVIEW SET

Octave Designations

A. Write eighth notes on the staff for each pitch as specified by the octave designation. *Be sure to include proper stem and flag direction.*

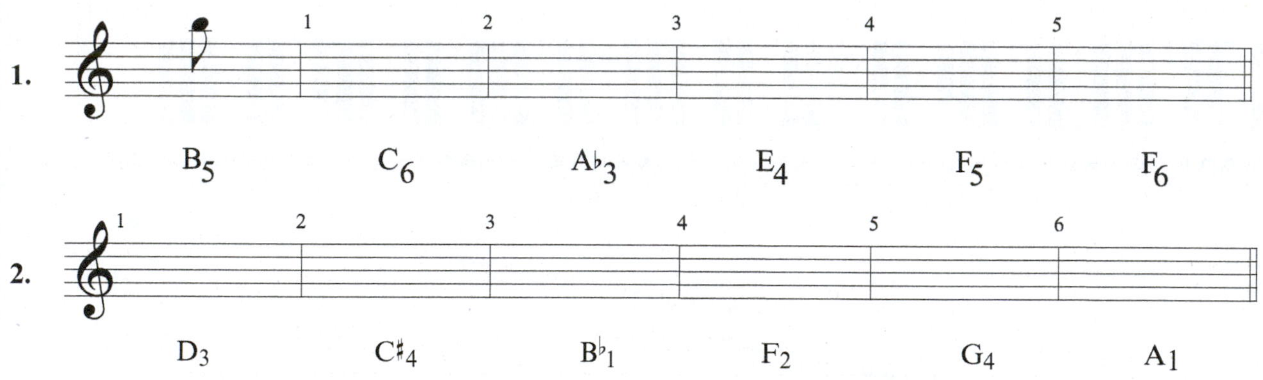

B. Provide the letter name and octave designation for each of the following pitches.

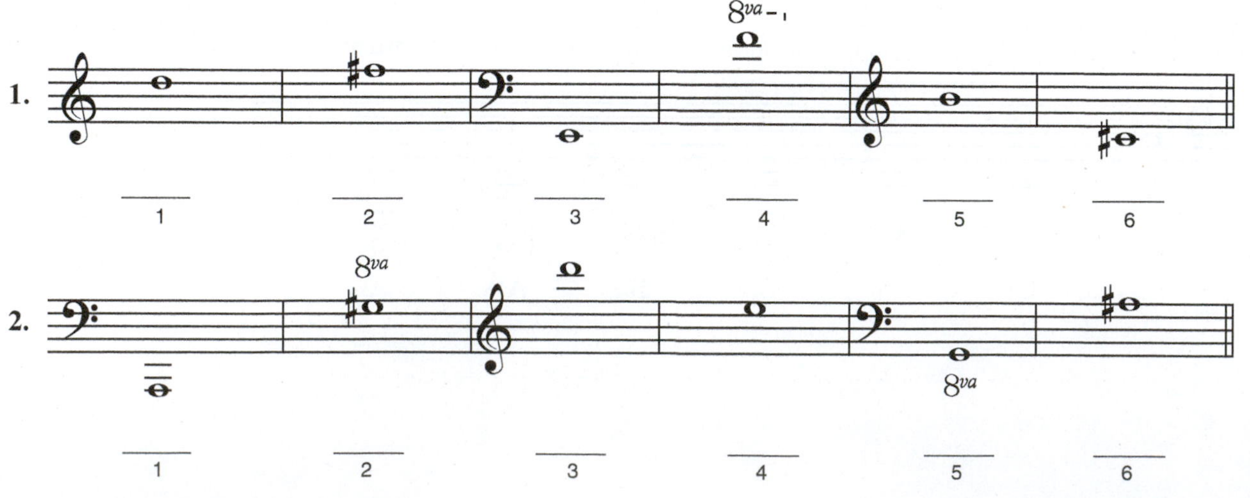

Complete Building Skills 3-2 on page 75

MUSICIANSHIP 3-1

Keyboard: Locating Pitches

A. Seated at the keyboard, play the two lines that follow. Begin with middle C, in the center of the piano keyboard; next, locate and play Cs that are one, two, and three octaves higher. Each pitch C will be to the immediate left of the lower of the paired black keys. Use your right index finger for each pitch. Do not slide to the right on the piano bench as you reach for the higher notes; remain in the center of the piano and *lean* to the right as necessary. In the second line, the same pitches occur in a random order.

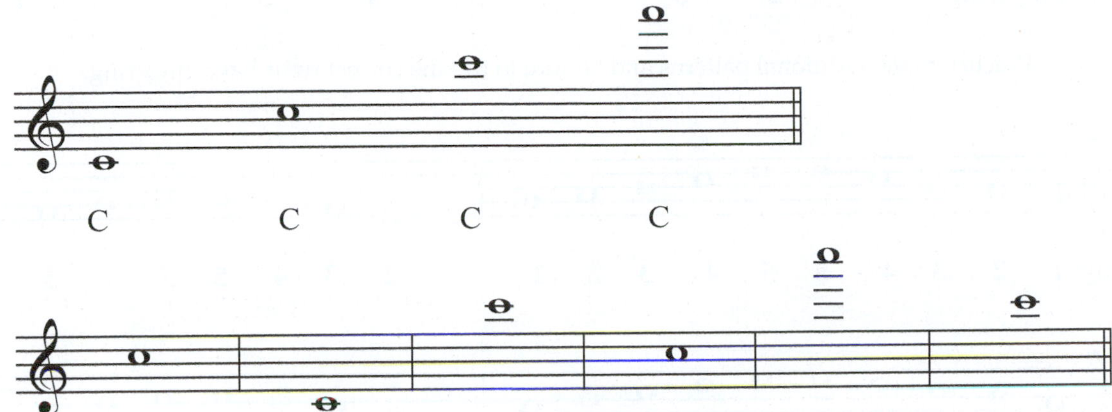

Locate the pitch F immediately above middle C (the white key to the left of the three black keys). Play this pitch, which is the first F notated in the next example. Play the other Fs in descending order. Use the index finger of your left hand and lean to the left as you play. In the second line, the Fs occur in random order.

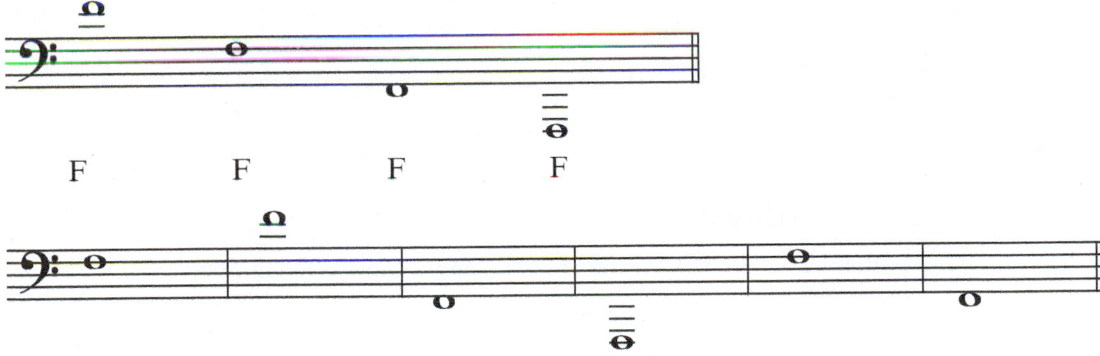

B. These exercises consist of stepwise five-pitch patterns. Refer to the diagram below for right- and left-hand finger numbers used in fingering patterns in the exercises.

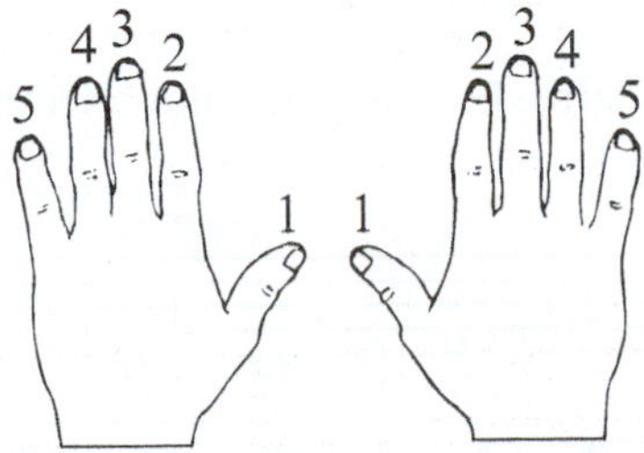

Right-Hand Patterns

These exercises include various arrangements of only the white notes. Play the patterns and experiment with the same pitches in different octaves.

Practice these additional patterns and be sure to use the correct right-hand fingering.

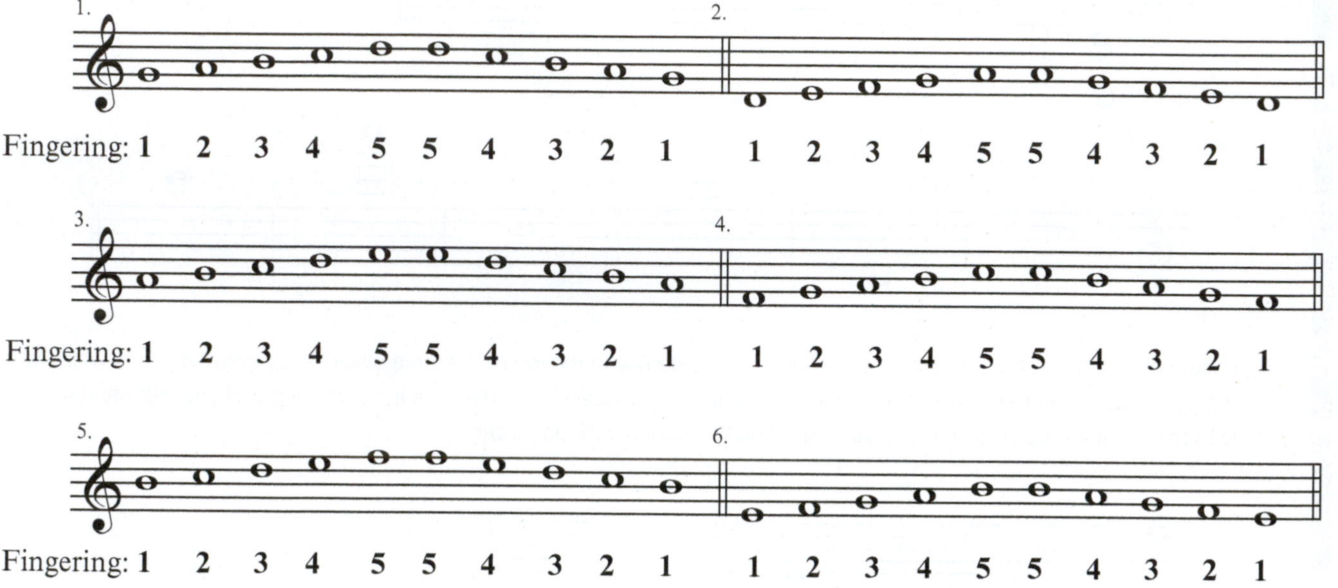

Left-Hand Patterns

Left-hand patterns begin with the little finger (5) and ascend to the thumb (1).

Try these left-hand patterns. Be sure to use the correct fingering.

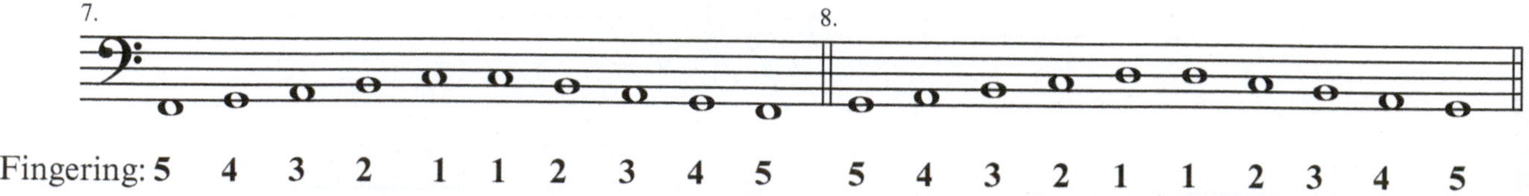

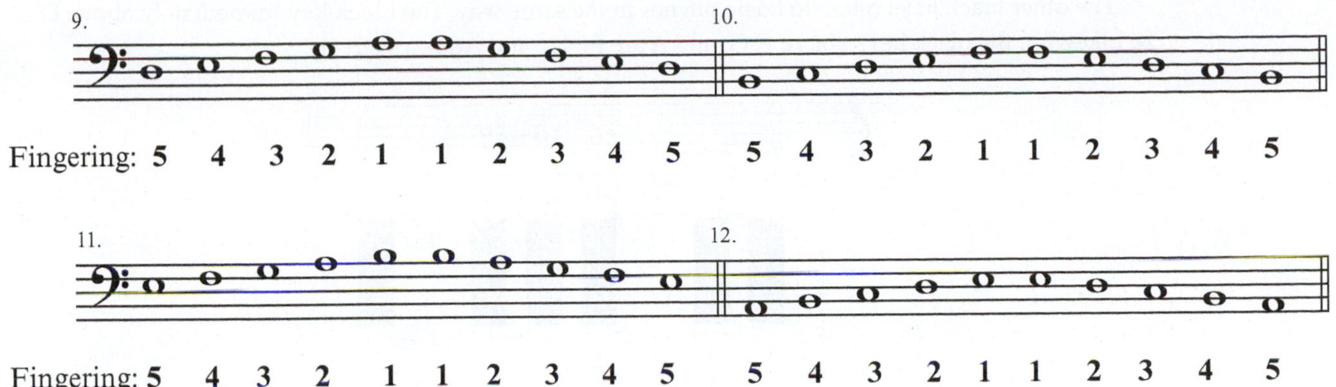

Creative Activity: Improvise a melody using a five-finger pattern as the basis for your composition. Be sure to keep the correct finger position as you play. Practice with both right-hand and left-hand patterns.

Accidentals

Basic pitches are regularly altered to sound higher or lower. **Accidentals** are symbols that appear before the note itself and indicate a half-step alteration in pitch. The three most common accidentals are the *sharp*, the *flat*, and the *natural*.

The Sharp

The **sharp** sign (♯) indicates that a basic pitch (white note) is raised one half step. If we want a pitch one half step higher than C, for example, it will be produced by the black key to the immediate right of the white key, C. The name of this new pitch is C-sharp (C♯). Notice that the sharp sign appears *before* a note on the staff. If we write it in words, the sharp sign appears *after* the letter name.

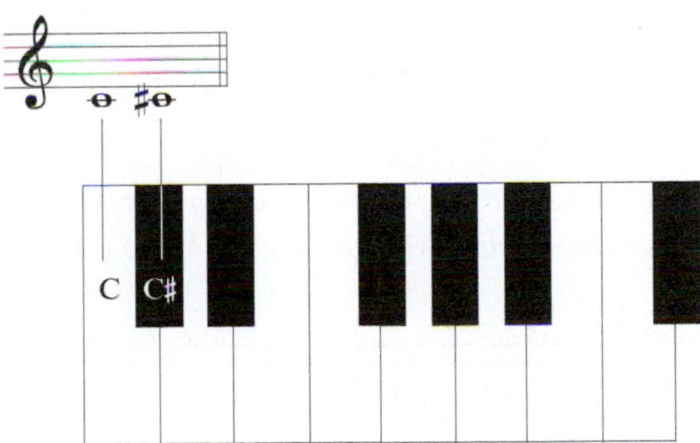

The pitches C and C♯ represent two completely different musical tones. Locate the pitches on the keyboard and sing along. Focus on the difference between a whole and a half step. The first two pitches in the figure below are C and C♯; this interval is a half step. The second interval is C and D—a whole step. Finally, listen to the pitches C–C♯–D for a series of two half steps. Locate the pitches on the keyboard and play along.

The other black keys relate to basic pitches in the same way. The black key immediately above D is D♯. Likewise, the black keys above F, G, and A are F♯, G♯, and A♯, respectively.

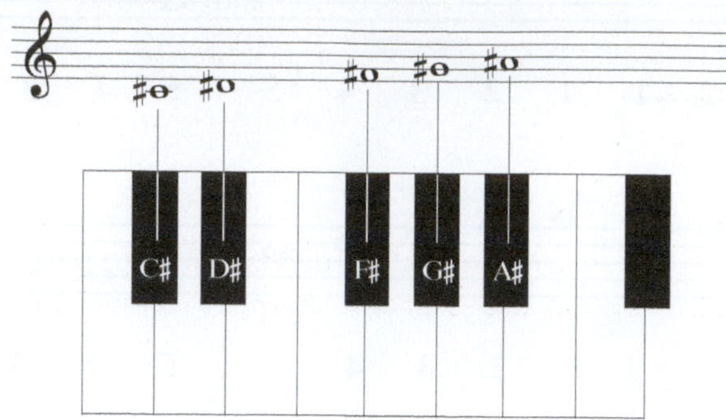

The Flat

The **flat** sign (♭) indicates that a basic pitch is lowered one half step. The pitch D is played with the white key to the immediate right of C. The pitch D♯ is the black key to the immediate right of D. Finally, D-flat (D♭) is the black key to the immediate left of D.

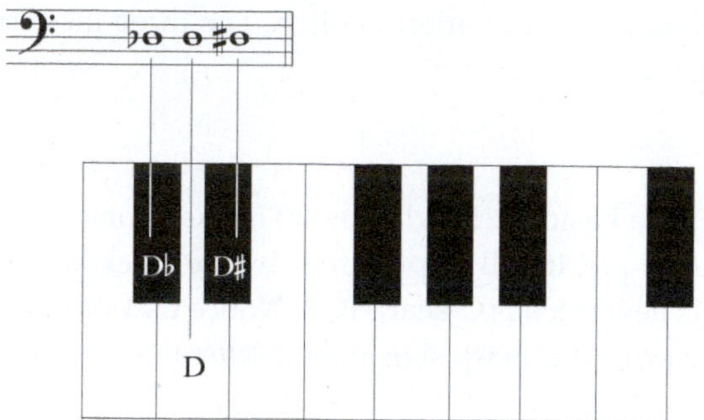

The Natural Sign

The term *natural* in music usually refers to one of the seven basic pitches. The **natural sign** (♮) cancels the previous flat or sharp and indicates a return to the original basic pitch.

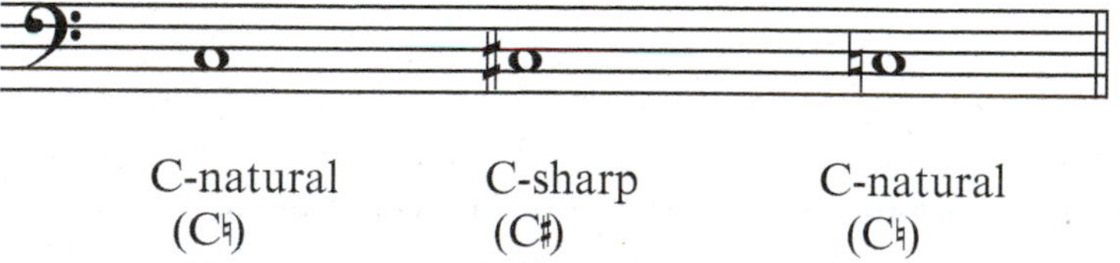

C-natural (C♮) C-sharp (C♯) C-natural (C♮)

CANCELING AND RESTORING ACCIDENTALS. Accidentals affect individual notes and carry throughout the measure. In the next example, the third pitch is C♯. Because the sharp sign would be in effect for the entire measure, it is necessary to use a natural sign to return to the basic pitch C for the sixth pitch. Accidentals in the second measure are used in a similar way. Play through the following examples, paying careful attention to the use of accidentals.

Original Melody

Franz Liszt, Waldersrauschen

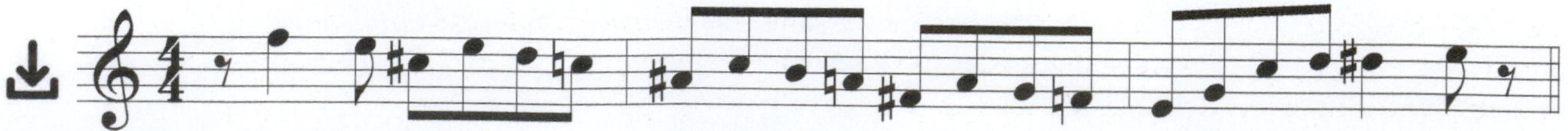

The same melody without canceling accidentals

Double Sharps and Double Flats

Basic pitches can be raised or lowered a whole step through the **double sharp** (𝄪) or **double flat** (𝄫) signs. While C♯ is played on the black key above C, C-double sharp (C𝄪) lies yet another half step higher—the same key used for the pitch D.

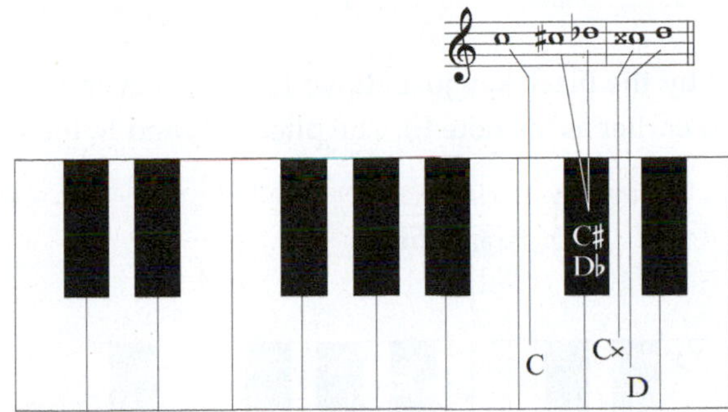

The pitch C♭ is produced by the white key below C (the same one used for B); C-double flat (C𝄫) is found yet another half step lower—the black key also used for B♭.

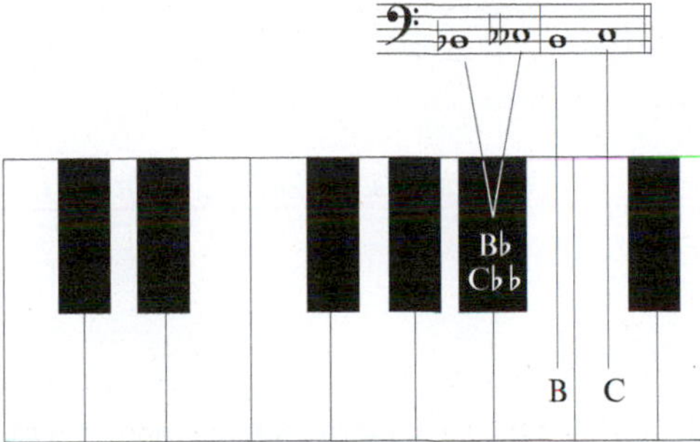

Enharmonic Equivalents

Although the pitches D, D♯, and D♭ produce different sounds, the same sound can be notated on the staff in a number of ways. Notice, for example, that D♭ is produced by the same key earlier labeled C♯. Obviously, since the two pitches employ the same key, the sounds are identical.

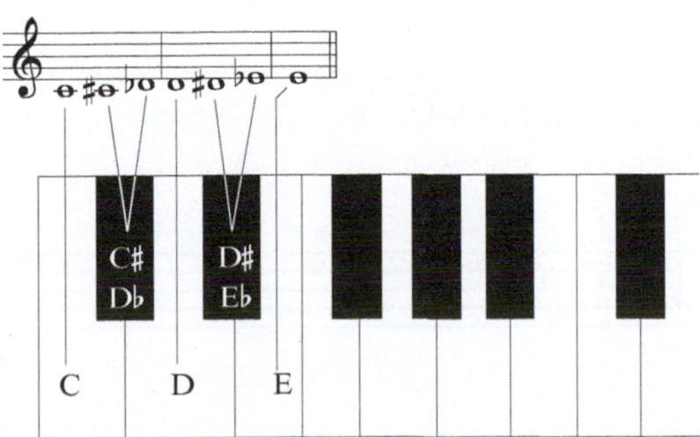

Equivalent pitches such as C♯ and D♭, which *sound* the same but are *notated* differently, are known as **enharmonics**. Composers choose spelling based on key or context. We will learn later how these notes tend to resolve based on the way they are spelled.

Another pair of enharmonic equivalents, F♯ and G♭, is identified in the next example. These two pitches are the same in sound, but are written in different places on the staff.

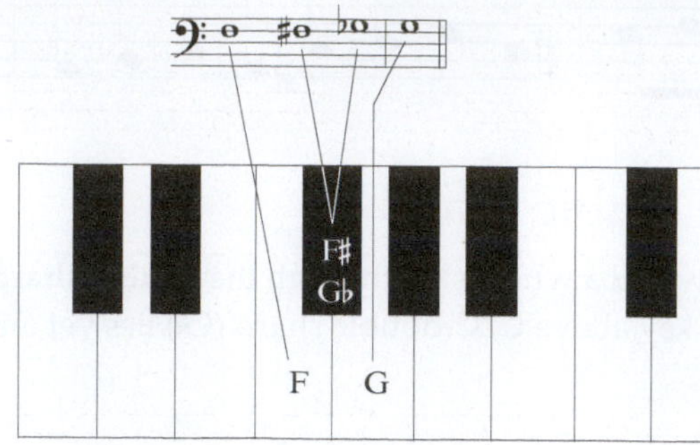

The pitch F♯ is produced by the black key just above F; F♭, however, is a white key—the one just below F (which was identified earlier as the note E). The pitches F♭ and E, therefore, are enharmonics.

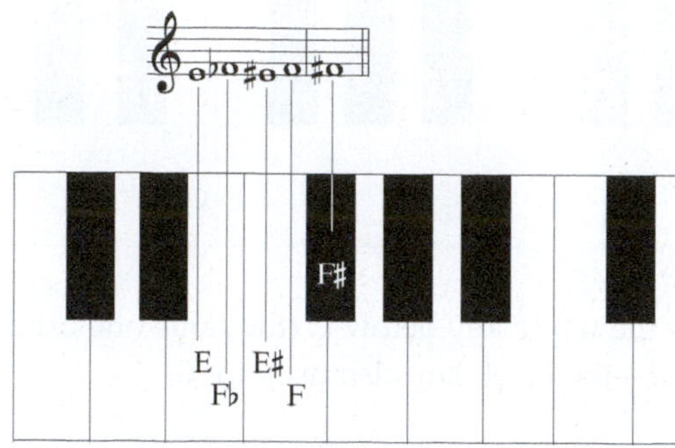

For class discussion or assignment: please do not remove these pages

REVIEW SET

Enharmonics

A. For each pitch, provide one harmonic equivalent. In some cases, more than one answer will be correct. Use the blanks to identify the letter names of the two pitches.

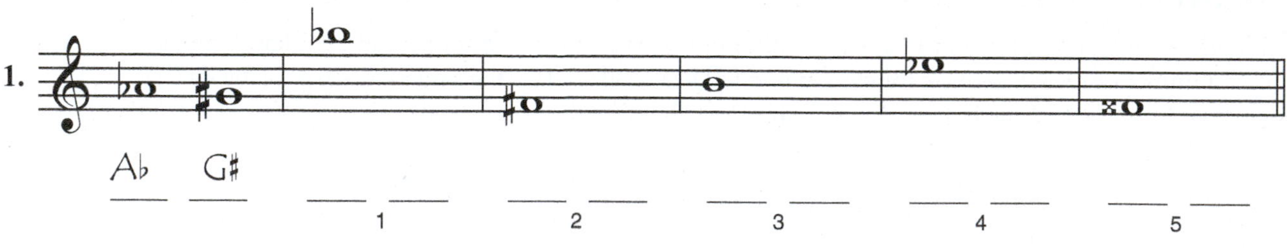

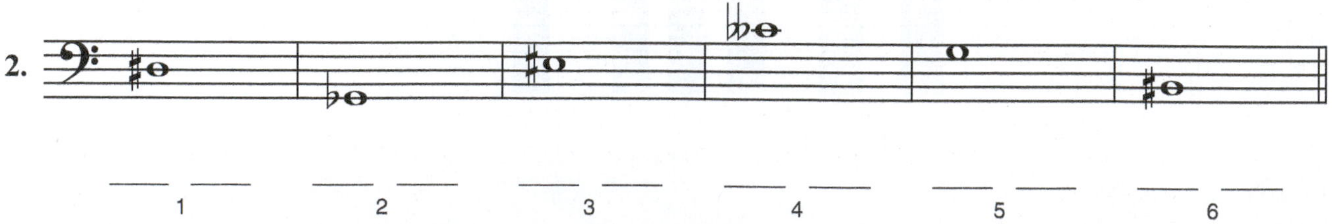

B. Some of these pairs of pitches are enharmonic equivalents; others are not. Write the note name of each pitch below the staff. Make a check mark in the measure if pitches are enharmonic equivalents.

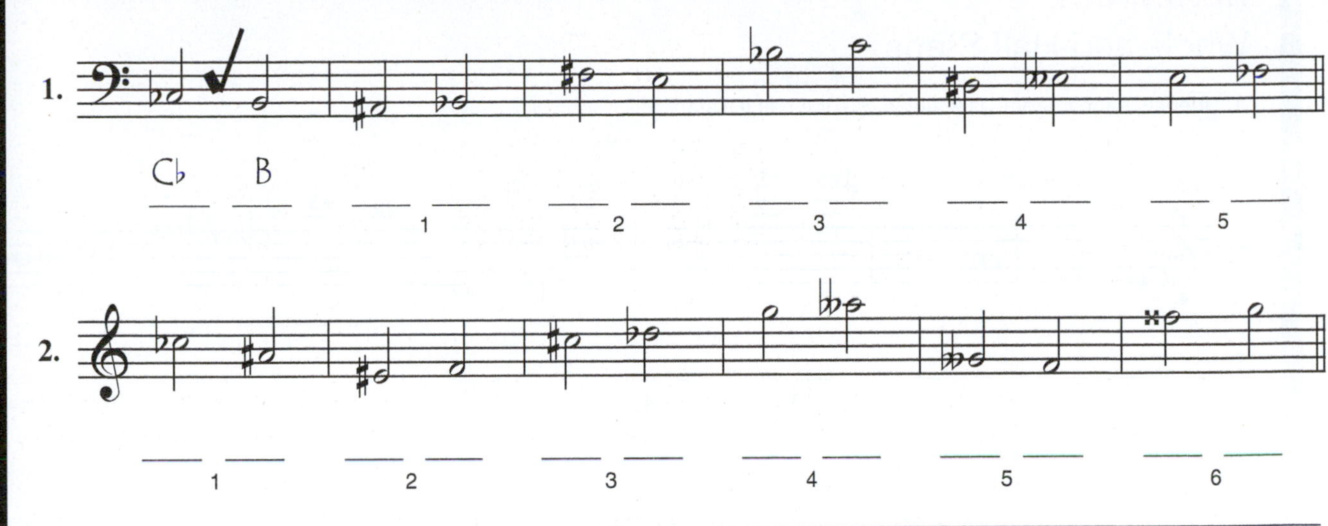

Diatonic Pitches

The term **diatonic** usually refers to pitches within a given scale system. Pitches that are diatonic are within the scale; those outside it are **nondiatonic** or **chromatic**. If the key is C major, the pitches of the C major scale are diatonic; any pitch outside the scale is chromatic (even if it is an enharmonic version of a diatonic pitch).

Scale of C Major

Diatonic and Chromatic Half Steps

Two categories of half step occur in Western music. If the interval involves pitches with *different* letter names (F♯ and G, for example), the half step is diatonic. A **chromatic half step**, on the other hand, exists between pitches with the *same* letter name (such as F and F♯). All of the intervals in the next line are half steps; note the important difference between those identified as diatonic and the others that are chromatic.

Both diatonic and chromatic half steps appear in melodies, but chromatic half steps are *never* used in writing major scales.

For class discussion or assignment: please do not remove these pages

REVIEW SET

Whole and Half Steps

A. Identify each interval as a whole (W) or a half (H) step.

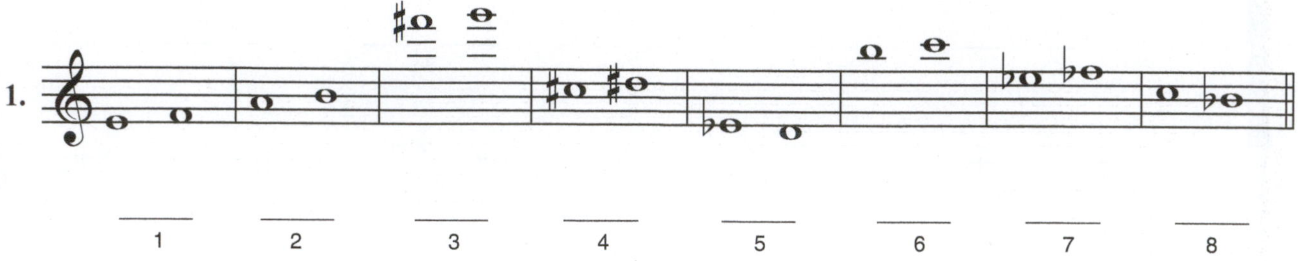

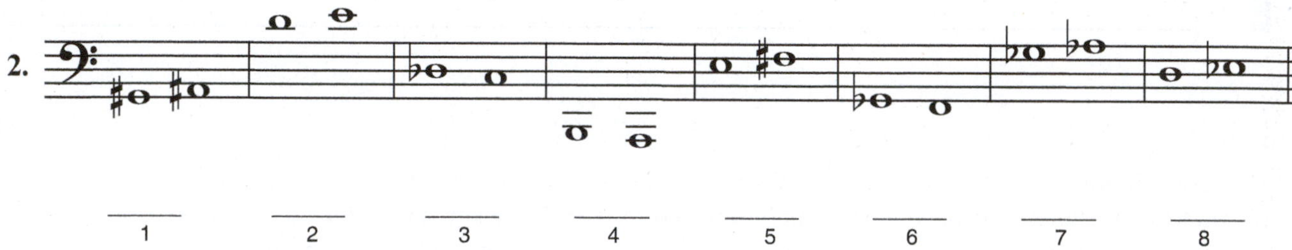

B. Write notes that are half or whole steps above or below the given pitch as specified. Provide letter names for both pitches. Remember that in letter-name notation, the accidental follows the letter (for example, F♯ and B♭).

For class discussion or assignment: please do not remove these pages

REVIEW SET

Diatonic and Chromatic Half Steps

A. Several intervals are given in the next lines. In the blank, write "D" if the half step is diatonic and "C" if it is chromatic. Write "W" if the interval is a whole step.

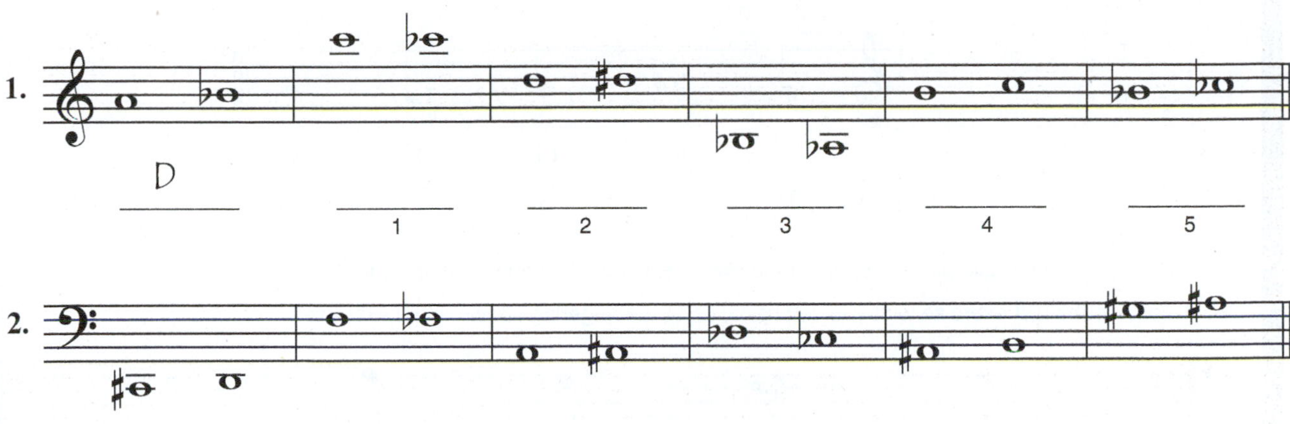

B. Write whole steps, diatonic half steps, or chromatic half steps *above* the given pitch.

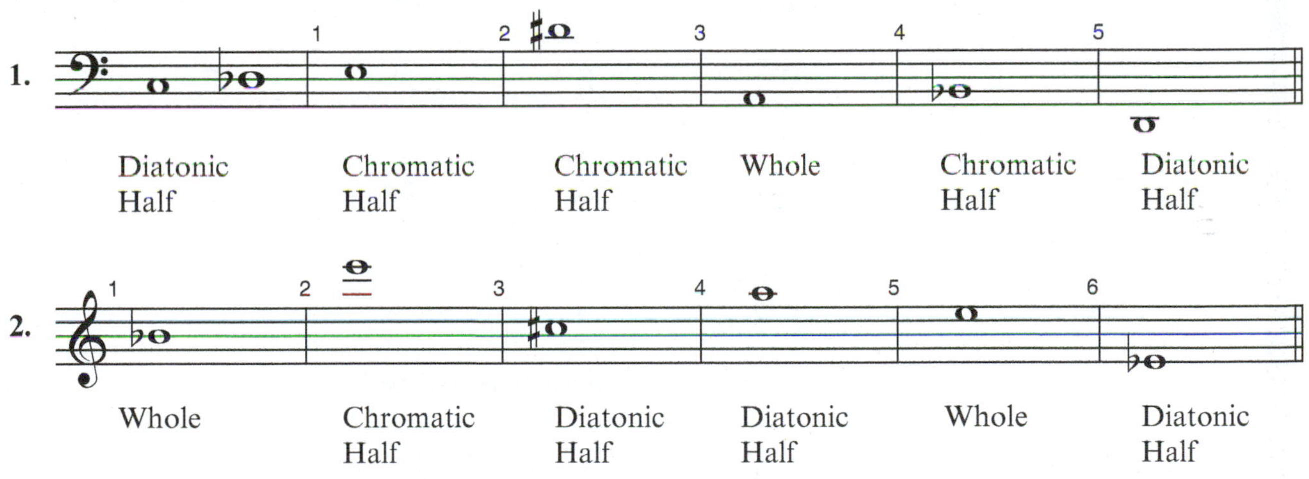

Complete the same exercise, now writing intervals *below* the given pitch.

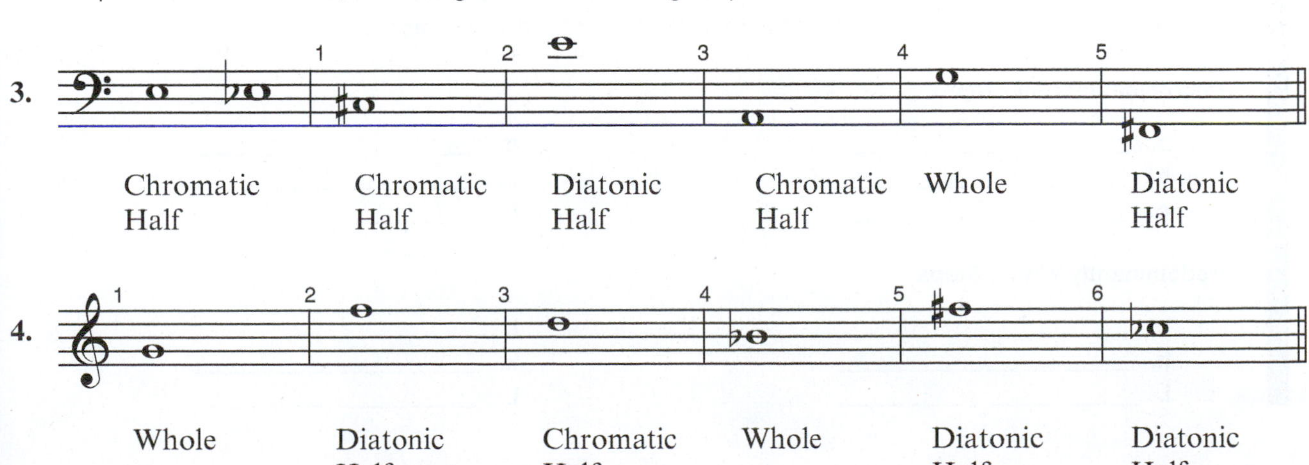

MUSICIANSHIP 3-2

I. Keyboard: Half and Whole Steps

A. Begin with one of the basic pitches (a white key on the keyboard). Using the third finger of your right hand play this pitch, then play one a half step higher (use the fingering 3–4). Return to the basic pitch (4–3), play a half step lower with your index finger (2), then end with the fingering 2–3. Practice this pattern slowly at first and increase speed until you are playing all five pitches in a single motion (3–4–3–2–3).

Move to another basic pitch and repeat the exercise. Gradually add whole steps into the same finger patterns.

B. Duplicate the last exercise with your left hand, using the fingering shown in the example.

Choose different octaves and a variety of white keys for beginning your exercise.

II. Ear Training: Hearing Half and Whole Steps

In this exercise, you will hear a series of ascending or descending intervals for identification. To provide immediate reinforcement, the answers are given in Appendix D. Identify the interval as whole or half step.

There are four intervals per line. This dictation material is available on the website.

Predominantly Half Steps

a. ______ ______ ______ ______
b. ______ ______ ______ ______
c. ______ ______ ______ ______

d. ______ ______ ______ ______
e. ______ ______ ______ ______
f. ______ ______ ______ ______

Predominantly Whole Steps

g. ______ ______ ______ ______
h. ______ ______ ______ ______
i. ______ ______ ______ ______

j. ______ ______ ______ ______
k. ______ ______ ______ ______
l. ______ ______ ______ ______

Whole and Half Steps

m. ______ ______ ______ ______
n. ______ ______ ______ ______
o. ______ ______ ______ ______
p. ______ ______ ______ ______
q. ______ ______ ______ ______
r. ______ ______ ______ ______

Directed Listening

Listen to each melody and identify the opening interval and last interval of each melody. The sound files are found on the website.

First Interval of the Melody	Last Interval of the Melody
Melody a: ______	______
Melody b: ______	______
Melody c: ______	______
Melody d: ______	______
Melody e: ______	______

Melodic Listening: Half Steps and Whole Steps

Sing the following melodies based on whole and half steps while the teacher plays. Listen for half steps versus whole steps as you sing.

Calligraphy

Notating Accidentals

Accidentals precede the note they affect and appear close to the notehead on the same line or space. In calligraphy, the sharp symbol is similar to the number sign (#), however, the cross bars of a sharp symbol slant up to the right. A flat sign is like a lowercase letter b. Of the many possible approaches to notating a natural sign, perhaps the simplest is a figure of two interlocking uppercase letters L (with the second of them upside down).

Sharp Flat Natural

When you write notes with accidentals, place the sharp, flat, or natural on the left side, proportional in size, and close to the notehead.

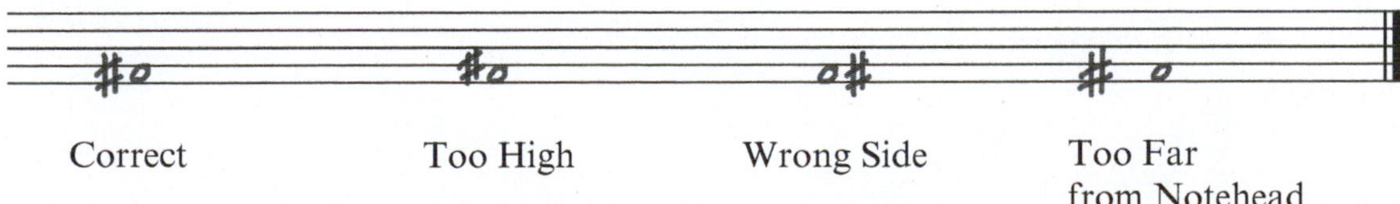

Correct Too High Wrong Side Too Far from Notehead

Remember, the accidental comes before the notehead when in notation. If we write it in words, we write it after the note name.

Complete Building Skills 3-1 on page 73

Name ________________________

Page may be removed

Building Skills 3-1

Whole and Half Steps

A. **Identify these intervals as whole step (W) or diatonic (DHS) or chromatic half step (CHS). Sit at the piano and play each note pair. Listen carefully to begin to hear the difference between the two.**

B. **These exercises include musical lines with pairs of pitches circled. Indicate whether the circled pitches are a whole step (W), half step (H), or *neither* (N). Listen to each musical example.**

W. A. Mozart, Sonata No. 12 in F Major, K. 332 adapted

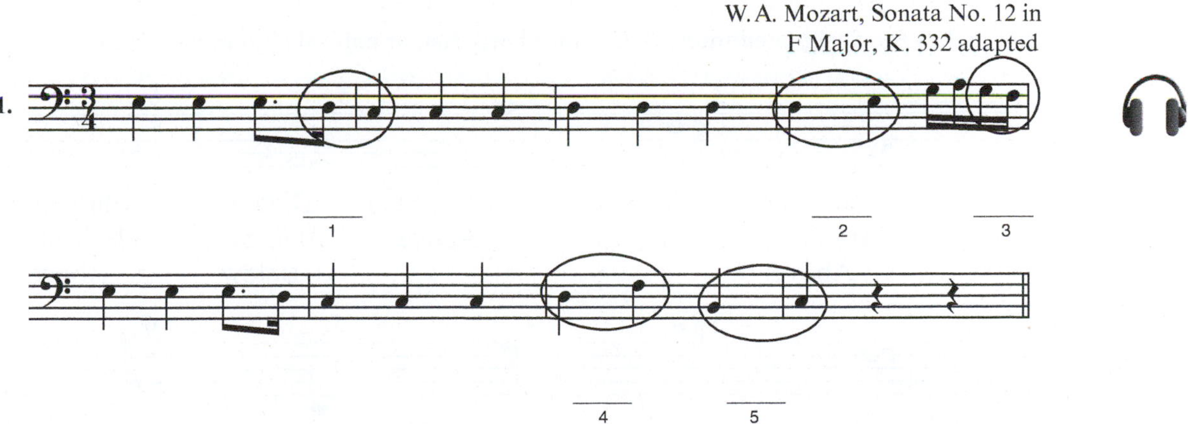

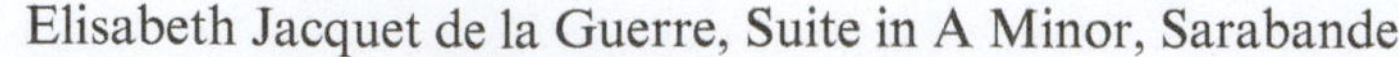

2.

___ 1 ___ 2

___ 3 ___ 4 ___ 5

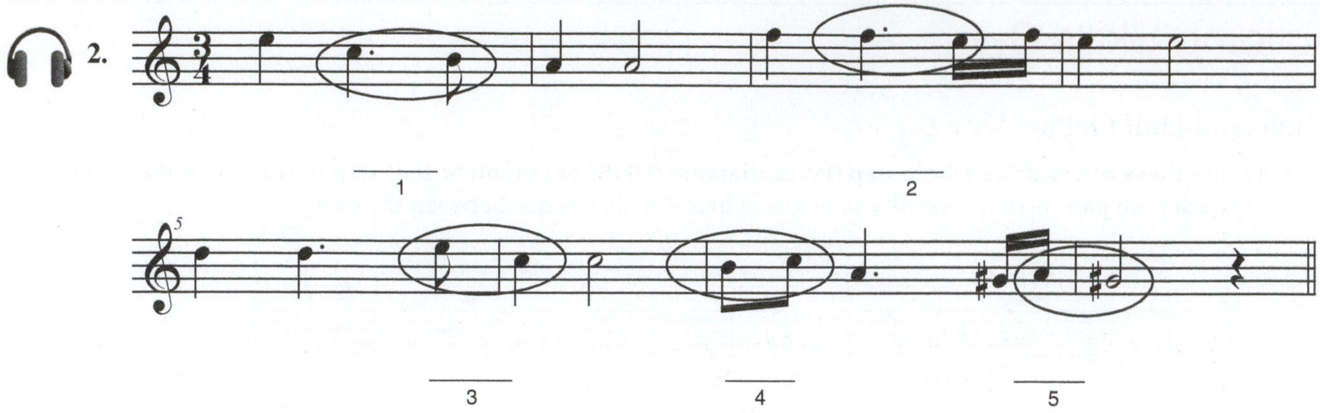

Japanese Traditional, "Cherry Blossoms"

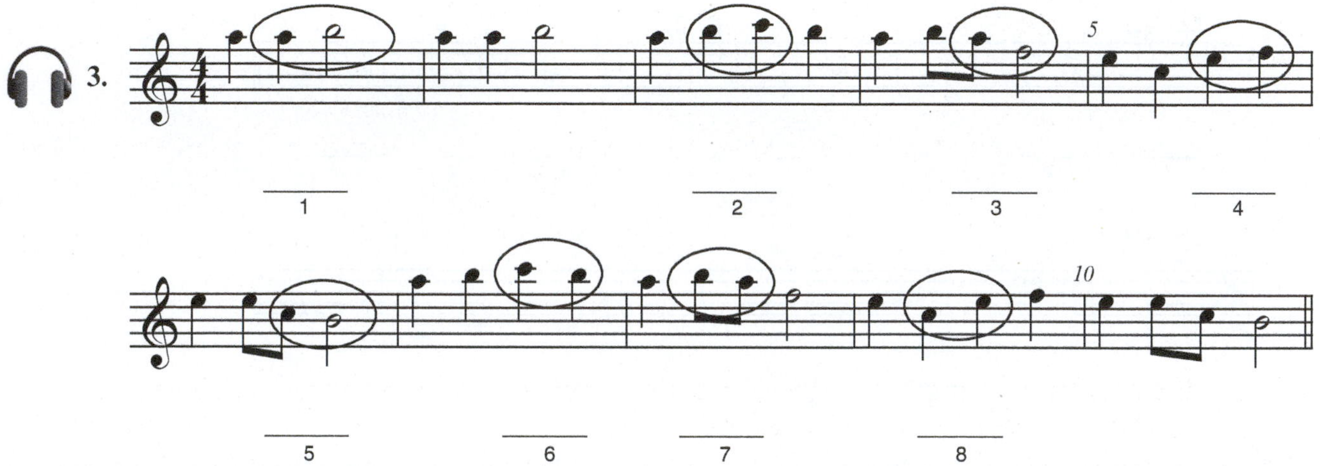

3.

___ 1 ___ 2 ___ 3 ___ 4

___ 5 ___ 6 ___ 7 ___ 8

C. **Add a pitch that makes the designated interval. Use the sharp, flat, or natural sign as necessary.**

Name ______________________

Page may be removed

Building Skills 3-2

Enharmonics and Octave Designation

A. **Write eighth notes that create the designated intervals. In some cases, more than one answer may be correct.**

B. **Using a half note, write pitches that are enharmonic equivalents with those given. In some cases, more than one answer is correct.**

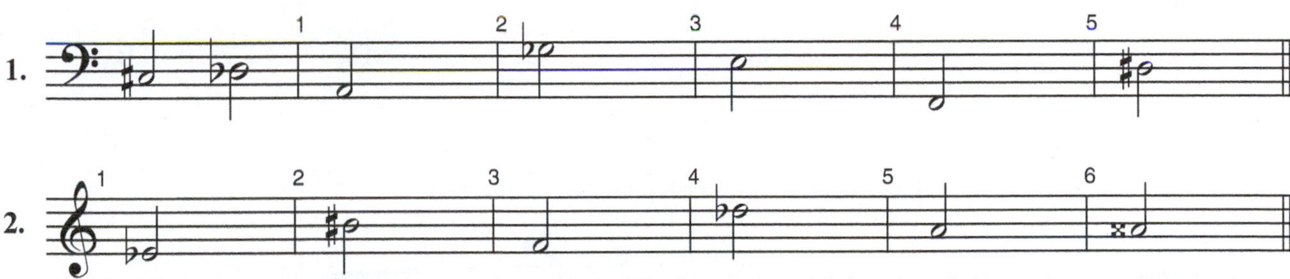

C. **Write the name and octave designation for each pitch. Because accidentals do not affect octave designation, only basic pitches are used in these lines.**

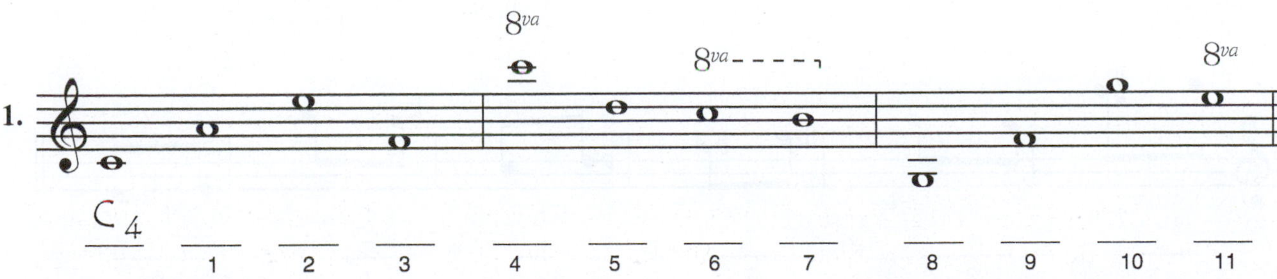

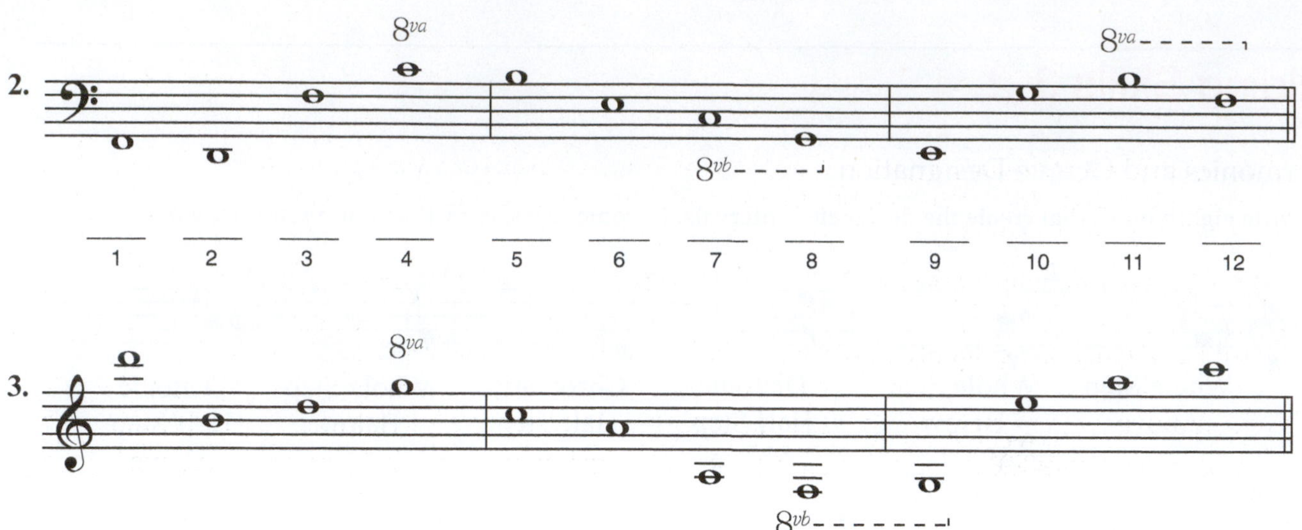

D. **Using the clef provided (and the octave sign as appropriate), notate the specified pitch. Use quarter notes.**

E. **Identify the given intervals as half step (H), whole step (W), or *neither* (N).**

Name ______________________

Page may be removed

Creative Projects • Chapter 3

A. **Compose two melodies that progress mainly by whole and half step. Follow the given rhythmic plan and the directions provided. Notice that some pitches are given. Identify your intervals as whole step (W), half step (H), or an interval of another type (N).**

Prepare to play your tune for the class or have your instructor perform it for you.

Ascend gradually using mainly whole and half steps with occasional repetition.

1.

Alternate mainly half and whole steps in a gradually descending pattern.

2.

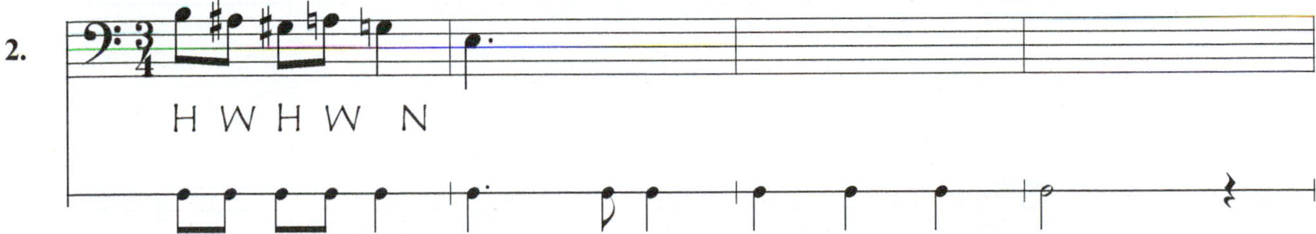

B. **Rewrite each of the two melodies as directed in the captions above the staff. Add accidentals as necessary. There may be two possibilities for notation.**

Name ____________________

Page may be removed

Analysis in Context 1 • Chapter 3

Rimsky-Korsakov wrote "Flight of the Bumblebee" for his opera *The Tale of Tsar Saltan*. Even though it was only an interlude between scenes in the opera, it is a very familiar work because of its frequent use in today's popular culture.

Study the score below and answer the questions that follow.

46
50
55
59
pp
63
67
71
75
f
78
dim.
82
8va
86
90

Name ______________________

Page may be removed

1. According to the time signature, how many beats are in each measure? What note value equals one beat?

2. What is the note name and octave designation of the first note in measure 1?

3. Label all the intervals in measures 1 and 2 (Diatonic half step (DHS), Chromatic half step (CHS), or Whole step (W)).

4. In what measure does the first clef change occur? What is the new clef?

5. Circle all the clef changes in the score.

6. Put a box around examples of an octave leap in the melody.

7. Most of the piece is comprised of half steps. Find two 4-measure long passages that are all whole steps.

8. Name two measures that include an example of a canceling accidental.

9. How many whole steps occur in measure 76? Where?

10. Considering the title of the piece, why do you think Rimsky-Korsakov chose to use the half step as the prevailing interval?

Chapter 4
Simple Meters

Essential Terms and Symbols

accent (>)
alla breve
anacrusis
beat subdivision
common time (𝄴)
cut time (𝄵)
duple meter
dynamic accent
meter
metric accent
natural metric accent
pickup
quadruple meter
simple beat division
simple meter
syncopation
tenuto (–)
triple meter

Western music moves primarily in measures of two, three, or four beats. Although intricate groupings of a dozen or more beats are common in some cultures (India and Indonesia, for example), traditional Western musicians have been content with only a few simple patterns. In the late nineteenth century, influences from other cultures began to broaden the possibilities, but most music heard today is conservative rhythmically.

Regardless of the number of beats in a measure, all beats are *not* equal in importance. The word "not" was italicized in the last sentence so you would give it more stress when reading. When beats in music are emphasized or stressed it is called an accent. An **accent** is a musical stress.

Metric Accent

Music in the West is based on recurring patterns of strong and weak beats called **meter**. Accents that create different meters are called **metric accents**. Further, meters are classified as either *simple* or *compound*. The beat in a **simple meter** is represented by a simple (undotted) value such as the quarter note. Simple meter is further defined by the even subdivision of the beat into two parts.

You can feel the effect of meter by singing the beat on a single pitch or counting aloud with a steady pulse. Count "one-two" four times, for example. Speak more loudly or sharply on "one" than on "two." This exercise creates the effect of a meter with one strong and one weak beat in each measure.

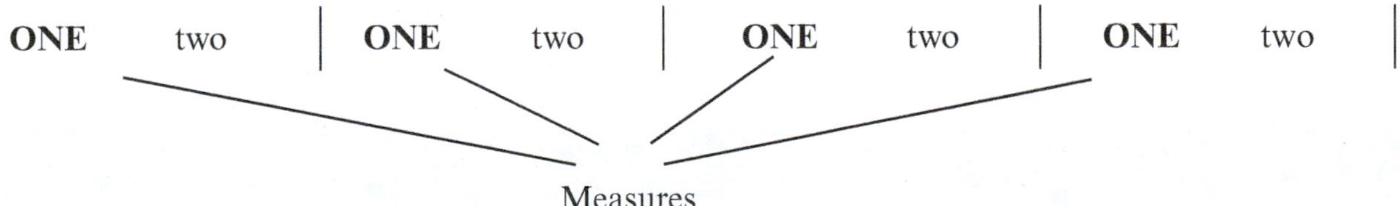

Next, create a meter with a three-beat pattern: strong-weak-weak. Again, say or sing at least four of these groups. Stress the metric accent on the first beat of each measure.

ONE two three | **ONE** two three | **ONE** two three | **ONE** two three ||

"You and Me" by Jason Wade and Jude Cole has a three-beat, strong-weak-weak pattern.

"You and Me"
Words and Music by
JASON WADE and JUDE COLE

Triple Meter

The metric pattern in the previous example is known as **triple meter**. As we discussed, any note value can represent one beat. The two lines that follow, with quarter-note and half-note beats, respectively, sound the same.

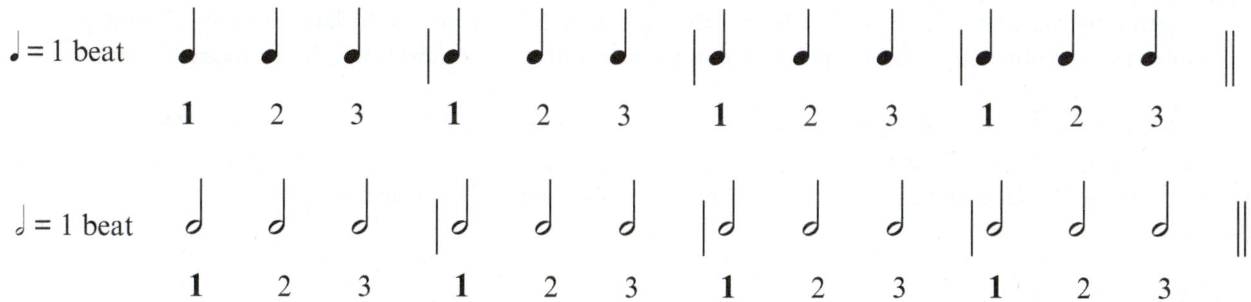

ANACRUSIS. Many melodies, like "You and Me," begin with a strong beat; others however, start with an incomplete measure called an **anacrusis** (or **pickup**). You may know the triple-meter song "The Star Spangled Banner?" Because the first syllable of text ("oh") is less important than the second syllable ("Say"), the musical setting begins with an unaccented beat. The song begins not with beat 1, but with beat 3.[1] The triple-meter sequence starts on the word "Say." When a composition begins with an anacrusis, the final measure is also incomplete—containing only the beats missing from the first measure. In other words, the value of the anacrusis is subtracted from the last measure. Because the song begins on beat 3, the last measure contains only beats 1 and 2.

Tap along as you listen or sing the tune, stressing the first beat of every measure.

[1]Musicians make a distinction between "song," a term that designates music with text, and other references to "work," "composition," "piece," "movement," and so on, that may or may not be "songs."

Using a half-note beat, only the appearance of the notation is different; a performance would sound the same.

Listen to "The Star Spangled Banner" two times. On the first playing, follow the notation with the quarter-note beat; on the second, read the half-note beat score. In both cases, sing along with the recording and feel the triple meter.

Duple Meter

In addition to a triple metric plan, composers often use a strong-weak or **duple meter** pattern. In both meters in the next example, the quarter note is the beat. The first beat of each measure is accented. Tap each rhythm pattern and accent the first beat of every measure.

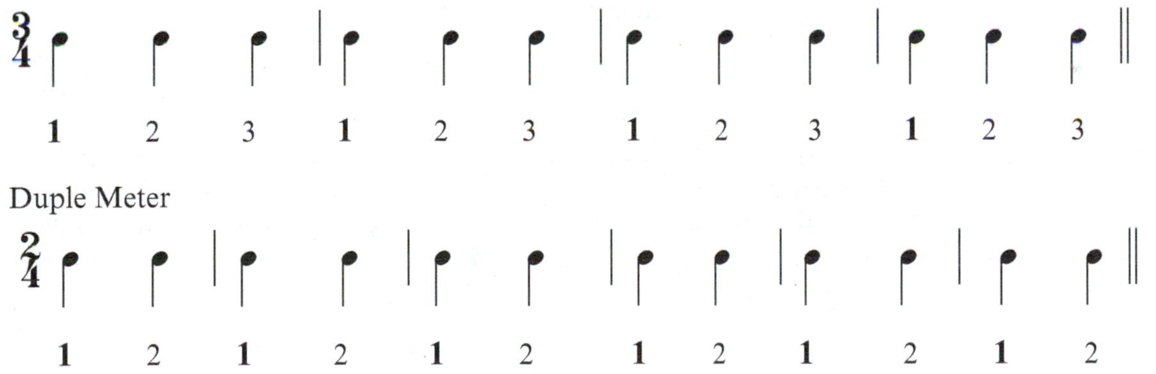

Another familiar melody is the opening to the Rondo Alla Turca by Wolfgang Amadeus Mozart. The melody is written in duple meter and the original composition has a quarter note beat. Feel the accents of duple meter as you sing along with the next two examples.

Mozart, Sonata No.11, K.331, Mvt. III, 'Rondo Alla Turca'

Mozart, Sonata No.11, K.331, Mvt. III, 'Rondo Alla Turca'

Quadruple Meter

A **quadruple meter** has four beats in each measure. Differences exist, however, between two measures (four beats) in a duple meter and one measure of quadruple meter (also with four beats). In quadruple meter, the first beat is accented and the third beat is accented, but *less so* than the first.

We will use two symbols to illustrate this emphasis. The symbol > is a **dynamic accent** and indicates a significant stress; another symbol, called **tenuto (–)** (lengthening), emphasizes the lesser accent.

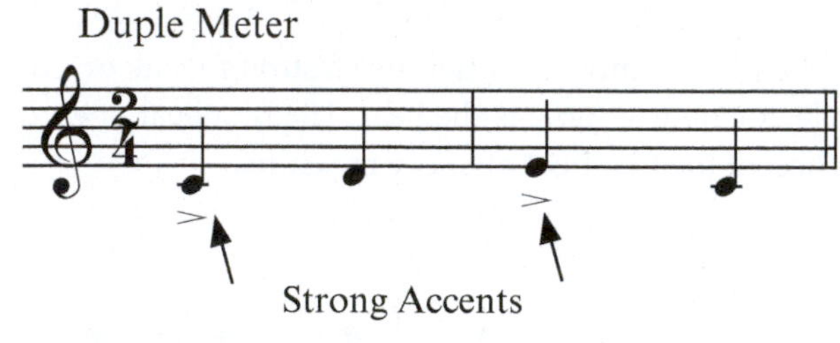

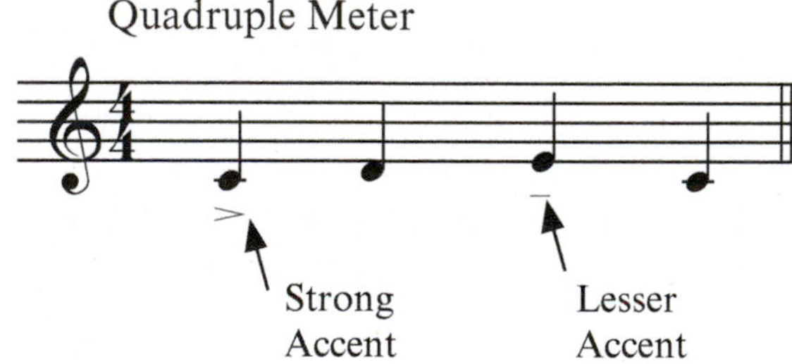

Equivalent Meters

The song "Twinkle, Twinkle, Little Star" might be written in either duple or quadruple meter. Sing the melody both ways, performing the accents carefully to differentiate between the two versions. Listen to the audio file on the website at least twice. When you listen the first time, follow the duple-meter score in the first example. Accents occur every other beat. On the second playing, read the quadruple-meter notation and feel the stronger and lesser accents on beats one and three.

Duple Meter

Quadruple Meter

Rest Notation

When an entire measure is silent, composers and arrangers use the whole rest—regardless of the actual number of beats in the measure. If the meter is duple with quarter-note beats, for example, the whole rest indicates a measure of silence. The same is true for triple meter. Using a half rest in duple meter or a dotted half rest in triple meter (assuming the quarter-note beat) is incorrect.

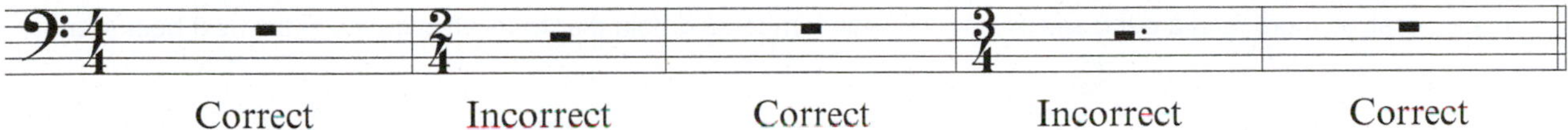

In a measure of quadruple meter with a quarter-note beat, observe correct and incorrect arrangements of quarter rests.

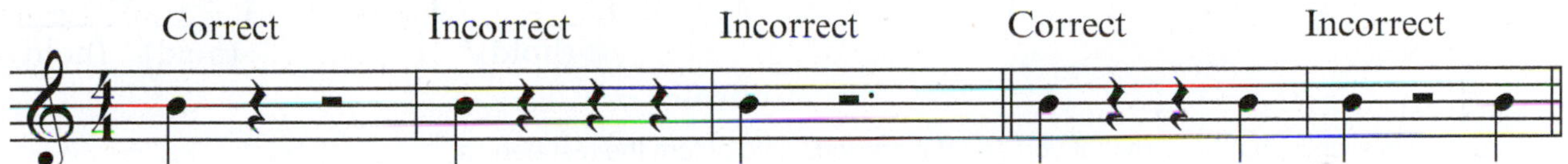

While performers could probably read the "incorrect" choices in the last example, the more accurate notation takes into account the division of the measure into two parts.

For class discussion or assignment: please do not remove these pages

REVIEW SET

Meter

A. These examples provide the beat value but do not include the time signature. Identify the meter (duple, triple, or quadruple) in the blank on the right.

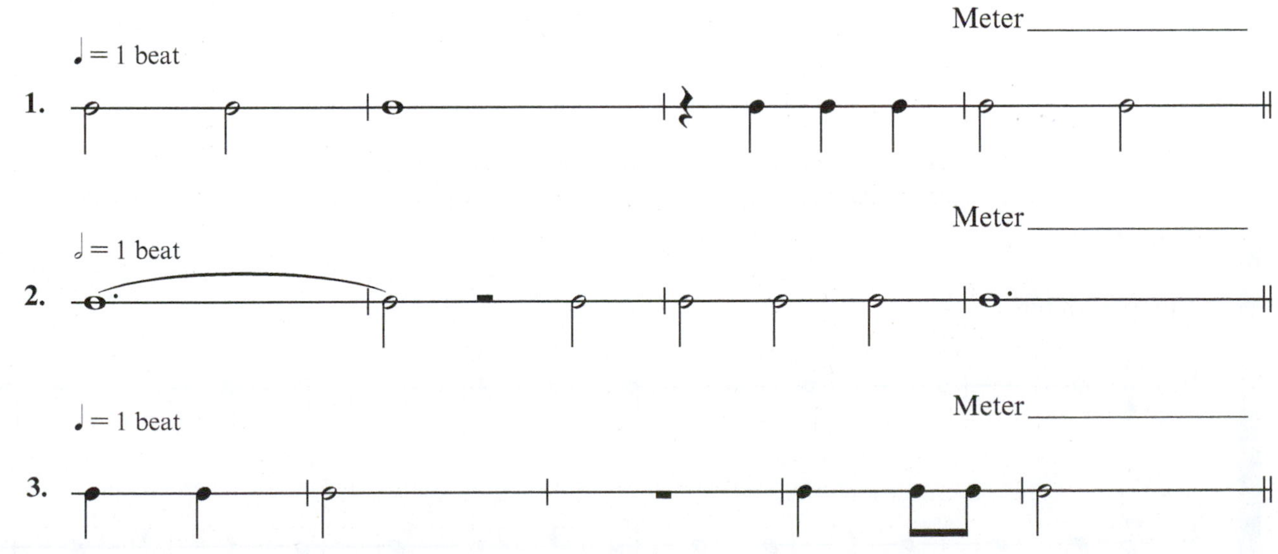

B. Identify the appropriate time signature for each of the meters shown in the last example.

1. ________ 2. ________ 3. ________

TRICKS OF THE TRADE

Using Counting Syllables

The system of counting syllables presented in this text represents a variety of methods. For now, we will concentrate on the counting system that uses numbers to indicate beats in the measure. Say or sing the beat numbers as shown:

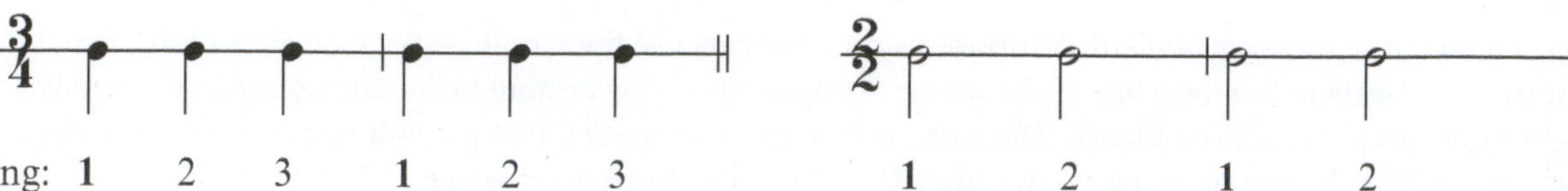

If a note receives more than a beat, say or sing the beat number and hold that tone while counting the next beat silently.

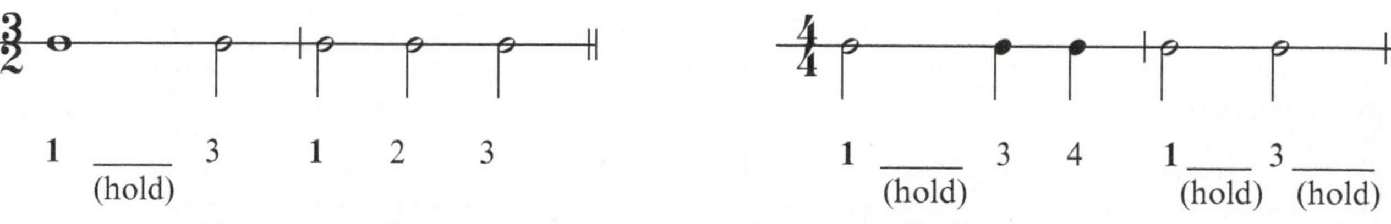

Count rests silently, but be sure that you end the previous note before the rest begins.

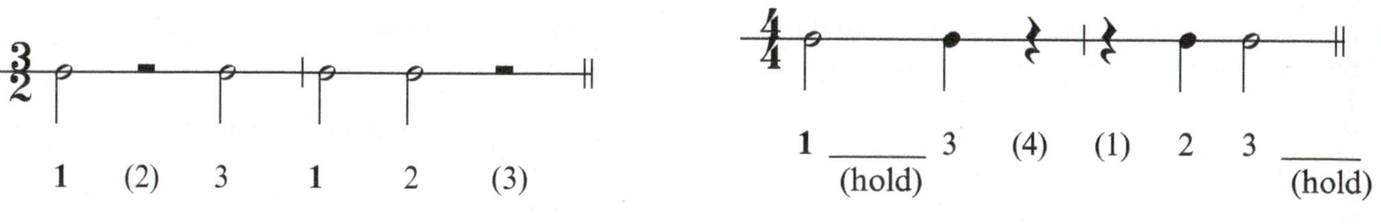

MUSICIANSHIP 4-1

Rhythmic Reading: Duple, Triple, and Quadruple Meters

These eight-measure passages are for performing individually or in class. First, review *Tricks of the Trade: Using Counting Syllables*. Sing the examples or play them on an instrument. Clapping or tapping is not as useful because longer tones cannot be sustained.

Duple Meter

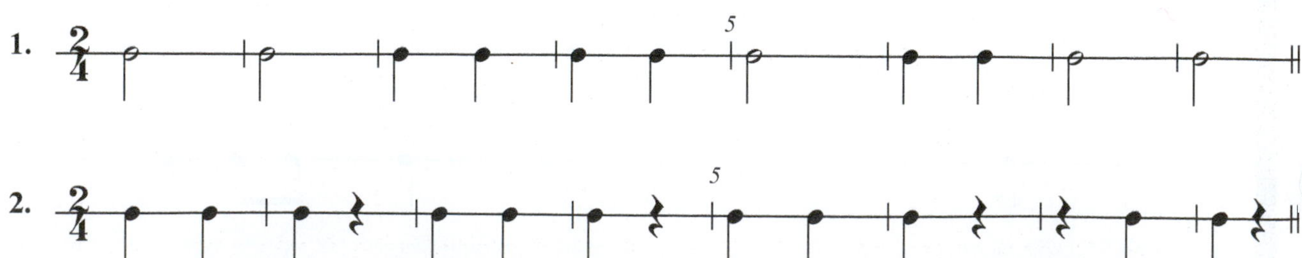

3. 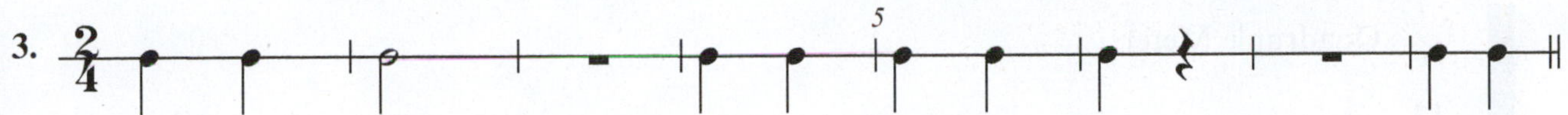

4.

5.

6.

Triple Meter

7.

8.

9.

10.

11.

12.

Quadruple Meter

13.

14.

15.

16.

17.

18.

Complete Building Skills 4-1 on page 103

Beat Division and Subdivision

Notes and rests of one, two, three, and four beats combined with notes of smaller values provide substantial rhythmic variety. **Simple beat division** means that the beat divides into two smaller, but equal, parts. A quarter-note beat, for example, divides into two eighth notes. The quarter note receives one beat; the two eighth notes each receive one-half beat.

The melody from the first movement of Mozart's *Eine Kleine Nachtmusik* has both beat and divided-beat notation. The first pitch receives a full beat; the first two pitches in the second measure, however, share a divided beat.

Mozart. Eine Kleine Nachtmusik, K. 525, Allegro

If the half note is the beat, the simple division is two quarter notes.

Eine Kleine Nachtmusik could also be written using a half-note beat.

Mozart, Eine Kleine Nachtmusik, K. 525, Allegro

Listen to *Eine Kleine Nachtmusik* several times. First, just sing along and feel the quadruple meter. Next, tap the beat as you listen and be conscious of the divided beats in nearly every measure. Finally, tap the beat division (eighth notes) while you sing from the printed score.

Mozart. Eine Kleine Nachtmusik, K. 525, Allegro

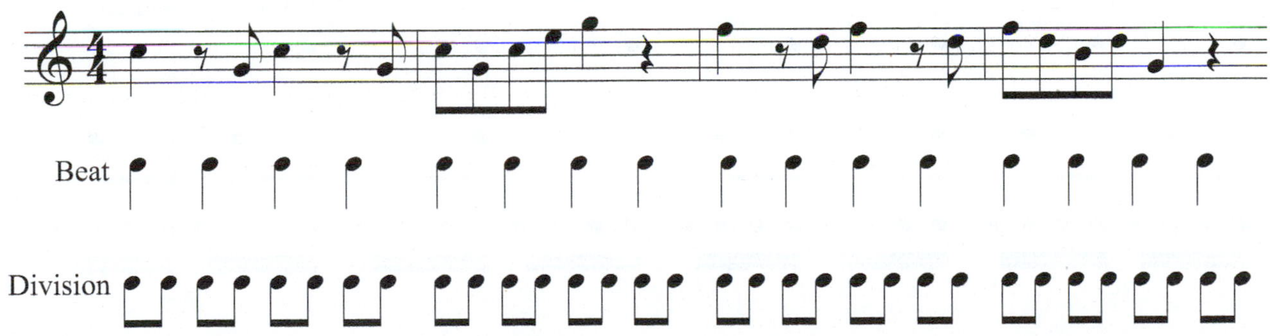

BEAT SUBDIVISION. Composers use values smaller than the division through **beat subdivision**—a sectioning of the beat into four equal parts. If the half note is the beat, for example, the division is the quarter note; the subdivision is the eighth note.

Beat Division Subdivision

The same principle applies when the quarter note receives the beat. Two eighth notes represent the division, and four sixteenth notes represent the subdivision.

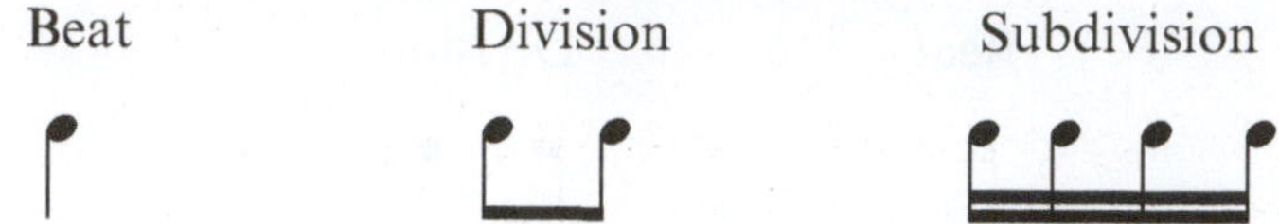

You are already familiar with the melody from the "The Stars and Stripes Forever" march by John Phillip Sousa. This melody includes an interesting mix of the beat, division, and subdivision. The meter is duple; in the passage that follows, the quarter note receives one beat.

Follow the score while listening to a performance. When you hear the song for the first time, tap or sing the beat (quarter note). Listen again and sing or tap the beat division (eighth notes). Finally, listen a third time and tap the beat subdivision (four sixteenth notes to each beat).

John Philips Sousa, "Stars and Stripes Forever"

Beat

Division

Subdivision

5

9

For class discussion or assignment: please do not remove these pages

REVIEW SET
Beat Division and Subdivision

A. Some of these measures are incomplete. Where necessary, add *one note* at the end of the measure. Some measures are complete even though they include blank spaces.

1. 

2. 

3. 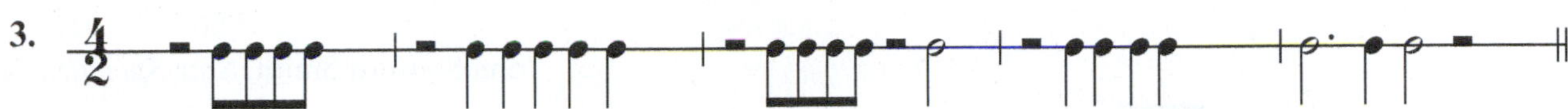

Add one rest as necessary to the incomplete measures in these two lines.

4. 

5. 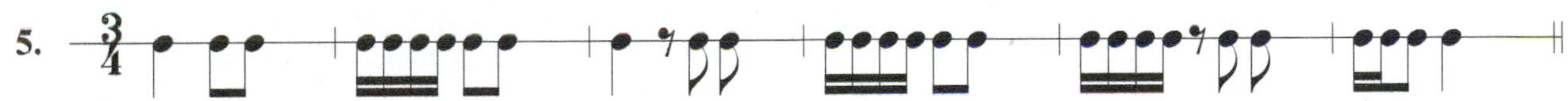

B. For each time signature given, provide the metric pattern (duple, triple, or quadruple) as well as the note receiving the beat, the beat division, and the subdivision. Write a word in the first blank, one note in the second blank, two notes in the third, and four notes in the fourth blank.

	Metric Pattern	Beat	Division	Subdivision
Example 3/4	Triple	♩	♫	♬♬
1. 2/2				
2. 4/4				
3. 3/2				

Meters with an Eighth-Note Beat

While uncommon in jazz and popular styles, meters with an eighth-note beat appear frequently in traditional music literature. If the eighth note receives one beat, a quarter note has the value of two beats; the sixteenth note receives one-half beat.

Study this adapted notation of "The Star Spangled Banner" using an eighth-note beat (compare with page 84). The time signature is $\frac{3}{8}$, the accent pattern is triple, and the eighth note receives one beat.

The notation of "Eine Kleine Nachtmusik" with quarter- and half-note beats appears on page 90. Compare the notation when an eighth-note beat is employed. The eighth note receives the beat; the sixteenth note receives half a beat.

Alla Breve and Common Time

Symbols may be used to represent meters in the time signature. The meter $\frac{2}{2}$, for example, is duple with a half-note beat. Composers often substitute the symbol ¢, termed ***alla breve*** (and less formally, **cut time**), for $\frac{2}{2}$. The letter C, in popular reference to **common time**, may be substituted for $\frac{4}{4}$.

A Step Further

Conducting

Traditional conducting patterns are helpful for enhancing coordination and ensuring accuracy of performance. Conduct with your right hand (whether you are right- or left-handed) and keep the beat in front of your body. The first beat of any complete metric pattern is downward; other motions depend on the accent pattern. A conductor conveys musical style such as the difference between a march and a lullaby through their arm motion (rigid or smooth, for example). Study the conducting patterns shown here for complete measures of duple, triple, and quadruple meter.

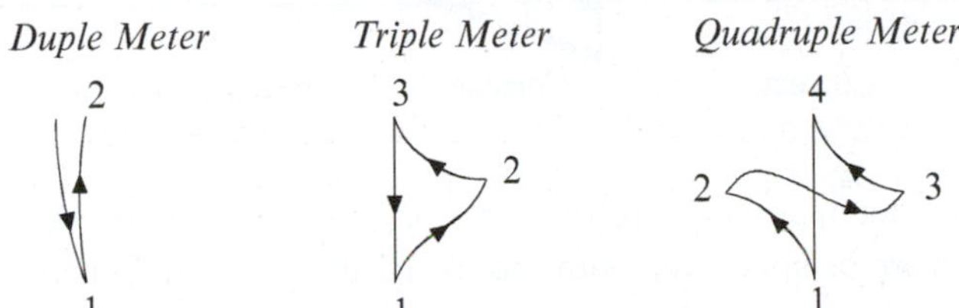

Finally, be aware that ensemble members discern the tempo through the conductor's preparatory beat or beats (the anacrusis). This movement precedes the actual first note of music, but at the intended tempo. If a passage is in $\frac{3}{4}$, for example, the conductor's preparatory motion will be upward—beat 3. In $\frac{4}{4}$ with a quarter-note anacrusis, the conductor would provide the motion for beat 3 (to the right); the performers enter on beat 4 (upward).

For class discussion or assignment: please do not remove these pages

REVIEW SET

Time Signatures

A. For each time signature shown, write a word in the first blank that identifies the accent pattern (duple, triple, or quadruple meter); in the second blank, write the note that will receive one beat.

		Accent Pattern	Beat			Accent Pattern	Beat
Example:	$\frac{3}{4}$	Triple	♩	4.	$\frac{4}{8}$	______	______
1.	$\frac{4}{2}$	______	______	5.	$\frac{3}{2}$	______	______
2.	$\frac{3}{8}$	______	______	6.	$\frac{2}{2}$	______	______
3.	$\frac{2}{4}$	______	______	7.	$\frac{4}{4}$	______	______

B. Write a time signature that corresponds to the given meter and unit of beat.

1. ______ triple meter eighth-note beat
2. ______ duple meter quarter-note beat
3. ______ quadruple meter half-note beat
4. ______ duple meter half-note beat
5. ______ quadruple meter eighth-note beat
6. ______ duple meter eighth-note beat
7. ______ triple meter quarter-note beat
8. ______ triple meter half-note beat

Calligraphy

Beaming

The purpose of beaming is to identify beat groups. Place beams about an octave above or below the note heads and make them thicker than stems (see page 33 for information on the proper placement of stems). If the notes ascend or descend, slant the beam accordingly.

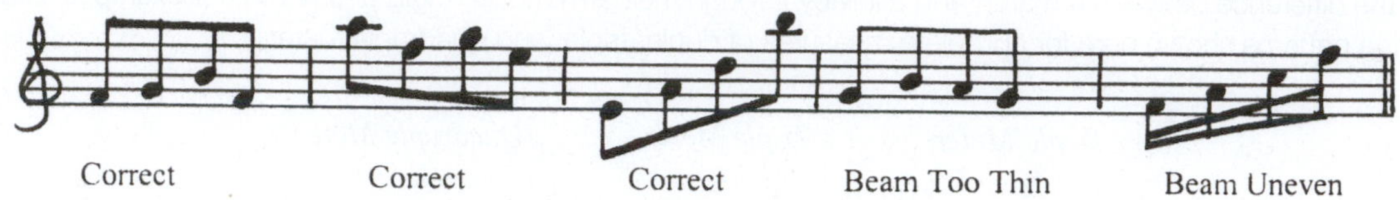

In simple meters with a quarter-note beat, groups of two eighth and four sixteenth notes are commonly beamed together. Likewise, beat groups are beamed even with mixed eighth- and sixteenth-note patterns. If a beam does not begin on the beat, however, beaming may not be appropriate.

Groups with fewer than one beat are usually not beamed unless a dotted note precedes or follows the group.

Occasionally in a meter like $\frac{3}{4}$, the entire measure may be beamed—again, depending on the tempo and style of the music.

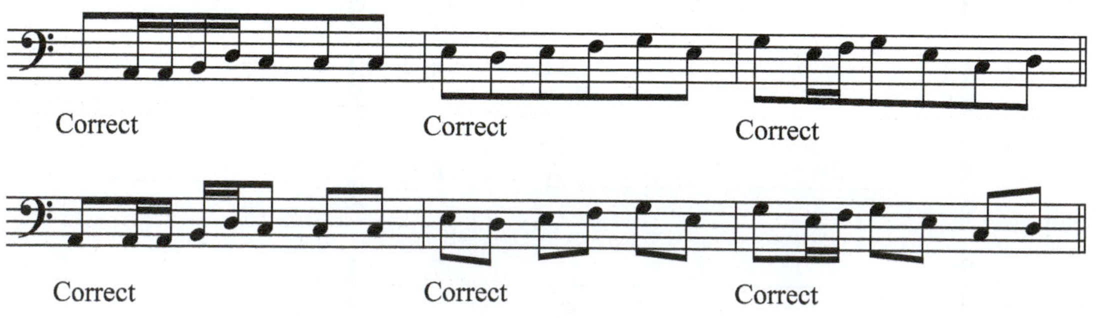

TRICKS OF THE TRADE

Counting Syllables

Whether your instrument is piano, guitar, or flute, singing rhythms is a basic skill. On page 90 we discussed performance of beat and multiple-beat passages. In this section we've provided three different methods of counting the beat division and subdivision shown in the following examples. Practice the various methods—your instructor may have a preference for a particular approach. Remember to count rests or ties silently.

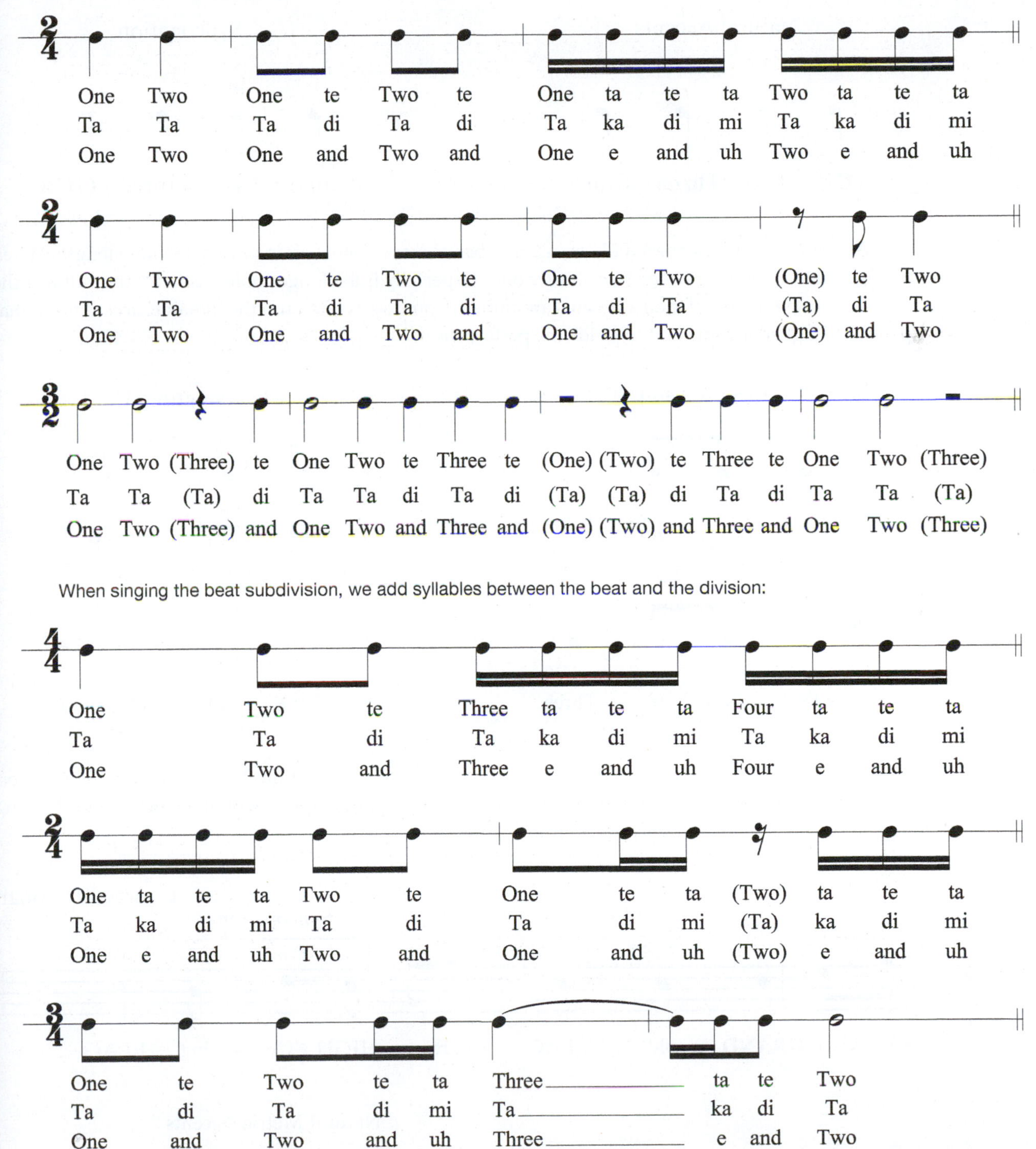

Syncopation

The accent pattern and manner of beat division form only a rough outline of rhythmic structure. To make music, composers must provide variety within this system. One means of varying metric structure is with **syncopation**—the intentional realignment of accents.

In quadruple simple meter, there is a strong accent on the first beat, and a lesser accent on the third beat. These are the **natural metric accents**. If the emphasis is suddenly shifted to the second or fourth beats, however, the effect is animated.

We can create a syncopated effect in a number of ways. One way is to vary the note length. When a longer note appears between two shorter ones (especially if the longer note has twice the value of the shorter ones), the natural metric accents are shifted. Composers often use the dynamic accent to dramatize the realigned accents and to guide the performer.

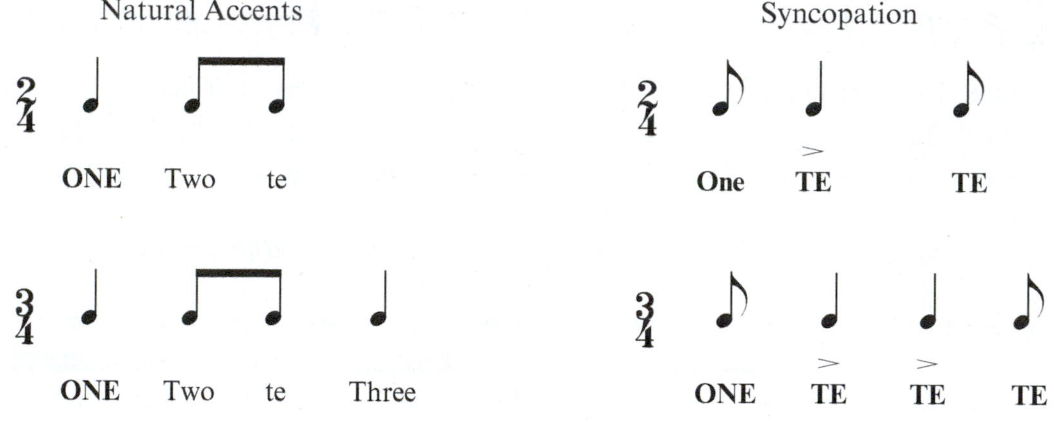

The song "You're a Grand Old Flag" includes a typical syncopation figure. Listen to the two versions of this tune on the website. In the first version, syncopation appears on the words "high FLY-ing flag." The second version uses only natural accents.

Complete Building Skills 4-2 on page 105

MUSICIANSHIP 4-2

I. Rhythmic Reading: Beat, Division, and Subdivision

Using different tempos, perform the passages that follow. Conduct and use an appropriate counting method as demonstrated in *Tricks of the Trade: Counting Syllables* on page 97

9.
10.
11.
12.
Quadruple Meter
13.
One Two and Three Four One Two and Three Four and One Two and Three Four and
One Two te Three Four One Two te Three Four te One Two te Three Four te
Ta Ta di Ta Ta Ta Ta di Ta Ta di Ta Ta di Ta Ta di
One Two Three (Four) (One) Two and Three Four (One) Two and Three Four
One Two Three (Four) (One) Two te Three Four (One) Two te Three Four
Ta Ta Ta (Ta) (Ta) Ta di Ta Ta (Ta) Ta di Ta Ta
(One) Two and Three Four and One Two Three (Four)
(One) Two te Three Four te One Two Three (Four)
(Ta) Ta di Ta Ta di Ta Ta Ta (Ta)
14.
15.
16.

17.

18. 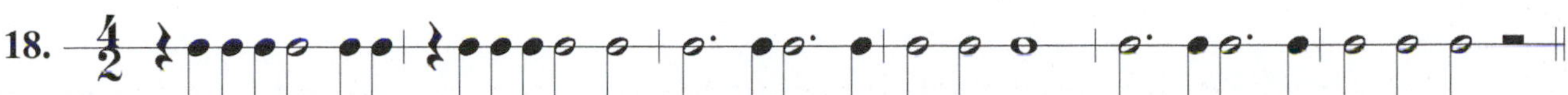

II. Ear Training: Meter Identification

A. Your instructor will play a number of phrases in simple meters (also available on the text website). Listen to each melody and identify the meter as "duple" or "triple." For our present purposes, consider duple and quadruple meters to be equivalent. The answers appear in Appendix D of the text.

a. ______________ **e.** ______________
b. ______________ **f.** ______________
c. ______________ **g.** ______________
d. ______________ **h.** ______________

B. Sing the following tunes to yourself. First, determine whether or not the melody begins with an anacrusis (the first text syllable may be useful). Check the appropriate box (yes or no). Next, identify the meter (duple or triple) as you did in the last problem and write this word in the second blank. See Appendix D for the answers.

	Anacrusis		Meter
	yes	*no*	
1. "The Star-Spangled Banner"	_____	_____	____________
2. "Mary Had a Little Lamb"	_____	_____	____________
3. "Amazing Grace"	_____	_____	____________
4. "Yankee Doodle"	_____	_____	____________
5. "The Marine's Hymn"	_____	_____	____________
6. "America"	_____	_____	____________
7. "Happy Birthday to You"	_____	_____	____________
8. "London Bridge"	_____	_____	____________

Name ______________________

Page may be removed

Building Skills 4-1

Duple, Triple, and Quadruple Meters

A. Observe the given time signature and add barlines. Each line is complete as written—none includes an anacrusis.

1. 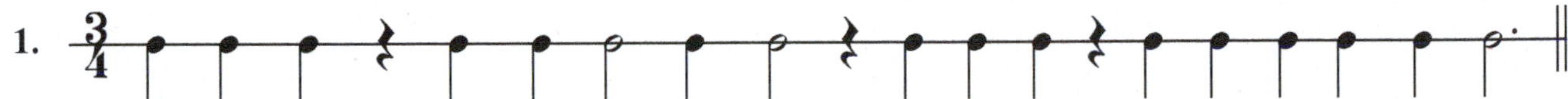

2. 

3. 

4. 

5. 

6. 

B. These examples are from music literature. Add barlines.

G. F. Handel, *Water Music (Minuet)*

1. 

Jean Sibelius, *King Christian Suite*

2. 

C. **For the notes and rests given, provide the value in beats or fractions of beats.**

1. 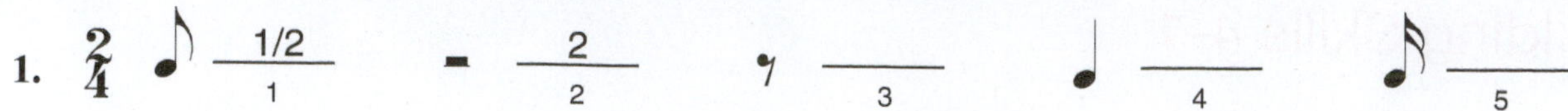

2. ______ 1 ______ 2 ______ 3 ______ 4 ______ 5

3. ______ 1 ______ 2 ______ 3 ______ 4 ______ 5

4. ______ 1 ______ 2 ______ 3 ______ 4 ______ 5

5. ______ 1 ______ 2 ______ 3 ______ 4 ______ 5

D. **Continue the lower voice as an accompaniment to the upper part. Align beats vertically as in the given measures. In your added voice, use notes and rests that are a *beat or more* in duration. Prepare to perform your duet for the class either as a two-hand exercise, or with a classmate performing it with you.**

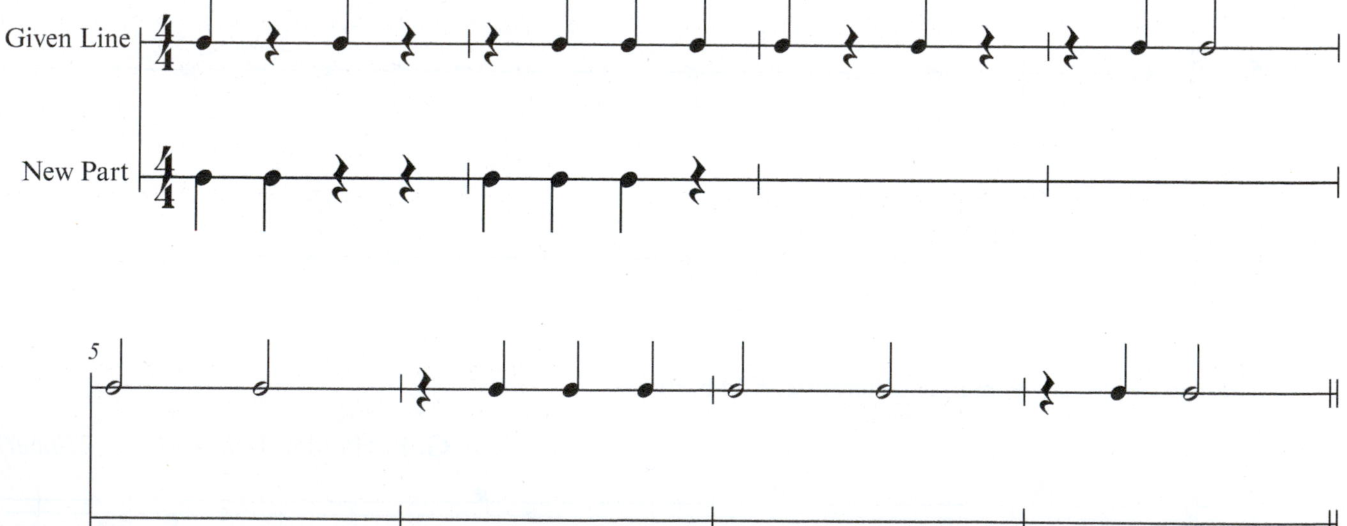

Name ________________________

Page may be removed

Building Skills 4-2

Simple Meters

A. **Add barlines. If a line begins with an anacrusis, both the first and last barlines are given. Tap and say the rhythm syllables while keeping a steady tempo.**

1. 

2. 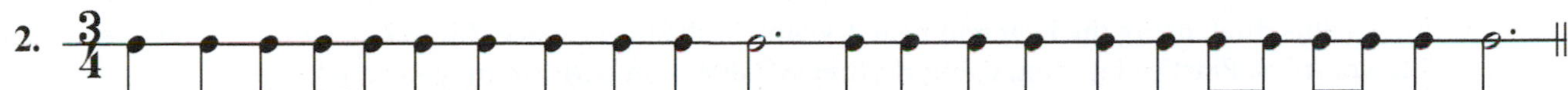

3. 

4. 

5. 

6. 

7. 

8. 

B. **These passages are from music literature. Add barlines as in the previous exercise.**

César Cui, *The Statue at Czarskoe-Selo*

1. 

Giacomo Puccini, *Manon Lescaut*

2. 

Folk Song, "Shoo Fly, Don't Bother Me"

3. 

C. **Continue this duet, using the beat and beat division in the lower voice. Align beats carefully between upper and lower lines. Practice tapping, using rhythm syllables and performing your duet.**

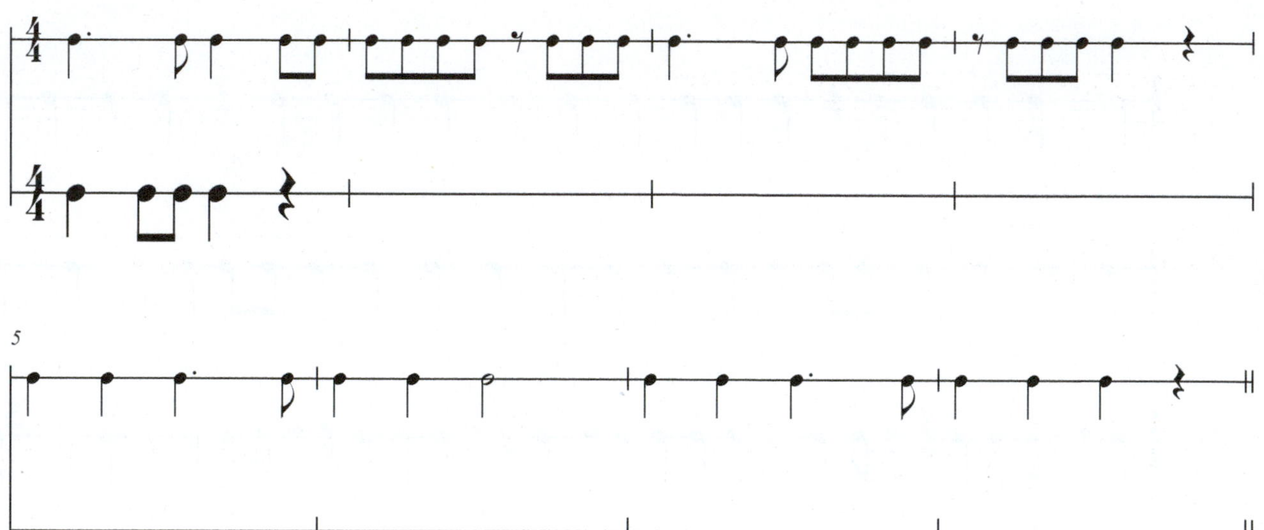

Name ____________________

Page may be removed

Creative Projects Chapter 4

A. **These exercises involve transcription (see page 86) from one meter into an equivalent meter. The accent pattern will remain unchanged, but for the transcription, you will need to halve or double the note values.**

B. **Create rhythmic settings for the poem "Tyger, Tyger" by William Blake. The duple-meter version has been started for you and the slashes in the text indicate recommended barlines. Prepare to perform your composition for the class by saying the text in tempo to the rhythm patterns you choose.**

Duple Meter

Ty-ger/Ty-ger/burn-ing/bright–;/
In the/fo-rests/of the/night-/
What im-/mor-tal/hand or/eye/
Could frame/thy fear-/ful sym-/me-try//

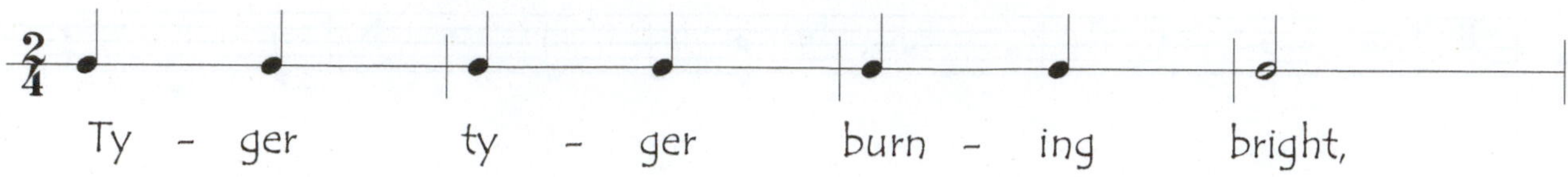

Triple Meter

Using the same poem, "Tyger, Tyger," rewrite the line using triple meter. The first line has been given to you.

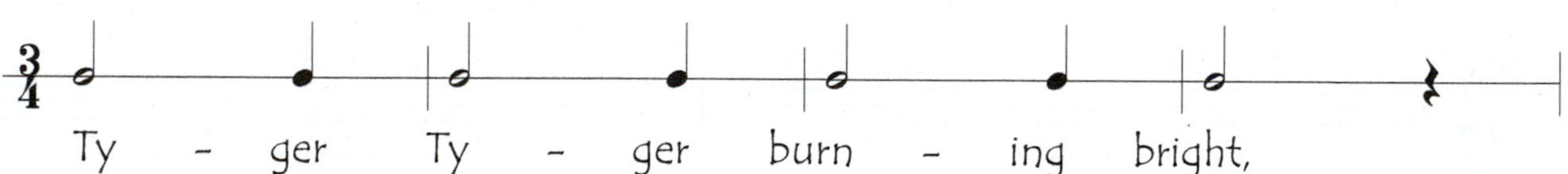

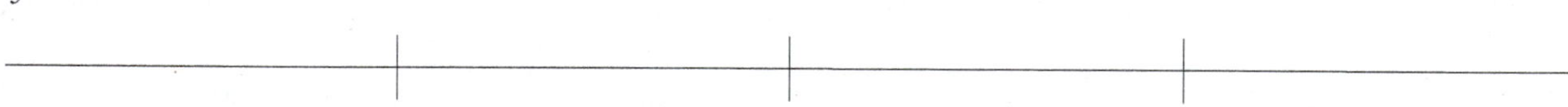

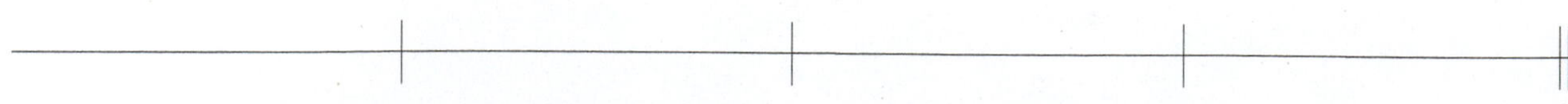

Name ____________________

Page may be removed

Analysis in Context • Chapter 4

George Frideric Handel's composition, *The Water Music Suite I,* is a collection of short movements for small orchestra written at the request of King George I of England. Some of the work was originally intended for outdoor performance, and the work was first performed on a Royal Cruise on the River Thames in 1717.

Use the score below to answer the questions that follow.

"Horn Pipe" from *Water Music Suite I,* HWV 348 No.9
George Friderick Handel

1. What is the time signature?
2. Is this movement in duple, triple, or quadruple meter?
3. What note value gets the beat in this time signature?
4. What note values represent the division and the subdivision of the beat?
5. Write in the counting syllables below the violin I/oboe part on the score. (When finished, count the rhythm syllables out loud while you listen to the recording.)
6. Write in the counting syllables below the violoncello (cello) part. (Listen to the audio file on the website and say the rhythm syllables out loud.)
7. Is the violoncello part composed mostly of the beat, the division of the beat, or the subdivision of the beat?
8. What does the term syncopation mean?
9. In what measure do you find an example of syncopation?
10. Name two equivalent time signatures and identify their beat values.

Chapter 5
Major Scales and Keys

Essential Terms and Symbols

caret symbol (ˆ)
cautionary accidental
circle of fifths
courtesy accidental
dominant
fermata (𝄐)
fifth
key
key signature
melody
scale
scale degree
subdominant
supertonic
tonality
tonic
transposition

Composers in virtually all parts of the world organize music so that the listener can follow transformations of a pattern of pitches throughout the course of a work. A **melody** is a group of pitches, often with a clear rhythmic identity, that the listener hears as complete. A **scale** is the melodic system on which a melody is based. We might also think of a scale as the table of contents for a melody. Outside the Western world, there are many different scales—some with intervals smaller than a half step. In the traditional system of Western music, however, scales fall into one of only two categories: major or minor. Major scales and keys will be discussed in this chapter; minor scales and keys will be covered in Chapter 8.

The Major Scale

Scales are distinguished by the number of pitches and the intervals found between successive pitches. Traditional Western scales, for example, have seven different pitches: five whole steps and two half steps in various arrangements. We traditionally end a scale with an eighth pitch—an octave above or below the first. In the major scale, half steps lie between the third and fourth and between the seventh and eighth (final) pitches while the other intervals are whole steps.

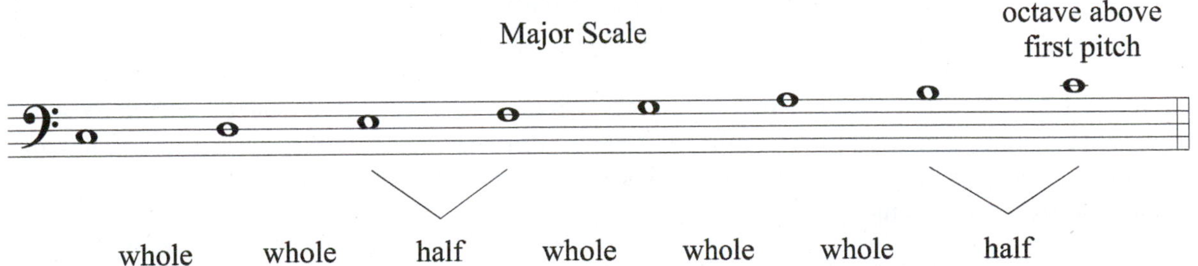

Scales can be written and practiced in both ascending and descending forms.

Listen to the ascending and descending major scale on the website. Follow the musical notation and keyboard diagram as you listen. The symbol 𝄐 is a **fermata** and indicates that the note should be held longer than its metric value.

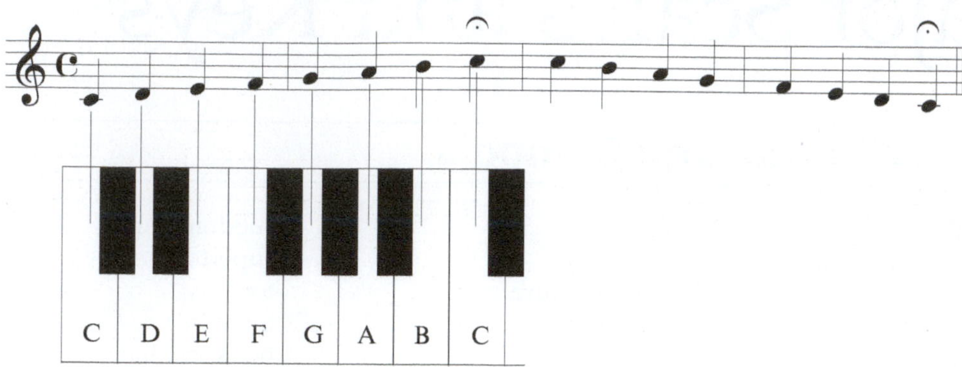

We frequently hear full ascending or descending scales in melodies. The first excerpt is by the Italian composer Luigi Boccherini (1743–1805). The first pitch of the scale (C) appears in two different octaves and is also the first and final pitch. The second phrase, by George Frideric Handel (1685–1759), also starts and ends on C but descends through the scale.

THE TONIC. The first pitch of a scale is important because it is the central tone toward which other pitches gravitate. This first pitch is called the **tonic** (from the Greek word for "weight"). Scales are named for their tonics; the tonic of the C major scale is the pitch C. Both pitches C in the next example are correctly labeled "tonic."

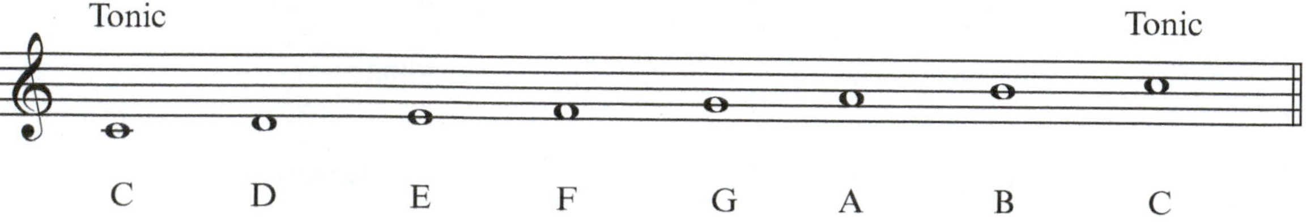

Scale Degrees

Order is important in understanding scales; accordingly, each pitch is assigned a scale-degree number to designate its relationship to the tonic. As we have discussed, the tonic is the first scale degree. The second **scale degree** is the second pitch of the ascending scale; the fourth scale degree is the fourth pitch, and so on.

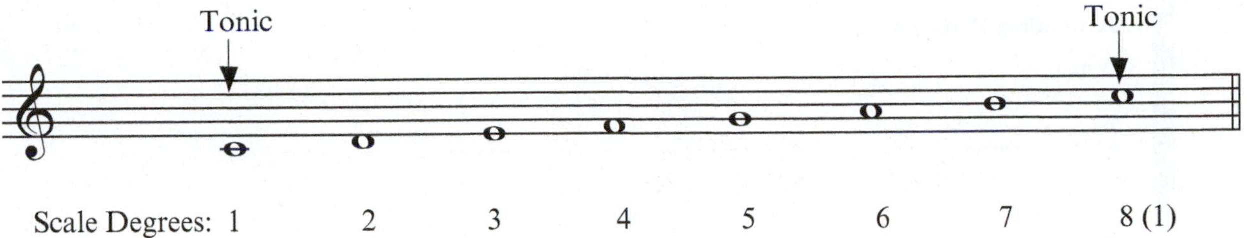

THE CARET SYMBOL. We often employ the **caret symbol (^)** to stand for or emphasize the words "scale degree." The symbol above the number $\hat{1}$ denotes the first scale degree; for example, the third scale degree can be specified by the symbol $\hat{3}$. Regardless of the octave, pitches in a given scale have the same scale-degree number. In the C major scale, the pitch E is always $\hat{3}$, and the pitch B in any octave of the C major scale is $\hat{7}$.

SCALE-DEGREE NAMES. Just as the first scale degree is known as the *tonic*, others have names that reflect their relationship to this central pitch. The second scale degree is the **supertonic**; the seventh scale degree is the *leading tone* (because it leads back to the tonic). Other scale-degree names lack such obvious associations. We will discuss these terms and their historical meanings further in Chapter 11.

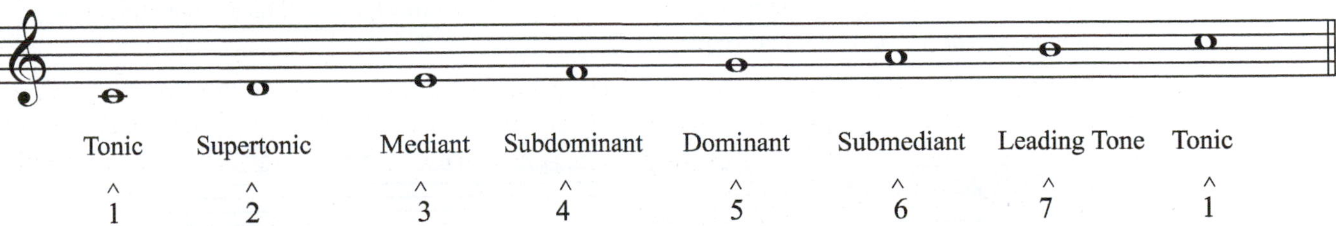

MUSICIANSHIP 5-1

Ear Training: Major Modes

Navigate to the audio files for this section on the website. You will hear patterns of three pitches that employ scale degrees $\hat{1}$, $\hat{2}$, and $\hat{3}$. Listen to each pattern and determine whether the mode is major or other. Answer "M" for major, and "O" for other. Answers are found in Appendix D.

Ascending Patterns

1. _____ 1 _____ 2 _____ 3 _____ 4 _____ 5 _____ 6

2. _____ 1 _____ 2 _____ 3 _____ 4 _____ 5 _____ 6

Descending Patterns

1. _____ 1 _____ 2 _____ 3 _____ 4 _____ 5 _____ 6

2. _____ 1 _____ 2 _____ 3 _____ 4 _____ 5 _____ 6

Ascending and Descending Patterns

1. _____ 1 _____ 2 _____ 3 _____ 4 _____ 5 _____ 6

2. _____ 1 _____ 2 _____ 3 _____ 4 _____ 5 _____ 6

Transposing Major Scales

If a musical work is based on the C major scale, the composition will be constructed so that the listener hears the pitch C as more important than any of the others. **Transposition** is the process of moving a series of pitches to a different tonic, but maintaining the original pattern of intervals. Any melody can be transposed; we will begin, however, with complete scales.

Scale transposition is a two-step process. First, write in noteheads from a new given tonic through to a note an octave above. Second, check the interval pattern and add accidentals if necessary. If we want to transpose the C major scale to begin on the pitch D, for example, D will be the new tonic. Begin by writing in noteheads between octave pitches D.

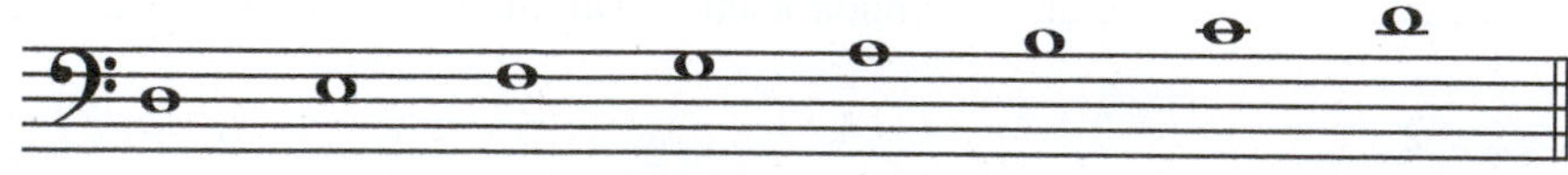

D Major Scale?

Note, however, that the interval between scale degrees $\hat{2}$ and $\hat{3}$ is a whole step, not a half step. To correct this problem, we can raise the pitch F to F♯.

After this change, pitches $\hat{1}$–$\hat{6}$ of the D major scale now conform to the interval pattern.

The final pitches of the scale, $\hat{7}$–$\hat{8}$, need adjustment since the half step is between $\hat{6}$ and $\hat{7}$—not pitches $\hat{7}$ and $\hat{8}$. Making the pitch C into a C♯ changes both intervals and creates a transposed major scale on D.

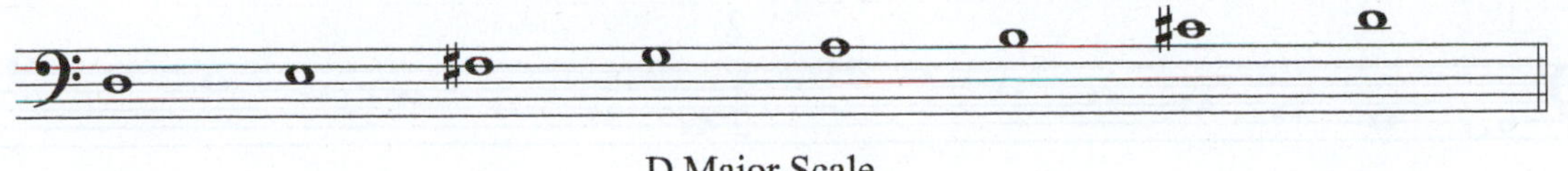

D Major Scale

The D major scale requires two accidentals—F♯ and C♯. Other scales require different accidentals. The E♭ major scale, for example, begins on E♭ and must also have B♭ and A♭ to replicate the pattern.

E♭ Major Scale

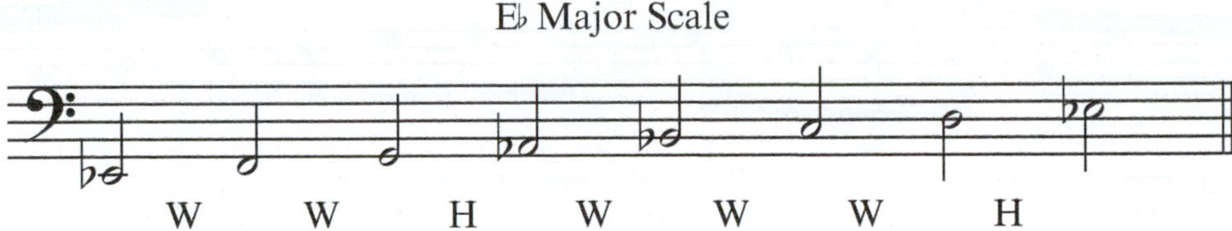

Five of the basic pitches must be made sharp in a B major scale.

B Major Scale

For class discussion or assignment: please do not remove these pages

REVIEW SET

Scale Transposition

A. These pitches are degrees $\hat{1}$–$\hat{5}$ in various major scales. The first pitch is tonic in all cases. If necessary, add sharps or flats to complete the interval pattern. Play each answer on the piano when finished.

Add accidentals as necessary to construct major scales.

B. These pitches may or may not conform to the major-scale pattern. If the scale is major, write "major" in the blank; if the scale is *not* major, write "other." For an added challenge, show what accidentals you would add to correct the "other" answers, transforming them to a "major" pattern.

Complete Building Skills 5-1 on page 129

MUSICIANSHIP 5-2

Sight Singing: Major-Scale Patterns

Two general methods are often used to sight sing. One is to sing the scale-degree numbers for each pitch in the line of music you are reading. The other, called *solfège*, is to sing specific syllables for each pitch.

Number Systems. Sight singing in either system may be performed using the tonic pitch of any key as 1. This system is called *movable numbers*. Another method, the *fixed number* method, uses the number 1 for the pitch C regardless of key.

Solfège Systems. Singing using solfège is also described using the same criteria as the number systems. In movable DO solfège, the syllables are assigned to specific scale degrees.

Movable DO Solfège

Degree in Scale	Solfège Syllable
1	do
2	re
3	mi
4	fa
5	sol
6	la
7	ti

Fixed DO Solfège

In fixed DO solfège, the syllables are assigned to generic pitch classes based on C as DO and do not change regardless of scale. There are many variants on this system that make it flexible for more complex musical contexts.

Fixed DO Solfège

Pitch Class	Solfège Syllable
C	do
D	re
E	mi
F	fa
G	sol
A	la
B	ti

A. Use scale-degree numbers or a solfège method as recommended by your instructor and sing these ascending patterns within major scales. Use a different octave as necessary and practice by beginning on other tonic pitches as well. As shown in the example, set a tempo, play the first pitch on the piano, and sing the notes—first ascending (as written), then descending. Test your accuracy by playing the first note on the piano after you have performed the pattern. If necessary, play each pitch *after* you have sung it.

These patterns center on scale degrees $\hat{1}$–$\hat{3}$.

Written

1.

2.

B. Sing scale degrees $\hat{1}$–$\hat{5}$ in these lines (and use the same method to begin on other tonics). Play the tonic pitch on the piano, then sing the first five scale degrees, both ascending and descending.

1.

2.

C. Sing through the following exercises using only the solfège syllables or numbers as indicated.

Solfège

1.	do	re	mi	fa	sol	la	ti	do						
2.	do	re	mi	re	mi	fa	sol	la	sol	fa	mi	re	do	
3.	do	re	mi	fa	sol	fa	mi	fa	mi	re	do			
4.	do	ti	do	re	mi	fa	sol	la	ti	do	re	mi	re	do
5.	do	re	mi	re	mi	re	mi	fa	sol	la	sol	ti	do	

Numbers

1.	1	2	3	4	5	6	7	1			
2.	1	2	3	4	3	4	5	6	7	1	
3.	1	7	1	2	3	4	5	4	3	2	1
4.	1	2	3	4	5	6	5	4	3	2	1
5.	1	2	3	2	3	2	3	4	5	7	1

Major Keys

Music theorists disagree about the best definitions of words such as *key* and *tonality*. We could make certain distinctions between the two terms depending on context, but for our purposes, **key** and **tonality** both denote the psychological perception that the tonic pitch is more important than any of the others. The skillful composer creates the sensation of tonality; listeners perceive it. If the scale is G major, the *key* and the *tonality* are both G major. Likewise, where A♭ is the tonic and the scale is major, the key and tonality are A♭ major.

If a composer wants to create a feeling for the key of E major, the pitches of that scale will predominate in the melody and harmony. The scale of E major includes four accidentals: F♯, C♯, G♯, and D♯.

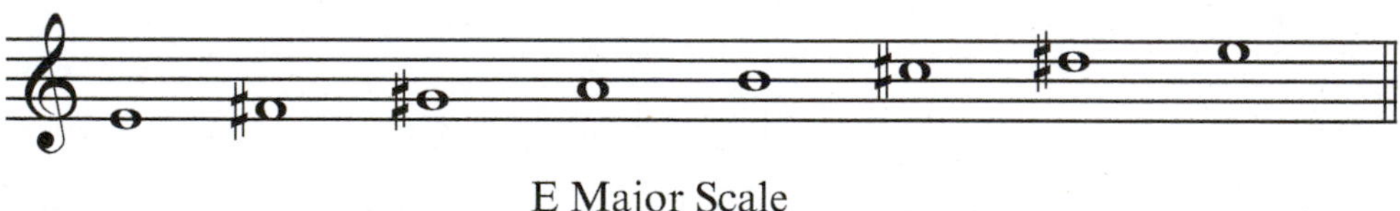

E Major Scale

When the E major scale (for example) is used in a composition, a sharp sign will be necessary for every F, C, G, and D. Rather than employing accidentals each time these pitches are used, however, composers identify them at the beginning of a composition in a *key signature*.

Key Signature

A **key signature** is a list of the accidentals associated with a given key. These accidentals are given at the beginning of a composition and placed between the clef sign and time signature. While the time signature is only shown in the first measure of a score, the key signature is displayed at the beginning of each line.[1] Accidentals in a key signature are *always* in effect unless canceled.

To understand the value of a key signature in clarifying notation, consider the following melody in A♭ major.

[1] In jazz and popular music, editors often treat the time and key signatures the same way: they are given at the beginning of the composition and *not* repeated unless a change occurs.

Ludwig van Beethoven, Sonata in A♭ Major

Melody with Accidentals

With a key signature, the flatted pitches are specified at the beginning of the line. This example is the same as the previous one, but the accidentals are now in the key signature. More importantly, the accidentals that are outside the key stand out to the performer. The notation has added clarity.

Melody with Key Signature

NULLIFYING A KEY SIGNATURE. Performers assume that accidentals stated in the key signature are *always* in effect. Any cancellation of an accidental in the key signature is in effect only for that measure; when the music moves past the next barline, the key signature is again in force. In the Beethoven example shown above, the D natural is notated in measures 1 and 3. The composer provided the D-flat accidental in measure 4 to confirm the return to the key. This **cautionary or courtesy accidental** is not necessary because the D-flat is found in the key signature, but is often supplied as a reminder.

In the next melody, the key is D major and the pitches F and C are assumed to be sharp.

Peter I. Tchaikovsky, "Waltz of the Flowers"
from *The Nutcracker*

In measure 9 of Tchaikovsky's waltz, the D♯ is outside the key signature and the sharp sign raises the basic pitch a half step. Tchaikovsky wanted the pitch C-natural to begin the next measure, but because the key signature specifies C♯, a natural sign nullifies the sharp. The A♯ added in measure 13 affects all the pitch A's in that measure.

CAUTIONARY ACCIDENTALS. In measure 9 of the last example, Tchaikovsky used the sharp sign to indicate a D♯. In the next measure, however, the sharp is cancelled by the barline, returning any pitch D back to D-natural. The composer employed a **cautionary or courtesy accidental** to remind the performer of the original D-natural.

Order of Sharps and Flats

There is a set order for the sharps or flats in key signatures. If the key signature has sharps, one sharp will always be F♯; two will be F♯ and C♯; and so on. With flats, the sequence is just as rigid; one flat will always be B♭; two will be B♭ and E♭; and so on.

Most students find it convenient to learn the order of flats first since they spell out the word "BEAD" plus the additional pitches "GCF." Sharps occur in the reverse of this order. Learning the order of flats, therefore, produces the order of sharps if the sequence is reversed.

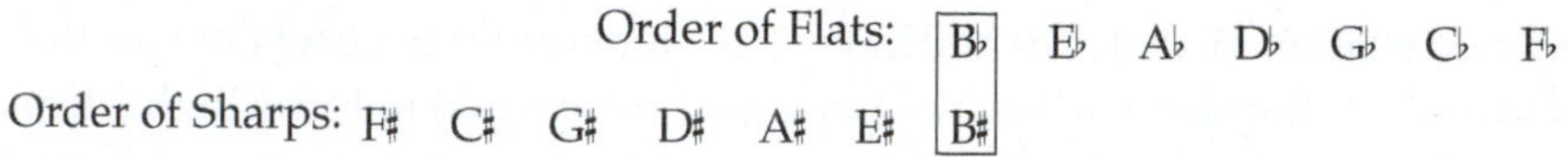
Order of Flats: B♭ E♭ A♭ D♭ G♭ C♭ F♭
Order of Sharps: F♯ C♯ G♯ D♯ A♯ E♯ B♯

When a key signature is written on the staff, the sharps and flats appear from left to right in the order given above—generally alternating between higher and lower choices of octave.

The key of C major has no sharps or flats; this fact is reflected in the key signature.

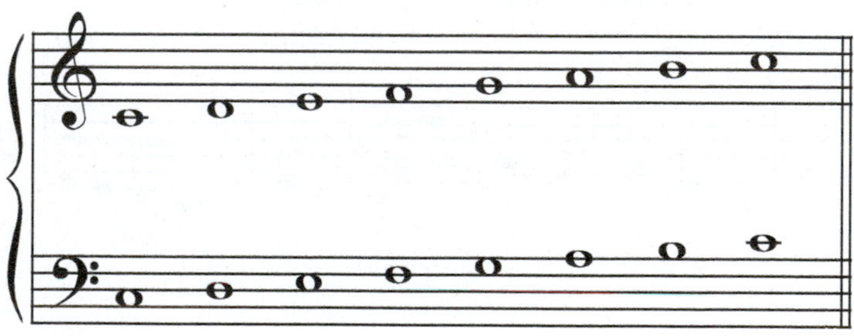

C Major Scale

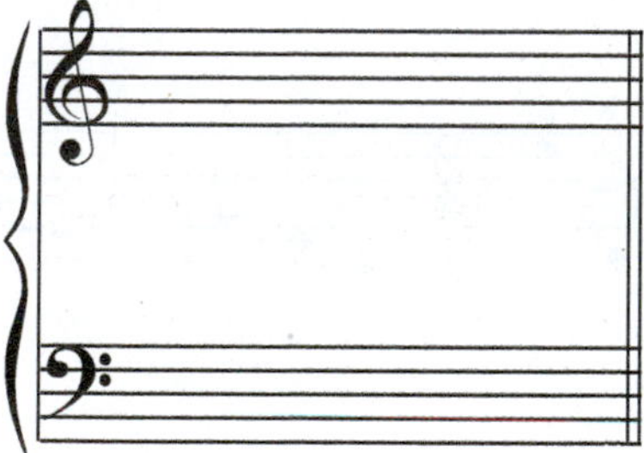

Key Signature: C Major

The key of C♯ major has all seven sharps in its scale and key signature. Notice the placement of the seven sharps on the grand staff.

C♯Major Scale

Key Signature: C♯Major

The key of C♭ major includes all seven flats in its signature.

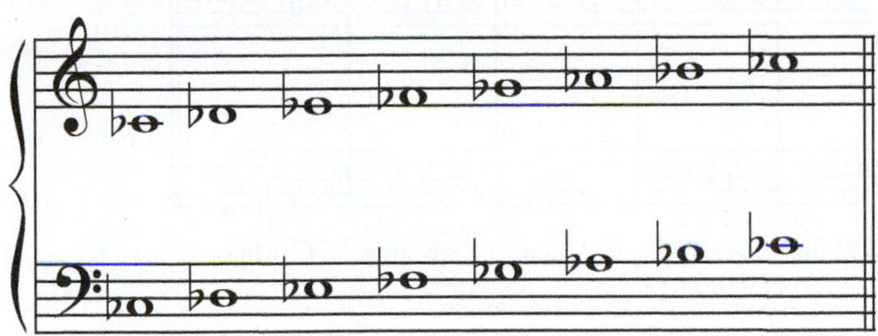

C♭ Major Scale

Key Signature: C♭ Major

You may find it helpful to remember that the C scales represent the extremes in key-signatures:

- C major — no sharps/no flats
- C♯ major — seven (all) sharps
- C♭ major — seven (all) flats

The position of sharps and flats on the staff is fixed; as a result, performers expect the key signature to be in that order on the score. Remember that accidentals in a key signature may appear just above the top line or just below the bottom one, but *never* on a ledger line. Study the paired examples and compare the correct/incorrect methods of key signature placement.

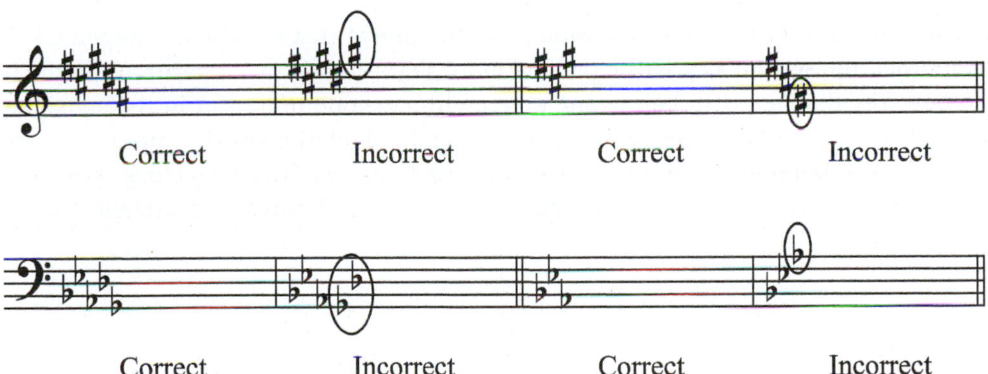

Major Key Signatures

Memorize the 15 major key signatures shown in the next example. Use *various drill websites*, such as www.musictheory.net or www.teoria.com, apps, flash cards, or the best method for you personally.

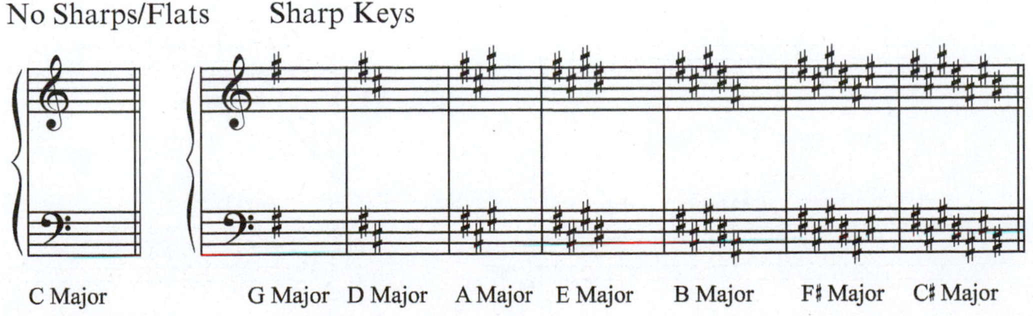

The Circle of Fifths

As we will discuss later in more detail, the **dominant** and **subdominant** relationships are among the most important in traditional tonal music. The intervals between the tonic and the dominant above it, and also between the tonic and subdominant below it are called **fifths** because they are comprised of five diatonic steps.

The dominant is a fifth above the tonic; the subdominant, a fifth below. When a key is a fifth above another, the second key will have one more sharp in its key signature than the first. Likewise, a new key that is a fifth below one given will have one more flat in its key signature. The **circle of fifths** is a way of understanding and using these relationships—one that is especially favored by jazz and popular musicians. Beginning with C major at twelve o'clock on a circle, moving clockwise, add a sharp at each step. Starting from C♯ major and moving counterclockwise, omit one sharp at each step.

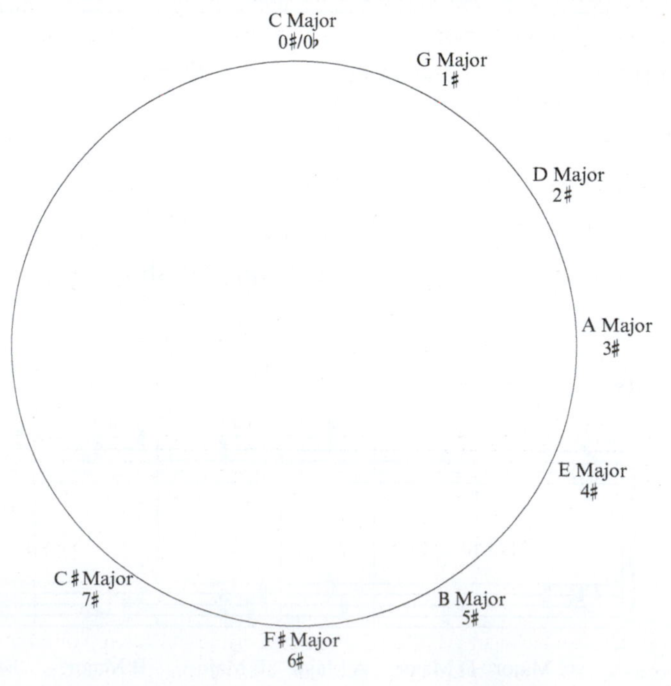

While we recommend that you memorize key signatures, you can rely on the circle of fifths for verification. If you want to find the signature of the key of A major, for example, this is clearly a sharp key since, with one exception (F), flat keys have "flat" in their names. Begin with G major (one sharp), move clockwise to D major (two sharps), and the next key clockwise is A major with three sharps.

Flat keys appear on the circle of fifths moving counterclockwise from C major. A fifth below C is F (with one flat); the next key counterclockwise from F major adds another flat and is B♭ major, and so on.[2] Notice that three enharmonic major keys are also apparent on the circle.

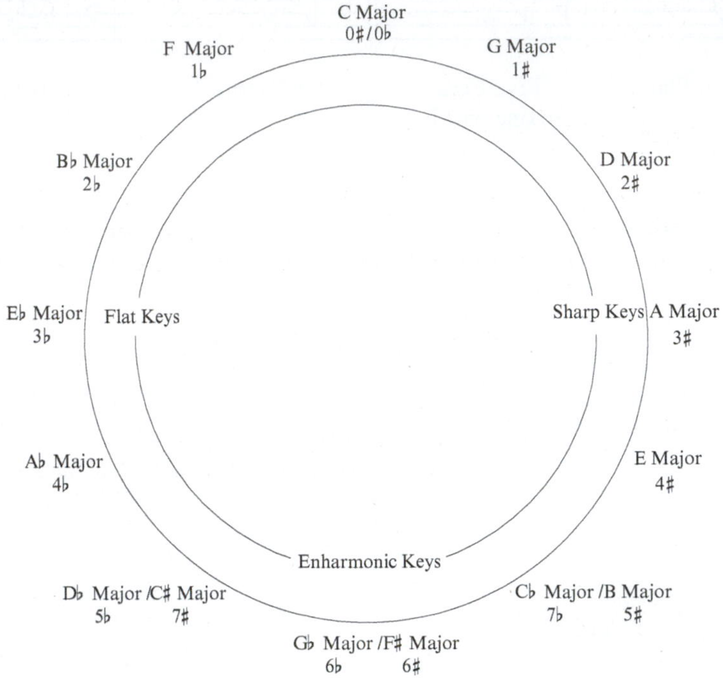

TRICKS OF THE TRADE

Learning Key Signatures

If you take the time to memorize the 15 major key signatures, you will find your future work in music fundamentals much easier. For some students, merely associating the key names with the appropriate accidentals will be sufficient. For others, making written lists or flash cards will help.

Although you should eventually rely on memory alone, as long as you know the order of sharps and flats, several "tricks" may help you in the beginning.

- **Sharp Keys.** In sharp keys, the key name is a diatonic half step above the last sharp. If a key, for example, has five sharps, A♯ will be the last sharp (because we know the order of the sharps). The key name, B, is a diatonic half step above this last sharp. Reversing the process, if we want to know the key signature of B major, a diatonic half step below B is A♯, which will be the last sharp. Because A♯ is the fifth sharp, the key of B major has five sharps.

[2]Remembering that flat keys (except F major) include "flat" in their names will help you avoid mistakes like naming "B major" as the fifth counterclockwise from F major. We would also ensure that any fifth calculated on the circle has seven half steps (discussed in Chapter 6, page 150).

- **Flat Keys.** The formula is different for flat keys (making these "tricks" less valuable than memorization). In flat keys, the key name is the *next-to-last* flat in the order of flats. If we want to know the key signature of D♭ major, for example, we know that D♭ (which is the fourth flat) is the next-to-last flat. The key has *five* flats: B♭, E♭, A♭, D♭, and G♭. Reversing the process, if we know that a key has five flats, we know that G♭ is the last flat (through the order of flats), then the next-to-last flat is D♭ and this is the name of the key.

There are two exceptions to the process of determining flat keys: C major, which has no sharps or flats, and F major, which has one flat. Remember also that considering sharp keys, only F♯ and C♯ major have "sharp" in the key name. With the exception of F major, all flat keys have "flat" in the key name.

For class discussion or assignment: please do not remove these pages

REVIEW SET

Major Key Signatures

A. List the order of flats.

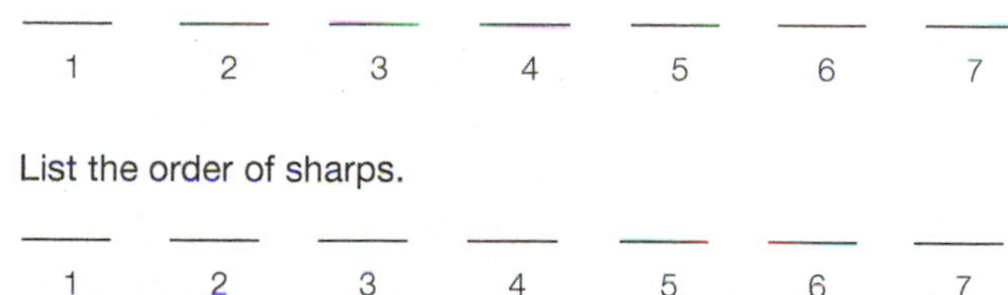

List the order of sharps.

____ ____ ____ ____ ____ ____ ____

1 2 3 4 5 6 7

B. Provide the key signature for each example.

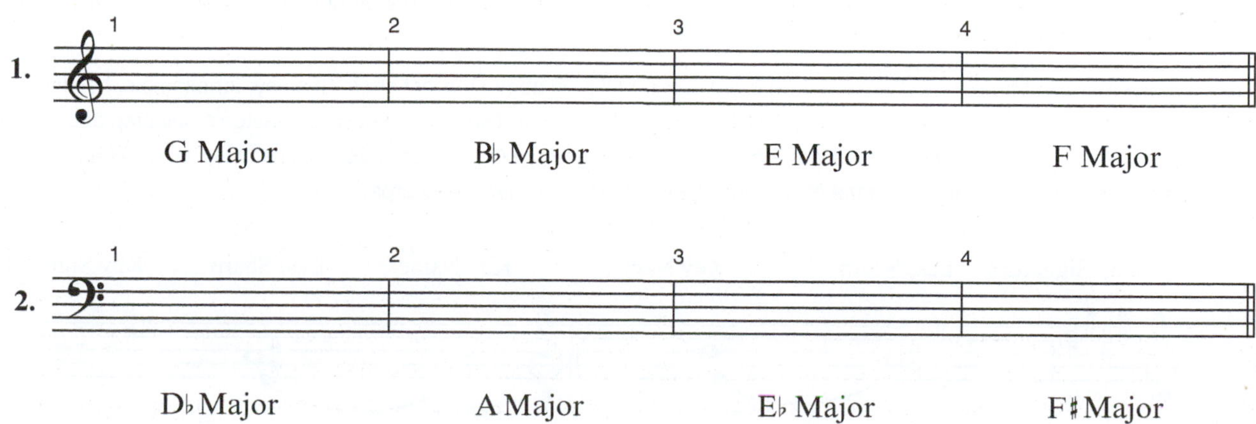

C. Write the pitch specified by the given scale degree and key. Include an accidental if necessary.

Complete Building Skills 5-2 on page 131

MUSICIANSHIP 5-3

I. Keyboard: Major Scales

In keyboard studies, major scales are learned in groups according to conventional fingering patterns. While the C major scale begins with the thumb in the right hand, for example, the scale of F major is best started with the fourth finger (to avoid using the thumb on a black key). The first group of scales shares the same right-hand fingering pattern (the thumb is numbered "1"):

fingering: 1 2 3 1 2 3 4 5

Play the first three scale degrees with the thumb through middle fingers (1–3). For the fourth pitch, turn your thumb under to end with fingers 1 through 5 (thumb through little fingers). Descending, simply retrace your path: fingers 5–4–3–2–1, then the third finger over the thumb for the final three pitches.

For the left hand, begin with your left little finger ("5") and continue upward through the thumb. For the final three pitches, bring your third finger over the thumb and end with third, index, and thumb:

fingering: 5 4 3 2 1 3 2 1

Descending, use the thumb, index, and third fingers, then bring your thumb under for scale degrees $\hat{5}$–$\hat{1}$.

For the present, your goal is to play scales one octave with each hand separately. Set a slow tempo that allows you to play without interrupting the beat.

Group I Scales

C major	G major
A major	D major
E major	

II. Sight Singing: Major Scales and Stepwise Patterns

A. Use scale-degree numbers, solfège, or pitch names to sing major scales, both ascending and descending. Play the tonic pitch on the piano (in another octave if necessary), match this pitch, then sing the complete ascending scale. Play the tonic an octave higher, then sing the descending scale. Finally, check the final pitch against the piano. Choose a variety of scales within your range.

B. These are short melodic patterns that progress stepwise, ascending and descending. Play the first pitch on an instrument, sing the pattern using the method recommended by your instructor, then check the last pitch against the piano. Each line is in a different key. As always, perform in whatever octave your voice range dictates.

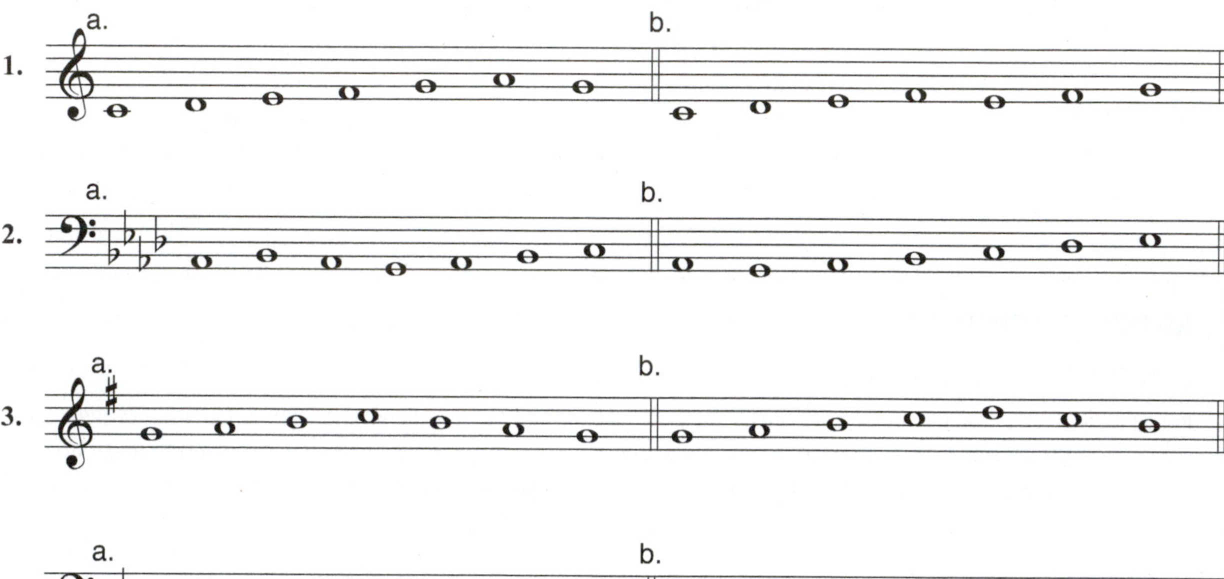

C. These phrases have the same melodic patterns as those in the previous exercise, but include simple rhythms as well. Practice the rhythm separately using counting syllables. When you can perform rhythms accurately, set a comfortable tempo and sing the melody from beginning to end.

D. These longer melodies are still stepwise, but they comprise two phrases.

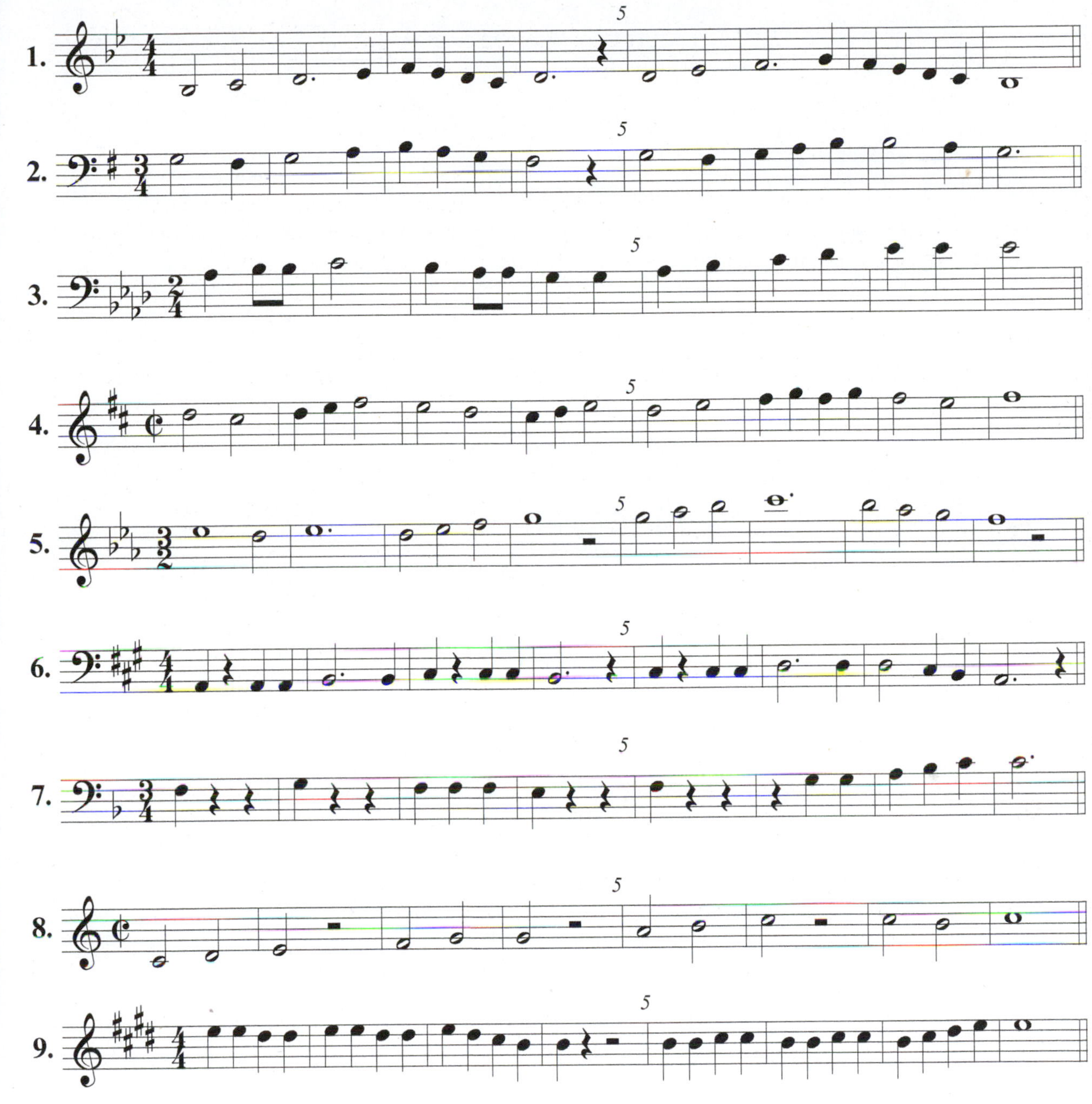

Name ______________________

Page may be removed

Building Skills 5-1

Major Scales and Keys

A. **Identify these patterns as "major" or "other" (if the scale is not major).**

B. **Construct major scales on each of these tonics. Use accidentals as necessary.**

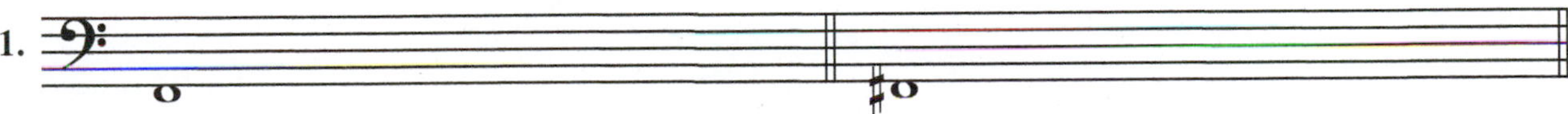

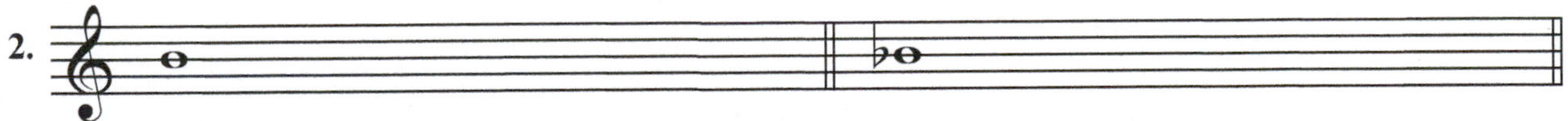

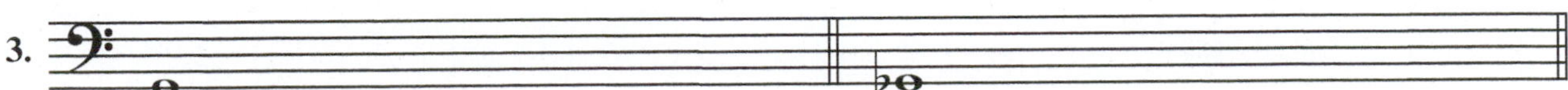

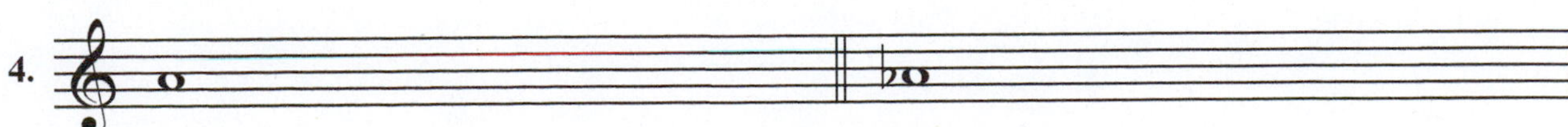

Name ____________________

Page may be removed

Building Skills 5-2

Scales and Scale Degrees

A. Identify the major keys represented by the following signatures.

______ 1 ______ 2 ______ 3 ______ 4 ______ 5 ______ 6

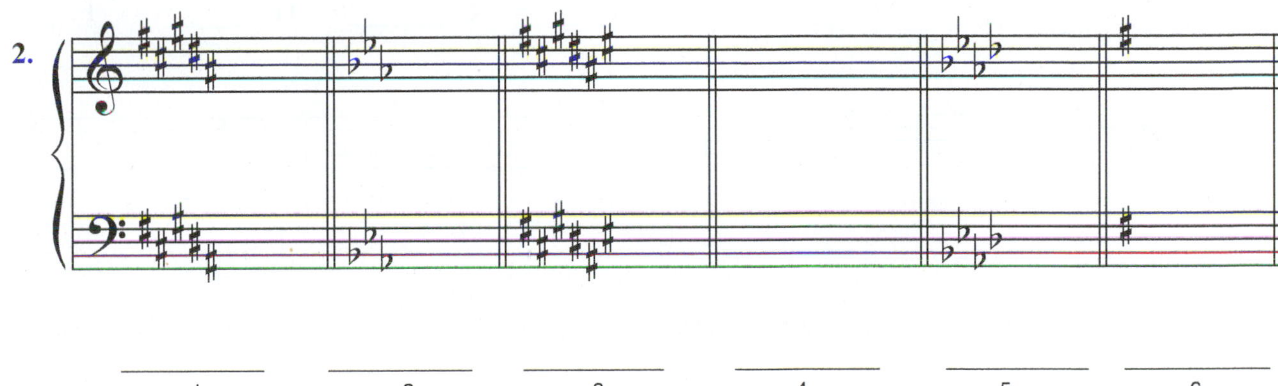

______ 1 ______ 2 ______ 3 ______ 4 ______ 5 ______ 6

B. Provide scale-degree numbers for the given pitches and keys. In the lower blank, write the scale-degree name ("supertonic," "submediant," and so on).

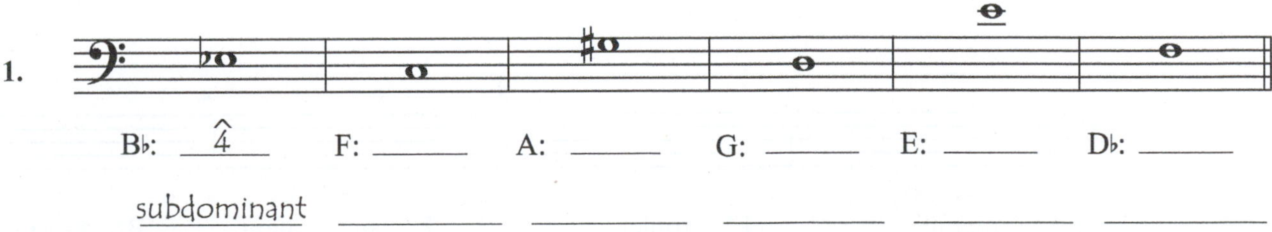

B♭: $\hat{4}$ F: ______ A: ______ G: ______ E: ______ D♭: ______

subdominant ______ ______ ______ ______ ______

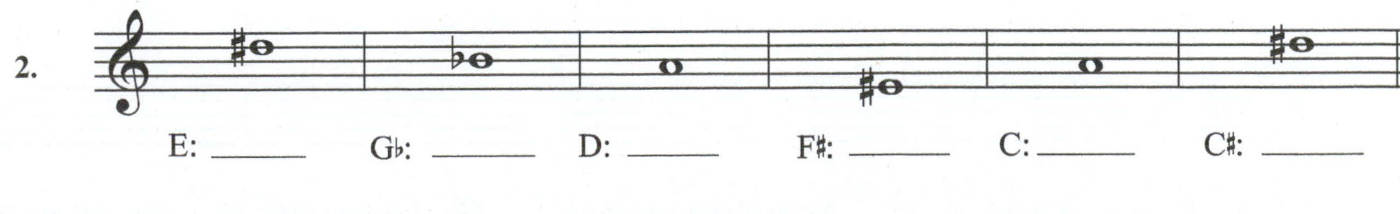

E: ______ G♭: ______ D: ______ F♯: ______ C: ______ C♯: ______

______ ______ ______ ______ ______ ______

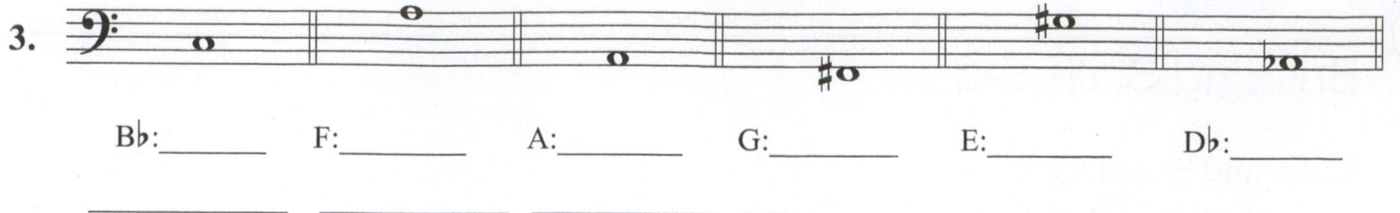

C. **A single pitch can serve various roles in different keys. For each pitch and key given, write the appropriate scale degree.**

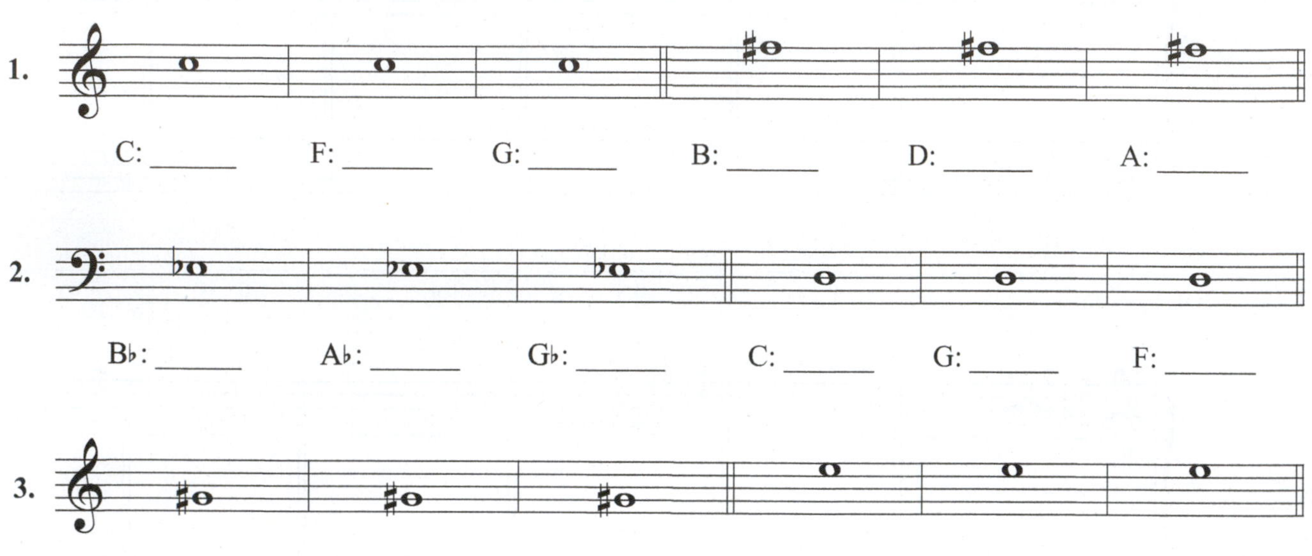

D. **Given the key and scale-degree name, notate the appropriate pitch (include an accidental if necessary).**

(any octave)

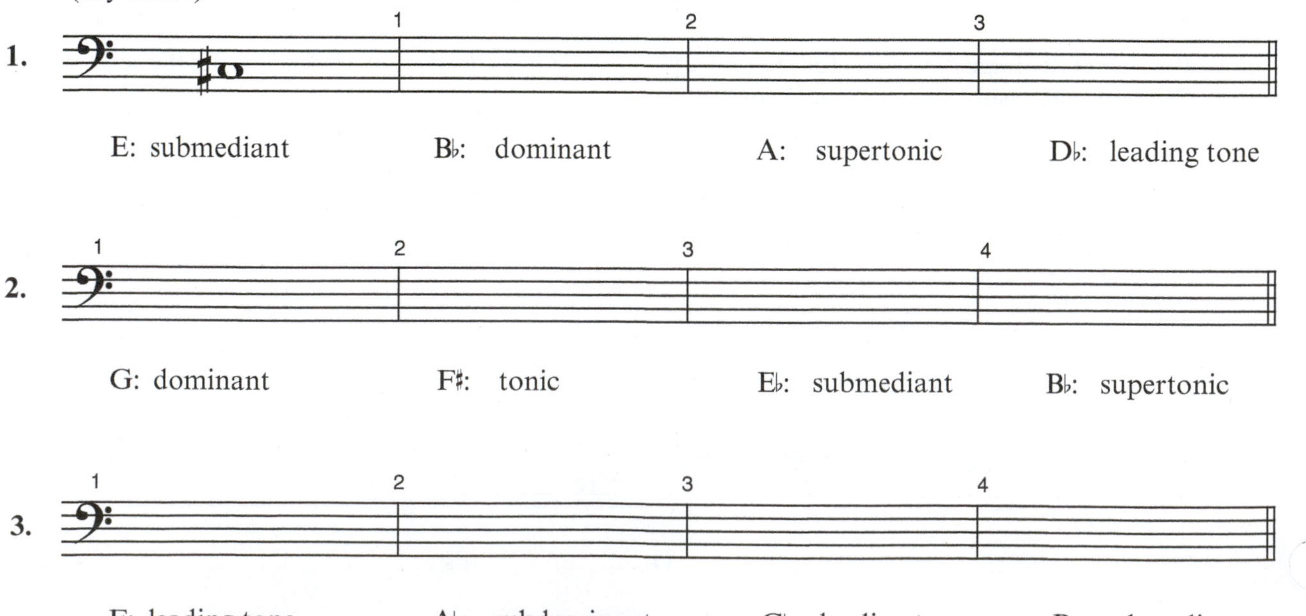

F: leading tone   A♭: subdominant   G♭: leading tone   B: submediant

Name ______________________________

Page may be removed

E. **Several sequences of adjacent pitches are given. Below each sequence, *circle* the one key name that is *not* appropriate. The pitches C–D–E–F, for example, would be possible in the keys of C major and F major, but *not* G major (where the F would be F♮).**

Name ______________________

Page may be removed

Creative Projects • Chapter 5

Compose phrases that conform to the given guidelines. Be sure to write in the key signature before you begin. Use only pitches within the key (although you may repeat pitches at your discretion).

- Practice and prepare to perform your melodies for the class.

A Major, use mostly dotted quarter and eighth-note rhythms, end on $\hat{3}$.

B♭ Major, use half and quarter notes with at least one pitch B♭ in each measure, end on $\hat{2}$.

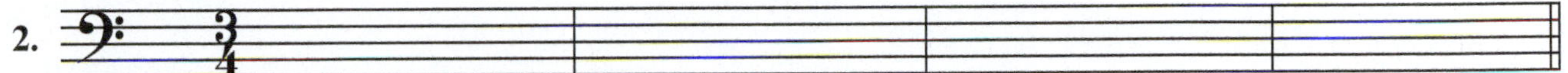

E Major, five-measure phrase, use mainly quarter and half notes with a number of similar rests, end on $\hat{5}$.

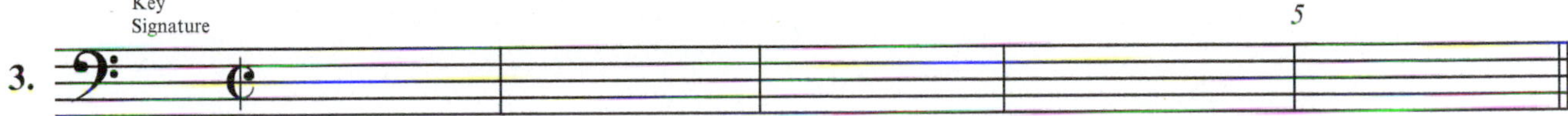

D Major, use half and whole notes and rests, end on $\hat{1}$.

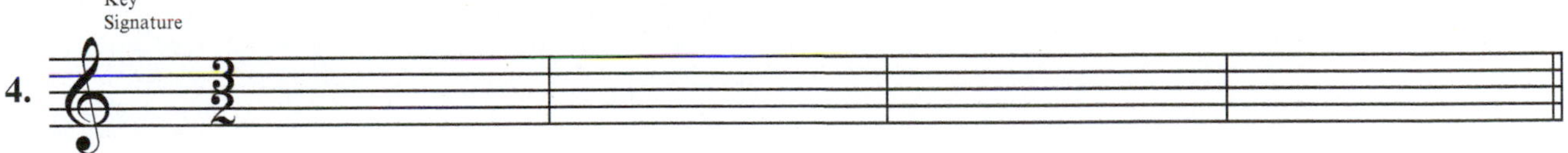

F Major, use repeated sixteenth notes that change every measure; end on any pitch you choose.

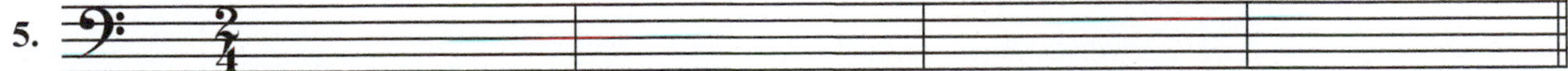

B Major, use rhythms of your choice, end on $\hat{1}$.

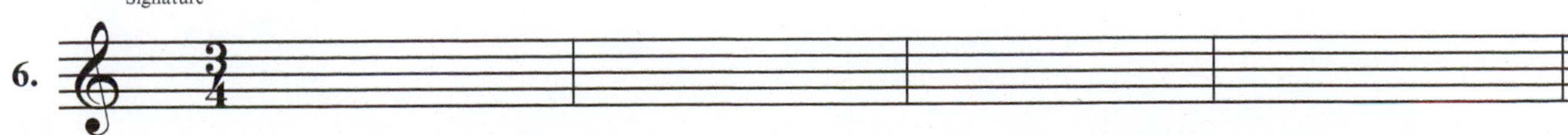

Name ______________________

Page may be removed

Analysis in Context 1 • Chapter 5

Muzio Clementi (1752–1832) was a highly regarded keyboardist, composer, and teacher. He also pursued business interests as a publisher, and eventually purchased a failing piano manufacturing company in London. He used his skill and reputation as a performer and composer to market his instruments in Europe.

Sonatina

Muzio Clementi
Op. 36, No. 2

19
f
24
p
29
cresc.
f
34

Name ______________________

Page may be removed

1. In what key is this piece written?

2. Write in the note names, scale degree numbers, and solfège above the treble clef melody in measures 1–4.

3. Name the scale degrees found in beats 1 and 2 of measure 2 on the treble clef staff.

4. In what other measures do you find this scale degrees? Circle all occurrences in both the treble and bass clef staves.

5. Study measures 6 through 15. What consistent non-diatonic pitch is found in these measures?

6. Label the note names below the bass clef staff in measures 16–22.

7. Are there any nondiatonic pitches in those measures? If yes, what are they?

8. Label the scale degrees of the melody above the treble clef staff in measures 26 and 27.

9. Are there more whole steps or half steps in these measures, or are they equal in number of occurrences?

10. Study the melody line and associated scale degrees in measures 31 to the end. Other than the key signature, how does Clementi craft the melody to confirm that this piece is in the original key (your answer to question 1)?

Name ____________________

Page may be removed

Analysis in Context 2 • Chapter 5

The following excerpt includes the verse and chorus from the song "Hey There Delilah" released by the Plain White T's in 2006. It reached number 1 on the Billboard charts and was nominated for several Grammys. After listening to the song on the webpage, answer the questions that follow.

HEY THERE DELILAH

HEY THERE DELILAH
Words and Music by TOM HIGGENSON
Copyright © 2005 WB MUSIC CORP.,
FEARMORE MUSIC and SO HAPPY PUBLISHING.
All Rights Administered by WB MUSIC CORP.
All Rights Reserved.
Used By Permission of ALFRED MUSIC.

8
—you look so pret-ty, yes you do.
Times Square can't shine as bright as you. —
I swear it's
8
12
true.
Hey there, De-li - lah, don't you wor-ry a-bout the dis - tance, I'm — right
12
15
there. If you get lone - ly, give this song an-oth-er lis - ten. Close your eyes. —
15
18
Lis-ten to me voice, it's my dis - guise. —
I'm by your side.
18

Name ______________________

Page may be removed

1. In what key is this piece written?
2. In what measure does the tonic first appear in the melody line?
3. Are there any accidentals used in this song? If so, give specific measure numbers.
4. Label the solfège in measures 5–9. How many half steps are in this opening line? How many whole steps?
5. What pitches of the D major scale are used in the melody line within measures 25–27?
6. What is the time signature of this song? Write in counting numbers for measures 16, 18, and 21.
7. Label the scale degree names in measures 21 and 22 (tonic, supertonic, etc.).
8. Is syncopation used in the piano line in this song? If yes, give specific measure numbers.
9. Label all of the pitches in the bass line in measures 9–12 with solfège syllables. Does this line create step-wise motion?
10. Why do you think this song was so popular? Feel free to include your thoughts on melody, lyrics, and performance.

Chapter 6
Intervals

Essential Terms

augmented interval
compound interval
diminished interval
double flat 𝄫
double sharp 𝄪
doubly augmented interval
doubly diminished interval
harmonic interval
interval quality
interval size
inverted interval
major interval
major-scale comparison
melodic interval
minor interval
perfect interval
prime
simple interval
tritone
unison

Melodies differ in many respects, such as rhythm, key, and mode. Another major difference between melodies is the manner in which they move from one pitch to the next. As we have discussed, the distance between two pitches is termed an *interval.* While a melody may include many different sizes of intervals, one or two of them are used more often.

The two melodies below both employ about the same range of intervals—basically stepwise with the use of wider intervals for dramatic effect. While we also can hear the "classical" symmetry of the Mozart melody and the "pop" rhythms of the Mars tune, the intervals are predictable and typical of Western music.

W. A. Mozart, Sonata in F Major, K. 332

"Just The Way You Are," Bruno Mars

Both the Mozart and Bruno Mars melodies have a narrow range of interval sizes. Listen to Adele's "Skyfall" for an example of a melody that uses larger intervals.

Adele Adkins, "Skyfall"

One of the reasons we study intervals is to understand and compare differences among musical styles and systems. Whether the music is pop, classical, or contemporary, the terminology in this chapter will build a vocabulary that will help us talk about and understand those differences.

Interval Size

A **melodic interval** is one that occurs between two consecutive pitches (as in the previous examples). If the interval is **harmonic**, the two pitches occur simultaneously.

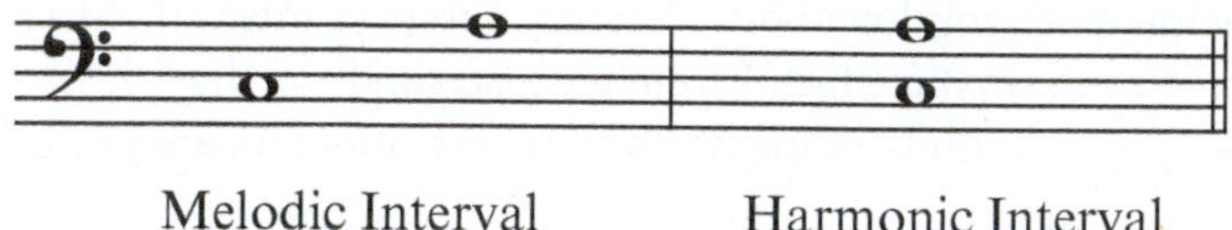

Melodic Interval Harmonic Interval

The **size** of an interval is determined by counting the number of steps (lines and spaces) between two pitches. To identify the interval size, begin with the lower pitch (whether the interval is melodic or harmonic) and then count lines and spaces, ending with the upper pitch. If the upper pitch is one line or space above the lower pitch, the interval is a *second;* if the higher pitch is two lines or spaces above, the interval is a *third*. In determining interval size, any accidentals associated with pitches are not counted.

When pitches are four and five steps apart, the intervals are a *fourth* and a *fifth*, respectively. These intervals shown are harmonic.

Sixths have six steps between pitches; if there are seven steps, the interval is a *seventh*. The intervals shown are melodic.

OCTAVES AND UNISONS. As we discussed previously, an octave is a duplication of pitch name either higher or lower. The **unison** (also called **prime**) is a duplication of the same pitch (*including* accidentals in this case) and in the same octave. Observe that in the notation of a harmonic unison (between two instruments, for example), the two pitches must touch; otherwise, we would read them as melodic.

You may have noticed that seconds, fourths, sixths, and octaves (the even-numbered intervals) involve a line *and* a space. Odd-numbered intervals such as the unison, third, fifth, and seventh occur over lines *or* spaces.

For class discussion or assignment: please do not remove these pages

REVIEW SET

Interval Size

A. Construct **harmonic** intervals **above** the given pitch. Do not employ accidentals.

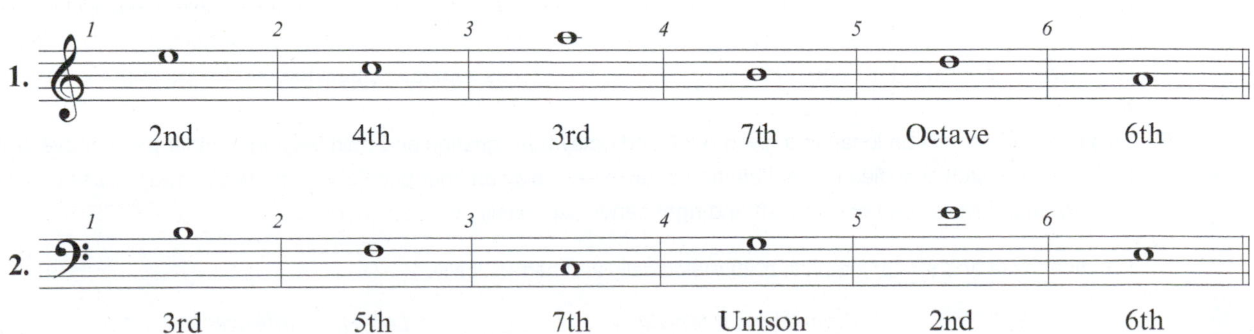

Now construct **melodic** intervals, but write the second pitch ***below*** the one given.

B. Identify the size of each interval.

A B C D E F

MUSICIANSHIP 6-1

Keyboard: Interval Size

A. Begin this exercise with lines B1–B2 from the preceding Review Set (above). Locate the octave of each line; using the right hand only, play both pitches left to right (melodic intervals) or two pitches together (for harmonic intervals). Repeat this exercise using only the left hand. When you can play the pitches separately, play them in tempo from the beginning to the end of each line.

B. This exercise centers on locating a given pitch and octave designation and then playing another pitch above or below it. First play the pitch specified in the identified octave; next, play another pitch above or below. You will use only the white keys for this exercise and only the left and right hands separately (not both together).

Practice these and similar intervals both melodically and harmonically.

Right-Hand Intervals

1. Third above G_5
2. Fourth below C_3
3. Fifth below B_5
4. Seventh above D_4
5. Second above E_6

Left-Hand Intervals

6. Fourth below F_1
7. Octave above A_0
8. Sixth above G_3
9. Sixth below C_2
10. Fifth below B_3

Use this table for piano fingering.

Interval Fingering Patterns

Interval	Right Hand Ascending	Right Hand Descending	Left Hand Ascending	Left Hand Descending
Second	1–2	5–4	5–4	1–2
Third	1–3	5–3	5–3	1–3
Fourth	1–4	5–2	5–2	1–4
Fifth and wider	1–5	5–1	5–1	1–5

Interval Quality

Interval size is a general way of classifying sounds as seconds, sixths, octaves, and so on. Two intervals classified as the same size, however, may sound different. The following intervals, for example, are *seconds,* yet the two sounds are distinct.

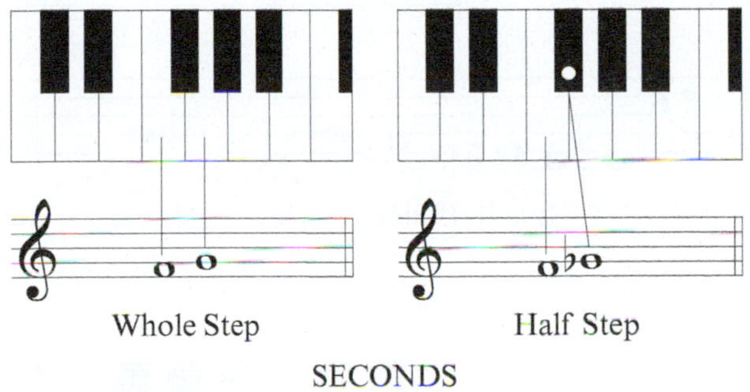

Identifying an interval's *quality* as well as size provides an exact description of the interval.

Perfect Intervals

Some of the terms we use in Western music originated in the ancient world. For early musicians, the term "perfect" meant a sound that was symmetrical, stable, and appropriate for use at the most important points in a composition. For us today, the term "perfect" is little more than one category of intervals. The octave, unison, fourth, and fifth, for example, can be classified as **perfect intervals**. Other interval sizes belong to the major/minor category and are *never* classified as perfect (see page 155).

PERFECT UNISON AND PERFECT OCTAVE. A unison is the sounding of the same pitch in the same octave. When two tones are notated identically (F and F, for example, or A♭ and A♭), the interval is classified as a *perfect unison* (abbreviated P1). Likewise, when the same pitch name is notated an octave above or below a given pitch (including the duplication of any accidental), the interval is a *perfect octave.*

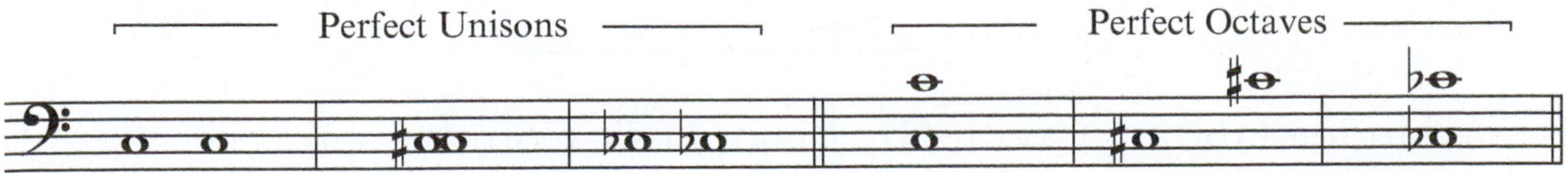

Perfect octaves are separated by 12 half steps.

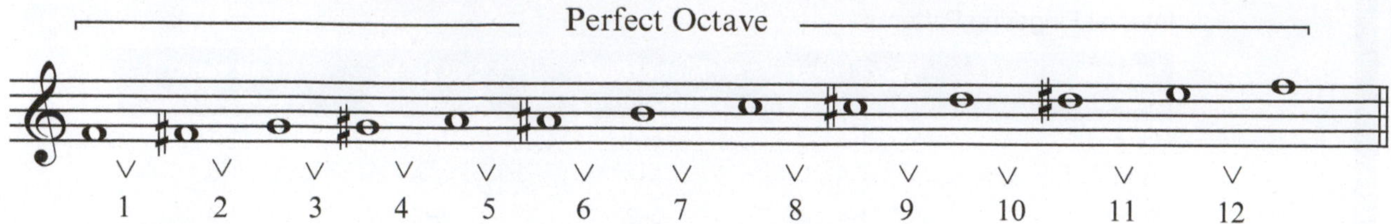

PERFECT FOURTHS AND FIFTHS. Pitches a fourth apart are perfect in quality if there are five half steps between them. Fifths are classified as perfect when the two pitches are separated by seven half steps.

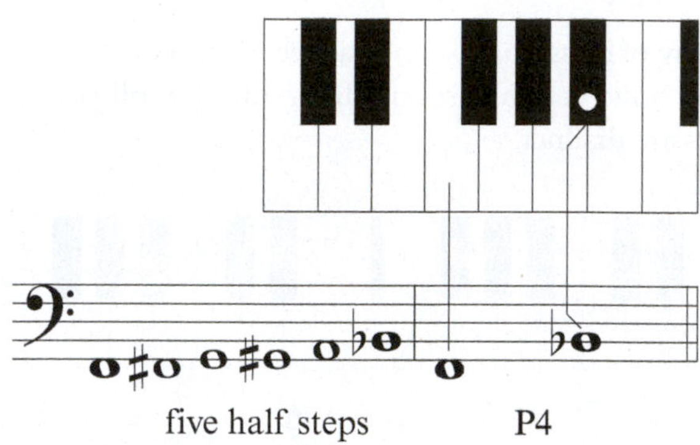

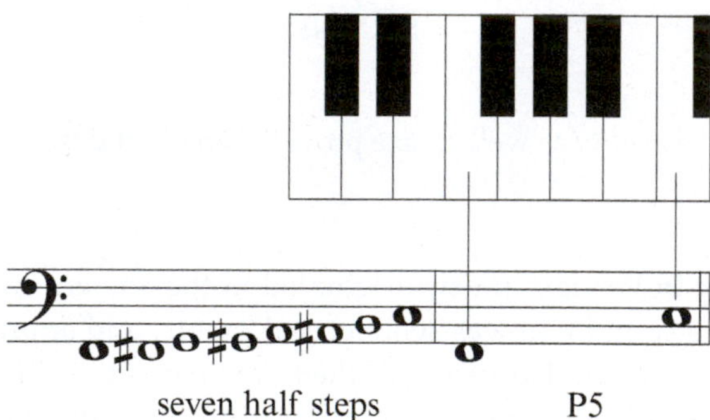

Review the widths (sizes) in half steps of the four perfect intervals.

Perfect Intervals

Interval	Size in Half Steps
P1	0
P4	5
P5	7
P8	12

Understanding Quality by Major-Scale Comparison

Fortunately, we do not need to count half steps to determine interval quality. **Major-scale comparison**, in which we view the upper pitch of an interval in the major scale represented by the lower pitch, is the fastest and most accurate method of interval construction and identification. Major-scale comparison rests on the following principle:

If the upper pitch of a unison, octave, fourth, or fifth is diatonic in the scale of the lower pitch, the quality is perfect.

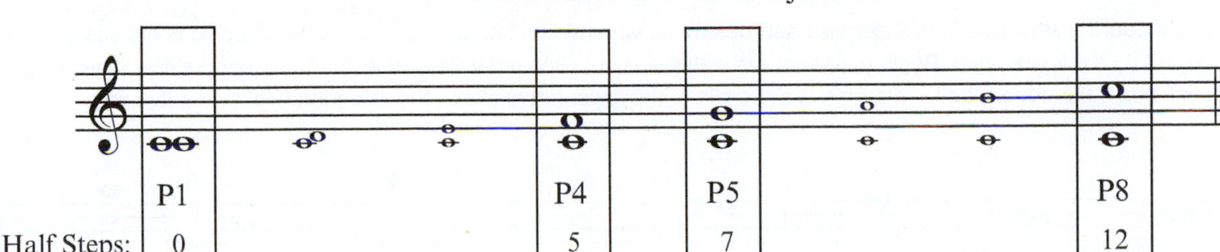

AUGMENTED AND DIMINISHED INTERVALS. If an octave, unison, fourth, or fifth is not perfect, then it is either wider or narrower than the corresponding perfect interval. An interval size of one, four, five, or eight that is one half step less than perfect is **diminished** in quality (abbreviated "d"). A similar interval that is one half step larger than perfect is **augmented** ("A").[1]

Major-scale comparison requires no counting and is generally faster and more reliable than other methods used for identifying intervals. In the next example, the three fifths shown are perfect, diminished, and augmented. We recognize the first interval as perfect (P5) because the upper pitch (A) is diatonic in the key of D major (the lower pitch). In the second example, the fifth is diminished (d5). Again, we note that the pitches D–A make a perfect fifth; this second interval (D–A♭), however, is a half step smaller than perfect and therefore is diminished (d5). The last fifth is wider than perfect and is augmented in quality (A5).

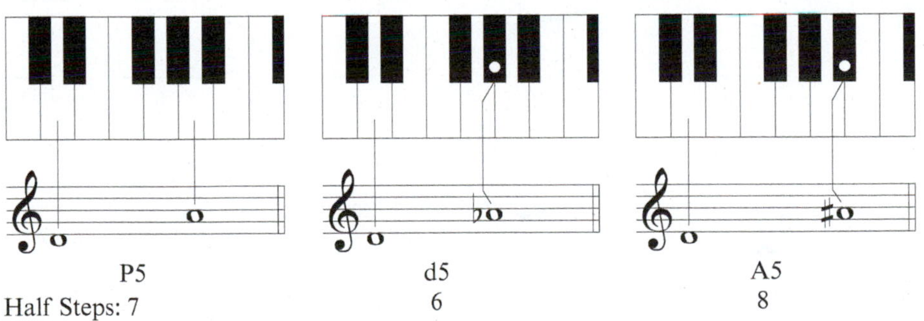

An octave or prime that is augmented or diminished is theoretically possible, but rare. We will not include these intervals in the present studies.

[1] Diminished intervals are identified in some sources with a circle symbol (°5). Likewise, a plus sign can designate an augmented interval (+5). Because these symbols have other meanings in analysis, we will use letters in this text.

For class discussion or assignment: please do not remove these pages

REVIEW SET

Quality in Perfect Intervals

A. Analyze the fourths and fifths in this exercise and determine whether the upper pitch is or is not diatonic in the scale represented by the lower pitch. Begin your analysis with the lower pitch regardless of which pitch occurs first. Check the "Diatonic" box if the upper pitch is diatonic in the scale of the lower pitch; check the "Nondiatonic" box if it is not.

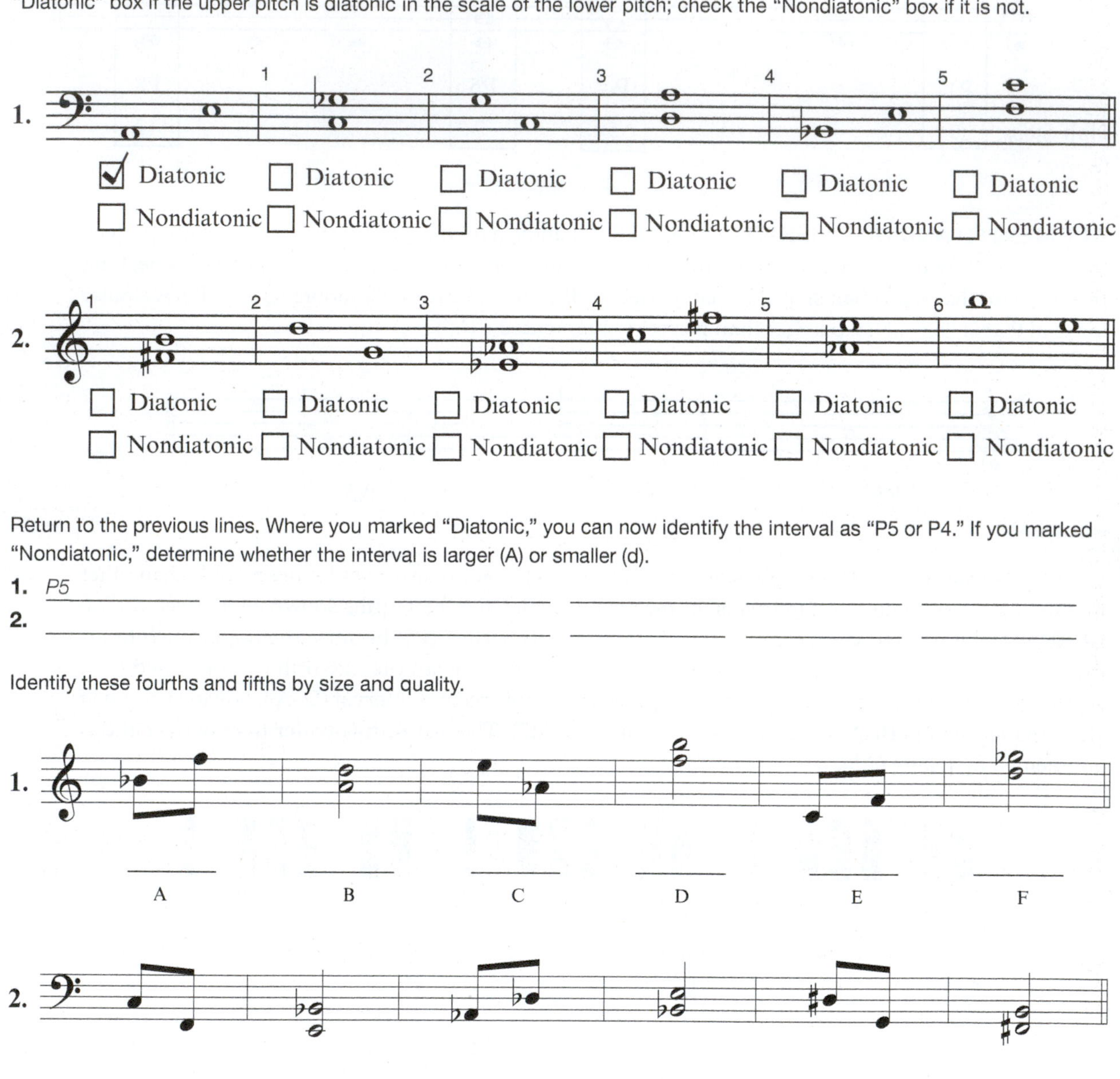

B. Return to the previous lines. Where you marked "Diatonic," you can now identify the interval as "P5 or P4." If you marked "Nondiatonic," determine whether the interval is larger (A) or smaller (d).

1. *P5* ______ ______ ______ ______ ______ ______

2. ______ ______ ______ ______ ______ ______

C. Identify these fourths and fifths by size and quality.

MUSICIANSHIP 6-2

Ear Training: Perfect Intervals

These exercises center on perfect intervals: unisons, octaves, fifths, and fourths. Listen to the interval played, then respond by entering "P1," "P8," "P4," or "P5" in the blank. There are six lines with six problems in each line. (See Appendix D for answers.)

1.	______	______	______	______	______	______
	1	2	3	4	5	6
2.	______	______	______	______	______	______
	1	2	3	4	5	6
3.	______	______	______	______	______	______
	1	2	3	4	5	6
4.	______	______	______	______	______	______
	1	2	3	4	5	6
5.	______	______	______	______	______	______
	1	2	3	4	5	6
6.	______	______	______	______	______	______
	1	2	3	4	5	6

CONSTRUCTING PERFECT INTERVALS. We can use major-scale comparison to construct intervals as well as to identify them. Begin by writing the appropriate size above the given pitch, adjusting the upper pitch *if necessary*. Study the two problems that follow.

Write the pitch G (the size) above D (the given pitch). Next, check G against the scale of D major. Because G is diatonic in D major, the interval is perfect.

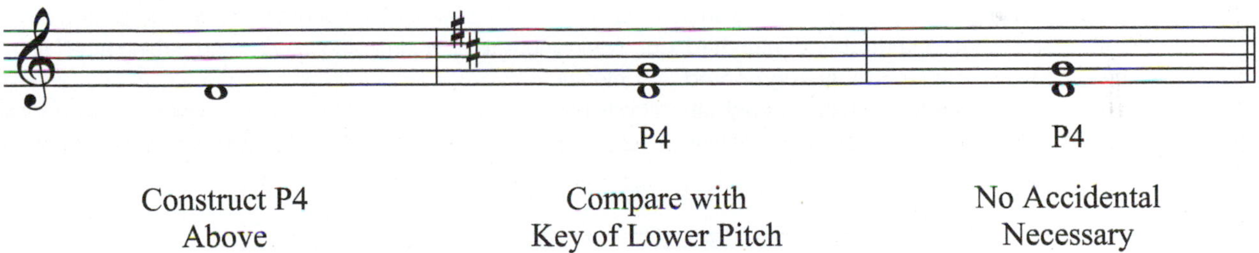

Verify your major-scale comparison by counting half steps. Because we want a perfect fourth, there will be five half steps between pitches.

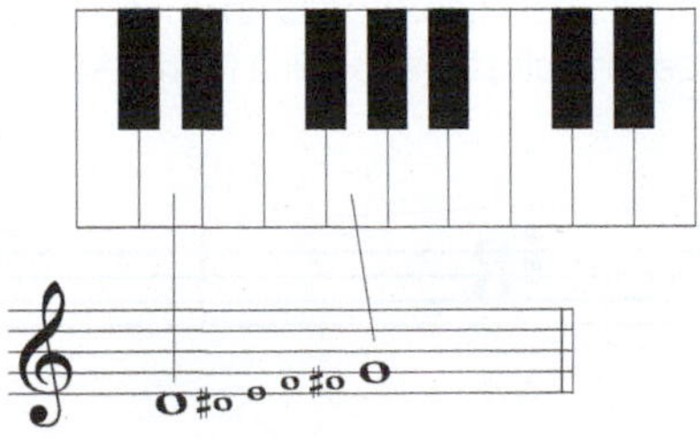

Write the pitch B above E. Compare this fifth with the scale of E major. The pitch B is diatonic in E major, so we know that the E–B fifth is perfect. Because we want a diminished, rather than a perfect fifth, we lower the B to B♭.

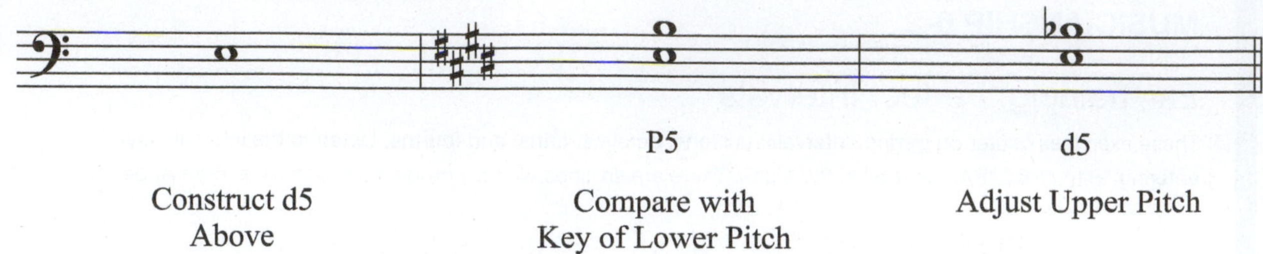

Again, we can verify half steps if desired. In a diminished fifth there should be six half steps between pitches.

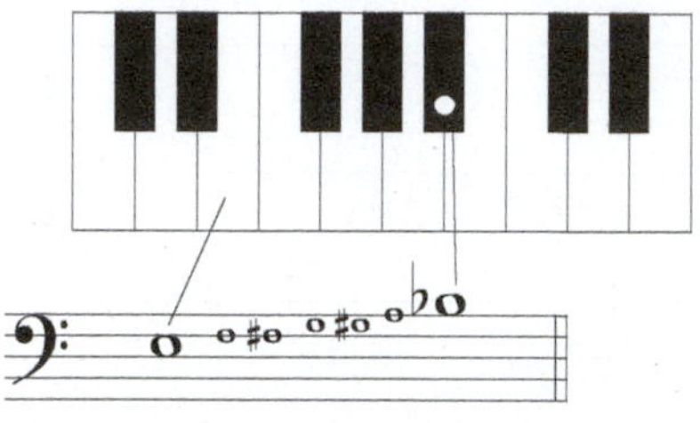

A Step Further

Doubly Augmented and Diminished Intervals

Although rare, an interval will occasionally be smaller than diminished or wider than augmented. If an interval is a half step smaller than diminished, it is **doubly diminished** (dd). Beginning with an augmented interval and adding a half step more between pitches results in a **doubly augmented** (AA) interval.

The interval from B to F is a diminished fifth (with six half steps between pitches); if the two pitch names remain the same, and if we decrease this interval by another half step, it becomes a *doubly diminished fifth* with only five half steps.

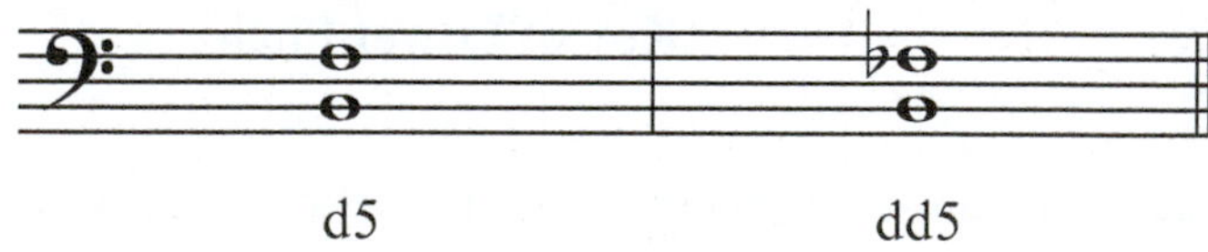

d5 dd5

Likewise, the interval C to F♯ has six half steps and is an augmented fourth. A **double sharp**, 𝄪 raises a pitch two half steps. The interval C to F𝄪 (with seven half steps) is still a fourth—this time *doubly augmented.*

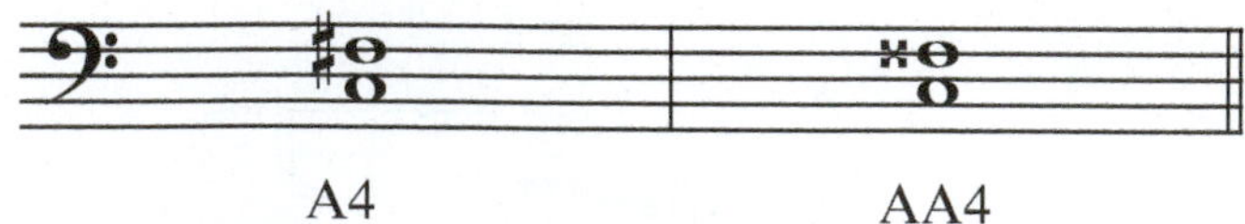

A4 AA4

While the C–F𝄪 interval sounds the same as C–G (a perfect fifth), composers and arrangers notate music from a theoretical standpoint and not by sound alone. Choices in notation are based on the direction of the line.

Complete Building Skills 6-1 on page 167

Major/Minor Intervals

Fourths, fifths, octaves, and unisons can be classified as perfect in quality; the remaining interval sizes can *never* be classified as perfect. Instead, seconds, thirds, sixths, and sevenths are in the **major/minor** category of interval quality.

The *major second* (M2) includes two half steps between pitches. Notice that a major second is equivalent to a whole step.

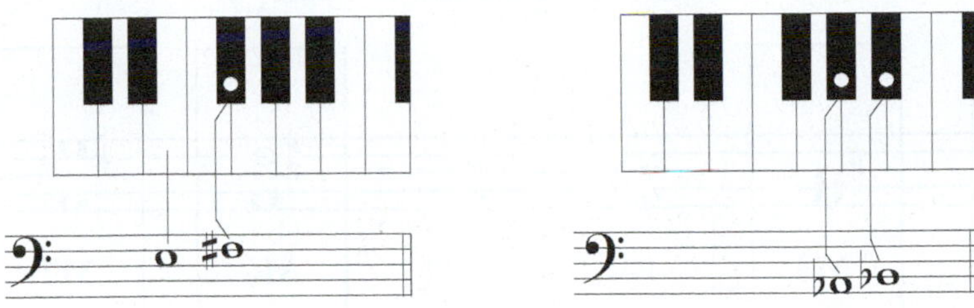

Major Seconds

The *major third* (M3) has four half steps between pitches.

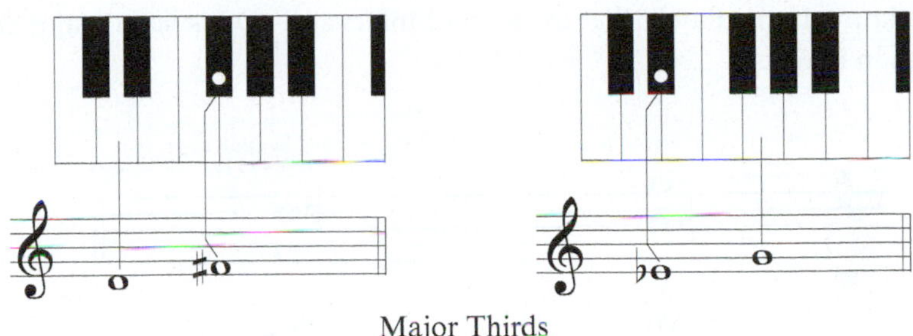

Major Thirds

A *major sixth* (M6) comprises nine half steps.

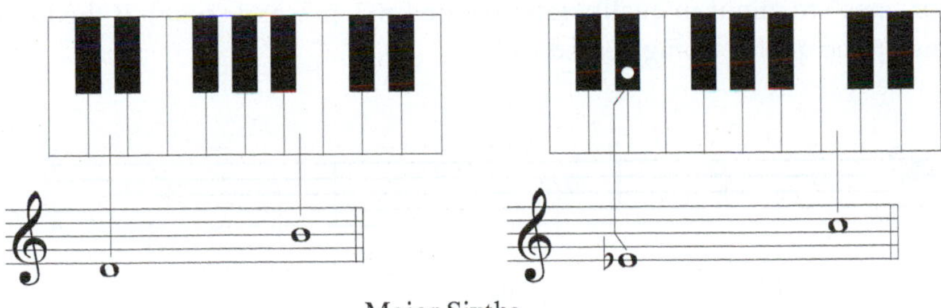

Major Sixths

Finally, the *major seventh* (M7) has 11 half steps between upper and lower pitches.

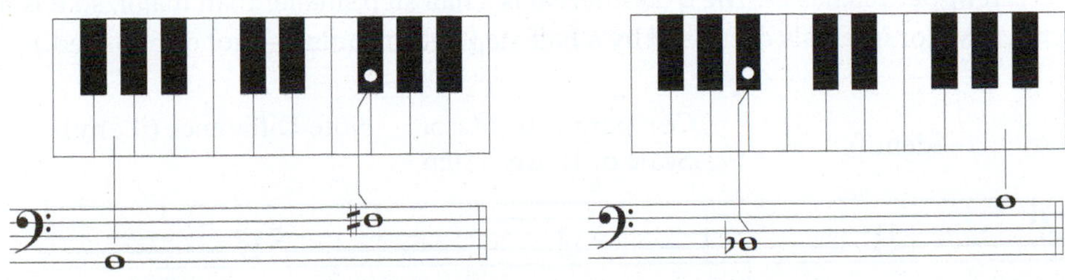

Major Sevenths

The half-step count is useful for comparison and verification of major intervals, but, as with the perfect category, the key signature of the lower pitch is a faster method of identification. The guideline for using major-scale comparison is identical in principle to the one for perfect intervals:

> If the upper pitch of a second, third, sixth, or seventh falls within the major scale of the lower pitch, the quality is major.

Major Intervals in the Major Scale

	P1	**M2**	**M3**	P4	P5	**M6**	**M7**	P8
Half Steps:		2	4			9	11	

Both intervals in the next example are sixths. When you know the key signatures thoroughly, you can tell almost at a glance that the first interval (B♭–G) is a *major* sixth because G is a diatonic pitch in B♭ major. Likewise, we know immediately that the second interval (F–D♭) is *not* a major sixth, since D♭ is not one of the pitches in F major.

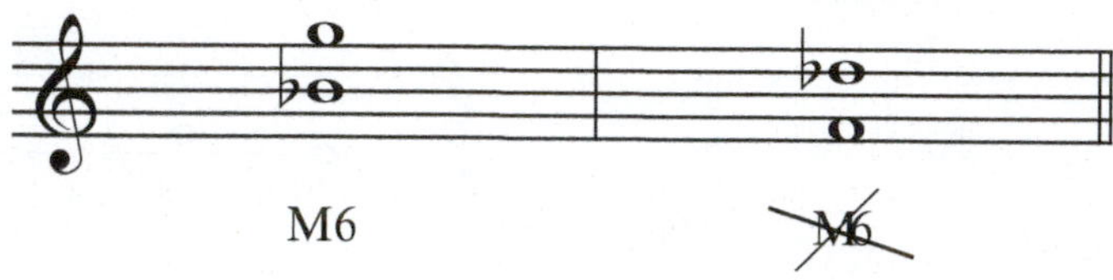

MINOR AND AUGMENTED INTERVALS. Seconds, thirds, sixths, and sevenths that are one half step smaller than major ones are minor in quality (abbreviated m2, m3, and so on). If the interval is a half step wider than major, the quality is augmented (A3).

We can identify major and minor intervals precisely by comparing them to the major scale of the lower pitch. In the next example, we know that the given third is *not* major because the scale of B major has a D♯. The given upper pitch is D♮. The B–D♮ interval is a half step smaller than major, so it is minor in quality. (*Remember:* Major intervals decreased by a half step become minor—not diminished.)

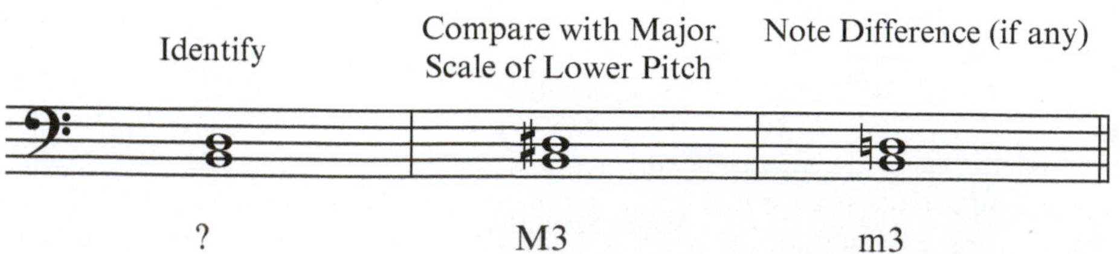

In the next example, we know that C major has an A♮—not an A♯. Because this interval is a half step wider than a major sixth, the interval is augmented.

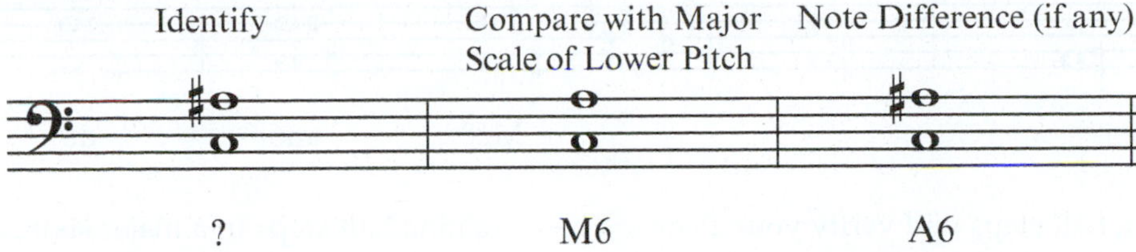

DIMINISHED INTERVALS. The only similarity between perfect and major/minor interval categories is that both can be augmented or diminished in quality. As we have discussed, major intervals decreased by a half step become minor. If a minor interval is narrowed by *another* half step, it becomes diminished.

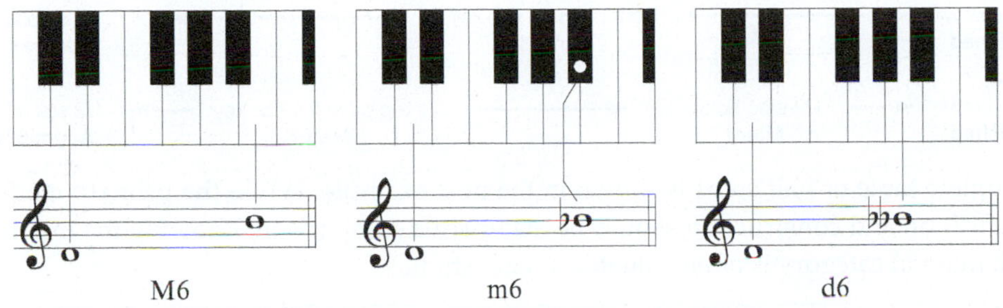

To construct major/minor intervals and their variants, we also rely on major-scale comparison. If we need to write a minor, diminished, or augmented interval, we adjust the upper pitch of the major interval accordingly. Note the procedure outlined in the next two problems.

First, write the pitch G that is a seventh above A. Next, check this pitch against the key signature of A major. Because G♯ is a diatonic pitch in A major, we must adjust the G accordingly.

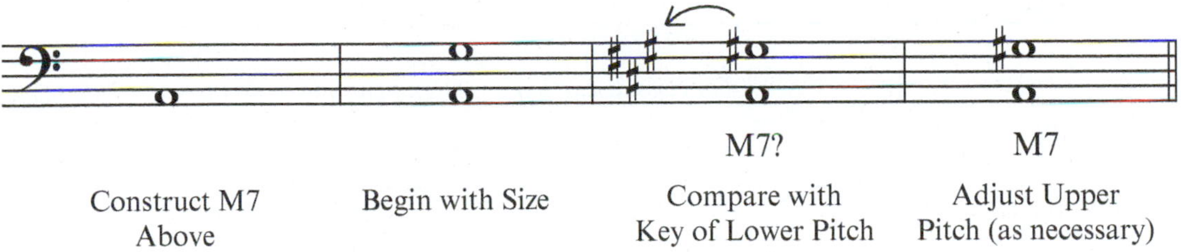

If you are unsure of your answer, you can double check by counting half steps. The upper pitch of a major seventh is 11 half steps above the lower.

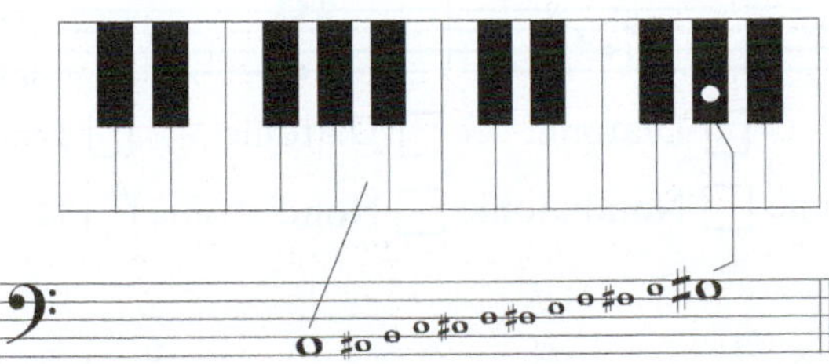

For this problem, use the same initial process: notate a sixth above F♯. Comparing the upper pitch to the scale of F♯ major, a sixth that is major would be D♯. Since we want a *diminished sixth,* we must lower the upper pitch by *two* half steps. The first half-step decrease makes the sixth minor; the second creates the diminished quality.

Counting half steps will verify your answer. There are nine half steps in a major sixth; eight in a minor sixth; and seven in our diminished sixth.

The major-scale comparison will allow you to calculate the quality of intervals quickly and precisely. Use the following chart as a guide:

The complete table of half steps is shown in the next example. While the primary method of interval identification and construction should be major-scale comparison, knowing the number of half steps in each interval category is often valuable in later studies.

Interval	Half Steps Between Pitches	Interval	Half Steps Between Pitches
P1	0	P5	7
m2	1	m6	8
M2	2	M6	9
m3	3	m7	10
M3	4	M7	11
P4	5	P8	12
A4/d5	6		

For class discussion or assignment: please do not remove these pages

REVIEW SET

Major and Minor Intervals

A. Check the "Diatonic" or "Nondiatonic" box according to whether the upper pitch of these intervals is or is not in the major key represented by the lower pitch.

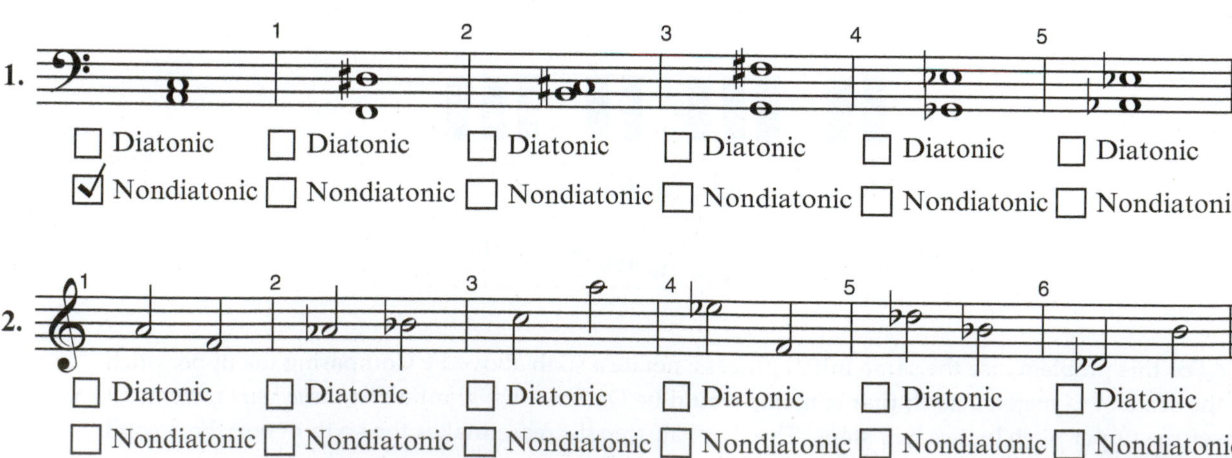

B. Return to your answers in the previous exercise. Where you chose "Diatonic" or "Nondiatonic" you can now identify the interval specifically as "m3," for example. If you chose "Nondiatonic," determine whether the interval is larger than or smaller than the corresponding diatonic interval.

1. *m3* __________ 1 __________ 2 __________ 3 __________ 4 __________ 5

2. __________ 1 __________ 2 __________ 3 __________ 4 __________ 5 __________ 6

C. Identify these seconds, thirds, sixths, and sevenths by size and quality.

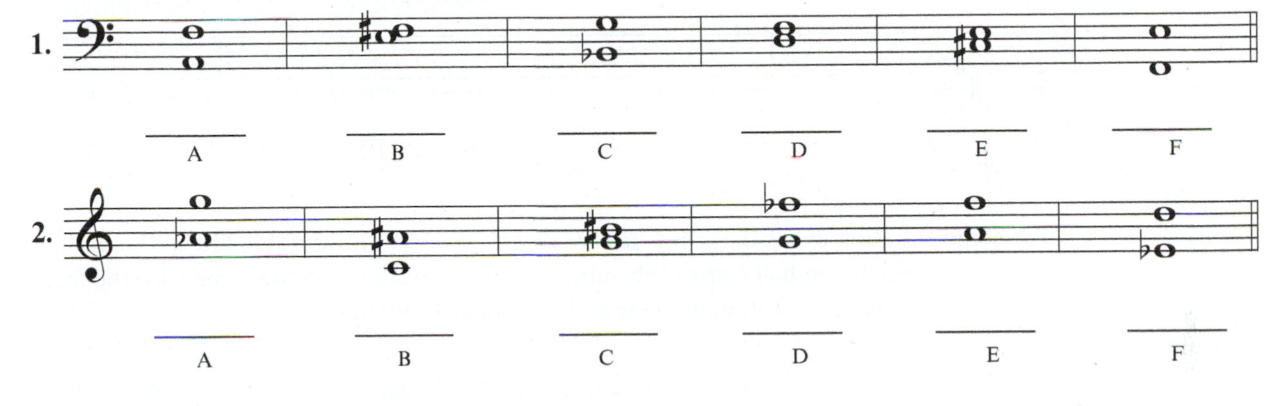

Complete Building Skills 6-2 on page 169

Guidelines for Interval Construction and Identification

Historically, the first accidentals were used to avoid an interval that was considered "unseemly" in the Middle Ages. The **tritone** (called "the devil in music" because of its unstable nature) is, for our purposes, either an augmented fourth or a diminished fifth. While we will discuss the tritone further in later chapters, notice that these *enharmonic intervals* are written differently, but sound the same. We can notate a tritone above the pitch D, for example, as either an augmented fourth (D–G♯) or a diminished fifth (D–A♭). Listen to the sound of the tritone on the course website.

Tritones

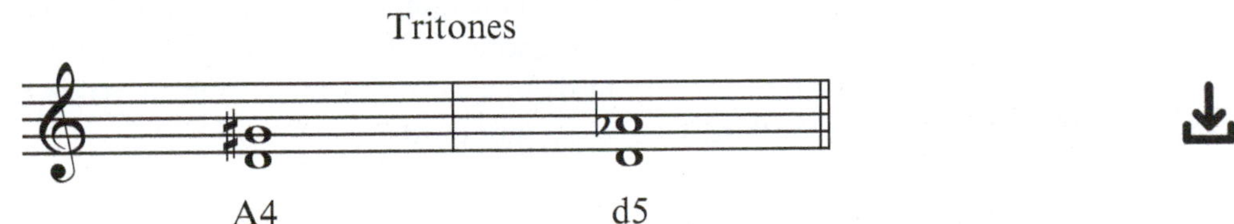

While the two intervals in the last example sound the same, one is a fourth and the other a fifth. We would never use them interchangeably in notation.

SIMPLE AND COMPOUND INTERVALS. An interval that spans an octave or less is termed **simple**. If the interval is larger than an octave it is **compound**. An octave plus a second is a compound interval termed a *ninth;* an octave plus a third is a *tenth,* and so on.

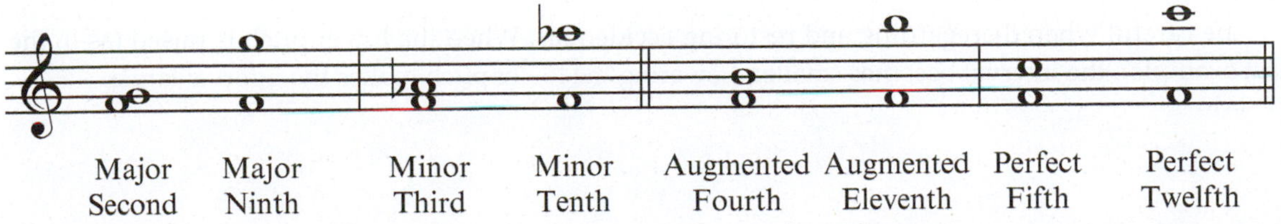

Even though the interval size maybe greater than an octave, the quality remains the same as its reduced version (within an octave).

INTERVAL EXCEPTIONS. In some cases, the lower pitch of an interval may not correspond to one of the 15 major key signatures. The interval E♯–B♯, for example, is a problem because there is no key of E♯major and we have nothing for comparison. If both pitches are affected by the same accidental, however, the accidentals can be ignored. If we need to calculate the interval between E♯ and B♯, we can ignore the sharps and instead calculate the interval between E and B in the usual manner.

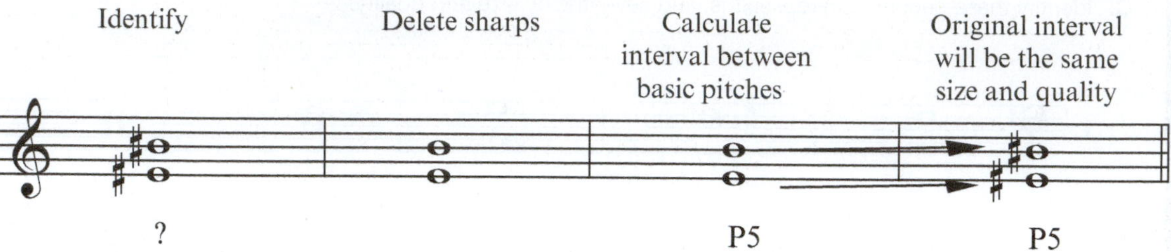

The same situation exists if our pitches are E𝄫 and B𝄫. (A **double flat** is like a double sharp. This symbol lowers a pitch two half steps.) When basic pitches are altered in the same way, the interval size and quality are unchanged (although the sound, of course, is different).

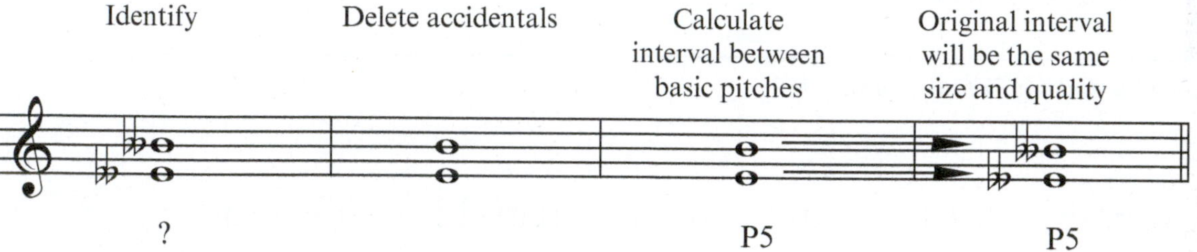

DISREGARDING AND RESTORING ACCIDENTALS. When two pitches of an interval are not affected by the same accidental and the lower pitch does not correspond to one of the major keys, a second approach may be helpful. First, disregard the accidental of the lower pitch so that it represents a major key; next, calculate quality in the usual way. Finally, adjust the result to reflect the accidental disregarded earlier. If we are concerned with the interval G♯–B, for example, we have no basis of comparison since G♯ is not a major key. If we ignore the sharp, however, we can use our usual process to calculate the interval G–B as a major third. Now add back the G♯, which makes the interval smaller. If the interval G–B is a major third, G♯–B is a minor third.

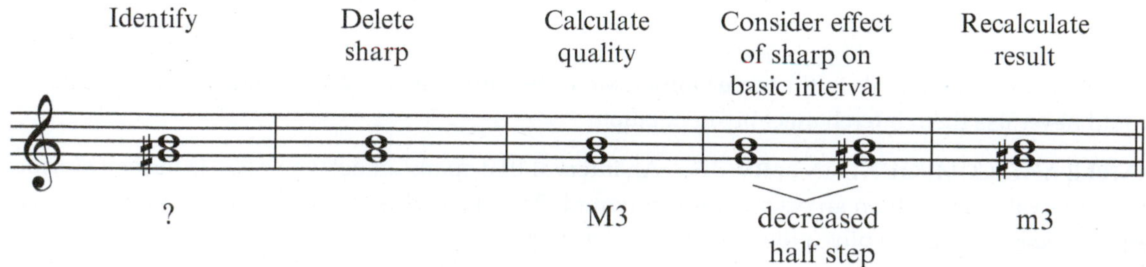

Be careful when disregarding and restoring accidentals. When the lower pitch is raised (as in the last example), the interval becomes smaller. Lowering the lower pitch makes the interval larger.

For class discussion or assignment: please do not remove these pages

REVIEW SET

More Complex Intervals

A. Construct these intervals *above* the given pitch. If the lower pitch does not correspond to one of the major keys, use another method to build the interval.

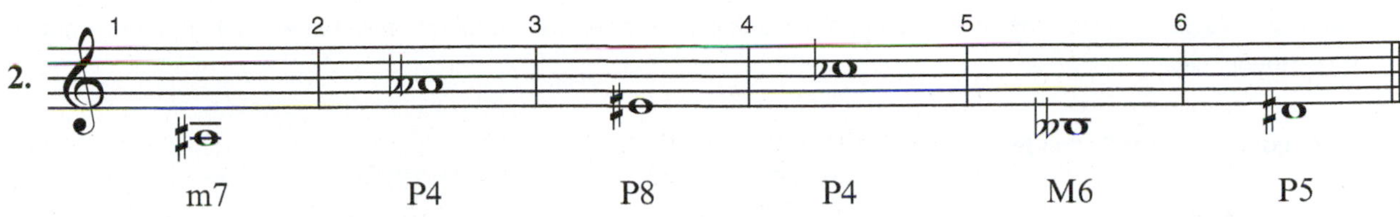

B. Identify these intervals by size and quality.

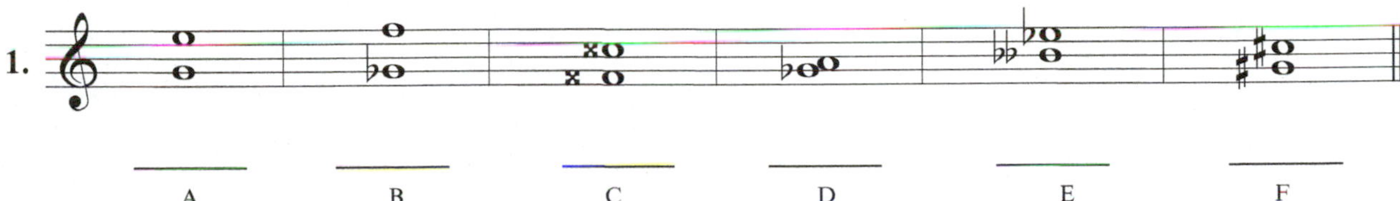

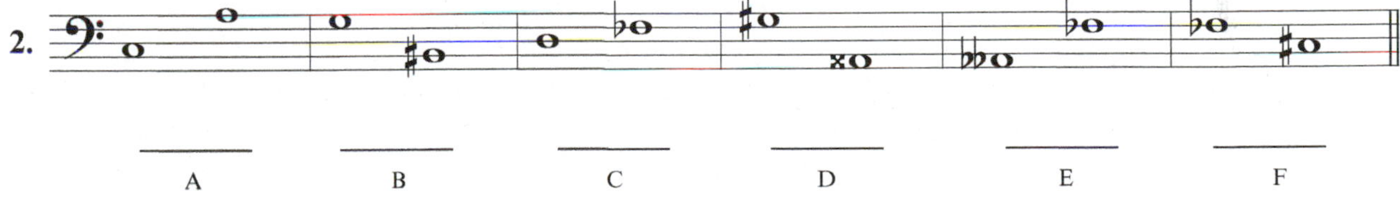

MUSICIANSHIP 6-3

I. Keyboard: Intervals

A. Follow the procedure detailed on page 294 to complete this exercise. Refer to Parts B1 and B2 of the preceding Review Set and play each interval in both lines at the keyboard. Do not play black keys with your thumb. The exact fingering will depend on the size of the interval; however, you should use two different fingers in all cases. Practice with both left and right hands.

B. Locate the correct octave and play each interval at the keyboard. Avoid playing black keys with your thumb.

Right-Hand Intervals	*Left-Hand Intervals*
1. M6 above D5	**6.** m7 below A_1
2. m3 below $C\sharp_3$	**7.** m2 above F_4
3. M7 above B_5	**8.** M6 below E_3
4. m6 above E_2	**9.** M3 below C_5
5. M2 above $F\sharp_3$	**10.** m6 above $E\flat_2$

II. Ear Training: Hearing Interval Quality

In Chapter 3, you differentiated between whole and half steps. These intervals, of course, are also known as major and minor seconds, respectively. This section invites you to compare major versus minor intervals. Use appropriate quality and size labels (M2, m2, M3, m3). Listen to the interval (played both melodically and harmonically), and write your answer in the blank. See Appendix D for answers. Additional ear training exercises can be found on websites such as Teoria.com and musictheory.net.

Major and Minor Seconds

	1	2	3	4	5	6
a.						
b.						
c.						

Major and Minor Thirds

	1	2	3	4	5	6
d.						
e.						
f.						
g.						

Major and Minor Seconds and Thirds

	1	2	3	4	5	6
h.						
i.						
j.						
k.						

The intervals in the next lines will be dictated by your instructor (or you can listen to the audio files on the website). These problems combine perfect intervals (P1, P8, P4, and P5) with the major and minor seconds and thirds from earlier exercises.

Perfect Intervals and Major and Minor Seconds, and Thirds

a. ______ ______ ______ ______ ______ ______
1 2 3 4 5 6

b. ______ ______ ______ ______ ______ ______
1 2 3 4 5 6

c. ______ ______ ______ ______ ______ ______
1 2 3 4 5 6

d. ______ ______ ______ ______ ______ ______
1 2 3 4 5 6

Interval Inversion

The word "inversion" suggests some change in a relationship. An inverted triangle, for example, is one that has been turned upside down and rests on its point.

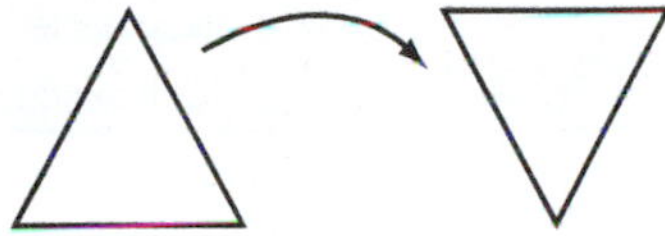

Similarly, an **inverted interval** is one in which the original upper/lower positions of the two pitches have been reversed. Inversion can be accomplished in either of two ways:

1. Raise the lower pitch an octave so that it now appears on top.
2. Lower the upper pitch an octave so that it now appears on the bottom.

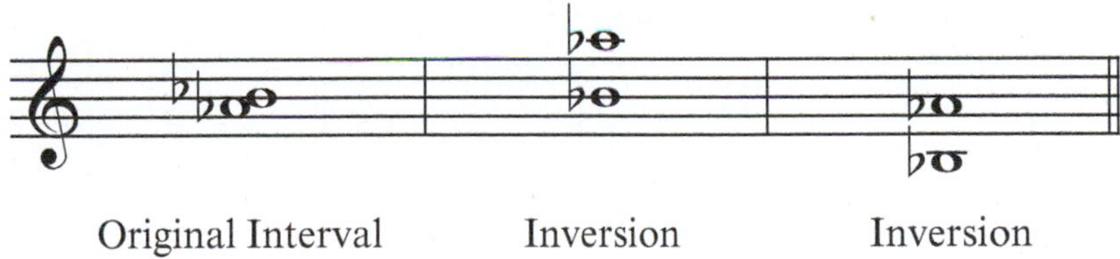

When intervals are inverted, size and quality usually change. In the previous example, the major second of the original interval inverts to become a minor seventh. Notice the inversions in the next example. With the exception of perfect intervals, size and quality *both* change.

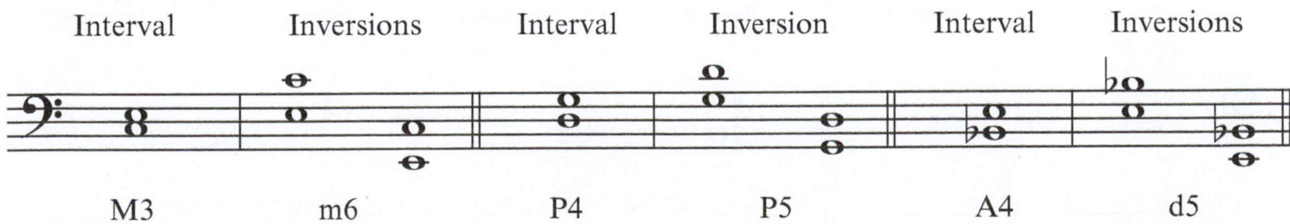

Changes in interval size and quality that result from inversion are predictable. Seconds invert to sevenths, thirds to sixths, and so on. Likewise, quality inverts logically. While perfect intervals remain perfect when inverted, major intervals invert to minor, minor to major, diminished to augmented, and augmented to diminished.

INTERVAL SIZE		
Original Size	⟶	Becomes
seconds		sevenths
thirds		sixths
fourths		fifths
fifths		fourths
sixths		thirds
sevenths		seconds

INTERVAL QUALITY		
Original Quality	⟶	Becomes
major		minor
minor		major
perfect		perfect
diminished		augmented
augmented		diminished

For class discussion or assignment: please do not remove these pages

REVIEW SET

Interval Inversion

Name the first interval size and quality. Invert the interval and identify the resultant size and quality.

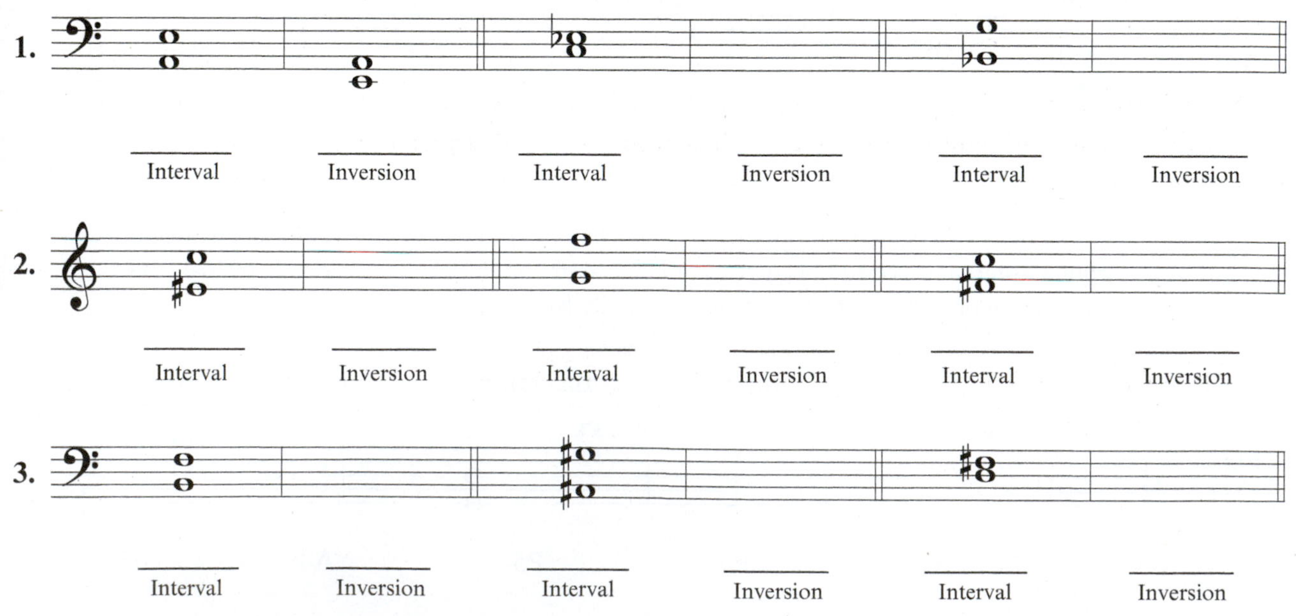

Writing Intervals Below a Given Pitch

We have discussed how to write intervals above a given pitch by beginning with the key signature and comparing the upper pitch to that scale. When we need an interval below a given pitch, however, the key signature is unknown. If we want a major sixth below A, for example, the correct pitch could be C major, C♭ major, or C♯ major.

To find the major sixth below A, we could count down nine half steps.

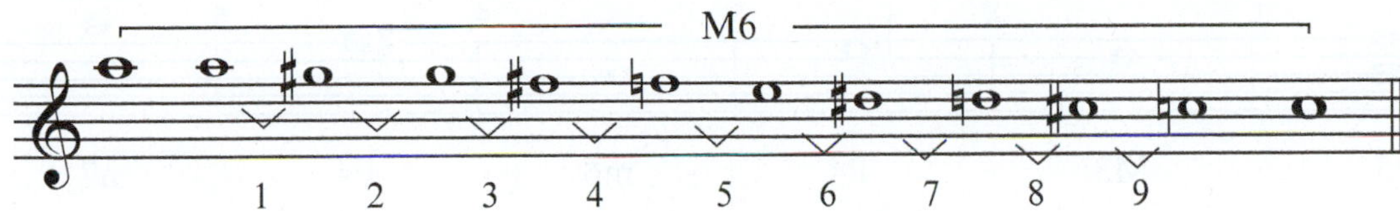

Counting half steps, however, is both slow and rich in the potential for error. Nine half steps below the pitch A can also result in the pitch B♯—a diminished seventh below A.

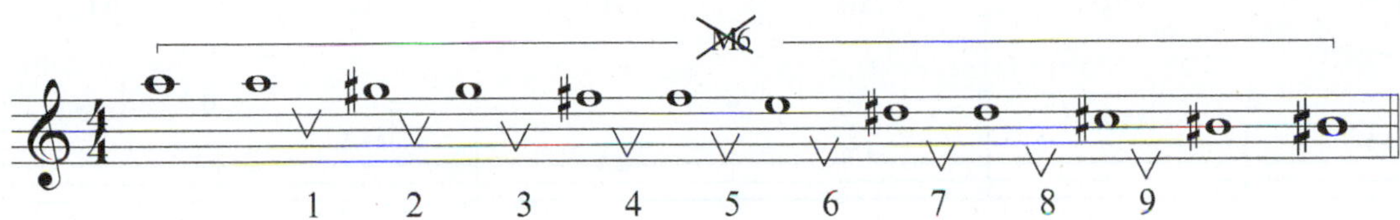

To construct a *minor* sixth below A, for example, notate the pitch C to establish the interval size. The next step is to calculate interval quality in the usual way, from bottom to top; from C up to A is a major sixth. But because we wanted a *minor* sixth, change the C to C♯.

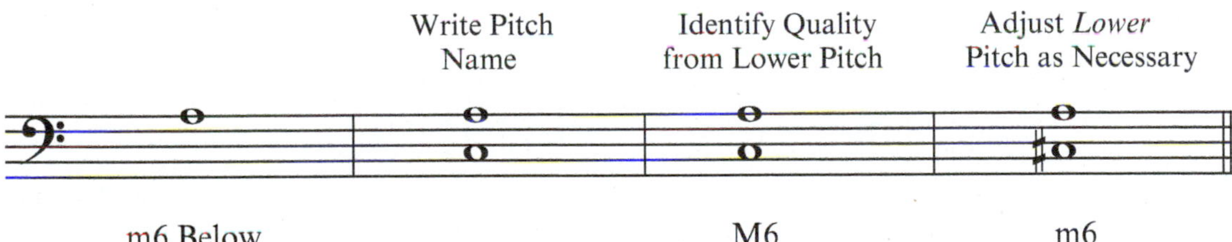

INTERVAL INVERSION. We know that intervals invert in a predictable way. To construct a major sixth below F using this method, begin with the inversion: a minor third. Construct the minor third above F in the usual way, then notate it below. The result is a major sixth.

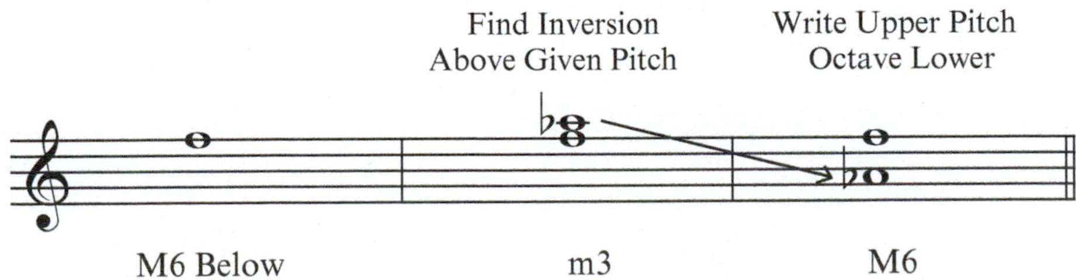

For class discussion or assignment: please do not remove these pages

REVIEW SET

Writing Intervals Below a Given Pitch

Construct the specified interval below the given pitch. Do not change the given pitch.

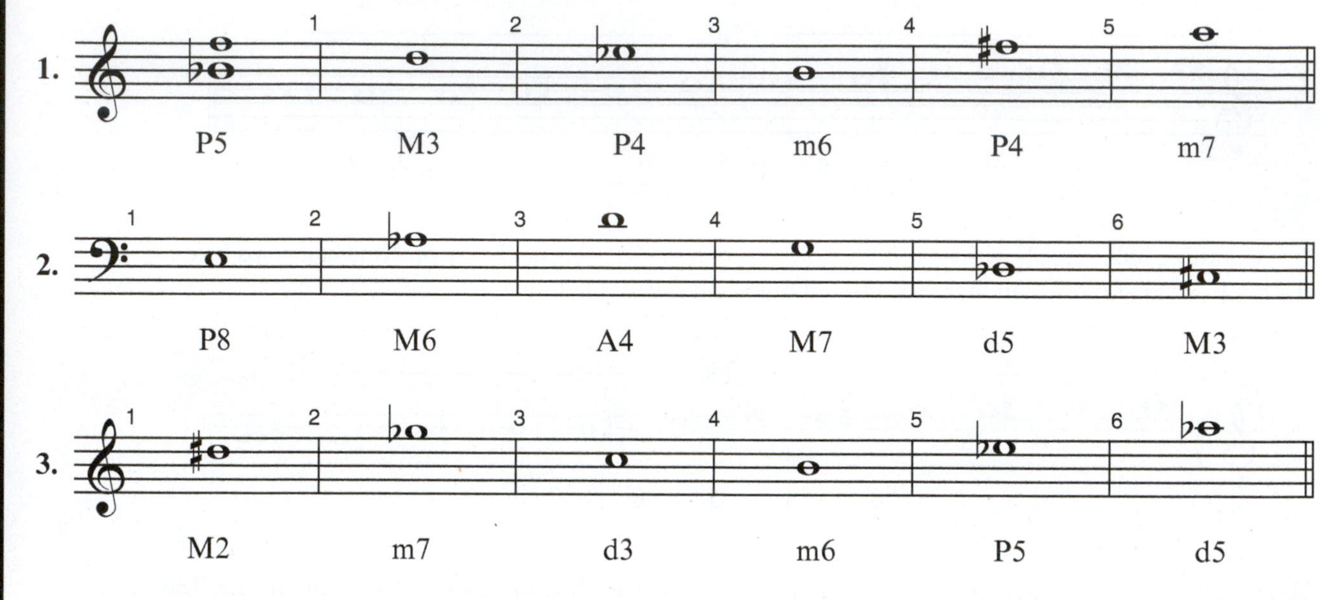

Complete Building Skills 6-3 on page 171

Name ______________________

Page may be removed

Building Skills 6-1

Intervals

A. Identify the interval size.

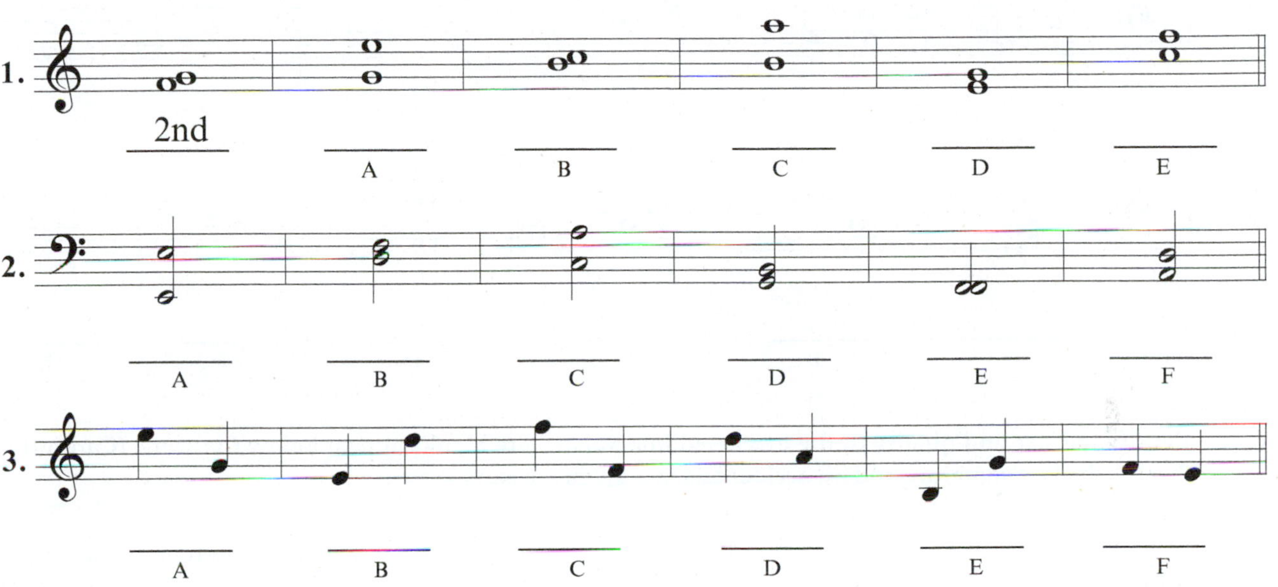

B. Provide a second pitch that produces the specified interval (size and quality) *above* the one given. This exercise includes perfect, augmented, and diminished intervals.

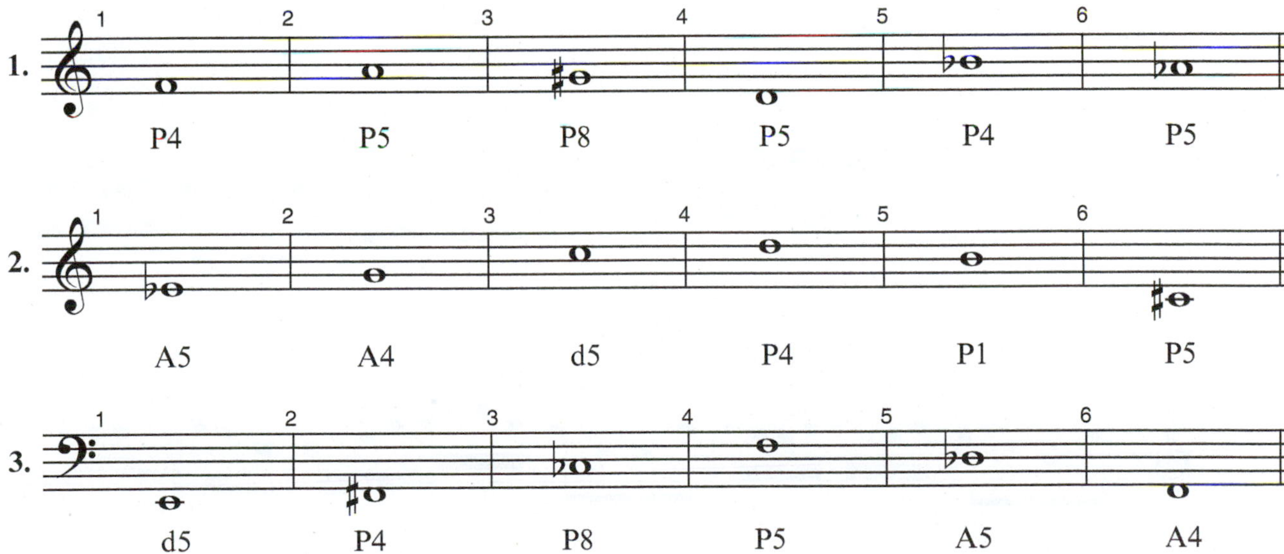

C. **Identify these intervals by size and quality.**

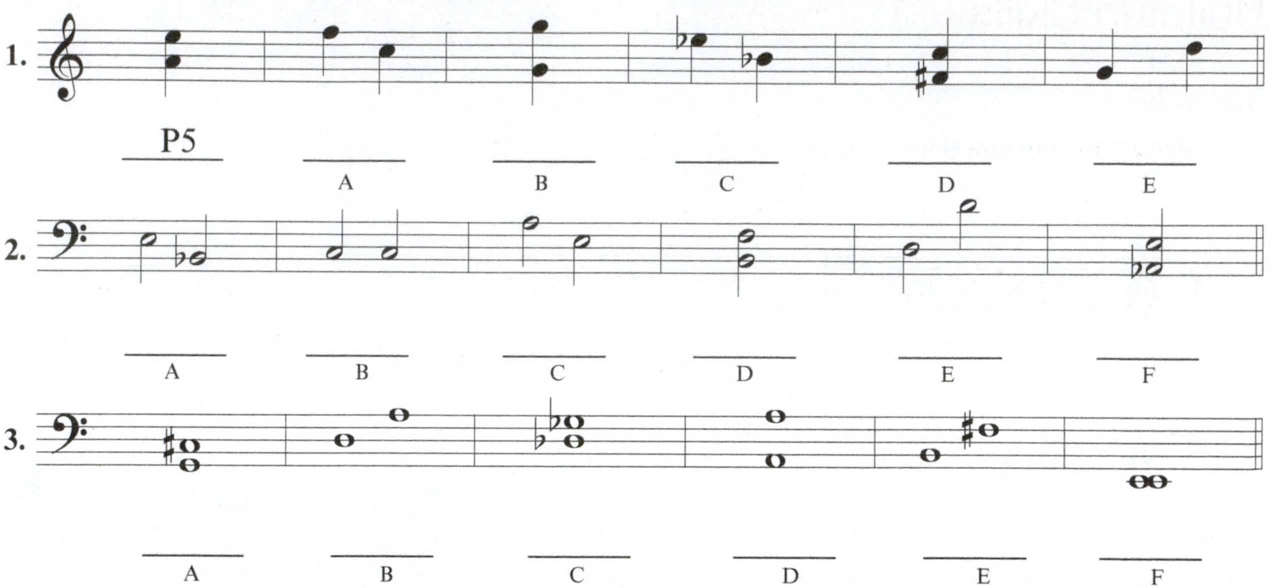

D. **Identify the size and quality of the bracketed intervals where blanks appear below the score. (Carefully observe the key signature and all accidentals in a given measure.)**

Name ______________________

Page may be removed

Building Skills 6-2

All Intervals

A. **Identify the following intervals by size and quality.**

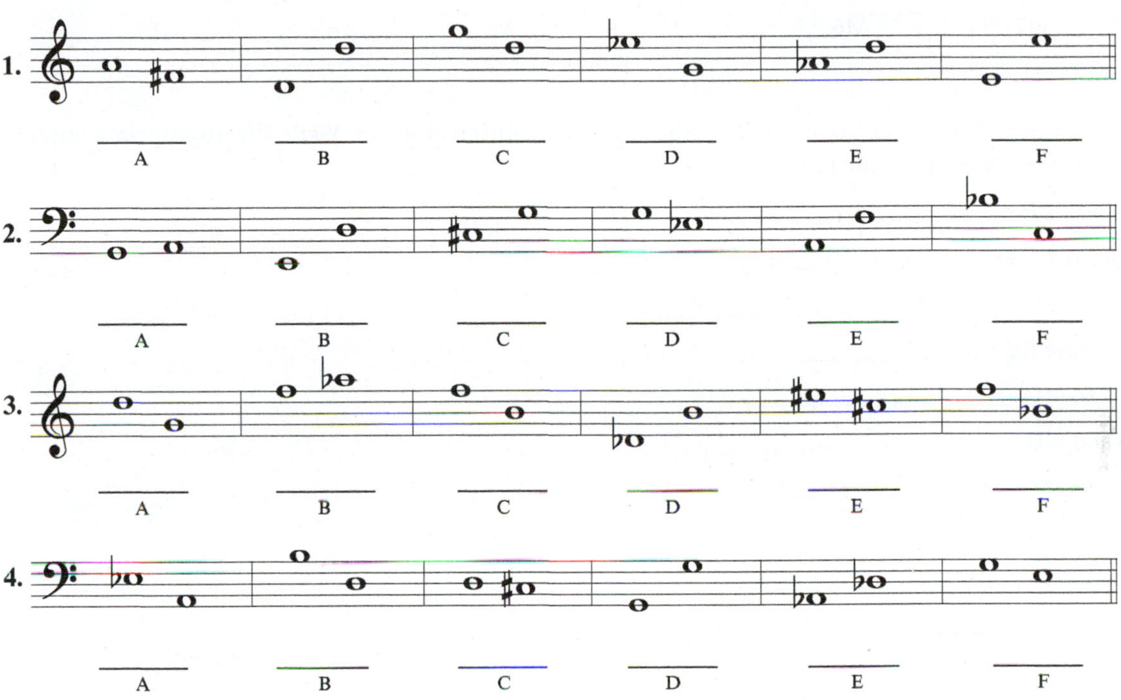

B. **Construct the named intervals above the given pitch.**

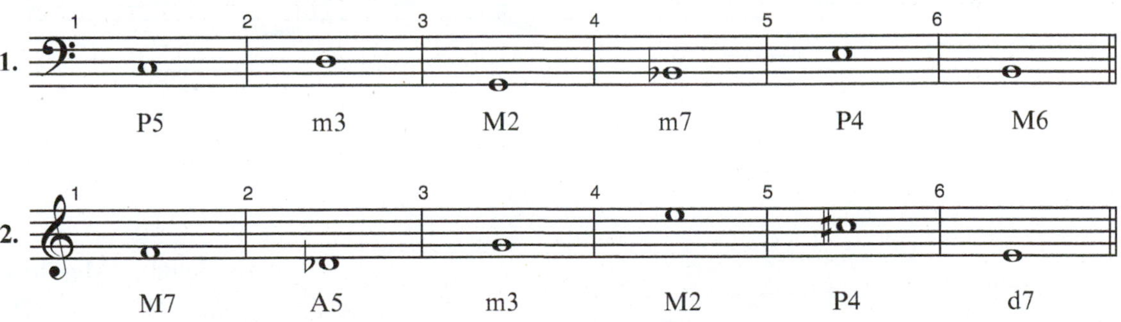

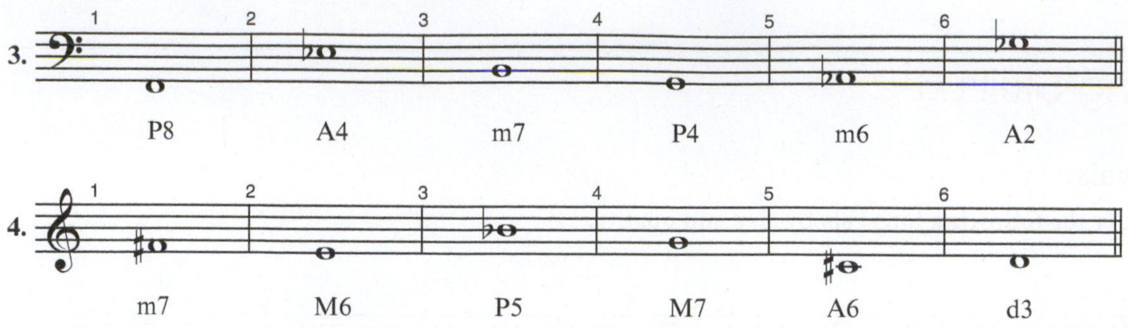

C. **Name the pitch that creates the interval without using manuscript paper. Write the appropriate letter (with an accidental if necessary) in the blank.**

1. M2 above B_3 ____________________
2. M6 above D_2 ____________________
3. A2 above $E\flat_5$ ____________________
4. m3 above $C\sharp_5$ ____________________
5. P5 above C_4 ____________________
6. d5 above D_3 ____________________
7. M3 above $E\flat_4$ ____________________
8. d7 above B_4 ____________________
9. m6 above D_5 ____________________
10. A4 above $C\sharp_2$ ____________________

D. **In the blanks below each staff, identify the bracketed intervals by size and quality. Remember to consider the key signature and accidentals when determining interval quality.**

Richard Wagner, *Tristan and Isolde*

Amy Beach, "Meadow-Larks"

2.

1 2 3 4 5

Name ______________________

Page may be removed

Building Skills 6-3

Interval Inversion

A. **Construct harmonic intervals *below* the given pitches.**

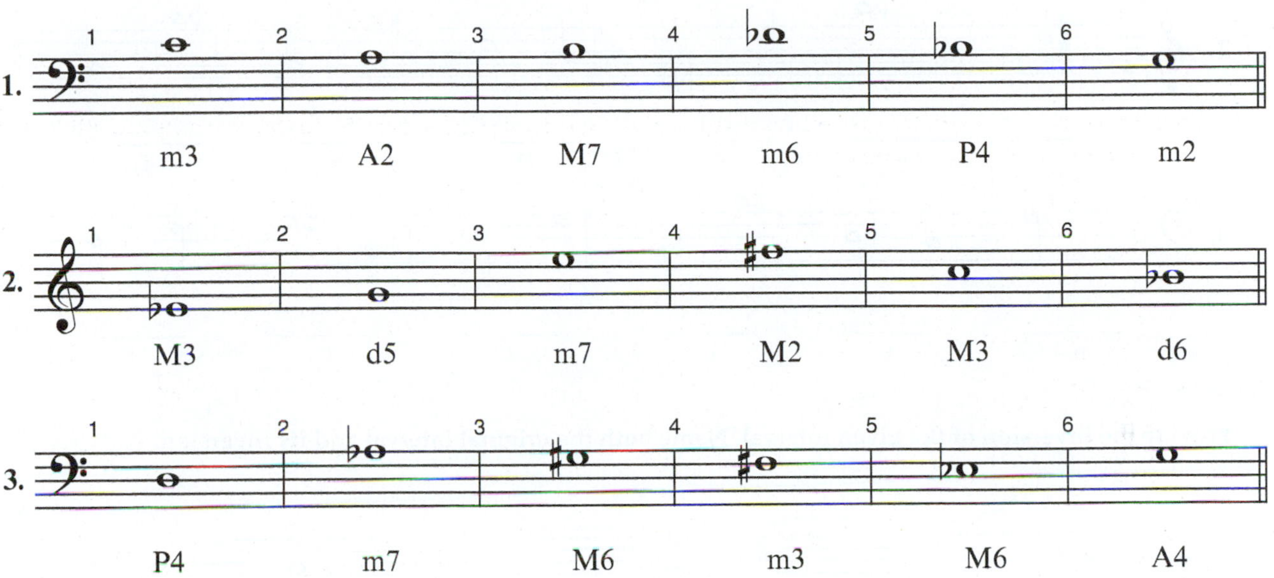

B. **These intervals are compound. Construct harmonic intervals *above* the given note.**

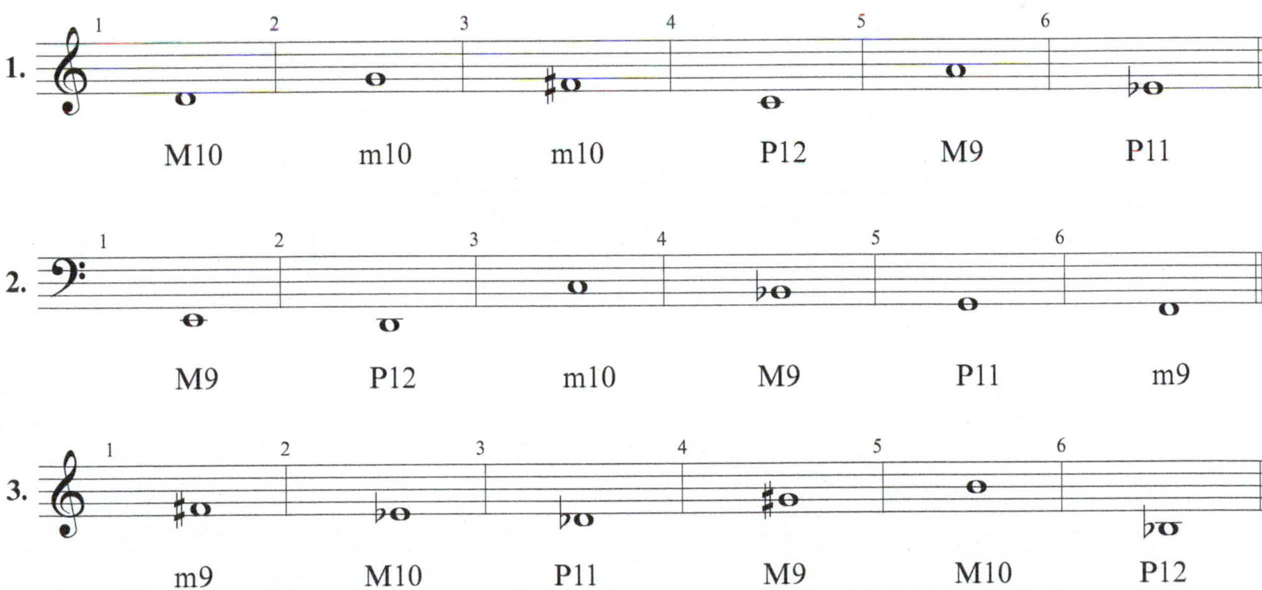

C. **Identify these intervals by size and quality.**

D. **Provide the inversion of the given interval. Name both the original interval and its inversion.**

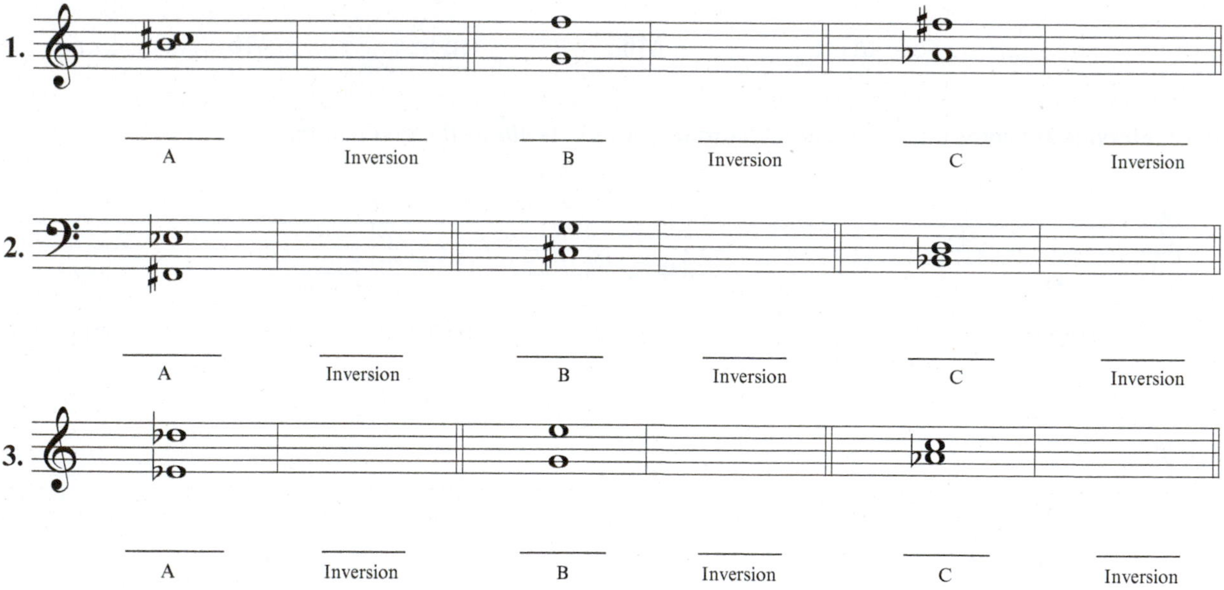

Name ____________________

Page may be removed

E. Analyze the melodic intervals between all pairs of consecutive pitches in these melodies.

American Folk Song, "Bury Me Not"

1.

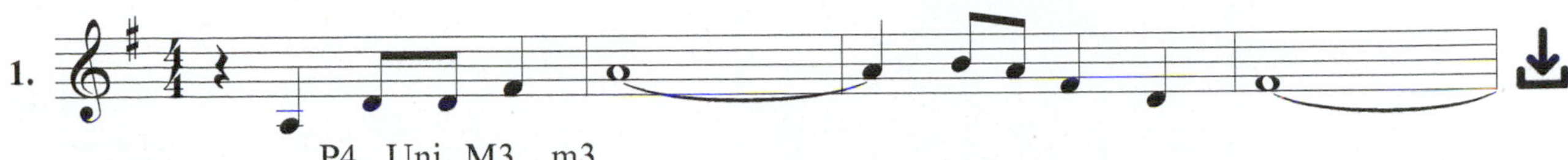

a. How many different interval sizes occur in this melody? ____________________

b. What is the smallest interval (quality and size)? ____________________ The largest? ____________________

c. Including the intervals provided, which interval occurs most frequently?

d. Comment on one interesting feature of this melody.

Maurice Ravel, *Valse Nobles et Semtimentales*

2.

a. How many different interval sizes occur in this melody? ____________________

b. What is the smallest interval (quality and size)? ____________________ The largest? ____________________

c. Including the intervals provided, which interval occurs most frequently?

d. Comment on one interesting feature of this melody.

Welch Folk Song, *The Ash Grove*

3.

a. How many different interval sizes occur in this melody? ____________________

b. What is the smallest interval (quality and size)? ____________________ The largest? ____________________

c. Which interval occurs most frequently?

d. Comment on one interesting feature of this melody.

Name ______________________

Page may be removed

Creative Projects • Chapter 6

Write melodies emphasizing the suggested intervals. Where you place these designated intervals is more important than how many you use. Balance an ascending leap with descending stepwise motion (or the reverse). Limit your lines to diatonic pitches, beginning and ending on the tonic.

1. E Major. Emphasize major sixths in the melody.

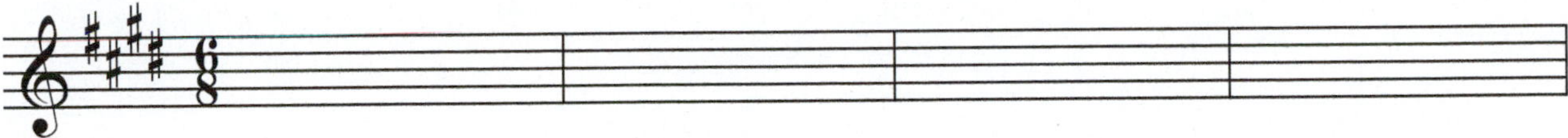

2. F Major. Emphasize perfect fifths in the melody.

Name ______________________

Page may be removed

Analysis in Context 1 • Chapter 6

Composed by Gustav Mahler at the turn of the 20th century, the song cycle *Kindertotenleider* is based on five poems written by Friedrich Rückert. Rückert wrote these particular poems following the death and illness of several of his children. "Nun will die Sonn' so hell aufgeh'n" (Now the sun wants to rise so brightly) is the first song in the cycle. After listening to the audio file on the website, answer the questions that follow.

Nun will die Sonn' so hell aufgeh'n!

Gustav Mahler, *Kindertonlieder*

p
Nun will die Sonn' so hell auf - geh'n,
9
pp
als sei kein Un - glück, kein Un - glück die Nacht ge-
15
p
scheh'n! Das Un-glück ge - schah nur mir al - lein!
29
p
Die Son - ne, die Son - ne, sie schei - net
35
all - ge - mein! Du muBt nieht die
49
Nacht in dir ver - schränken, muBt sie ins
53
ew' - ge Licht, ins ew' - - - ge Licht ver - sen -
59
ken! Ein Lämplein ver - losch in mei - nem Zelt!
72
mf
p
Heil! Heil sei dem Freu - den-licht der Welt,
79
sf
dem Freu - den - licht der Welt.

1. Look up the translation of the word *Kindertotenlieder*. How is this reflected in Mahler's use of nondiatonic pitches in the melody line?

2. Based on your listening, what does the symbol mean in the first full measure?

3. Label all of the melodic intervals in measures 11–15 directly in the score. What interval is used most frequently?

4. Give the measure number(s) where the largest interval occurs. Identify the interval by size and quality.

5. Circle all melodic minor seconds found in the score. Why do you think minor seconds are so prevalent?

6. What is the highest pitch used in measures 35–36? ______ What is the lowest pitch used in measures 35–36? ______ What is the interval between those two pitches?

7. Label all of the melodic intervals in the final phrase (measures 79–82). What is the largest interval? ______ What is the smallest interval? ______

8. Look up a translation for the text of the excerpt. How does the placement of the rests in measure 74 emphasize the meaning of the text?

Chapter 7

Compound Meters

Essential Terms and Symbols

𝄆 𝄇	compound meter	natural beat division
borrowed beat division	duplet	triplet

Simple and compound meters are central to the Western system of rhythmic organization. In Chapter 4 we discovered that the beat in simple meter is a note that may be divided into two equal parts. The beat in **compound meter** is a *dotted note;* dotted notes divide naturally into three parts. This fact is the essence of the difference between simple and compound meters.

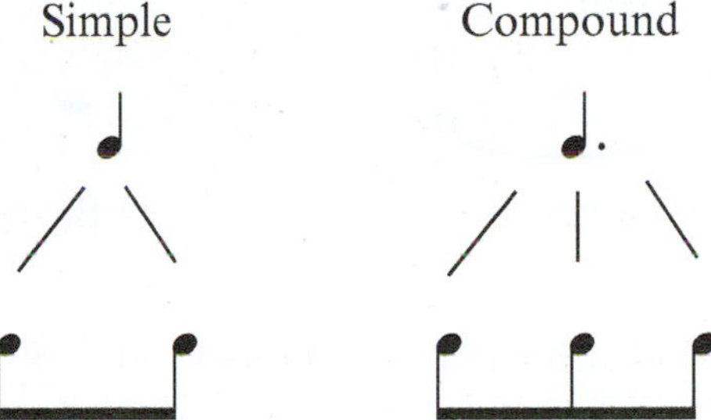

Just as the half note can be used as the beat in simple meter, a *dotted half note* can be used as the beat in compound meter.

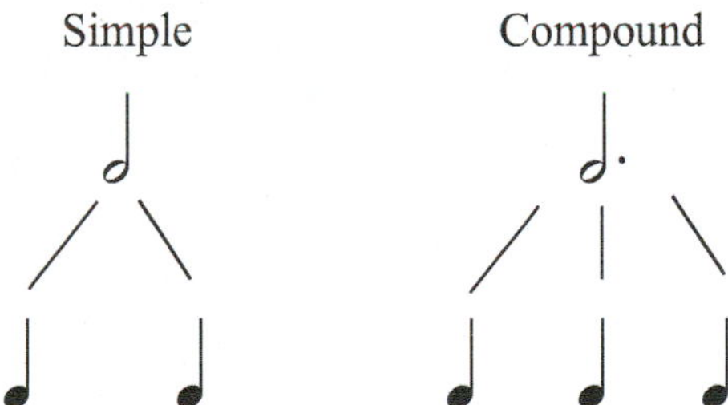

The dotted eighth-note beat is relatively rare, but follows the same pattern, dividing into three sixteenth notes.

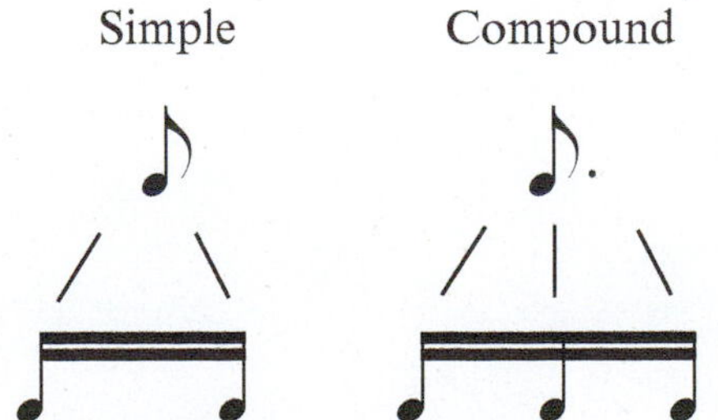

Note Values in Compound Meters

In compound meters, notes and rests receiving more than one beat represent values as they do in simple time (two, three, and four times the beat, for example). If the beat is a dotted quarter note, the dotted half note receives two beats; the dotted whole, four beats.

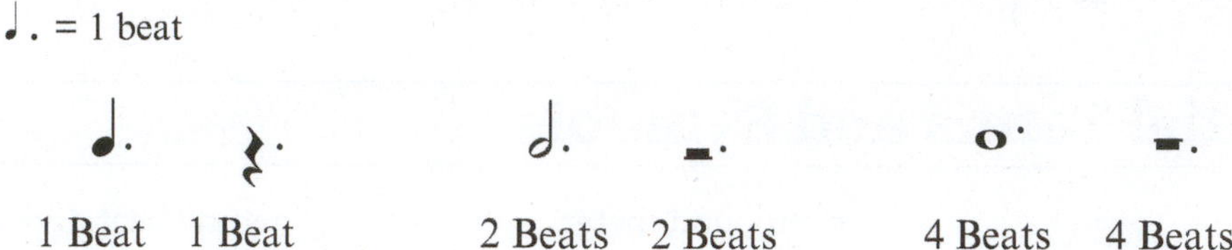

We have no single symbol to represent a unit of three beats in compound meter. While a single dotted note may have three beats in simple meter, tied notes are necessary in compound meters. Notice in the next example that the larger value precedes the smaller. Also, remember that a whole rest is appropriate for an entire measure of silence in any meter.

When the meter is compound, notes and rests of lesser value are often *thirds* and *sixths* of a beat. If the beat is a dotted quarter note, for example, a single eighth note or rest has the value of one-third of a beat. An undotted quarter note or quarter rest receives two-thirds of a beat.

If the dotted half note is the beat, the symbols are different, but the values are the same.

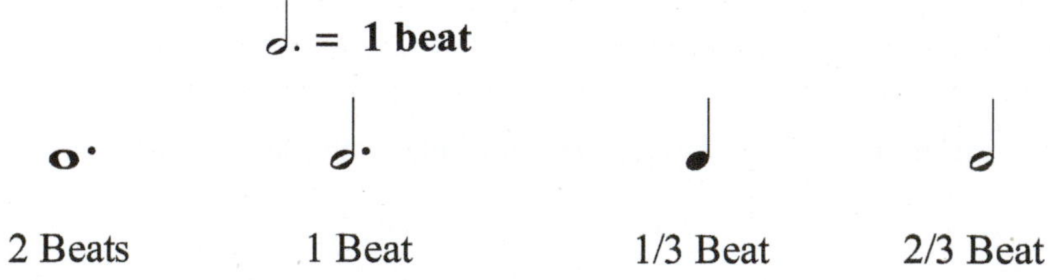

For class discussion or assignment: please do not remove these pages

REVIEW SET

Note Values in Compound Meters

While our goal is to read and understand musical patterns, this exercise centers on individual values given the dotted quarter or dotted half-note beat. Write the appropriate values in the blanks.

♩. = 1 beat

1. 𝄽. ____ A　　𝄼. ____ B　　♩ ____ C　　𝅗𝅥. ____ D

2. ♩. ____ A　　𝅝. ____ B　　𝄾 ____ C　　♩ ____ D

𝅗𝅥. = 1 beat

3. 𝄽 ____ A　　𝅗𝅥 ____ B　　𝅝. ____ C　　♩ ____ D

4. 𝄼. ____ A　　𝄼 ____ B　　𝅗𝅥. ____ C　　𝄻. ____ D

Compound Time Signatures

The upper number of the time signature gives the accent pattern and the lower number stands for the unit of beat. If the beat is a quarter note, for example, the lower number is 4. In compound meters, however, the beat is a dotted note and we have no number to represent this value.

2 over ♩ = 2 over 4　　　2 over ♩. = 2 over ?

To solve the problem of representing the lower number of a compound time signature, composers do not tell us which note gets the beat, but the note that is the beat *division*. When there are two dotted quarter notes in the measure, there are *six* eighth notes in the measure. The number 6 completes the time signature.

The time signature for a duple meter where the beat is a dotted quarter note is $\frac{6}{8}$. If the meter is triple, the signature is $\frac{9}{8}$; if quadruple, it is $\frac{12}{8}$.

Division 3
Beat
= 9/8

4
= 12/8

Compound time signatures lose much of their mystery when you remember that the top number is *three times* the number of beats and that the lower number represents the division of the beat.

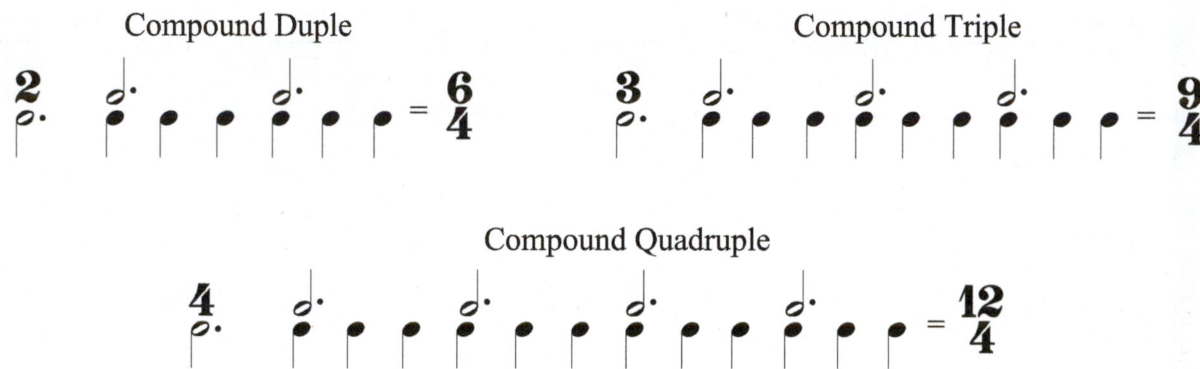

Just as we can hear immediately whether music is in simple or compound meter, the time signature also conveys this same information. A simple rule and a single exception differentiate simple from compound time signatures:

> If the upper number of the time signature is divisible by 3, the meter is compound. In this case, the beat will be a dotted note and will divide into three parts. *Exception:* A meter with 3 as the top number is always simple.

The upper number of a compound time signature will always be divisible by 3 (except 3 itself, which is the exception). Compound time signatures are represented principally by the upper numerals 6, 9, and 12.

Note the information provided by the following compound time signatures.

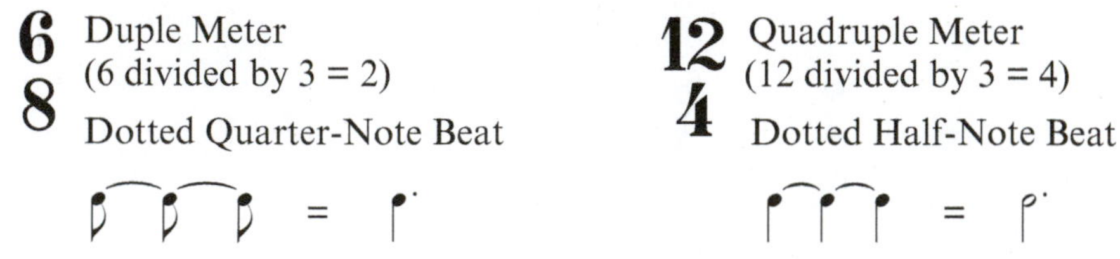

"I Won't Give Up" is a popular song in compound duple meter. There are two beats per measure with the beat divided into three equal parts. Listen to "I Won't Give Up" at least twice. The first time, tap the duple accent pattern of the melody. Each measure has one strong and one weak beat. As you hear the song a second time, tap the underlying beat division (represented by eighth notes in this notation).

Jason Mraz, "I Won't Give Up"

Look at the first eight measures of "Three Blind Mice" written in two different time signatures. Assuming that the tempo remains the same, the two transcriptions would sound exactly alike. (The symbol 𝄆 𝄇 indicates that material between the double bars is to be repeated.) "Three Blind Mice" can also be notated using a dotted half or dotted eighth-note beat.

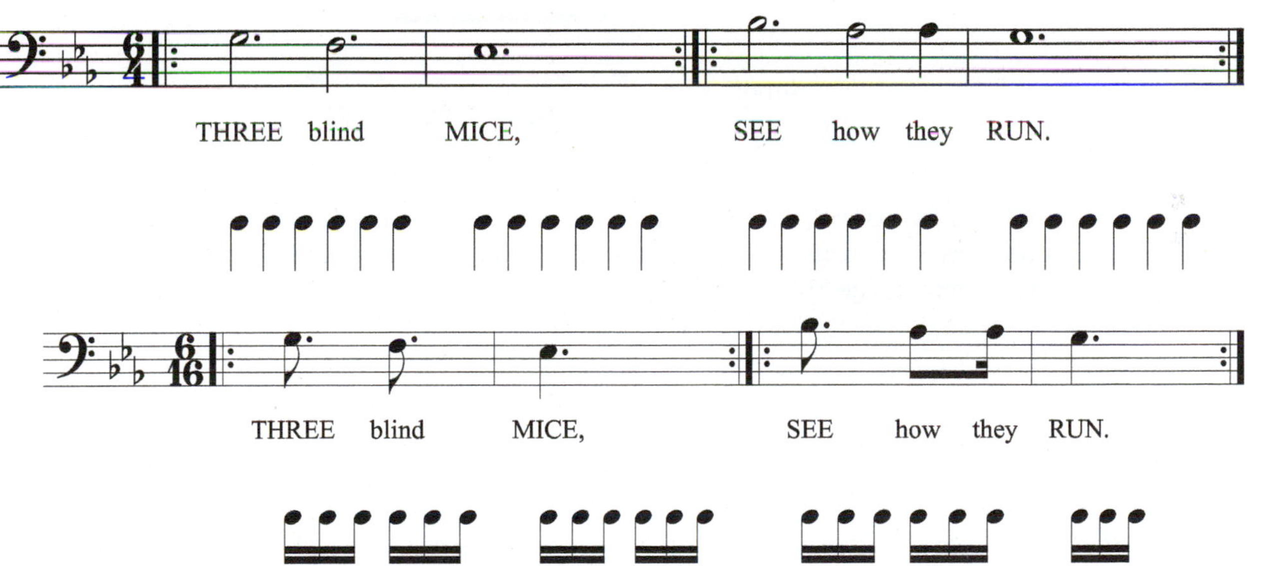

Beat Subdivision

Although the beat in compound meter divides into three parts, the subdivision is still divisible by *two*. If the beat is the dotted half note, for example, it divides into three quarter notes; each quarter note is equivalent to two eighth notes, so the subdivision is six eighth notes.

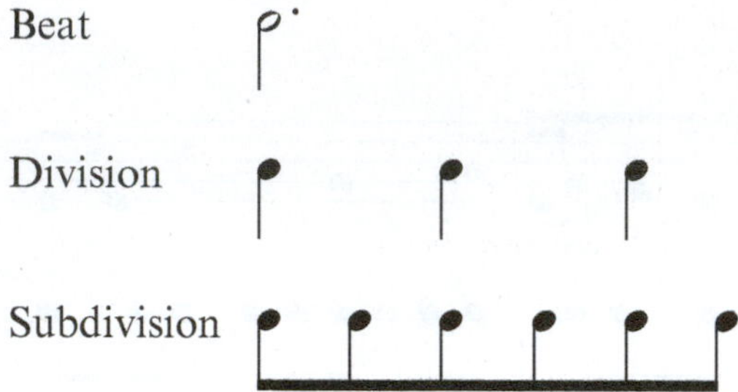

Other compound beats subdivide in a similar manner. The dotted quarter-note beat divides into three eighth notes and subdivides into six sixteenth notes.

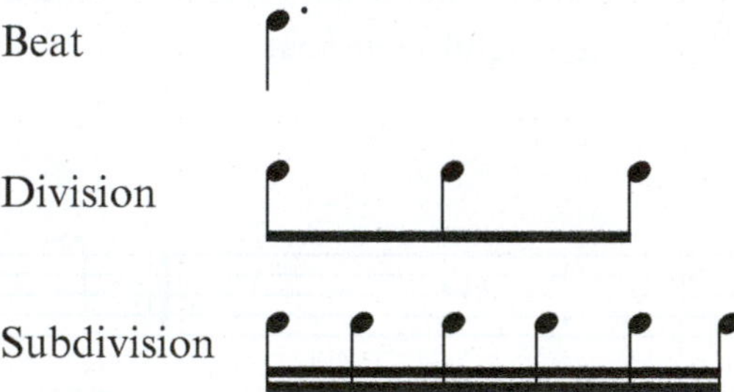

CONDUCTING IN COMPOUND METERS. Because accent patterns in compound meters are the same as the three employed in simple meters, we can use the same basic two-, three-, and four-beat conducting patterns (page 95).

TRICKS OF THE TRADE

Meter Signatures

Below is a chart of the more common compound meters.

Meter Signature	Beats per Measure	Value That Equals One Beat	Equivalent Rest	Sample Measure
6/8	2	Dotted quarter note		6/8
9/8	3	Dotted quarter note		9/8
12/8	4	Dotted quarter note		12/8

Other note values, including the dotted eighth note and the dotted half note, can be used as the beat in compound meter, but they are much less frequent. The chart below indicates other time signatures that may be used in compound meter.

Complete Building Skills 7-1 on page 199

For class discussion or assignment: please do not remove these pages

REVIEW SET

Compound Meters

A. For each meter signature given, provide the structure (simple or compound), the accent pattern (duple, triple, or quadruple), and then write the note value that gets one beat.

1.

	$\frac{4}{4}$	$\frac{6}{4}$	$\frac{4}{2}$	$\frac{3}{8}$	$\frac{9}{8}$
Structure:	Simple	______	______	______	______
Pattern:	Quadruple	______	______	______	______
Beat:	♩	______	______	______	______
		1	2	3	4

2.

	$\frac{6}{8}$	$\frac{3}{4}$	$\frac{12}{4}$	$\frac{2}{2}$	$\frac{3}{2}$
Structure:	______	______	______	______	______
Pattern:	______	______	______	______	______
Beat:	______	______	______	______	______
	1	2	3	4	5

B. Provide a meter signature that corresponds to the given description.

1. ______________ simple duple meter, quarter-note beat

2. ______________ compound triple meter, dotted half-note beat

3. ______________ compound duple meter, dotted quarter-note beat

4. ______________ compound quadruple meter, dotted quarter-note beat

Calligraphy

Beaming in Compound Meters

Groups of two and four equal values are most often beamed together in simple meters, but groups of three and six are more common when the meter is compound. Music editors vary in their approaches to beaming the subdivision. In the next passage, for example, the beaming on the left accentuates duple meter; the notation on the right emphasizes the beat division. Tempo is the most influential factor in such a choice (although both notations are correct).

As always, beaming clarifies beats or groups of beats. In the example that follows, the pattern on the left is readable, but the beaming suggests simple meter ($\frac{3}{4}$). The second notation clarifies the two beats in $\frac{6}{8}$.

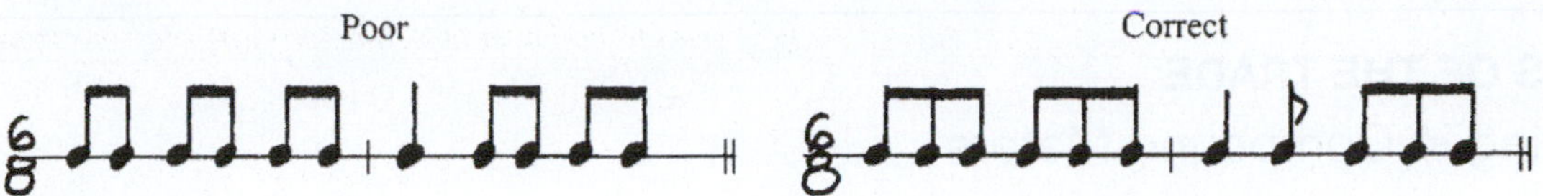

Depending on the values employed, there are many correct beaming combinations in compound meters. However, groups that contain less than or more than one beat are usually not beamed.

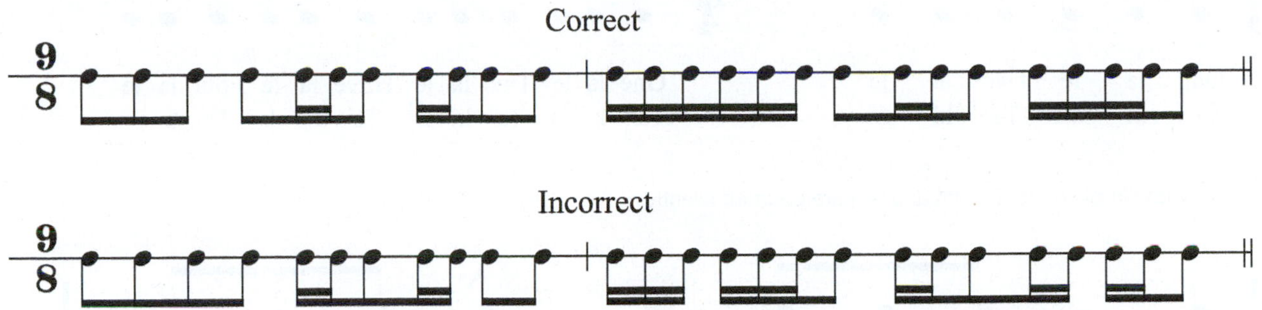

As in simple meters, complete beat groups can be beamed together regardless of the number of notes involved.

Correct

Music editors today often use beams to complete beat units that include rests. The older notation, shown in the first example, is also acceptable.

More Modern Notation

Complete Building Skills 7-2 on page 201

TRICKS OF THE TRADE

Counting in Compound Meters

In compound meter, notes on the beat are counted with the beat number just as they are in simple meters. Because the beat divides into three parts, however, we use a different set of syllables for the division.

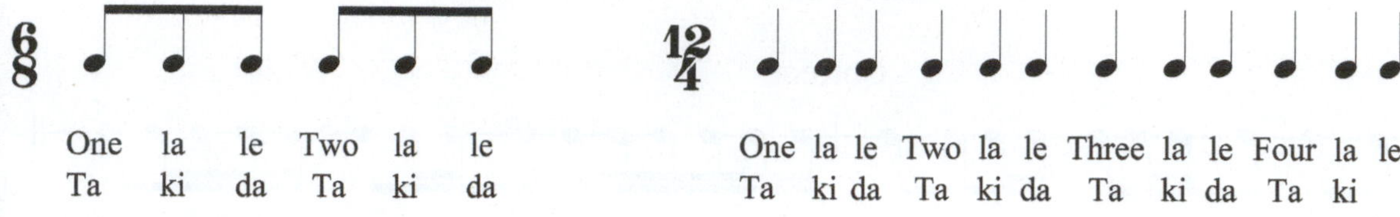

As with simple meters, rests and ties are counted silently.

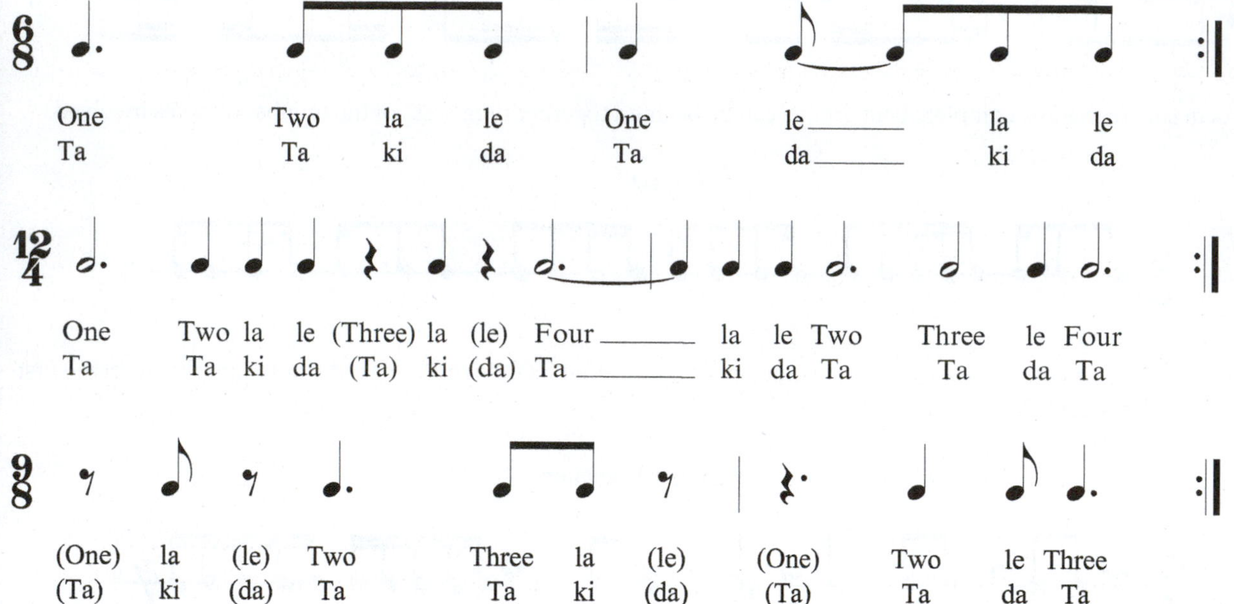

Since the beat division further breaks into two subdivisions, in the first counting methods we use the syllable "ta" or "va" as we do in simple meters. In the Takadimi counting system each subdivision has a unique syllable.

MUSICIANSHIP 7-1

Rhythmic Reading: Compound Meters

Set a slow tempo and perform these eight-measure phrases using counting syllables.

Beat and Beat Division

1.

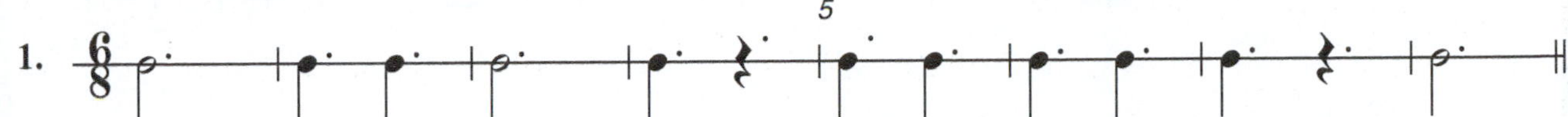

2.

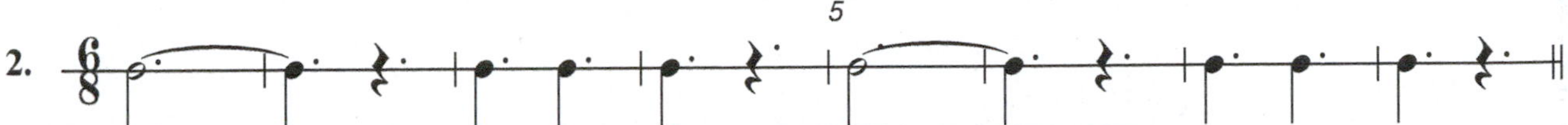

3.

4.

5.

6.

7.

8.

9.

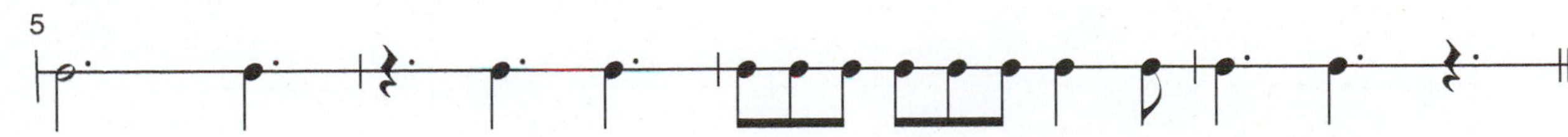

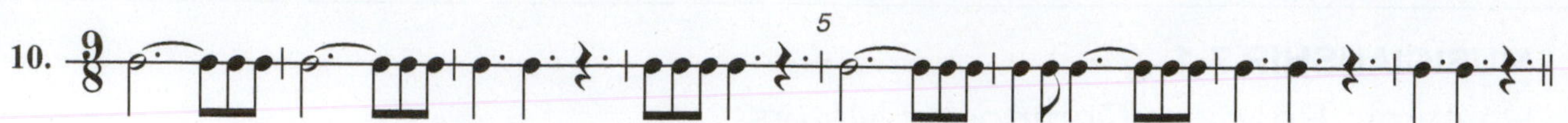

11. 12/8

12. 12/8

13. 12/8

14. 12/8

Meters with Dotted Half-Note Beat

15. 6/4

16. 9/4

17. 6/4

18.
9
4
5
19.
12
4
5
20.
12
4
5
Including Beat Subdivision
21.
6
8
5
22.
6
8
5
23.
9
8
5

Borrowed Division

We have outlined how Western composers choose either a two-part or three-part beat division. Once the time signature is in place, performers interpret the symbols accordingly. Even though a simple or compound meter has been chosen for the composition as a whole, there may be occasions when the contrasting division is desired.

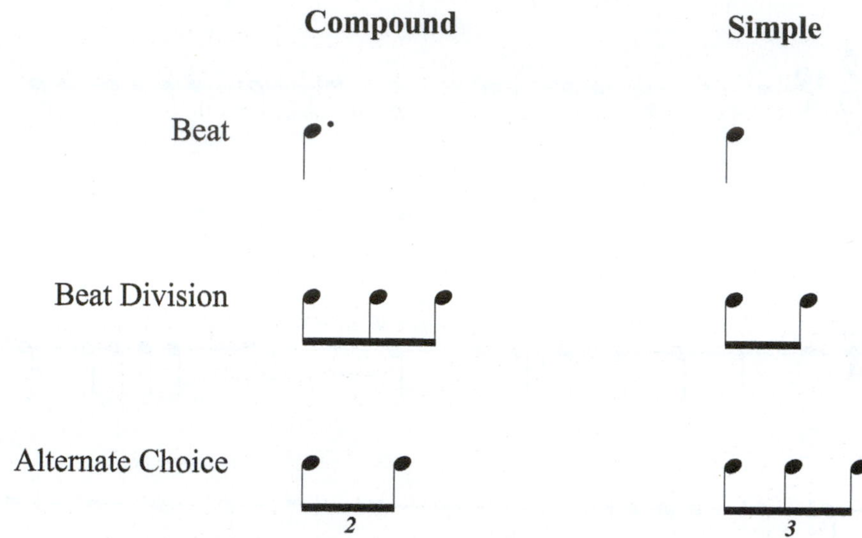

In addition to the **natural beat division** in compound meter, such as $\frac{6}{8}$, composers may want a temporary two-part division. Traditional music notation includes a means of "borrowing" the two-part division from a simple meter or, in a simple meter, the temporary use of the three-part division from a compound meter.

THE TRIPLET. In a simple meter such as $\frac{2}{4}$, the beat is a quarter note that divides into two eighth notes. For a three-part division, we can mark the three notes with the numeral 3 to indicate a **triplet** figure—three notes in the time of two. The eighth notes in the triplet are played *faster* than those of the natural division.

In other simple meters, the triplet is performed in the same way. In $\frac{4}{2}$, for example, the beat divides into two quarter notes; the borrowed division is a quarter-note triplet.

In $\frac{3}{8}$, the natural beat division is two sixteenth notes; three sixteenths as a triplet are played on one beat.

A popular tune that employs a triplet figure is "New York State of Mind." Listen for the three-part beat division that occurs on the words "takin' a" and "I'm in a." Compare the speed of the eighth-note triplet to the natural divisions that occur on the words "River line." In this notation, the triplets are eighth notes.

"New York State of Mind"
Words and Music by
BILLY JOEL

If the half note is the beat, the division is two quarter notes; the **borrowed beat division** is a quarter-note triplet.

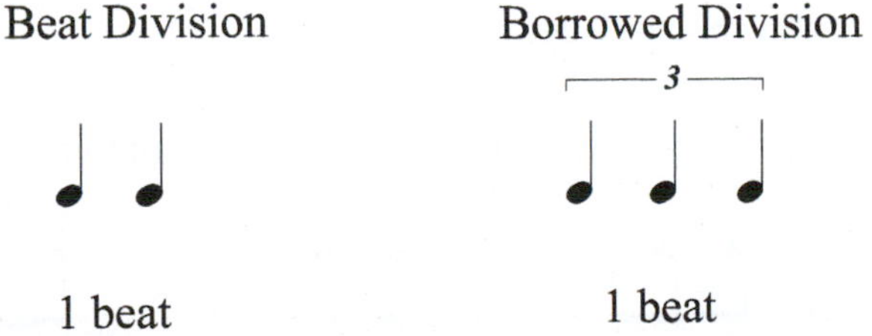

An alternate notation of "New York State of Mind" is in *alla breve* ($\frac{2}{2}$). The half note is the beat in the next example; the *borrowed division* is the quarter-note triplet.

"New York State of Mind"
Words and Music by
BILLY JOEL

The numeral 3 *must* appear with a triplet figure (otherwise, the notes are performed over a beat and a half). Whether the numeral is accompanied by a curved line (a *slur* in musical parlance), a bracket, or no symbol at all is largely a matter of tradition. Engravers most often use a slur with eighth-note triplets and a broken bracket with quarter-note figures.

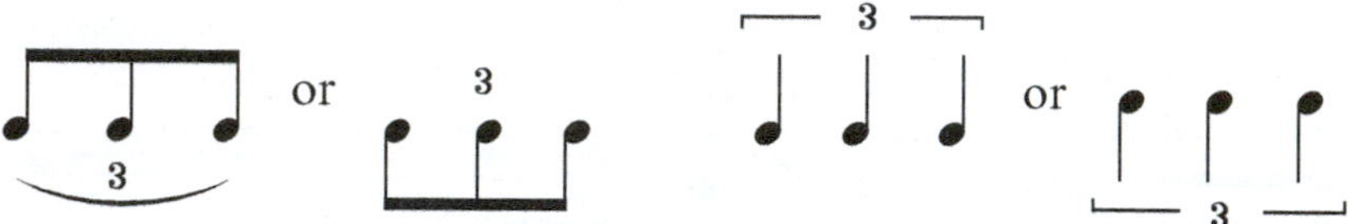

THE DUPLET. The triplet effects a three-part beat division in simple meter; the **duplet** fulfills the opposite role in a compound meter. The division of the beat in $\frac{9}{8}$, for example, is three eighth notes. Two eighth notes alone do not have a full beat's value. Placing the number 2 above or below the two eighth notes, however, tells the performer to slow them down so that they occupy a full beat.

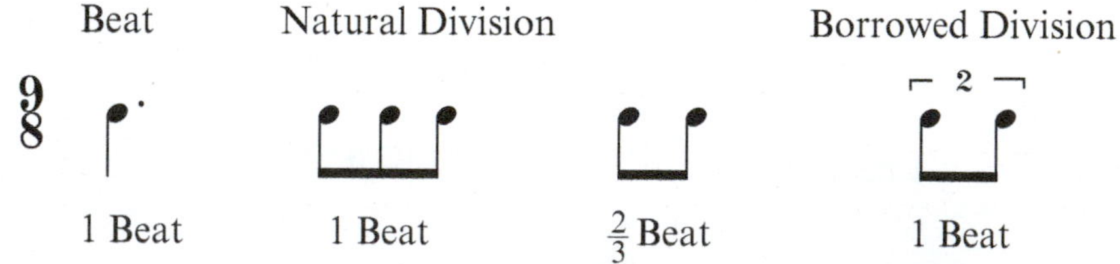

This passage, by the Russian composer Peter Ilyich Tchaikovsky (1840–1893), juxtaposes natural division in the first two measures with borrowed division (duplets) in the measures immediately following.

Peter Ilyich Tchaikovsky, Symphony No. 5

For class discussion or assignment: please do not remove these pages

REVIEW SET

Borrowed Division

A. For the following meters, write the note or notes that receive the beat, the beat division, and the borrowed division.

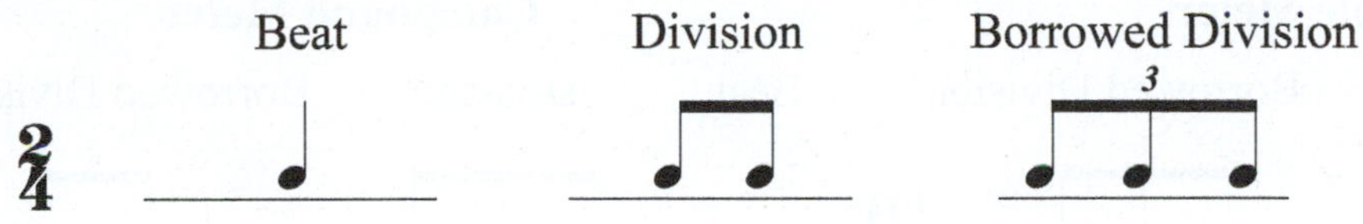

2. ¢ ________ ________ ________

3. 3/8 ________ ________ ________

4. 12/8 ________ ________ ________

B. Place barlines in these examples at the appropriate points.

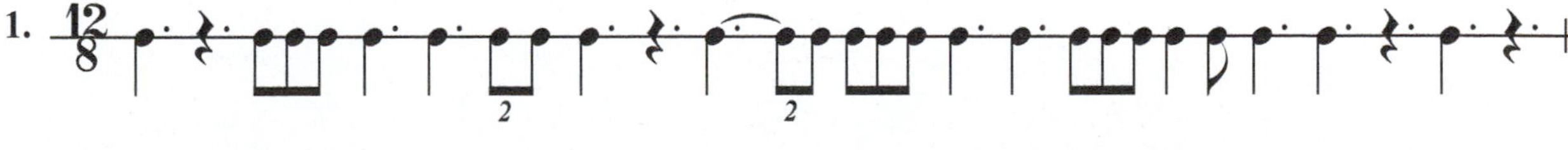

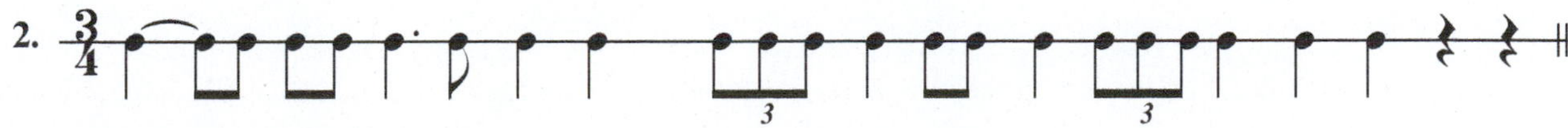

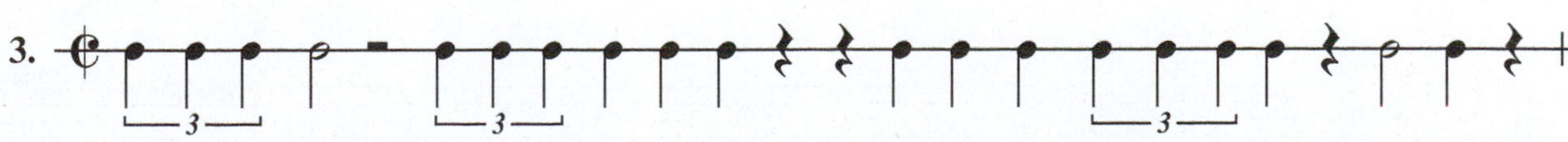

TRICKS OF THE TRADE

Counting the Borrowed Division

One of the advantages of the counting systems we have presented in this text is the flexibility when borrowed division occurs. Study the following examples.

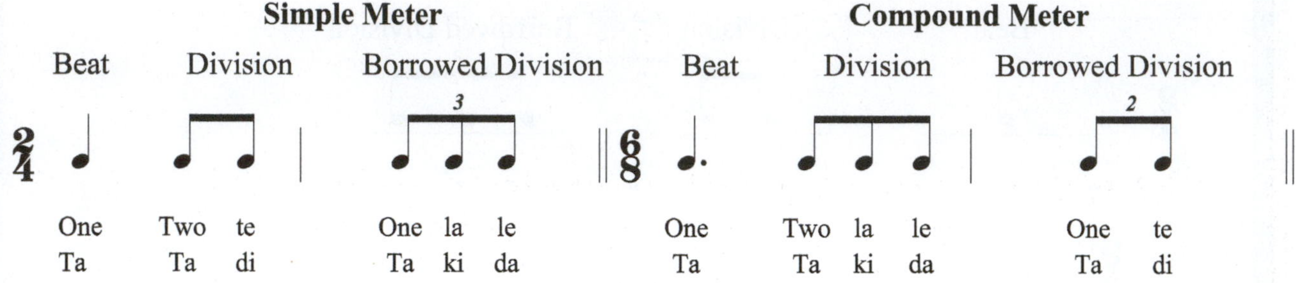

Notice in the next example that, although the notation is different, the music sounds the same. Likewise, the counting syllables are identical.

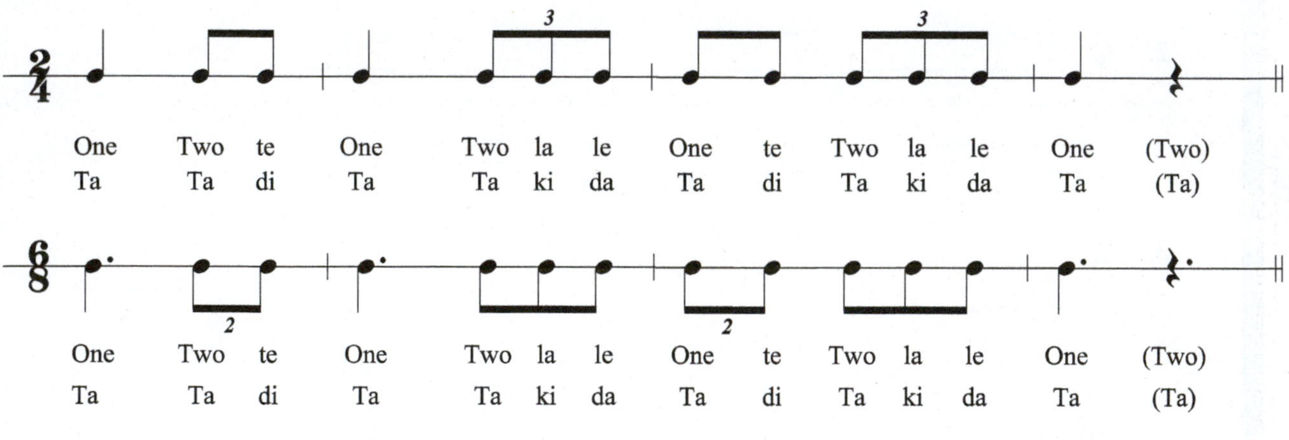

Complete Building Skills 7-3 on page 203

MUSICIANSHIP 7-2

I. Rhythmic Reading: Borrowed Division

These rhythmic-reading phrases include the borrowed division. Count the rhythm syllables while tapping each rhythm pattern. (Sound files for examples 1–9 are available on the website.)

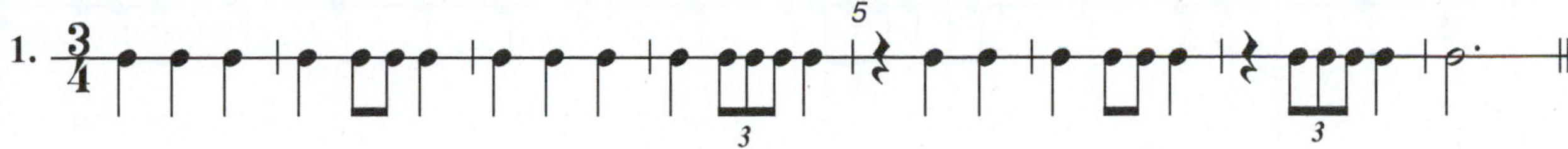

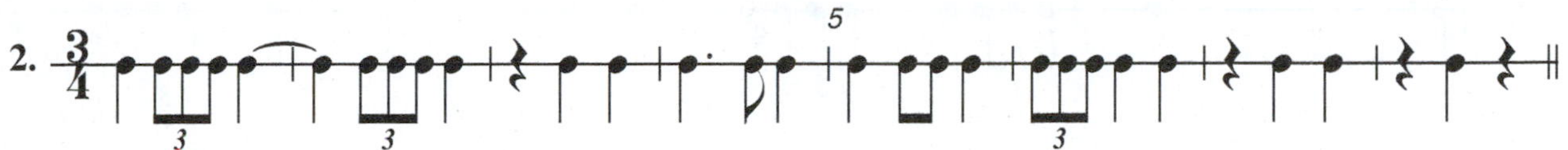

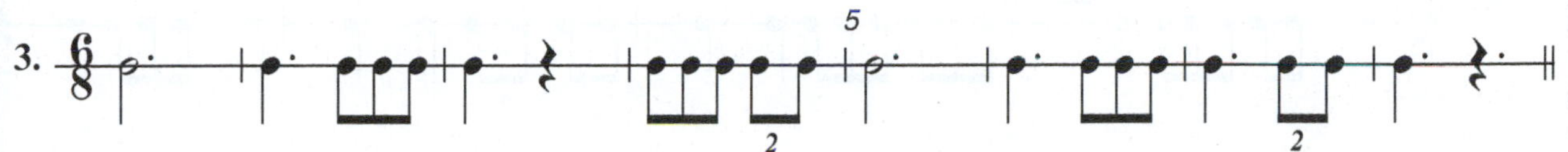

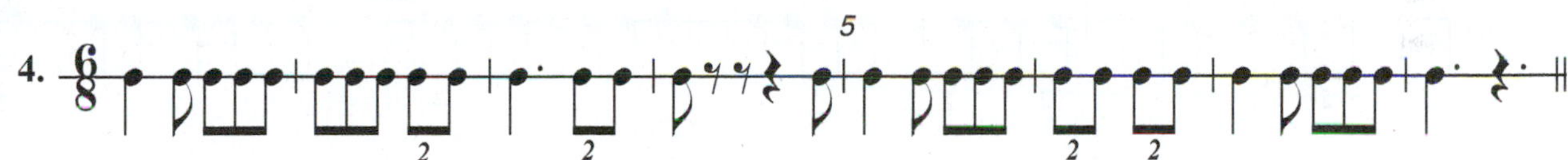

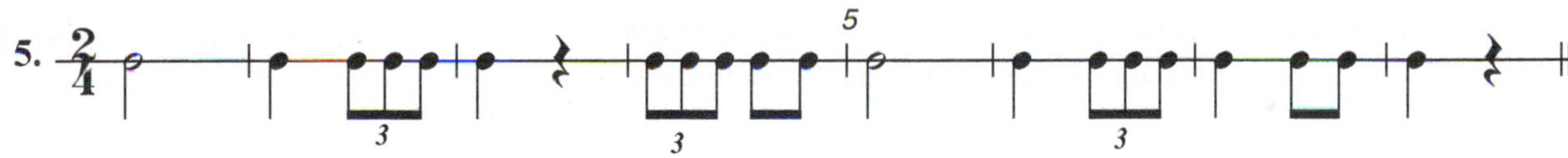

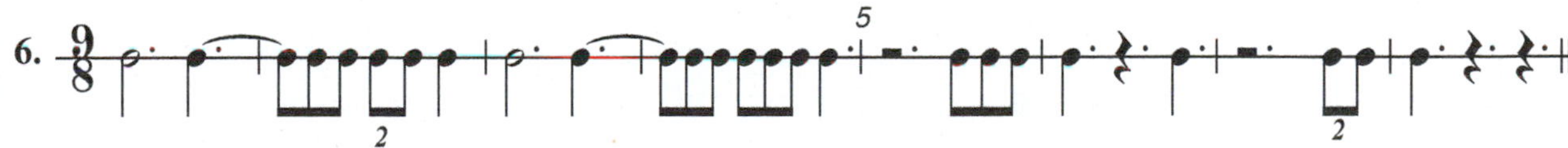

7.

8.

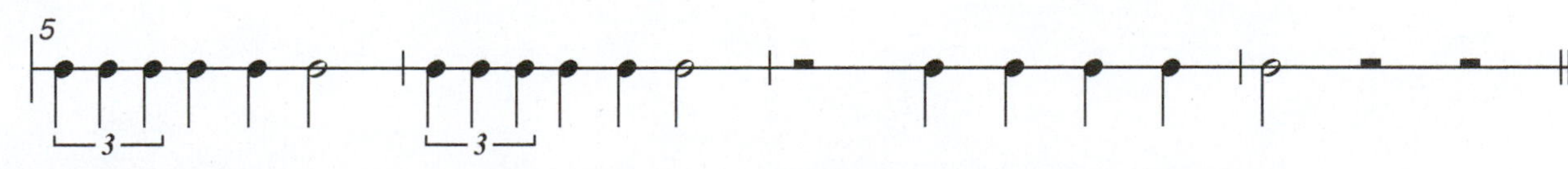

II. Ear Training: Simple and Compound Meters

Your instructor will play a number of melodies in various duple and triple meters. Listen for the beat division, then write the word "simple" or "compound" on the blank. See Appendix D for answers.

Duple Meters

a. ______________ e. ______________
b. ______________ f. ______________
c. ______________ g. ______________
d. ______________ h. ______________

Triple Meters

a. ______________ e. ______________
b. ______________ f. ______________
c. ______________ g. ______________
d. ______________ h. ______________

Name ______________________

Page may be removed

Building Skills 7-1

Note Values in Compound Meters

A. **Provide one note that has the beat value indicated.**

♩. = 1 beat

1. ______________ 1 ______________ $\frac{1}{3}$ ______________ $\frac{2}{3}$ ______________ 2

♪. = 1 beat

2. ______________ 2 ______________ $\frac{2}{3}$ ______________ 1 ______________ $\frac{1}{3}$

In these lines, write *rests* that have the beat value specified.

𝅗𝅥. = 1 beat

3. ______________ $\frac{1}{3}$ ______________ 1 ______________ 2 ______________ $\frac{2}{3}$

♩. = 1 beat

4. ______________ 1 ______________ $\frac{2}{3}$ ______________ $\frac{1}{3}$ ______________ 2

B. **Some of these measures are incomplete. Where necessary, add *one rest* (simple or dotted) to complete the measure.**

1. 

2. 

3. 

4. 

5. 

6. 

C. **Add barlines to these examples.**

French Folk Song, "Nearby to My Dear One"

Robert Schumann, "Hunting Song"

D. **Complete the upper voice of this rhythmic duet using similar patterns.**

Name ______________________

Page may be removed

Building Skills 7-2

Compound Meters

A. For the meters listed, write the notes that constitute the beat, division, and subdivision.

	Meter	Beat	Division	Subdivision
1.	$\frac{4}{4}$	_____	_______	__________
2.	$\frac{6}{8}$	_____	_______	__________
3.	$\frac{3}{8}$	_____	_______	__________
4.	$\frac{9}{4}$	_____	_______	__________
5.	$\frac{3}{2}$	_____	_______	__________

B. Add barlines to these examples where appropriate.

Modest Mussorgsky, *Pictures at an Exhibition*

India, *Krishna*

G. F. Handel, Concerto Grosso

Johannes Brahms, Trio

4.

Medieval England, "Summer Is A-Coming In"

5.

Name ______________________

Page may be removed

Building Skills 7-3

Borrowed Division

A. Complete this table of meters and values.

	Meter	*Beat*	*Division*	*Borrowed Division*	*Subdivision*	*Accent Pattern*
1.	______	quarter note	______	______	______	Quadruple
2.	______	______	______	two beamed eighth notes (duplet, 2)	______	Triple
3.	$\frac{9}{4}$	______	______	______	______	______
4.	______	______	______	______	four beamed eighth notes	Duple
5.	______	______	three beamed eighth notes	______	______	Quadruple
6.	$\frac{3}{8}$	______	______	______	______	______
7.	______	half note	______	______	______	Quadruple
8.	______	______	______	three beamed eighth notes (triplet, 3)	______	Duple

B. **Some of these measures are incomplete. Where necessary, add one note at the end of the measure.**

C. **Provide barlines for these passages. Where there is an anacrusis, both the first and final barlines are given.**

Creative Projects • Chapter 7

A. The upper line of this score is beamed incorrectly. Use the middle line to revise the notation to show correct notation that reflects the meter. (The first measure is completed.) In the lowest line, write a new voice that moves generally more slowly than the given line. Align beats vertically.

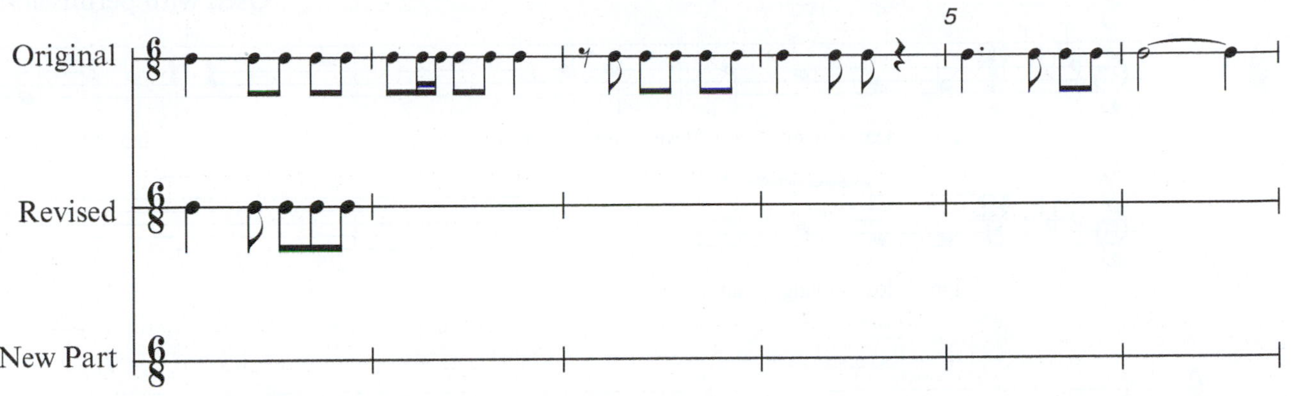

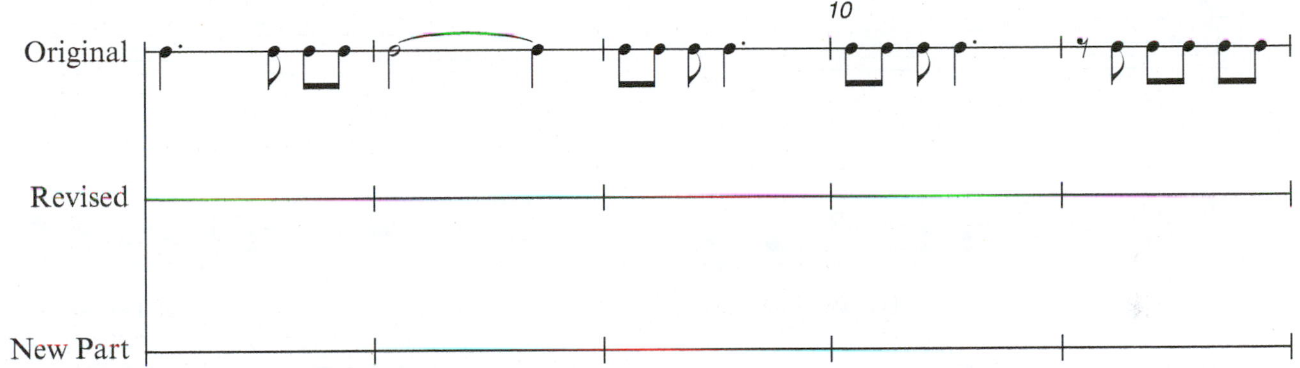

B. **This blues song "I'll Be Home Soon" is given in $\frac{12}{4}$ and with a key signature of A♭ major. In the lower line, transcribe the notation to a more conventional $\frac{12}{8}$.**

I'll Be Home Soon

"I'll Be Home Soon," Andrew Hannon.
Used with permission.

Name ______________________________

Page may be removed

C. **Write a 16-measure rhythmic solo (to be sung, played on one note of an instrument, or clapped). You may find it convenient to consider composing four 4-measure phrases with one or more of them repeated. Write the solo in triple meter with a simple beat division. Employ borrowed division in several measures but avoid overly complicated rhythms in general. Practice your composition to perform for the class.**

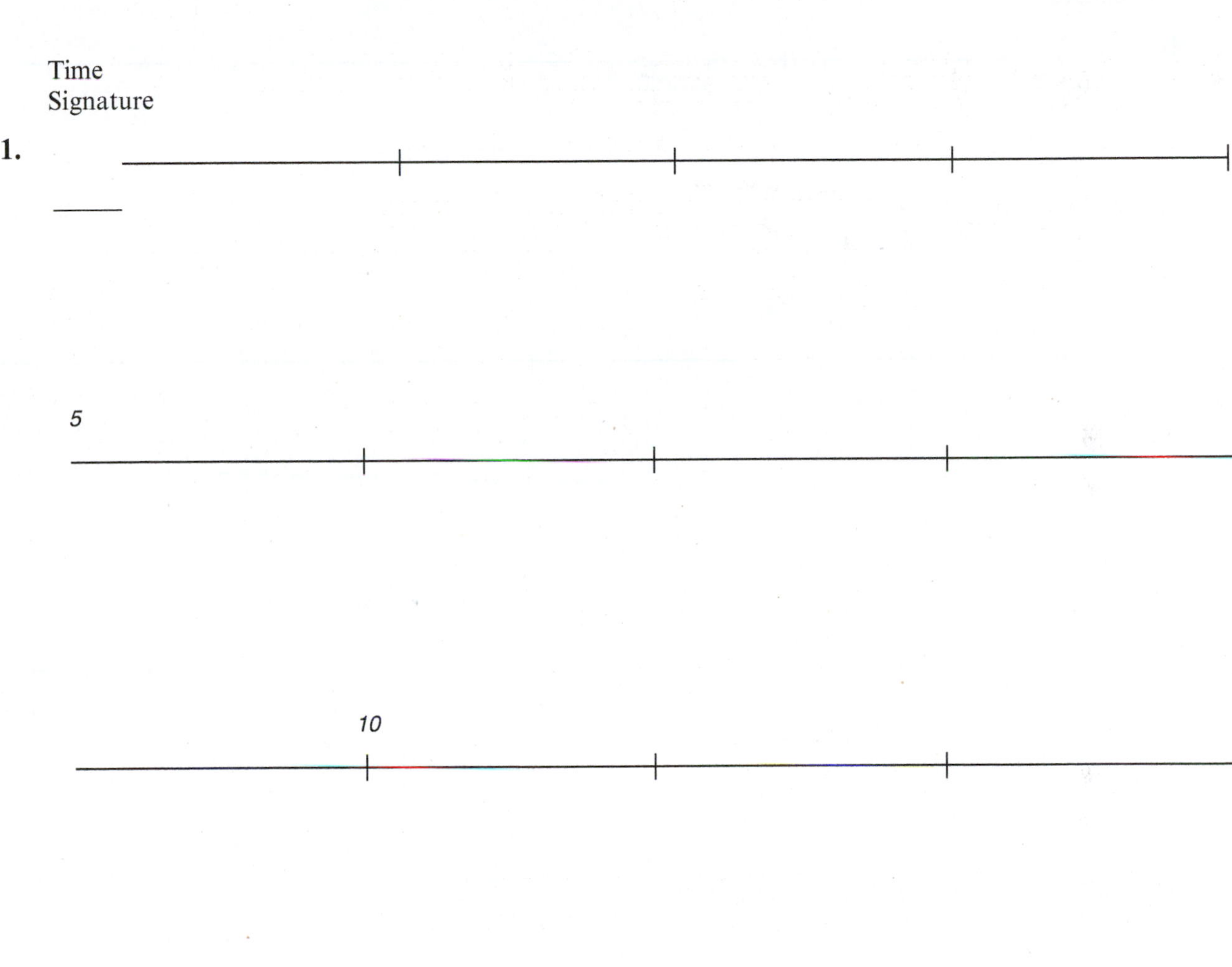

D. **Compose a second solo in compound meter and with a similar structure to the first solo. Be sure to use borrowed divisions.**

Solo in Compound Duple Meter

Time Signature

1.

5

10

15

Name ______________________

Page may be removed

Analysis in Context 1 • Chapter 7

Gustav Holst (1874–1934) was a composer, trombonist, and a teacher of composition and organ in England. He composed operas, ballets, symphonies, chamber music, and songs. He became the Commander of all the English Army Bands during the First World War. The fourth movement of his work "The Second Suite in F Major for Military Band" includes a melody of the English country dance "The Dargason." We will focus on how he uses that folk melody to create a whole movement. Listen to the two melodic excerpts below to familiarize yourself with the main theme. Then search a YouTube recording to listen to the whole movement as you answer the study questions.

Gustav Holst, Second Suite in F for Military Band, IV. Fantasia on the "Dargason"

Gustav Holst, Second Suite in F for Military Band, IV. Fantasia on the "Dargason"

1. **In what key is this movement written?**

2. **Write in the solfege syllables/scale degree numbers for the folk tune melody as played by the oboe and bassoon.**

3. **Identify the type of meter used in this song (i.e., simple triple).**

4. **What note gets the beat in this meter?**

5. **Write out the 2-measure long rhythm pattern that is used repeatedly throughout this work.**

6. **Write out one counting method for the rhythm referenced in the previous question (i.e., takadimi counts). (Write it below your answer to question 5.)**

7. Label the melodic intervals in the oboe part.

8. Listen to the recording on the website. Clap and count along with the recording, listening for the repetition of the 8-measure melody shown above.

9. There are examples of borrowed divisions in this movement. Listen to the recording and see if you can locate their arrival. Write down the counter number for the location in the audio file.

10. The melody is restated many times in the movement. How does Holst keep it interesting? Describe things that change in the music each time you hear the tune.

Chapter 8
Minor Scales and Keys

Essential Terms

augmented second
harmonic minor
leading tone
major mode
mediant
melodic minor
minor mode
minor scale
mode
natural minor
parallel major
parallel minor
relative major
relative minor
subtonic

Major and Minor Modes

As we use the term in this text, **mode** is the "flavor" or "affect" of a scale. Although the tonic is the most important pitch, the third scale degree, also known as the **mediant**, serves a pivotal role as well. The mediant defines the affect of a scale as being major or minor. A **major mode** is created when the third degree is two whole steps above the tonic. In the **minor mode**, the first and third scale degrees are separated by a whole step plus a *diatonic* half step.

Study the notation and keyboard diagrams. The pitch C is the tonic in both cases; the mode is defined by the mediant pitch.

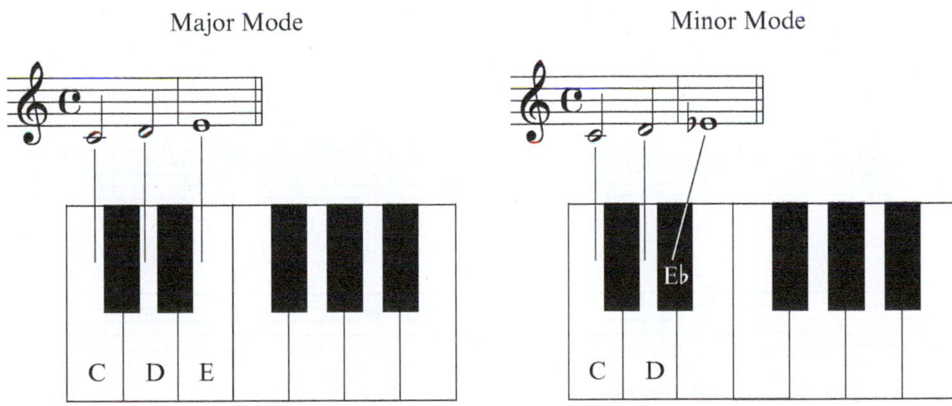

Now listen to "Brother John" played first in the major mode (as you probably know it), then in the minor mode. Notice that although only the third (mediant) scale degree is different, the two "flavors" are distinct.

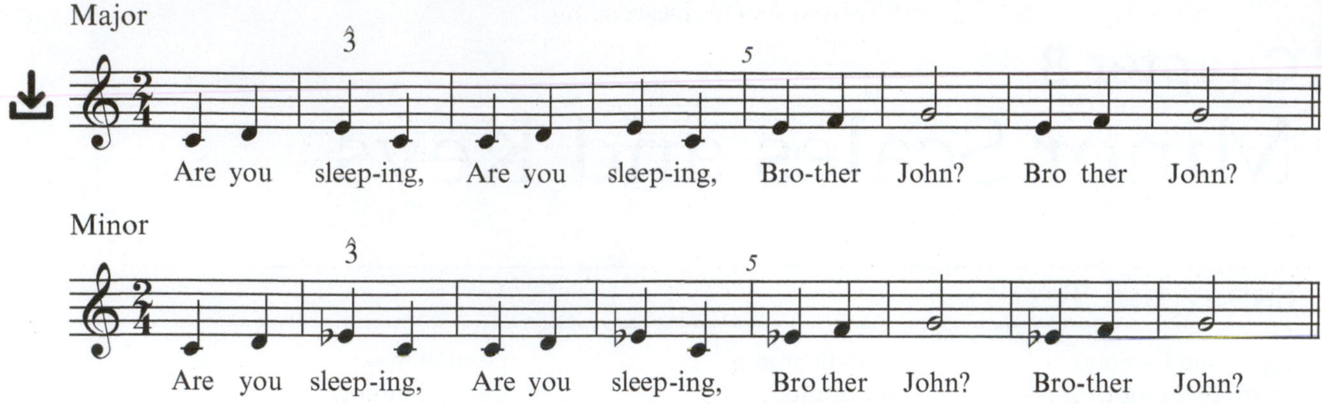

Major and minor scales were among the *last* melodic patterns to gain acceptance as Western musical traditions evolved between the sixth and sixteenth centuries. By about 1675 these two scales had become so popular with composers that other possibilities known as church modes (see Appendix E), so prominent in early music, fell into disuse. While Western melodies are now rich and varied, for two hundred years (roughly 1675–1875), composers limited themselves to only major and minor scales.

Minor Scales

One **minor scale** is found on the white keys of the piano beginning on the pitch A. Listen to the ascending and descending minor scale. Follow the score and the keyboard diagram as you listen. After the scale you will hear Handel's "Joy to the World" played in minor.

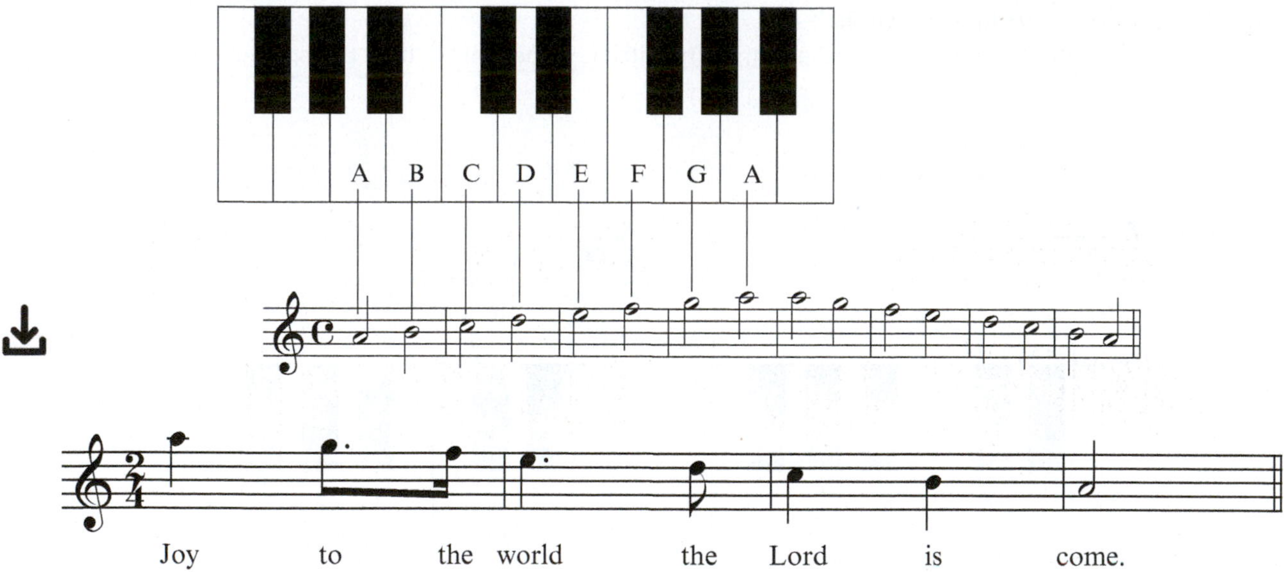

Like the major scale, the minor scale has a fixed pattern of intervals—one that you will need to memorize: W H W W H W W. The two half steps in the next example are marked with a bracket; they fall between the second and third and between the fifth and sixth scale degrees.

Minor Scale: Ascending

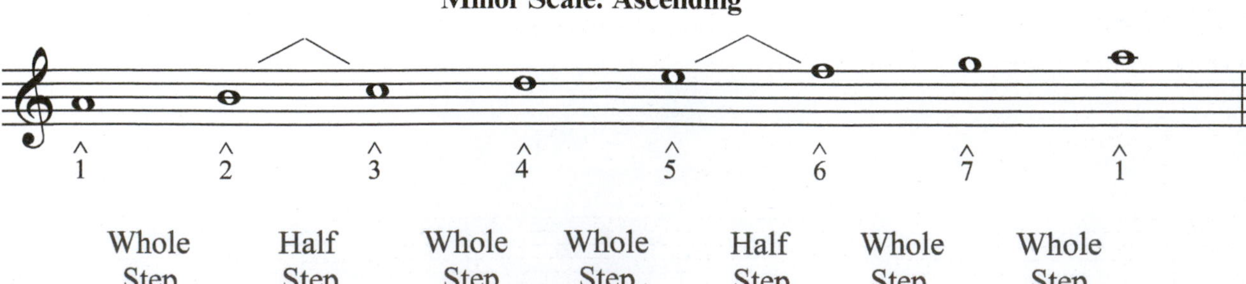

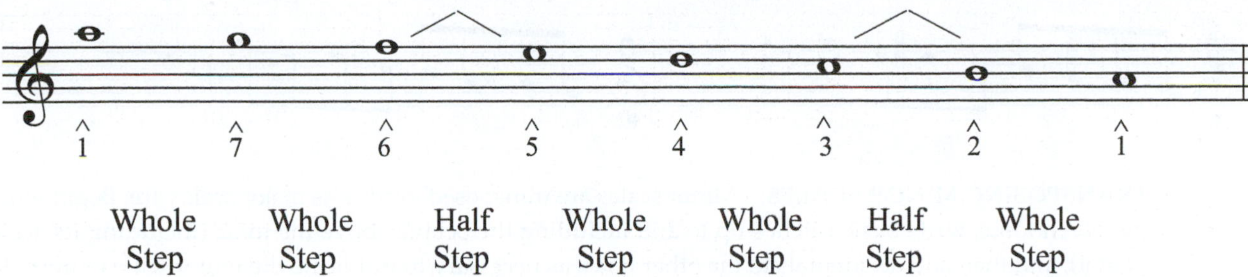

Study the differences between the C major and C minor scales, and between the A major and A minor scales shown in the next example. Notice that scale degrees 3, 6, and 7 are lowered in the minor scale.

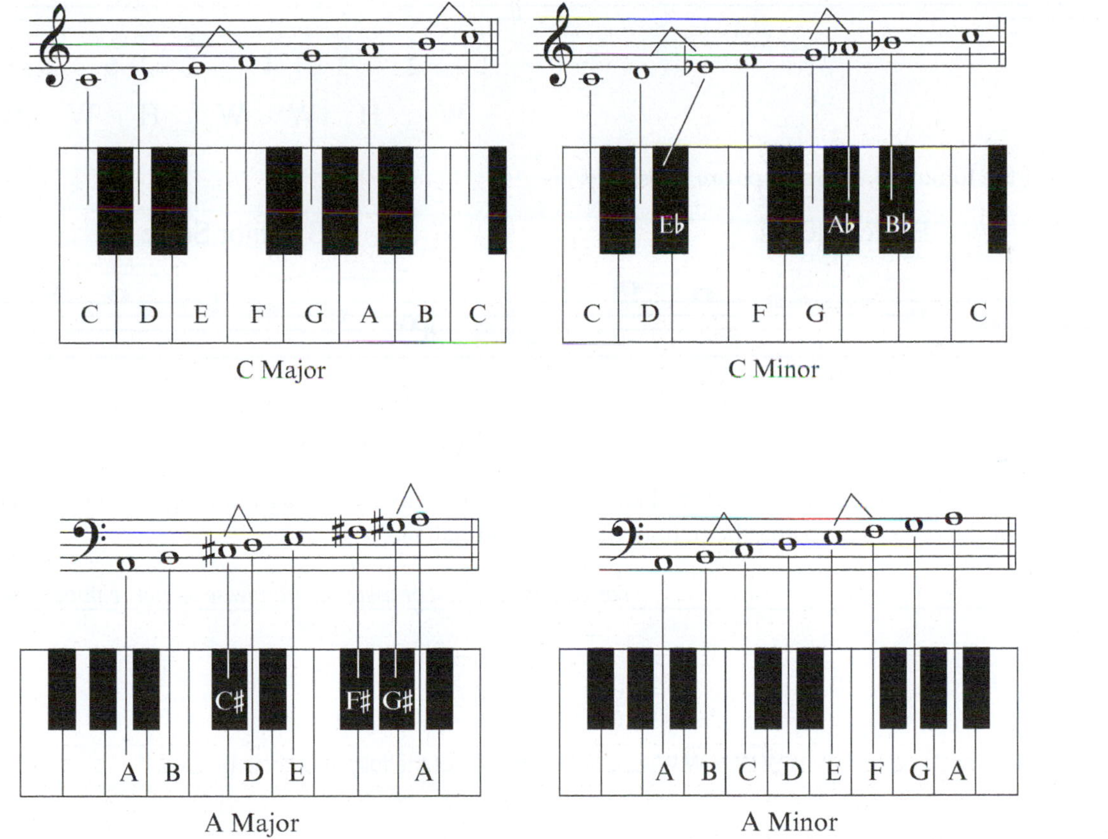

The Parallel Relationship

When major and minor keys have the same tonic, their relationship is termed **parallel**. This relationship is complementary; C major is the parallel major of C minor; C minor is the parallel minor of C major. If we know the name of the major key, finding the parallel minor requires little effort. Likewise, the key of G major is the parallel major of G minor.

TRANSPOSING MINOR SCALES. Minor scales are transposed exactly as major scales are: Begin with the given tonic, write basic pitches up to and including the octave above the tonic (including its accidental), and then add accidentals to the other notes as necessary to duplicate the minor scale pattern. If the tonic is D, for example, a B♭ is necessary to create a minor scale.

If the tonic is B, two sharps are necessary.

While minor scales are recognized and used more effectively through key signatures, center your work for the present on using the pattern of whole and half steps.

For class discussion or assignment: please do not remove these pages

REVIEW SET

Minor Scales

A. Duplicate the minor scale pattern (W H W W H W W) beginning on each of the following tonic pitches.

1. 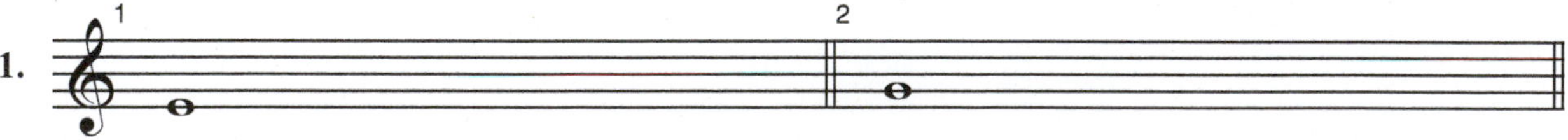

2. 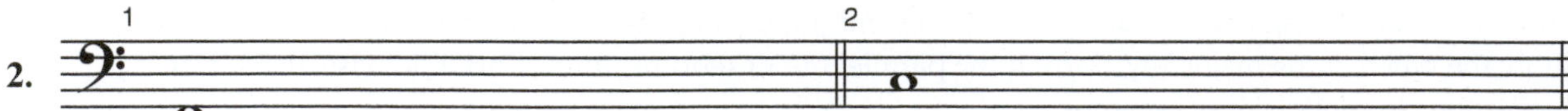

3. 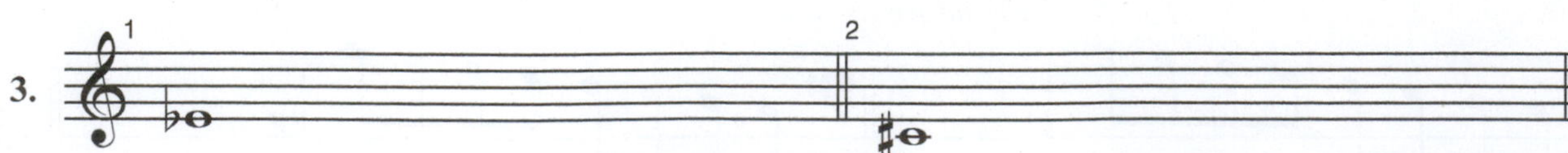

B. Identify these scales as "major" or "minor." Write the appropriate term in the blank.

1.

______ 1 ______ 2

2.

______ 1 ______ 2

3.

______ 1 ______ 2

Minor Key Signatures

From writing out the whole- and half-step patterns, you may have noticed that the keys of C major and A minor have the same key signature (no sharps/no flats). This means that there are *two* keys with identical pitch content—one of these is major, the other, minor.

The Relative Relationship

Major and minor keys with the same key signature share a complementary *relative relationship*. The key of C major, for example, is the **relative major** of A minor; A minor is the **relative minor** of C major.

The following figure shows the signatures for all fifteen minor keys. Notice that the order of sharps and flats and their placement on the grand staff are the same as those for major key signatures.

No Sharps/Flats

C Major

a minor

Relative Pairs of Key Signatures

Sharp Keys

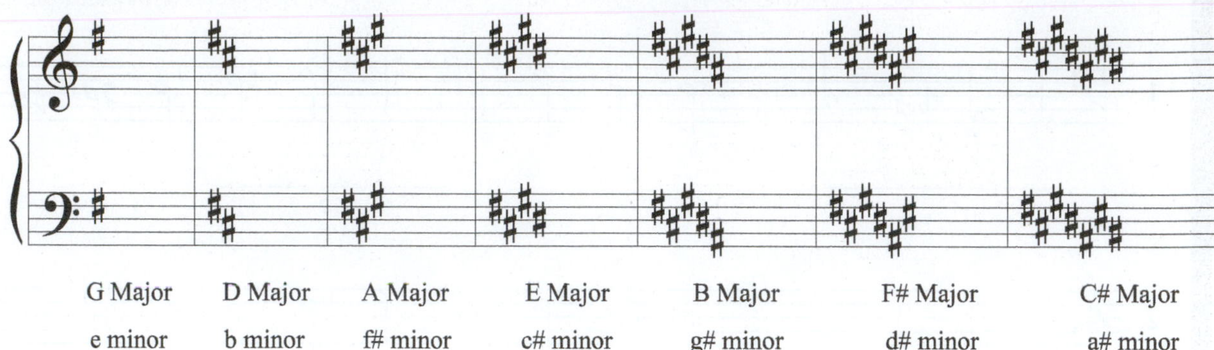

Flat Keys

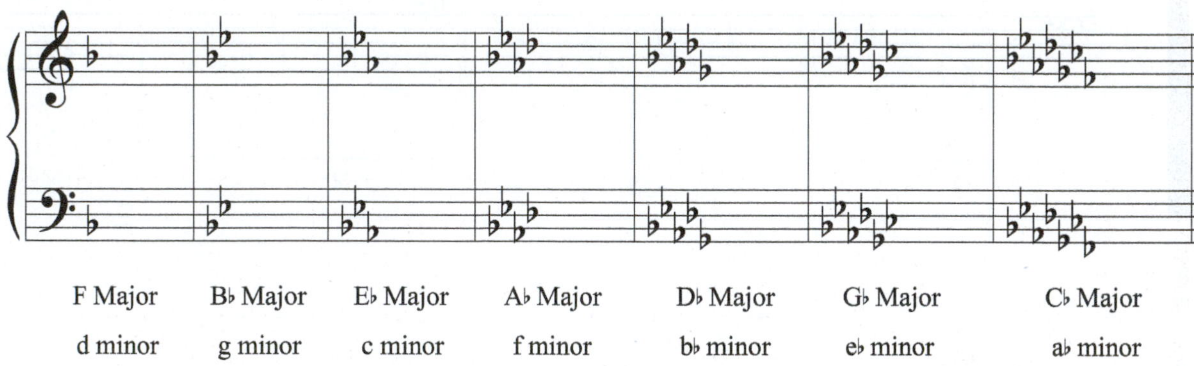

Remember that scale degrees are identified in minor just as they are in major; the third degree of a minor scale is $\hat{3}$, the sixth is $\hat{6}$, and so on. We indicate a minor key with a lowercase letter. The designation b: $\hat{2}$ refers to the pitch C♯; in the key of G minor, E♭ would be labeled g: $\hat{6}$.

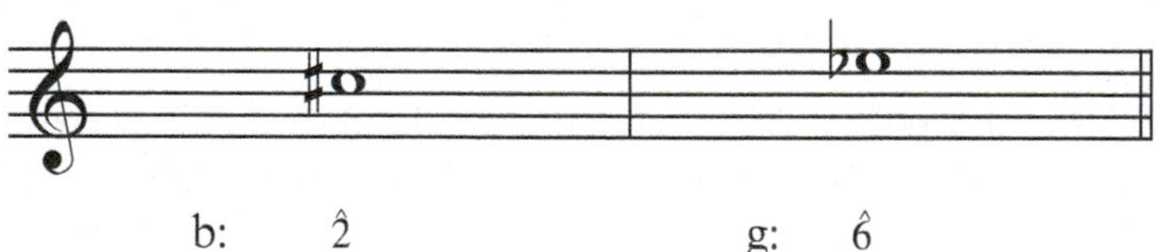

TRICKS OF THE TRADE:
Parallel Major and Minor Keys

A parallel minor key will always have three more flats or sharps than the corresponding major key. If the major key is C, for example (no flats/no sharps), we know by this guideline that C minor has three flats.

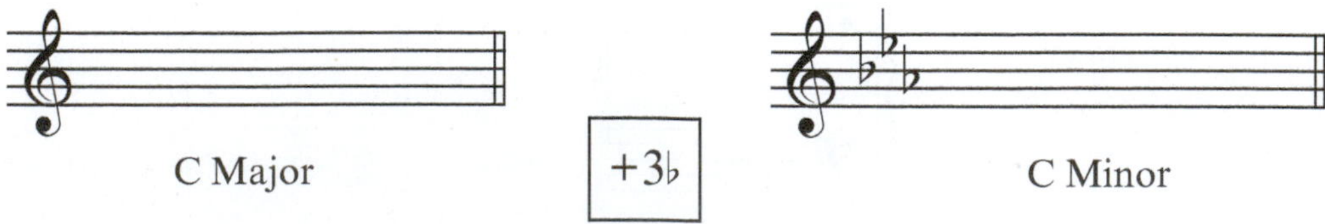

While the first example is straightforward, consider the keys of E major and E minor. In determining key relationships, it helps to think of sharps and flats as positive and negative numbers. If we have four sharps (E major) and add three flats (i.e., cancel three sharps), one sharp remains and establishes the signature of the parallel minor key.

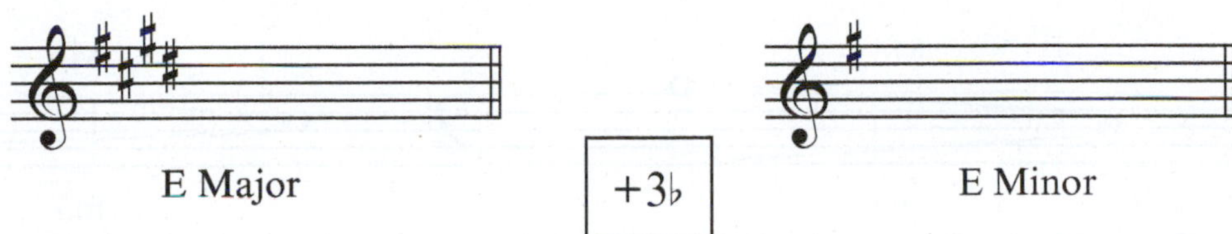

If the major key is E♭ (three flats), the parallel minor has six flats.

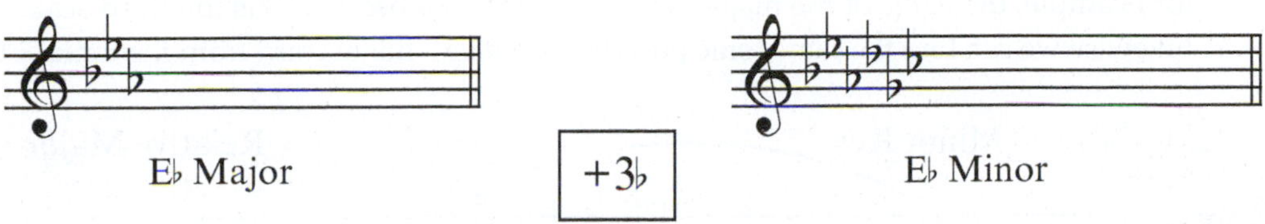

The process works equally well in reverse. Given a minor key, add three sharps to arrive at the signature of the parallel major.

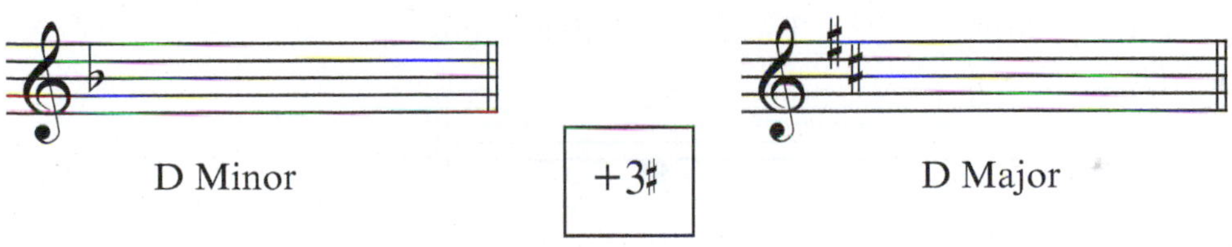

DETERMINING RELATIVE MINOR KEYS. Relative major and minor keys *do not* have the same tonic. A relative minor key is simply a rearrangement of the pitches found in the corresponding major key; the tonic of the minor is the sixth scale degree of the major. To find the relative minor of C major, for example, count up to the sixth degree.

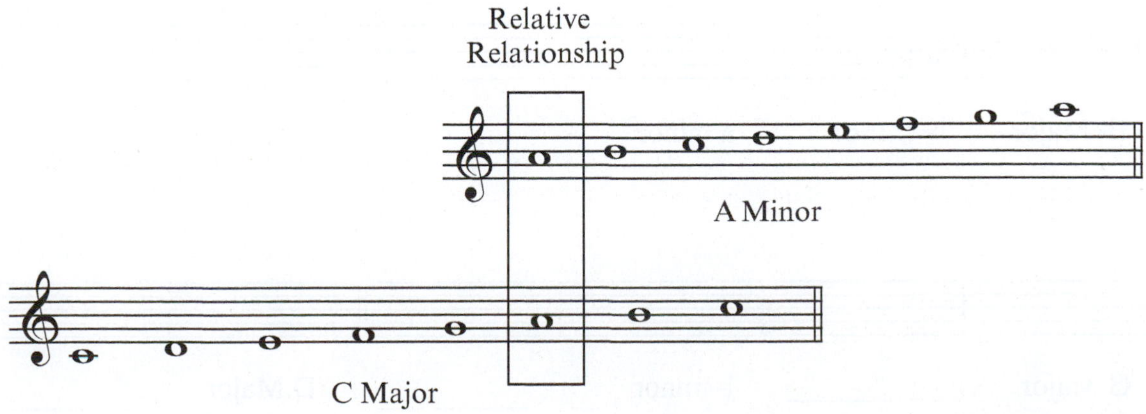

When we locate a relative minor key through the sixth scale degree of the major, we must be careful to use the *key signature* of the major key. The relative minor of A major, for example, is F♯ minor—not F minor; the relative minor of D♭ major is B♭ minor.

The tonic of a relative minor can be viewed as lying a major sixth *above* the tonic of the major. Likewise, the same pitch name is found a minor third *below* the tonic of the major key.

DETERMINING RELATIVE MAJOR KEYS. Should you need to find the relative major of a given minor key, remember that the name of the tonic is also the mediant pitch of the minor. If we are given B minor, for example, the name of the major key will be D major because D is the third scale degree in B minor. Likewise we can find the same tonic pitch by *ascending* a minor third from the tonic of the minor key.

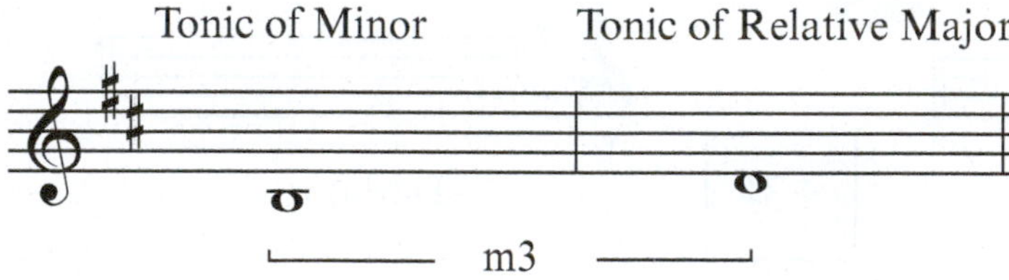

For class discussion or assignment: please do not remove these pages

REVIEW SET

Parallel and Relative Keys

A. For each major or minor key given, provide the key name of the *parallel* key. Enter the key signature of *both* keys.

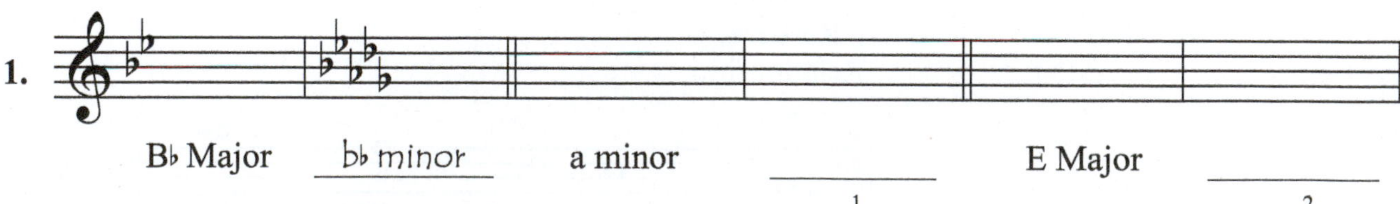

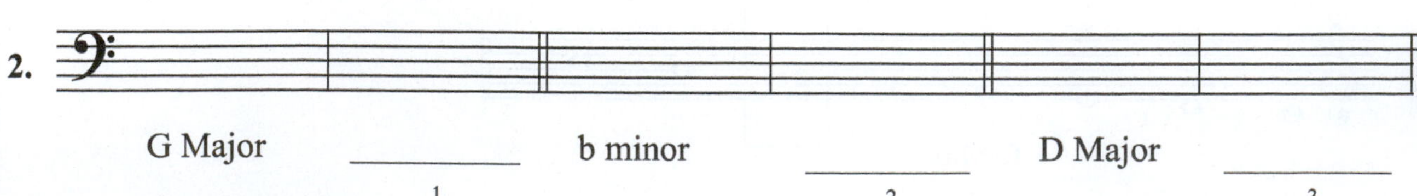

3. 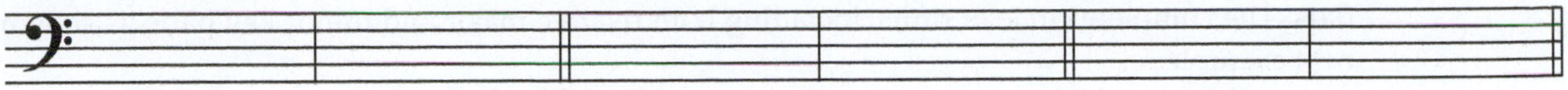

A♭ Major ________ d minor ________ C♯ Major ________

1 2 3

B. Given the name of a major key, provide the key signature and the tonic of the relative minor (both major and minor keys will have the same key signature).

1. 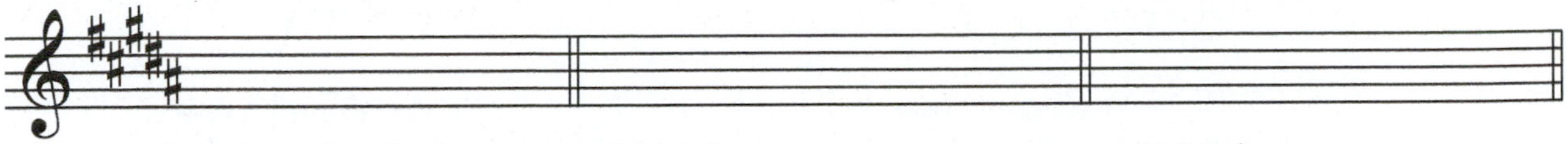

B Major g♯ minor F Major ________ A♭ Major ________

1 2

2. 

E♭ Major ________ G Major ________ D♭ Major ________

1 2 3

3. 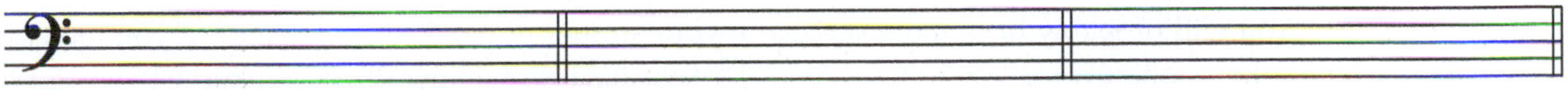

B♭ Major ________ C♯ Major ________ F♯ Major ________

1 2 3

Complete Building Skills 8-1 on page 233

THE CIRCLE OF FIFTHS IN MINOR KEYS. As is the case with major keys, clockwise movement by ascending perfect fifths produces each successive new minor key on the sharp side.

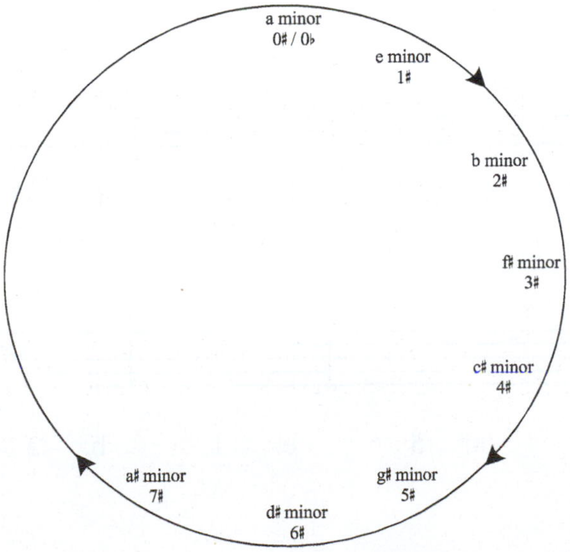

Moving counterclockwise by descending fifths highlights minor keys with increasing numbers of flats. The complete circle of fifths, including both relative major and minor key pairs, is shown in the next example.

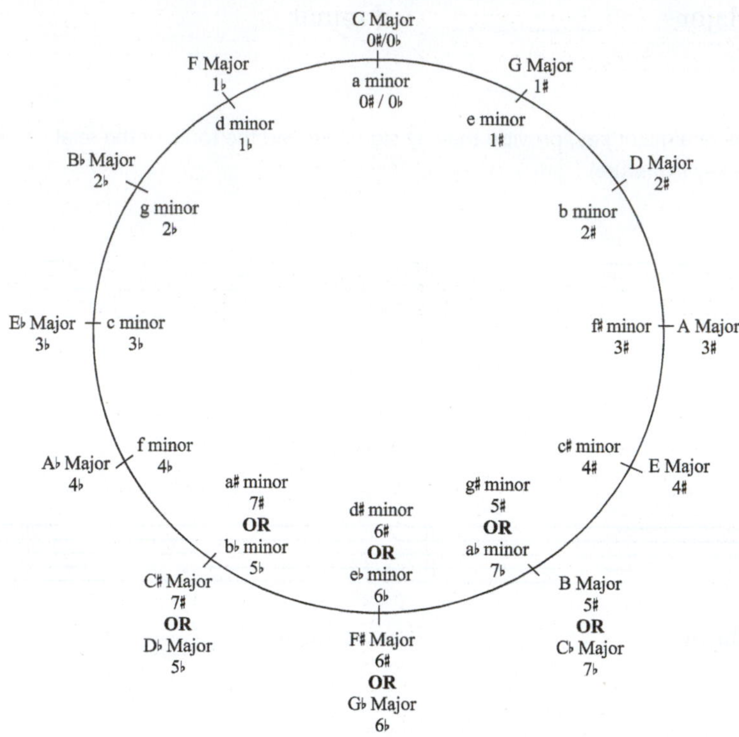

You will probably have more success in your studies of music fundamentals if you memorize the minor key signatures as you did for the major key signatures. However, if you know the major key signatures thoroughly, you can quickly find a minor key signature by associating it with a related major key.

For class discussion or assignment: please do not remove these pages

REVIEW SET

Scale Degrees in Minor Keys

A. Provide the pitch indicated by the scale-degree symbol within the given key. Use an accidental as necessary. Refer to the table of key signatures on page 215, use the circle of fifths or another method as needed.

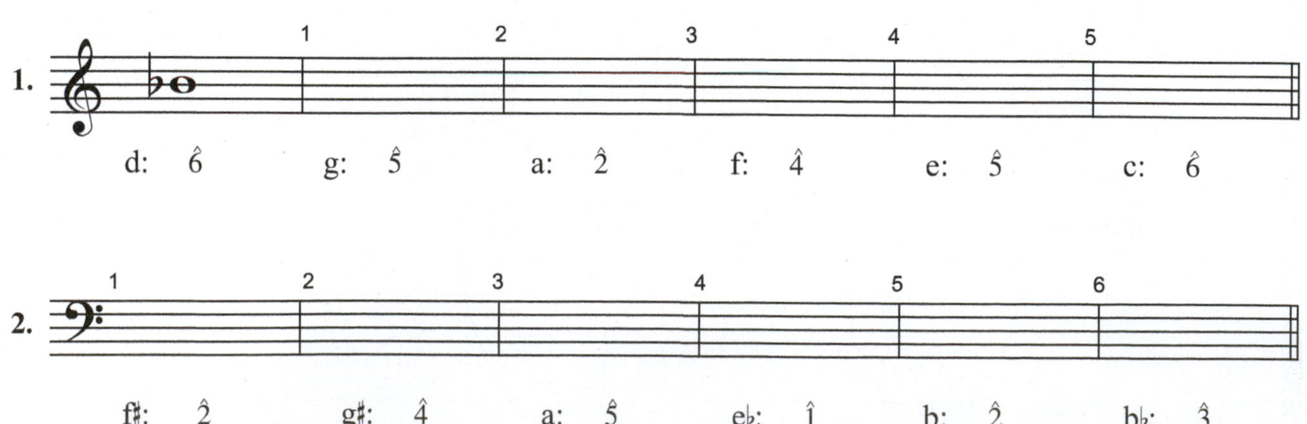

B. Given the pitch and minor scale designations, provide the scale degrees.

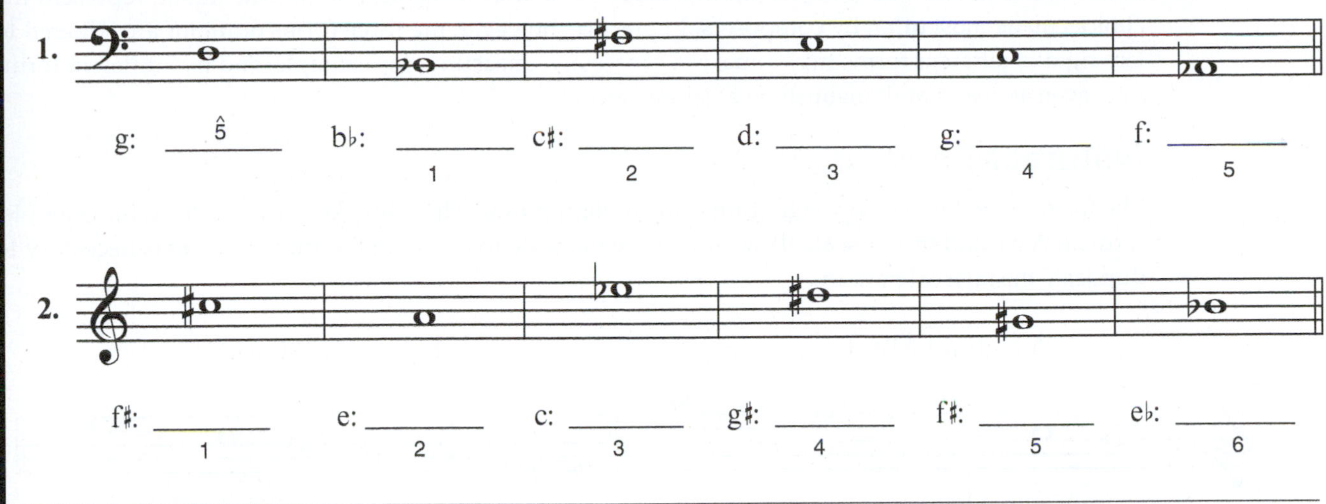

Complete Building Skills 8-2 on page 235

MUSICIANSHIP 8-1

Keyboard: Patterns in Minor

Fingering patterns for minor scales parallel those for major keys. In this exercise, we will practice five-finger scale patterns. Begin with your thumb (right hand) or fifth finger (left hand). Ascend and descend using both hands separately. While we will cover all major scales in keyboard studies, these are the only exercises in minor presented in the text.

The same fingering pattern is applicable to these minor scales as well:

A minor	no sharps/flats	D minor	one flat
E minor	one sharp	G minor	two flats
B minor	two sharps	C minor	three flats
		F minor	four flats

Variations in Minor

While Western composers did not alter the interval pattern of major scales, three different forms of minor are common. These forms, known today as *natural, harmonic,* and *melodic* minor, represent the choices made most often by composers. In practice, however, the three forms of minor are adhered to less rigidly; different forms may appear in consecutive measures, for example, and two different forms may even appear simultaneously in adjacent voices.

Natural Minor

The form created by the key signature is the **natural minor**. The white keys from A to A, for example, form an A natural minor scale. If we transpose the scale to begin on the pitch E, an F♯ is necessary to duplicate the interval pattern.

LEADING TONE AND SUBTONIC. In addition to the characteristic third degree, the most important difference between major and natural minor concerns the seventh scale degree. As we discussed in Chapter 5, the **leading tone** is a pitch that lies a diatonic half step below the tonic. In a natural minor scale, the seventh scale degree is a whole step below the tonic; we refer to this pitch as a **subtonic**.

Harmonic Minor

Since the Renaissance era in music (ca. 1450–1600), Western composers have favored the stronger pull of the leading tone to the tonic as opposed to the subtonic (found in natural minor). Even when writing in minor keys, composers often create a leading tone simply by raising the seventh scale degree a half step.

This new scale is known as **harmonic minor** because it includes the leading tone.

A Natural Minor

A Harmonic Minor

The following excerpt is from an invention composed by J. S. Bach. The piece is in the key of D minor, and the pitch C# is used consistently. This excerpt is based on the D harmonic minor scale.

J.S. Bach, Invention in D minor

To construct a harmonic minor scale, begin with *natural minor* (the key signature or interval pattern), and then raise the seventh degree a half step.

G Harmonic Minor   B♭ Harmonic Minor

For class discussion or assignment: please do not remove these pages

REVIEW SET

Natural and Harmonic Minor Scales

A. Several ascending natural minor scales are shown. Rewrite each scale as harmonic minor (i.e., raise the seventh scale degree).

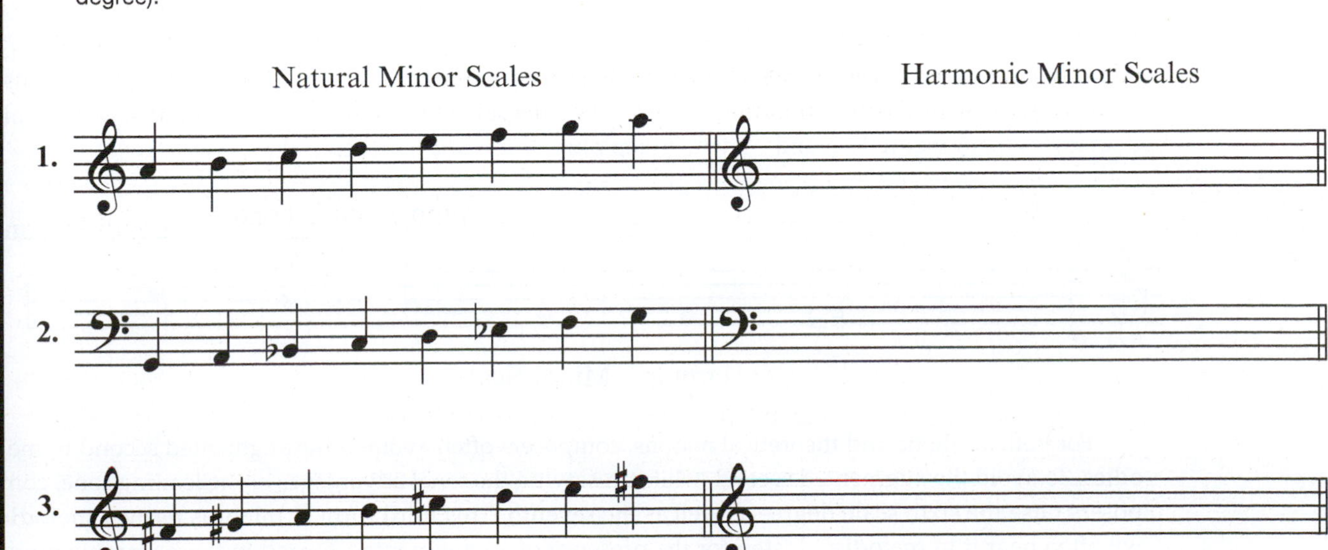

B. Write harmonic minor scales on these tonics. Begin with the key signature from natural minor (or use the W H W W H W W pattern if you have not mastered minor key signatures), then raise the seventh degree a half step to become a leading tone.

Optional Key Signature

1. 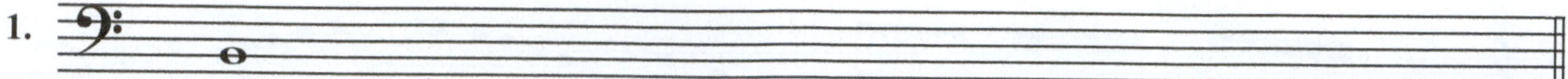

2. 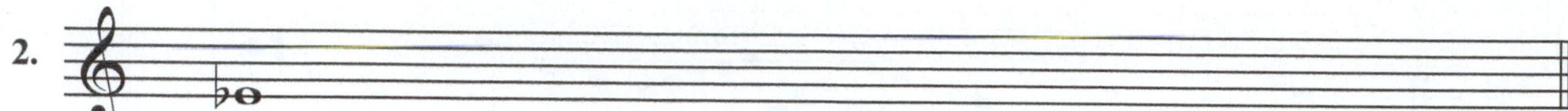

3. 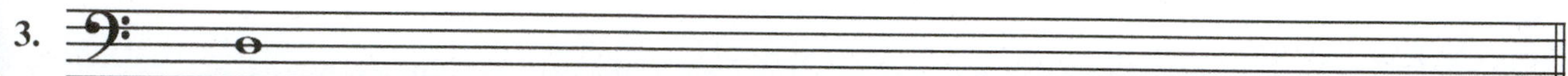

C. These ascending scales may be major, natural minor, or harmonic minor. Write the appropriate term in the blank.

Melodic Minor

Although the raised seventh scale degree in the harmonic minor scale provides a leading tone, it also creates a stylistic problem in traditional music. The interval between the sixth and raised seventh scale degrees is an **augmented second**—a whole step plus a *chromatic* half step.

C Harmonic Minor Scale

For both aesthetic and theoretical reasons, composers often avoided the augmented second in melodies. To avoid the augmented second, while preserving the tonal advantages of the leading tone, composers raise the sixth scale degree as well as the seventh. This third form of minor is termed **melodic**; we often hear it in melodies. Listen for the presence of an augmented second in the harmonic minor scale and its absence in the melodic minor.

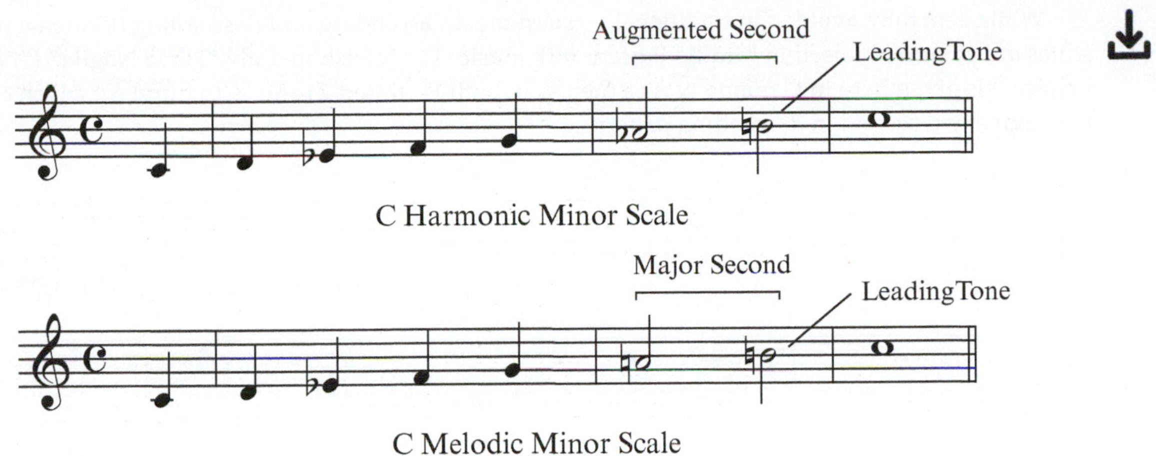

DESCENDING MINOR SCALES. Major, natural minor, and harmonic minor scales are written the same whether ascending or descending. Melodic minor, however, has two forms. The ascending form, with raised sixth and seventh, has already been discussed. When descending, the leading tone is not a factor (it no longer "leads" to anything); accordingly, melodic minor has a subtonic and natural sixth scale degree as does natural minor. Remember that scales are theoretical materials; the forms we use in performance reflect goals and tendencies in music.

Traditional Ascending and Descending Forms of Minor

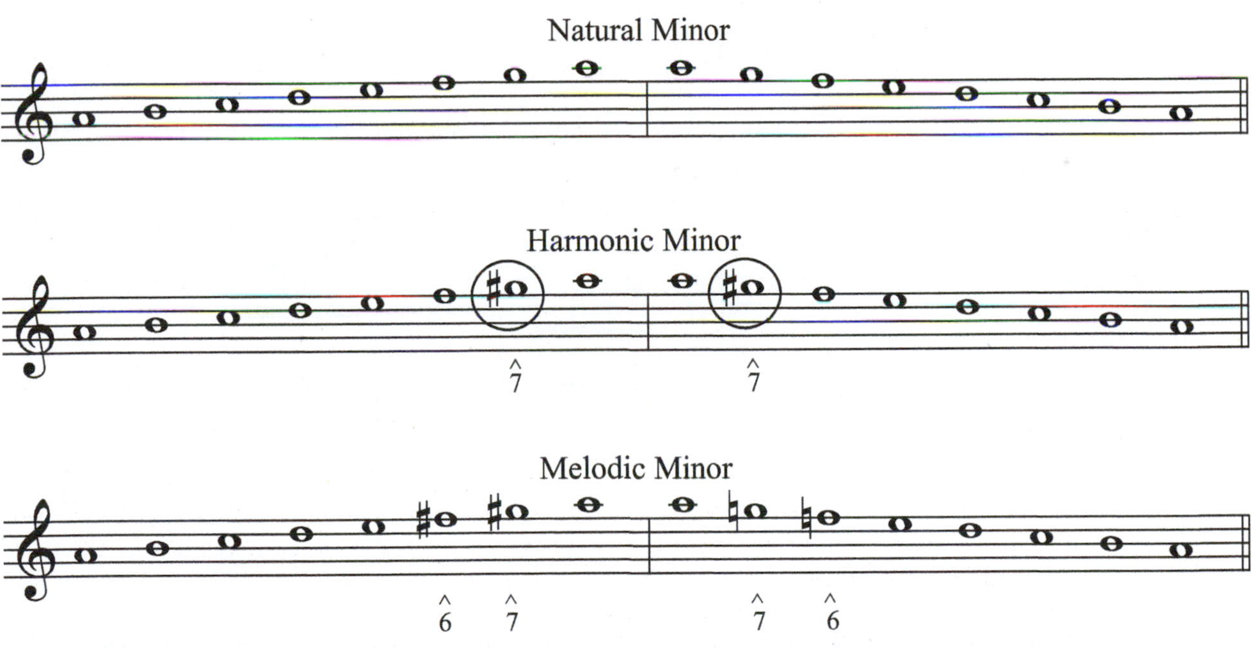

In the next example by the Italian composer Antonio Vivaldi (1678–1741), notice that the key is G minor. The opening figure outlines a natural minor scale; while the next two beats represent the melodic minor ascending pattern.

While generally avoided in traditional Western music, ascending and descending harmonic minor scales are commonly used in Middle Eastern folk music. The Jewish melody "Hava Nagila" ("Let Us Rejoice") is given here in G minor. Notice the use of both F♯ (raised $\hat{7}$) and E♭ (natural $\hat{6}$), which create the augmented second in descending patterns.

Jewish Folk Song, "Hava Nagila"

The Polish-French composer Frédéric Chopin (1810–1849) wrote the following passage in which both the leading tone and subtonic are used.

Frédéric Chopin, Mazurka in G Minor, Op. 67, no. 2

To further compare major and minor, listen to four different versions of the carol "The First Noel." The first line is in major as we usually hear it. The lines that follow are heard in natural, harmonic, and melodic minor, respectively. While the pitch content of each line is different, we still recognize the melody; this indicates that there are more similarities between major and minor scales than there are differences.

For class discussion or assignment: please do not remove these pages

REVIEW SET

Minor Scales

A. Write ascending minor scales as indicated. Begin with a key signature and add accidentals as necessary.

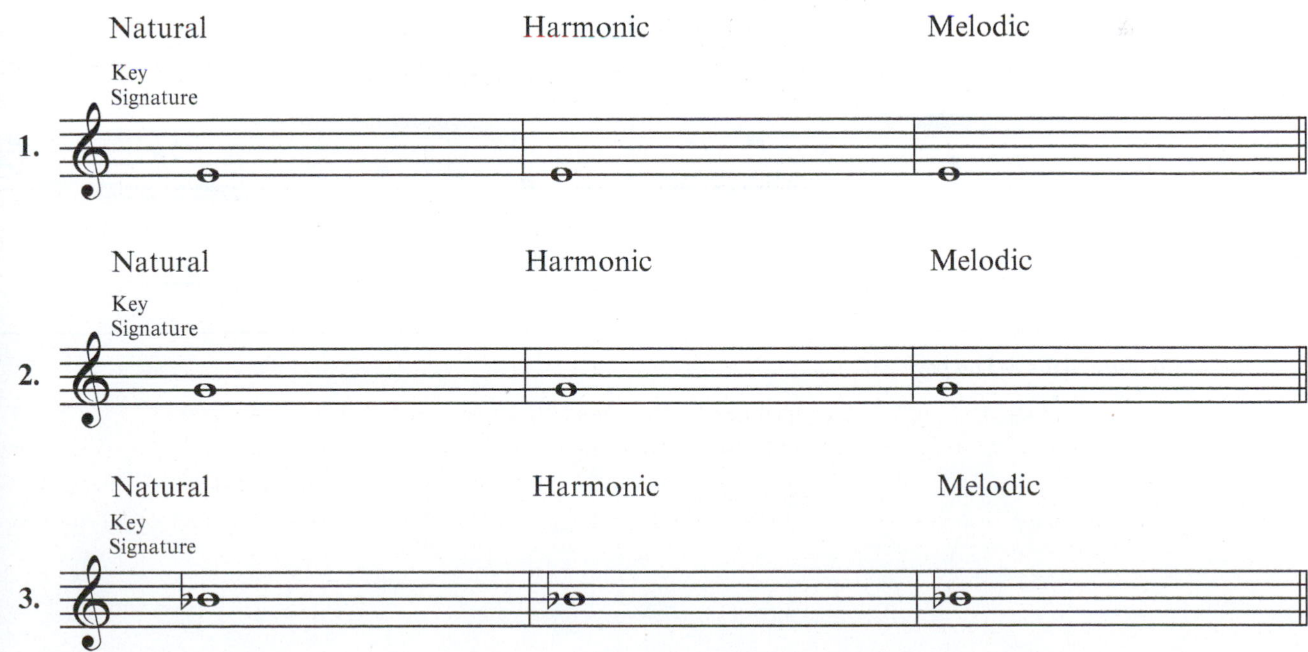

B. Write ascending and descending melodic minor scales. Begin by writing the ascending and descending natural minor and then alter $\hat{6}$ and $\hat{7}$ in the ascending form.

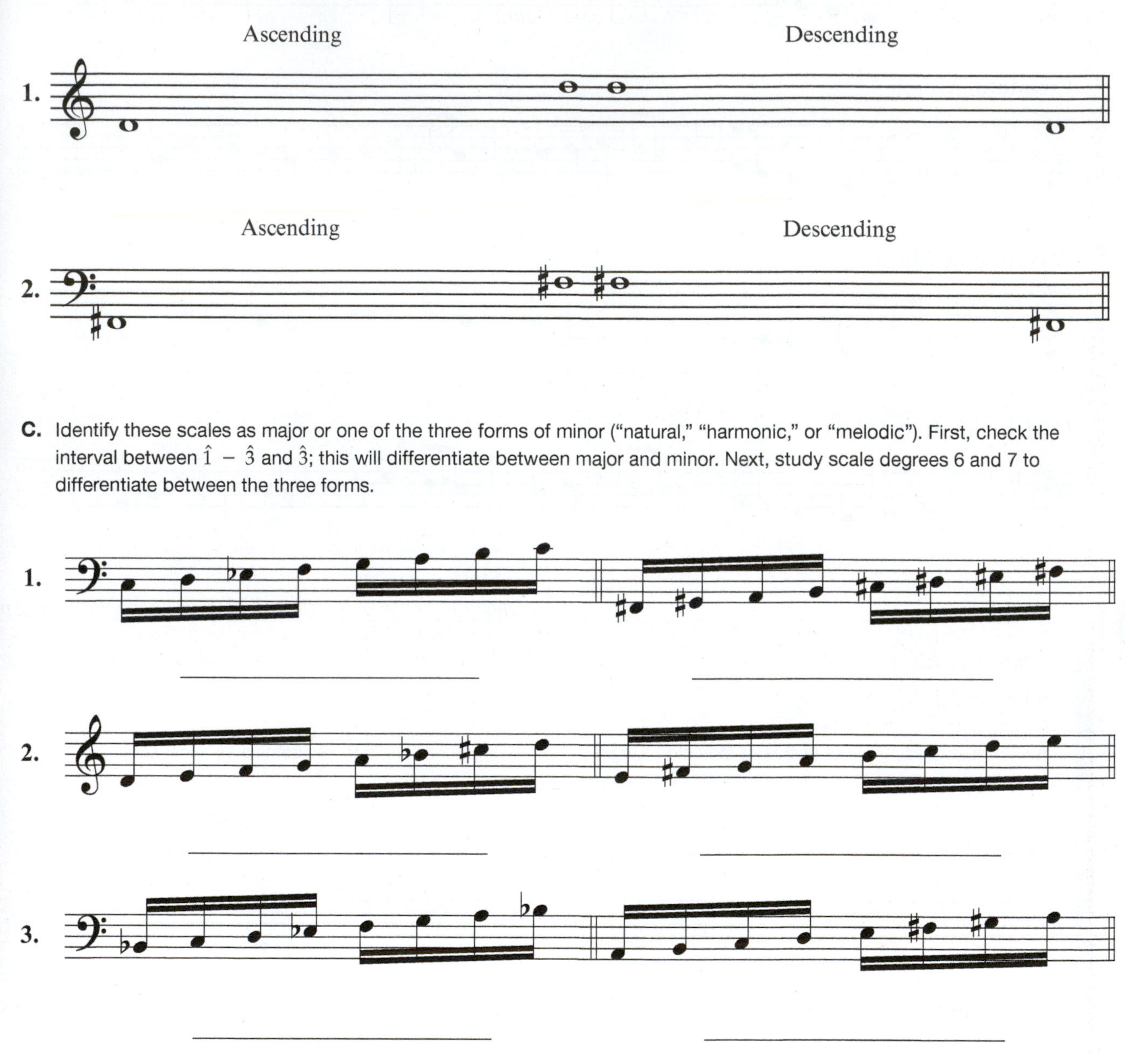

C. Identify these scales as major or one of the three forms of minor ("natural," "harmonic," or "melodic"). First, check the interval between $\hat{1}$ – $\hat{3}$ and $\hat{3}$; this will differentiate between major and minor. Next, study scale degrees 6 and 7 to differentiate between the three forms.

Complete Building Skills 8-3 on page 237

MUSICIANSHIP 8-2

Ear Training: Hearing Major and Minor

A. Listen to each pitch pattern, focusing on scale degree 3. Write "M" for major and "m" for minor in the blanks below. (See Appendix D for answers.)

Ascending

1. ______ 1 ______ 2 ______ 3 ______ 4 ______ 5 ______ 6

2. ______ 1 ______ 2 ______ 3 ______ 4 ______ 5 ______ 6

Descending

3. ______ 1 ______ 2 ______ 3 ______ 4 ______ 5 ______ 6

4. ______ 1 ______ 2 ______ 3 ______ 4 ______ 5 ______ 6

Various

a. ______ 1 ______ 2 ______ 3 ______ 4 ______ 5 ______ 6

b. ______ 1 ______ 2 ______ 3 ______ 4 ______ 5 ______ 6

B. Listen to the ascending and descending passages based on scale degrees $\hat{1}-\hat{5}$ in major or minor. Some of the patterns are stepwise; others are unordered. In all cases, however, the tonic is the first and final pitch you will hear. Write "M" in the blank if the mode is major and "m" for minor.

Scale Degrees 1–5 in Major and Minor

a. ______ 1 ______ 2 ______ 3 ______ 4 ______ 5 ______ 6

b. ______ 1 ______ 2 ______ 3 ______ 4 ______ 5 ______ 6

c. ______ 1 ______ 2 ______ 3 ______ 4 ______ 5 ______ 6

C. Scale degrees $\hat{5}-\hat{8}$ are equally important when differentiating among the three forms of minor. If you hear a leading tone, for example, the scale is harmonic or melodic. If there is a subtonic, the scale is natural minor. The stepwise patterns in this set represent the *final* four pitches in an ascending scale ($\hat{5}-\hat{8}$). Here you are asked to determine only whether the scale has a leading tone (write "LT") or subtonic (write "ST").

Listening for Leading Tone and Subtonic

a. ______ 1 ______ 2 ______ 3 ______ 4 ______ 5 ______ 6

b. ______ 1 ______ 2 ______ 3 ______ 4 ______ 5 ______ 6

c. ______ 1 ______ 2 ______ 3 ______ 4 ______ 5 ______ 6

MUSICIANSHIP 8-3

Sight Singing: Patterns in Major and Minor Scales

Considering the first five scale degrees of major and parallel minor keys, only $\hat{3}$ is different. Using scale-degree numbers or the syllable method suggested by your instructor, sing the following five-pitch patterns in major (for example, movable-do solfège: do–re–mi–fa–sol) and parallel minor keys (movable-do solfège: do–re–me–fa–sol).

- Practice singing the major scale in various keys. These examples demonstrate either scale degree numbers or movable-do solfège:

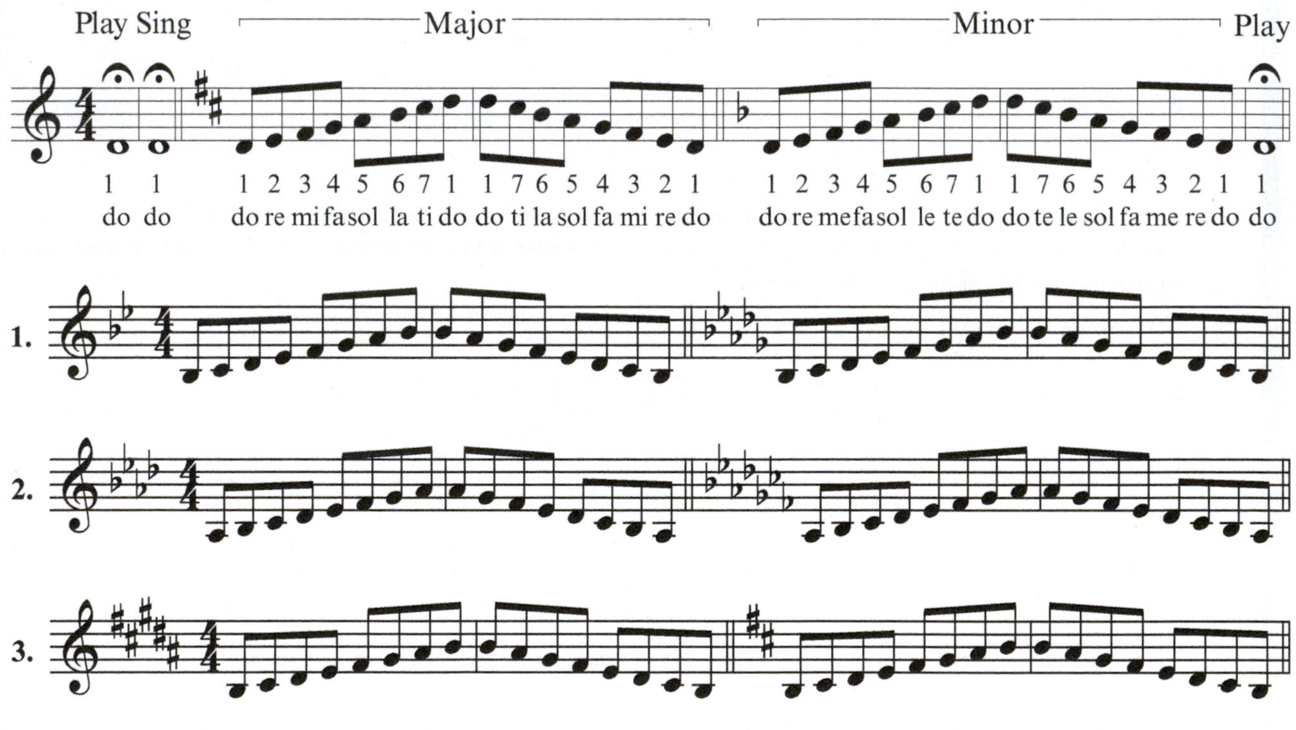

- Practice these skills in the context of short melodies. Experiment with singing each example in the parallel minor. Explore the various minor scale forms.

2.
3.
4.
5.
6.
7.
8.

Name ______________________

Page may be removed

Building Skills • 8-1

Parallel and Relative Keys

A. **For each given major or minor key, provide the name of its relative key and write the key signature for both keys in the treble and bass staves.**

	Key	Relative Major/Minor	Key Signature
1.	E♭ Minor 	______________	
2.	F Major	______________	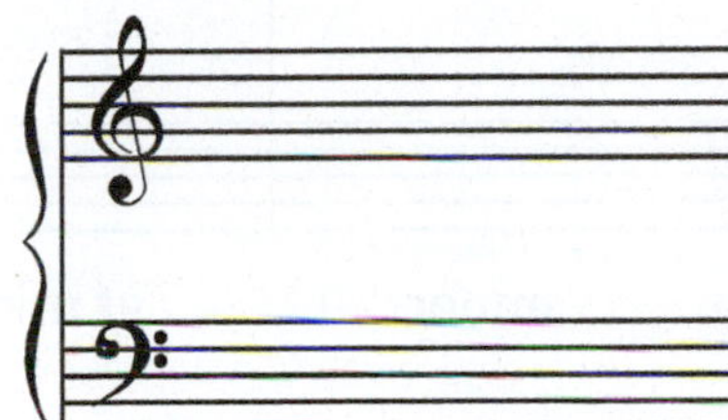
3.	C Minor	______________	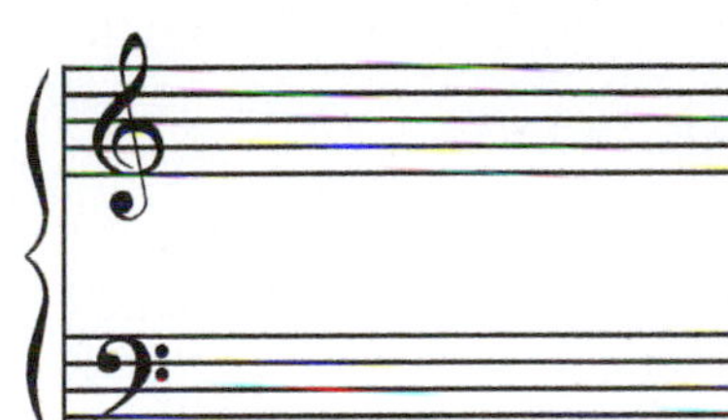
4.	A♭ Major	______________	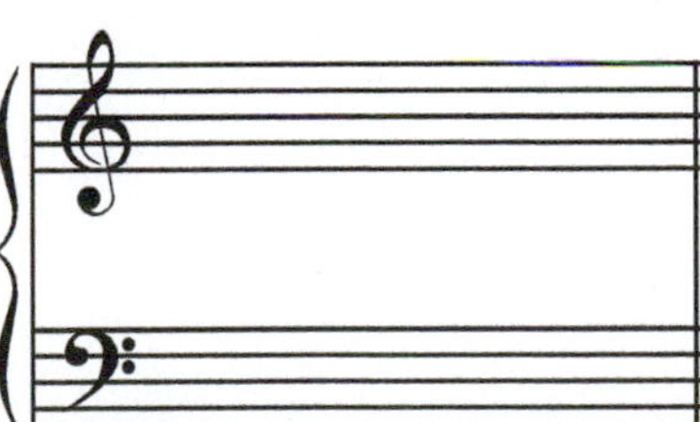
5.	G♯ Minor	______________	
6.	D♭ Major	______________	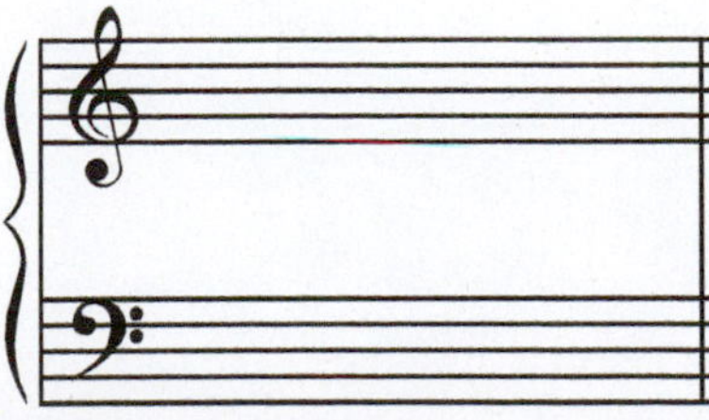

B. **Provide the signatures of the specified minor keys in both treble and bass staves.**

1.

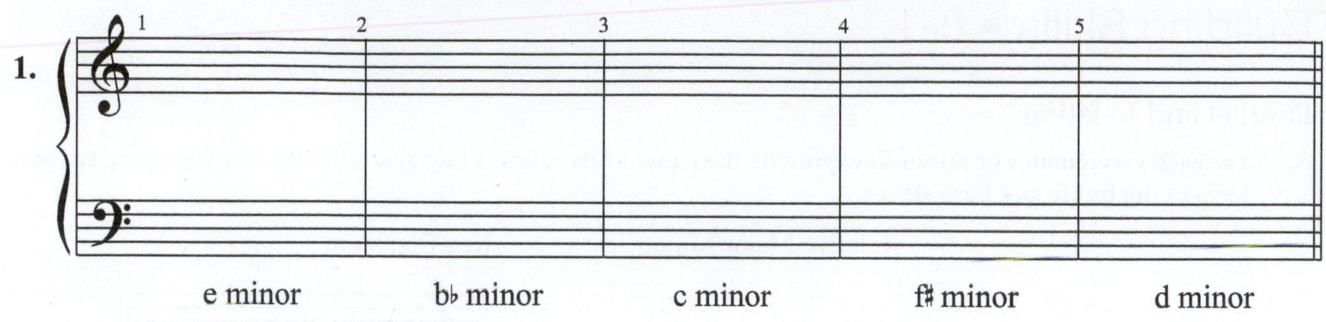

2.

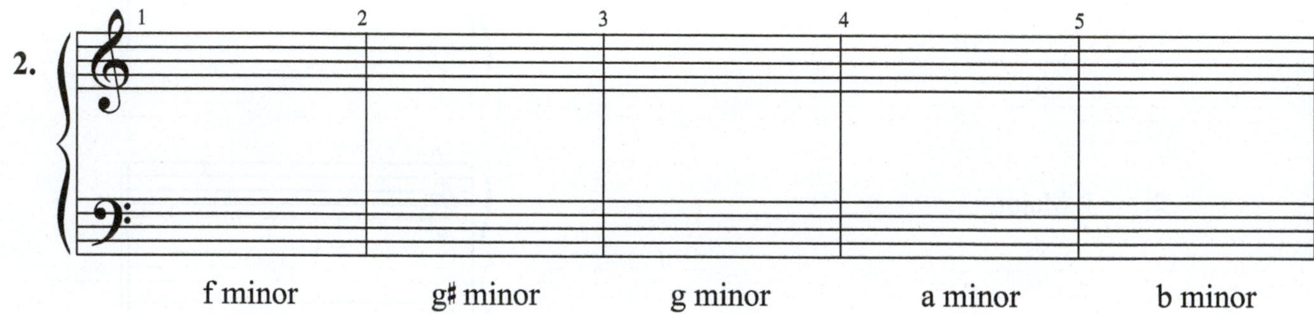

Name ________________________

Page may be removed

Building Skills • 8-2

Minor Scales

A. **Construct these natural minor scales. Add accidentals as necessary.**

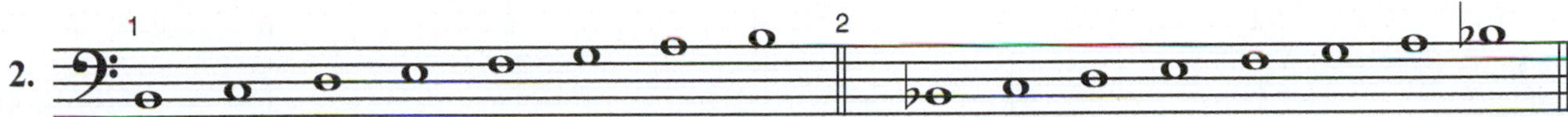

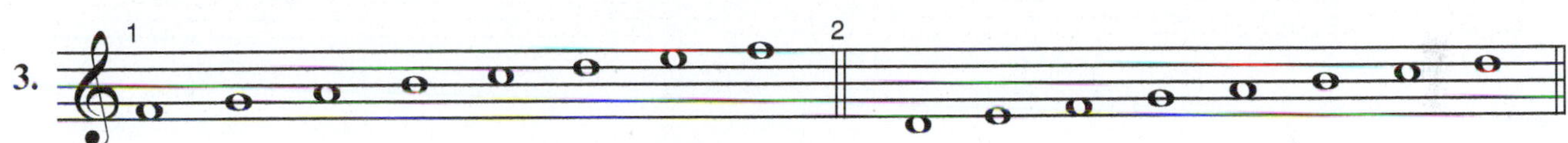

B. **Identify the scale-degree number of the given pitches in the specified minor. There are three pitches in each key.**

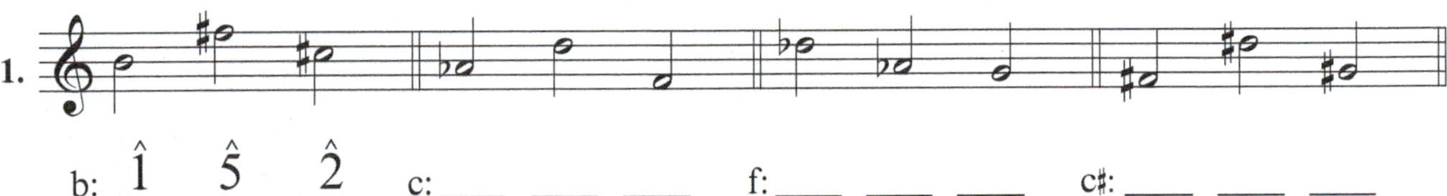

b: $\hat{1}$ $\hat{5}$ $\hat{2}$ c: ____ ____ ____ f: ____ ____ ____ c♯: ____ ____ ____

e: ____ ____ ____ g: ____ ____ ____ f♯: ____ ____ ____ b♭: ____ ____ ____

a: ____ ____ ____ g♯: ____ ____ ____ a♭: ____ ____ ____ e♭: ____ ____ ____

C. **In these minor keys, provide the pitch indicated by the scale-degree name. Add an accidental if necessary.**

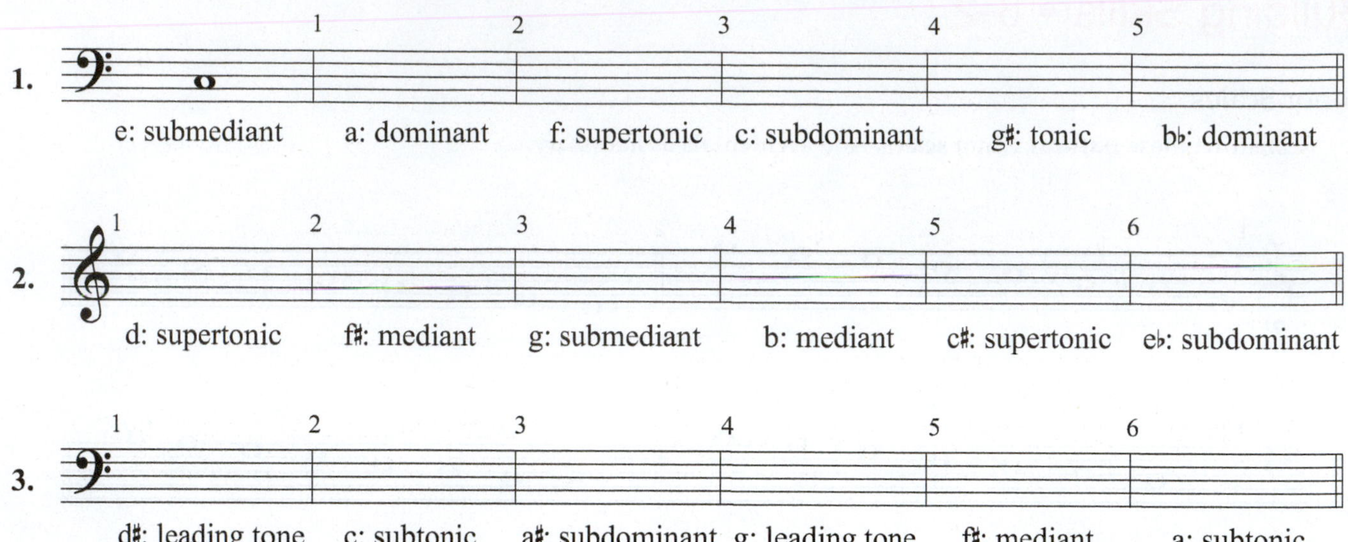

Name ______________________

Page may be removed

Building Skills • 8-3

Natural, Harmonic, and Melodic Minor Scales

A. Identify these scales as major or one of the three forms of minor. Sing or play your answers as you work.

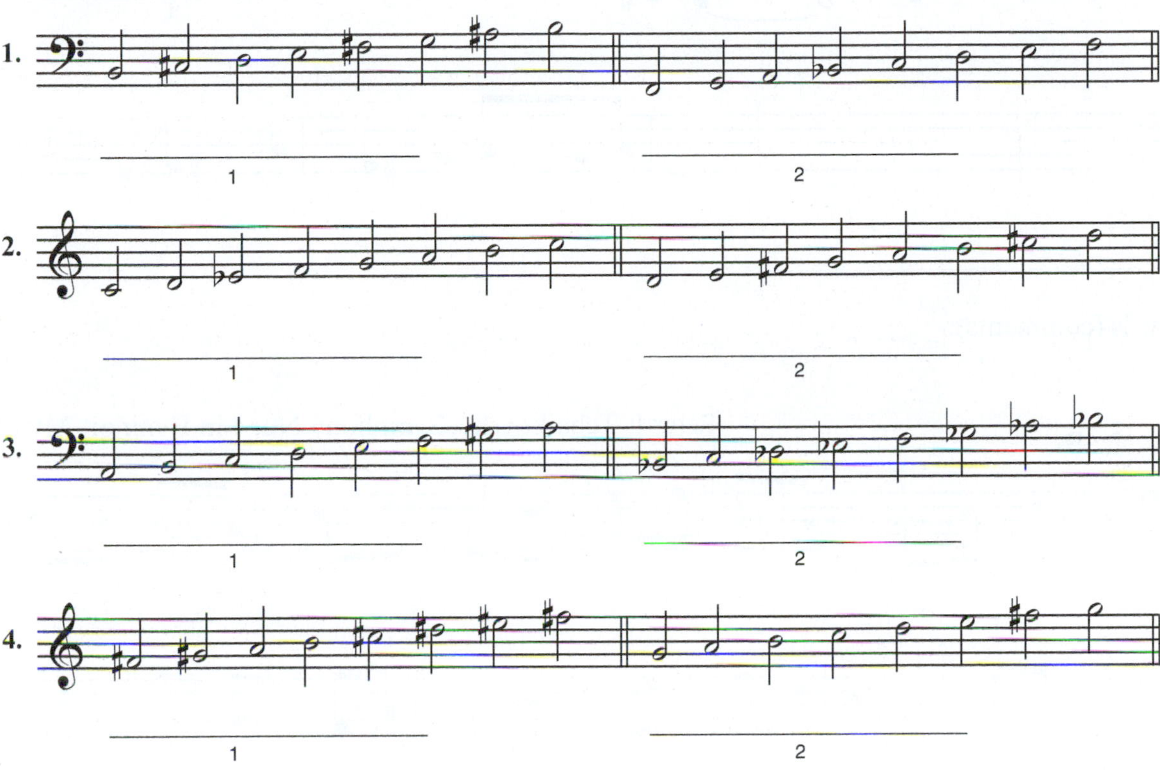

B. Construct the following minor scales. Use a key signature and add accidentals as necessary. Write only the ascending forms for natural and harmonic minor; provide both ascending and descending forms for melodic minor.

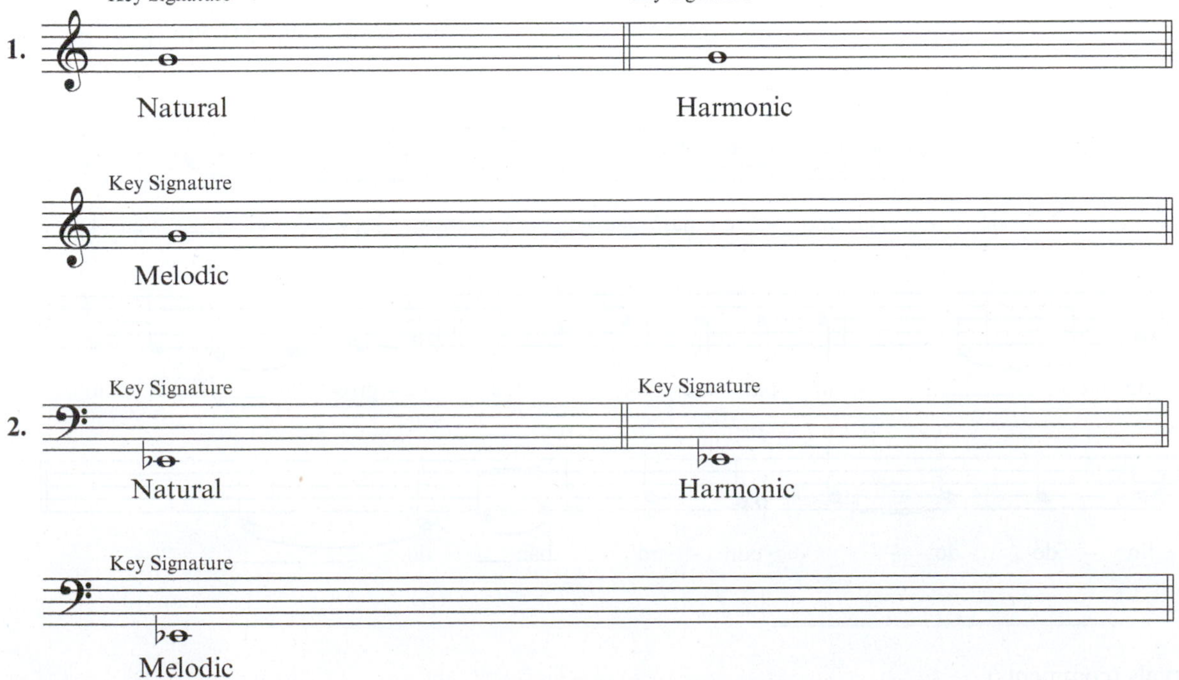

C. **These melodies are constructed from a major scale or minor scale. The tonic pitch is specified (it may not be the first pitch). Analyze the scale and identify it as major, natural minor, harmonic minor, or melodic minor. In addition, study the interval types present in the melody and summarize your findings in a few sentences.**

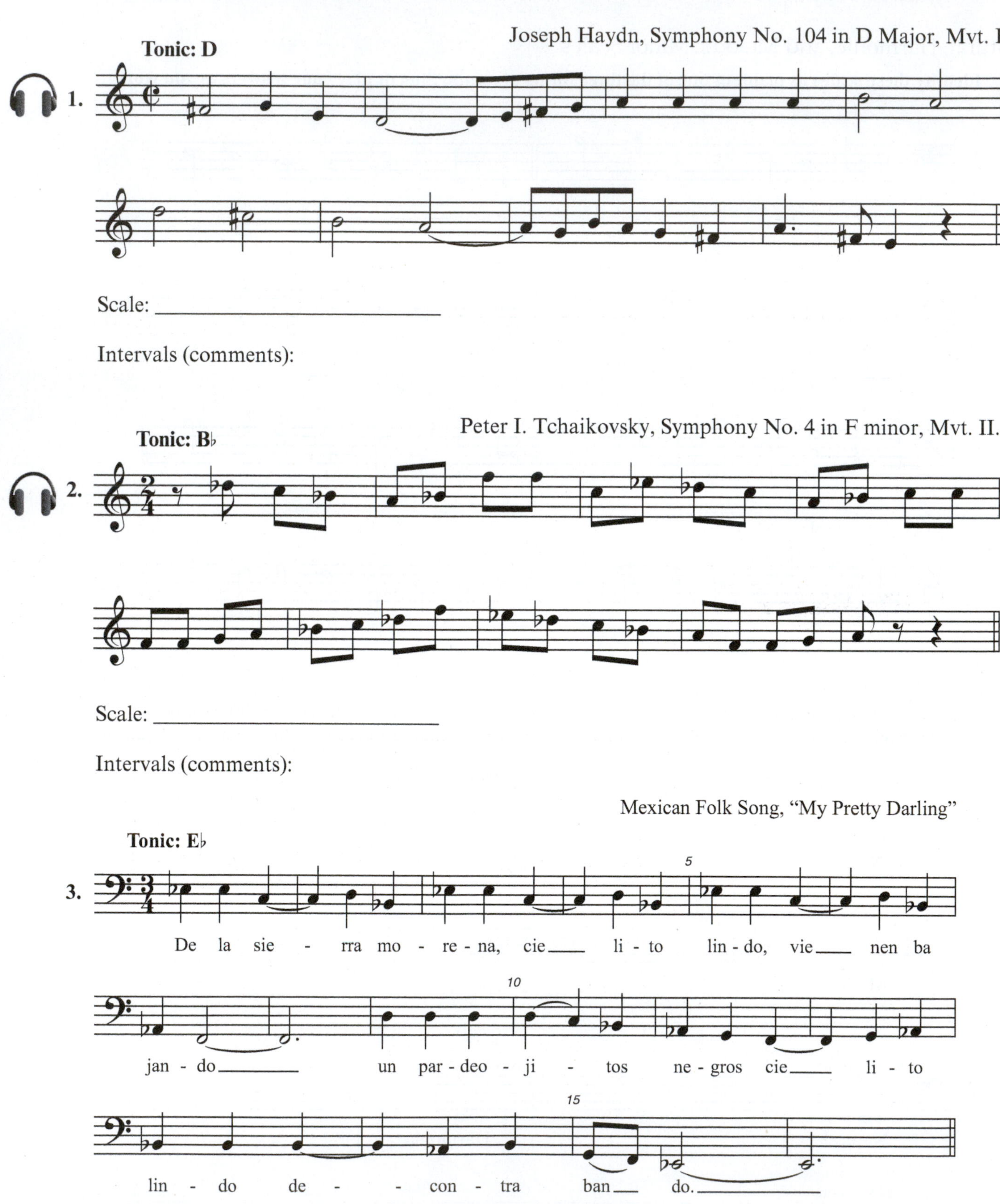

Scale: ______________________________

Intervals (comments):

Name ______________________

Page may be removed

D. **Each fragment can be heard in the context of one or more major or minor keys. While a few fragments are included in the scale of only one scale form, most can be heard in two or more. Identify up to three possible keys for each fragment. If keys you identify are minor, provide the form as well.**

E. **Each of these eight-measure melodies represents a major key or one of the forms of minor. Determine the key based on the key signature, the prominent pitches, and any accidentals present.**

1.

a. Key ____________________

b. Mode and Form (if minor) ____________________

2.

a. Key ____________________

b. Mode and Form (if minor) ____________________

3.

a. Key ____________________

b. Mode and Form (if minor) ____________________

4.

a. Key ____________________

b. Mode and Form (if minor) ____________________

Name ______________________

Page may be removed

F. **Write the scales indicated. In some cases, you will first need to determine the appropriate tonic pitch. Begin with a key signature and add accidentals as necessary. Play your answer on the piano when you've finished with the notation.**

1. The parallel minor of C major (natural form)
2. The parallel minor of E major (harmonic form)
3. The parallel major of B minor
4. The relative minor of E♭ major (melodic form)
5. The relative minor of B♭ major (natural form)
6. The relative major of D♯ minor
7. The parallel minor of A major (harmonic form)
8. The relative minor of F major (harmonic form)

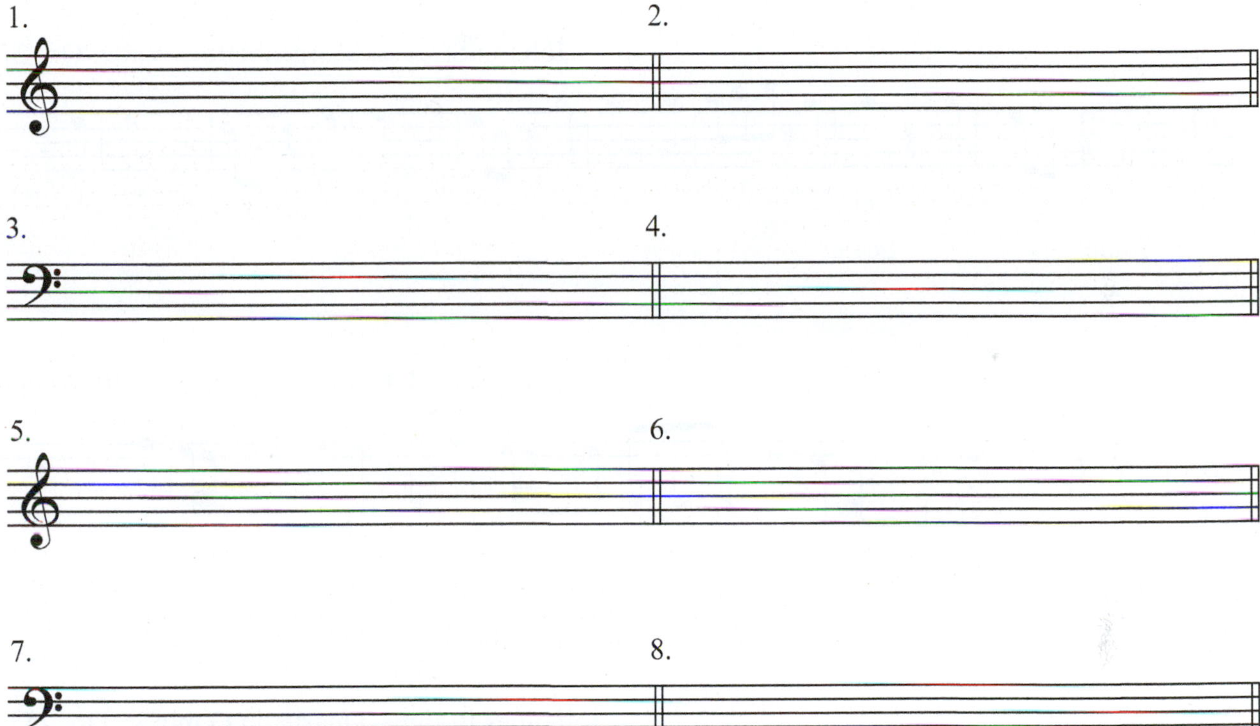

G. These phrases are in major or one of the forms of minor. Determine the tonic pitch from studying the key signature, pitch content, and metric accents. Next, indicate whether the phrase is major or minor (include the form if minor).

Name ______________________

Page may be removed

Creative Projects • Chapter 8

A. **Complete the given melodies in the specified keys. If the melody is in minor, be sure to emphasize characteristic pitches in ascending or descending passages. Some pitches at phrase endings are given. As you have done in other composition exercises, make your melody basically stepwise, with occasional leaps for emphasis and variety. Work out your melodies on another sheet before copying the final versions here. Prepare to perform your melodies for the class.**

B. Create a setting of the poem "The Great Way" by the thirteenth-century Chinese priest known as Wu Men.

> The Great Way has no gate;
> there are a thousand paths to it.
> If you pass through the barrier,
> you walk the universe alone.
>
> —Wu Men

Use the space below to plan the rhythm and meter as you have done in earlier chapters. The lines can be set with or without an anacrusis (or a combination of lines with and without). Treat each pair of lines as a four-measure phrase (like those in exercise A on the previous page) and feel free to use repetition. Make the last beat of each four-measure phrase fill the entire measure (or the second half of a measure in quadruple meter).

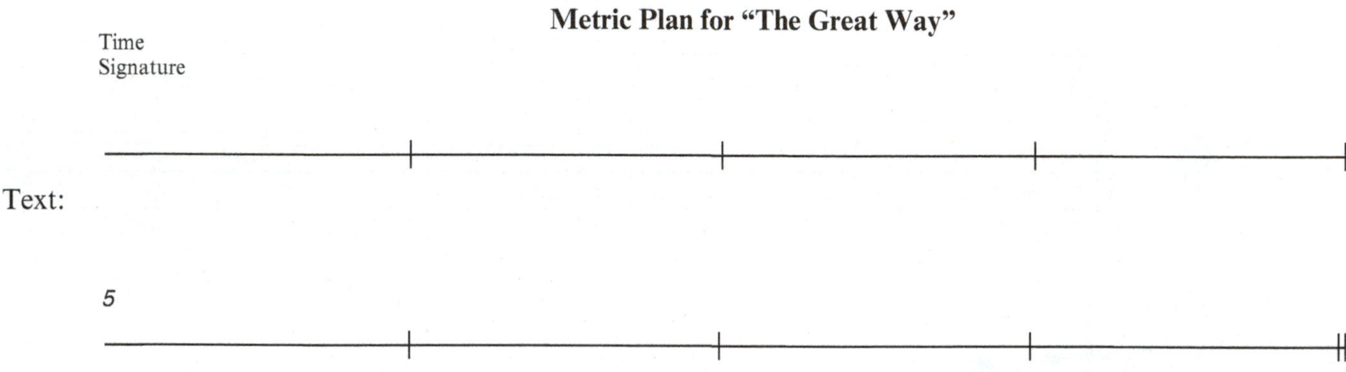

Now you are ready to write a melody. Notice that the second and fourth lines end with a period while the first and third have a semicolon and comma, respectively. Consider using the first or third scale degrees at the end of stronger phrases and other pitches for the intermediate pauses. Use stepwise movement with occasional leaps. Complete a draft on another page before copying the final version here.

"The Great Way"

Music by:______________________
Text by Wu Men

Key Signature Time Signature

Text:

Text:

Text:

Name ______________________

Page may be removed

Analysis in Context 1 • Chapter 8

Composed in the late 1500s, "Flow My Tears" was originally written for voice and lute. The vocal line includes several repeats, and performers often add ornamentation for phrases that are repeated. Listen to several performances of this vocal standard before answering the questions that follow.

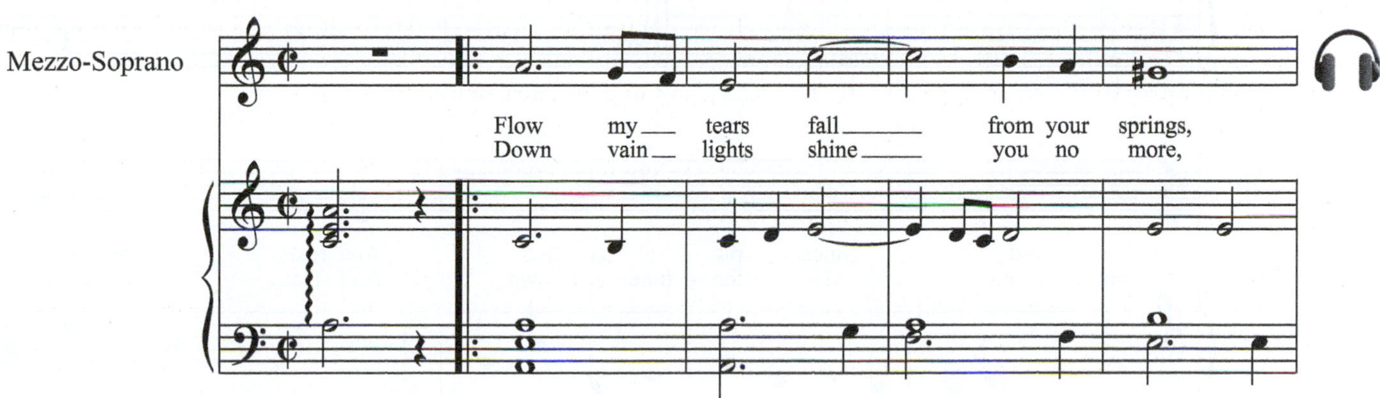

16
Mezzo
lorn. Nev - er may my woes be — re -
close. From the high - est spire of — con -
21
Mezzo
liev - ed, Since pit - y is fled, And tears, and sighs,
tent - ment, My for - tune is thrown, And fear, and grief,
26
Mezzo
and groans my wea - ry days, my wea - ry days Of all
and pain for my de - serts, for my de - serts Are my
31
Mezzo
joys have de - priv - ed. Hark you sha - dows
hopes since hope — is gone.

Name ______________________

Page may be removed

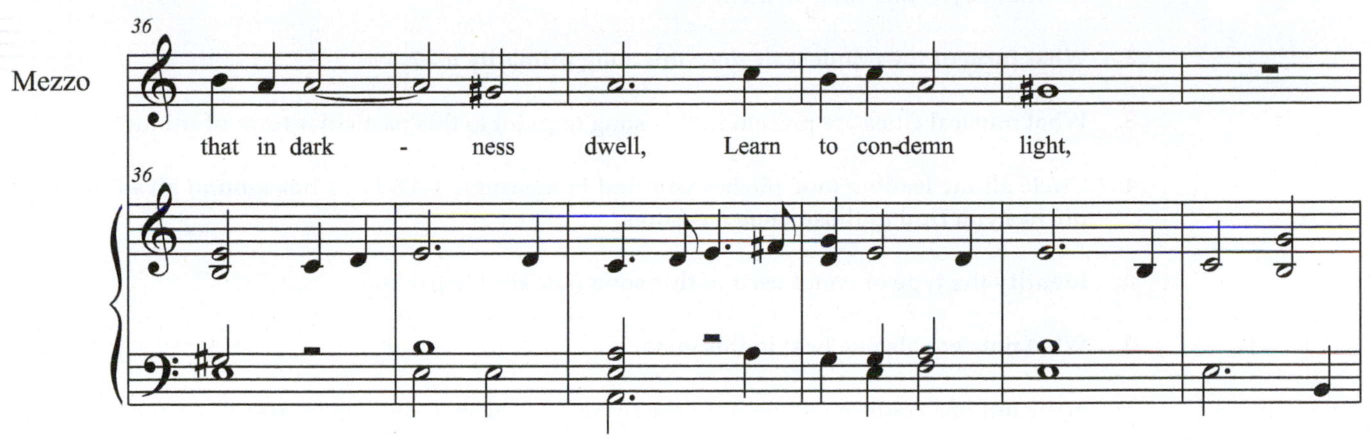

1. In what key is this song written?
2. What form of the minor scale does this song primarily use?
3. What musical clues are present in this song to point to this particular form of minor?
4. Circle all the leading tone pitches you find in measures 1–17. Put a box around all subtonic pitches you find in those same measures.
5. Identify the type of meter used in this song (i.e., simple triple).
6. What note equals one beat in this meter?
7. Write out one counting method for the rhythm of the melody in measures 11–17 (i.e., takadimi counts).
8. What is the relative major key to this song's key signature?
9. Does the melody in measures 18–21 seem to be in the established minor key or in the relative major key? Why?
10. Write in the scale degree numbers above the melody in measure 42 to the end. Discuss the composer's treatment of scale degrees 6 and 7 in measure 48, and the surprise accidental in measures 49 and 50. Consider the text when crafting your answer.

Chapter 9
Introduction to Form

Essential Terms and Symbols

al fine
antecedent phrase
cadence
chorus
consequent phrase
da capo
dal segno (𝄋)
D.C.
double period
D.S.
fine
first ending (⌈1 :‖)
form
melodic cadence
motive(s)
period
phrase group
progressive melodic cadence
refrain
second ending (⌈2)
sequence
terminal melodic cadence
thirty-two-bar song form
verse
verse and refrain form

Form is the shape of a musical work in time. We can measure form over the span of a few beats or even several hundred measures. We trace form in smaller segments, called *motives.* Lengthier forms, on the other hand, depend in large part on changes of key. In this chapter we introduce and discuss melodic forms—common models that shape and combine one or more phrases.

Building Phrases

While there are many exceptions (depending on meter, tempo, and other factors), the most common phrase length is four measures. Phrases introduce musical material and then carry the listener to a goal called a *cadence.* A **cadence** is a musical pause; a **melodic cadence** is usually the final pitches in a phrase.

PROGRESSIVE MELODIC CADENCE. When the cadential pitch is the second, fifth, or seventh scale degree, the melodic cadence is **progressive**; at least one more phrase will follow. A progressive melodic cadence is like a comma in sentence construction. The pause provides an intermediate division but we know that the statement is incomplete.

The first phrase in the melody of Beethoven's ninth symphony is progressive. Metric position and note length emphasize the cadence on the pitch E ($\hat{2}$).

Ludwig Van Beethoven, Symphony No. 9, IV

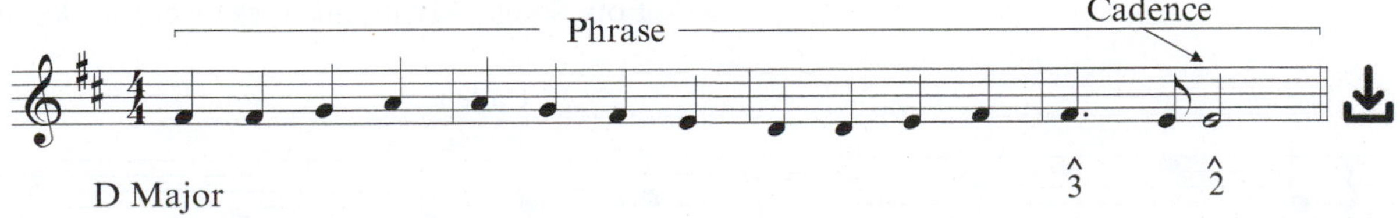

Written nearly two hundred years after Beethoven's symphony, the first phrase of "I Won't Give Up," by Jason Mraz, ends with a similar phrase (measure 4). Like Beethoven, Mraz uses both metric accent and note length to dramatize the progressive cadence on the second scale degree.

Jason Mraz, "I Won't Give Up"

TERMINAL MELODIC CADENCES. While a progressive melodic cadence assures the listener that another phrase will follow, a **terminal melodic cadence**—ending on the tonic or mediant pitch ($\hat{1}$ or $\hat{3}$)—is a point of relative finality and more like a period in a sentence. The first phrase of the Quintet for Clarinet and Strings by Wolfgang Amadeus Mozart (1756–1791) ends with the tonic pitch, which is a terminal melodic cadence.

W. A. Mozart, Quintet for Clarinet and Strings in A Major. K581, I

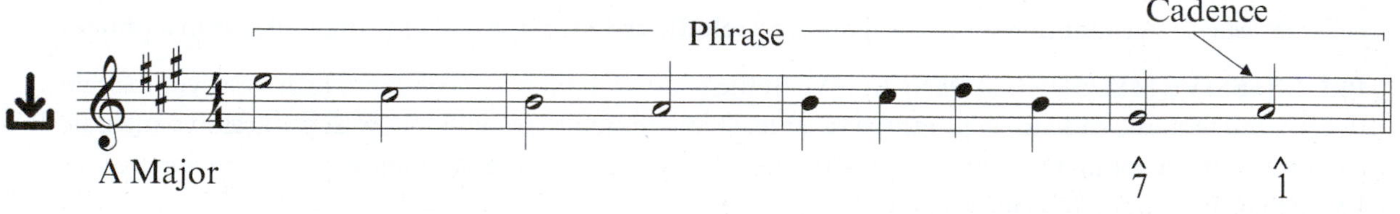

Even though more of the song follows, we would consider the first cadence of "My Bonnie Lies Over the Ocean" to be terminal because it ends on $\hat{3}$—a pitch associated with the tonic.

Folk Song, "My Bonnie Lies Over the Ocean"

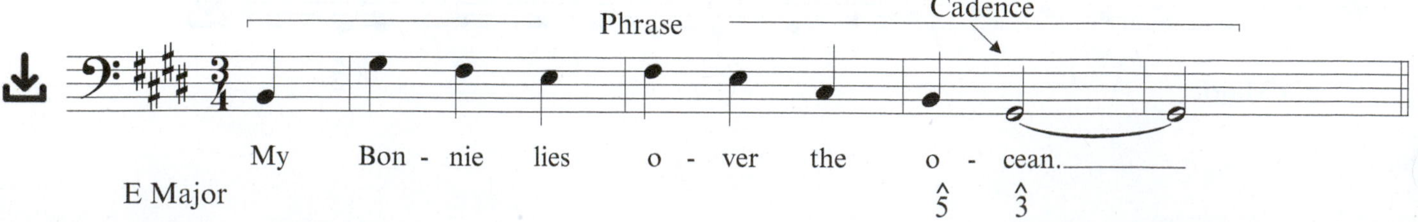

While "My Bonnie" ends on the mediant pitch, the tonic is the final pitch in the Mozart.

For class discussion or assignment: please do not remove these pages

REVIEW SET

Progressive and Terminal Melodic Cadences

Determine the *major* key of each phrase. Next, enter the scale degree of the cadential (circled) pitch and write "progressive" or "terminal" as appropriate. *Remember:* All keys are major.

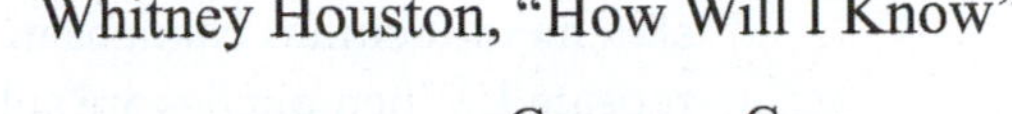
Whitney Houston, "How Will I Know"

Key: _______ Scale Degree: _______

Melodic Cadence: ___________

Joseph Haydn, Symphony No. 104, IV

Key: _______ Scale Degree: _______

Melodic Cadence : ___________

Welsh Folk Song, "The Ash Grove"

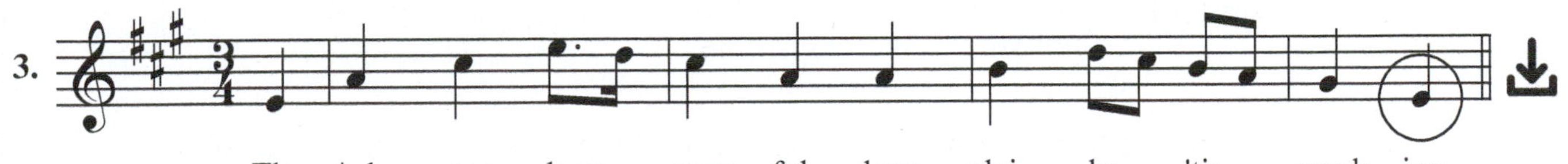

Key: _______ Scale Degree: _______

Melodic Cadence : ___________

Unifying and Extending Phrases

The smallest element used to create a melody is called a **motive**. In the development of a phrase, and especially when two or more phrases are connected, composers use motives in one or more of several ways: *repetition, variation, sequence,* and *contrast*.

Repetition

To generate a phrase, composers may state a motive and then simply repeat it. Even when another statement includes changes in rhythm, if the pitches remain essentially the same, the motive has been repeated. When pitches are substantially different, on the other hand, new material represents *variation* or *contrast* (discussed later in this section).

The opening phrase of Beethoven's first symphony is little more than a reiteration of three pitches: C–G–B. The third and fourth statements of the three-pitch motive are altered rhythmically to generate momentum toward the cadence.

Beethoven, Symphony No. 1, I

Repetition of motives is a consistent feature of many styles of music. Brahms' "Weigenlied" is similar to Beethoven's phrase in its consistent return to a single pitch.

Brahms, "Weigenlied," mm2-10

Variation

Composers may unify a phrase by stating a motive, then providing one or more variations. To perceive a variation, however, we must hear the second and subsequent statements of the motive as clearly related. In his Concerto for Piano in B♭ major, German composer Johannes Brahms (1833–1897) states a motive and then reverses its direction. The comparable rhythmic values tie the two statements together into a complete phrase.

Johannes Brahms, Concerto in B♭ for Piano, Op. 83, I

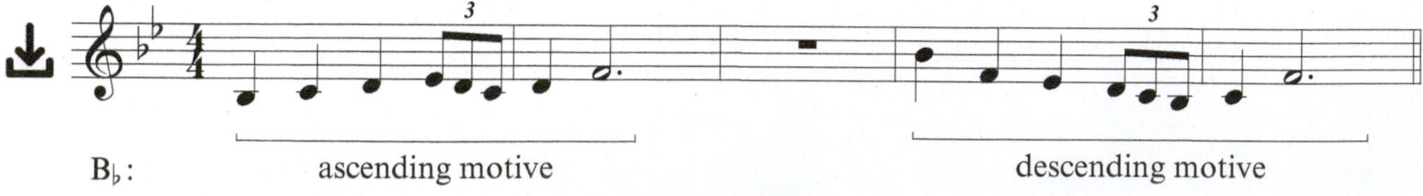

The Neapolitan song "Santa Lucia" begins with a two-measure motive followed by a variation. The characteristic leap of a fourth that defines the motive is reduced to a leap of a third in the variation.

Neapolitan Song, "Santa Lucia"

Sequence

A **sequence** occurs when a motive is immediately restated at a new pitch level in the same voice. We identify sequence by ascending or descending motion and also by the interval between the first pitch of the original motive and the first pitch of succeeding variations. In the next example, the sequenced motive ascends by step to the progressive cadence.

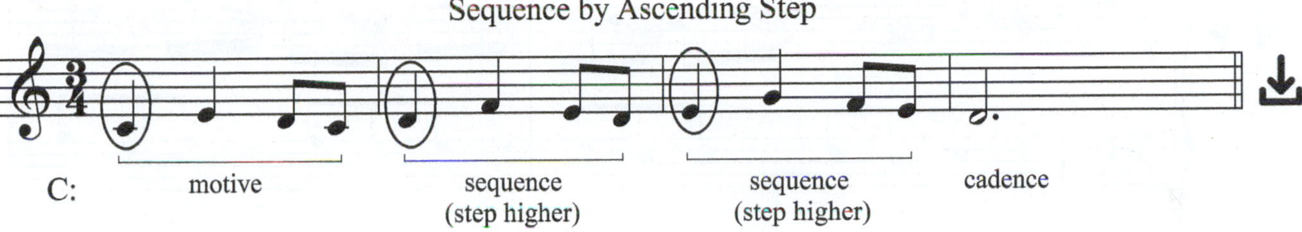

Sequences are also commonly found descending by step.

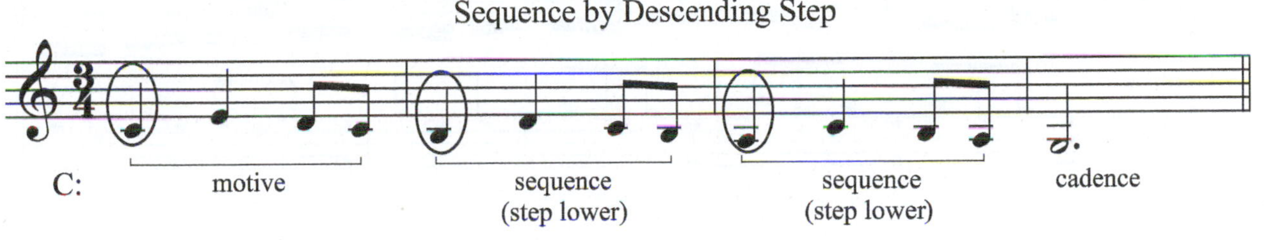

An ascending or descending sequence may also occur by larger intervals. In the next example, the first phrase grows through a descending sequence by third; the second phrase is based on an ascending sequence by fourth.

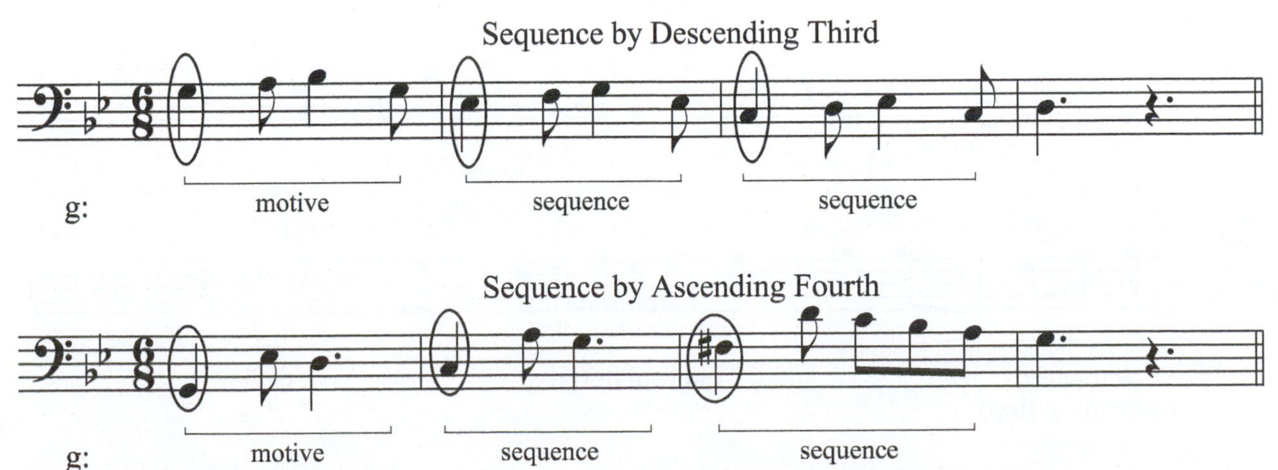

This phrase from a concerto by the German composer George Frideric Handel (1685–1759) is an example of an ascending sequence by step. As is common in sequential passages, the third repetition of the pattern is varied to create momentum toward the cadence.

George Frideric Handel
Concerto Grosso in A minor, Op. 6, No. 4

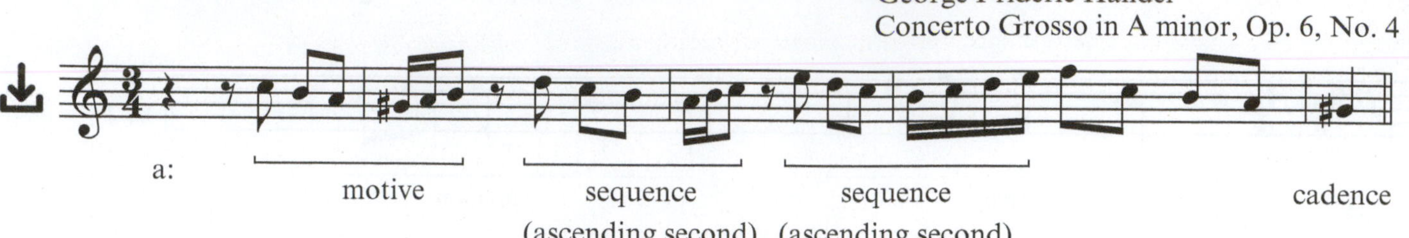

The melody from Bach's Brandenburg Concerto no. 5 includes both an ascending and a descending sequence.

J.S. Bach, Brandenburg Concerto no. 5 in D Major, BWV 1050

In Mozart's Concerto for Clarinet, the ascending sequence by step is followed by new material to prepare for a terminal cadence in D major.

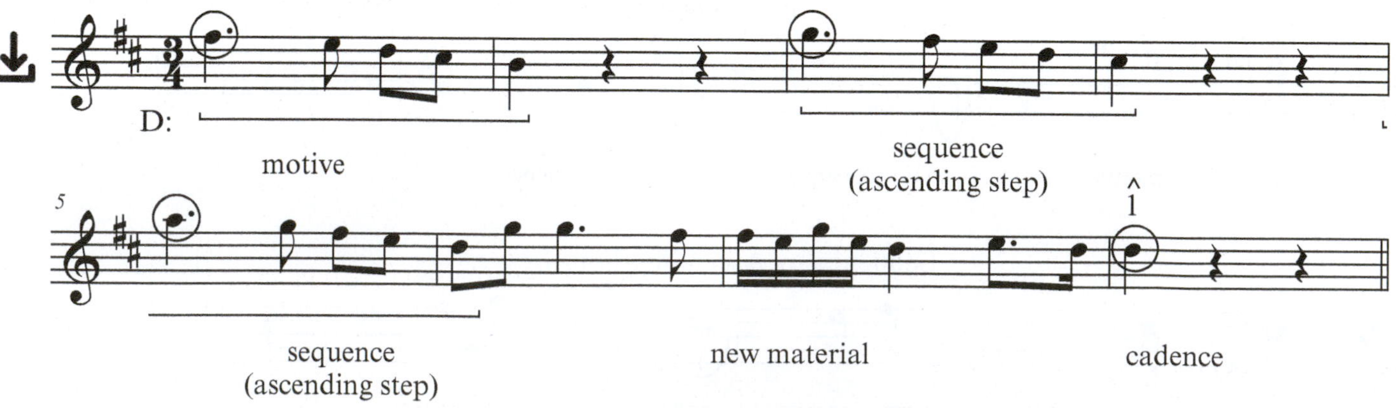

All three of the previous examples show sequence by step (Handel and Mozart ascending; the melody from the Bach includes both descending and ascending).

Contrast

In the passage that follows, notice how the motives are repeated and varied in the first and second phrases. In addition, the second phrase provides contrasting material to the opening phrase.

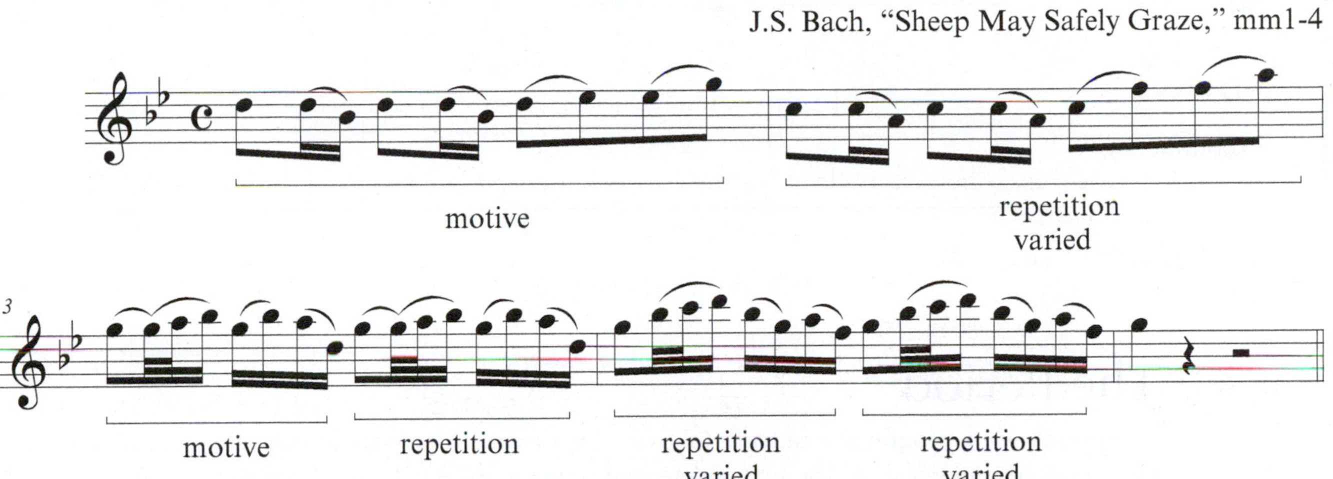

Bach combines repetition with contrasting material in this four-measure phrase.

J.S. Bach, March in D major

Repetition, variation, sequence, and contrast are tools employed to build phrases. In the next section, we will discuss how these same techniques can unify *groups* of phrases.

For class discussion or assignment: please do not remove these pages

REVIEW SET

Shaping Phrases

Comment on the opening motive and explain how this material grows to complete the phrase (repetition, variation, sequence, or contrast). If sequence is present, identify the direction and interval. Identify the cadence (circled) as terminal or progressive.

Robert Schumann, "Scenes from Childhood"

Pachabel, Canon in D (Bass Line Only)

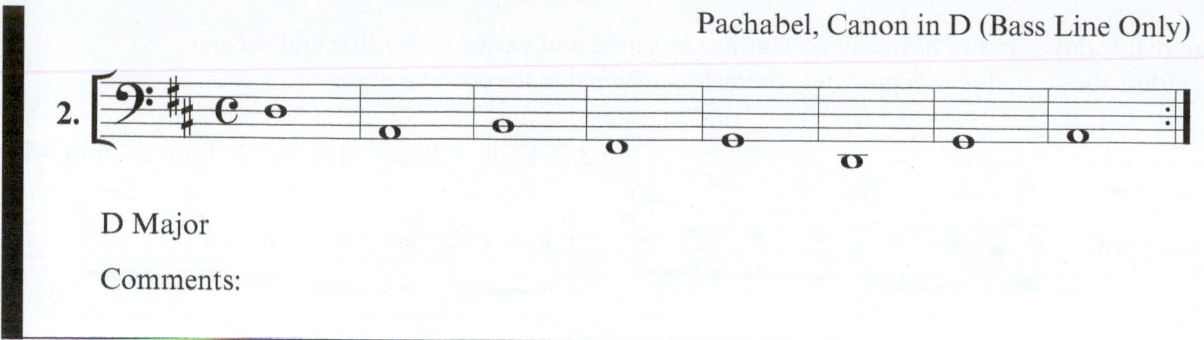

D Major

Comments:

Complete Building Skills 9-1 on page 267

The Period

Composers use a progressive cadence followed by a terminal cadence to help the listener hear two phrases as one longer unit. The first and second phrases of Beethoven's "Ode to Joy" form a longer passage of eight measures. Listen to the example on the website and notice that the only difference between these two phrases is in the final measure. The melodic material is the same; only the cadential pitches are different. Still, we hear the progressive cadence in measure 4 as a halfway point (a relatively weaker pause) and the terminal cadence in measure 8 as a completion (stronger in effect).

Ludwig Van Beethoven, Symphony No. 9, IV
"Ode to Joy"

When two phrases have a weaker–stronger arrangement of cadences (as in the last example), the form is known as a **period**. The weaker phrase of a period is termed the **antecedent phrase**; the stronger and concluding phrase is the **consequent phrase**. Periods are relatively easy to identify because (at least for our purposes) the first cadence will be progressive and the second will be terminal.

Periods are extended by the same techniques that we discussed in phrase structure: repetition, variation, sequence, and contrast. The periodic structure of Beethoven's "Ode to Joy," for example, emerges from repetition. The folk song "Frère Jacques" ("Are You Sleeping?") is also a period. The two phrases are each eight measures long (not uncommon when the meter is duple). The first (antecedent) phrase concludes on $\hat{5}$; the second (consequent) provides contrasting material and ends on the tonic.

French Folk Song, "Frere Jacques" ("Are You Sleeping?")

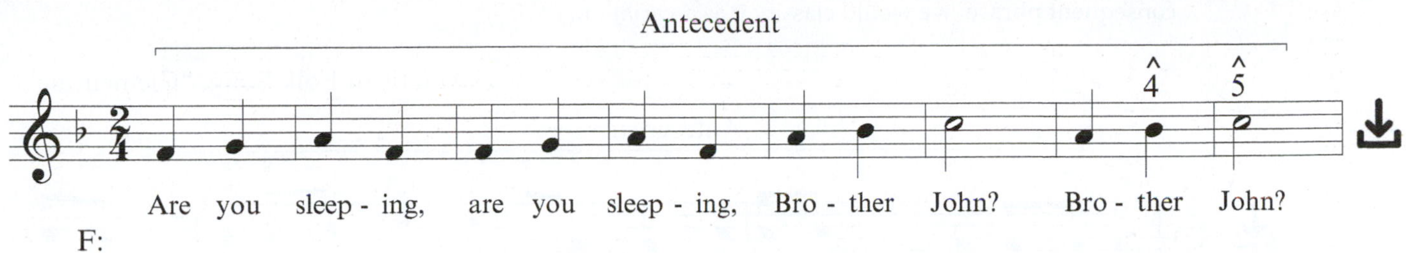

In triple or quadruple meter, phrases are often four measures in length. The excerpt from Haydn's Sonata has a conventional period structure based on repetition. The antecedent phrase ends with a progressive cadence on the dominant in C major, while the consequent phrase ends with a terminal cadence on the tonic.

Haydn, Sonata in C Major, III, Hob.XVI:35, mm1-8

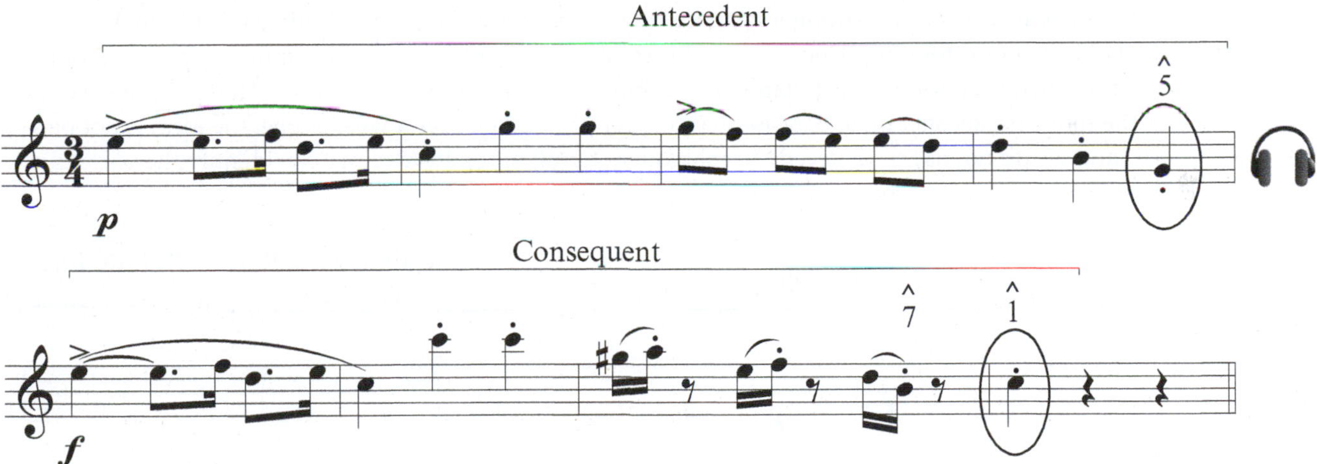

The verse portion of the song "Clementine" is another example of period structure. It features antecedent and consequent phrases ending on $\hat{2}$ and $\hat{1}$, respectively. Due to the rhythmic similarities in the consequent phrase, we would classify it as a variation.

American Folk Song, "Clementine"

Phrase Group

We've defined period phrase structure as two phrases that have an antecedent–consequent relationship. When related phrases have a weak–weak structure rather than a weak–strong structure, the term **phrase group** is more appropriate. In a phrase group, both phrases may have the same cadences (both strong or both weak), or a stronger cadence may precede a weaker one. While we could make many subtle distinctions, for our purposes, two phrases that do not make a period comprise a phrase group.

The Australian folk song "Botany Bay" begins with a group of two phrases. The first phrase ends on the tonic; the second, on $\hat{5}$. Because the stronger phrase precedes a weaker one, the form is not periodic and we do not use the antecedent–consequent terminology. Instead, we can identify the phrases as "first" and "second," respectively.

The first cadence in "For He's a Jolly Good Fellow" ends on $\hat{3}$ (in a strong metric position) followed by the tonic pitch. Both of these melodic ending pitches represent a terminal cadence. The second phrase also ends on a terminal cadence. This combination creates a phrase group and the melodic structure is based on repetition.

English Folk Song, "For He's a Jolly Good Fellow"

Composers often coordinate metric and melodic elements so that cadences are clear. Notice that in each of the preceding examples, all cadences occur on the beat. While this is not always the case, such metric emphasis is a reasonable expectation.

Some phrase groups have three, rather than two, phrases. Listen to the English folk song "The Oak and the Ash" while you study the score. The first two phrases are similar and close with progressive cadences, while the third provides contrast and ends with a terminal cadence.

English Folk Song, "The Oak and the Ash"

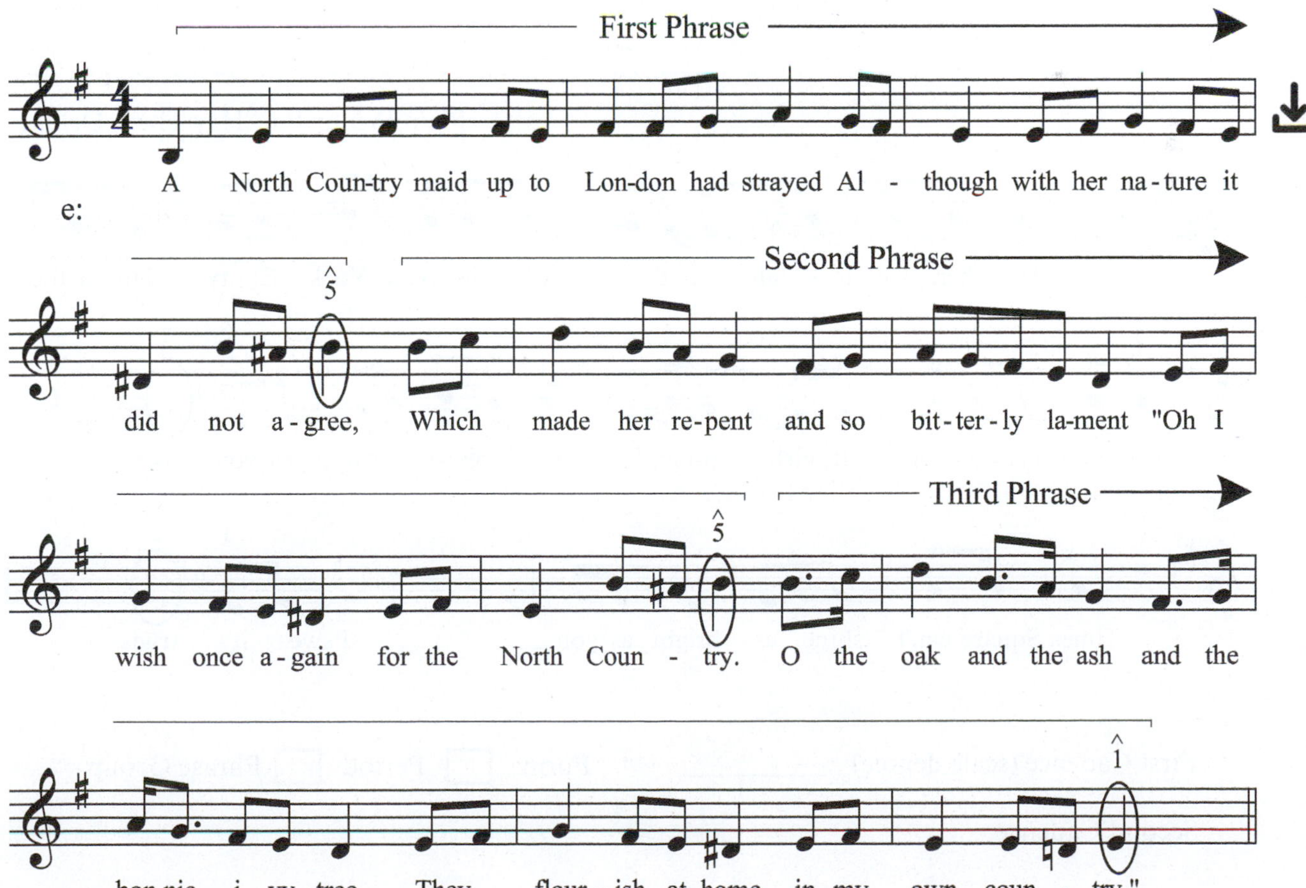

For class discussion or assignment: please do not remove these pages

REVIEW SET

Periods and Phrase Groups

Cadences in the following melodies are circled. Identify the cadences as relatively stronger ("S") or weaker ("W") depending on the scale degree. Use this information to determine whether the passage is a period or a phrase group and check the appropriate box.

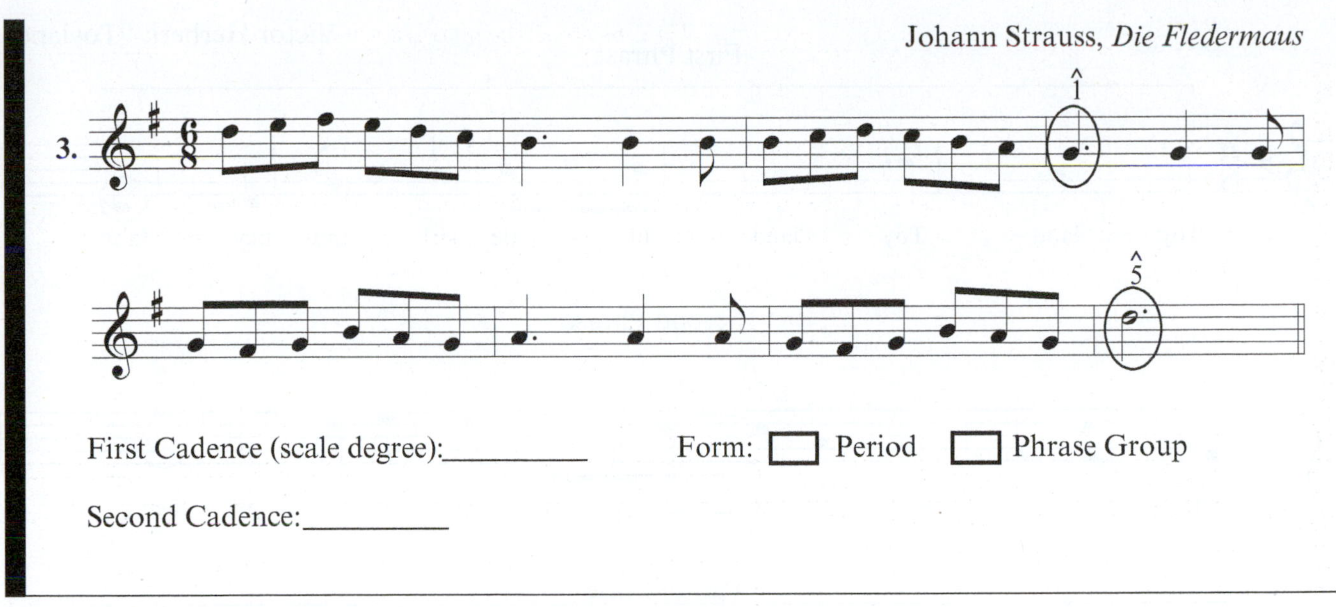

Complete Building Skills 9-2 on page 269

Double Period

Four phrases are often combined to form a **double period**. There are numerous types of double periods, but one of the most common is a chain of four phrases with a weak–weak–weak–strong cadence structure (a phrase group plus a period). The first, second, and third phrases end with a weaker, progressive cadence ($\hat{2}$, $\hat{5}$, or $\hat{7}$) and the final cadence ends with a strong, terminal cadence ($\hat{1}$ or $\hat{3}$). A common double period is illustrated in the diagram below. The first two phrases comprise a phrase group (weak–weak); the second two phrases are a period (weak–strong).

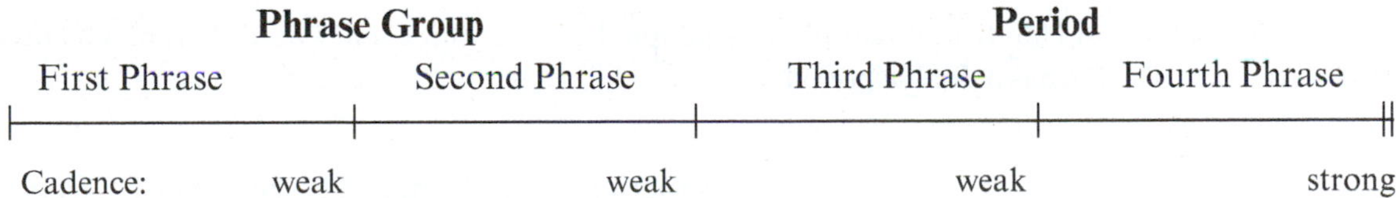

Irish-American film and stage composer Victor Herbert (1859–1924) was also a founder of the American Society of Composers, Authors, and Publishers (ASCAP). His song "Toyland" is from a hit 1903 musical. The first three phrases have progressive melodic cadences; the final phrase ends on the tonic.

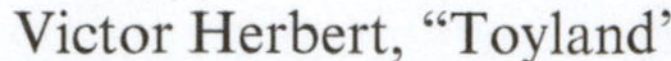

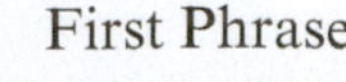

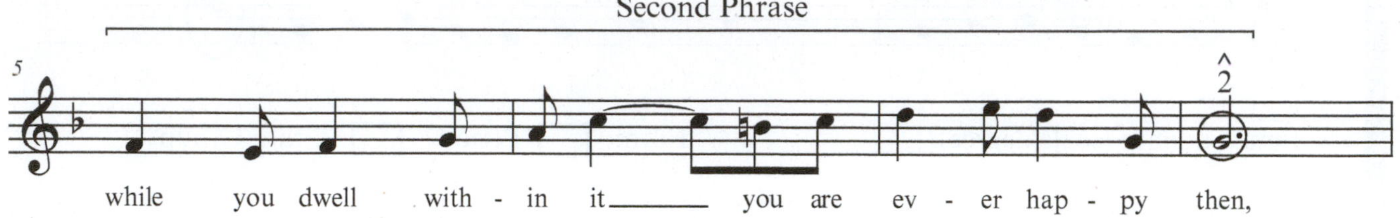

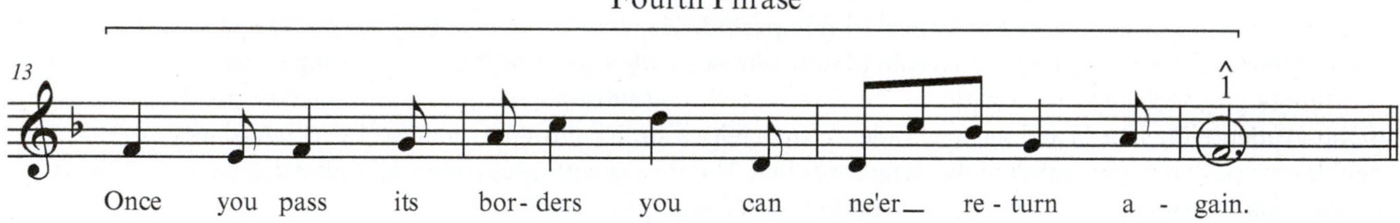

The Irish ballad "A Handful of Laurel" was adapted as "The Streets of Laredo" in nineteenth-century America. The form is a double period.

American Folk Song, "The Streets of Laredo"

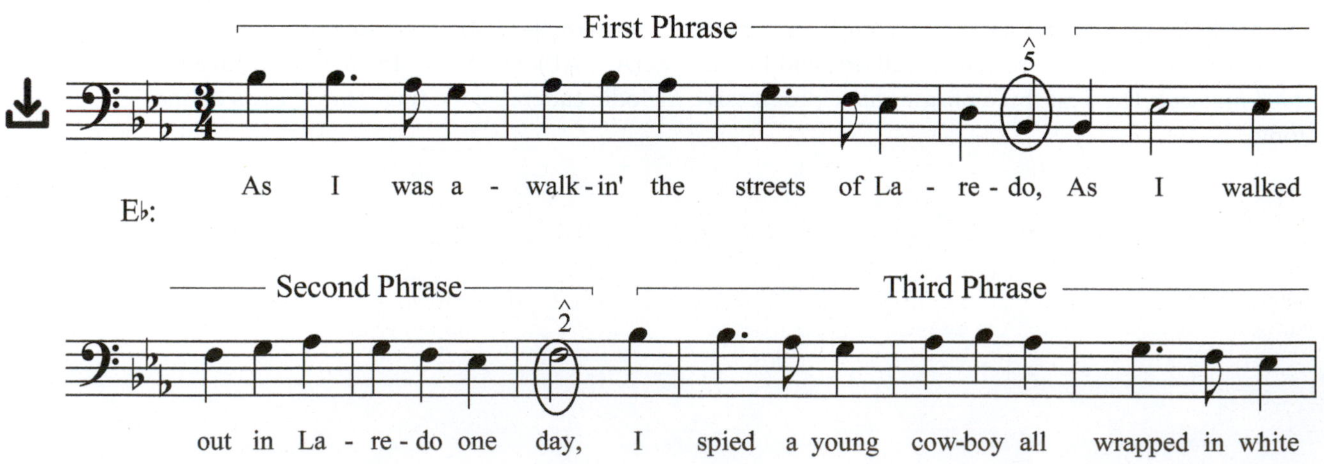

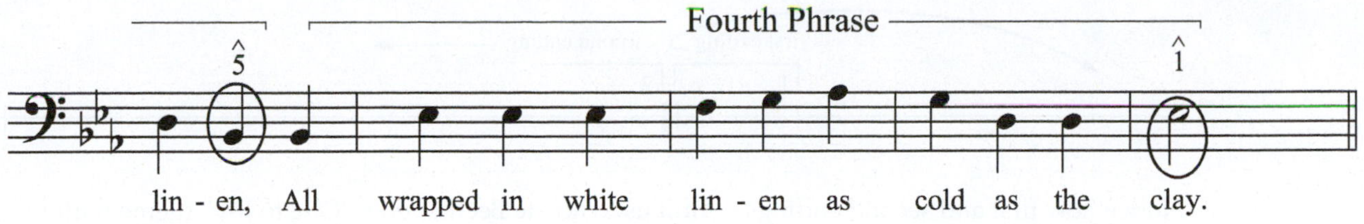

Another type of double period features a weak–strong–weak–strong phrase arrangement. The "Ode to Joy" theme from Beethoven's Ninth Symphony is cast in this form.

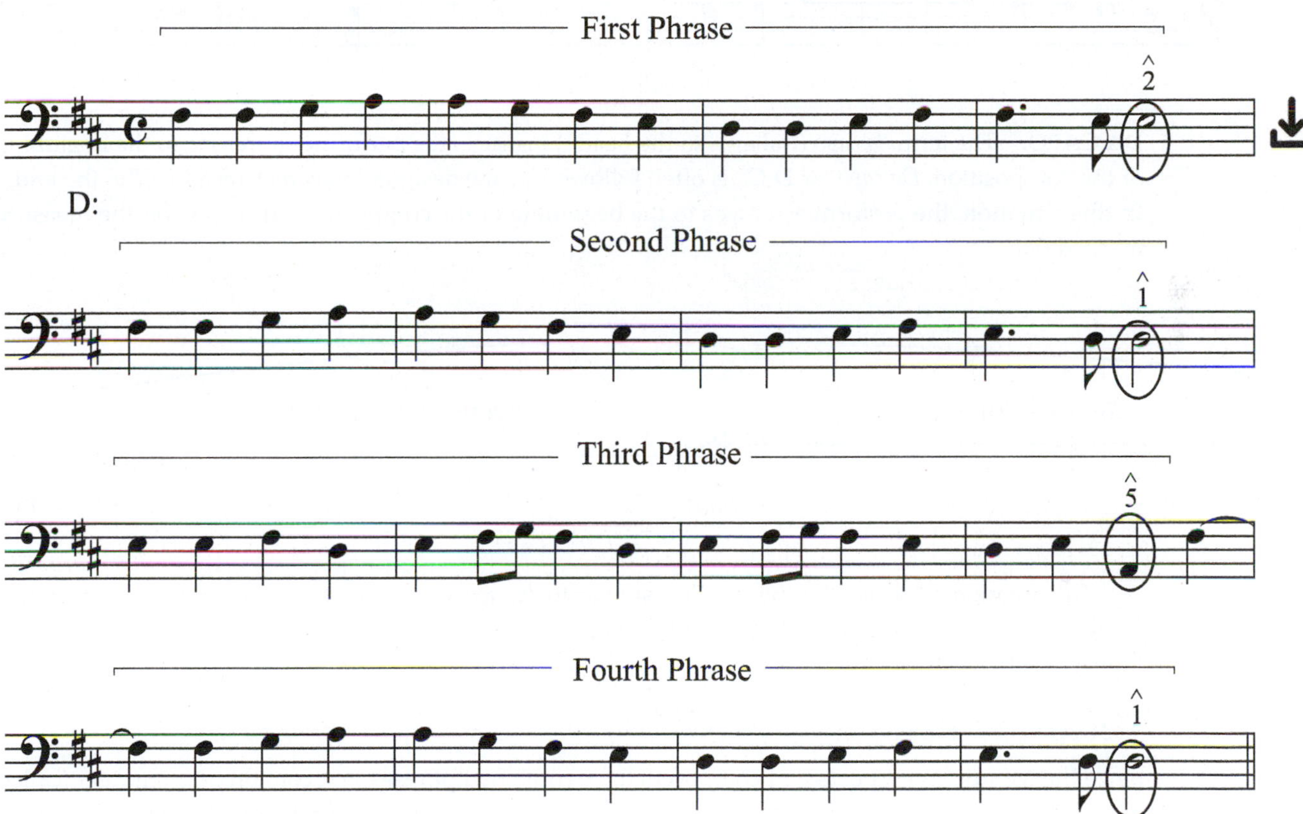

Other Forms

Two simple forms that abound in folk and popular music are *thirty-two-bar song form* and *verse and refrain*. Because two special types of repeat notation, *first and second endings* and *da capo*, are common in these and other forms, however, we will turn to them first.

FIRST AND SECOND ENDINGS. Earlier, we discussed repeat signs in notation (𝄆 𝄇) (refer to page 183). Another common practice, **first** and **second endings**, is used to streamline the notation of material that is different only at the cadence. The familiar repeat sign is used at the end of the first section, but there are two choices for the final measure. Performers play through to the first ending the first time; the second time through, the measure or measures of the first ending are omitted and the performer moves on to the second ending.

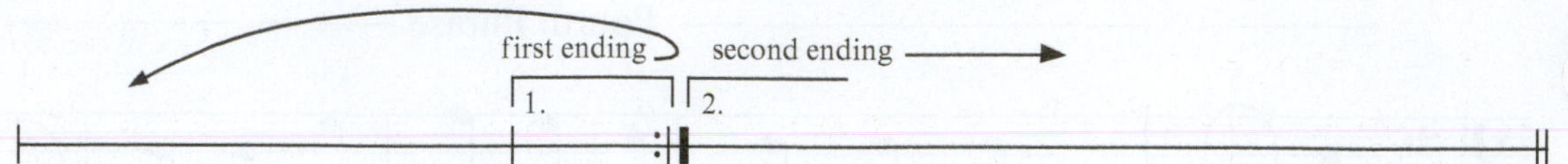

Notice how first and second endings permit us to notate Beethoven's "Ode to Joy" theme with five, rather than eight measures. The notation without these repeats appears on page 263.

Beethoven, "Ode to Joy"

DA CAPO. The term *da capo* (Italian, "to the head") instructs the performer to return to the beginning of the composition. *Da capo*, or **D.C.**, is often followed by the designation *al fine*, meaning "to the end." In this situation, the performer returns to the beginning of the composition and ends on the measure marked *fine*.

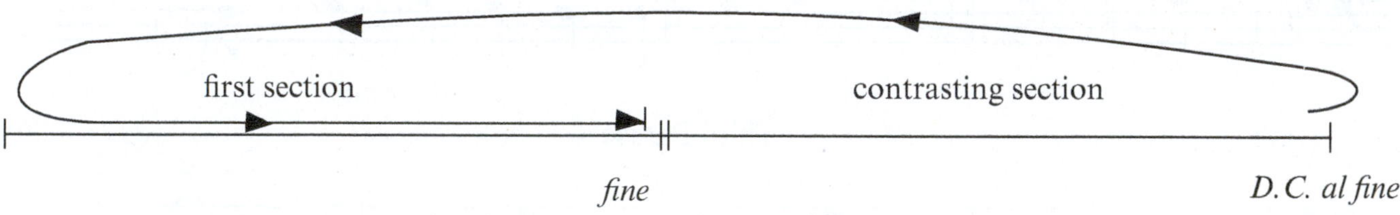

The notation *dal segno* ("to the sign") is similar to *da capo*, but instructs the performer to return to a designated point in the music marked with a special symbol (𝄋). The abbreviation "**D.S.** *al fine*" is common as well.

Verse and Refrain

Since the Middle Ages, poets and composers have combined phrases that contain different text (called **verses**) with one or more additional phrases that repeat the same text—a **refrain** (also termed **chorus**). **Verse and refrain form** appears in Christian hymns, patriotic and folk songs, rock, jazz, and many other styles. Sometimes the verses and refrain are similar in melodic and rhythmic material; in other cases, they contrast markedly.

In the sea chanty "Mermaid Song" the verse is an eight-measure phrase group. Notice that there is different text for each of the three verses given. The refrain ("Oh, the ocean waves may roll . . .") is sung three times to the same text. An extra two measures (repetition) provide a more definitive ending.

Sea Chanty, “Mermaid Song”

Name ______________________

Page may be removed

Building Skills • 9-1

Phrases and Cadences

A. **In each case, the cadence is the last pitch of the phrase. Identify the scale degree of this pitch in the specified key and indicate whether the cadence is progressive or terminal.**

Franz Schubert, Impromptu

1. 

B Minor

B: ________

Cadence Type: ______________

Hector Berlioz, *Roman Carnival*

2. 

C Major

C: ________

Cadence Type: ______________

Arcangelo Corelli, Sonata in E Minor

3. 

E Minor

e: ________

Cadence Type: ______________

African Folk Song, "Water Has Gone from the Village"

4. 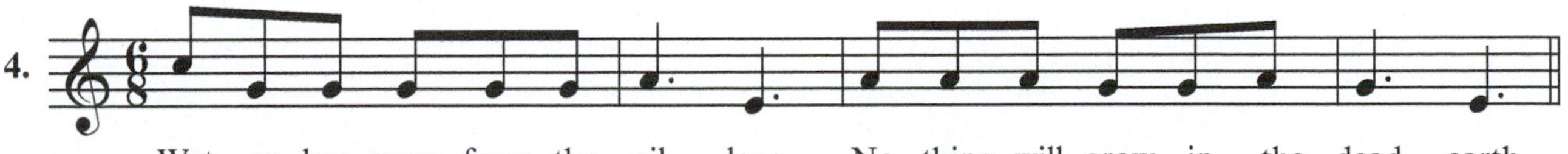

C Major

C: ________

Cadence Type: ______________

B. **Review each of the four phrases in part A. Identify a principal motive and label it in the music. In a few sentences, explain how the motive is used in the phrase (repetition, variation, sequence, or contrast, for example).**

1.

2.

3.

4.

C. **Continue the given motive in sequence as directed. End in the fourth measure with a pitch that makes a progressive or terminal cadence as specified. When you are finished, play each example, focusing on the sequence and the cadence.**

1. Descending sequence by third — progressive

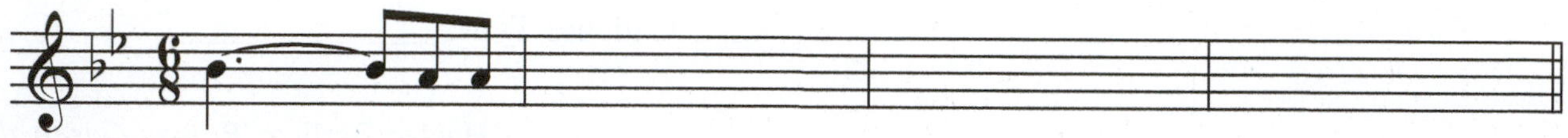

2. 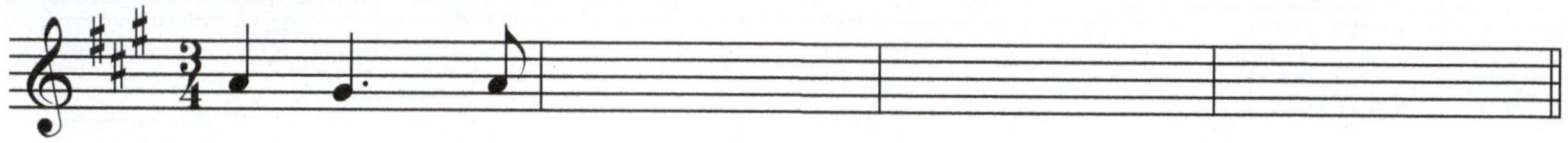 Ascending sequence by second — progressive

3.  Ascending sequence by second — terminal

4. Ascending sequence by third — terminal

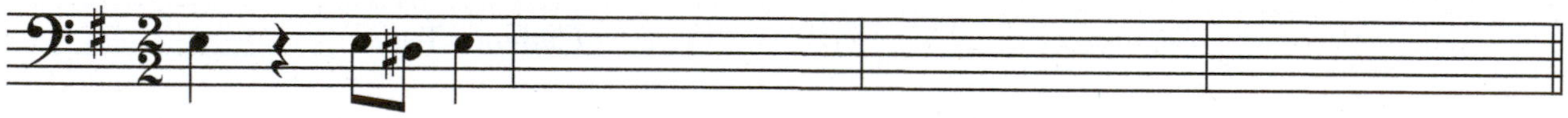

Name ______________________________

Page may be removed

Building Skills • 9-2

Period and Phrase Group

Listen to the melodies on the website. Comment on each example, being sure to include the following information:

A. **cadence for first and second phrases;**

B. **structure of the melody (period or phrase group);**

C. **the relationship of melodic material between the first and second phrases (repetition, variation, sequence, contrast).**

Giovanni Battista Bononcini, "Per la gloria d'adorarvi"

Comments:

Robert Schumann, "Wild Rider"

A Minor

Comments:

American Civil War Song, "The Cruel War"

3.

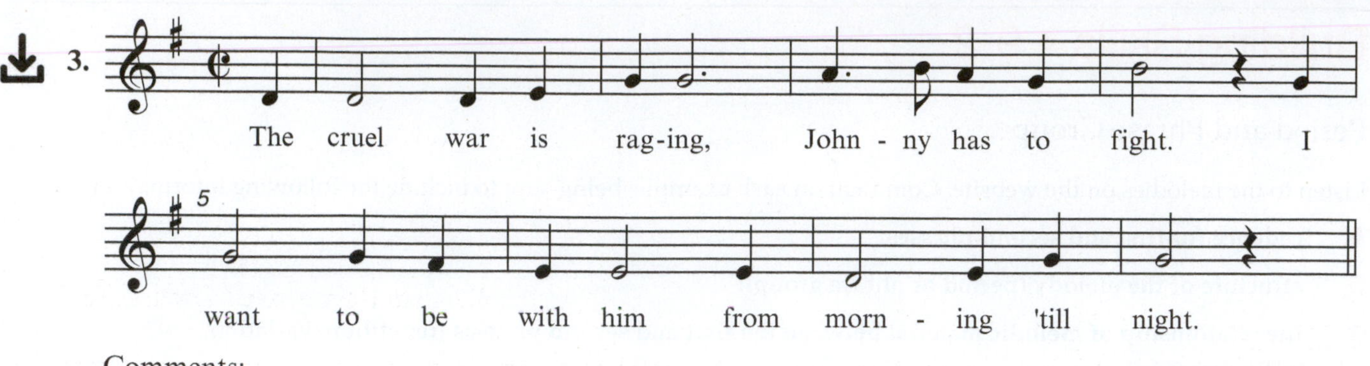

Comments:

Joseph Haydn, Symphony No. 104

4.

Comments:

Name ____________________

Page may be removed

Building Skills • 9-3

Double Period and Other Forms

Examine the composition to determine the structure of phrases, cadences, melodic materials and their development, and the overall form. Cadential pitches are circled. Explain your conclusions in a paragraph.

German Folk Song, "Three Lilies"

1.

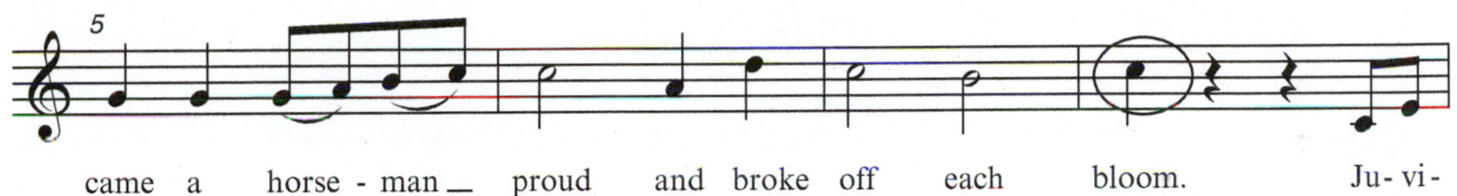

Conclusions:

Creative Projects • Chapter 9

This project takes you through several steps to setting a text in double period form. Because we have not yet discussed harmonic flow (Chapters 11 and 12), you may want to create patterns that are mainly stepwise. Do your work on other paper and copy it here when you have the music in final form.

A. Within the meter specified, complete a rhythmic draft of the lines below. Include the text (an American hymn) beneath the notation. Each line begins with an anacrusis (shown in the text with a slash /). The final syllable in each pair of lines (boldfaced) is "ing" and will be a melodic cadence on the third beat, so plan your rhythm to make this point coincide with the metric accent.

When/tyrants tremble, sick with fear,
And/hear their death knells ring**ing**;
When/friends rejoice both far and near,
How/can I keep from sing**ing**?

In/prison cells and dungeons vile,
Or/thoughts to them are ring**ing**;
When/friends by shame are undefiled,
How/can I keep from sing**ing**?

Rhythmic Plan

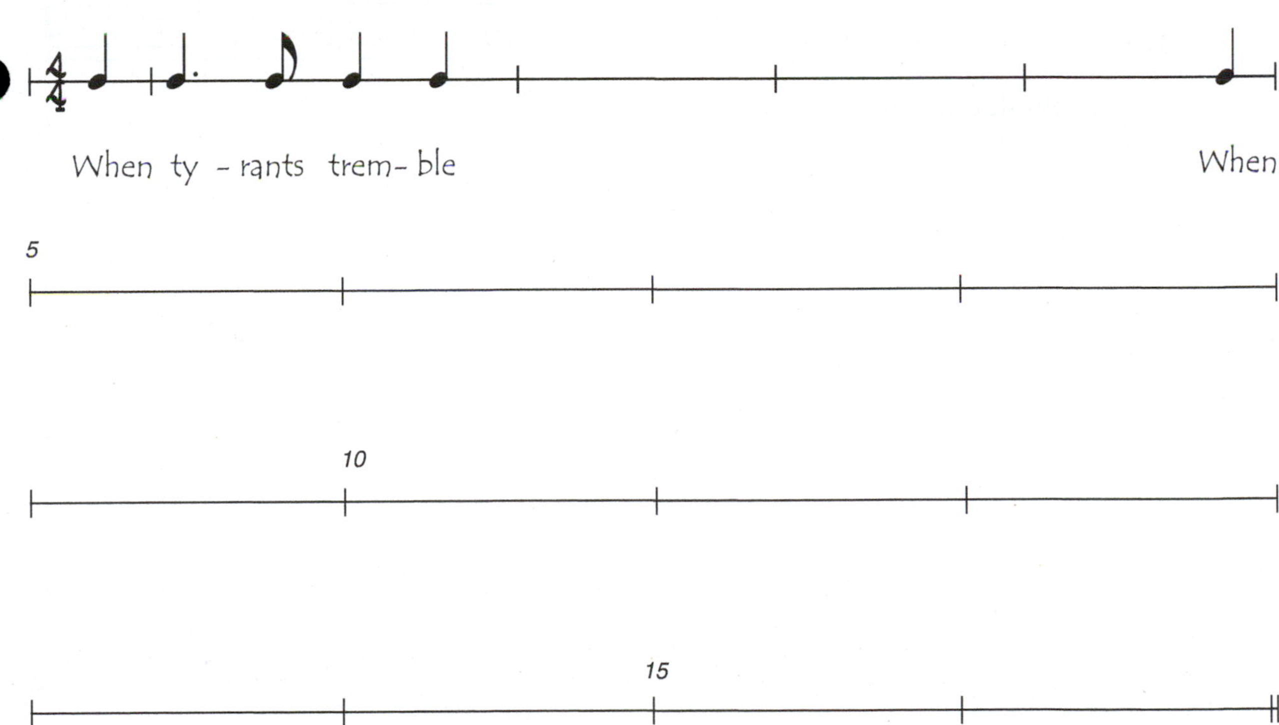

In F major, compose the first phrase of the melody using your rhythmic plan (include the remaining text as well). The first notes are again given. Use a progressive cadence for the first phrase. Employ repetition, variation, sequence, or contrast to complete the first phrase.

First Phrase

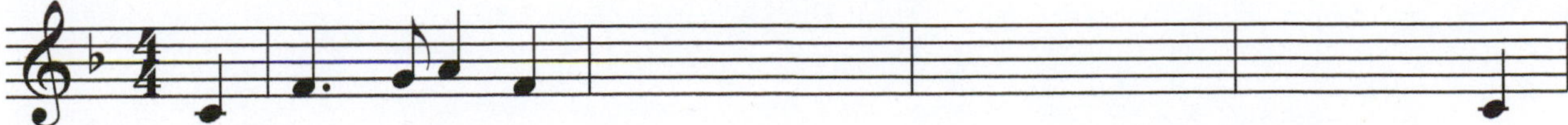

Make the second phrase identical to the first, except make the cadence terminal (F or A in this case).

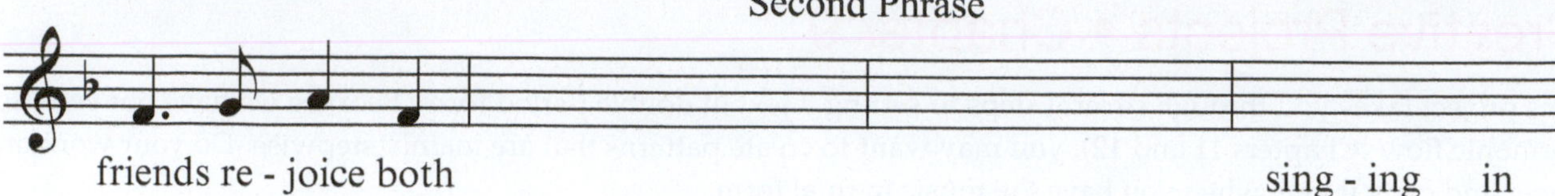

Compose contrasting material for the third phrase. Use only pitches in the F major scale, but begin "In/pri-son" with pitches *other* than C and F. Again, conclude with a progressive cadence.

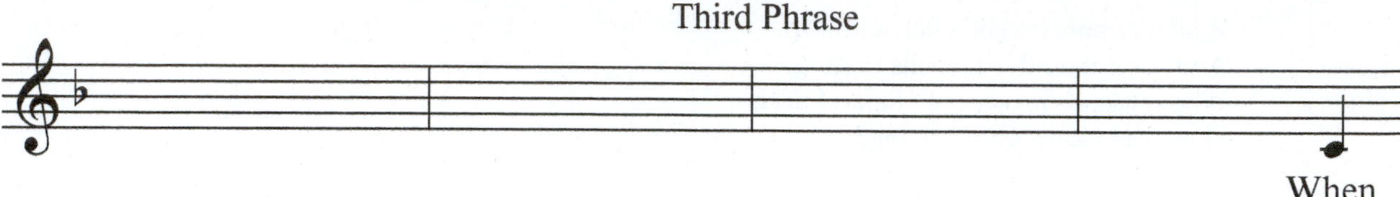

The simplest ending for the song is to repeat the second phrase with the terminal ending.

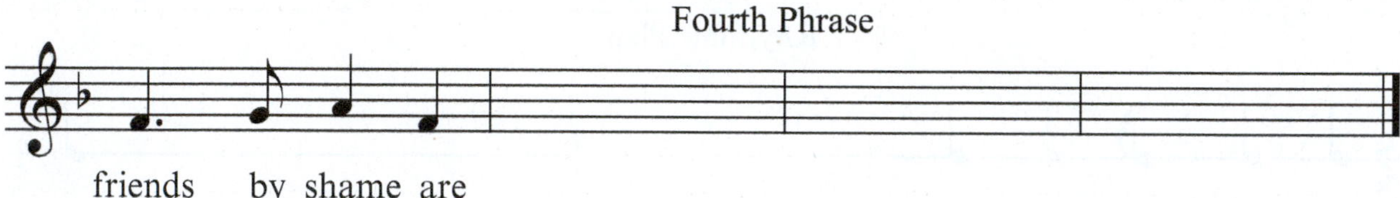

Name ______________________

Page may be removed

B. **Copy your entire song in this space, including clef, key signature, time signature, and lyrics. Identify cadences with scale-degree numbers.**

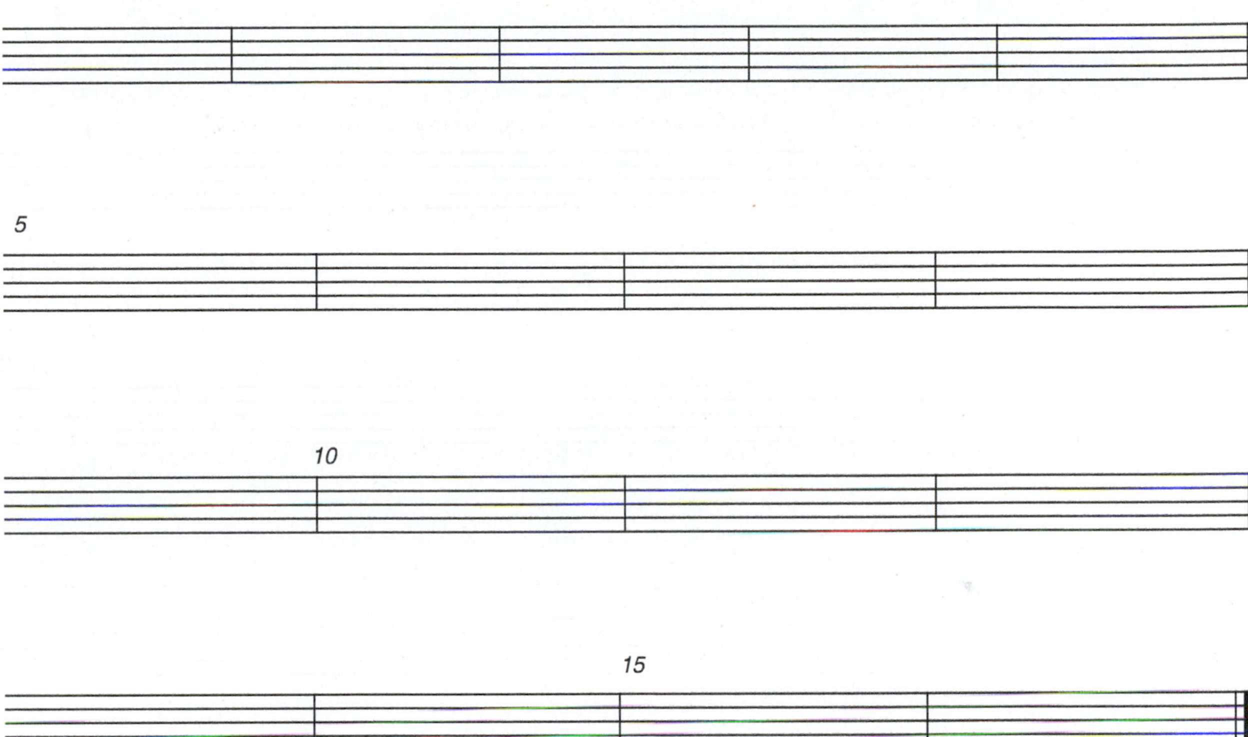

C. **Use your setting of "How Can I Keep from Singing" as a model and set these lines from the Irish ballad "Cold Winter Shadow" as a double period in the key and meter of your choice. Use the same weak–strong–weak–strong cadential structure of the first song, or a more common weak–weak–weak–strong pattern. As before, pairs of lines will constitute a musical phrase. For the most regular effect, each line begins with an anacrusis (although other possibilities exist) and a rhythmic plan of four 4-measure phrases. Copy your complete song (with lyrics) on the next page.**

Cold Winter Shadow

When a cold winter shadow I cast on the ground,
And frost from the foothills is creeping all around;
I now and then glance down the road towards the town,
In a kind of a hope you'll be coming on down.

It must have been November when I left you to the train,
I watched your carriage disappear in the lonely western rain;
And I wiped the rain from off my face and turned the way I'd come,
And drove our old spring wagon thru the hills near Edmonton.

Cold Winter Shadow

Name ______________________________

Page may be removed

Analysis in Context 1 • Chapter 9

The aria "Lascia ch'io Pianga" is from Handel's opera Rinaldo. Opera arias in the Baroque Period present opportunities for the composer to highlight contrasting dramatic and emotional aspects of the characters and story. On the repeat of the first section, the soloist was given the opportunity to add embellishments to the original melodic line, showcasing their virtuosic talent.

G.F. Handel, Lascia ch'io pianga

17
p
f
la du - ra sor - te e che so - spi - ri la li - ber - tà.
mf
23
f
3
p
Fine
31
f
p
Il duol in - fran - ga ques - te ri - tor - te de' miei mar - ti - ri sol
p
37
f
D.S. al Fine
per pie ta, si, de' miei mar - ti - ri sol per pie - tà.

Name ______________________________

Page may be removed

1. What is the term for the symbol at the end of the score?
2. What does that symbol mean to the performer?
3. What does the term "fine" mean in measure 30?
4. What is the starting key of the aria?
5. Scan the score to determine what other keys the aria moves through. Mark them in the score.
6. Label the scale degrees in the vocal line and cadence type in measure 8.
7. Label the scale degrees in the vocal line and the cadence type in measure 14.
8. Continue labeling the cadences (and melodic scale degrees) in measures 22 and 30.
9. It is common for the middle section of a DaCapo aria to provide contrast to the first section. Study the section in measures 31–42. Discuss what elements create contrast in this section (for example, you might consider the key, melodic line, and rhythm).
10. Study the lyrics in both sections. How does Handel use the music to relate the mood of the text in both sections?

Chapter 10
Triads

Essential Terms

arpeggiated
arpeggiation
augmented triad
bass
chordal
closed position
diminished triad
fifth
first inversion
harmony
major triad
minor triad
open position
resolution
root
root position
second inversion
tertian triad
third
triad

Harmony is a vertical arrangement of pitches that occurs simultaneously with melody, rhythm, and form. Of several fundamental elements that separate Western music from that of other cultures, this concept of a predictable harmonic pattern is one of the most important.

The basic unit of Western harmony is the **triad**—a collection of three pitches. A **tertian triad** is constructed of thirds. Although other types of triads exist, the tertian triad is the most common in Western traditional music.

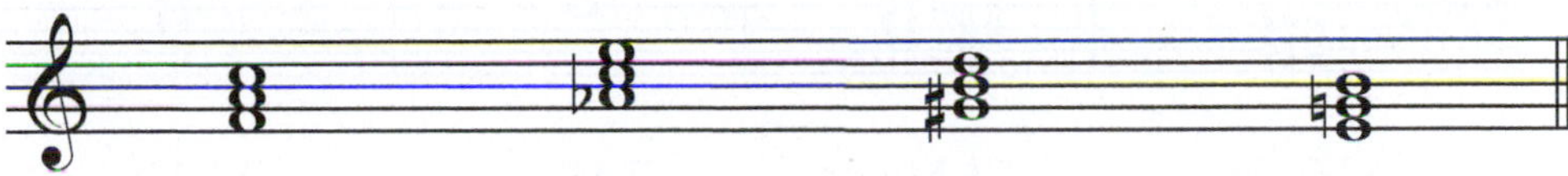

Tertian Triads

Think of triads as having three elements: *root, third,* and *fifth*. The **root** is the lowest of the three pitches when the triad is spaced over consecutive lines and spaces (as in the next example). The terms **third** and **fifth** refer to interval sizes above the root.

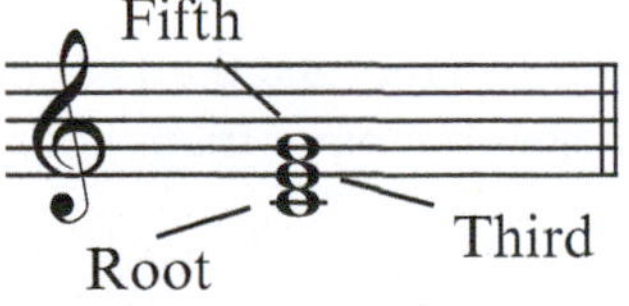

ROOT POSITION. The **bass** is the lowest sounding pitch. When the root of a triad is also the bass (as in the previous examples), the triad is in **root position**. When the root is not the bass, the triad is *inverted*. We will cover inverted triads later in this chapter.

Triad Quality

Like intervals, triads occur in several different qualities—each with a distinct "flavor." The quality of a triad is determined by the qualities of the component intervals. The intervals formed between the root and third, root and fifth, and third and fifth of the triad all contribute to our understanding of a triad's quality.

Major and Minor Triads

A root-position triad is **major** if the lower third is major and if the fifth is perfect. If these conditions are met, the upper third will always be minor.

Major Triad

Triads are identified by two factors: (1) the pitch name of the root and (2) the quality. The triad in the last example is identified as A♭ major. The root name is A♭; the quality is major. Notice the identification of other root-position triads below.

USING KEY SIGNATURE TO DETERMINE TRIAD QUALITY. Notice that each of the major triads in the last example corresponds to the key signature of the root pitch. We can check the intervals between root and third and between root and fifth for verification, but note this rule:

If the third and fifth of a triad are diatonic pitches in the major key of the root, the triad is major.

A triad is **minor** if the interval between root and third is a minor third and the interval between root and fifth is perfect. Note that both major and minor triads have a perfect fifth. The two qualities are differentiated by the lower third.

Minor Triad

Concerning minor triads, we can state another rule:

The third and fifth of a minor triad correspond to the *minor* key represented by the root.

We can also view a minor triad as major with a lowered third.

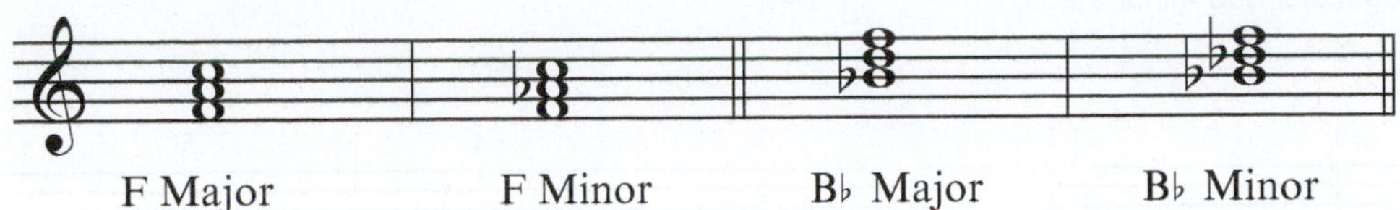

The lower third of a triad imparts the characteristic modal flavor (just as the third scale degree differentiates major and minor scales). When the lower third is major, the effect is major; if minor, we hear the mode as minor.

ARPEGGIATION. The pitches in the previous example are notated to sound at the same time (a **chordal, or block chord** performance). In a melody, triads are often **arpeggiated**—that is, sounded in succession. Play the arpeggiated and block chords in the next example in order to understand the difference between the arpeggiated and chordal major and minor triads.

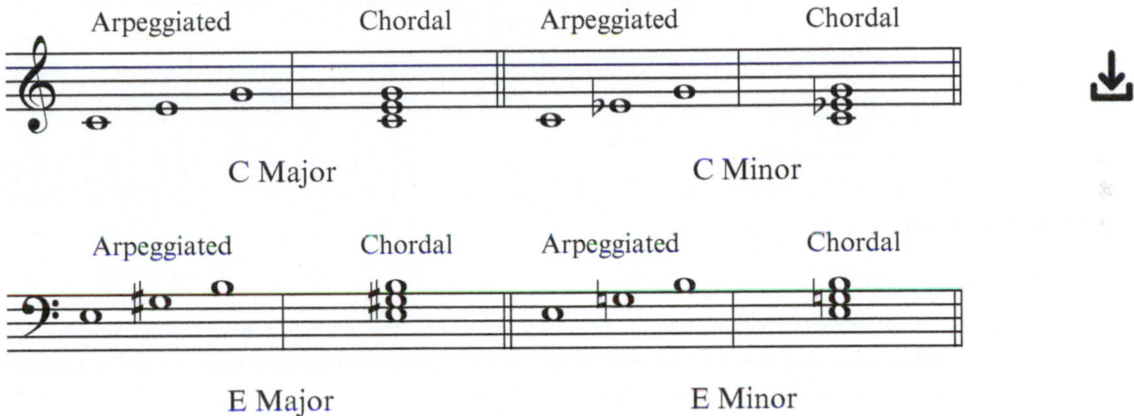

For class discussion or assignment: please do not remove these pages

REVIEW SET

Major and Minor Triads

A. Identify the following triads by root name and quality (either major or minor). Compare the third of the triad to the major key signature of the root; if the third is diatonic, the triad is major. Otherwise (in the current context), the third is lowered and the triad is minor.

B. Construct the following major and minor triads.

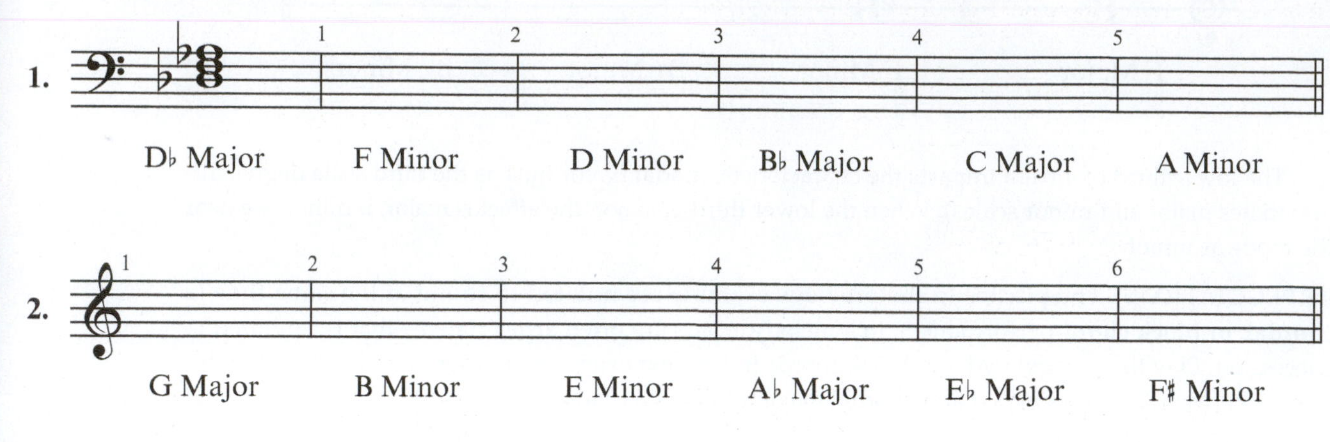

MUSICIANSHIP 10-1

Ear Training: Major and Minor Triads

Your instructor will play a number of root-position major and minor triads or you can listen to the recording. These triads are first arpeggiated, then played as a chord. Listen to the chord, then write "M" if the triad is major or "m" if minor. Check your answer and move on to the next problem. (See Appendix D for answers.)

a. ______ ______ ______ ______ ______ ______
1 2 3 4 5 6

b. ______ ______ ______ ______ ______ ______
1 2 3 4 5 6

c. ______ ______ ______ ______ ______ ______
1 2 3 4 5 6

d. ______ ______ ______ ______ ______ ______
1 2 3 4 5 6

Diminished and Augmented Triads

Major and minor triads have a perfect fifth between root and fifth. In a **diminished triad**, the lower third is minor and the fifth is diminished. The upper third is minor as well.

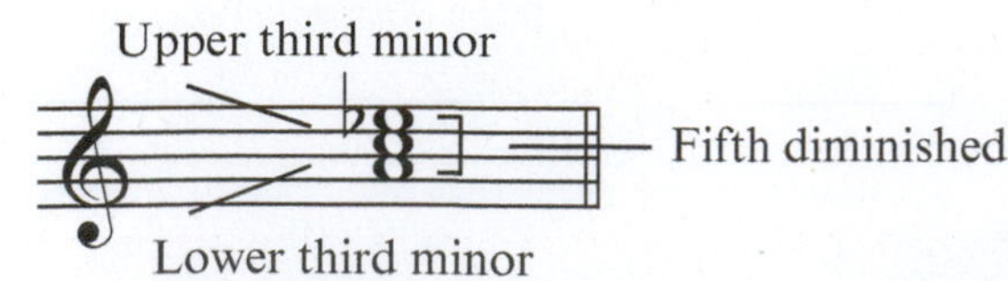

Using key-signature comparison for construction and identification, think of a diminished triad as minor with a lowered fifth. If you are not comfortable with minor key signatures, a diminished triad may also be viewed as major with lowered third *and* fifth.

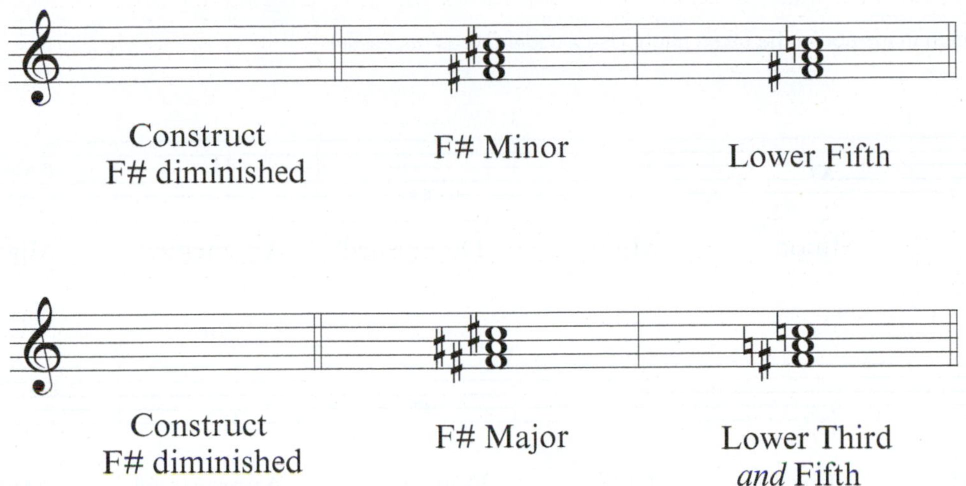

An **augmented triad** has a major third between root and third and an augmented fifth between root and fifth. The upper third is major.

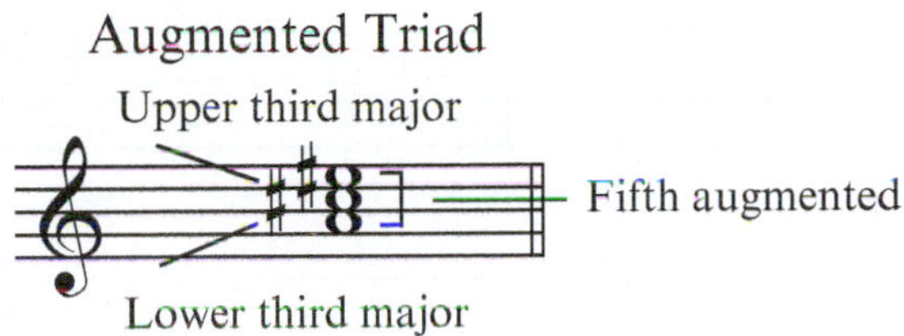

Many students will find it convenient to recognize and construct augmented triads beginning with major, then raising the fifth a half step.

Identifying and Constructing Triads

We can construct and identify any triad by referring to the major key signature of the root. As shown in the next table, notice that triads of all four qualities can be related to a major key signature. Minor and diminished triads can also be related to the minor key signature of the root.

Major Key Signature of Root	Minor Key Signature of Root
Major Triad: Third and fifth are diatonic	*Minor Triad:* Third and fifth are diatonic
Minor Triad: Lower third	*Diminished Triad:* Lower fifth
Diminished Triad: Lower third and fifth	
Augmented Triad: Raise fifth	

For class discussion or assignment: please do not remove these pages

REVIEW SET

Constructing and Identifying Triads

A. Construct root-position triads above the given pitch. Use accidentals as necessary.

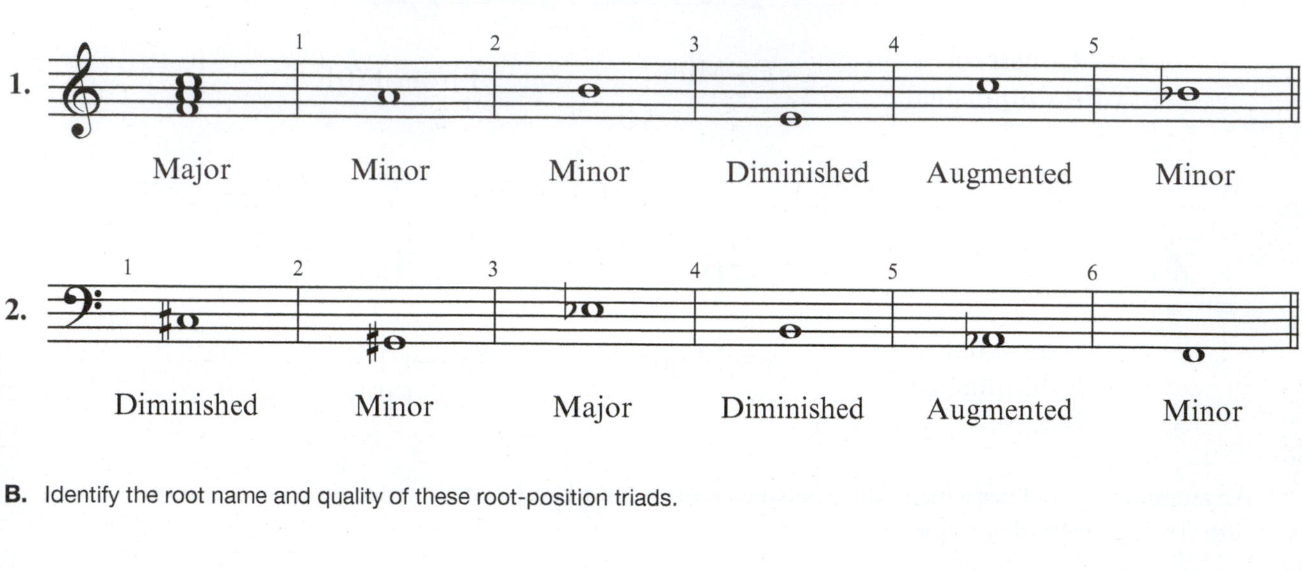

B. Identify the root name and quality of these root-position triads.

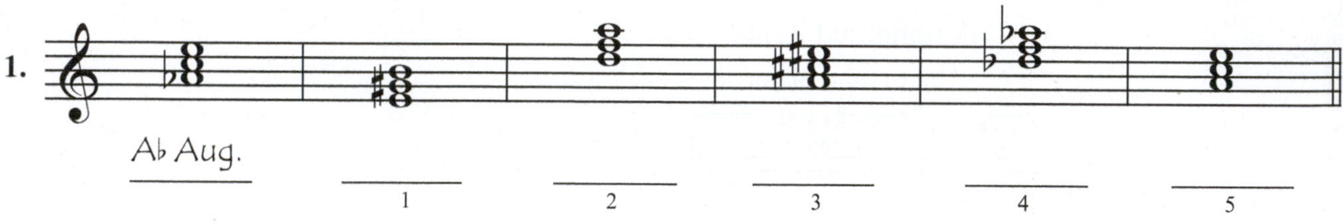

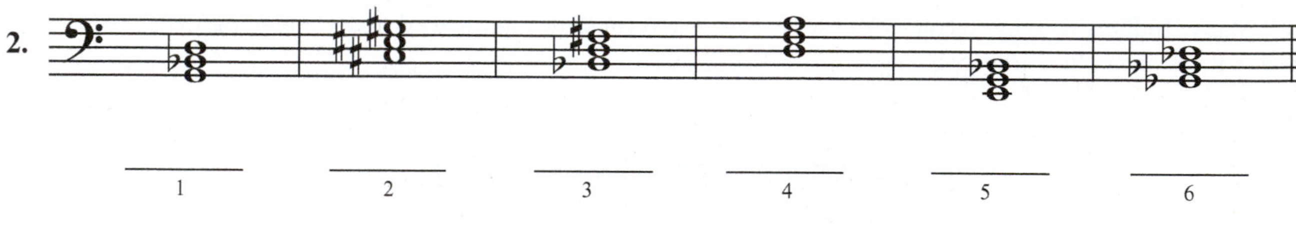

Triads and Stability

In tonal music, as discussed further in Chapter 12, some pitches are active and have a pronounced tendency to move to a stable sound—a process called **resolution**. A diminished triad, for example, has a strong need for resolution due to the tritone between the root and fifth. Major and minor triads, with a perfect fifth, are heard as more stable. In tonal music, augmented triads have neither stability nor a tendency to resolve; accordingly, they are rarely heard in traditional music.

Listen to the four triad qualities: major, minor, diminished, and augmented.

Complete Building Skills 10-1 on page 297

MUSICIANSHIP 10-2

I. Ear Training: Triads of All Qualities

Listen to the triads played and identify the quality as "M" for major, "m" for minor, "d" for diminished, or "A" for augmented. (See Appendix D for answers.)

Triads: All Qualities, Part I

1. ______ ______ ______ ______ ______ ______
1 2 3 4 5 6

2. ______ ______ ______ ______ ______ ______
1 2 3 4 5 6

3. ______ ______ ______ ______ ______ ______
1 2 3 4 5 6

Triads: All Qualities, Part II

1. ______ ______ ______ ______ ______ ______
1 2 3 4 5 6

2. ______ ______ ______ ______ ______ ______
1 2 3 4 5 6

3. ______ ______ ______ ______ ______ ______
1 2 3 4 5 6

II. Keyboard: Root-Position Triads

Play root-position major, minor, diminished, and augmented triads beginning on various roots. With the right hand, use the fingering 1-3-5; with the left, 5-3-1. With each hand, playing separately, arpeggiate the triad, then sound the three pitches together as a chord. At first, you may want to play triads that are notated in this chapter (see pages 283 and 286, for example). The goal, however, is to begin with a given root, then play all four triad qualities.

Inverted Triads

Just as an interval is sometimes inverted, the relationship between the root and the bass of a triad is flexible. As we discussed in the previous section, a triad is in root position when the lowest sounding pitch is also the root. If the root appears *above* the bass, however, two new arrangements of the same triad are possible. These new versions—one with the third in the bass, the other with the fifth in the bass—are termed *first inversion* and *second inversion*, respectively.

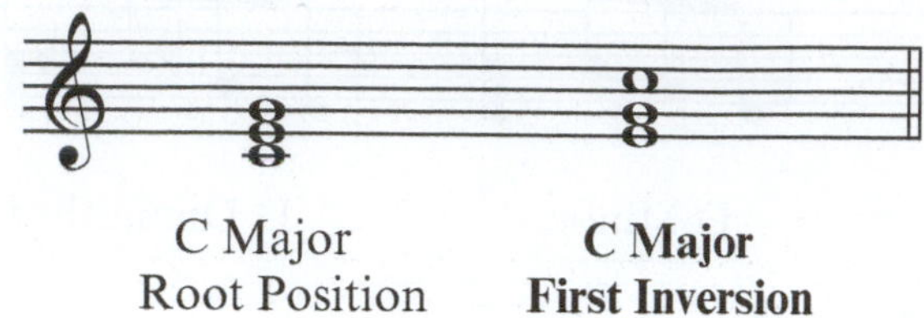

First and Second Inversions

A triad is in **first inversion** when the third of the triad is in the bass (the lowest sounding note). In inverted triads, we know that the root is above the bass, but whether it is the highest or the middle pitch is not a factor. Note that triads are identified by their root name and quality, regardless of any inversion.

For acoustical reasons, the perfect fifth above the root in a root-position triad is especially stable. Notice that in first inversion, a sixth and a third appear above the bass. (The labeling of intervals within the inversion, called figured bass, is further discussed in Chapter 11.)

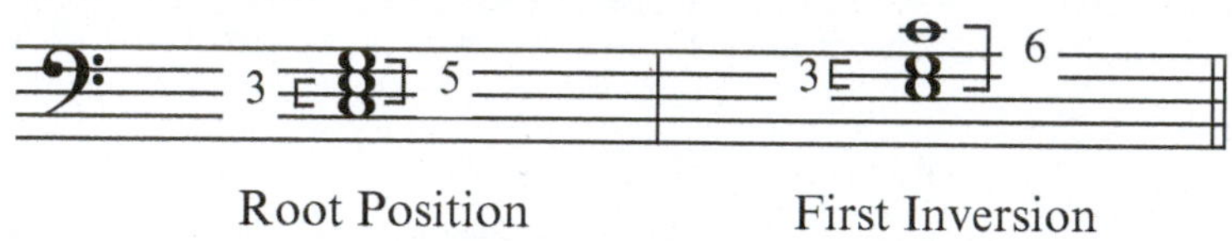

SECOND INVERSION. If the fifth of a triad is in the bass, the triad is in **second inversion**. In second inversion, intervals of a fourth and a sixth are formed above the bass.

In Western classical music, second-inversion triads are particularly unstable and are handled very carefully in only a few stereotypical patterns.

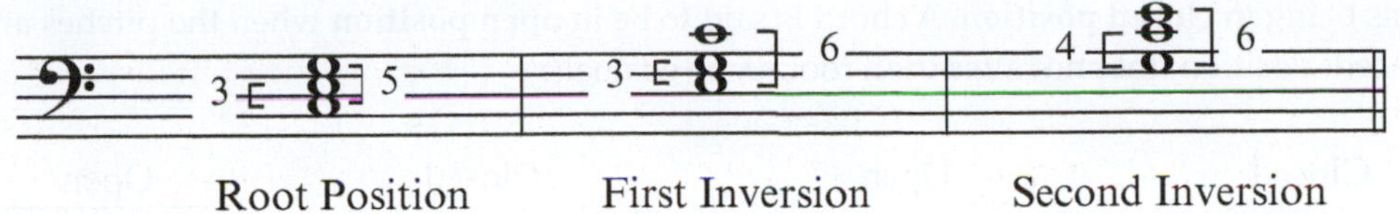

Root Position First Inversion Second Inversion

CONSTRUCTION OF INVERTED TRIADS. Construct a first-inversion triad by first drafting a triad in root position and then rearranging pitches so that the third is in the bass. To construct a D minor triad, begin with root position, then rearrange the pitches with the third as the lowest sounding pitch.

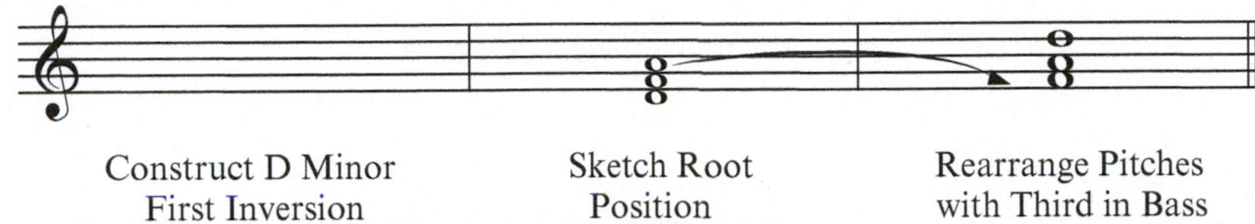

Construct D Minor First Inversion | Sketch Root Position | Rearrange Pitches with Third in Bass

For second-inversion triads, use the same construction and identification process. To construct a second-inversion B♭ minor triad, first write the triad in root position, then rearrange the pitches so that the fifth is the lowest sounding pitch.

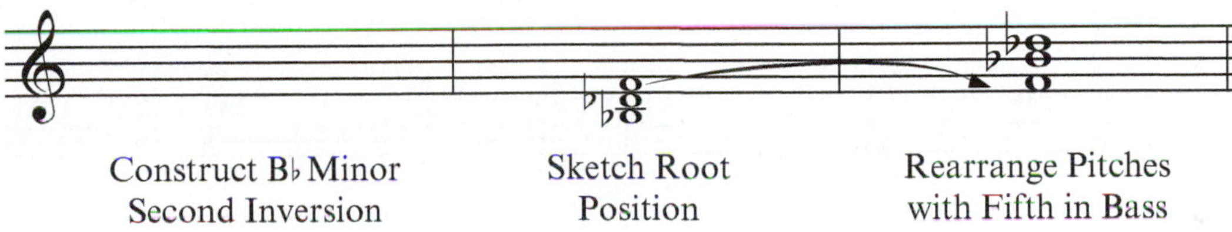

Construct B♭ Minor Second Inversion | Sketch Root Position | Rearrange Pitches with Fifth in Bass

IDENTIFYING INVERTED TRIADS. Before identifying an inverted triad, first draft or visualize it in root position. Once this is done, identify the root name and quality.

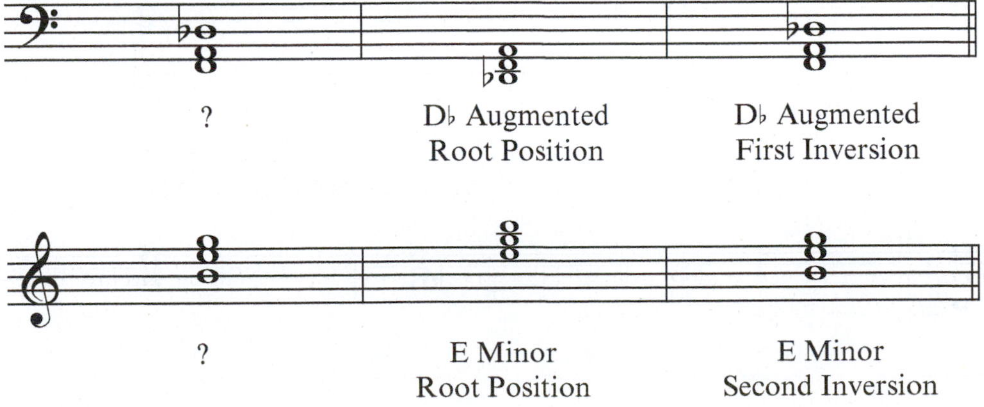

OPEN AND CLOSED POSITION. When triad elements are within the span of an octave, the chord is described as being in **closed position**. A chord is said to be in **open position** when the pitches are more widely spaced. Position does not alter triad root name or quality.

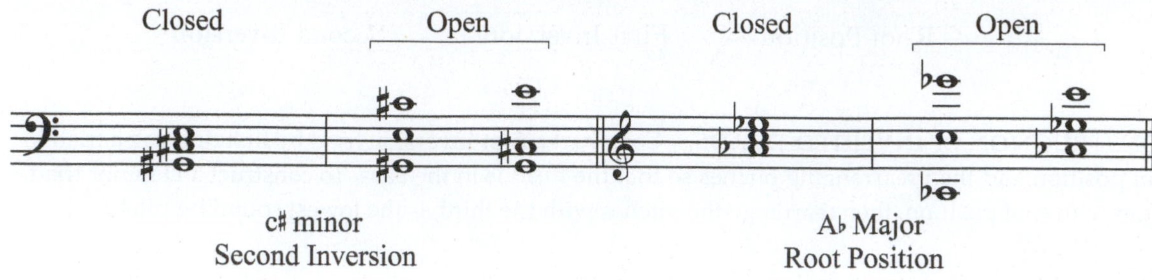

For class discussion or assignment: please do not remove these pages

REVIEW SET

Root-Position and Inverted Triads

A. Identify these root-position and inverted triads by root name quality (top blank) and inversion (bottom blank). In the middle blank, identify the spatial position as "closed" or "open." Use the blank measure to rearrange the triad in root position.

1.

Triad: B Dim. ________ ________ ________

Spatial Position: Closed ________ ________ ________

Inversion: 2nd ________ ________ ________

2.

Triad: ________ ________ ________ ________

Spatial Position: ________ ________ ________ ________

Inversion: ________ ________ ________ ________

3.

Triad: ________ ________ ________ ________

Spatial Position: ________ ________ ________ ________

B. Construct the following triads. Use the first measure to construct the triad in root position. If indicated, use the second measure to invert the same chord. There are many correct possibilities for open spacing.

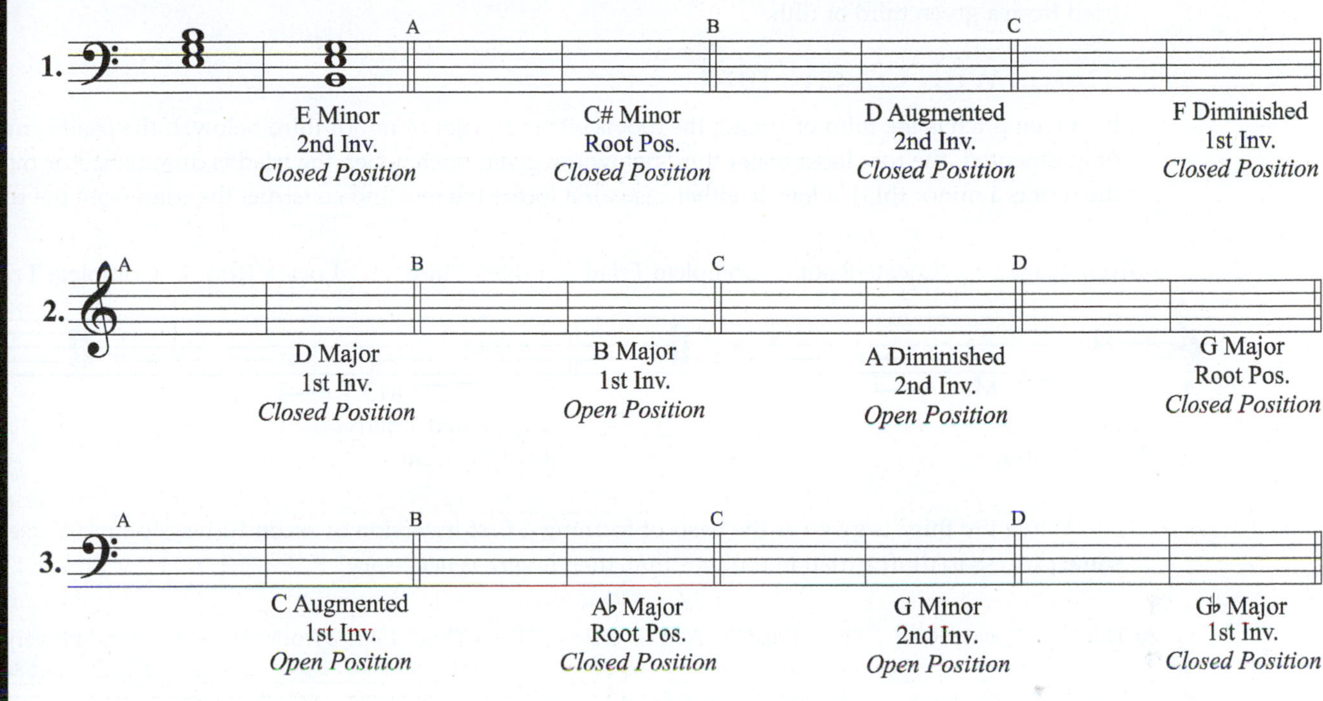

Complete Building Skills 10-2 on page 299

MUSICIANSHIP 10-3

Ear Training: Hearing Triad Quality

Identify the triad quality. Some of these triads are inverted; others are in root position. All, however, are in closed position. You will hear the triad arpeggiated, then sounded as a chord. Write an appropriate letter in the blank ("M" for major, "m" for minor, "d" for diminished, or "A" for augmented). (See Appendix D for answers.) Additional ear training exercises on triad quality are found on the web site.

1. ______ ______ ______ ______ ______ ______
1 2 3 4 5 6

2. ______ ______ ______ ______ ______ ______
1 2 3 4 5 6

3. ______ ______ ______ ______ ______ ______
1 2 3 4 5 6

4. ______ ______ ______ ______ ______ ______
1 2 3 4 5 6

Constructing Triads with Given Third or Fifth

To this point, we have constructed triads from a given root. Sometimes, however, we need to spell a triad from a given third or fifth.

Triads with Given Third

If a given pitch is the third of a triad, the root is either a major or minor third below. If the triad is major or augmented, the root lies a major third below the given pitch; when the triad is diminished or minor, the root is a minor third below. In either case, first locate the root and construct the triad from the root.

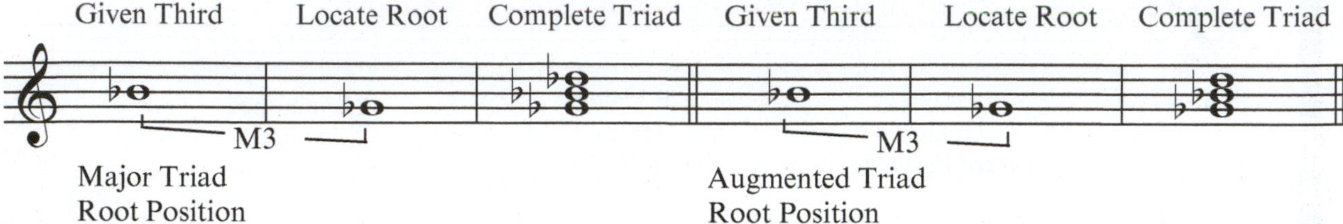

When the third is given as the basis of forming a first-inversion or second-inversion triad, use the same process to draft a triad in root position, then invert as necessary.

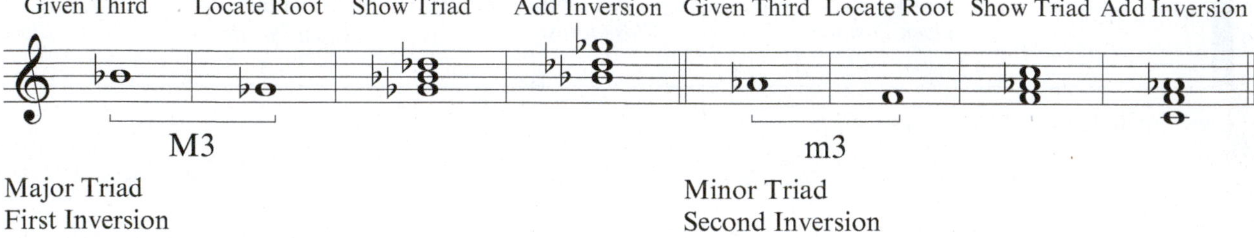

Triads with Given Fifth

The process for constructing triads with a given fifth is only slightly different from that for a given third. If the triad is major or minor, the root is a perfect fifth below the given pitch. If the triad is diminished, the root lies a diminished fifth below; if augmented, the root of the triad is an augmented fifth below.

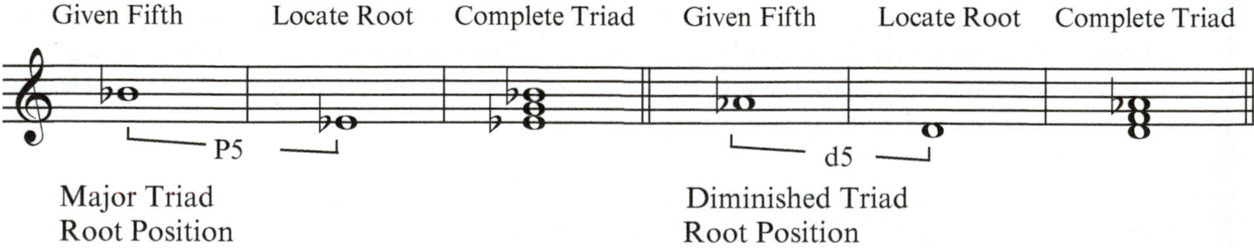

Once the complete triad in root position has been determined, you can write the root and third above the bass.

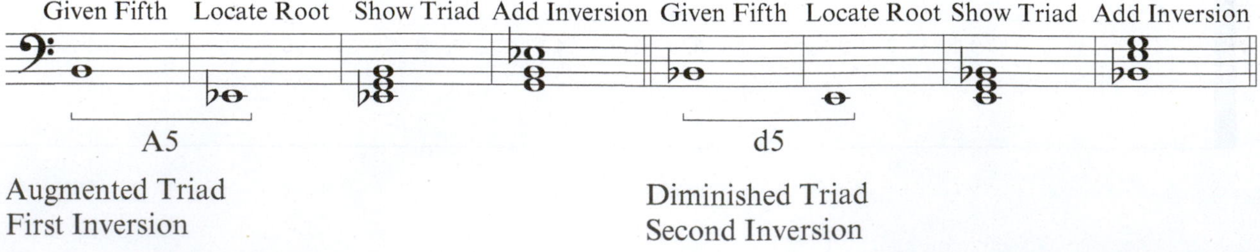

For class discussion or assignment: please do not remove these pages

REVIEW SET

Triads with Given Third and Fifth

From the given third or fifth, construct triads as indicated. Add accidentals as necessary. Use closed position. Use the first blank measure to write out the triad in root position before writing the inversion (if indicated).

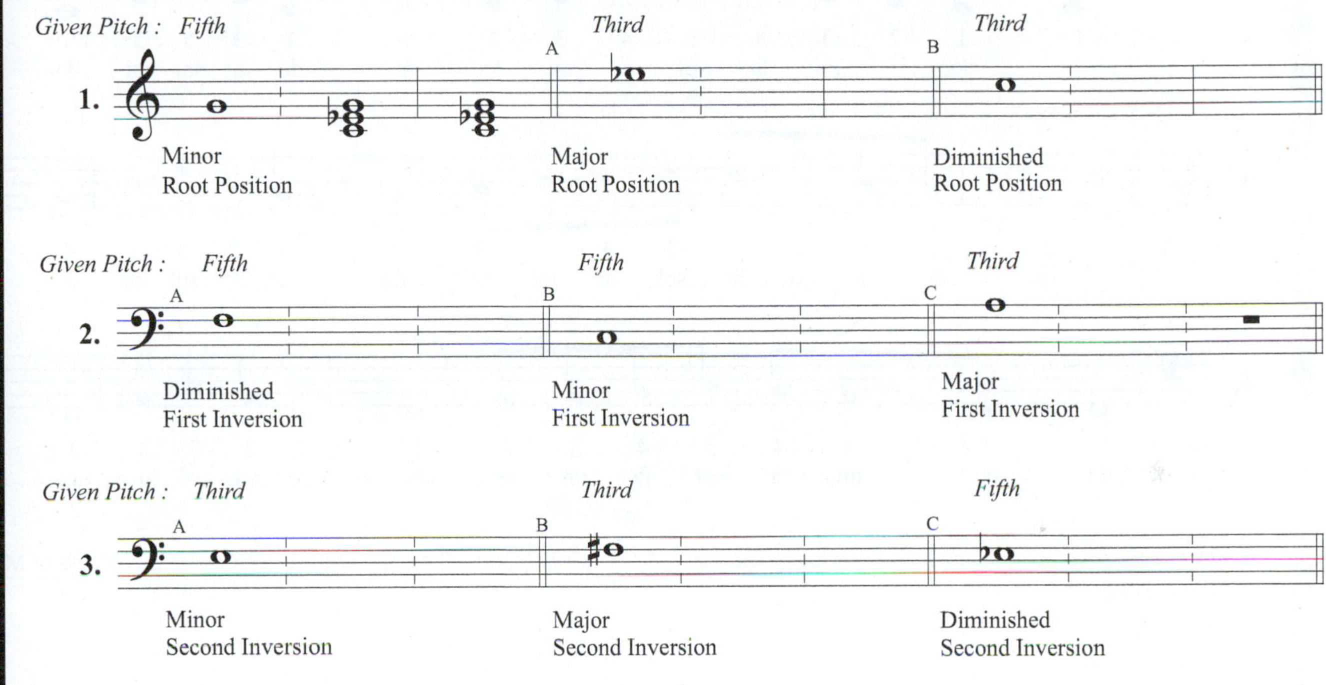

Complete Building Skills 10-3 on page 301

MUSICIANSHIP 10-4

I. Sight Singing: Major and Minor Triads

A. Practice singing major triads first by performing a stepwise pattern, then by singing just the scale degrees that outline a triad. Play the first pitch on the piano. Next, match this pitch and sing; $\hat{1}-\hat{5}$ (or do-sol) ascending and descending. Finally, sing $\hat{1}-\hat{3}-\hat{5}-\hat{3}-\hat{1}$ (do-mi-sol-mi-do) to outline a complete triad. While only four different keys are shown, you can practice these patterns throughout your range.

Procedure

1. 
1 1 2 3 4 5 4 3 2 1 1 3 5 3 1
do do re mi fa sol fa mi re do do mi sol mi do

2. 
1 1 2 3 4 5 4 3 2 1 1 3 5 3 1
do do re mi fa sol fa mi re do do mi sol mi do

3. 
1 1 2 3 4 5 4 3 2 1 1 3 5 3 1
do do re mi fa sol fa mi re do do mi sol mi do

4. 
1 1 2 3 4 5 4 3 2 1 1 3 5 3 1
do do re mi fa sol fa mi re do do mi sol mi do

B. Use the procedure outlined in the previous exercise, but sing minor triads. (The solfége for scale degree 3 changes to ME in minor keys.)

Procedure

II. Keyboard: Root-Position and Inverted Triads

Arpeggiate a root-position major triad followed by its inversions. Begin with major, then play the same triad in the parallel minor.

1. Major

Minor

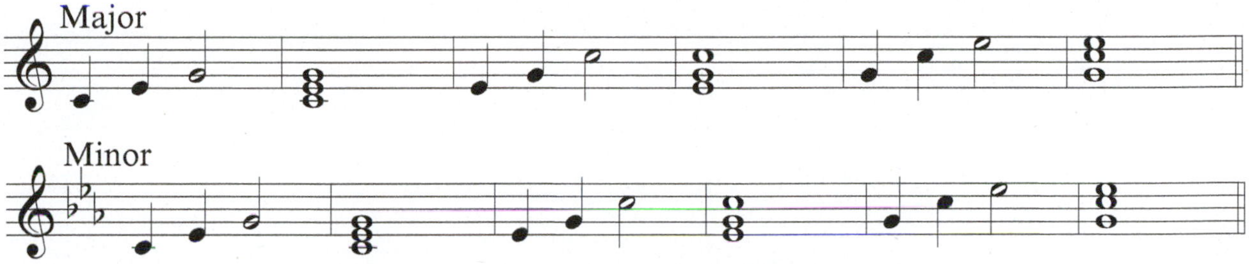

2. Major

Minor

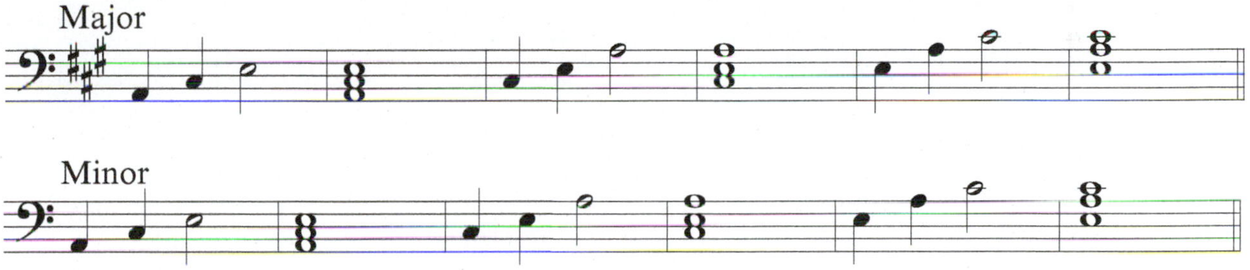

3. Major

Minor

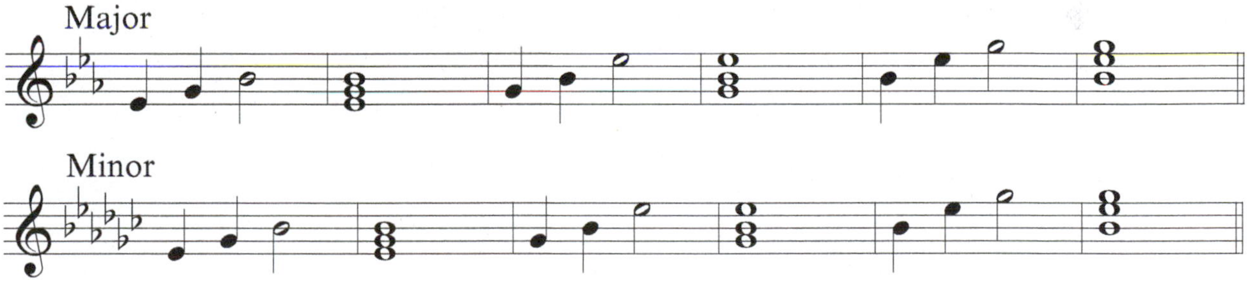

4. Major

Minor

Name ______________________

Page may be removed

Building Skills • 10-1

Root-Position Triads

A. *If necessary*, **add an accidental to the third, fifth, or third *and* fifth to create the given quality. Do not change the root.**

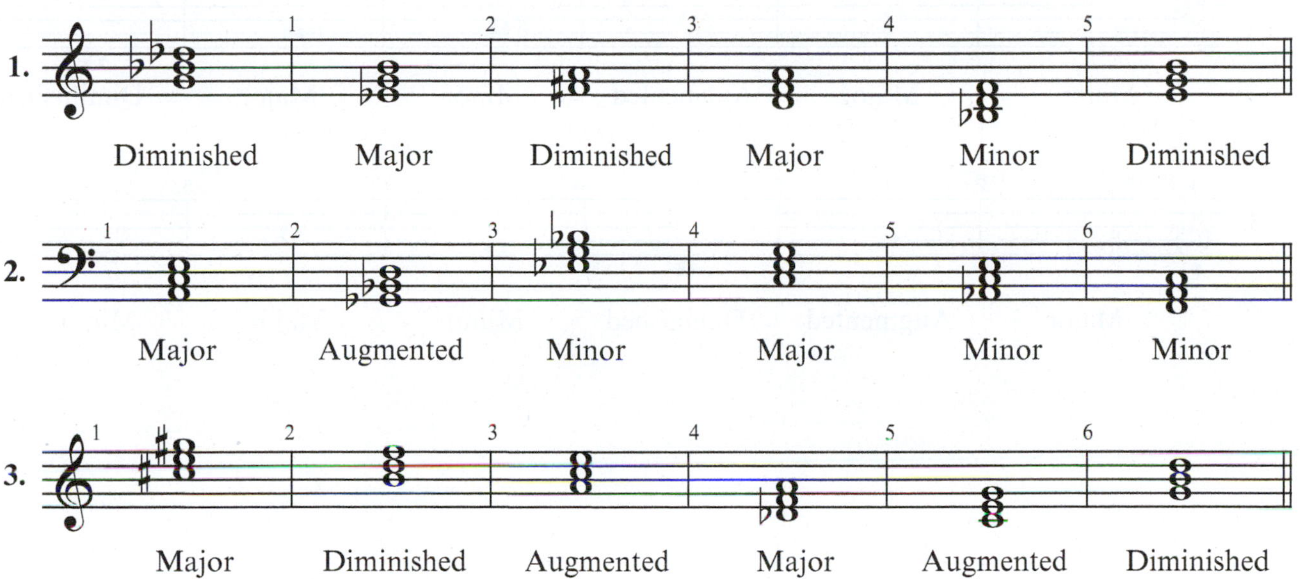

B. **Identify these triads by root name and quality.**

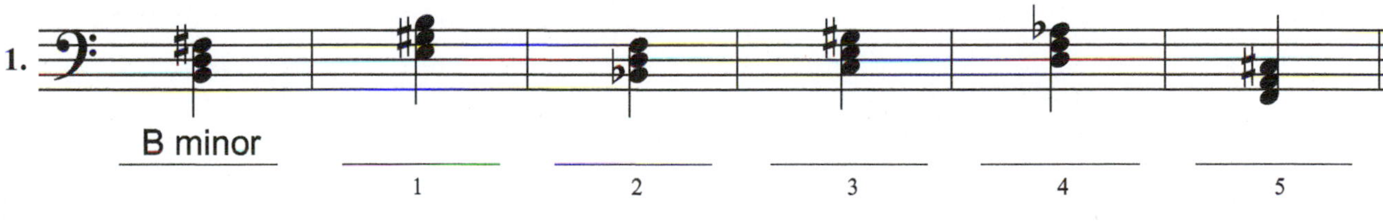

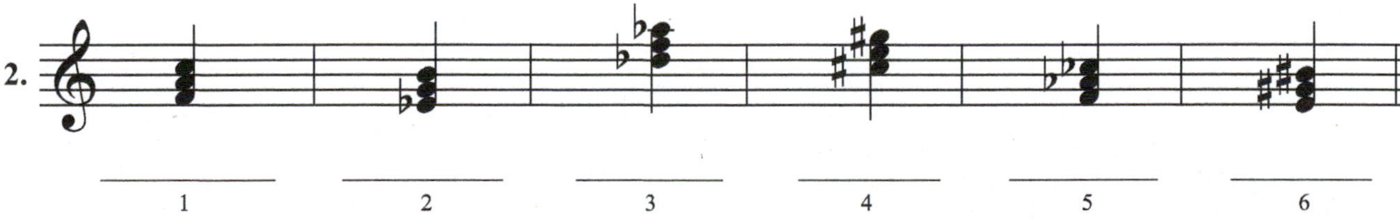

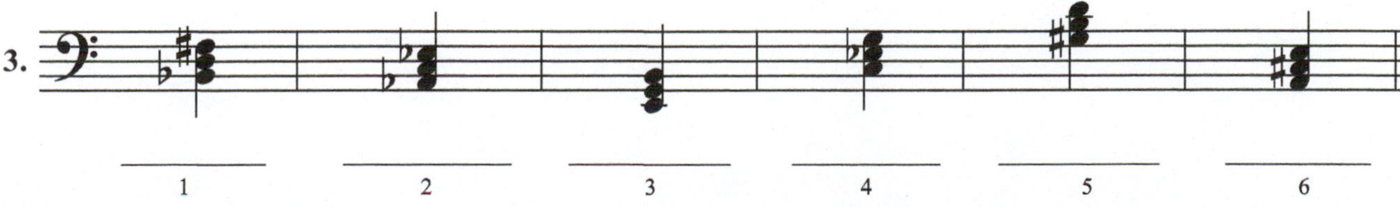

C. Construct root-position triads on each pitch. Add accidentals as necessary.

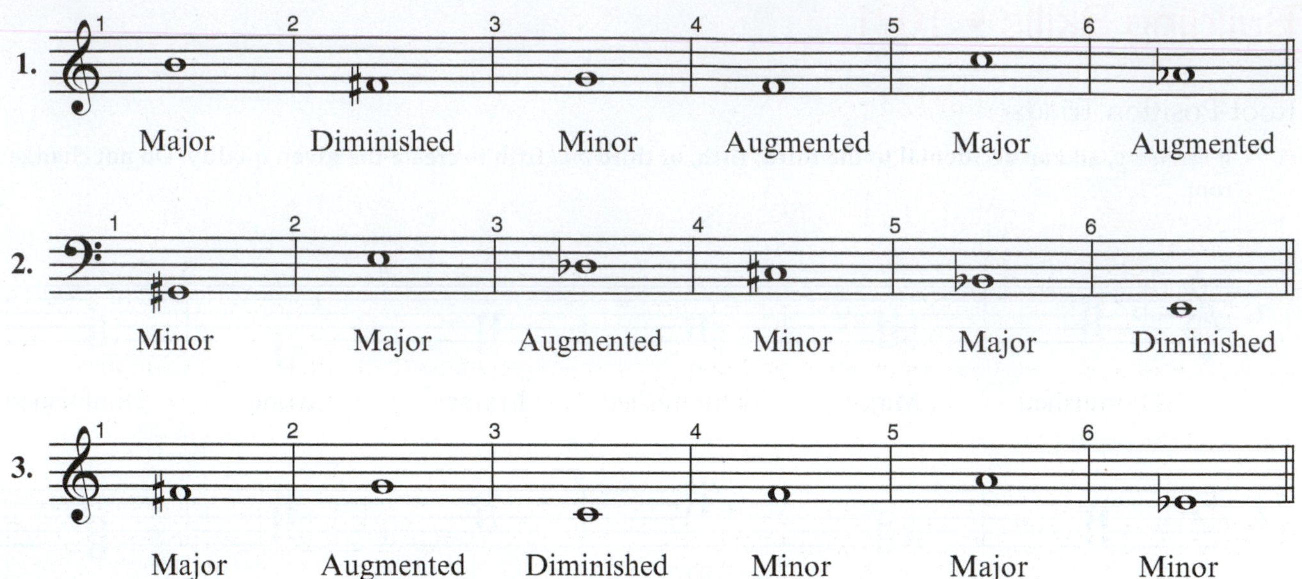

Name ______________________

Page may be removed

Building Skills • 10-2

Root-Position and Inverted Triads

A. Construct triads according to the specified root, quality, and inversion.

1. (treble clef)

	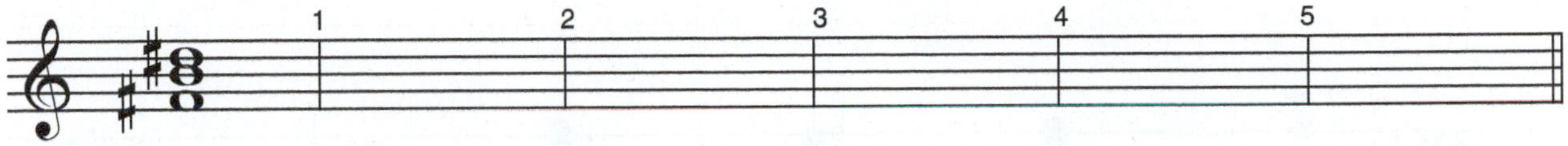 1	2	3	4	5
B Major 2nd Inversion	E♭ Minor 1st Inversion	D Major Root Position	F Augmented Root Position	B♭ Minor 1st Inversion	E Major Root Position

2. (bass clef)

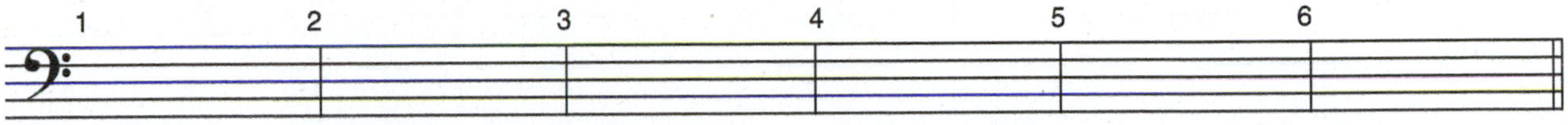 1	2	3	4	5	6
C Minor 1st Inversion	A♭ Minor 2nd Inversion	D♭ Major 1st Inversion	G Diminished Root Position	G Minor 2nd Inversion	E Diminished Root Position

3. (treble clef)

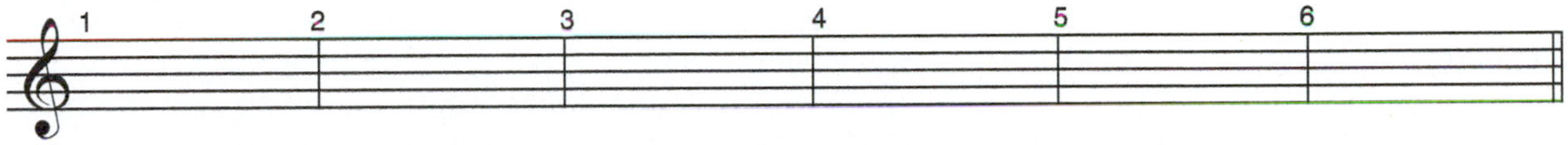 1	2	3	4	5	6
C♯ Diminished 1st Inversion	A Minor Root Position	G♭ Major 1st Inversion	B Diminished 1st Inversion	C Minor Root Position	F♯ Major 1st Inversion

4. (bass clef)

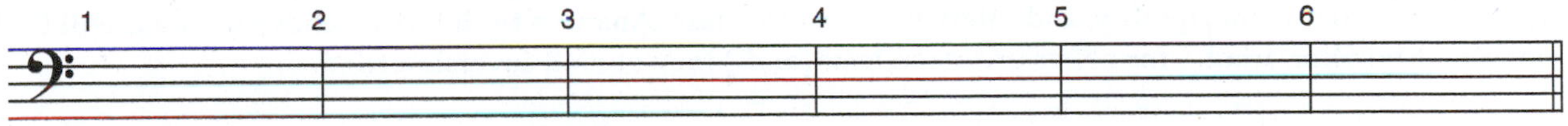 1	2	3	4	5	6
E Major Root Position	G♯ Minor Root Position	F Major 1st Inversion	B♭ Diminished 1st Inversion	D Major 2nd Inversion	A Major 1st Inversion

B. Identify these triads by root name, quality, and inversion.

2.

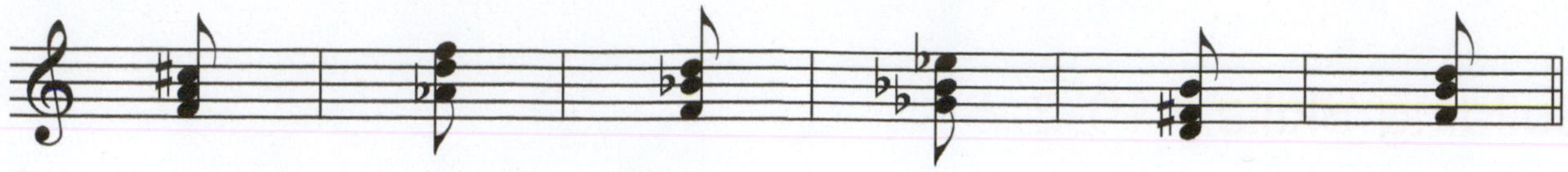

Root/Quality ______ ______ ______ ______ ______ ______

Inversion ______ ______ ______ ______ ______ ______

1 2 3 4 5 6

3.

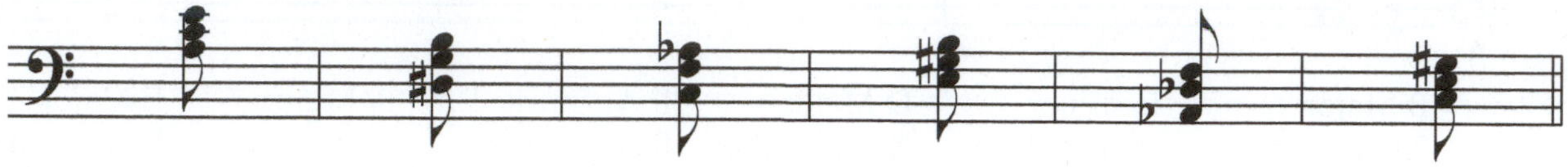

Root/Quality ______ ______ ______ ______ ______ ______

Inversion ______ ______ ______ ______ ______ ______

1 2 3 4 5 6

4.

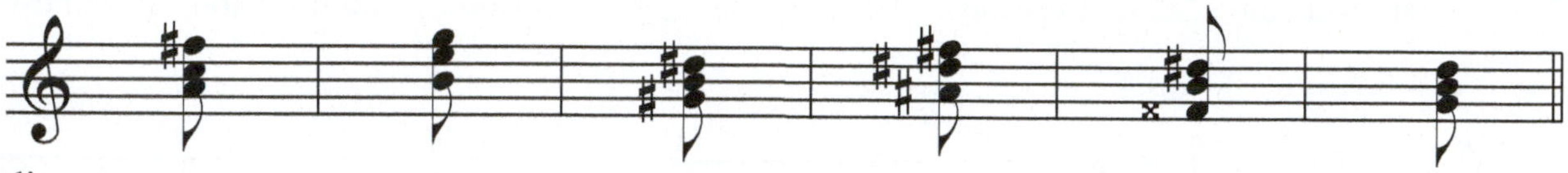

Root/Quality ______ ______ ______ ______ ______ ______

Inversion ______ ______ ______ ______ ______ ______

1 2 3 4 5 6

C. **Another way to look at triad inversion is through the intervals sounding above the bass. Identify these triads according to root name, quality, and intervals above the bass. Answers for intervals above the bass will be $^5_3$ for a root-position triad, $^6_3$ for a first-inversion triad, and $^6_4$ for a second-inversion triad.**

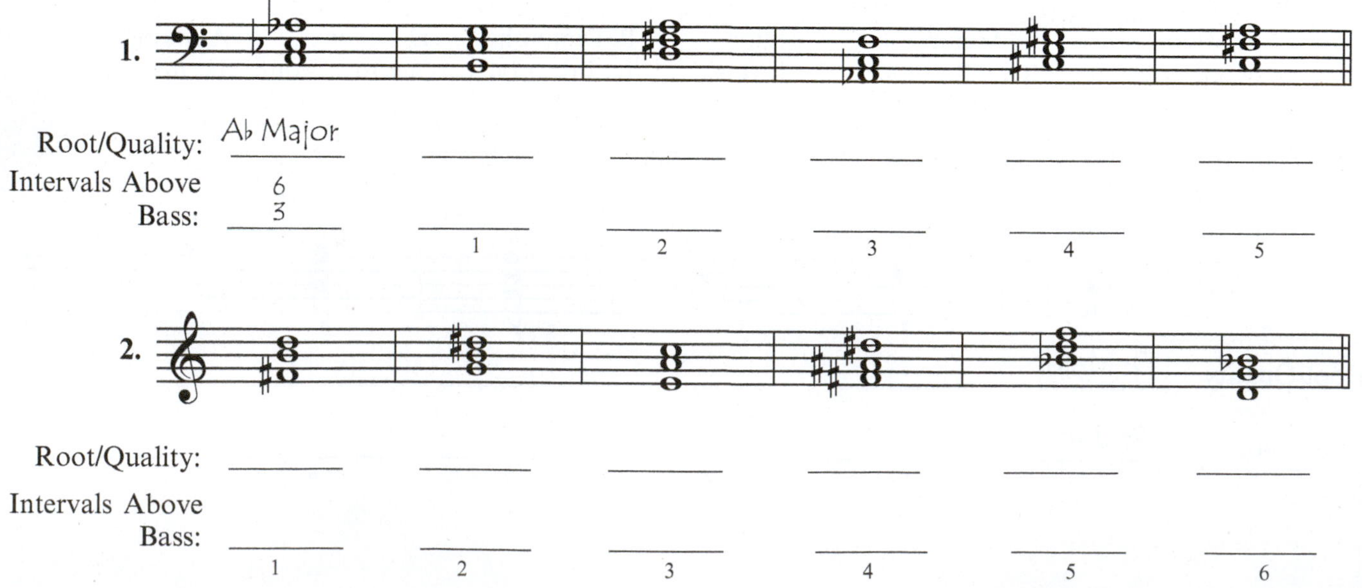

Name ______________________

Page may be removed

Building Skills • 10-3

Triads with Given Third or Fifth

A. **Construct root-position triads. Consider the given pitch to be the root, third, and fifth as specified. Add other pitches above and/or below the one given as necessary.**

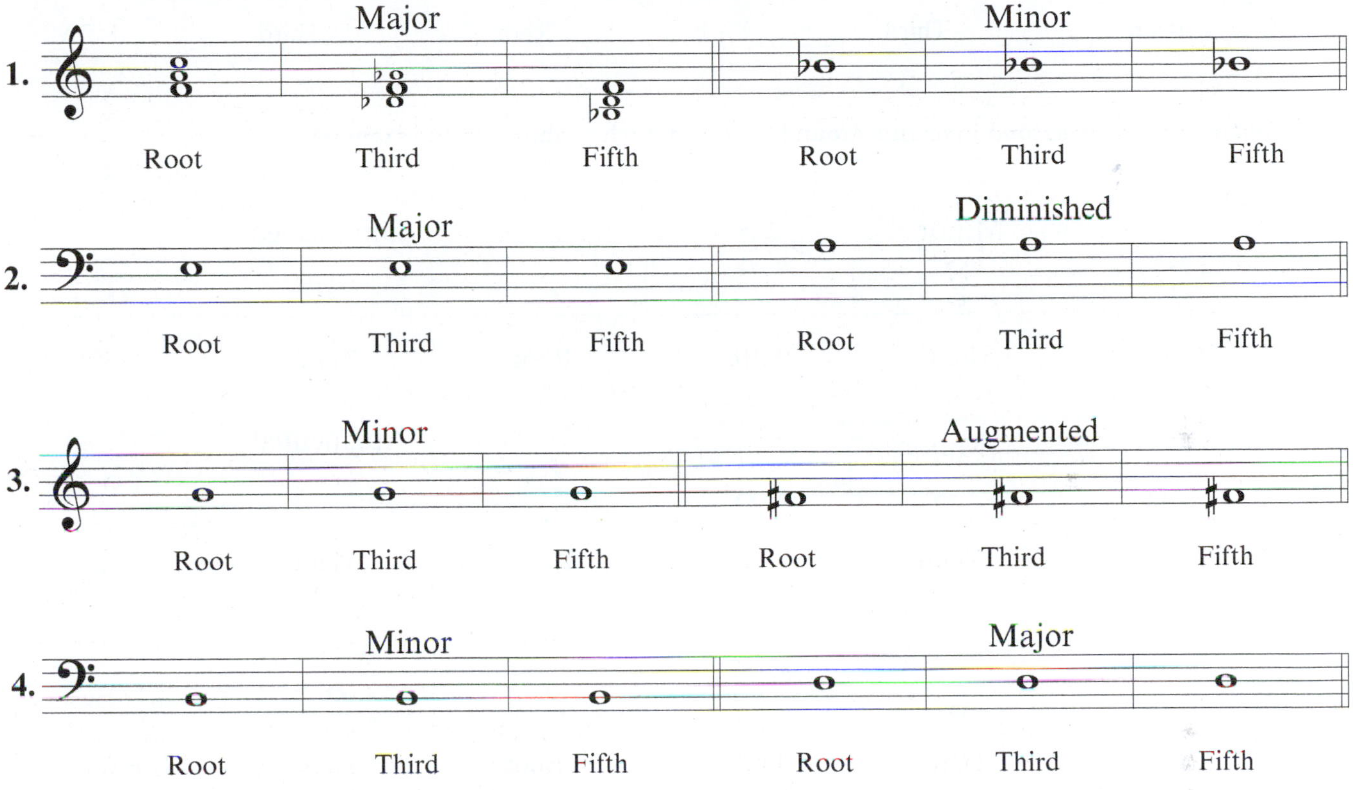

B. **Follow the process in the previous exercise, but construct these triads in first inversion. The given pitch can be the root, third, or fifth.**

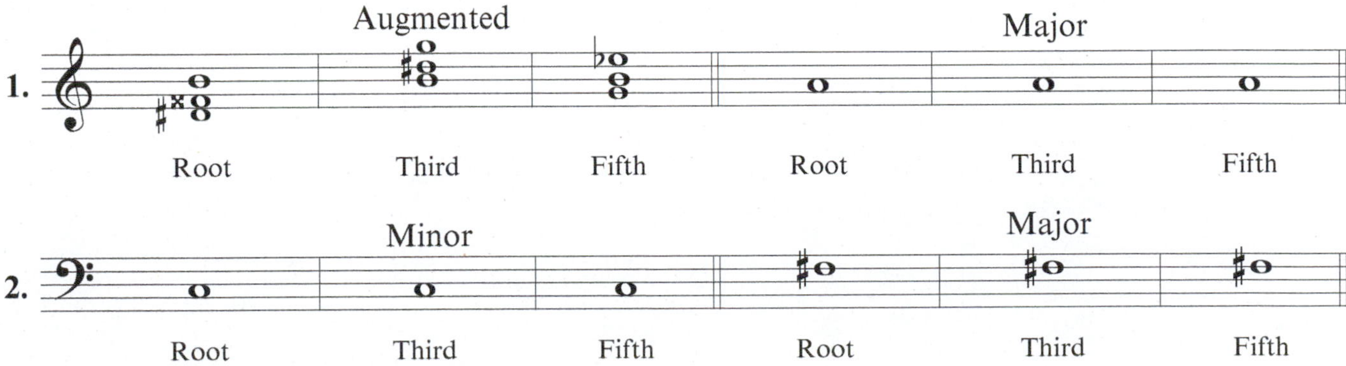

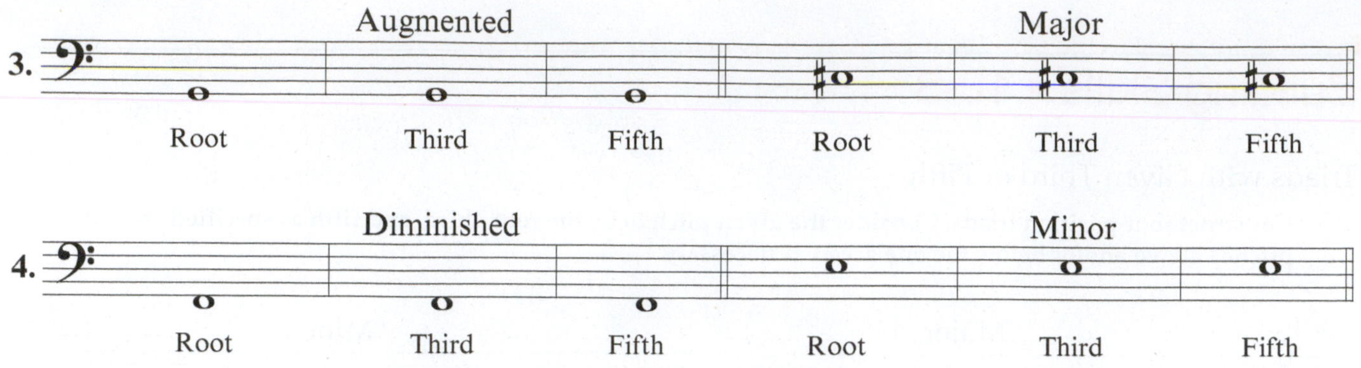

C. **Construct triads in second inversion around the given pitch as shown in the example.**

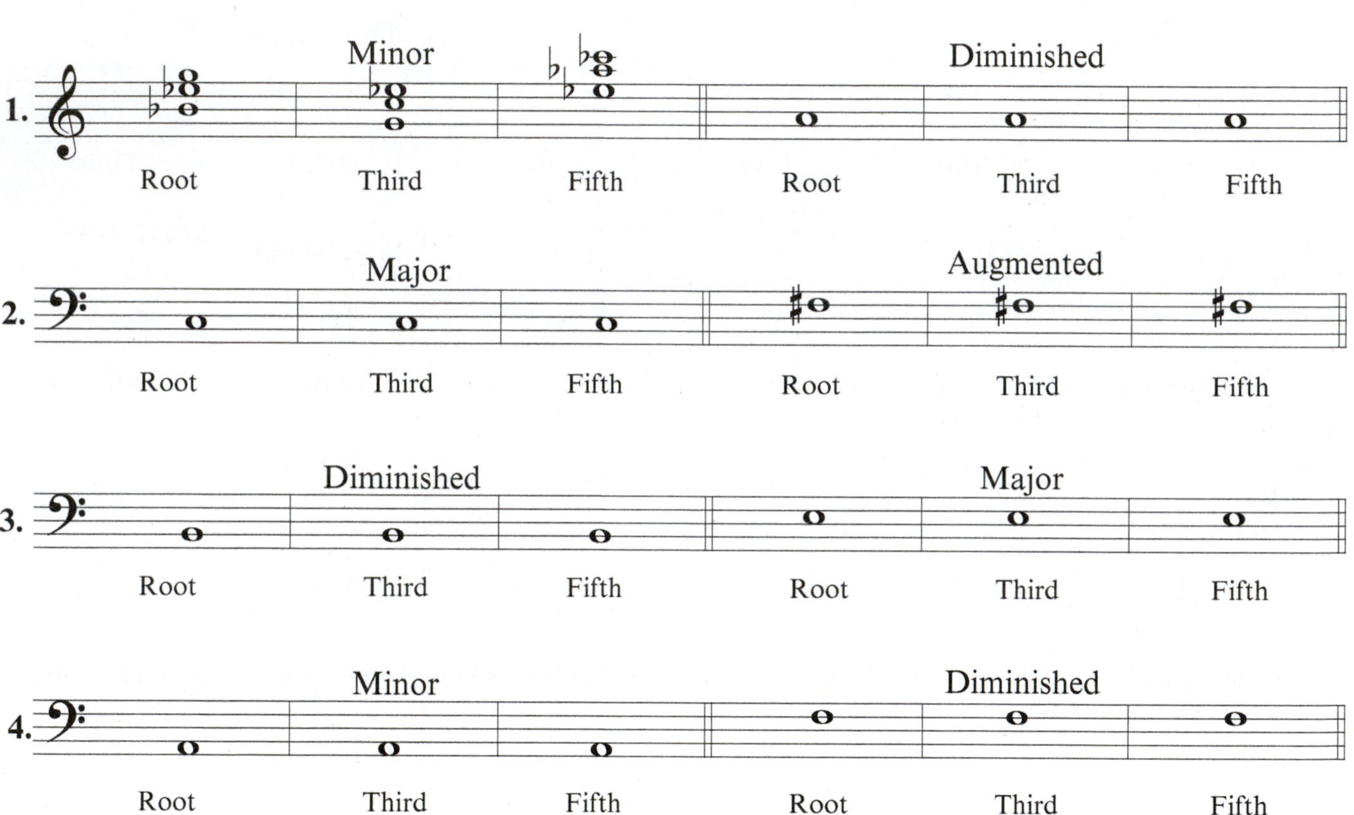

Name ______________________

Page may be removed

D. **Identify these arpeggiated triads by type and quality.**

E. **Write three pitches in each measure that outline triads as indicated. Use any order and octave placement, but create a different rhythmic pattern for each measure.**

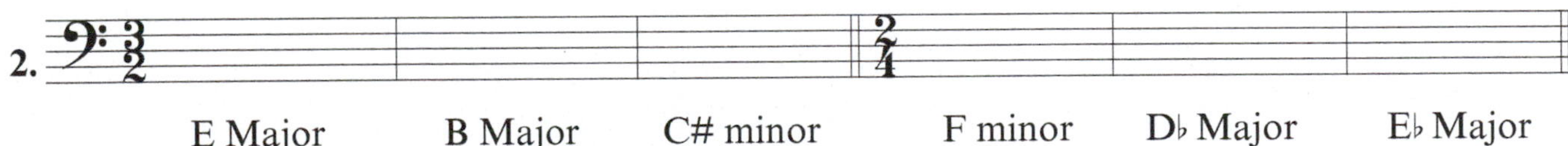

F. **Identify these root-position and inverted triads by indicating the intervals sounding above the bass ($^5_3$ for root position, $^6_3$ for first inversion, and $^6_4$ for second inversion).**

1.

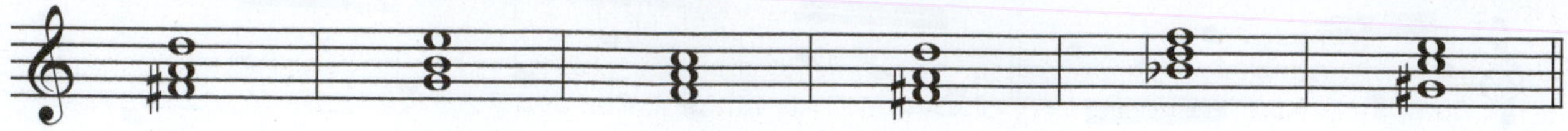

Root:	D					
Quality:	Major					
Intervals Above Bass:	$^6_4$	1	2	3	4	5

2.

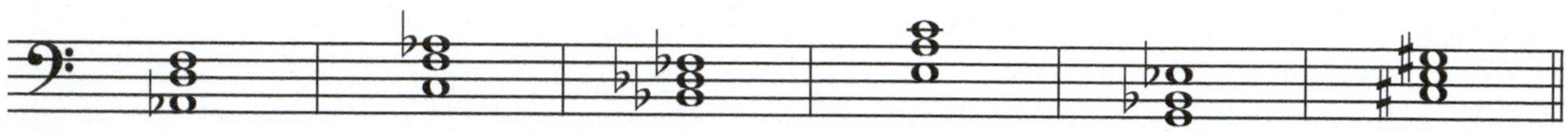

Root:						
Quality:						
Intervals Above Bass:	1	2	3	4	5	6

3.

Root:						
Quality:						
Intervals Above Bass:	1	2	3	4	5	6

Name ______________________

Page may be removed

Creative Projects • Chapter 10

Triads

A. **The brackets above the staves indicate arpeggiated triads in these melodies. Write the triad in root position on the lower staff. Name the triad root and quality in the blank. Be sure to take the key signature into consideration when identifying quality. Listen to the musical examples after you have inserted the triads.**

J.S.Bach, Suite No. 1 in G Major, BWV 1007, Courante (m. 19)

Beethoven, Piano Sonata no. 21 in C Major, op. 53 "Waldstein"

English Folk Song, "Early One Morning"

3.

Name ______________________

Page may be removed

B. **Compose an eight-measure period based on the triads specified in the lower staff. Limit your melody to pitches in the triad, but vary the order and rhythm as you see fit. End the first phrase with a progressive melodic cadence; use a terminal cadence for the second phrase. Prepare to perform your melody for the class.**

1.

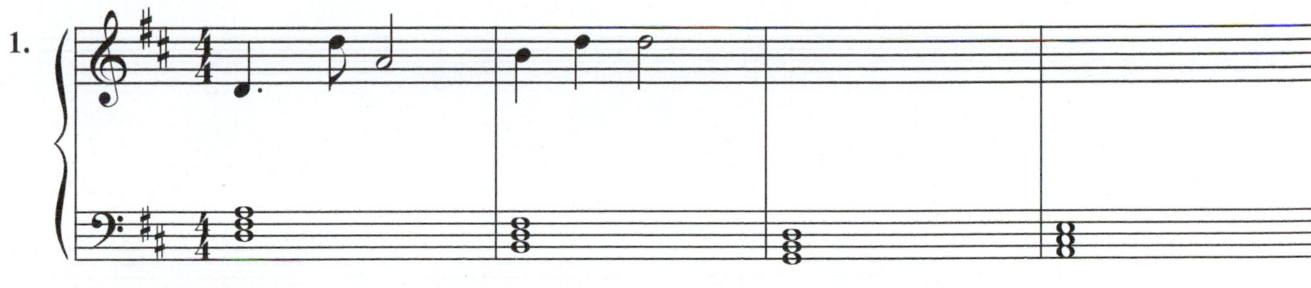

D Major

Moderate Speed

2.

C Minor

Waltz
3.
5
B♭ Major
Faster
4.
5
E Major

Name ______________________________

Page may be removed

Analysis in Context 1 • Chapter 10

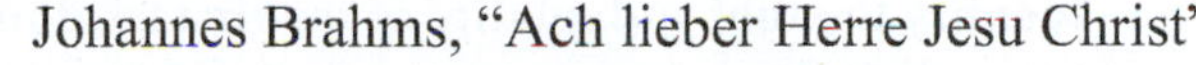

Johannes Brahms, "Ach lieber Herre Jesu Christ"

Soprano / Alto / Tenor / Bass

Ach lie - ber Her - re Je - su Christ, weil du ein Kind ge -

4

we - sen bist, so gib auch die - sem Kin - de - lein dein Gnad und auch den

8

Se - gen dein; ach Je - sus, Her - re mein, be - hüt dies Kin - de - lein.

1. The time signature for this chorale tells us that there are _________ beats in each measure and that a _________ note equals one beat.

2. In what key is this song written?

3. Identify the root and quality of the first triad in the chorale (i.e., major, minor, diminished, augmented). Begin by reading the note name on each staff from the bass up to the soprano. Arrange the note names in thirds to determine the root the chord is based on.

4. Using the same triad referred to in Question 3, determine whether the triad is in root position, first inversion, or second inversion.

5. Use the process in questions 3 and 4 to continue identifying the triad root, quality, and inversion for the remaining measures of the piece.

Chapter 11
Chords and Symbols

Essential Terms and Symbols

Arabic numerals
augmented triads (+)
chord
chord symbols
diatonic triads
diminished triads (°)
doubling
figured bass
implied triad
lead sheet
music theory
Roman-numeral analysis
spacing
subtonic
voicing

Triad and Chord Identification

The term "triad" refers to three distinct pitches stacked in consecutive thirds. A **chord**, is a collection of two or more pitches. The pitches of the triad may be arranged in different ways through doubling and voicing.

Doubling

With four or more voices and only three pitches in a triad, composers employ **doubling** by duplicating one or more of those pitches. Although identification of a triad is unchanged through doubling, the sound is different depending on many factors.

When a triad is spaced out over the grand staff, or when one of the three pitches is heard simultaneously in different octaves, a simple triad takes on new life. Listen and follow the score as the E minor triad expands through spatial variety and doubling.

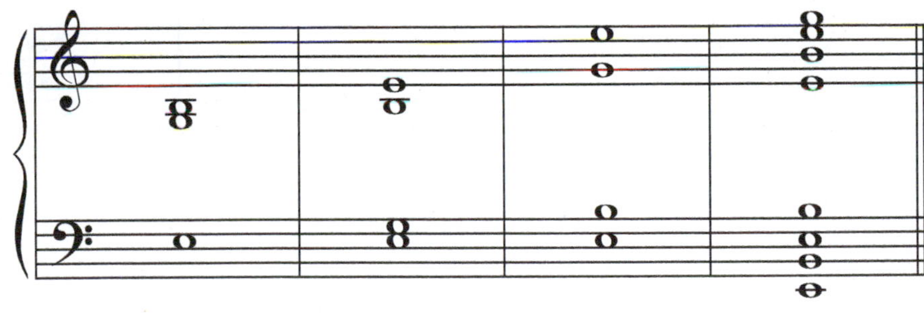

E Minor Triads

Voicing (also termed **spacing**) refers to both the choice of octave and to any doubling present in a triad or chord. In the next example, each D major chord is voiced with one pitch of the triad doubled and with various octave placements.

For class discussion or assignment: please do not remove these pages

REVIEW SET

Doubling

A. These chords have from three to five voices. In the blank, indicate which (if any) triad element (root, third, or fifth) is doubled. If the triad has only three voices, write "none"; if it has five voices, indicate which *two* elements are doubled.

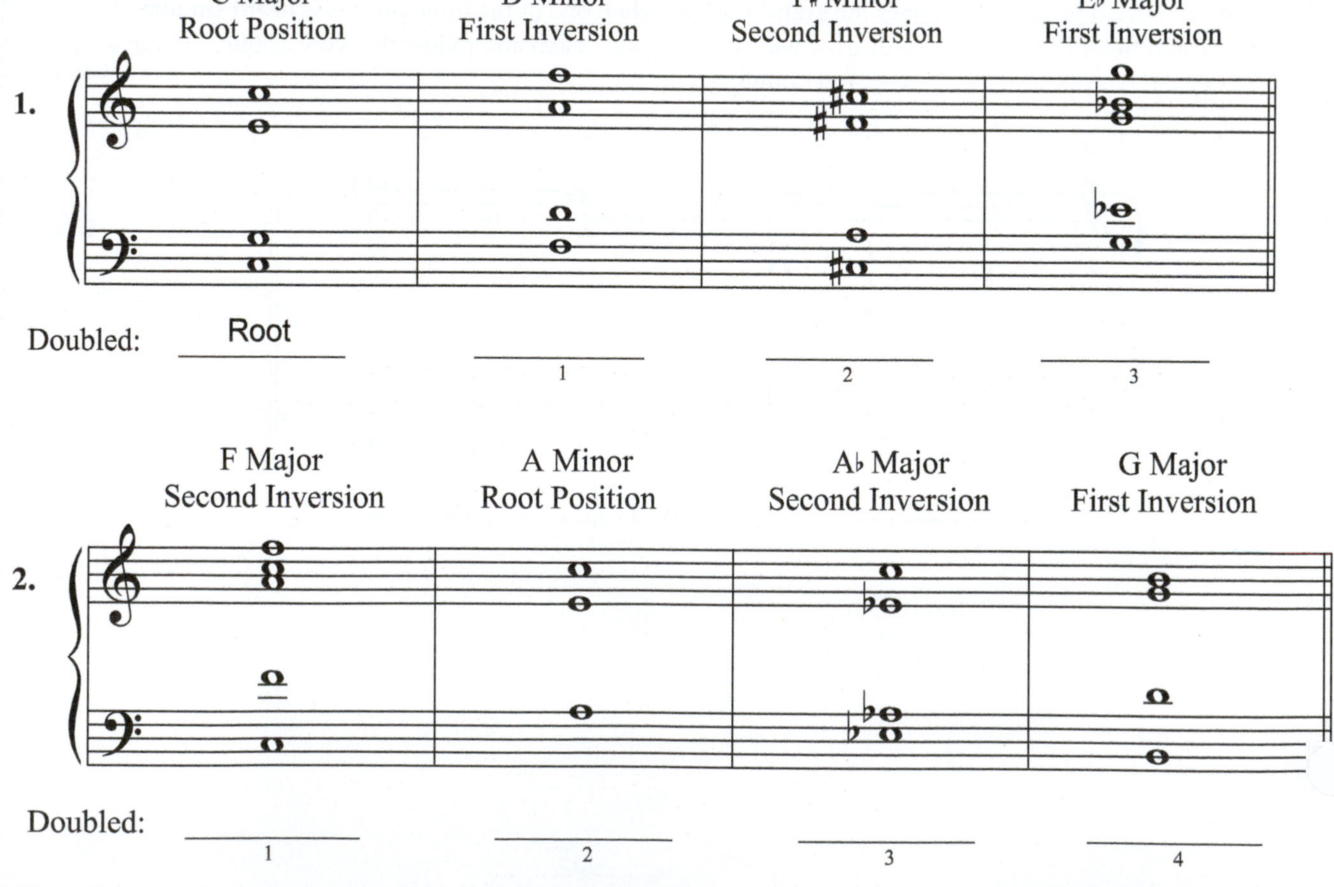

Identifying Chords

When triads and chords have more complex voicings (various spacings and doublings), one additional step precedes our usual identification process. Begin by *eliminating* octave duplications and pitch doublings to return the triad to its most basic structure. Consider the chord in the next example.

With *seven* pitches in this chord, we may not see at a glance that they all correspond to a B♭ major triad. If needed, use a work staff to notate the triad in closed position. Begin with *the original bass pitch* (in a different octave if you prefer). Your goal is to eliminate all but two triad elements and notate these above the bass.

After notating the bass, move upward through the remaining pitches that are not duplicated. Add new pitches *above the bass* on your work staff. The first pitch above the bass in our sample chord, for example, is another occurrence of the pitch D, so we will ignore it and move upward to the next pitch: the F in the treble clef. This is a new pitch, so add it above the D on your work staff.

The pitch B♭$_4$ above F$_4$ is new. Notate this pitch above the D and the F on the work staff. Because the remaining pitches in the treble clef duplicate those already notated on our work staff, we can identify the chord as B♭ major in first inversion.

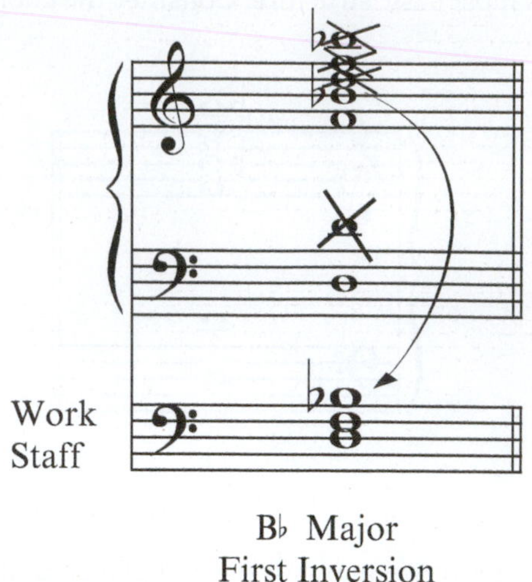

B♭ Major
First Inversion

After some experience, the lengthy process outlined in the preceding examples can be done mentally and within seconds. Discounting accidentals, there are only seven different triad possibilities. Within a short time, you will become so familiar with these spellings that you will recognize them instantly.

Diatonic Triads	
C E G	G B D
D F A	A C E
E G B	B D F
F A C	

Arpeggiation

Triads and chords are frequently broken up or *arpeggiated* in both melody and accompaniment. While traditional music is built of triads, we cannot always expect the three pitches to occur on the beat, simultaneously, or in root–third–fifth order. In identifying an arpeggiated triad, consider several consecutive beats if necessary.

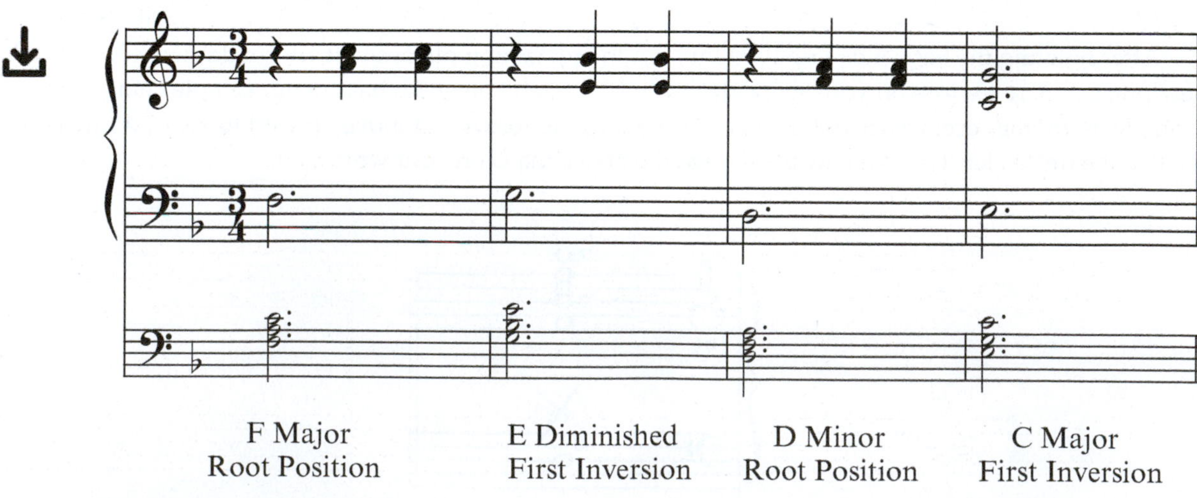

F Major
Root Position

E Diminished
First Inversion

D Minor
Root Position

C Major
First Inversion

Sometimes, several measures will elapse before the triad is clarified.

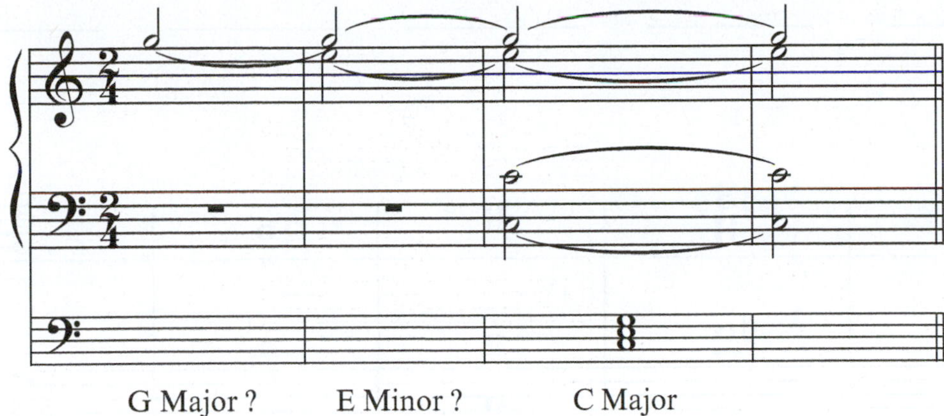

INCOMPLETE TRIADS. A triad is **incomplete** when the root and third are present with the fifth omitted. The root is always necessary to determine relationships with other diatonic triads. Likewise, the third must be present to clarify quality. But while the fifth fills out the sonority and is usually present, it is occasionally omitted. Add the abbreviation "(INC)" when the fifth is omitted.

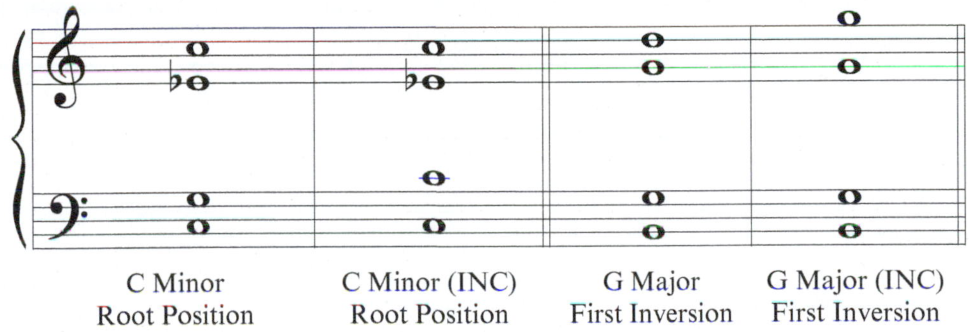

For class discussion or assignment: please do not remove these pages

REVIEW SET

Chords with Varied Spacing and Doubling

A. These chords include alternative doubling and spacing as well as implied triads. Identify the root name, quality, and inversion. Include the abbreviation "INC" with the root name if the triad is implied. Use the work staff if necessary.

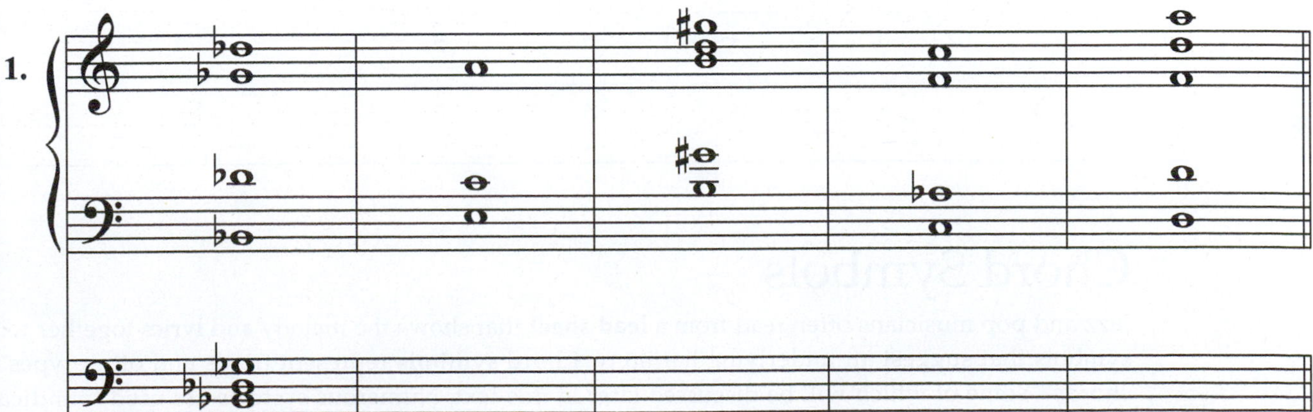

Root: Gb ______ ______ ______ ______

Quality: Major ______ ______ ______ ______

Inversion: 1st Inv. ______ ______ ______ ______

1 2 3 4

2.

Root: ______ ______ ______ ______ ______

Quality: ______ ______ ______ ______ ______

Inversion: ______ ______ ______ ______ ______

1 2 3 4 5

Complete Building Skills 11-1 on page 329

MUSICIANSHIP 11-1

Ear Training: Chord Quality

While listening to the audio on the website, identify these triads and chords as major ("M"), minor ("m"), diminished ("d"), or augmented ("A"). Write the appropriate answer in the blank. The performance is chordal. (See Appendix D for answers.)

1. ______ ______ ______ ______ ______ ______
   1 2 3 4 5 6
2. ______ ______ ______ ______ ______ ______
   1 2 3 4 5 6
3. ______ ______ ______ ______ ______ ______
   1 2 3 4 5 6
4. ______ ______ ______ ______ ______ ______
   1 2 3 4 5 6

Chord Symbols

Jazz and pop musicians often read from a **lead sheet** that shows the melody and lyrics together with symbols that suggest an underlying harmony. **Chord symbols** represent triads and other types of chords—some of which will be discussed later in this text. Numerous systems are used to indicate chords in jazz and popular music; each has advantages and disadvantages. Depending on the system, for example, a C major triad might be indicated in any of the following ways:

C CM C MA C MAJ

The system of chord symbols employed in this text is favored by many jazz and popular musicians today because it offers clarity. In an era when a professionally engraved font is available with computer software, jazz and popular musicians still prefer a hand-copied appearance. We will follow this preference in our examples.

Chord symbols represent root-position triads and chords. In actual practice, any pitch of the triad may appear in the bass (along with many others). An uppercase letter (along with any accidental) signifies a major triad. On a lead sheet, lyrics appear below the staff; chord symbols above it.

Augmented triads are rare (see Chapter 10), but we can specify them with the root letter and any accidental along with a plus sign (+), or the abbreviation "AUG."

If the triad is minor, add the abbreviation "MIN" or "–" to the root symbol.

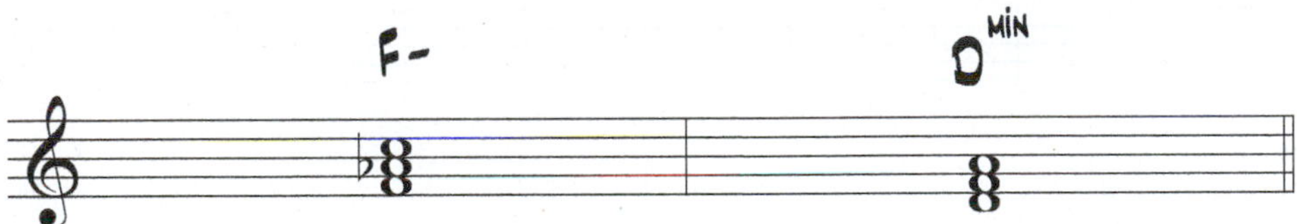

The symbol for a diminished chord clarifies a minor triad ("MI") with lowered fifth (♭5). The circle symbol (°) is also used to denote a diminished chord.

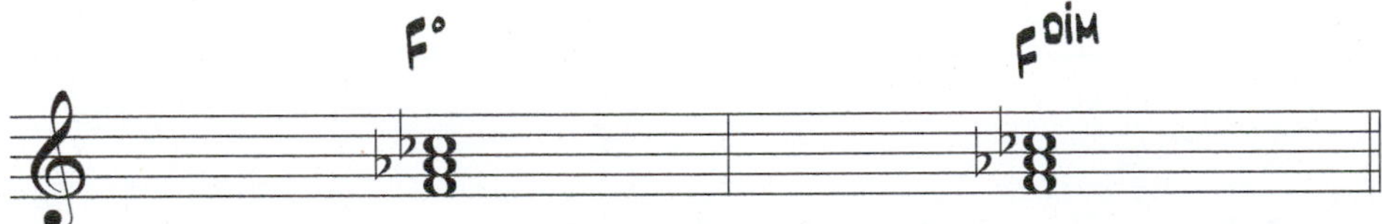

INVERSION In jazz and pop styles, often a bass pitch is not specified (letting performers work that out for themselves). To specify a bass, however, use a slash after the chord symbol followed by a letter to designate the bass pitch. This pitch may or may not be part of the chord.

For class discussion or assignment: please do not remove these pages

REVIEW SET

Chord Symbols

A. For each chord, provide an appropriate symbol *above* the staff as it would appear in jazz and popular music. If the third or fifth is in the bass, indicate this factor as well (E♭/G, for example).

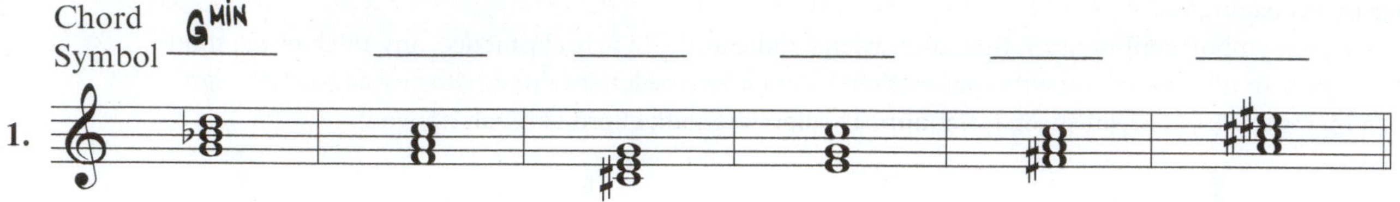

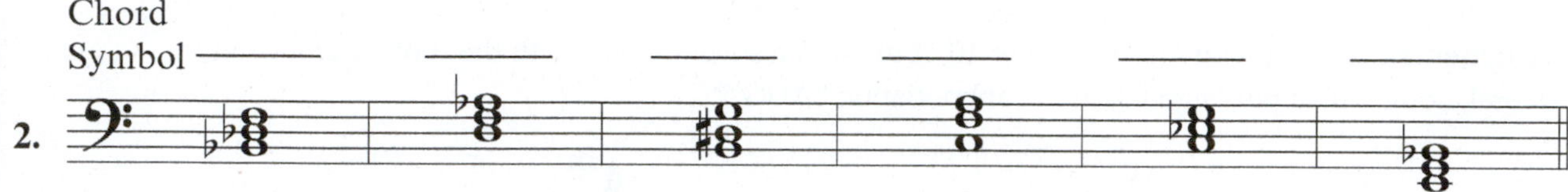

B. Construct chords that correspond to the following symbols. Add all necessary accidentals.

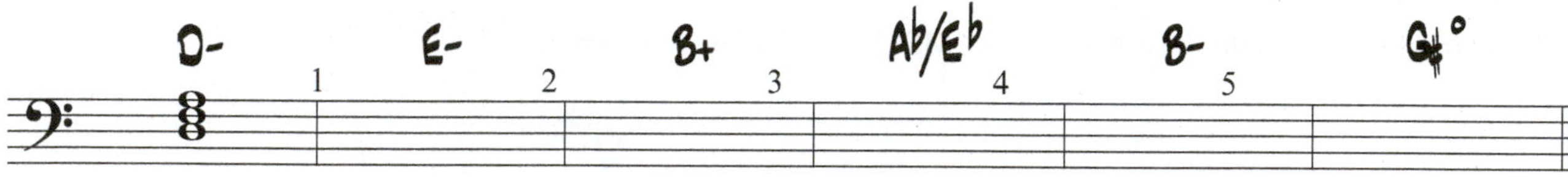

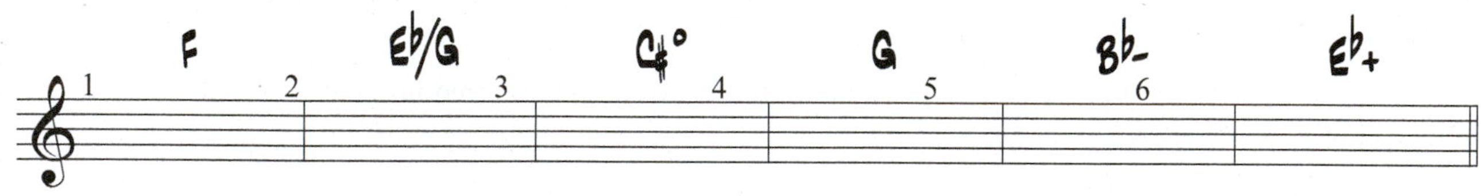

Roman-Numeral Analysis

Chord symbols serve well for jazz and popular music; only the triad root and quality are specified, allowing the performer to make most other decisions. In addition, a single chord symbol identifies one sound—regardless of the key and without concern for the chords coming before and after it. In C major, the symbol C stands for the tonic; if the key is G major, C identifies a triad built on the fourth scale degree, and so on.

In common practice music, tonality is so important that the system of chord identification centers on the relationships among triads within a key. Originating in nineteenth-century Germany, **Roman-numeral analysis** is a way of tracing relationships among triads and chords in tonal music.

Diatonic Triads in Major Keys

Using the scale-degree names introduced in Chapter 5, triads can be built on each pitch of a major scale; these are called **diatonic triads**. Remember that the designation "F": specifies F major.

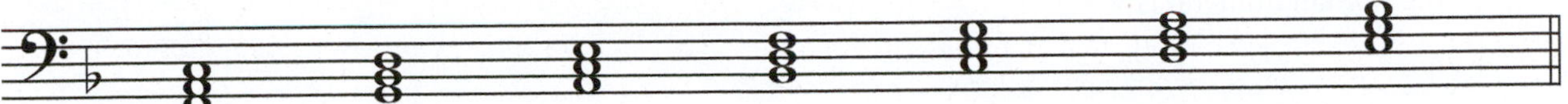

F: Tonic Supertonic Mediant Subdominant Dominant Submediant Leading Tone

If the key is B major, the same triad names designate different sets of pitches.

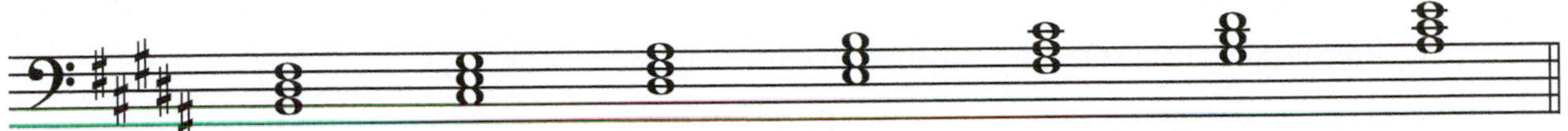

B: Tonic Supertonic Mediant Subdominant Dominant Submediant Leading Tone

Roman-numeral analysis provides similar information in a more compact form. Roman numerals from I through VII designate the triads built on the first through seventh scale degrees. More recently, theorists and composers have also included triad quality within the symbol, using "lowercase" Roman numerals for minor triads and the circle symbol for **diminished triads**. In any major key, I, IV, and V are major triads; ii, iii, and vi are minor; and vii° is diminished.

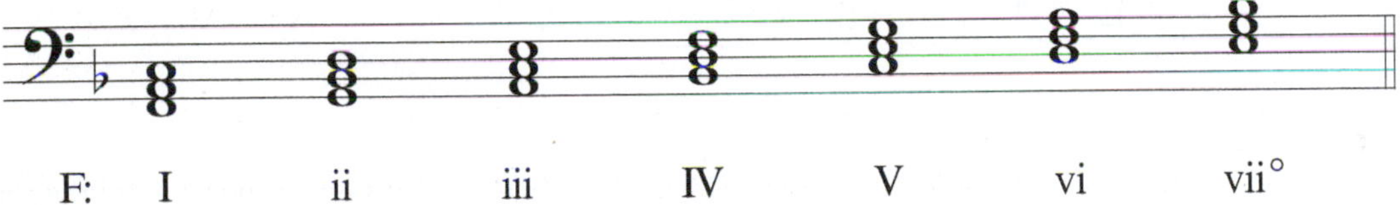

Unlike chord symbols, a key indication always accompanies Roman-numeral symbols; otherwise, they are almost meaningless. In B major the symbols themselves are identical to those in F major. The sounds they represent, of course, are completely different.

With the designation of a key, we can represent a particular diatonic triad or chord. The Roman-numeral symbol tells us both the quality and the relationship of the given chord to the tonic pitch.

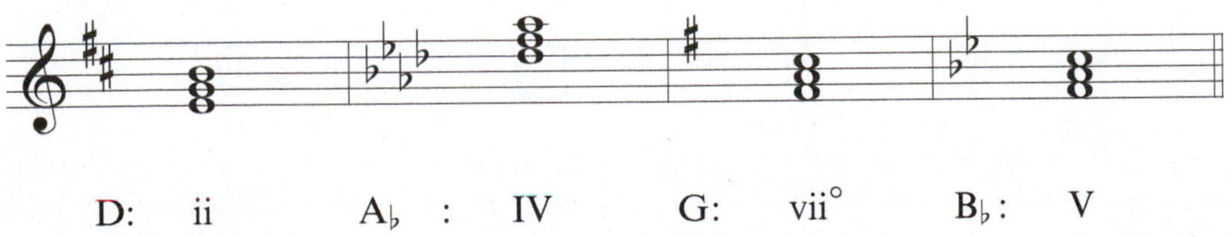

ROMAN-NUMERAL IDENTIFICATION. Using Roman-numeral symbols for identification, determine the scale degree of the root, then provide the appropriate symbol.

To identify a G–B–D triad in the key of D major, calculate the scale degree of the root G in the D major scale [$\hat{4}$], then provide the related Roman numeral (IV). If the same chord is identified in C major, the Roman numeral is V.

Roman-numeral analysis is unchanged by doubling and voicing.

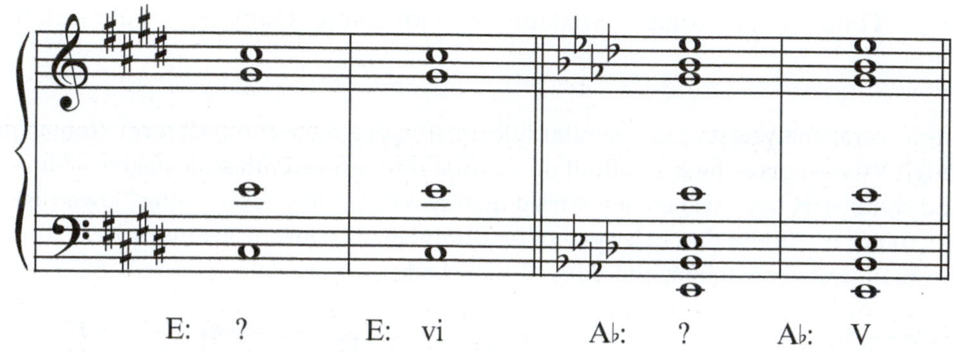

CHORD CONSTRUCTION FROM ROMAN-NUMERAL SYMBOLS. Roman-numeral symbols represent sounds just as notes and chord symbols do. From a given Roman-numeral symbol we can notate the corresponding pitches. Begin with the key signature, determine which scale degree corresponds to the symbol, then notate the root-position triad. In our present studies, the following rule is of extreme importance when constructing diatonic triads in major keys:

> Accidentals—outside the key signature—are *never* necessary for constructing diatonic triads in a major key.

Given the key of A major and the symbol vii°, begin by providing the key signature of three sharps (or be prepared to provide the necessary accidentals). Next, build a diatonic triad on G♯. Likewise, to construct the chord represented by the symbol F: iii, follow the same process: Provide the key signature, then notate the mediant triad in F major.

For class discussion or assignment: please do not remove these pages

REVIEW SET

Roman Numerals

A. Provide a Roman-numeral symbol for the given root-position triads. In the lower blank, write the triad term ("tonic," "supertonic," and so on). Two chords appear in each key.

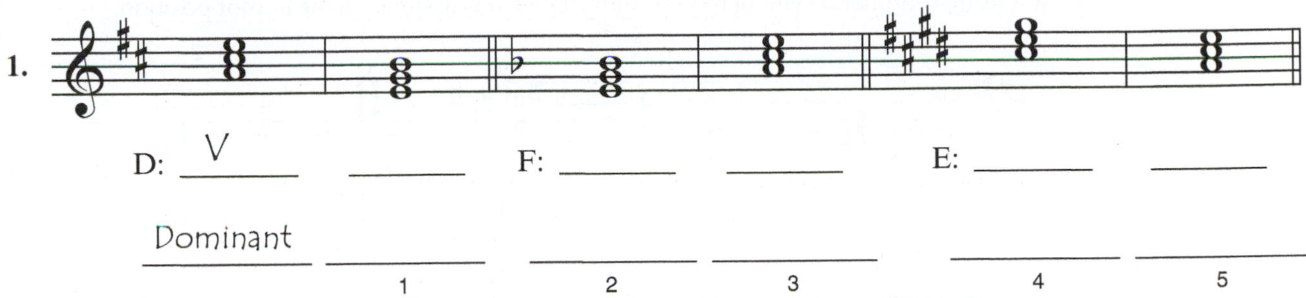

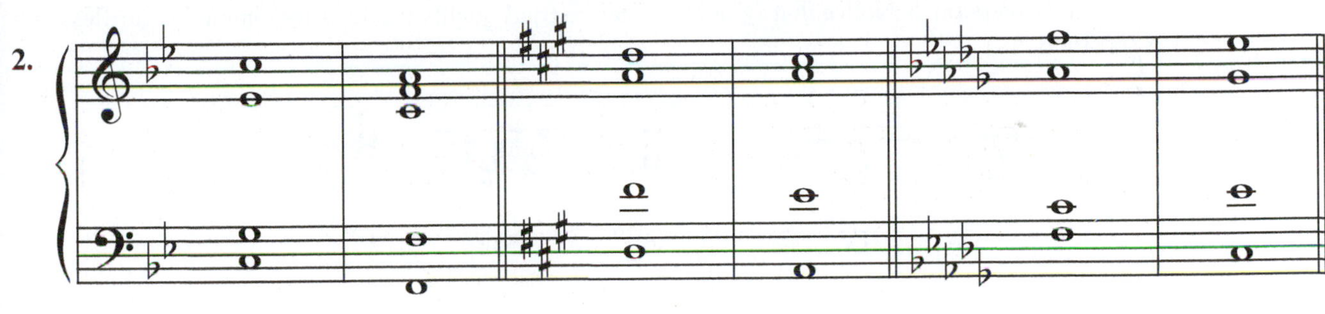

B♭: _____ _____ A: _____ _____ D♭: _____ _____

1 2 3 4 5 6

B. Construct root-position triads that conform to the key and Roman-numeral symbol. *Begin by providing the appropriate key signature*. Next, determine the scale degree indicated by the Roman numeral, then construct the triad. No accidentals outside the key signature are necessary. There are two chords in each key.

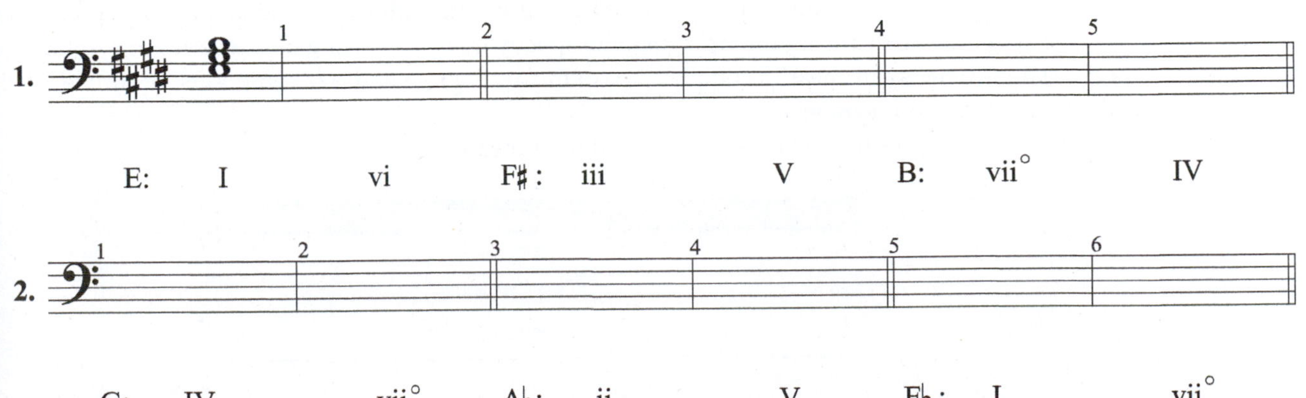

Figured-Bass Symbols

Seventeenth-century composers often provided only the melody and bass pitches, leaving details of the inner voices to the performer's discretion through improvisation. The lead sheet chord symbols we've studied are used today by jazz and pop composers. Along with the soprano and bass, however, seventeenth-century composers also added numbers below the bass to indicate intervals sounding above it. This system, called **figured bass**, uses **Arabic numerals** to indicate inversion. You will find that you are already familiar with figured bass from exercises in earlier chapters.

While triads in root position have a fifth and third above the bass, these numbers $\binom{5}{3}$ are understood. If a Roman-numeral symbol has no Arabic label, it is assumed to be in root position.

In first inversion, the third of the triad is in the lowest sounding voice. As a result, intervals of a sixth and a third appear above the bass $\binom{6}{3}$. In analysis, the numeral 3 is understood, making the label for first inversion, 6. Notice that symbols related to triad quality (° and ⁺) are retained regardless of bass position.

The fifth of the triad is in the lowest sounding voice in a second inversion triad. The label $^6_4$ indicates that intervals of a sixth and a fourth sound above the bass.

Individual diatonic triads can be identified precisely through Roman numerals and figured bass symbols, together with any additional symbol to specify quality. Viewing only a series of symbols, experienced musicians can "hear" a complete line of music. Popular and jazz composers, of course, do the same with their chord symbols.

This table reviews figured bass symbols and their meanings.

Figured Bass Symbols	Corresponding Bass Position
None	Root position
6	First inversion
$^6_4$	Second inversion

Follow the score as you listen to an edited version of the Lutheran melody "In God's Dear Name, I Close My Weary Eyes," harmonized by Johann Sebastian Bach (1685–1750). The passage is in G major and includes a variety of diatonic chords. Listen to the phrase at least three times. First, study the score as you listen. Next, view only the analytical symbols. Finally, listen a third time as you follow the score.

J. S. Bach, "In God's Dear Name, I Close My Weary Eyes"

For class discussion or assignment: please do not remove these pages

REVIEW SET

Figured Bass Symbols

A. Use Roman-numeral symbols and figured bass symbols to identify each chord in the key specified. There are two chords in each key. Visualize the triad in root position and without doublings.

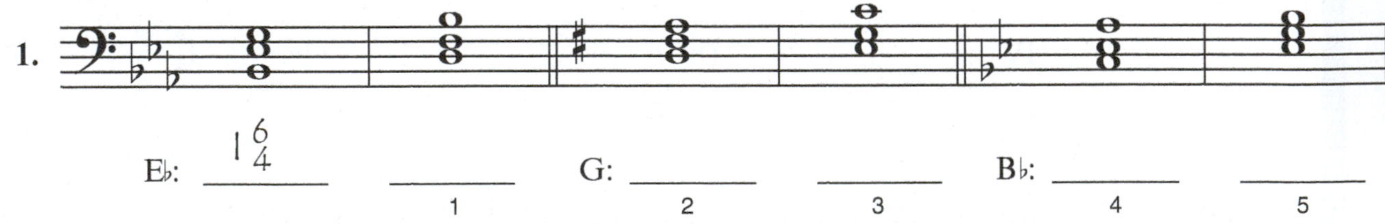

E♭: I 6/4 ____ ____ 1 G: ____ 2 ____ 3 B♭: ____ 4 ____ 5

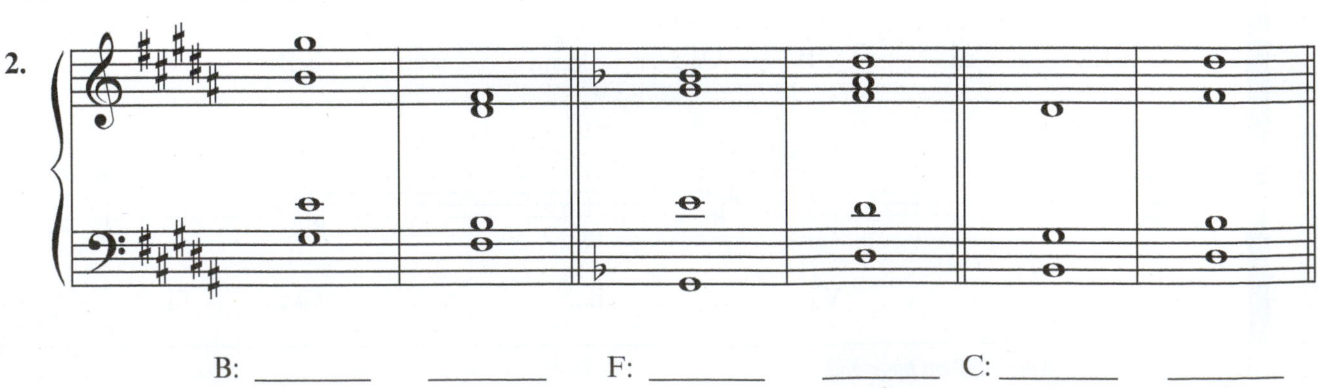

B: ____ 1 ____ 2 F: ____ 3 ____ 4 C: ____ 5 ____ 6

Construct the triad and provide the triad name.

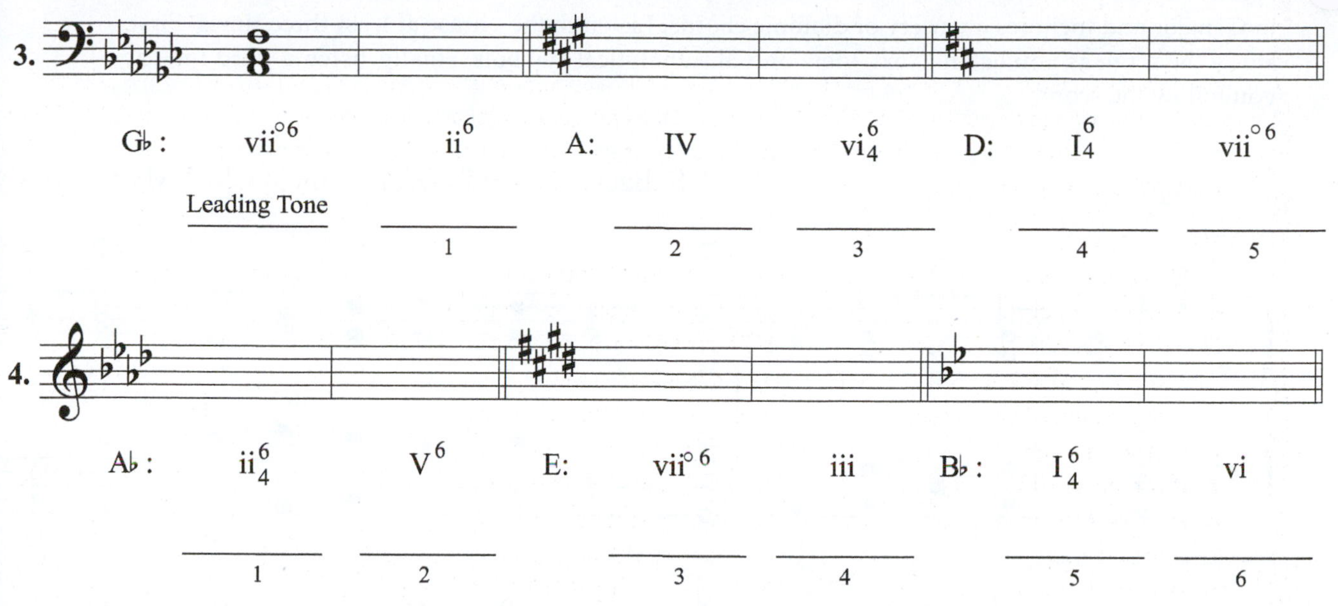

B. Reverse the process and construct triads from the given analytical symbol. Visualize or draft the triads in root position, then invert if necessary. There are two chords in each major key.

1. 1 2 3 4 5 6

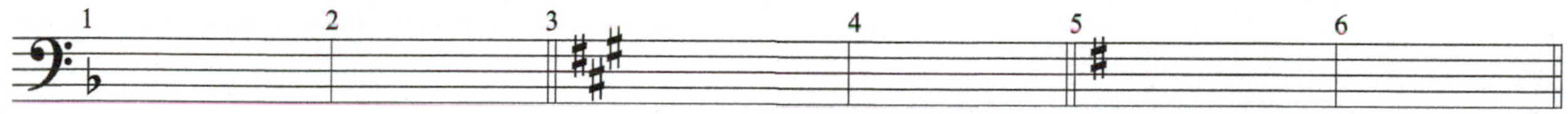

F: ii^6 V A: I IV G: vii$^{\circ 6}$ iii

2. 1 2 3 4 5 6

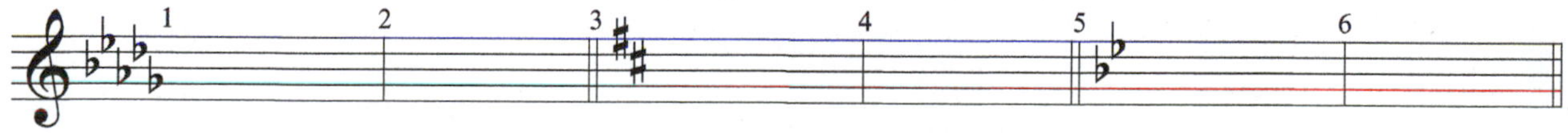

D♭: IV^6 vi D: ii vii$^{\circ 6}$ B♭: I$^6_4$ V

3. 1 2 3 4 5 6

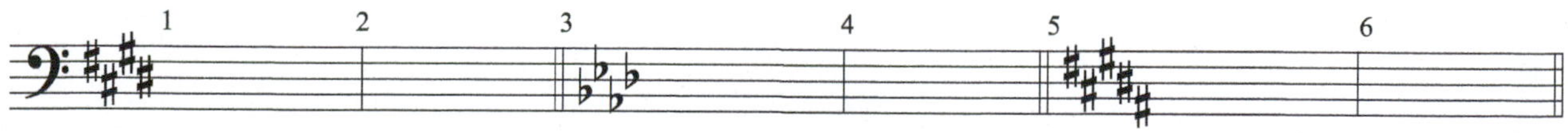

E: iii IV A♭: V^6 vii$^{\circ 6}$ B: vi V^6

4. 1 2 3 4 5 6

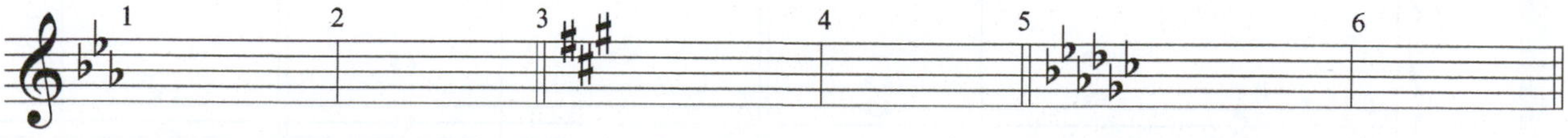

E♭: ii V$^6_4$ A: vii$^{\circ 6}$ vi G♭: iii IV$^6_4$

Complete Building Skills 11-2 on page 333

MUSICIANSHIP 11-2

Keyboard: Diatonic Triads in Major Keys

Playing individual diatonic triads is only slightly different from exercises you have done in previous chapters. Through visualization (do *not* notate triads on a staff), determine the appropriate root and play the triad in root position first. Follow this by inverting the triad if an inversion is indicated. Triads in several different keys are given, but you can repeat the exercise by substituting other keys.

Triad

1. B♭ major, first inversion
2. A minor, root position
3. E diminished, first inversion
4. F major, second inversion
5. E♭ augmented, first inversion
6. B minor, second inversion
7. G augmented, root position
8. F♯ major, second inversion
9. A♭ major, root position
10. D minor, first inversion
11. G♯ minor, root position
12. C minor, second inversion
13. B diminished, first inversion
14. A major, root position
15. G♭ major, second inversion
16. D augmented, first inversion
17. B major, second inversion
18. D♯ minor, root position
19. C♯ major, first inversion
20. G minor, root position

Diatonic Triads in Minor Keys

When the mode is minor, all triads except the tonic can appear in either of two qualities depending on the form of the minor scale in use. While the examples here illustrate possibilities within natural, harmonic, and melodic forms of minor, remember that composers virtually never adhere to any one form. The sixth scale degree may be raised in one chord and natural in the next; the same is true of the seventh degree.

Applying the minor key signature (without raised sixth and seventh scale degrees), the following triads result. Remember that the lowercase letter identifies a minor key, in this case, c minor.

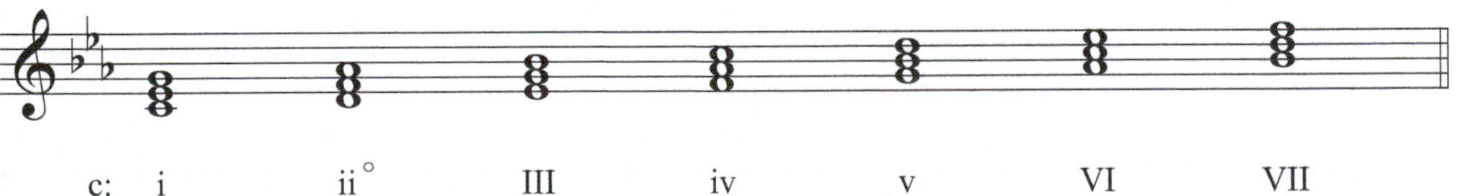

THE SUBTONIC TRIAD. A leading tone is, by definition, a diatonic half step below the tonic. In minor, however, as shown in the last example, the seventh scale degree is a *whole step* below the tonic. This pitch and the resulting major triad are called the **subtonic**.

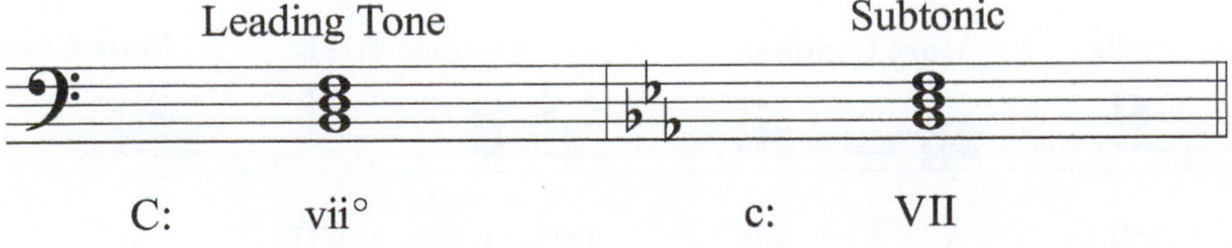

When the *raised* seventh is employed, three triads are affected. The mediant becomes augmented, the dominant is major, and the subtonic triad is replaced by a leading-tone triad.

If the raised six *and* seventh are used, three more triads are altered. The supertonic becomes minor (rather than diminished), the subdominant is major, and the submediant is diminished.

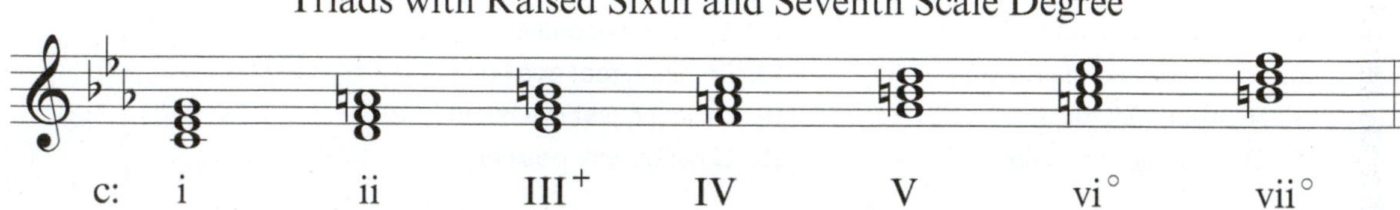

Although all of the chords in the last three examples are *possible,* the most common choices made by traditional composers are shown in the next example. The augmented mediant is rare; both the supertonic and the leading-tone triads are more commonly diminished.

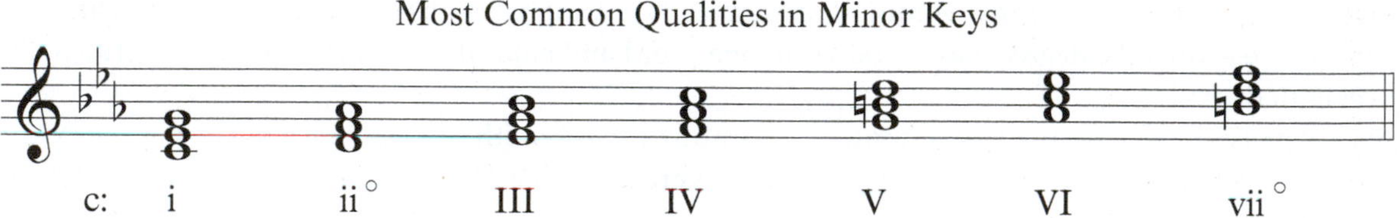

DOMINANT AND LEADING-TONE TRIADS IN MINOR. With occasional exceptions, the dominant triad is almost always major; the triad on the seventh degree is nearly always the diminished leading tone. Traditional composers liked the sound of the leading-tone pitch ascending to the tonic and they employed it in minor as well as major keys. Accordingly, observe this important rule when constructing dominant and leading-tone triads in minor keys:

> Dominant and leading-tone triads in minor require an accidental *outside* the minor key signature, which is the leading tone of the key. Remember, this "raised" seventh scale degree is also evidenced in the harmonic and melodic forms of the minor scale. The raised seventh scale degree in minor becomes the third of the dominant triad and the root of the leading tone triad.

Putting this rule into practice, check the construction of these two triads in D minor and F♯ minor.

For class discussion or assignment: please do not remove these pages

REVIEW SET

Triads and Chords in Minor

A. Provide a Roman-numeral analysis (including figured bass symbols).

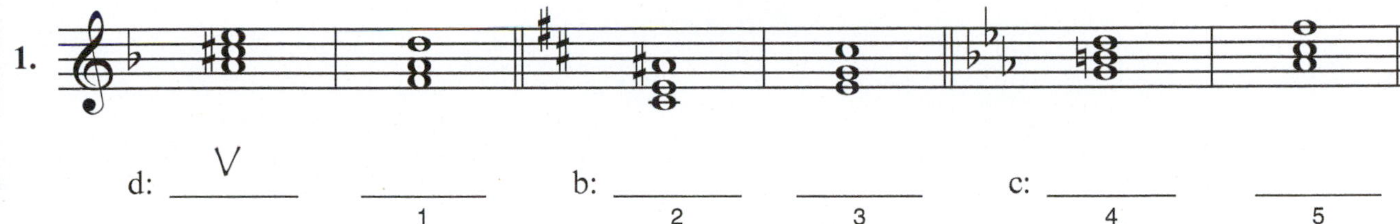

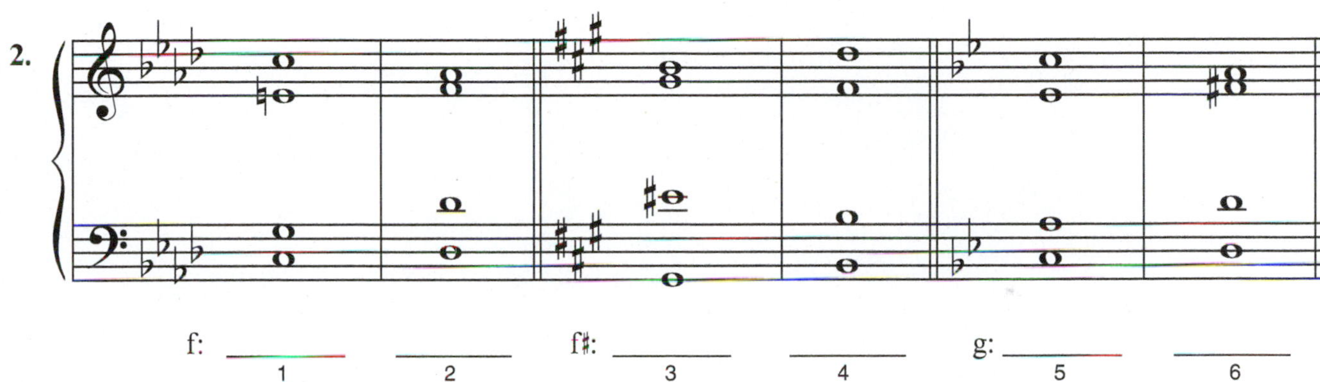

B. Begin by supplying the appropriate minor key signature, then construct triads that correspond to the Roman numerals. Remember that the Roman numeral specifies the quality of the triad and indicates whether you should use raised or natural $\hat{6}$ and raised or natural $\hat{7}$.

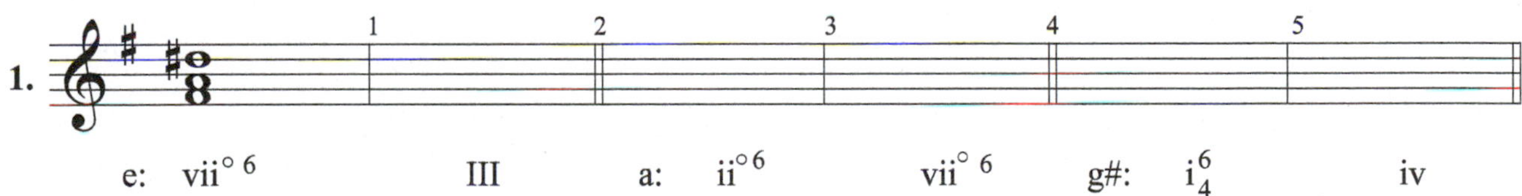

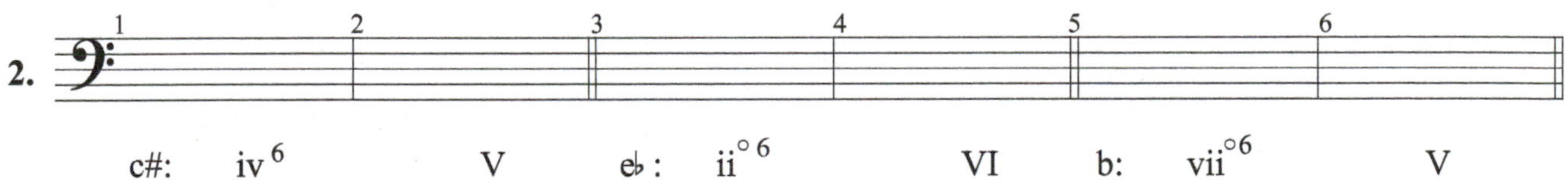

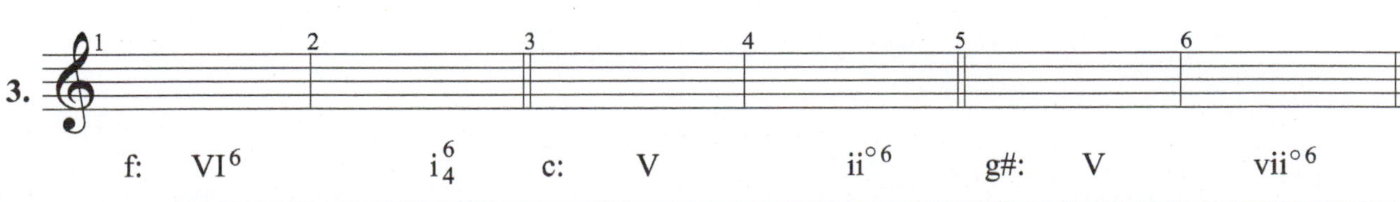

Complete Building Skills 11-3 on page 335

Building Skills • 11-1

Identifying Triads and Chords

A. In addition to implied triads, these chords include many different doublings and spacings. Identify root name, quality, and inversion. Include the abbreviation "INC" if the fifth is omitted from a triad. Use the lowest staff to renotate the chord as a triad (be sure to retain the original bass pitch).

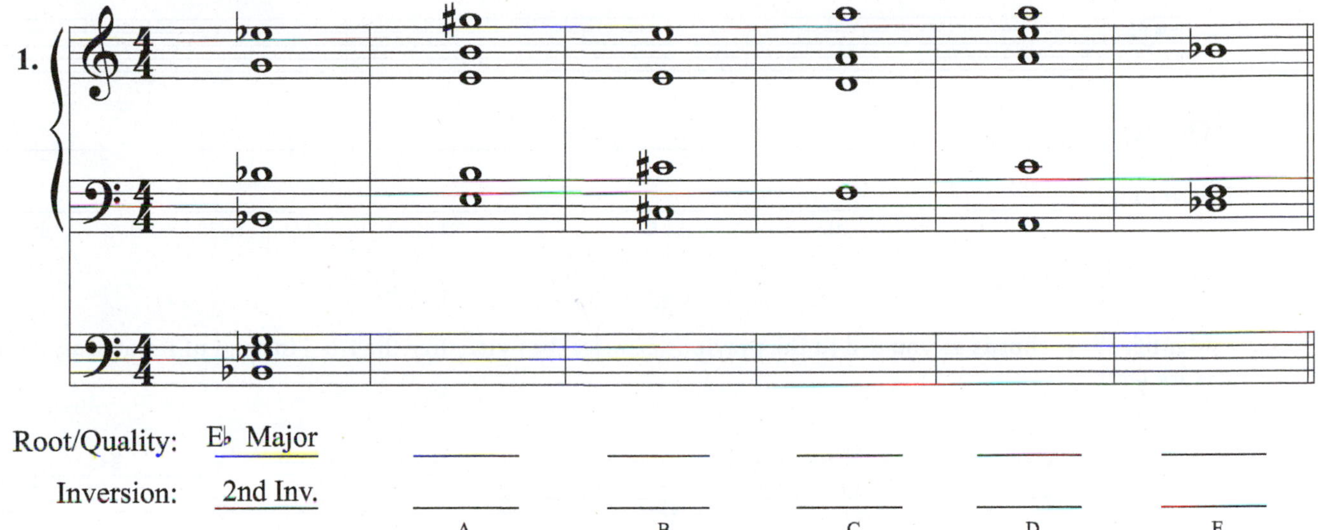

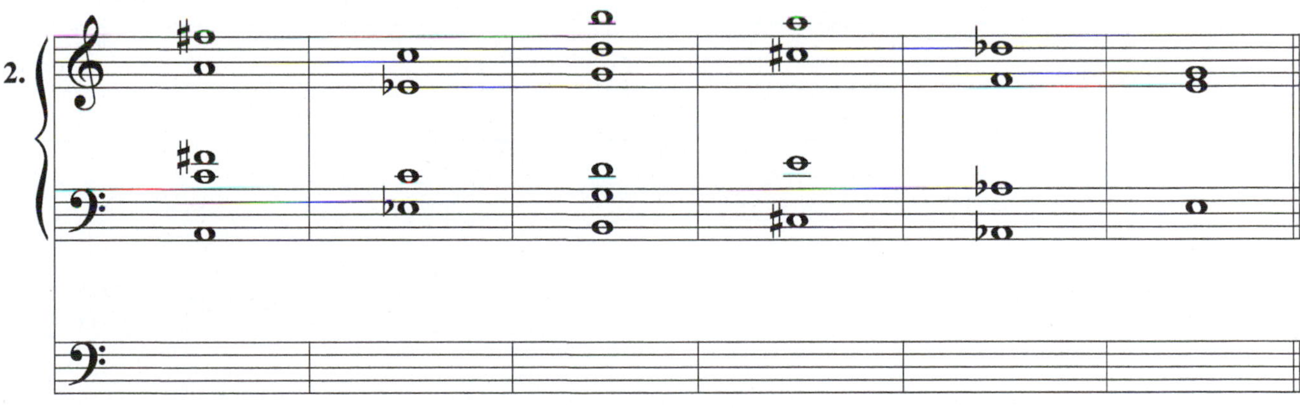

Root/Quality: ______ ______ ______ ______ ______ ______

Inversion: ______ ______ ______ ______ ______ ______

A B C D E F

Root/Quality: ______ ______ ______ ______ ______ ______

Inversion: ______ ______ ______ ______ ______ ______

A B C D E F

B. **Identify these chords as you did in the previous exercise, but visualize the triad instead of renotating it on a work staff.**

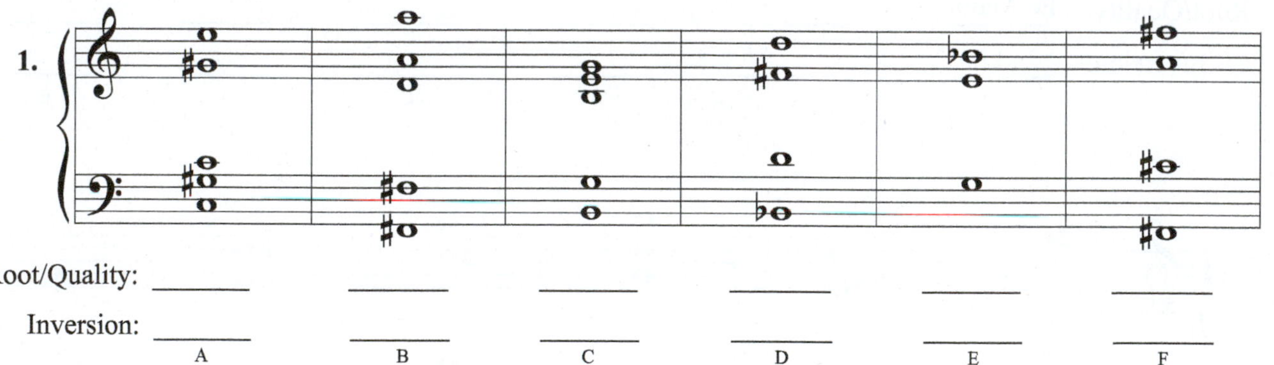

Root/Quality: ______ ______ ______ ______ ______ ______

Inversion: ______ ______ ______ ______ ______ ______

A B C D E F

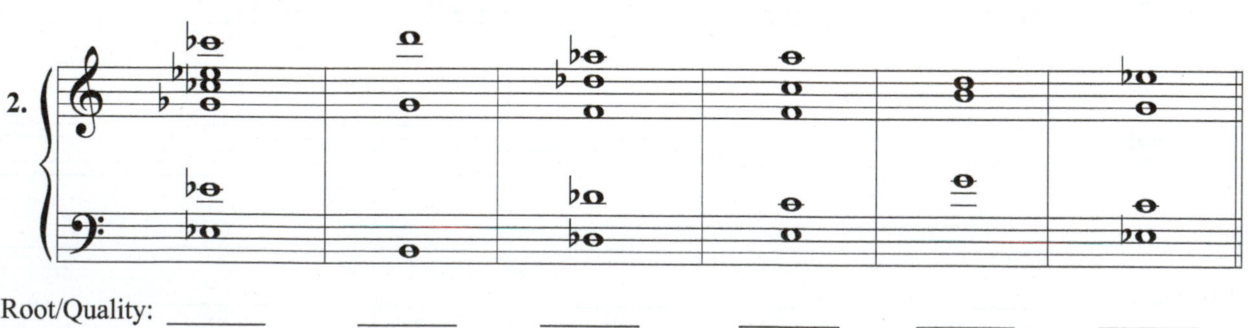

Root/Quality: ______ ______ ______ ______ ______ ______

Inversion: ______ ______ ______ ______ ______ ______

A B C D E F

Name ______________________________

Page may be removed

C. **These passages include triads that are arpeggiated. Identify them by root name and quality. (Be sure to take the key signature into account.)**

Name ______________________

Page may be removed

Building Skills • 11-2

Chord Symbols and Roman Numerals

A. **Construct triads as specified by the lead sheet symbol. Include all necessary accidentals.**

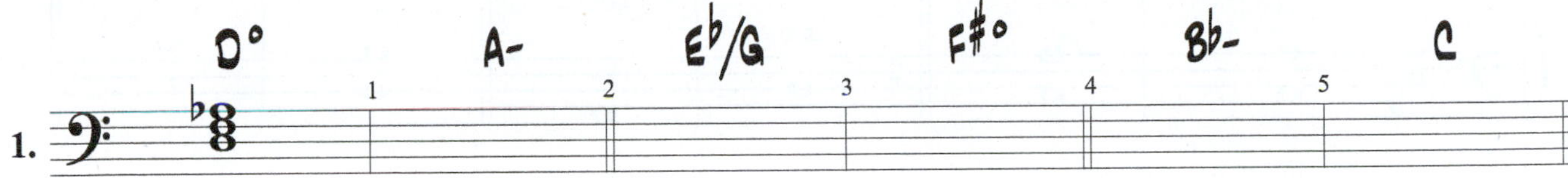

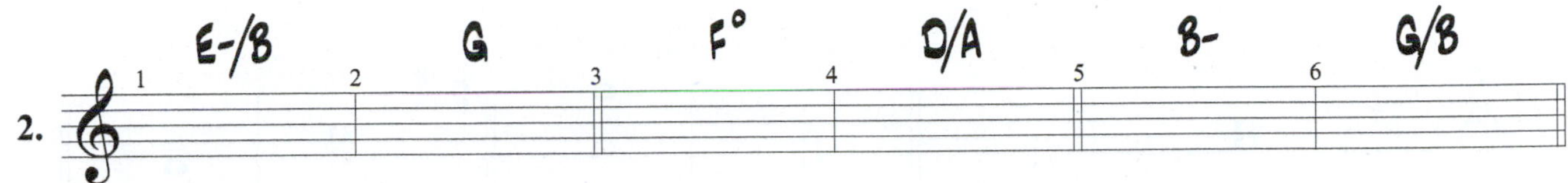

B. **Provide a chord symbol in the blank above the staff.**

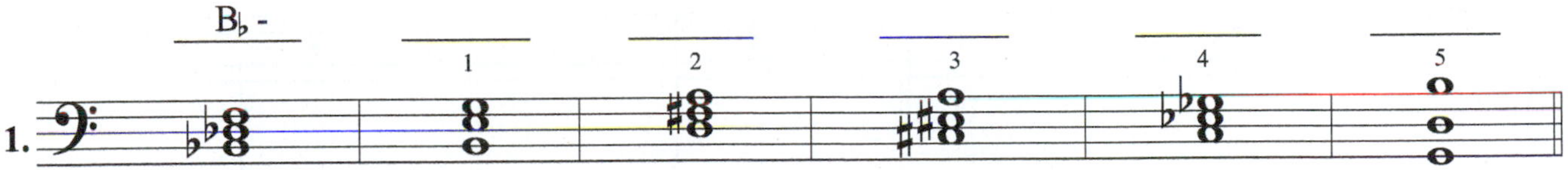

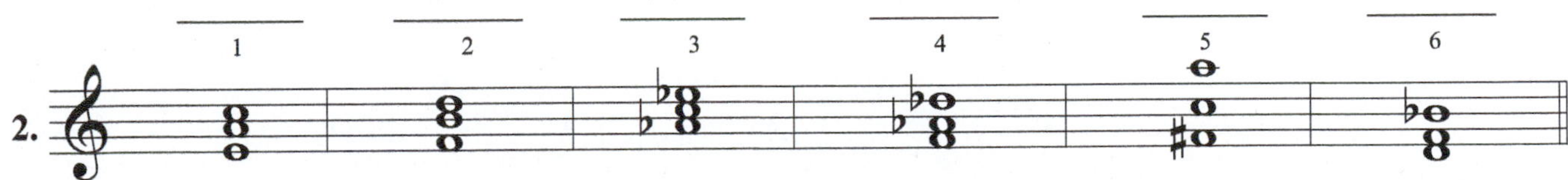

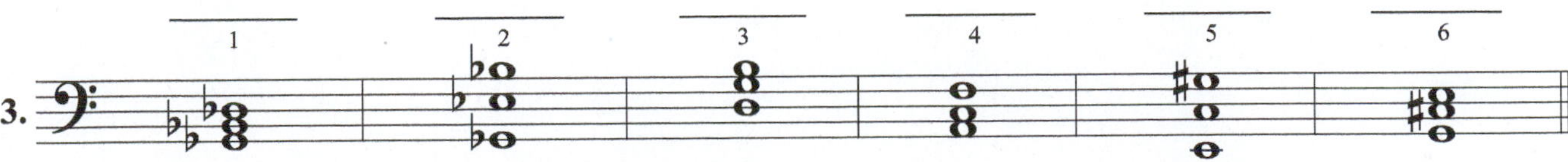

C. **Note the given key signature, then provide Roman numerals (and figured bass symbols) to identify the chord shown. Two chords are given in each key.**

1.

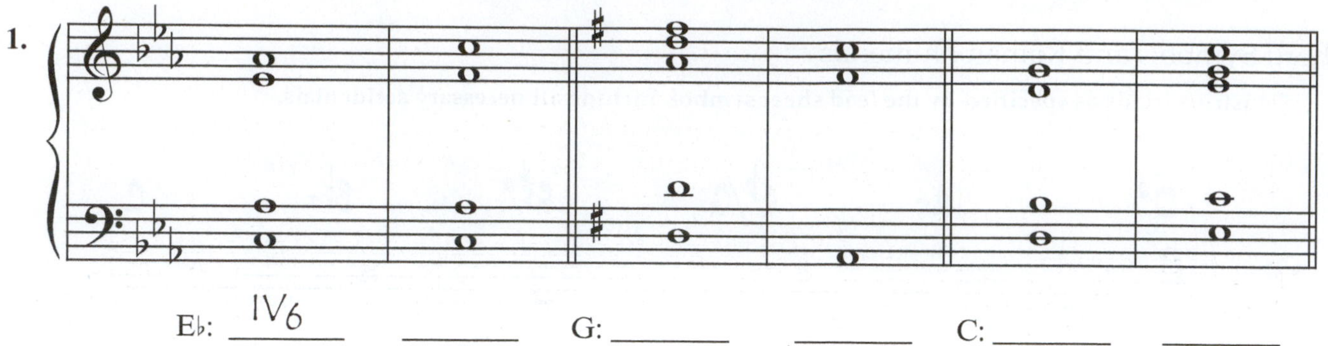

E♭: IV6 ______ ______ 1 G: ______ 2 ______ 3 C: ______ 4 ______ 5

2.

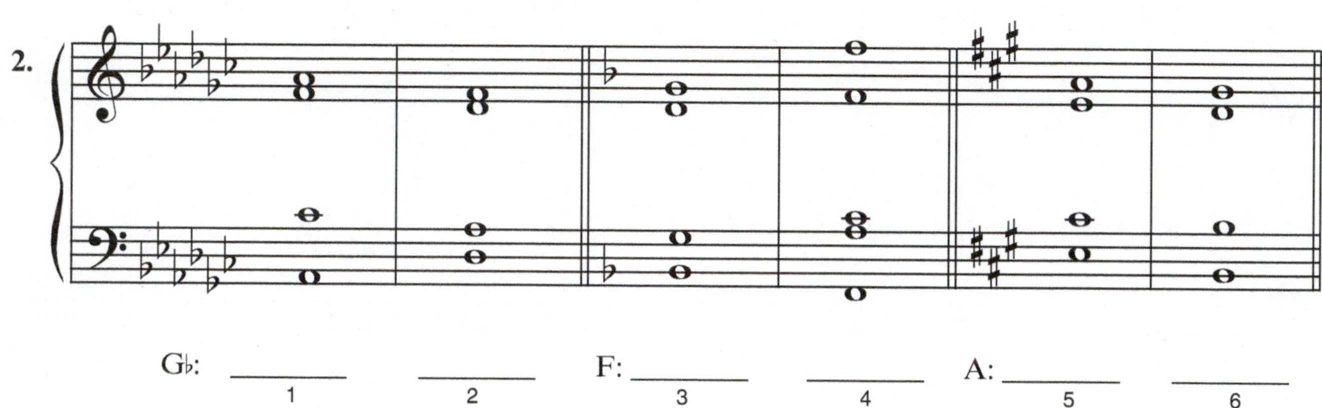

G♭: ______ 1 ______ 2 F: ______ 3 ______ 4 A: ______ 5 ______ 6

3.

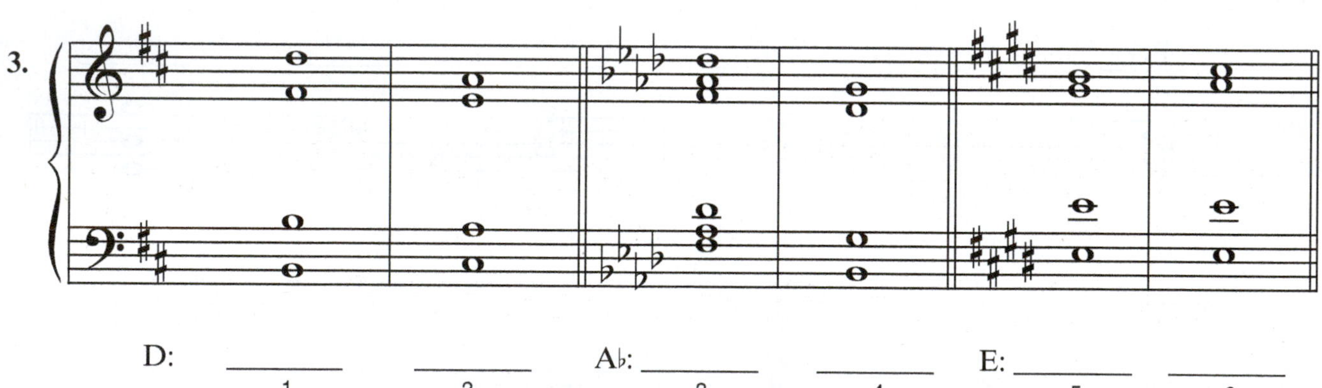

D: ______ 1 ______ 2 A♭: ______ 3 ______ 4 E: ______ 5 ______ 6

Name ________________

Page may be removed

Building Skills • 11-3

Roman Numerals in Major and Minor Keys

A. **Provide both a Roman numeral and a chord symbol for each chord in these frames. In the Roman-numeral blank, enter the precise designation including quality and figured bass symbols. With the chord symbols on the lower blank, describe the chord in terms of root name and quality and indicate inversion if necessary.**

B. **Provide the appropriate key signature and construct triads in major and parallel minor keys as indicated.**

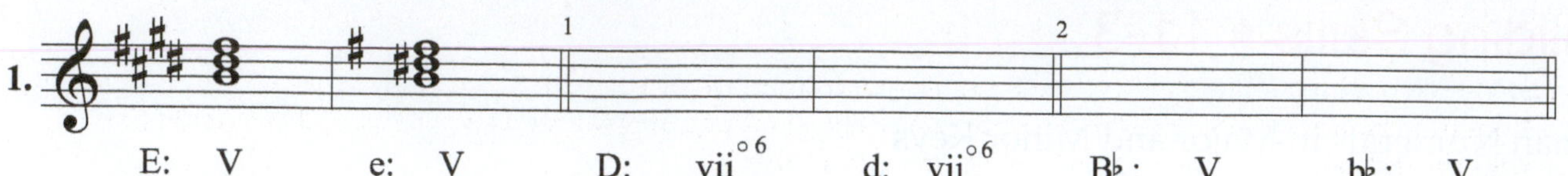

E: V e: V D: $\text{vii}^{\circ 6}$ d: $\text{vii}^{\circ 6}$ B♭: V b♭: V

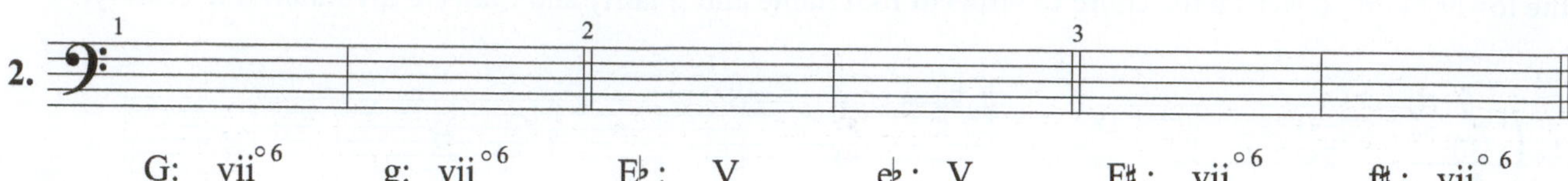

G: $\text{vii}^{\circ 6}$ g: $\text{vii}^{\circ 6}$ E♭: V e♭: V F♯: $\text{vii}^{\circ 6}$ f♯: $\text{vii}^{\circ 6}$

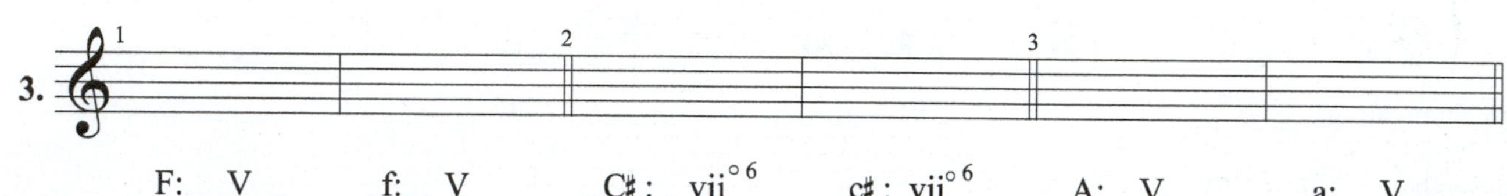

F: V f: V C♯: $\text{vii}^{\circ 6}$ c♯: $\text{vii}^{\circ 6}$ A: V a: V

C. **Provide an appropriate major or minor key signature and construct the triads (closed position) specified by the Roman-numeral symbol. Add accidentals where necessary.**

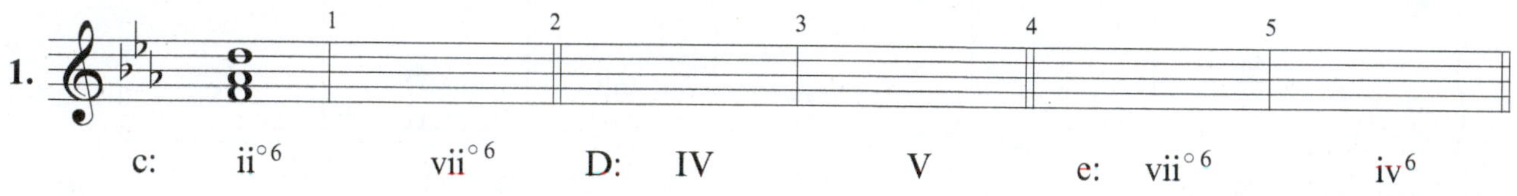

c: $\text{ii}^{\circ 6}$ $\text{vii}^{\circ 6}$ D: IV V e: $\text{vii}^{\circ 6}$ iv^{6}

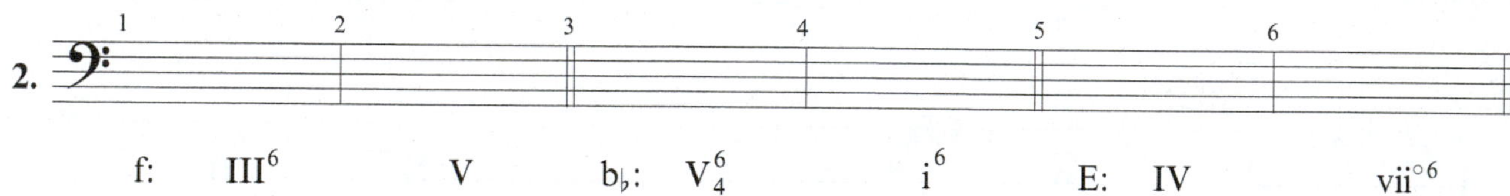

f: III^{6} V b♭: V^{6}_{4} i^{6} E: IV $\text{vii}^{\circ 6}$

D♭: ii^{6} vi f♯: $\text{vii}^{\circ 6}$ ii B: V^{6} I^{6}_{4}

Name ______________________

Page may be removed

Creative Projects • Chapter 11

A. **Use the work staff to reduce the chords to root-position or inverted triads. Next, in the blanks below provide a Roman-numeral symbol to identify each triad. The smaller notes (called *nonchord tones*) lie outside the harmony and can be excluded from your harmonic analysis.**

J. S. Bach, "The Star Proclaims the King Is Here"
Chorale Harmonization

g: i i6 ___ ___ ___ ___ ___ ___ ___
1 2 3 4 5 6 7

Dimitri Bortniansky, *St. Petersburg*

C: I I^6_4 ___ ___ ___ ___ ___ ___ ___
1 2 3 4 5 6 7

___ ___ ___ ___ ___
8 9 10 11 12

B. **Continue these melodies in the same style while conforming to the period or phrase-group structure indicated. First, complete the triads in the lower staff. Next, select tones from each chord that combine to make an effective melody. Pay special attention to cadential pitches; ideally, there should be only one pitch in the fourth and eighth measures.**

Name ________________________

Page may be removed

Analysis in Context 1 • Chapter 11

"Jenny Jenkins" was a popular courting song from colonial days. It is based upon traditional color symbolism, where red stands for sin, blue for faithfulness, white for purity. Subsequent verses ask about other colors. By asking the girl what color of dress she will wear, the suitor is looking for her quick wit and charm in respons to his questions.

Folk Song, "Jenny Jenkins"

1. In what key is this song written?

2. The first three and a half measures use a sustained G chord. List the names of the pitches that should be included in this chord.

3. Study the melody in measures 1–3. Circle the pitches in the melody that are part of the G major chord.

4. Using the same chord referred to in Question 2, use the lead sheet notation to determine if the chord is in root position, first inversion, or second inversion.

5. There is a chord change on beat 3 of measure 4 to D7. What notes are missing from the melody that must be included in the chord?

6. Using the same triad referred to in Question 4, determine whether the triad is in root position, first inversion, or second inversion.

7. On beat 4 of measure 7, what chord does the lead sheet indicate should be played?

8. Spell the chord referred to in the previous question.

9. The time signature for this folk song tells us that there are _______ beats in each measure and that a _______ note equals one beat.

10. Write out the rhythmic counts (i.e., takadimi) for measures 5–10.

Chapter 12
Tonality

Essential Terms

active pitch
consonance
contrapuntal
dissonance
dominant function
dominant seventh chord
harmonic functions
homophony
imitation
improvisation
major-minor seventh chord
melodic tendency
polyphony
predominant function
seventh chord
stable pitch
texture
tonality
tonic function

From infancy we hear music through a variety of media, television, and theater. In the process, we become so familiar with traditional melodic, rhythmic, and harmonic patterns that we soon learn to expect certain patterns with a wide range of musical styles. The expectations we develop over time are a combination of musical elements, such as **texture**, **tonality**, and **harmonic function**.

Texture

Texture in music is the complexity and design of individual voices as they contribute to the whole. In a sense, you can think of musical texture as we do the weave of cloth; the closer the weave, the more dense our perception of texture. Between the tenth and seventeenth centuries, much of Western music centered on a texture called polyphony.

A layering of voices that are *equal* in importance is called **polyphony**. In polyphonic compositional practice, several individual lines are crafted so that, while the composition forms a unified whole, two, three, or more individual lines are heard as equal in importance.

J. S. Bach is considered a master of traditional counterpoint. The excerpt shown in the next passage is based on **imitation**. This means that one voice enters, then, as if in a dialogue, the other voices enter with the same or similar material. The "a3" symbol at the top left of the score means that there are 3 "voices" that contribute to the texture. They are made visually apparent by stem direction (see measure 6). Listen to, or play the melody, of measures 1–5. Hum along to get to know this melody. Then listen to the whole example, making note of where you hear it again. The fact that you hear the melody in each voice adds to the independence of each line in the polyphonic texture.

J. S. Bach, Little Fugue in G Minor, BWV 578

Homophony

Composers often use a memorable melody in one voice with less important, accompanying material in the others. This "melody and accompaniment" musical texture, termed **homophony**, originated in the late sixteenth century and has been a prominent feature of Western music ever since. Homophony has been popular with musical styles that feature improvisation because we can compose a strong melody, suggest the chords, and let performers fill in the harmony.

Listen to the excerpt from "Standchen." The texture is homophonic. The passage shown includes only four different chords (d minor, B♭, g minor, and A); the meter is triple and the accompaniment part provides support for the moving melodic line.

Melodic Tendency

Composers create the effect of **tonality** by making the listener hear one of the 12 pitches as more important than the others. We can create this effect with melody alone, with harmony alone, or through a combination of melodic and harmonic means. As long as you stick to patterns that are well known and understood, composing tonal works "by ear" is not an insurmountable task.

The pitches in a well-constructed melody have a sense of momentum and order known as **melodic tendency**. More active pitches gravitate toward stable ones. **Stable pitches** are those in the tonic triad, while other pitches are relatively **active**. The pitches termed as active are often called tendency tones. In considering melodic tendencies, be aware that composers sometimes ignore them for the sake of creating a memorable phrase or to emphasize the text. Likewise, pitches that follow leaps are more likely to adhere to tendencies than those in a stepwise pattern.

Let's examine common tendencies in major keys. The leading-tone pitch has the strongest tendency and gravitates toward the tonic. Likewise, $\hat{4}$ usually falls to $\hat{3}$ (reinforcing the mode). The supertonic pitch ($\hat{2}$) has a weak tendency and may ascend to $\hat{3}$ or descend to $\hat{1}$. The sixth scale degree is also more ambiguous and may fall to $\hat{5}$ or ascend to $\hat{7}$ and on up to $\hat{8}$. View the next example as an illustration of tonal principles and not as strict rules of composition.

Melodic Tendencies in C Major

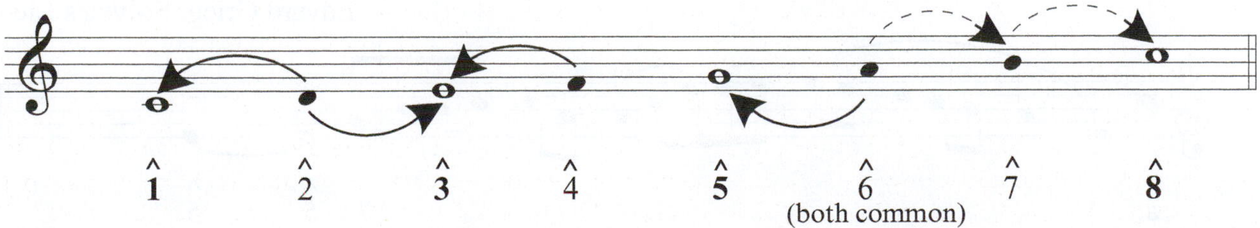

Whether we are aware of the underlying theory or not, melodic tendencies guide us when we sing or play "by ear." If tendencies are ignored repeatedly, the listener may hear the melody as rambling.

MELODIC TENDENCIES IN MINOR KEYS. Melodic tendencies in minor keys are more complicated because we have the choice between raised or natural $\hat{6}$ and raised or natural $\hat{7}$. In minor, the pitches of the tonic triad are stable, as they are in major. The second and fourth scale degrees, together with the raised sixth degree and the leading tone $\hat{7}$ also have the same tendencies as in major.

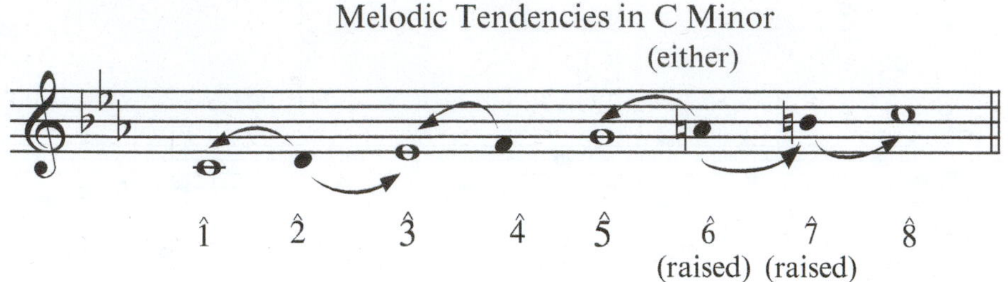

Both the subtonic pitch and the natural sixth scale degrees typically descend to $\hat{5}$.

Melodic Tendencies in C Minor

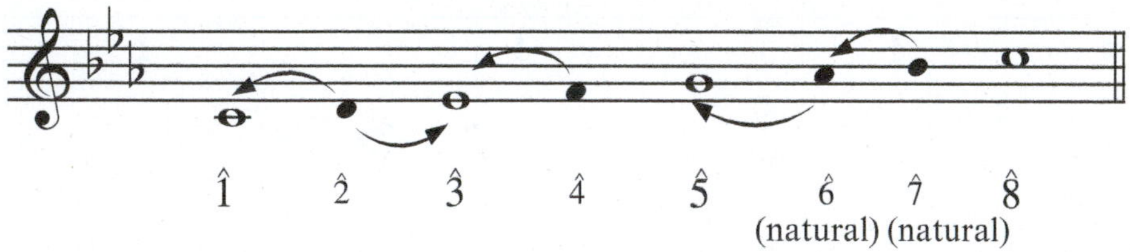

This phrase from the opera *Carmen* by Georges Bizet (1838–1875) is basically a descending scale fragment in D minor. Notice the use of the raised and natural $\hat{7}$ and natural $\hat{6}$. In measure 4, the C♯ functions as a leading tone and ascends to D. In measure 7, however, where the pitch A is the goal (a progressive cadence), Bizet uses the subtonic pitch (C♭).

George Bizet, Intermezzo from *Carmen*

On the other hand, composers often ignore melodic tendencies to furnish the pitch they consider musically, rather than theoretically, correct. This passage in A minor by Edvard Grieg (1843–1907) is similar to Bizet's descending scale, yet on the way down to a progressive cadence on E, Grieg uses the unresolved leading tone.

Edvard Grieg, Solveg's Lied

For class discussion or assignment: please do not remove these pages

REVIEW SET

Active and Stable Pitches

A. For each fragment given, label the scale degree above the last pitch. Determine whether the last pitch is active ("A") or stable ("S"). If the last pitch is active, use the blank frame to provide a stable pitch or pitches to which it would likely gravitate. Leave the frame blank if the last pitch is stable.

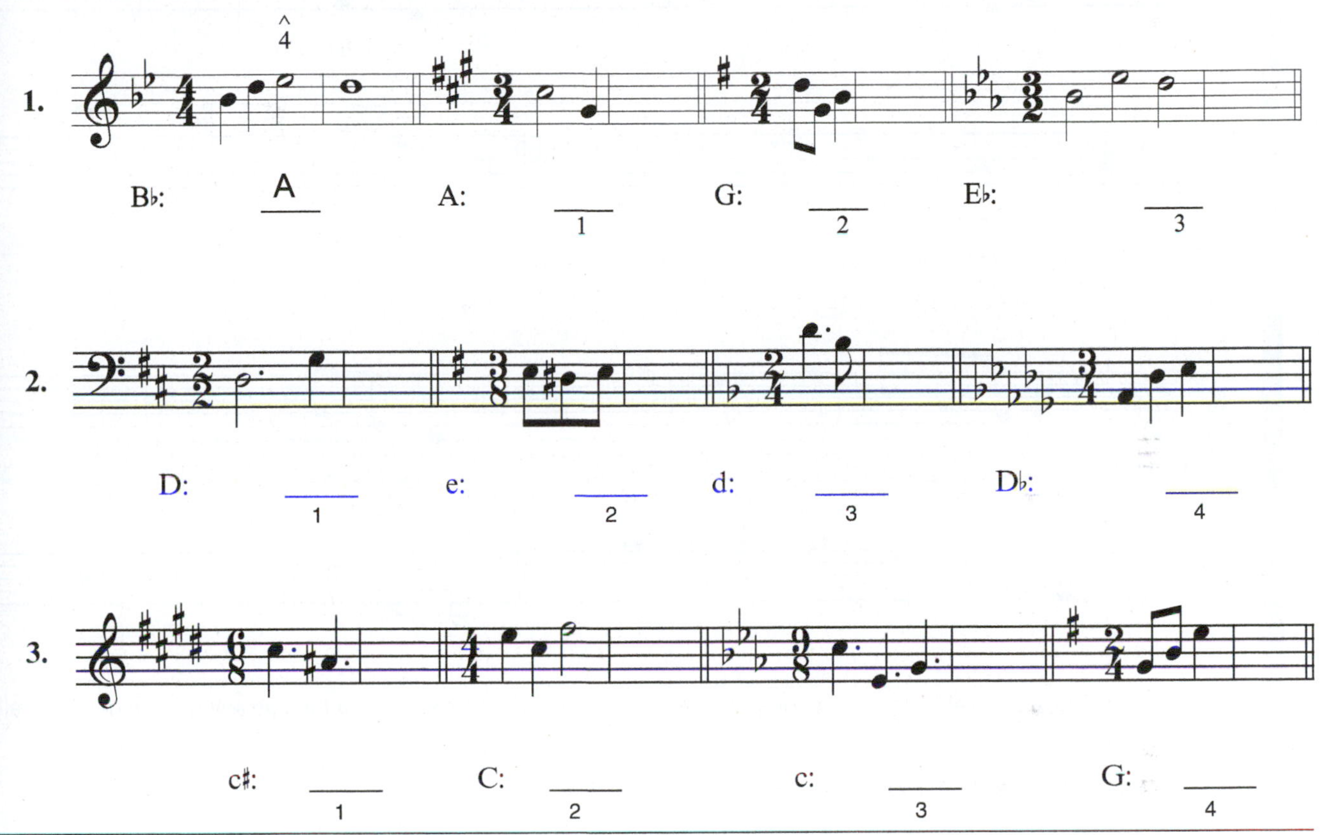

Complete Building Skills 12-1 on page 359

MUSICIANSHIP 12-1

Sight Singing: Tendency Tones

A. These exercises center on the tendency of the leading tone in major and minor keys. Begin by arpeggiating a tonic triad, descend to the leading tone, then resolve that pitch through a return to tonic. While the number of keys shown is limited, you can practice the same exercises throughout your range. Use a different octave as necessary.

Leading Tone: Major and Minor Keys

2. 1 2

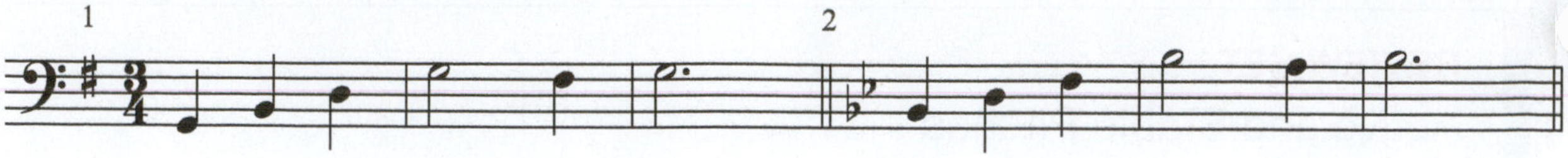

3. 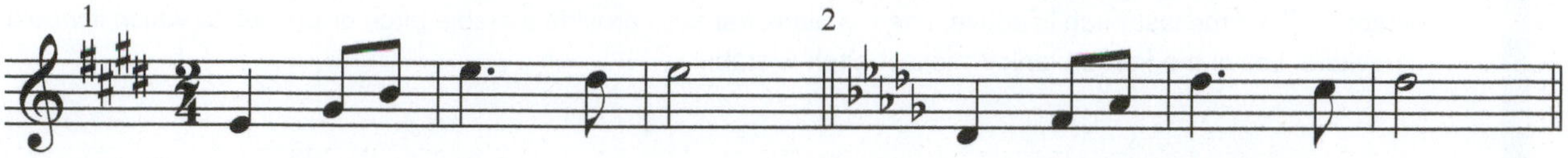 1 2

4. 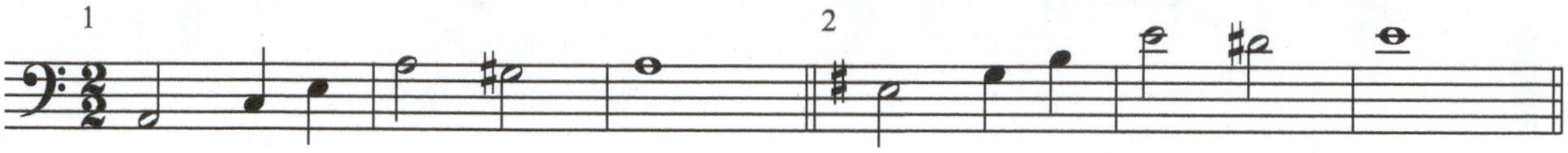 1 2

1 3 5 1 7 1
do me sol do ti do

5. 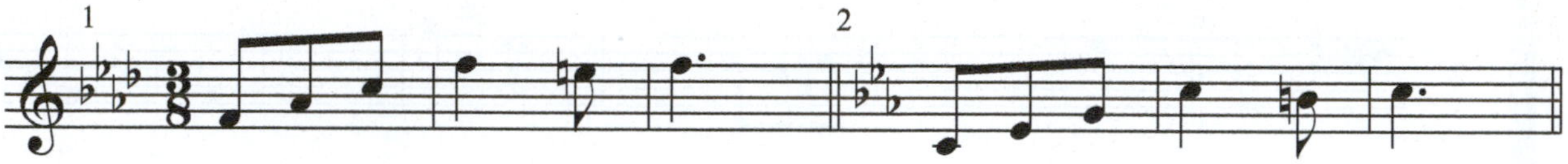 1 2

6. 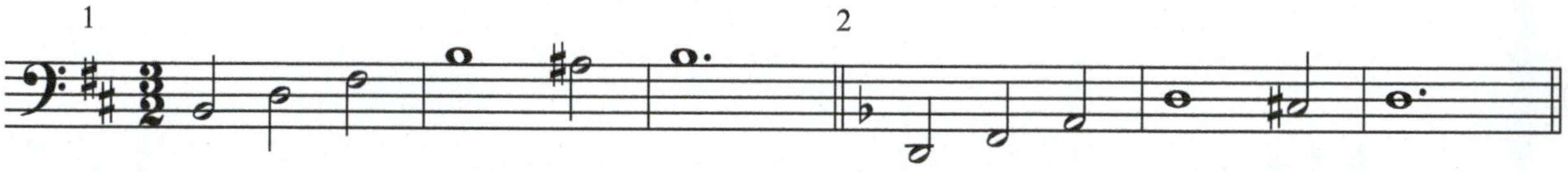 1 2

B. In these lines, arpeggiate a tonic triad, descend back to $\hat{5}$, then continue descending through $\hat{4}$ and its tendency to fall to $\hat{3}$. As in earlier exercises, practice the patterns in other keys in addition to those shown.

Fourth Scale Degree: Major and Minor Keys

Harmonic Function

A study of **harmonic function** focuses on the use of chords to create a sense of tonality.

Tonic, Predominant, and Dominant Functions

Western music centers on three different harmonic roles (or functions). Two or three functions, used over and over again, often form the basis of a musical work. In "classical" music, variety may come through embellishment and a wide variety of chords in each of the categories. But in popular music, as we have discussed, interest and variety more often spring from the performer. Whether the music is by Mozart or Maroon 5, tonality emerges from a variety of patterns of *tonic, predominant*, and *dominant function chords*.

TONIC FUNCTION. Just as the tonic pitch is stable, the **tonic function** is the goal of a chord progression. The tonic function is represented by the tonic triad and, less often, by the submediant. These two chords share two common tones (stable scale degrees 1 and 3) and thus can easily serve the same role. Compositions often begin with the tonic; they almost invariably end on tonic; and throughout a composition, the tonic is heard as an arrival, the goal of most intermediate chord progressions. If a phrase, period, or phrase group ends with the tonic triad and with the tonic pitch in the melody, we hear the arrival as especially strong.

In the next illustration, we can view the tonic as a point of arrival—the musical goal of a progression.

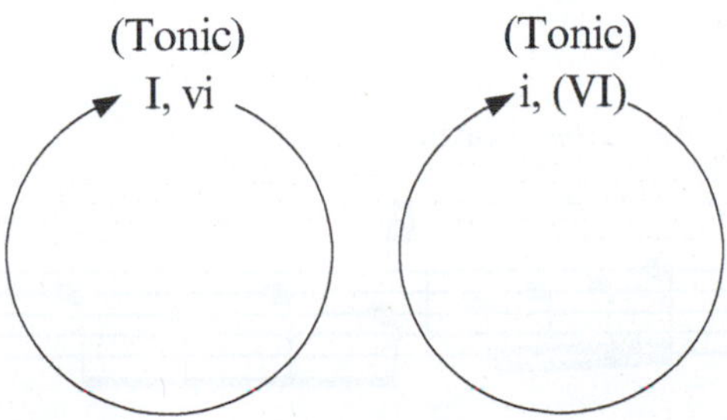

DOMINANT FUNCTION. While the tonic function is one of stability, the **dominant function** includes chords containing the leading tone and represents momentum. The dominant and leading-tone triads have equivalent dominant function and they both generally progress to the tonic. Like the tonic function chords, dominant function chords share two common tones, unstable scale degrees 7 and 2. The choice between chords within a function is usually made on the basis of an accompaniment pattern or the pitches present or absent in the melody.

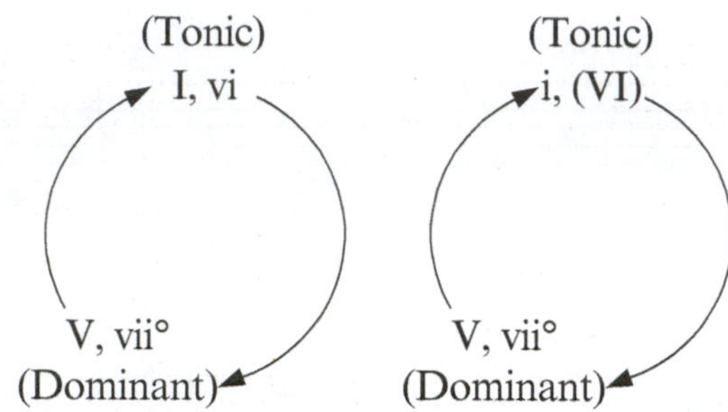

The interplay of tonic and dominant provides sufficient variety for shorter compositions. Listen to the Irish folk song "The Galway Piper" online. We could use a wider variety of chords, but the tonic and dominant functions (arrival–momentum–arrival) adequately support the melody.

With symbols, we can specify the same chords.

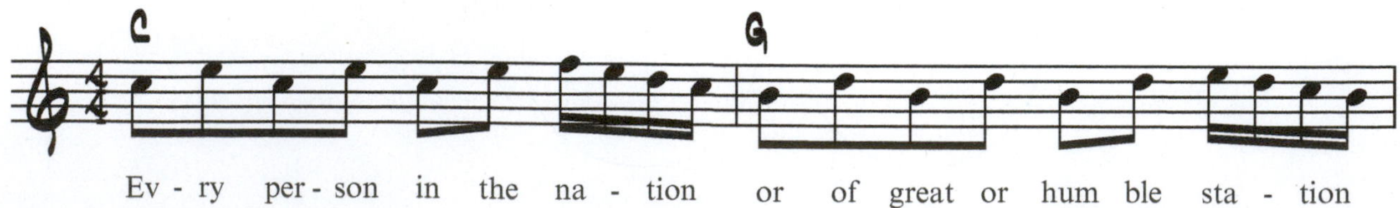

PREDOMINANT FUNCTION. The **predominant function** provides an intermediate point between the stability of the tonic and the momentum of the dominant. The supertonic and subdominant triads have predominant function and complete the cycle.[1] These two chords share common tones as well, scale degrees 4 and 6. In some instances, the vi can also lead to dominant chords, especially in popular music.

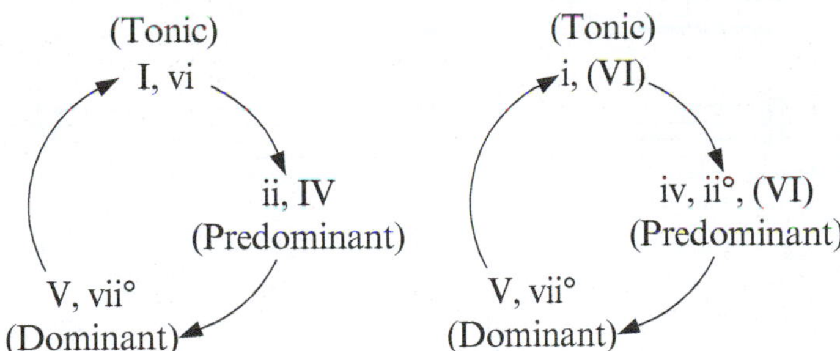

Many melodies in a variety of styles can be harmonized with only three chords. Look again at "Standchen" by Schubert. The key is D minor, and the use of the tonic, dominant, and subdominant chords is traditional. Notice how the passage ends with a tonic chord. The B-flat major chord is a VI chord and in the context of this progression it is functioning as a predominant.

The American folk song "Red River Valley" has much in common with "Standchen." Listen to a recording and notice how this folk song is less active rhythmically, but the repetition, sequence of harmonic function, and the variety of diatonic pitches are all about the same.

[1]Composers veer from harmonic function for variety or special effect. The progression I–IV–I is quite common—especially in the middle of a phrase.

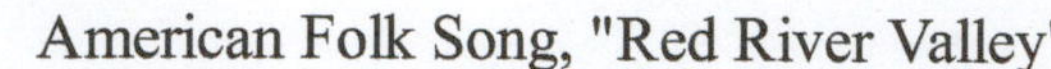

In its most simple form, a 12-bar blues progression is a series of three 4-measure phrases. While 8 of the 12 measures usually consist of tonic harmony, predominant and dominant functions maintain interest and clarify the tonality. In the hands of a skilled blues composer, melodic and harmonic colorations affect virtually every chord.

Swing! ♫ = ♩♪ (3)

Simple Blues Progression and Melody

B♭ B♭ B♭ B♭

B♭: I I I I

E♭ E♭ B♭ B♭

IV IV I I

F7 E♭ B♭ B♭

V^7 IV I I

For class discussion or assignment: please do not remove these pages

REVIEW SET

Harmonic Function

A. Write a triad that serves the indicated function. Begin by writing the appropriate key signature, supply a Roman-numeral symbol, and then notate the triad. Use accidentals as necessary.

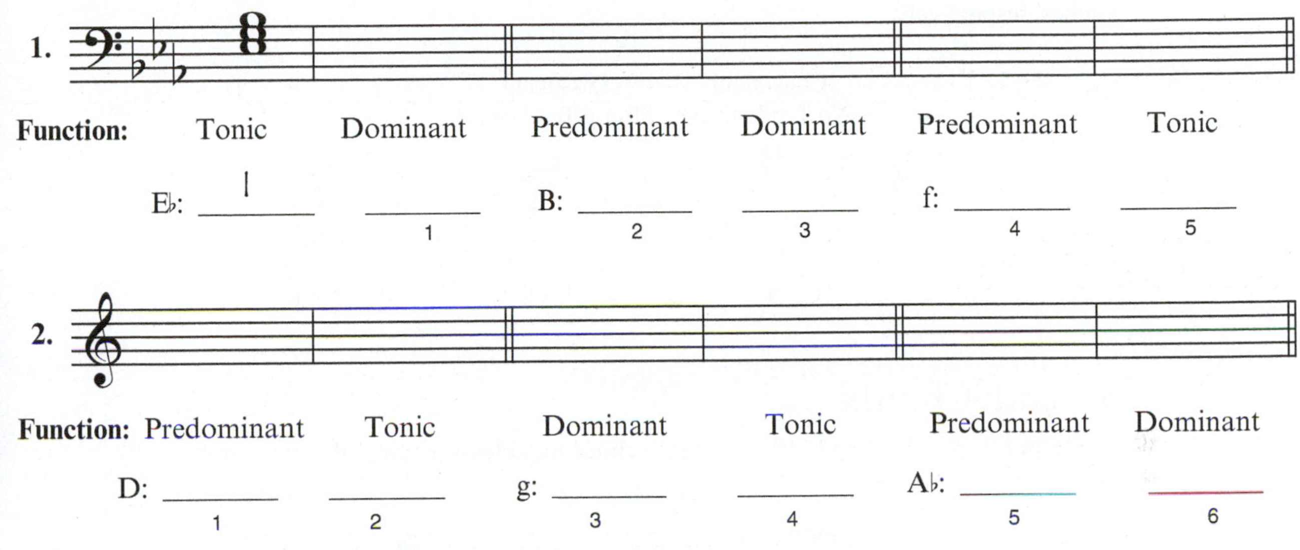

B. In addition to Roman-numeral symbols, identify the function of each chord in the given key. Write "tonic," "predominant," or "dominant" in the blank.

Complete Building Skills 12-2 on page 361

Harmonic Dissonance

A **consonance** in tonal music is an interval or chord that is stable; other pitches and chords move or resolve toward these consonances. When an interval or chord is active, with a tendency to resolve, it is termed a **dissonance**. The component intervals of a triad or chord determine whether it is consonant or dissonant. Major and minor tertian triads are stable because they include a perfect fifth. On the other hand, a diminished triad is dissonant because it contains a tritone. In the leading-tone triad, for example, the fourth and seventh scale degrees create momentum and resolve to tonic and mediant pitches, respectively.

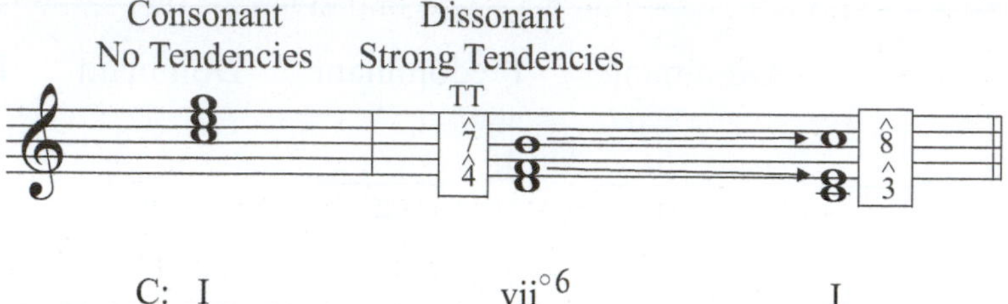

Seventh Chords

In addition to the third and fifth, a **seventh chord** includes a seventh above the root.

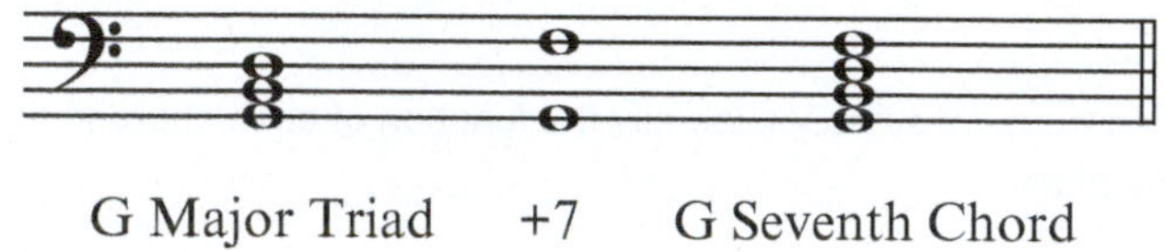

DOMINANT SEVENTH CHORD. Several different qualities are possible by adding a seventh above the bass of a diatonic triad. We identify quality by the structure of the triad and the quality of the seventh above the root. By far the most frequently used seventh chord occurs on the dominant pitch (5), a dominant function. The **dominant seventh chord** (also called a **major-minor seventh chord**) is a major triad with an added minor seventh.

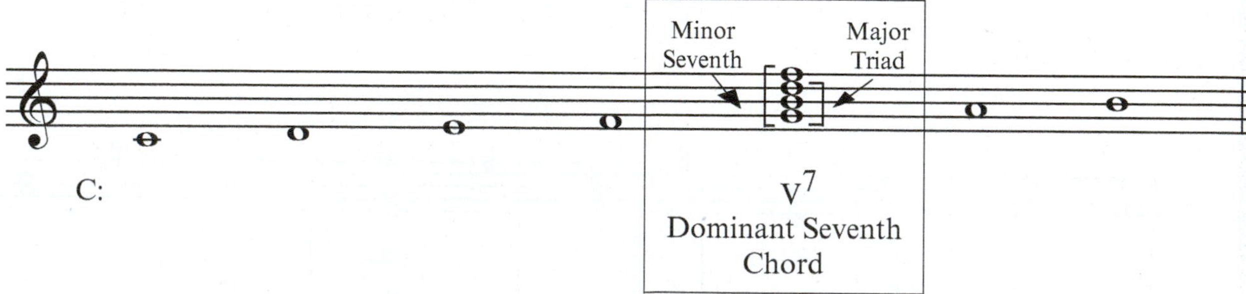

ANALYZING SEVENTH CHORDS WITH ROMAN NUMERALS. In analysis, we indicate a root-position seventh chord by adding the numeral 7 to the Roman-numeral symbol. The chords in the next example are dominant sevenths. Notice that the third of the dominant triad, as always, is raised in minor keys. This raised pitch is the leading tone.

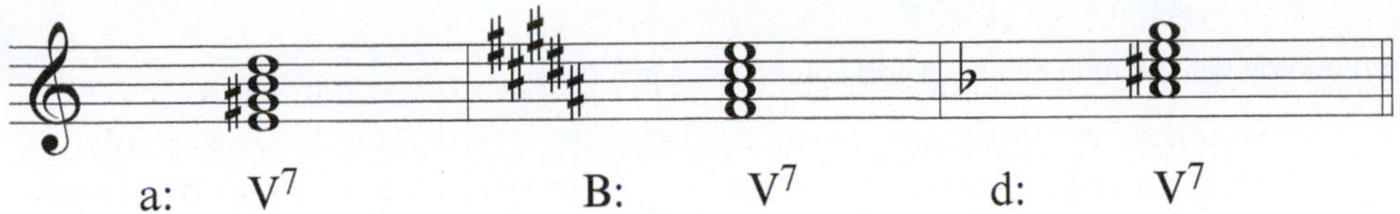

There are *three* inversions of a seventh chord because, in addition to root position, we can have the third, fifth, *or seventh* in the bass. The full designations for seventh chords in first, second, and third inversions are $\substack{6\\5\\3}$, $\substack{6\\4\\3}$, and $\substack{6\\4\\2}$. As with triads, however, abbreviated designations are more common. A seventh chord in first inversion is indicated by the numerals $\substack{6\\5}$, second inversion by $\substack{4\\3}$, and third inversion by $\substack{4\\2}$ (sometimes just as 2).

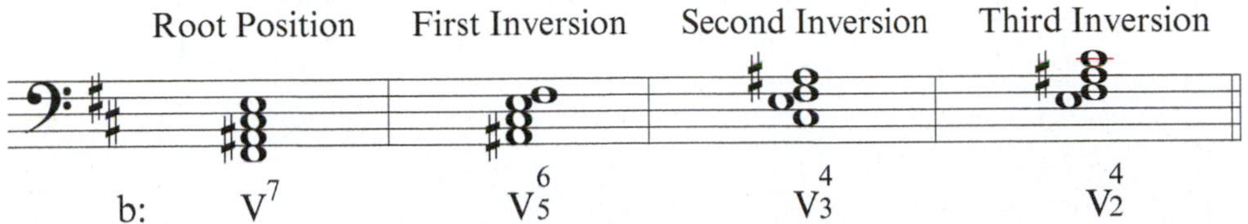

Review the abbreviated Arabic-numeral labels for triads and seventh chords.

Arabic Label	Chord Structure
None	Triad, root position
6	Triad, first inversion
$\substack{6\\4}$	Triad, second inversion
7	Seventh chord, root position
$\substack{6\\5}$	Seventh chord, first inversion
$\substack{4\\3}$	Seventh chord, second inversion
$\substack{4\\2}$	Seventh chord, third inversion

For class discussion or assignment: please do not remove these pages

REVIEW SET

Dominant Seventh Chords

A. Construct these chords in closed position. Many are dominant seventh chords, but others are simple triads. Add any necessary accidentals.

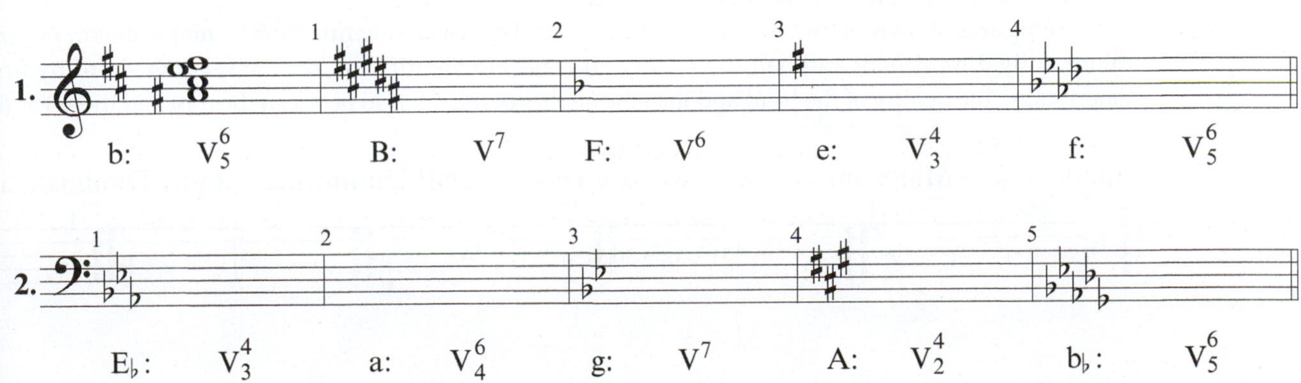

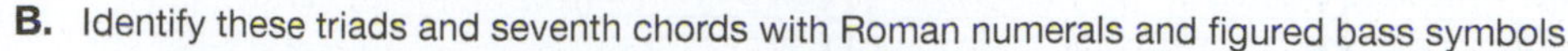

B. Identify these triads and seventh chords with Roman numerals and figured bass symbols.

1.

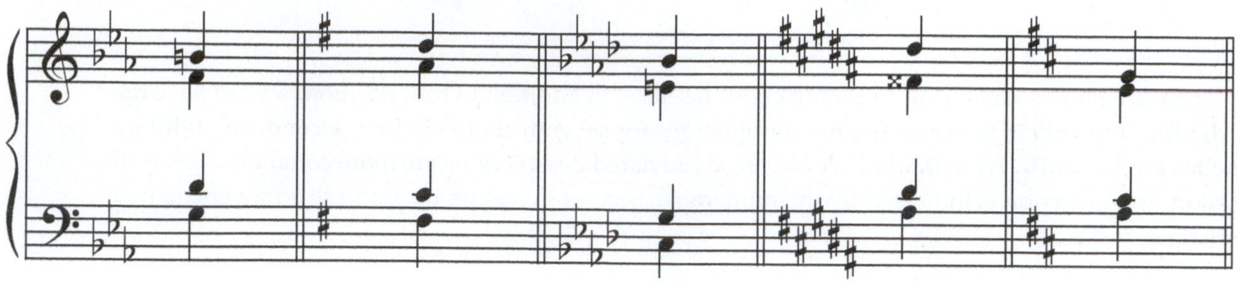

c: V7 G: ______ (1) f: ______ (2) g♯: ______ (3) D: ______ (4)

2.

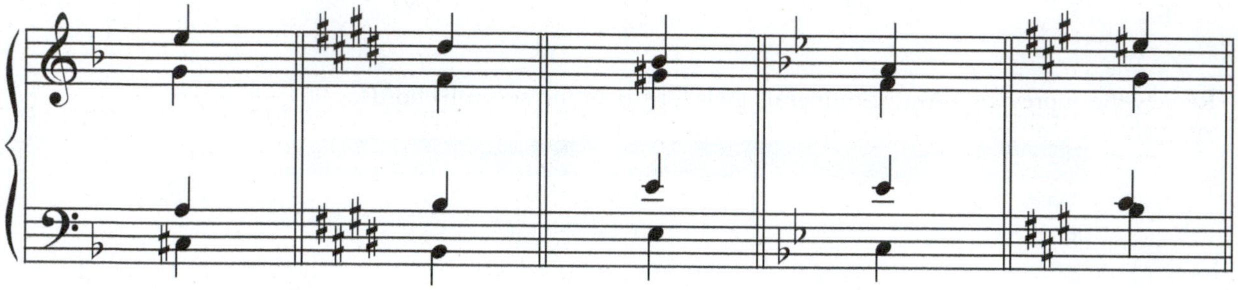

d: ______ (1) E: ______ (2) a: ______ (3) B♭: ______ (4) f♯: ______ (5)

Other Types of Seventh Chords and Symbols

In traditional music before about 1875, resolutions are predictable and notated precisely. At the end of the nineteenth century, however, a new attitude toward dissonance emerged in the music of European composers like Wagner, Debussy, and Mussorgsky. Using methods unthinkable a hundred years before, these composers often added dissonances to every chord (even the tonic). Furthermore, the dissonances were not intended to clarify tonality (as earlier composers used them), but to enhance color. By the late nineteenth century, it became fairly common practice for composers to extend the triad with an added seventh, thus creating new qualities of seventh chords.

The figures shown below indicate four additional types of seventh chords: major-major, minor-minor, fully diminished, and half diminished. It is best to identify the type of seventh chord by first determining the quality of the triad and then the quality of the interval between the root and the seventh.

Major-minor Minor-minor Major-major Half Diminished Fully Diminished

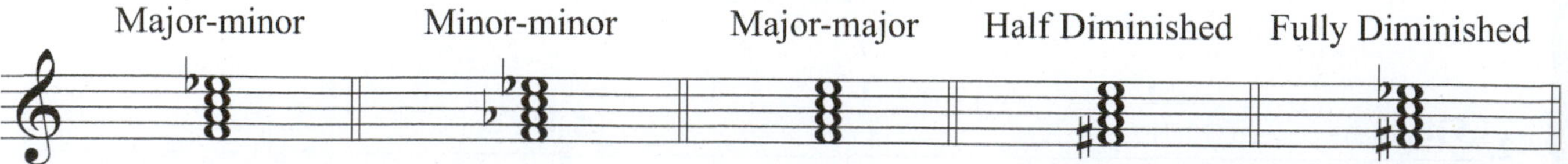

CHORD SYMBOLS FOR SEVENTH CHORDS. Regardless of the key signature, the suffix "7" added to a chord symbol (and without additional qualification) designates a major-minor (dominant) seventh chord. A chord designated "A7" would function in D major or minor; "C♯7" has dominant function in F♯ major or minor; "F7" functions in B♭ major or minor; and so on.

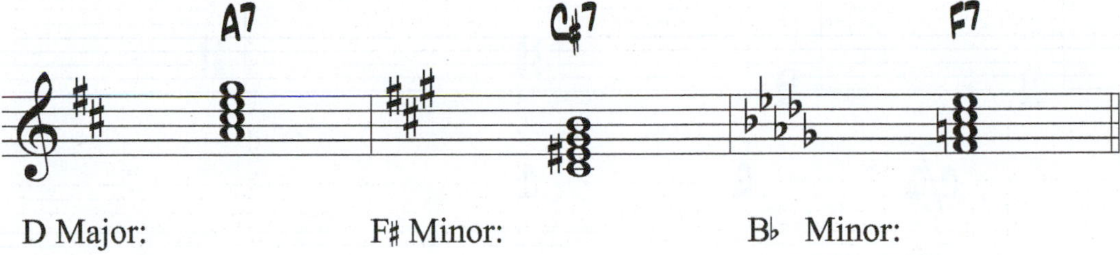

The commonly used lead sheet symbols for seventh chords are shown below. Notice that there are several ways to indicate types of seventh chords. You should be familiar with all of the symbols, as you will encounter the various types in musical literature.

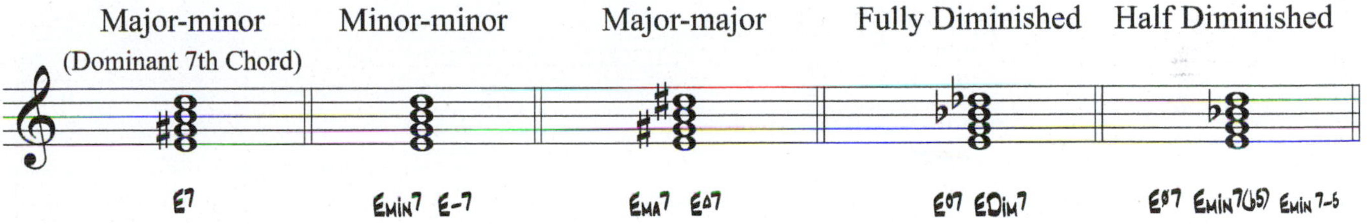

As we have discussed, composers may specify a bass pitch with the slash symbol:

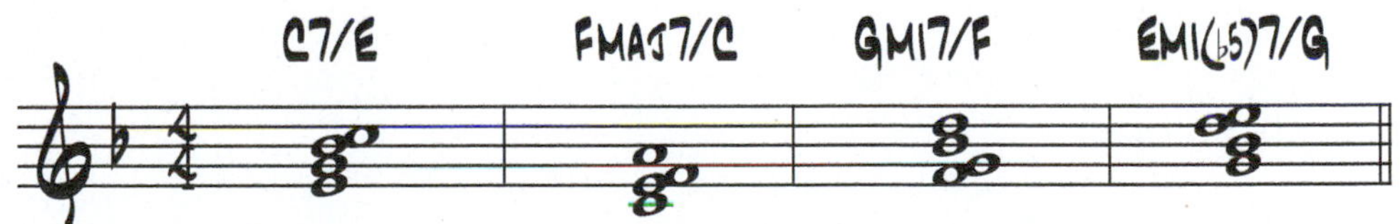

Remember that there are many different systems of chord-symbol notation; moreover, performers may substitute their own harmonization for the composer's original suggestions. Using the chord symbols discussed here, however, we can easily represent the harmony of "Stand By Me" by Ben E. King (1938–2015).

"Stand By Me", Ben E. King
C
Am
When the night has come and the land is dark, and the
5
F
C/G
G
C
moon is the on - ly light we'll see,

For class discussion or assignment: please do not remove these pages

REVIEW SET

Chord Symbols Including Sevenths

A. Notate triads and seventh chords indicated by the chord symbols. Add accidentals as necessary. Two chords are given in each key (with the key designation given for information only).

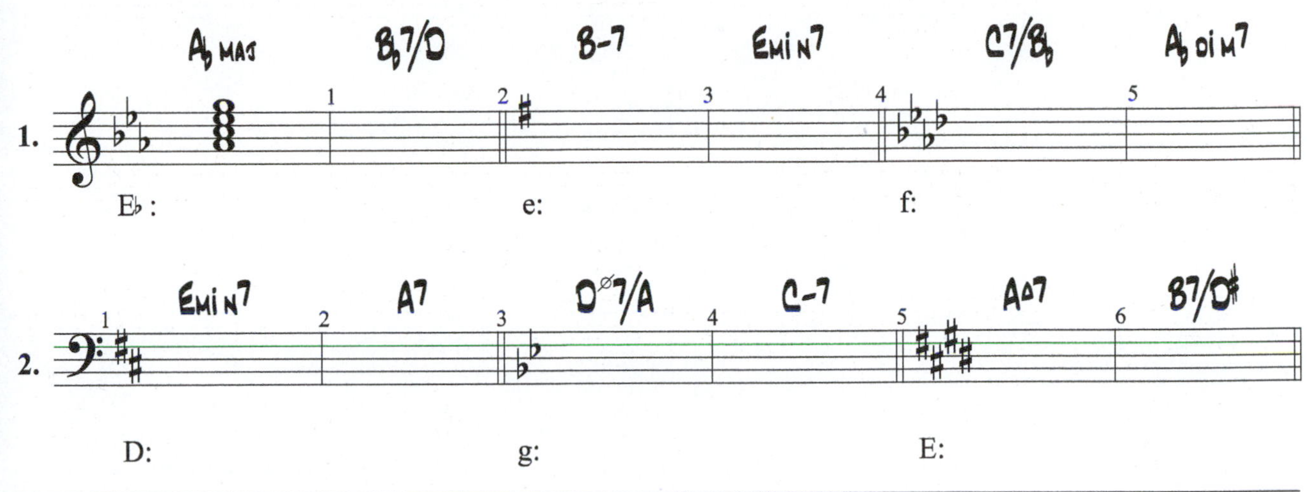

Complete Building Skills 12-3 on page 363

MUSICIANSHIP 12-2

Ear Training: Hearing Triads and Seventh Chords

This exercise will help you distinguish between triads and seventh chords. For each chord played, circle "Triad" or "Seventh." Some of the chords are in root position; others are inverted. You are asked only to identify the presence or absence of a seventh. (See Appendix D for answers.)

Arpeggiated Triads and Chords

1.	Triad Seventh 1	Triad Seventh 2	Triad Seventh 3	Triad Seventh 4	Triad Seventh 5	Triad Seventh 6
2.	Triad Seventh 1	Triad Seventh 2	Triad Seventh 3	Triad Seventh 4	Triad Seventh 5	Triad Seventh 6
3.	Triad Seventh 1	Triad Seventh 2	Triad Seventh 3	Triad Seventh 4	Triad Seventh 5	Triad Seventh 6
4.	Triad Seventh 1	Triad Seventh 2	Triad Seventh 3	Triad Seventh 4	Triad Seventh 5	Triad Seventh 6

Name ______________________

Page may be removed

Building Skills • 12-1

Melodic Tendencies

A. **For each tendency tone (circled) identify the scale degree in the upper blank. In the lower blank, indicate whether the resolution to the following pitch is "typical" or "less typical" according to the guidelines given on pages 344-345.**

B. **Identify the texture of the following passages as "homophony" (melody and accompaniment) or "polyphony" (equal melodies). Write the appropriate word in the blank.**

Texture ______________________

Texture ______________________

L. van Beethoven, Romanze from Sonatina no. 1

Texture ______________________________

3

J. S. Bach, Invention no. 4

Texture ______________________________

4

Name ______________

Page may be removed

Building Skills • 12-2

Harmonic Function

A. For the given chord, indicate whether the harmonic function is tonic ("T"), predominant ("PD"), or dominant ("D"). There are two chords in each key.

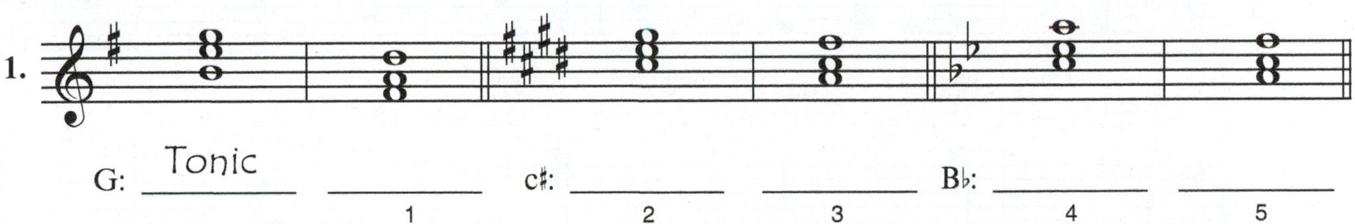

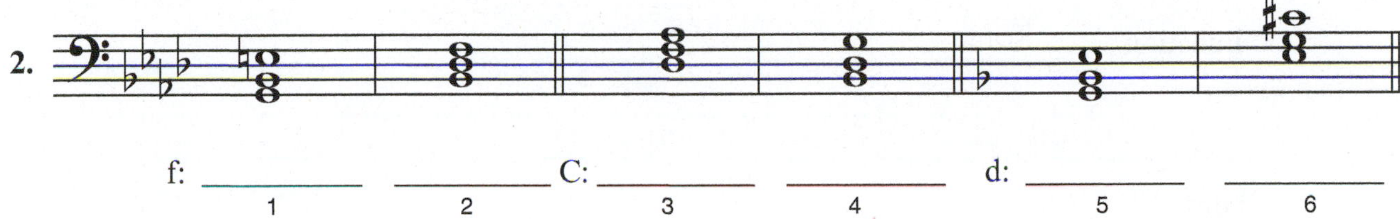

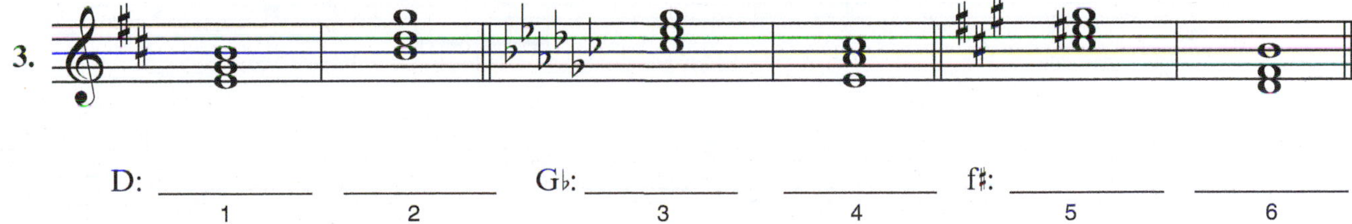

B. For each key listed, provide a key signature and then notate chords of predominant, dominant, and tonic function (in that order). There are two possible chords for each function; alternate between these choices.

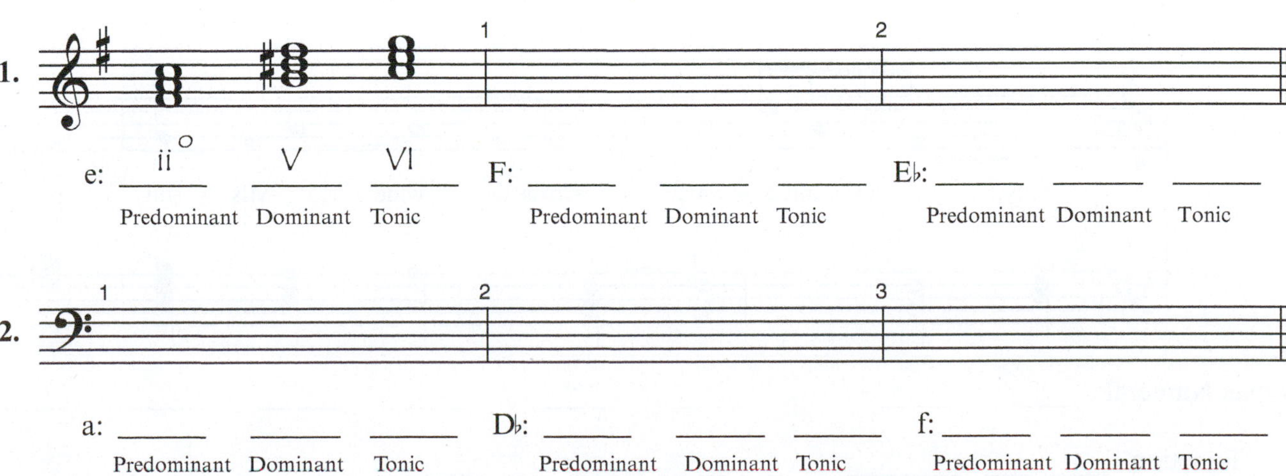

C. Study the melody and harmonic reduction of the song "Shenandoah." Determine the function of each chord in F major. Provide an appropriate Roman-numeral symbol in the upper blank and a word to describe the function in the lower one. Write a chord symbol in the blanks above the melody.

American Folk Song, "Shenandoah"

1.

Chord Symbols F ___ ___ ___ ___ ___

Oh, Shen-an - doah, I long to hear you. A - way, you roll-ing

Roman Numerals F: I ___ ___ ___ ___ ___

Function Tonic ___ ___ ___ ___ ___

1 2 3 4 5

Chords ___ ___ ___ ___ ___ ___

riv - er. Oh, Shen-an-doah I long to hear you. A -

Roman Numerals ___ ___ ___ ___ ___ ___

Function ___ ___ ___ ___ ___ ___

6 7 8 9 10 11

Chords ___ ___ ___ ___ ___ ___ ___ ___

way, I'm bound a - way, 'Cross the wide Mis - sou - ri.

Roman Numerals ___ ___ ___ ___ ___ ___ ___ ___

Function ___ ___ ___ ___ ___ ___ ___ ___

12 13 14 15 16 17 18 19

Name ______________________

Page may be removed

Building Skills • 12-3

Seventh Chords

A. **Begin by notating the appropriate key signature, then construct dominant seventh chords in closed position. Be sure to observe the correct inversions. Remember to add an accidental for the leading tone in minor keys.**

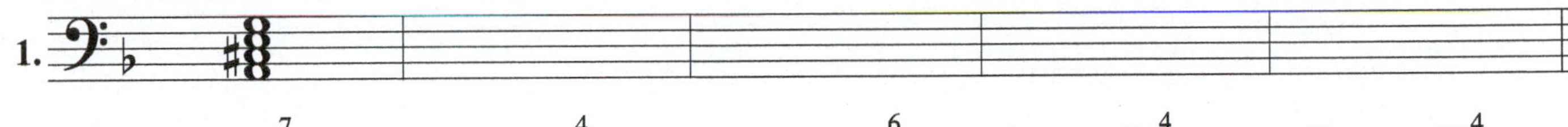

d: V^7 E: V^4_3 A♭: V^6_5 b: V^4_2 C: V^4_3

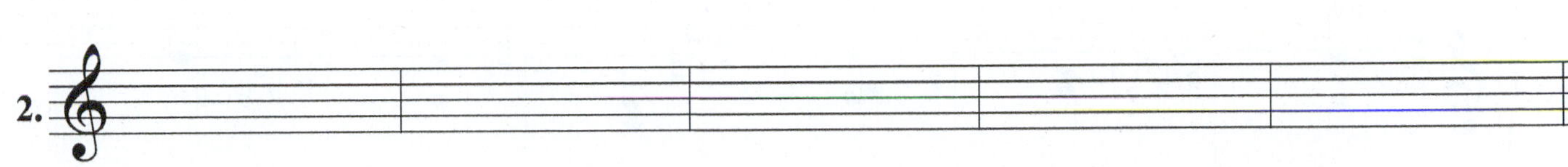

D♭: V^6_5 f: V^7 A: V^4_2 e: V^4_3 f♯: V^7

B. **Some of the root-position chords notated are triads, others are dominant seventh chords. Provide a chord symbol as appropriate.**

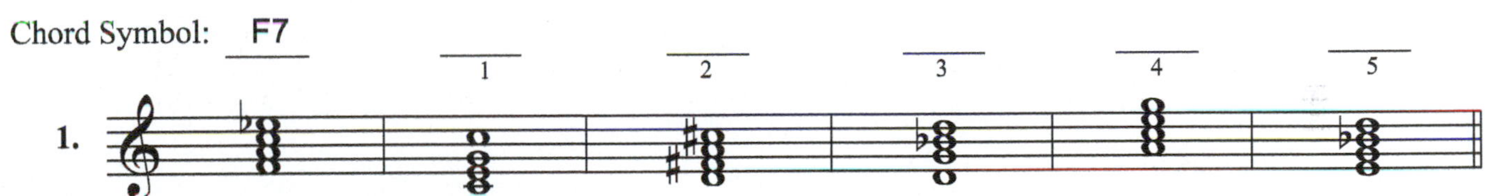

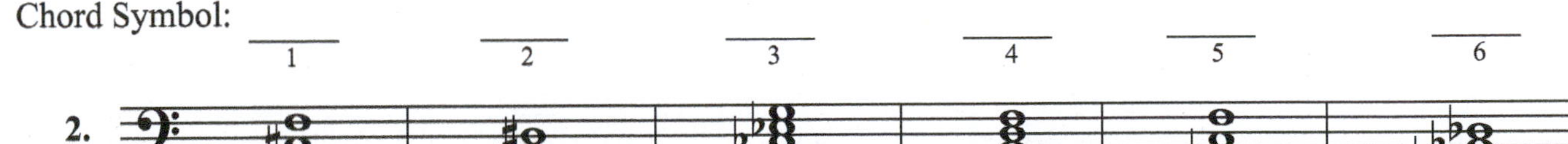

C. **Use Roman-numeral and figured bass symbols to identify these dominant seventh chords.**

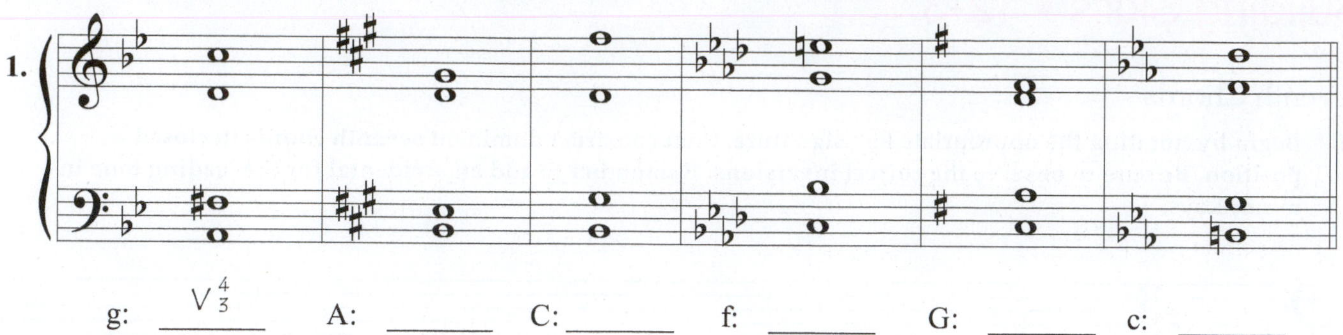

Name ______________________

Page may be removed

D. **Provide a chord-symbol analysis of the two melodies below, which are based on arpeggiated chords.**

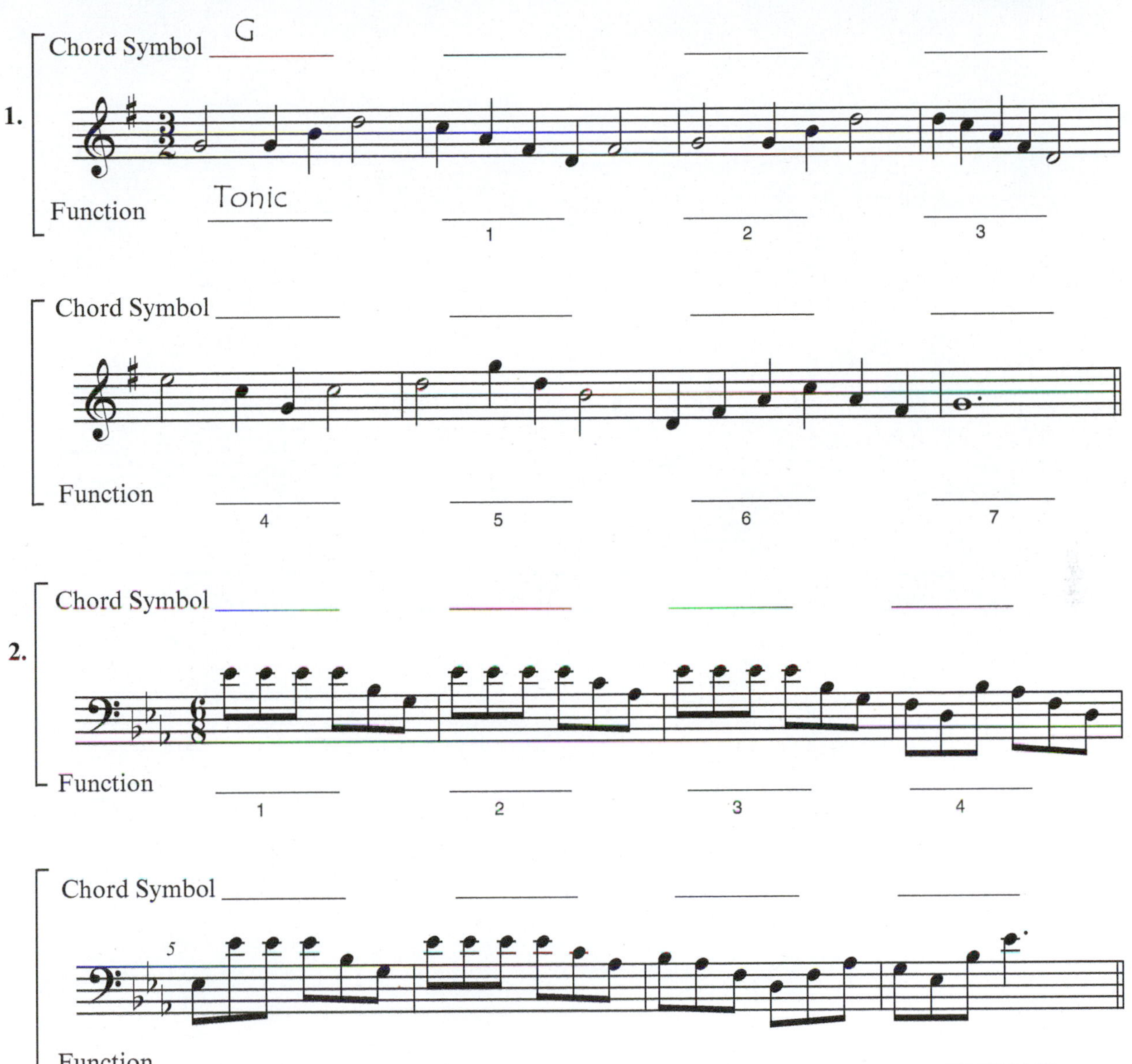

Name ______________________

Page may be removed

Creative Projects • Chapter 12

A. **For the following chord progression, compose a melody that focuses on triad outlines. Use any rhythmic patterns you want, but limit your melody to chord tones that follow the given progressions. No material is given for the third melody; follow the same guidelines with functional progressions and strong melodic cadences to compose a melody of your own design.**

B. **Choose one of the first two melodies in Exercise A and adapt it to set two verses of Emily Dickinson's poem "I Measure Every Grief" as a period. Each line of text should be two measures in length and each line begins with an anacrusis.**

Limit your melody to chord tones, but you may, however, fill in a third between two chord tones to create a stepwise line (see the sample phrase that follows). Complete all of your work on a sheet of manuscript paper with your name, date, and other information as specified by your instructor.

Set the second stanza exactly like the first, but write out the entire 16 measures. Include chord symbols as shown on this page. You need not indicate a chord for the beginning anacrusis, but others will be harmonized from the previous chord. Work out a draft before making the final copy.

I measure every grief I meet
With narrow, probing eyes;
I wonder if it weights like mine,
Or has an easier size.

I wonder if they bore it long,
Or did it just begin?
I could not tell the date of mine,
It feels so old a pain.

—Emily Dickinson (1830–1886)

THE POEMS OF EMILY DICKINSON, edited by Thomas H. Johnson, Cambridge, Mass.: The Belknap Press of Harvard University Press, Copyright © 1951, 1955 by the President and Fellows of Harvard College. Copyright © renewed 1979, 1983 by the President and Fellows of Harvard College. Copyright © 1914, 1918, 1919, 1924, 1929, 1930, 1932, 1935, 1937, 1942, by Martha Dickinson Bianchi. Copyright © 1952, 1957, 1958, 1963, 1965, by Mary L. Hampson.

Name ________________________

Page may be removed

Analysis in Context 1 • Chapter 12

Das Wohltemperierte Klavier, BWV 846-893 ("The Well-Tempered Clavier"), is a two-volume collection of preludes and fugues written by J.S. Bach. Each volume includes a Prelude and Fugue for each of 12 major and minor key pairings. The C Major Prelude featured here is the first piece in volume I.

J.S. Bach, Well-Tempered Clavier, Book 1, Prelude No.1

16
19
22
25
28

Name ______________________________

Page may be removed

1. What is the musical texture of the piece?

2. On average, how often do the chords change (every beat, every measure, etc.)? How do you know?

3. Determine the root, quality, and inversion of the chords in measures 1–15. Write your answers between the staves.

4. Review your answers to question 3. Write the corresponding Roman numeral analysis of the first four measures below the bass clef staff. Name the function (tonic, predominant, dominant) of each chord in these bars and discuss how this helps to define the key.

5. Consider the use of seventh chords in this piece. How many different types did you find? (List them here.)

6. Why do you think seventh chords are important to the harmonic goals of the piece?

7. Listen to a recording of the piece and sing the bass clef voice. Listen a second time and sing (or play) the soprano line—hold the highest pitch in each measure for four counts. This exercise shows us that although the visual shapes may appear to be all skips and leaps, each voice creates a smooth, almost connected line.

Chapter 13
Harmonization

Essential Terms

Alberti bass
alto
anticipation
authentic cadence
bass
copyright
deceptive cadence
half cadence
harmonic cadence
harmonic rhythm
melisma
neighboring tone (NT)
nonchord tones
passing tone (PT)
plagal cadence
public domain
range
soprano
swing
tenor
vocables
vocal range

Our goal in this final chapter is to draw together many of the topics discussed so that you can compose and notate your own songs as well as create arrangements of existing melodies. If you have mastered the material in the previous chapters, you will be prepared to do this. If your goal is to attain an understanding of the composer's art and to notate your own simple songs, this chapter will provide a beginning.

Harmonization

The process of harmonizing an existing melody requires a good deal of planning. These stages include an assessment of the *harmonic rhythm*, planning *harmonic cadences*, and dealing with *nonchord tones*. Each of these topics will be discussed in the following sections.

Harmonic Cadences

For many arrangers, defining cadences is the first step in harmonization. As we discussed earlier, a cadence is a musical point of rest. Melodically, a phrase that ends with $\hat{1}$ or $\hat{3}$ has a terminal effect; scale degrees $\hat{2}$, $\hat{5}$, and $\hat{7}$ are progressive. A **harmonic cadence** is the final two chords in a phrase. Cadences often involve two different harmonic functions: either (1) predominant and dominant or (2) dominant and tonic. Like melodic cadences, harmonic cadences are either progressive or terminal. Observing punctuation in the lyrics will usually help with musical divisions. A comma in the text may indicate a weaker, progressive cadence, while a period or exclamation point may indicate a more definitive one.

AUTHENTIC CADENCE. At a cadence, a progression from a chord of dominant function to the tonic (V–I or vii°–I) is termed **authentic**. In the song "For He's a Jolly Good Fellow," we can harmonize the end of the first phrase with an authentic cadence. Notice that the third scale degree occurs on the strong beat in the last measure, making this cadence relatively weaker than one where the tonic pitch falls on the strong beat.

"For He's A Jolly Good Fellow"

The first phrase of the song "Good King Wenceslas" ends with a similar authentic cadence. The dominant seventh is not necessary, but the dissonance and its resolution (also seen in the previous example) make the arrival of tonic even stronger.

"Good King Wenceslas"

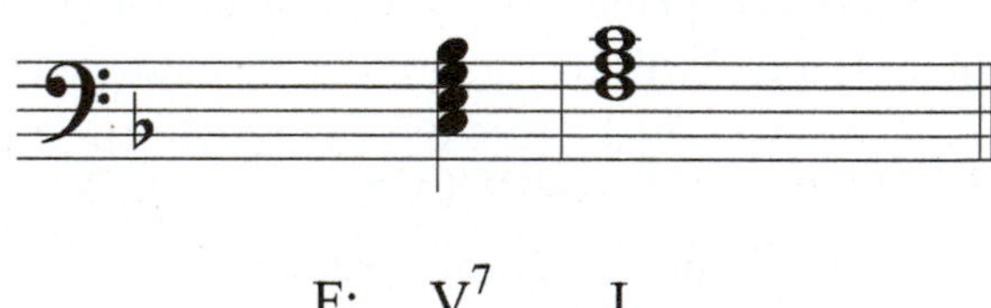

F: V^7 I

Authentic Cadence

When the leading tone serves as the chord of dominant function, the cadence is still authentic, but the effect is weaker.

"Good King Wenceslas"

F: vii$^{\circ 6}$ I

Authentic Cadence

All three examples of authentic cadences can be heard on the online resources. These formulas are examples of different types of authentic cadences that occur at the end of a phrase.

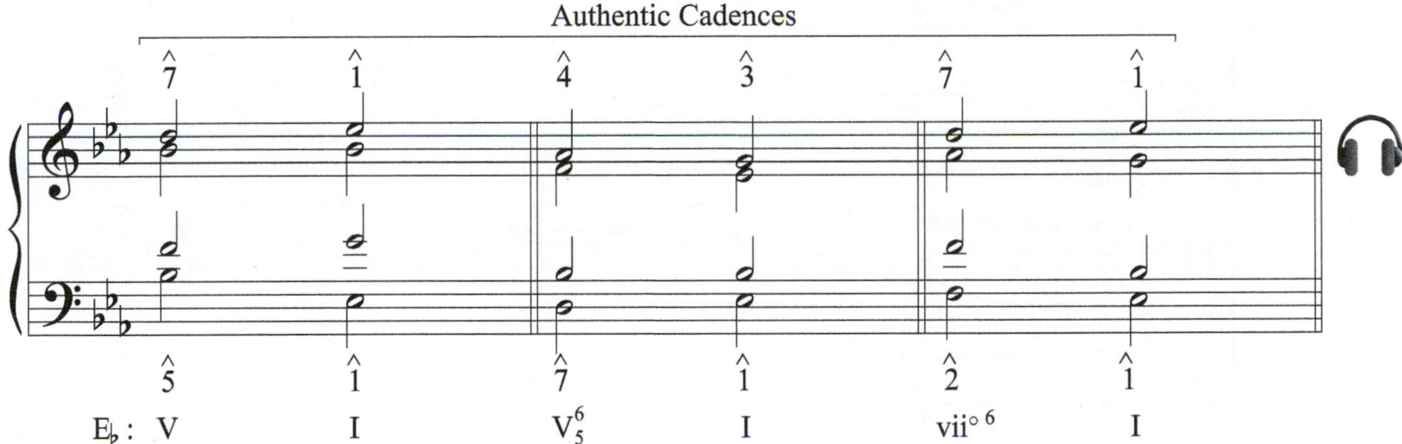

DECEPTIVE CADENCE. Composers may delay an arrival at the tonic with a V–vi cadence (V–VI in minor) known as a **deceptive cadence**. In this case, the submediant serves a tonic function, since we expect the tonic chord. (Refer to the discussion of harmonic function in Chapter 12.) Study the string quartet below and listen for the final cadence of the excerpt.

Haydn, String Quartet in d minor, Op. 76 No. 2, Movement II, mm.47-50

HALF CADENCE. Like a comma in language, the **half cadence** is a progression that ends on the dominant, leaving a need for continuation. Three versions of the half cadence are common:

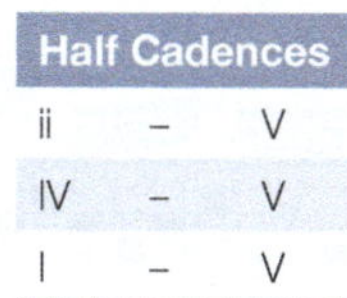

Half Cadences		
ii	–	V
IV	–	V
I	–	V

The first phrase of the Irish folk song "Gary Owen" ends with a I–V half cadence in C major.

"Simple Gifts," a Shaker hymn, includes a ii6/5–V half cadence.

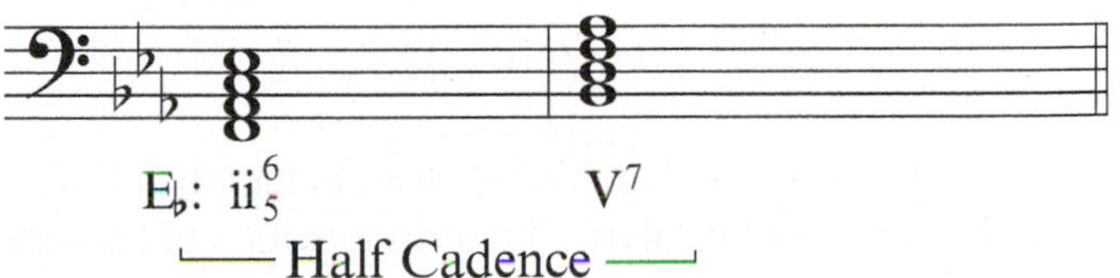

Traditional half cadences follow the same patterns. When the ii–V half cadence is used, it is frequently ii$_6$–V.

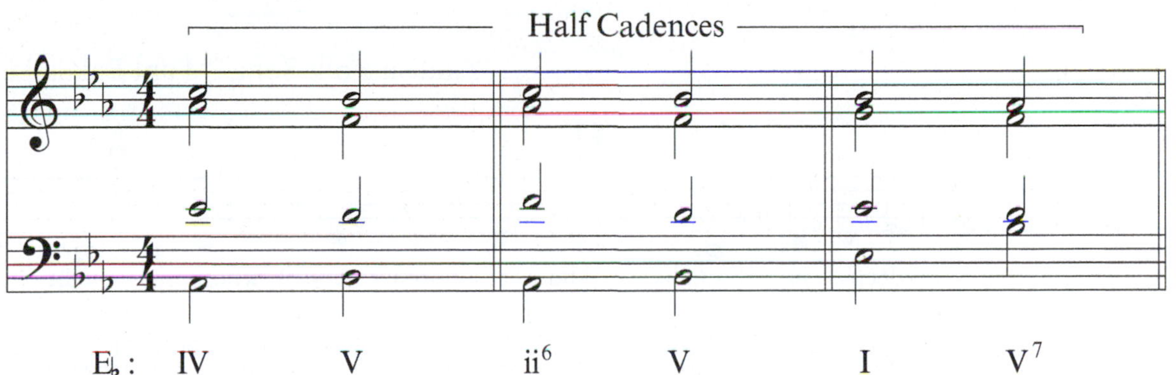

PLAGAL CADENCE. In a **plagal cadence**, the subdominant moves directly to tonic (IV–I). The familiar "A-men" ending used with hymns and other religious pieces is called a *plagal cadence.*

In the folk song "Michael Row the Boat Ashore," the first phrase ends with a plagal cadence; the period concludes with an authentic cadence. Listen to the song online and in addition to the plagal and authentic cadences, notice a relatively rare use of the mediant triad (iii) in measure 5. In this role, the mediant serves a tonic function.

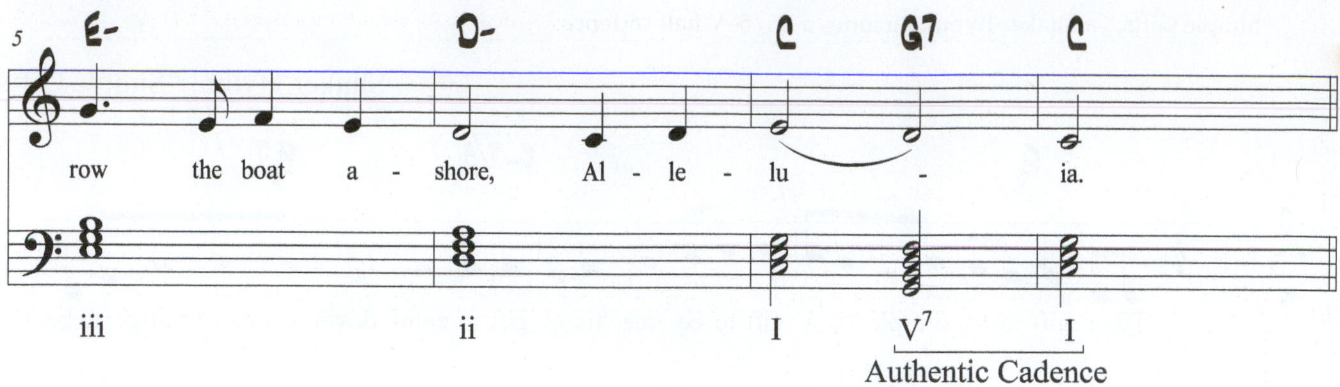

Folk songs are often four phrases in length and use a variety of cadences. The verse of the Yiddish melody "Tum Balalaika" ("Play Balalaika") is a combination of two periods. The first phrase ends with a half cadence (i–V) followed by one that is authentic (V^7–i). The second period is unusual in combining a plagal cadence with a final authentic formula. Both periods have antecedent/consequent structure. Notice how the contrast of the four cadences creates the effect of completeness.

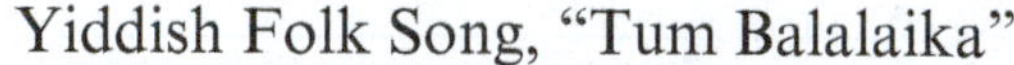
Yiddish Folk Song, "Tum Balalaika"

For class discussion or assignment: please do not remove these pages

REVIEW SET

Cadences

A. Identify each chord using Roman numerals and figured bass. Label the cadence type.

B. Provide chords, chord symbols, and Roman numerals that create the designated cadences in the given keys. There is more than one choice for some cadences; vary your selections.

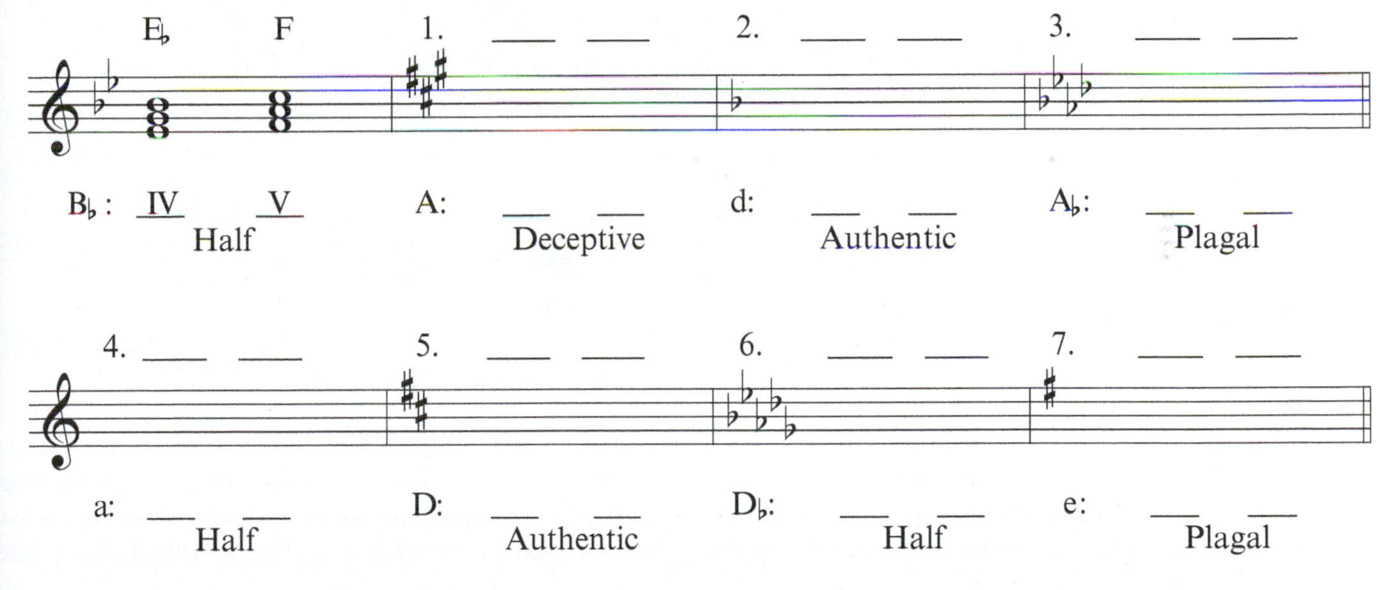

Planning Cadences in a Melody

Cadential planning is an essential first step in harmonization. The following examples use a relatively simple phrase with lyrics. As we have discussed, lyrics often tell us exactly where cadences appear and their relative strength. The spiritual "Go Down, Moses" begins with a repeated phrase in A minor. The cadence occurs at the first ending ("peo-ple | go!").

At first glance, we might follow the comma and insert a cadence into the second measure ("E-gypt's land"). Especially in $\frac{4}{4}$, however, four-measure phrases are more common, and in any event, the two pitches in question (C and A) do not permit any of the standard cadence types. If the possibilities for a cadence are not immediately apparent, take each pitch of the melody in turn as the root, third, and fifth of a triad. As shown in the next example, none of the possibilities for chords on the words "E-gypt's land" forms a traditional cadence.

The words "Let my people go!" end the phrase and coincide with the first cadence. The pitches G♯ (measure 3) and A (measure 4) eliminate all cadential possibilities except authentic and deceptive.

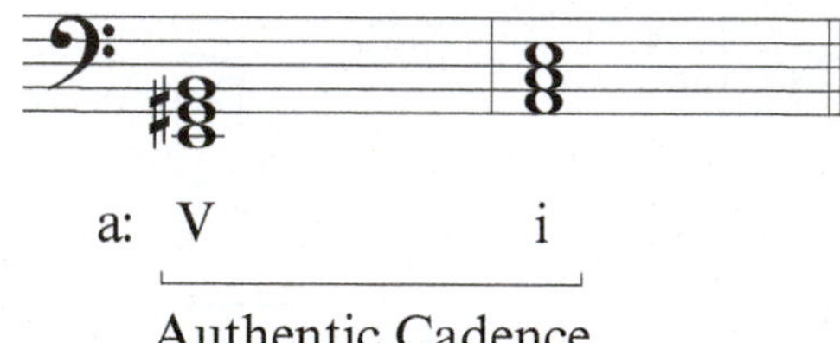

The folk song "Loch Lomond" presents a different cadential setting. In G major, the first phrase ends with the pitches E and D (measure 4), meaning that an authentic cadence is not one of the choices. Looking at the possibilities in the previous example, both plagal and half cadences (either ii–V or IV–V) are supported by the melody. Especially considering the comma in the text, the phrase is most effective with a half cadence.

Scottish Folk Song, "Loch Lomond"

We can also plan cadences for an entire poem by studying the text. Consider this setting of the final stanza from Alfred Lord Tennyson's "Lost Love." The poem concludes with these lines:

I hold it true whate'er befall;
I feel it when I sorrow most;
'Tis better to have loved and lost
Than never to have loved at all.

There are many possibilities for setting this text, but the punctuation supports a weak–weak–weak–strong double period. The key is F♯ minor with each line as a four-measure phrase. Text lines begin with an anacrusis, so we might be well advised to rearrange the lyrics to better represent our setting (cadences are boldfaced in the lines that follow). If you were composing your own melody, you would probably have already made this adjustment in the rhythmic plan.

I/hold it true whate'er **be-fall;** I
Half Cadence
feel it when I sor**row most;** 'Tis
Half Cadence
better to have loved **and lost** Than
Half Cadence
never to have loved **at all**.
Authentic Cadence

Our setting of "Lost Love" includes only the harmonic and melodic materials discussed in this text—those that you are prepared to analyze. Obviously, a more intricate and sophisticated version would be possible with more advanced materials. Remember also that, at this stage, we are choosing only cadences; harmony for the measures between these anchor points will be added later.

"Lost Love"

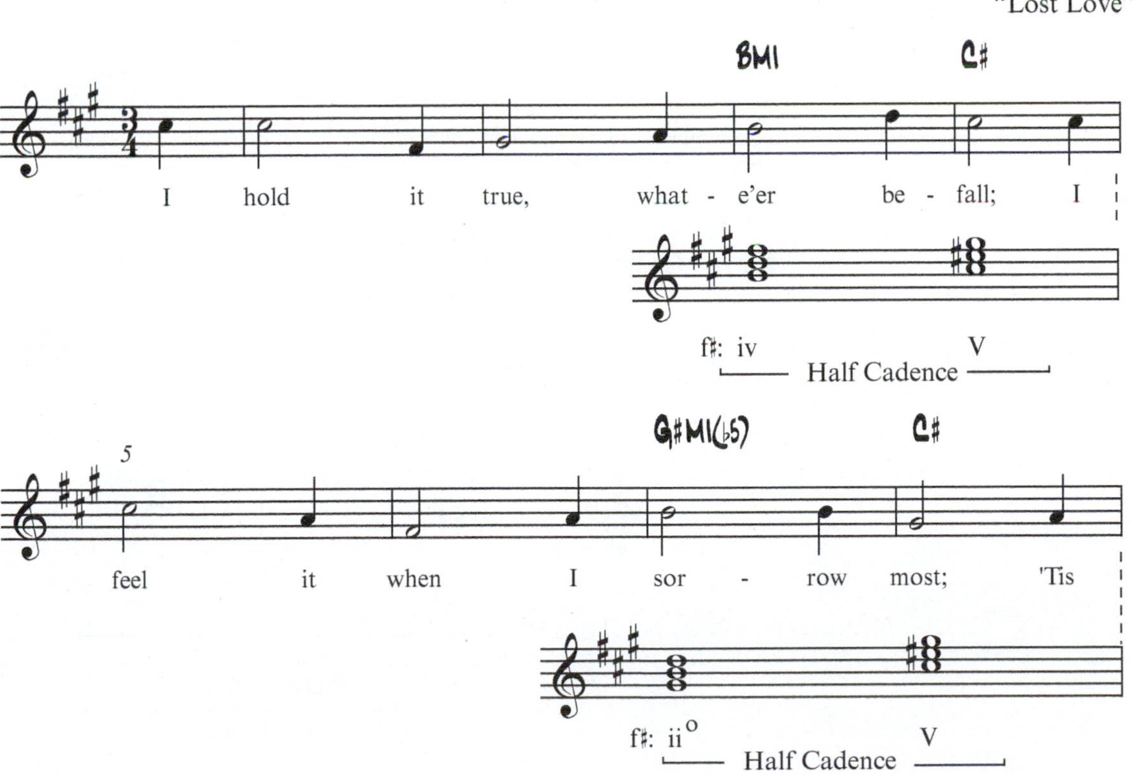

For class discussion or assignment: please do not remove these pages

REVIEW SET

Cadences

Analyze the final two chords (marked by blanks) and determine the final cadence. Identify the Roman numerals, the chord symbols, and the final cadence.

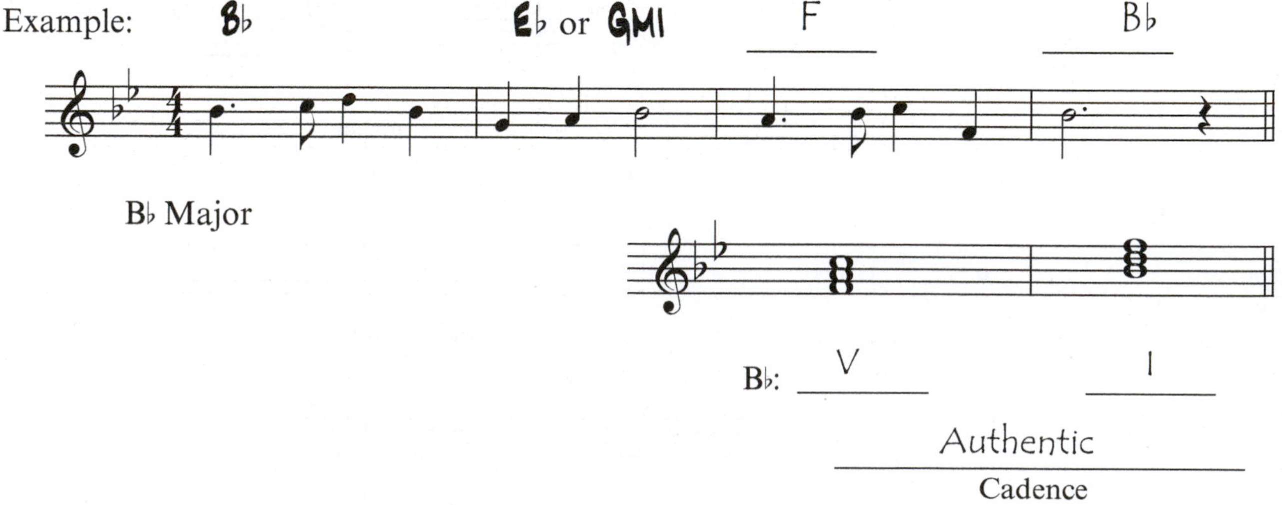

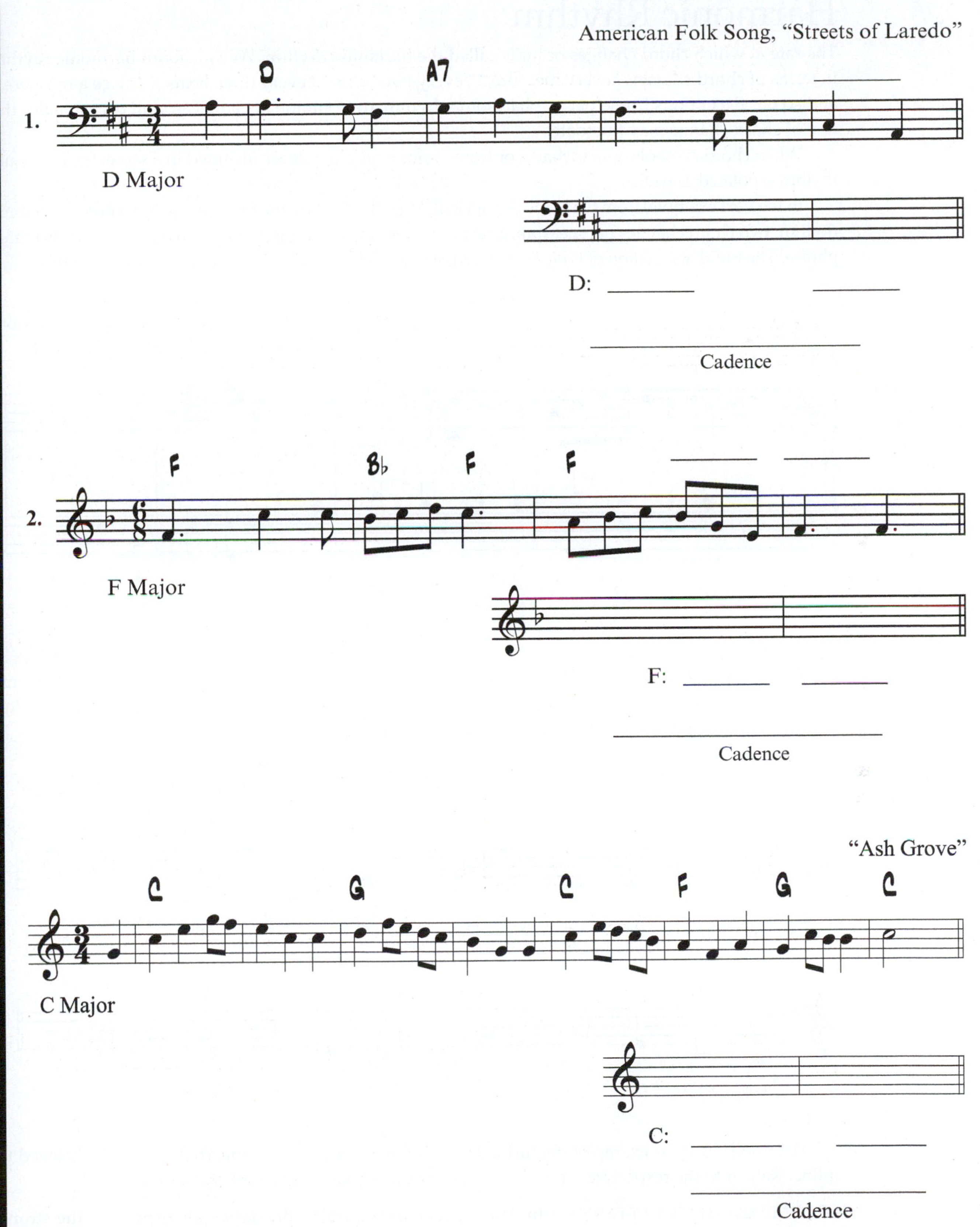

Complete Building Skills 13-1 on page 399

Harmonic Rhythm

The rate at which chord changes occur is called the **harmonic rhythm**. We talk about harmonic rhythm in terms of chord changes "every measure," "every two beats," "every three beats," "twice a measure," and so on. Exceptions in the pace of harmonic rhythm are common at cadences, and occasionally the rate of chord change may fluctuate.

When chord symbols, guitar charts, or Roman-numeral symbols are included in a score, the harmonic rhythm is notated as well.

In the next example, from the Piano Sonata in B♭ Major by Mozart, the final phrase has a faster harmonic rhythm: two chord changes per measure, or every two beats. Mozart used only two different chords in this phrase. The rapid alternation of tonic and dominant was very typical of Mozart's compositional style.

W. A. Mozart, Sonata in B♭ Major
K.333, III. Allegretto Grazioso

The folk song "Down in the Valley" has an unusually slow harmonic rhythm. In the 12 measures shown, there are only two chord changes (and only the tonic and dominant chords). Rather than being more specific, the best description for the harmonic rhythm is "slow."

American Folk Song, "Down in the Valley"

The previous three examples, featuring three different rates of harmonic rhythm, can be listened to online. Return to the respective scores and listen for the regularity of chord changes.

ACCOMPANIMENT PATTERNS. In dances, such as the waltz, the bass may appear on the strong beat with the full chord following on weaker beats. The cadences in this brief work by Franz Schubert (1797–1828) are all authentic. Since the final cadence is preceded by the only occurrence of a predominant function chord, we sense a stronger feeling of conclusion.

Franz Schubert, Dance

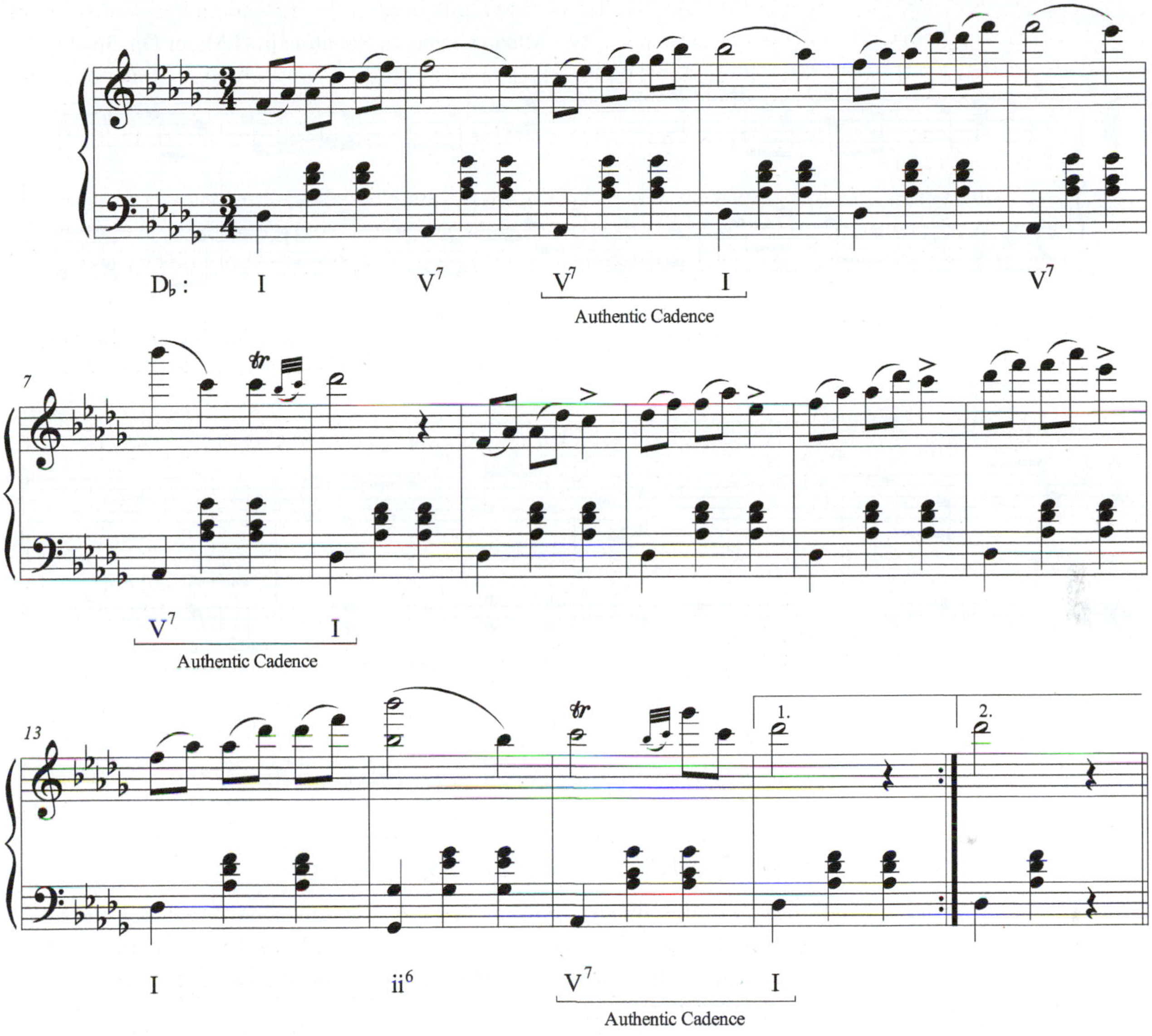
D♭: I
V7
V7
I
Authentic Cadence
V7
7
tr
V7
I
Authentic Cadence
13
tr
1.
2.
I
ii6
V7
I
Authentic Cadence

Especially in the eighteenth century, accompanying chords were arpeggiated in recurring patterns called **Alberti bass** (after the Italian composer Domineco Alberti, 1710–1746).

Alberti Bass Accompaniment

C: I
IV
V 7
I

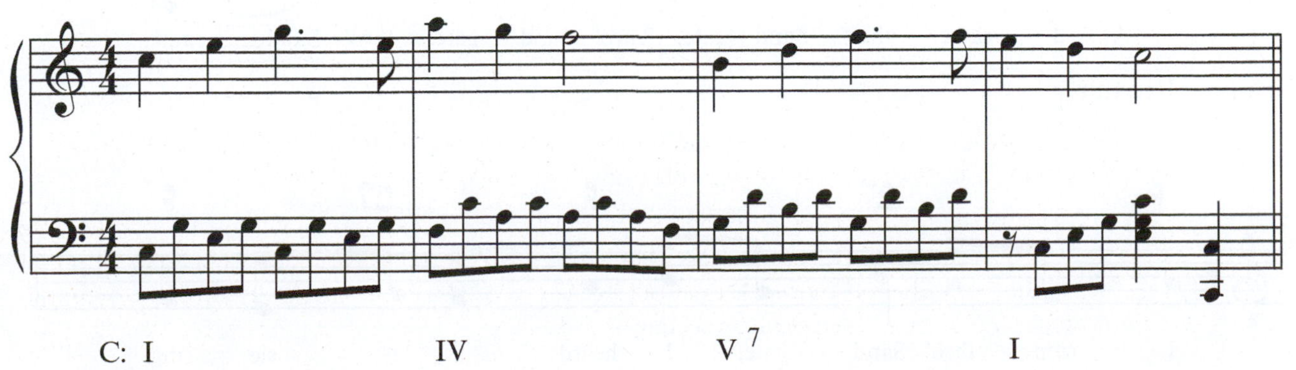

This phrase group is from the Sonatina in G Major, Op. 36, No. 2 by Muzio Clementi (1752–1832). Notice that the arpeggiated bass pattern changes to accentuate the two authentic cadences.

Muzio Clementi, Sonatina in G Major Op. 36, No. 2

Planning Harmonic Rhythm in a Harmonization

Planning harmonic rhythm is an important step in harmonization. The folk song "Weel May the Keel Row," for example, from eighteenth-century England, is based on triad outlines. The harmonic rhythm is one chord change per measure; any other choice would be difficult to harmonize. The acceleration in measure 7 is common before a cadence.

English Folk Song, "Weel May the Keel Row"

For class discussion or assignment: please do not remove these pages

REVIEW SET

Cadences and Harmonic Rhythm

A. Study the piano composition that follows. Provide a Roman-numeral analysis. Answer the questions that follow the score.

Robert Schumann, "The Wild Horseman"

1. Identify the cadences in measures 4 ____________________ and 8 ____________________.
2. What is the overall form of this passage? ____________________
3. Locate at least two different examples in the melody of typical melodic tendencies in A minor. Be prepared to explain.
4. Locate at least one instance in the melody of melodic tendencies ignored. How would you account for this apparent exception?
5. From a harmonic standpoint, why is the key of A minor so clear in this passage?
6. How would you describe the harmonic rhythm?

B. The Menuet in G Major, BWV Anh. 116 by J. S. Bach has two cadences. Supply a Roman-numeral analysis (ignore the smaller notes), identify the cadences, and comment on the harmonic rhythm. Consider the form of this passage as well.

J. S. Bach, Menuet in G major, BMV Anh. 116

Harmonizing a Melody

If you are harmonizing an existing melody, or if you want to make sure that your own melody has a strong tonal basis, begin by planning the cadences and the harmonic rhythm.

Nonchord Tones

Although we can create an interesting melody using only chord tones, **nonchord tones (NCT)**, pitches that lie outside the harmony, create interest and a smoother melodic line.

PASSING TONE. A **passing tone (PT)** fills in the interval of a third between two chord tones, creating a smoother melody. The song "Oh, What a Beautiful Morning" from the 1943 musical *Oklahoma*, includes several passing tones in the melody (circled and labeled "PT" in the lead sheet below). In measures 1–3 and 6–7, a passing tone connects two chord tones.

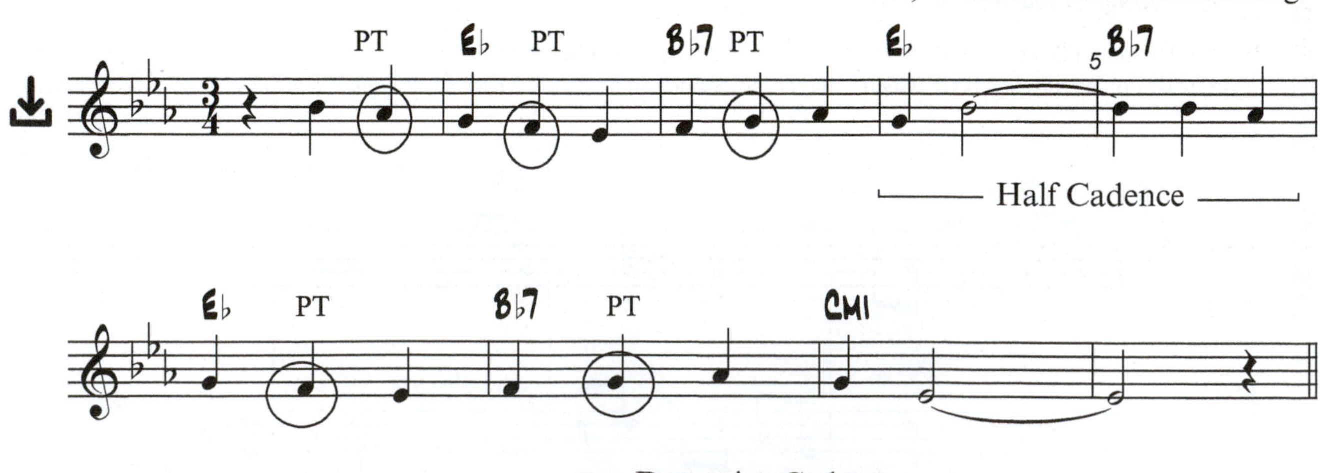

NEIGHBORING TONES. While a passing tone simply fills in a third with stepwise motion, the **neighboring tone (NT)** embellishes a pitch from above or below by step.

Georg Philipp Telemann, "1. Fantasie," TWV 40

ANTICIPATION. A pitch that arrives early, anticipating the next chord, is called an **anticipation**. Almost every measure in "Knowing You" (next example) has an anticipation (marked "ANT"). Anticipations are relatively easy to locate since they always precede the same pitch in the following harmony.

Beethoven, Sonata in G Major, Op.49, II Minuetto

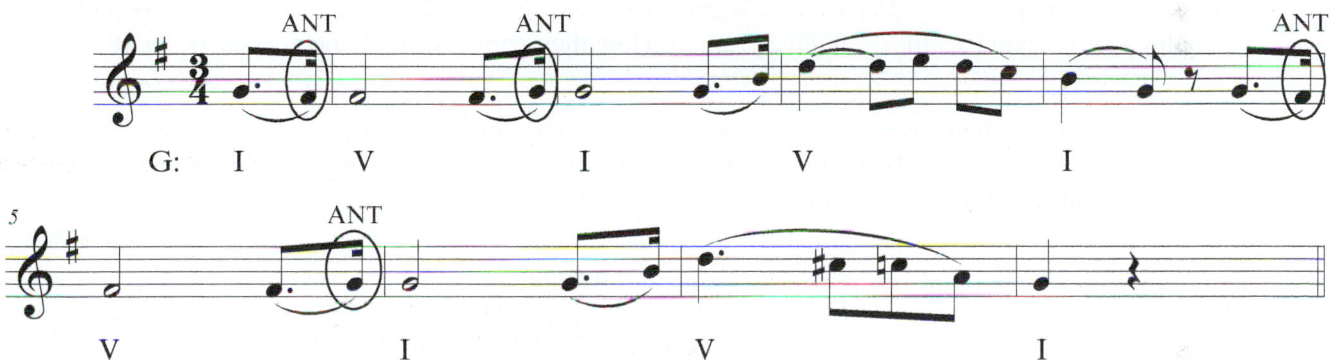

Vocal Ranges

A **vocal range** is a set of pitches that categorizes singers into one of four basic groups: **soprano**, **alto**, **tenor**, or **bass**. Notice in the next example that vocal ranges overlap; a soprano can sing some—but not all—of the pitches in the alto range (and vice versa); tenors can sing into the bass range; and so on. The ranges shown here are typical for trained amateur singers.

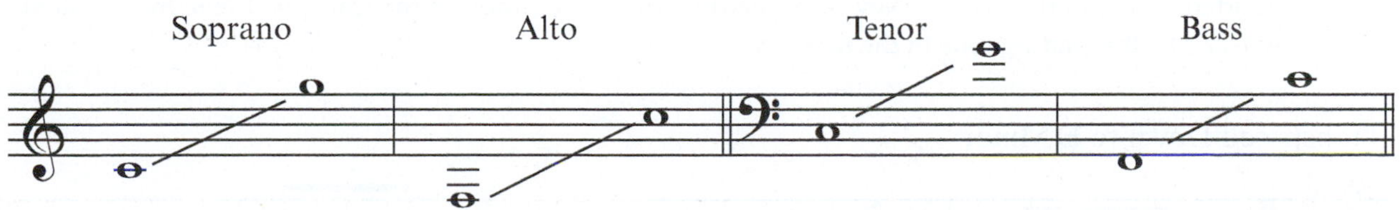

The soprano and tenor ranges are the same pitches, but an octave apart; the same is true of the alto and bass. If we write a melody with a soprano in mind, a tenor could probably sing it as well (an octave lower).

Keys and Transposition

If you are harmonizing an existing melody (as opposed to composing your own), begin by assessing the range. The melody that follows is a setting of a verse from Edgar Allen Poe's poem "The Bells." The mode is minor to reflect Poe's dark character rather than the cheerful text.

In addition to a vocal category, the term **range** refers to the distance between the highest and lowest pitches of a melody or vocal part. As written, the range of "The Bells" is rather wide—a perfect eleventh: E_4 to A_5.

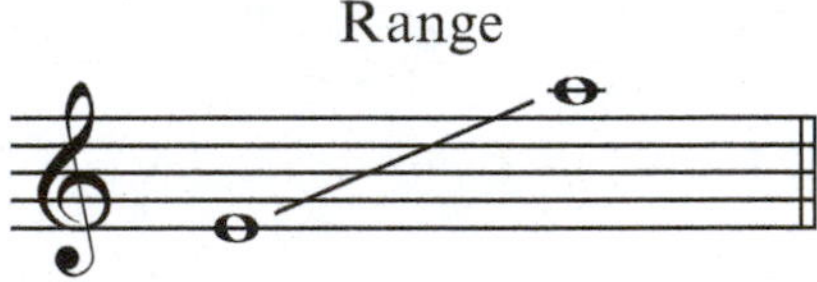

Some sopranos and tenors could sing the high A_5, but some could not. For an alto or bass, the range in the key of A minor is entirely impractical.

TRANSPOSING A MELODY. In order to fit a melody into a comfortable range, we can transpose the entire melody by changing the key signature, then duplicating the pitches higher or lower as we choose. Our setting of "The Bells" is transposed into the keys of E minor and F minor in the next example. The accidental (G♯) in the original key is the leading tone in A minor; in the transpositions, the accidental will *also* be the leading tone in the new keys.

Transposed Down to E Minor

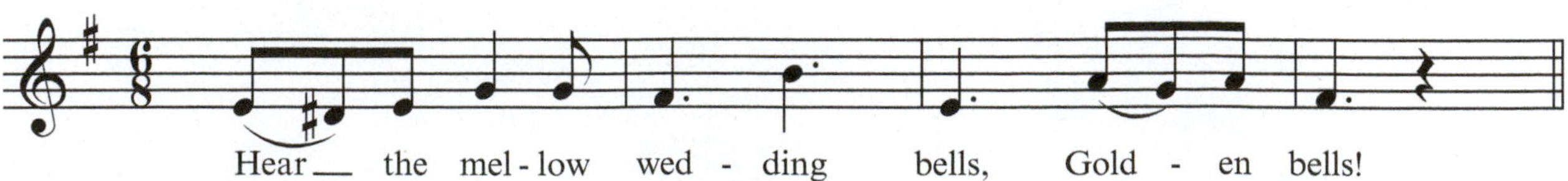

Transposed Down to F Minor

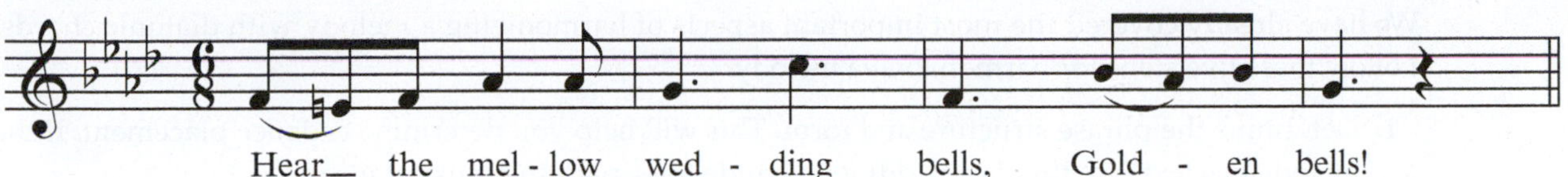

Except for accidentals, changing the key signature also duplicates the original intervals.

Returning to the Poe text, if we lower the range by a perfect fourth (to E minor), the highest pitch will now be E_5—well within the soprano range.

Transposed P4 Lower

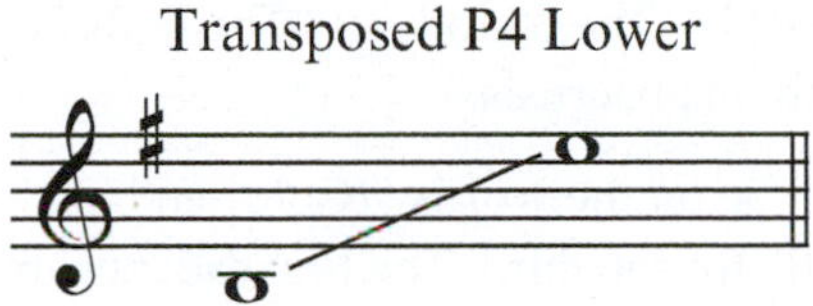

For a soprano/tenor setting of the Poe text, three keys make both the highest and lowest pitches viable: F minor, F♯ minor, and G minor.

Transposed Ranges

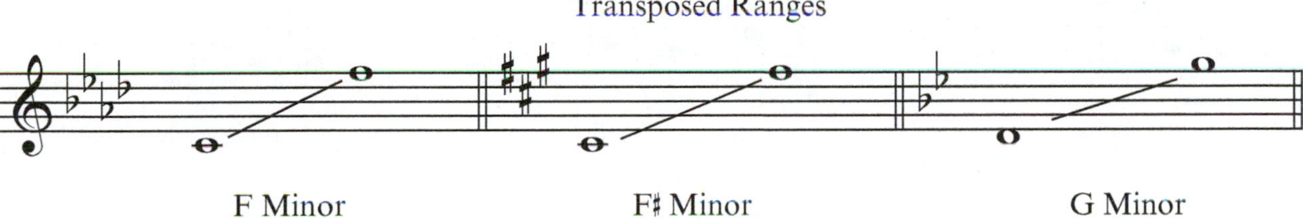

While any of the three keys is acceptable, our revision that follows is a transposition to G minor.

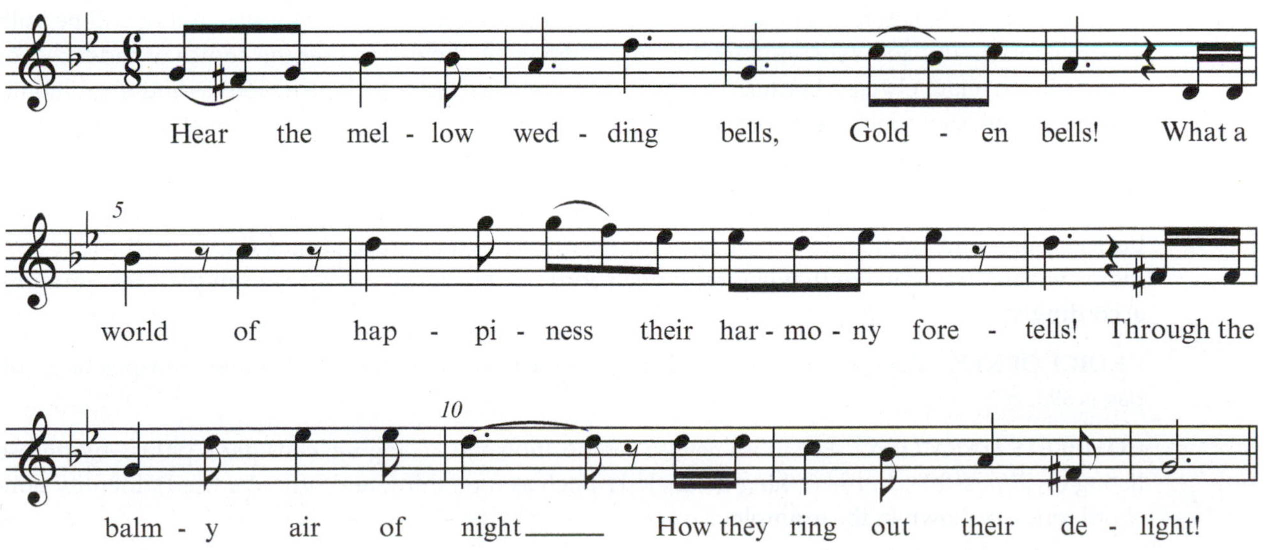

Planning the Harmony

We have already covered the most important aspects of harmonizing a melody with diatonic chords. Follow these five steps for harmonizing a melody.

1. Determine the phrase structure and form. This will help you determine cadence placement. If the melody has text, use this as an additional guide for separating musical ideas.
2. Plan the cadences for each phrase.
3. Determine the harmonic rhythm.
4. Consider your performers' range when choosing a key.
5. Use functional harmonic progressions that reinforce the key, focusing on dominant–tonic or predominant–dominant–tonic momentum.

PHRASE STRUCTURE AND FORM. The melody of "The Bells" is a group of three phrases; the second and third phrases begin with an anacrusis.

CADENCES. Our cadences will be on the words "(Gold)-en bells" for the first phrase, "fore-tells" in the second phrase, and "de-light!" for the third. The first cadence must be a half cadence because scale degree 2 is part of the dominant chord. The same is true for the pitches E♭ and D in the second phrase. The final phrase, however, with the pitches F♯ and G indicate the need for a strong authentic cadence.

The three cadences for "The Bells" form a weak–weak–strong phrase grouping that will be both effective in tonality and satisfying in structure. Remember, however, that the choice of cadences for "The Bells" is relatively easy because the phrase structure is regular and the melody is entirely diatonic. Even some folk songs include changes of key in one or more phrases. Further, chromatic pitches, which may complicate harmonic choices, are common in popular music.

HARMONIC RHYTHM. Without triad outlines and other clues, the harmonic rhythm can vary between one and two chord changes per measure. If two chord changes create a stronger harmony, we are free to make that choice; if one chord change seems better, we can plan the harmony accordingly.

CHOICE OF KEY. Review the choice of G minor in the previous section, "Keys and Transposition," on pages 390.

COMPLETE HARMONY. For those new to composition and arranging, consider a phrase-by-phrase listing of all possible chords (taking the melody pitch as root, third, and fifth of a triad). Identify nonchord tones as shown in the example.

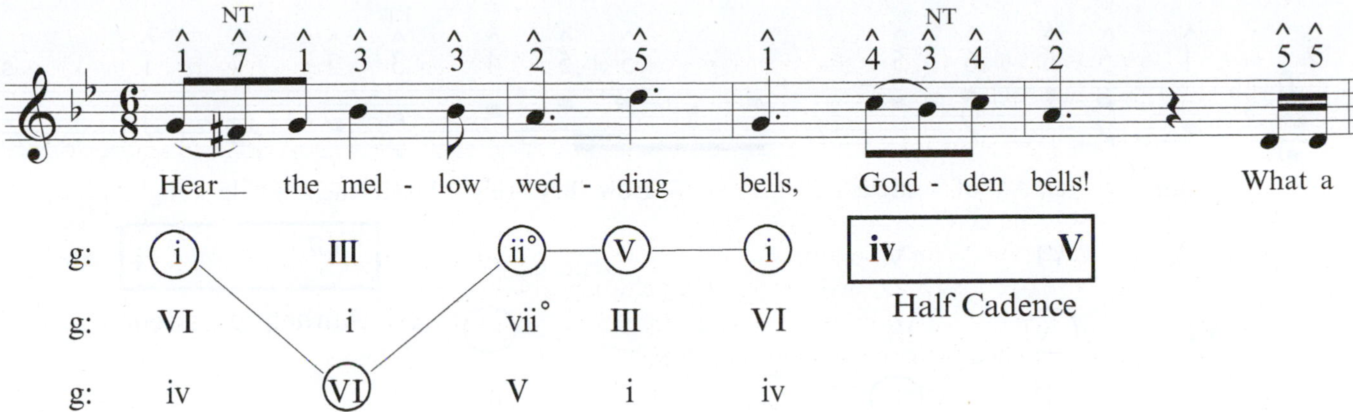

If we choose the circled chords in the previous example, the harmony is strong and varied. For a simpler harmonization, however, we can slow the harmonic rhythm and still effectively establish tonality.

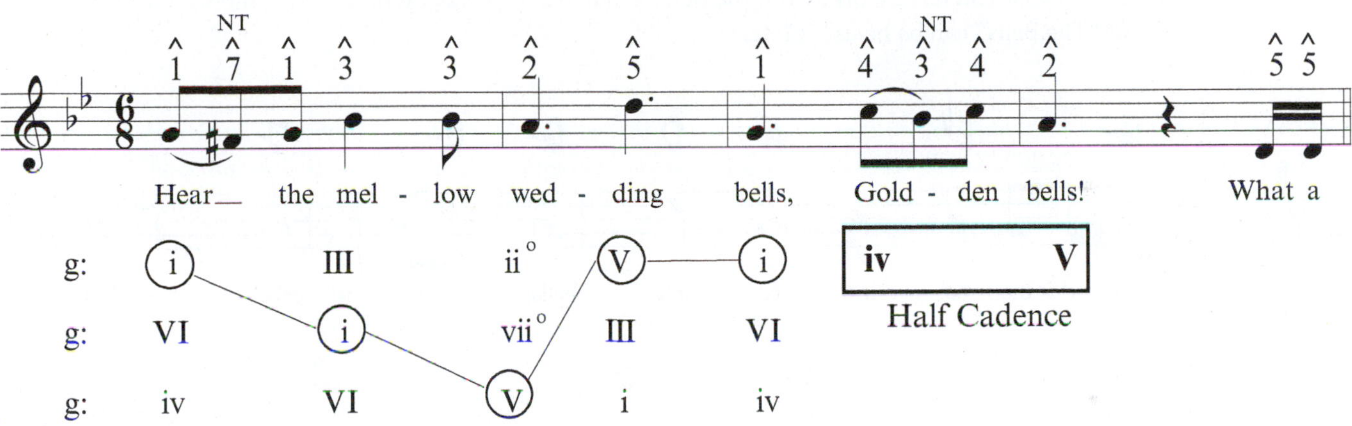

Either of the previous plans is acceptable (assuming that the other two phrases are harmonized consistently). The composer or arranger makes these choices—sometimes by ear—based on musical instincts and personal preferences.

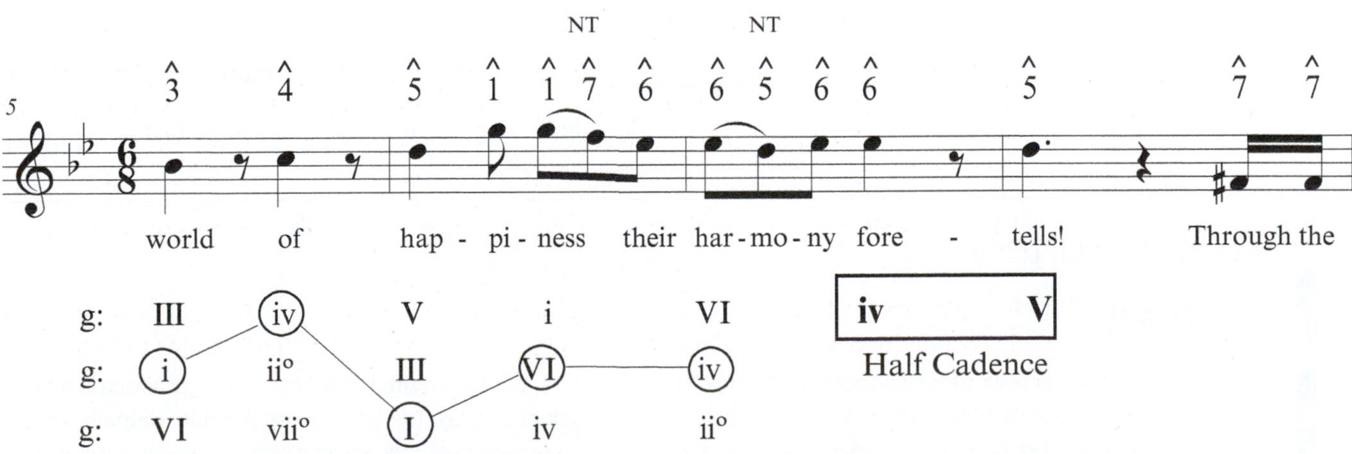

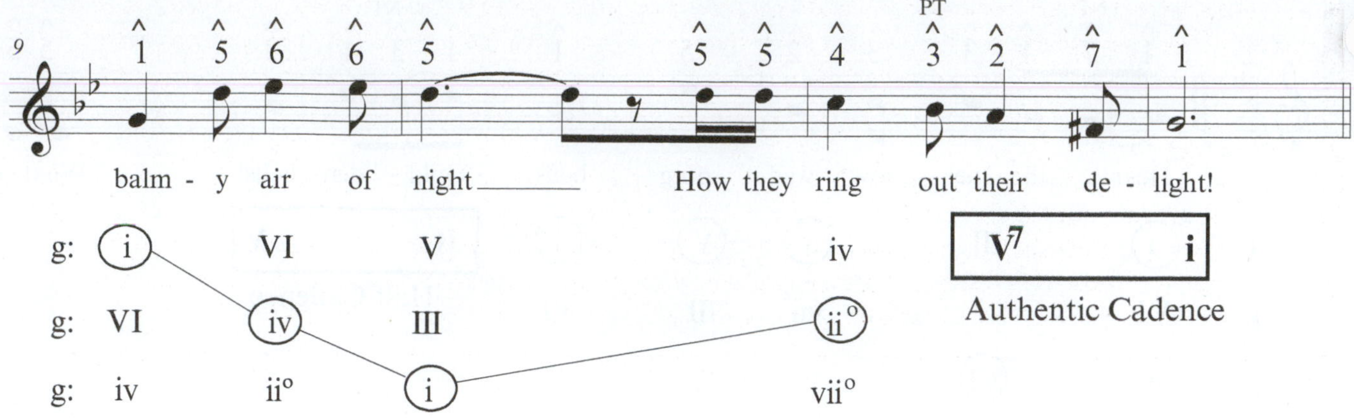

A final step should always include revision and editing. Do you like the consecutive predominants in measure 7 or do they constitute a "dead spot" where momentum slows? Is the progression i–iv–i in measures 9–10 a welcome break from movement through the three functions or would i–iv–V be preferable? Once you have worked out the details, make a lead sheet with chord symbols. Our final version of "The Bells" can be heard online.

A Step Further

Copyright

If you arrange a song or even compose your own, you need to know a bit about **copyright**. We cannot offer legal advice in a text, of course, but two aspects of copyright law are important for a song composer today. The first of these is **public domain**, which means that a work is *not* covered by copyright and can be used by the general public for any purpose—including profit. When the 1970s and 1980s folk-rock group Steeleye Span, for example, recorded a version of the British folk song "Seventeen Come Sunday," they needed no permission because the original song dates from the 1840s. On the other hand, if you want to arrange "Love Me Tender" (Elvis Presley's version of the folk song "Aura Lee"), you will need permission even though "Aura Lee" is in public domain. Your song is based on a later, copyrighted version.

When in doubt about whether a source is or is not copyrighted, assume that it is. If you have based your song on a notated score, contact that publisher and they will steer you to the owner of the rights. The original music of compositions dating from 1930 and before is probably in public domain; even in this event, your source may be a later arrangement that remains protected. Online resources (such as the Music Publisher's Association) are helpful. Copyright law is complicated and cannot be covered here in any detail.

The second question that often arises is: Should I copyright my original song? If you write a song on your own text and intend it for your personal or limited commercial use, you probably do not. Thanks to international copyright law, once you make a recording or notation of your music, it is copyrighted from that date. Should you want to register your title anyway (to be able to bring legal action against copyright violators, for example), you can do this online through the U.S. Copyright Office. After you apply (the forms are online), there is a nonrefundable fee whether your music is accepted for registration or not.

For class discussion or assignment: please do not remove these pages

REVIEW SET

Harmonization

A. A number of the chords in these harmonizations do not follow predominant, dominant, and tonic functions. Mark an "X" through the incorrect chord and propose another beneath it. Some of the cadences, too, are not traditional types. Replace these as well.

Simple Melody

American Folk Song, "Old Mac Donald"

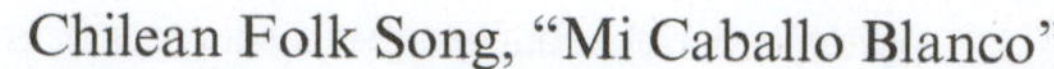

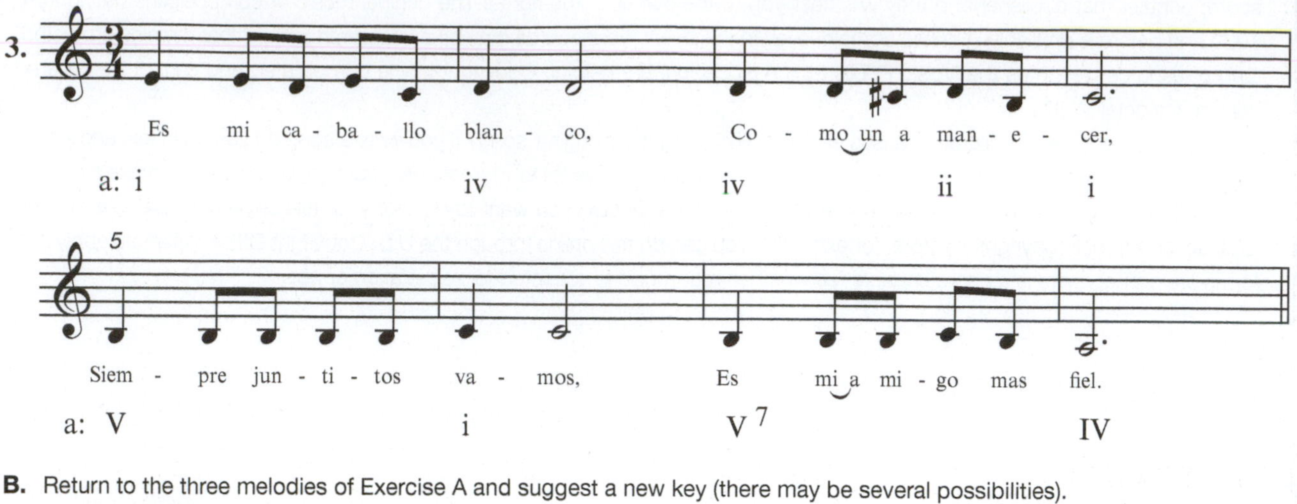

B. Return to the three melodies of Exercise A and suggest a new key (there may be several possibilities). Indicate whether your transposition would be up to the new key or down.

1. Melody 1 for *soprano*. Transpose from E major ___________ to ___________.
   up/down new key
2. Melody 2 for *alto*. Transpose from E♭ major ___________ to ___________.
   up/down new key
3. Melody 3 for *soprano*. Transpose from A minor ___________ to ___________.
   up/down new key

Complete Building Skills 13-2 on page 401

MUSICIANSHIP 13-1

Keyboard: Major Scales

Practice these scales using the fingerings given.

F Major

E♭ Major

A♭ Major

Name ______________________

Page may be removed

Building Skills • 13-1

Phrases and Cadences

A. **Provide block chords (with any necessary accidentals) and Roman numerals that represent the cadences specified. In the case of a half cadence, any of the three choices is correct.**

B. **These chords may or may not represent one of the cadence types in the specified key. Write the Roman numerals in the spaces below the staff and the lead sheet symbols above the staff. If the chords could make a cadence, identify the type (authentic, plagal, half, and so on). If the chords do not represent a cadence type, write "none."**

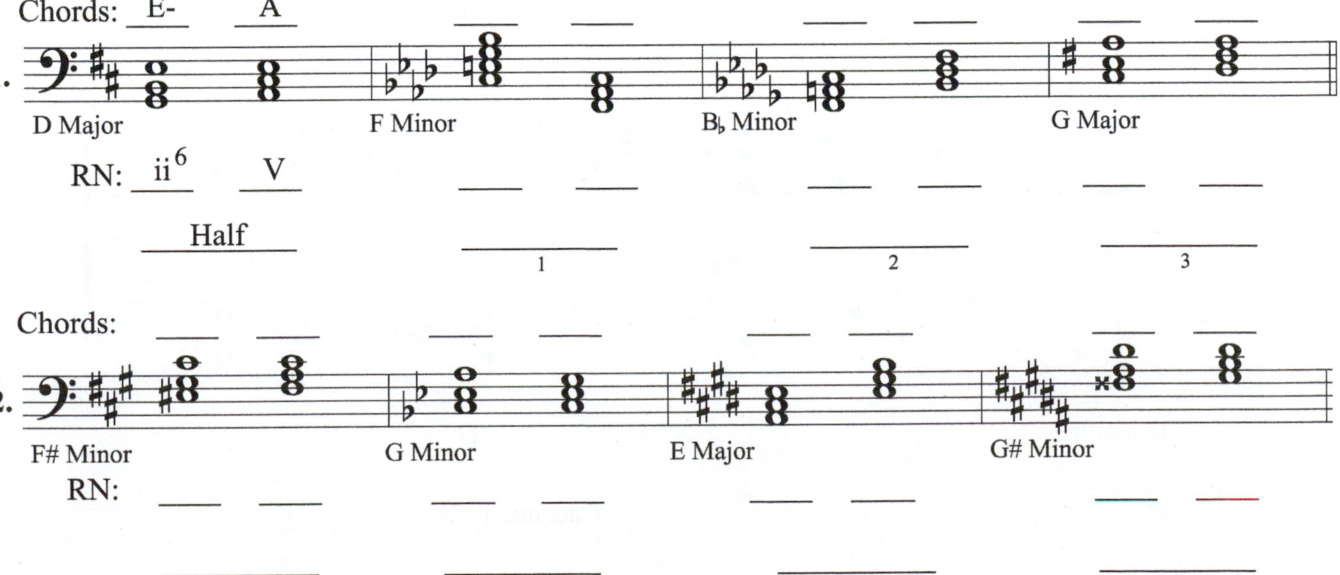

C. **Plan cadences for the following phrases. The final two chords are indicated by the blanks. In the key specified, list one possible cadence and provide Roman numerals. Ignore the smaller notes in your analysis.**

Franz Schubert, Impromptu

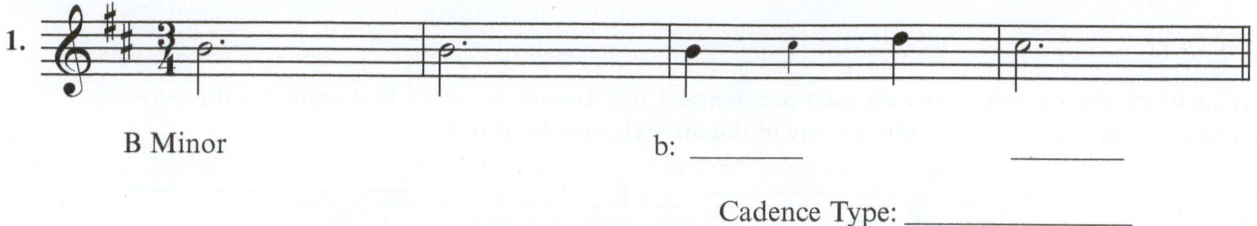

B Minor b: ________ ________

Cadence Type: ________________

Hector Berlioz, *Roman Carnival*

2.

C Major C: ________ ________

Cadence Type: ________________

G.F. Handel, "Hallelujah Chorus"

D Major D: _____ _____

Cadence Type: ________________

Name ______________________

Page may be removed

Building Skills • 13-2

Harmonization

Provide an analysis of these two-phrase melodies:

1. **Determine the harmonic rhythm. Study the given chord symbols or Roman numerals.**
2. **Describe the harmonic rhythm with one or more sentences. State a basic rate of harmonic flow and account for any exceptions.**
3. **Identify the cadences of both phrases and provide a term to identify the form.**
4. **Determine how the second phrase is related to the first: repetition, variation, sequence, or contrast (remembering that we perceive this relationship from the *beginning* of the second phrase).**

C Major

Australian Folk Song, "The Overlander"

Comments on Harmonic Rhythm:

Cadences: First Phrase ______________________ Second Phrase ______________________

Melody Form ______________________ Phrase Construction ______________________

Italian Folk Song, "The Maid of Sorrento"

D Major

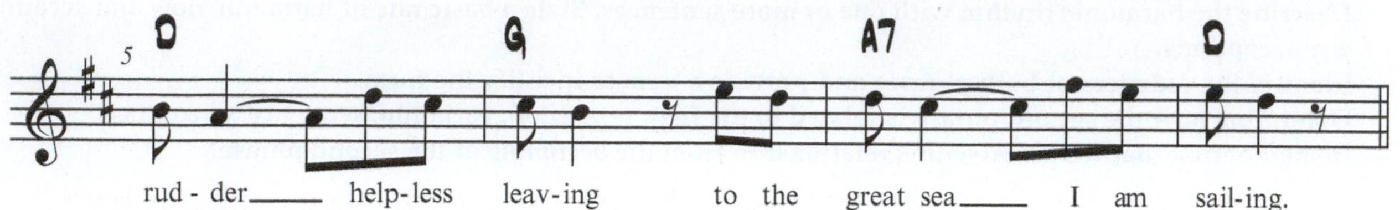

Comments on Harmonic Rhythm:

Cadences: First Phrase ______________________ Second Phrase ______________________

Melody Form ______________________ Phrase Construction ______________________

Name ______________________

Page may be removed

Creative Projects • Chapter 13

Harmonize the melodies provided. Analyze the melody and follow the steps listed on pages 391–394 (including transposition as needed). Provide chord symbols and identify cadences. Do your work on another sheet of manuscript paper.

Transpose for Soprano/Tenor Range if Necessary

"The Poor Ghost"
Words by Christina Rossetti (1830–1894)

D Minor

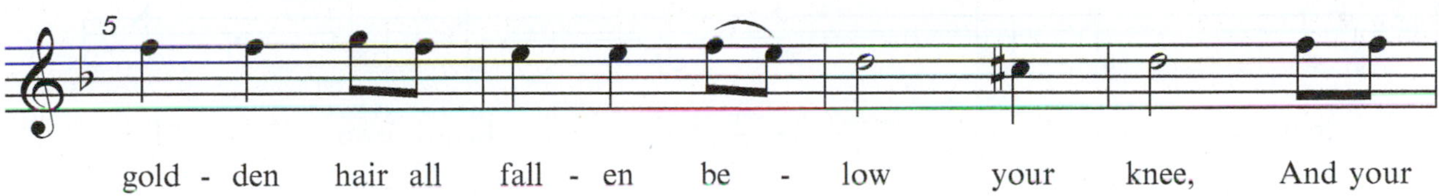

Transpose as Necessary for Alto/Bass Voices

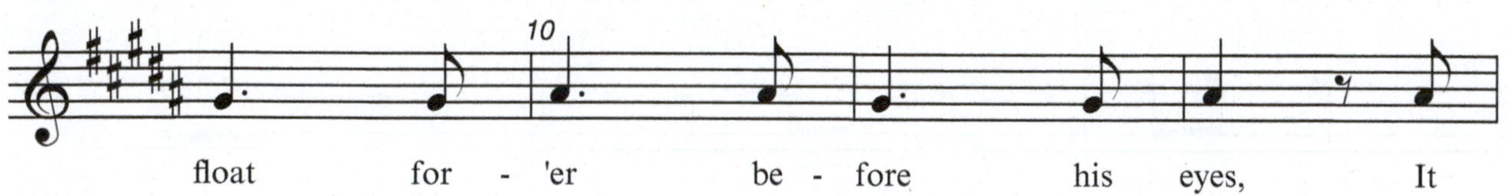

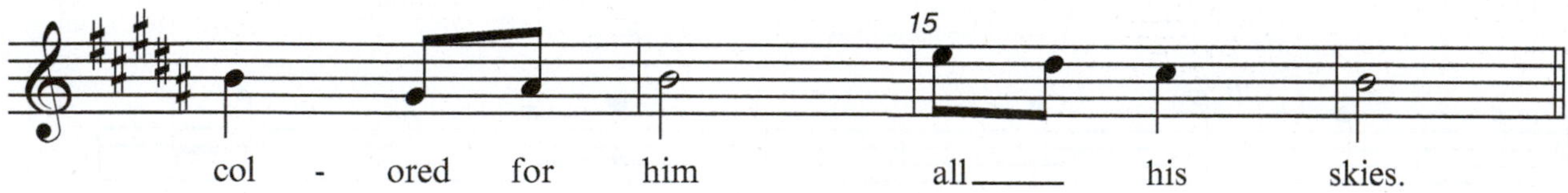

Name ______________________________

Page may be removed

Analysis in Context 1 • Chapter 13

"Caro mio ben" is an 18th century Italian art song, composed by Tommaso Giordani in 1783. Unlike much vocal music of this time, it was not composed as part of an opera. Instead, it was a concert piece to be performed on its own.

12
p
cor. Il tuo fe - del so - spira o -
12
f
p
16
mf
gnore, ces - sa, cru - del, tan - to ri - gor, ces - sa, cru - del, tan - to ri -
16
p
20
rit.
pp a tempo
mf
gor, tan - to ri - gor. Ca - ro mir ben, cre - dimi al - men, Sen - za di
20
rit.
f
pp a tempo
p
24
3
rit.
f a tempo
p dolce
f
te lan - gui - sce il cor. Ca - ro mio ben, cre - dimi al - men, sen - za di
24
rit.
f a tempo
p
mf

Name ____________________

Page may be removed

1. In what key does the song begin?

2. Listen to the first 12 measures of the song. Describe the melodic characteristics (stepwise, leaps or skips, mostly diatonic, chromatic pitches, etc.). What types of non-chord tones seem most prevalent given the traits you described above?

3. What cadence type is present at the beginning of measure 4?

4. What cadence type is present at the beginning of measure 8?

5. What type of cadence is found at the beginning of measure 12?

6. What is the primary melodic treatment in these first three phrases?

7. Listen to the complete song. What short melodic motive is the whole song based on?

8. The song has three main parts. Where does a new melodic idea begin? Compare and contrast it to the first melodic theme.

9. What is the vocal range of the song? Given the vocal range, what voice part (soprano, alto, tenor, or bass) would be best suited to sing this song?

10. On a separate piece of manuscript paper, transpose the vocal line only to suit the range of another voice part of your choosing.

Appendix A
The Nature of Sound

Essential Terms

acoustics
amplitude
duration
frequency
fundamental
harmonics
harmonic series
hertz (Hz)
noise
overtones
partials
pitch
psychoacoustics
sound waves
timbre
tone quality

In addition to measurable *physical* properties, sounds such as those of a clarinet or automobile horn make an impression on us psychologically. Duration, which can be measured with precision, is a physical property; the length of a particular sound might be two seconds, for example. Hearing a sound as loud, soft, or somewhere in between, on the other hand, is a relative psychological sensation. Exposed to the same sound, one listener might think it is loud; another might consider it relatively soft. **Acoustics** is the branch of science that deals with the physical properties of sound. **Psychoacoustics** is a relatively new field in which the psychological responses to sound are explored.

Sound Waves

Before sound can be transmitted, the air surrounding the sound source must be set into motion. On a violin, the vibrations of a string disturb the air molecules; on the flute, saxophone, and other wind instruments, the air inside the instrument's "tube" is set into motion. The vibrating string or column of air causes the surrounding air particles to be set into motion in regular patterns of vibration. These patterns of molecular motion are termed **sound waves**. Like waves in the water, sound waves travel spherically from the source, growing more and more faint until they die out completely. If the sound is a musical tone, the sound waves are regular and controlled; **noise** results when waves are irregular and uncontrolled. Counting the number of sound waves over a given time span measures the *frequency* of the sound.

FREQUENCY. **Frequency** is determined by the number of sound waves created by a vibrating string or column of air. We measure frequency over one second of time in *cycles per second* (cps); a more modern term is **hertz** (abbreviated "**Hz**"). Most musical tones register from about 50 Hz to 2000 Hz. A tone in the upper register of a flute is about 1600 Hz. The lowest sound on the double bass, on the other hand, is about 40 Hz. The limits of human audition fall between about 20 Hz and 20,000 Hz.

PITCH. The frequency of a sound produces the psychological response we call **pitch**. The greater the frequency, the higher the pitch; sounds with lower frequencies produce tones of lower pitch. An oscilloscope measures the frequency of sound waves. The first illustration that follows is of a relatively high pitch as it might appear on an oscilloscope. The second diagram is lower; the third is lower still.

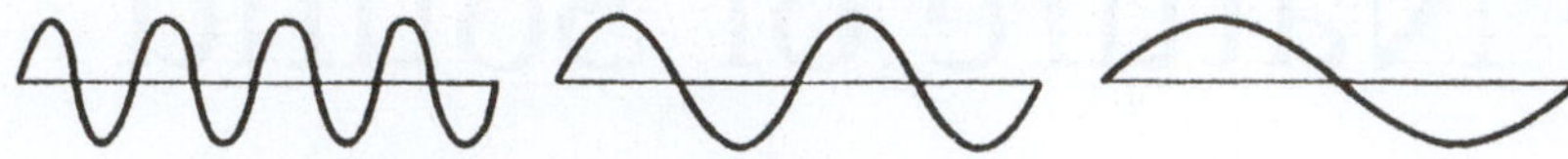

Amplitude and Intensity

Sounds differ not only in pitch, but in other aspects as well. The acoustical property known as *amplitude*, for example, plays a role in most musical works. **Amplitude** is the degree of disturbance in air molecules caused by the sound. We translate differences in amplitude into how we perceive a sound as being loud or soft. If a sound has relatively greater amplitude, that is, if it creates a relatively greater disturbance in the air particles, we perceive the sound as loud. Lesser amplitude creates the sensation of a softer tone. Notice that the two sounds represented below have the same frequency yet they differ in amplitude. The first would be the louder, the second, softer.

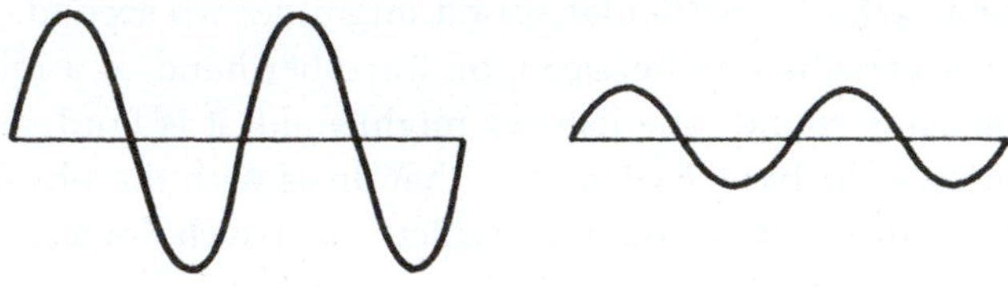

Timbre and Quality

Almost any musical sound is made up of many different frequencies—some relatively strong, others weaker. The various frequencies present in a tone are known as **harmonics**. A flute can be distinguished from a trumpet even if the sounds have identical frequency and amplitude. This is primarily because the harmonics present in the tone of a trumpet are greater in number and relatively stronger than those of the flute. Differences in harmonics largely determine the acoustical property known as **timbre**. We perceive differences in timbre (pronounced "tam-bar") as differences in **tone quality**—the corresponding psychological response. Even if we cannot see the performers, we can identify most orchestral instruments by the quality of their tones. The same phenomenon allows us to recognize a familiar voice over the telephone.

The Harmonic Series

One of the most important factors affecting tone quality is the *harmonic series*. When a tone is sounded on an acoustic musical instrument such as a flute or a trumpet, in addition to the **fundamental** (the lowest frequency heard), other, weaker frequencies are audible as well. The frequencies sounding above the fundamental are termed **partials**; the strength and quantity of these partials determine the quality and timbre of the musical tone. The higher frequencies above a fundamental are called **overtones**. The fundamental is included when counting partials, but excluded when counting overtones.

The **harmonic series** is a natural phenomenon that occurs when a sound source is set into motion. The relationship of partials and overtones to the fundamental is invariable. Each fundamental produces exactly the same range of partials and overtones. The harmonic series for the fundamentals C and A♭ are shown in the following examples. Harmonic series for other fundamentals are simply transpositions of these series.

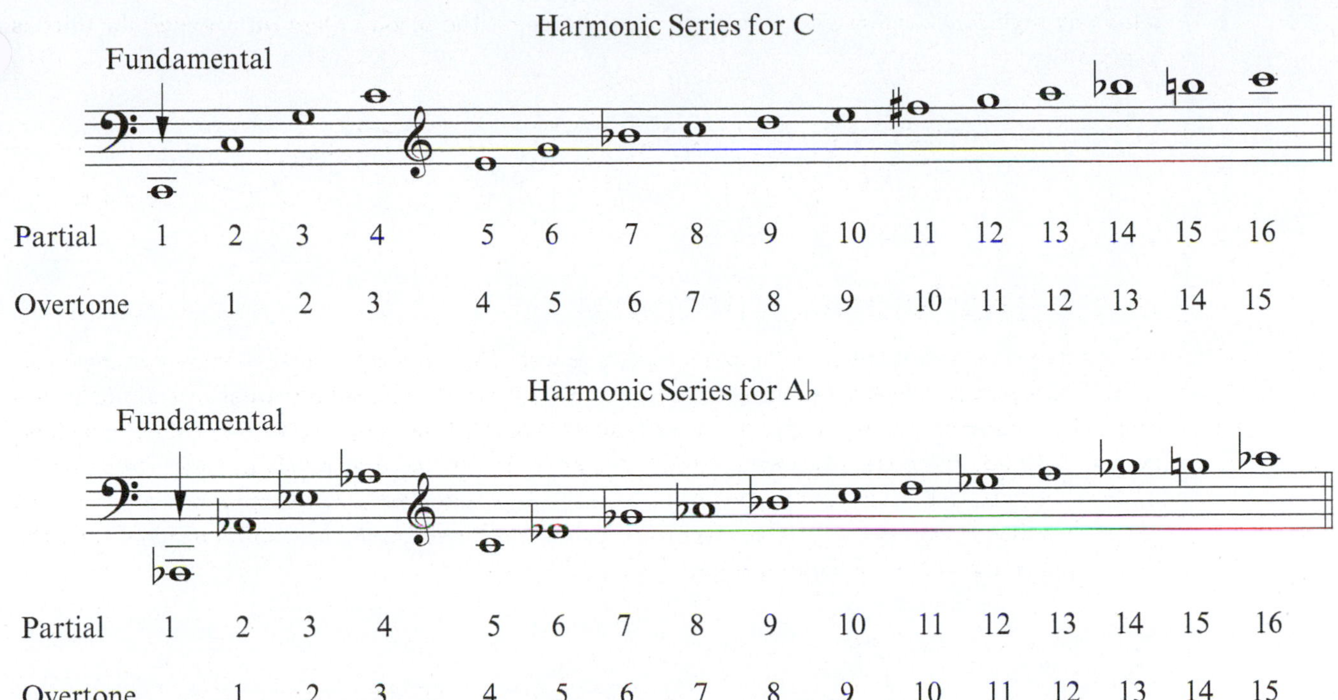

Duration and Length

Frequency, amplitude, and timbre cannot be measured precisely without the aid of electronic equipment. A fourth acoustical property, however, **duration**, can be calculated in minutes, seconds, or even smaller increments. The duration of a sound results in our perception of note length.

Appendix B

Terms and Symbols of Tempo and Expression

Essential Terms

crescendo decrescendo metronome tempo

One of the most complex aspects of notating music concerns nuance. Although the composer can designate a certain group of specific pitches and even the precise length of each note, the performer ultimately decides on certain less-exact parameters such as volume, articulation (the expressive manner in which tones and phrases begin, continue, and end), and enhancing effects such as vibrato (tonal pulsations). Over the centuries, composers developed a vocabulary of terms and symbols to aid the performer in understanding how to approach musical nuance. Many of the terms we continue to use are Italian—reflecting an almost total domination of Western music by Italian composers during the seventeenth and early eighteenth centuries.

Tempo

Tempo is the speed of the beat. Although many twentieth- and twenty-first-century composers use their native language to indicate tempo ("quick," "very slowly," "moderate," and so on), Italian terms are still common. Remember that terms for tempo are relative. The word *Andante* (Italian, "walking") is usually interpreted as a "walking speed," giving the performer only a general idea of the composer's intentions. Likewise, the Italian words *Lento* and *Presto* indicate slower and faster tempos, respectively.

THE METRONOME. Since the early nineteenth century, the **metronome**, a device for measuring a certain number of beats per minute, has given performers a more exact guide to the speed of the beat. Rather than relying on the performer's interpretation of general tempo indications, composers simply write the letters *M.M.* (for Maelzel metronome) followed by a note value and the number of those notes to be played in one minute. The letters *M.M.* are often omitted.

M.M. ♩ = 132   M.M. 𝅗𝅥 = 72   ♪ = 100   ♩. = 60

Dynamics

As with terms for tempo, indications of dynamic level are relative. Several Italian terms, shown in the next table, are often abbreviated to indicate volume.

Term	Meaning	Abbreviation
pianissimo	very soft	*pp*
piano	soft	*p*
mezzo piano	moderately soft	*P*
mezzo forte	moderately loud	*F*
forte	loud	*f*
fortissimo	very loud	*ff*

Gradual increases or decreases in volume are often shown with special symbols. A **crescendo** (<) indicates a gradual increase in volume; a decrease is marked by a **decrescendo** (>). The length of the crescendo and decrescendo symbols may indicate how quickly the change in volume takes place.

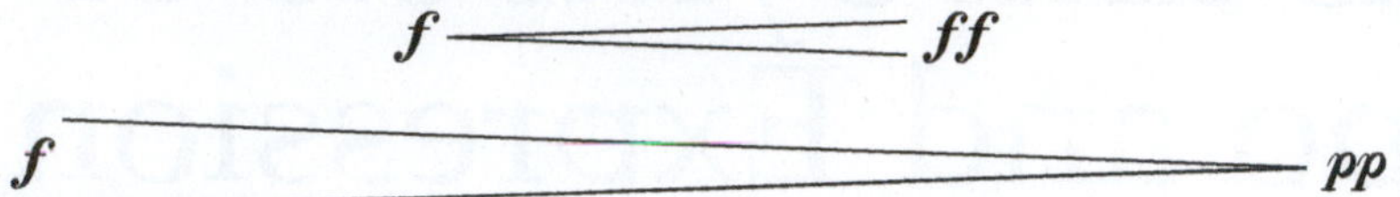

Expression

Composers often indicate a specific effect they want the performer to achieve, such as "tender," "detached," or "singing." Again, such terms are primarily Italian.

Short Glossary of Italian Terms

Tempo

accelerando, gradually speeding up
adagio, slow
allegretto, moderately fast
allegro, fast
andante, moderate, walking speed
largo, very slow
lento, slow (at ease)
moderato, moderate speed
presto, very fast
ritardando, gradually slowing

Expression

affettuoso, tender, with affect
cantabile, singing style
con gusto, with zest
crescendo, gradually louder
decrescendo, gradually softer
dolce, sweetly
forte, loud
fortissimo, very loud
legato, smooth, connected
marcato, marked, stressed
mezzo forte, moderately loud
mezzo piano, moderately soft
molto, much, greatly
pianissimo, very soft
piano, soft
poco, a little
subito, suddenly
sempre, always

Appendix C
The C Clefs

Essential Terms

alto clef
mezzo-soprano clef
movable C-clef
soprano clef
tenor clef

In addition to the treble and bass clefs discussed in Chapter 2, another clef is often encountered both in the music of the past and in instrumental music today. The **movable C-clef** (𝄡) locates the pitch C on the line that runs through the center of the symbol.

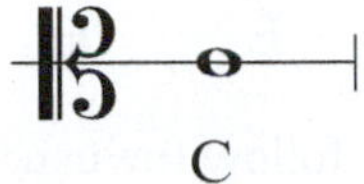

In modern orchestral music, the *alto* and *tenor clefs* remain a common way to avoid excessive ledger lines.

Alto and Tenor Clefs

The **alto clef** identifies the third line as the pitch C. In the orchestra, the viola reads its part entirely in alto clef.

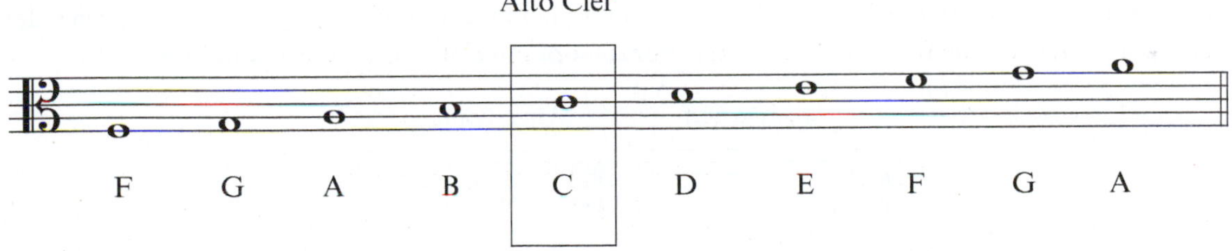

On the alto clef, the lines are F, A, C, E, and G; the spaces are G, B, D, and F.

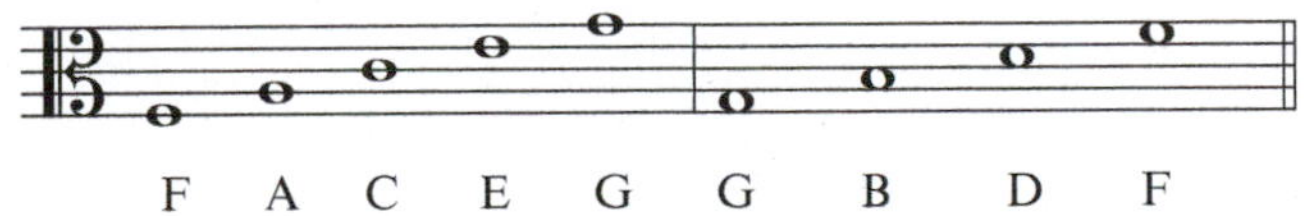

When needed, ledger lines function in the C clefs just as they do in the treble and bass clefs.

Joseph Haydn

Notice the placement of accidentals on the staff in the alto clef.

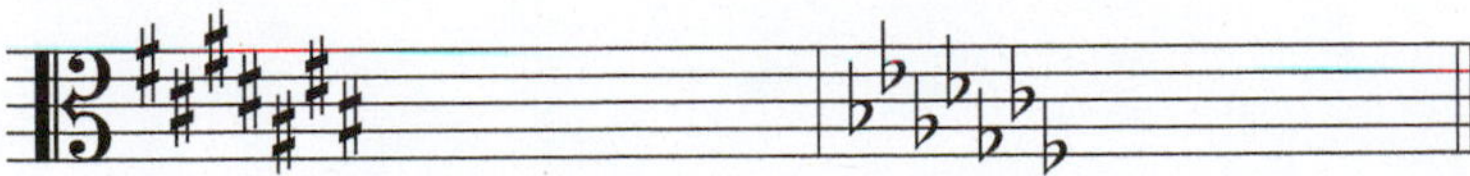

TENOR CLEF. On the **tenor clef**, the *fourth* line is the location of the pitch C. Advanced performers on cello, trombone, and bassoon all encounter parts written in tenor clef.

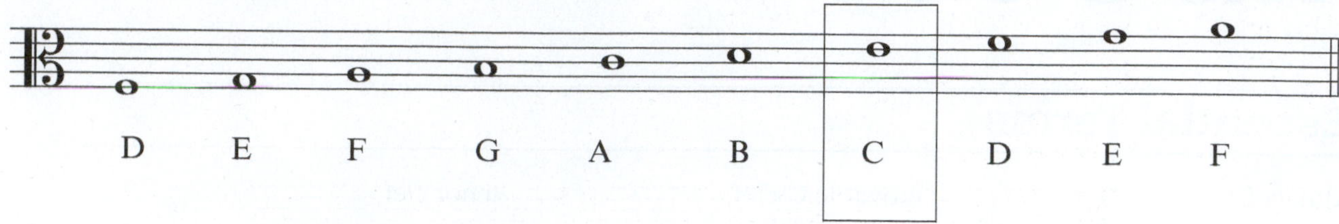

Lines on the tenor clef are D, F, A, C, and E; the spaces are E, G, B, and D.

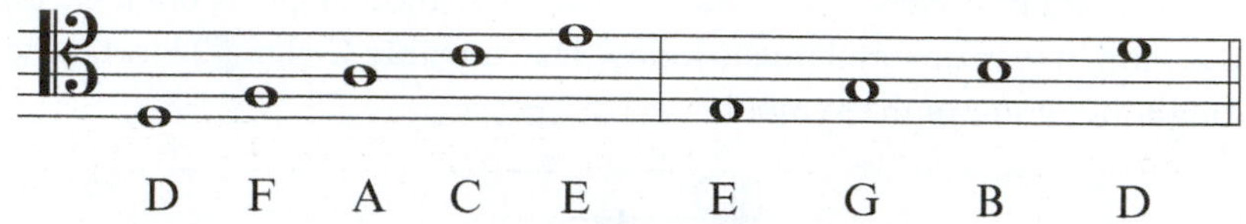

Accidentals in a tenor-clef key signature follow the usual pattern.

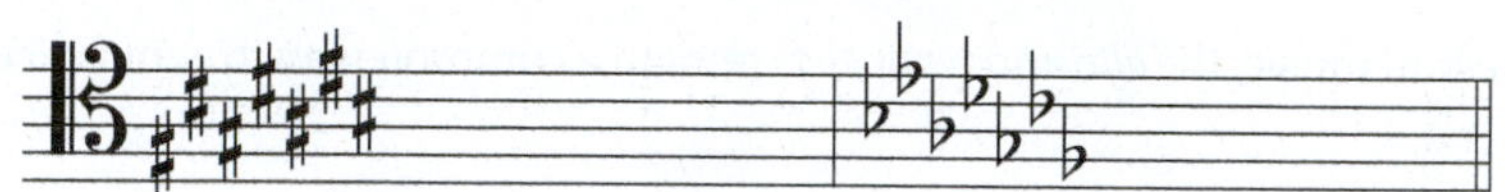

Soprano and Mezzo-Soprano Clefs

While rarely found in notation today, other C clefs were common in music until the late nineteenth century. Those who study music professionally are expected to read music in *any* clef. The **soprano clef** locates the pitch C on the first staff line; on the **mezzo-soprano clef**, C is on the second line.

Complete Building Skills C-1 on page 417

Name ____________________

Page may be removed

Building Skills • C-1

Alto and Tenor Clefs

A. **Write the pitch name beneath each note.**

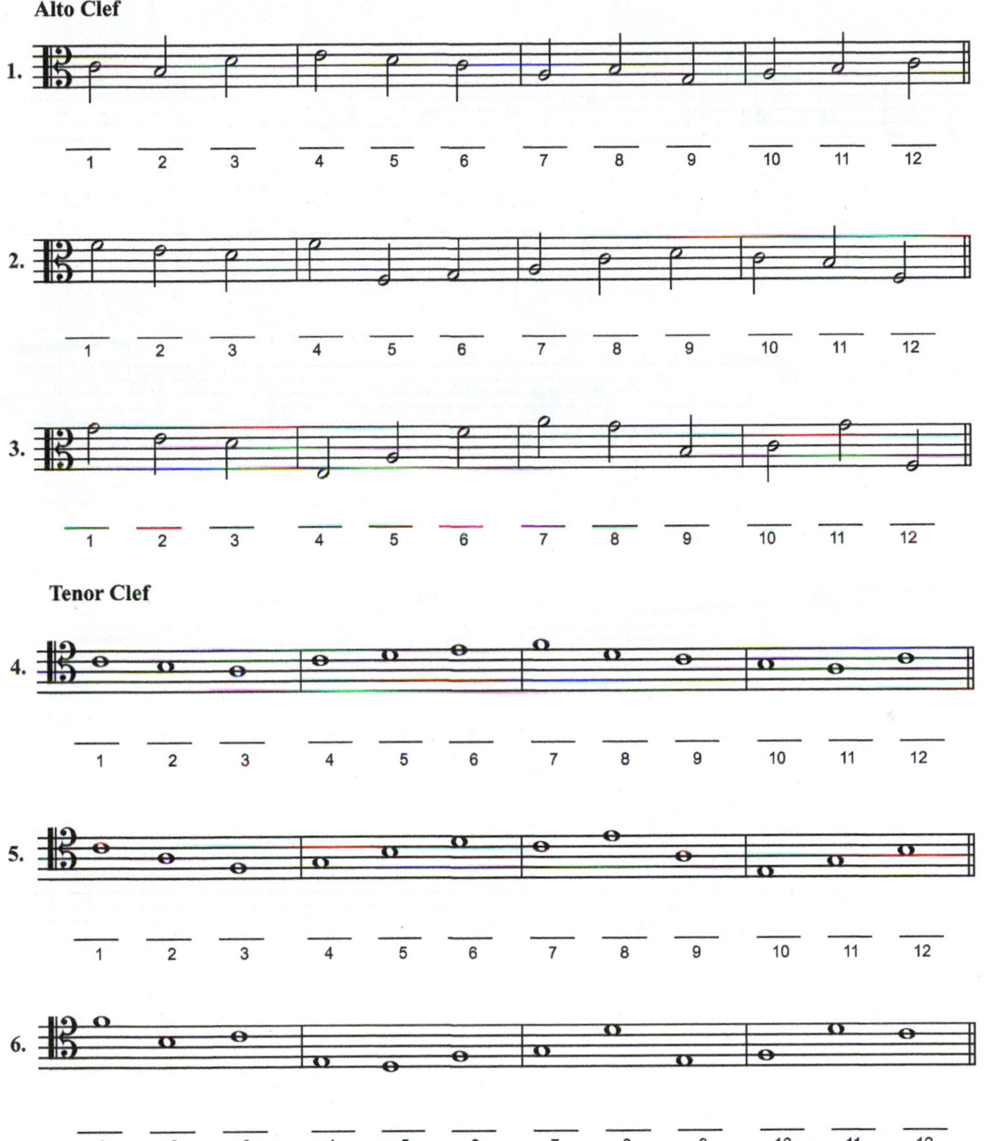

B. These lines include rhythmic values. Identify each pitch in the blank below it. Do not include accidentals.

Alto and Tenor Clefs

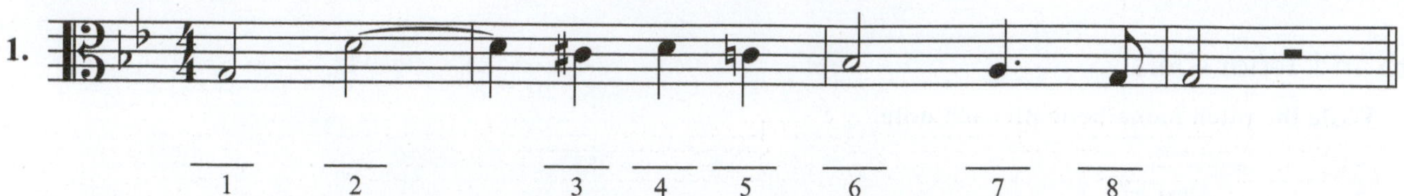

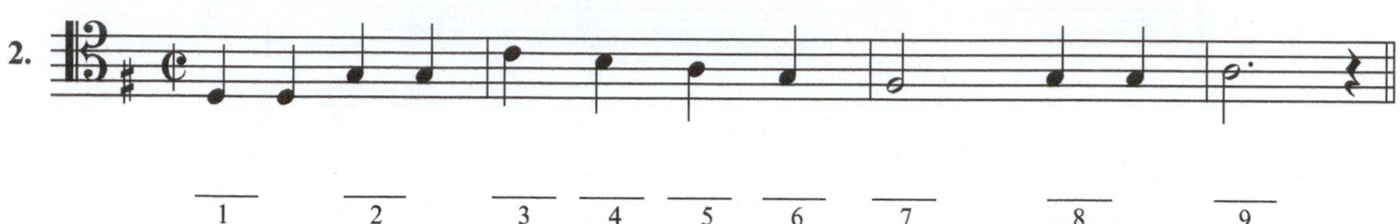

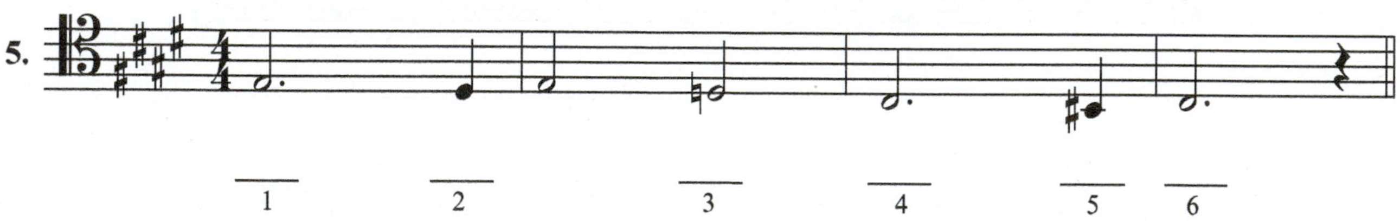

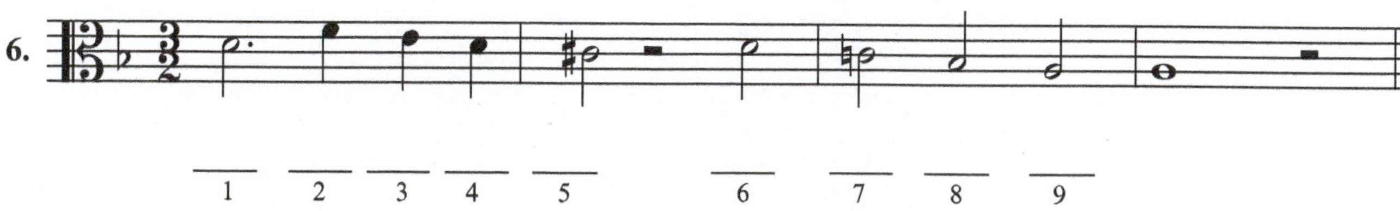

Name ____________________

Page may be removed

C. **Where blanks appear, name the note in the given alto or tenor clef. You do not need to provide accidentals with the note name.**

D. **The upper line of this passage is the viola part from the second movement of Haydn's Quartet in G Minor. On the lower line, rewrite this part in bass or treble clef (as indicated) retaining the original octaves. Include all dynamics and other markings in your revision. The curved lines over and under notes in the viola part tell the performer how to group notes by up and down movements of the bow; in measure 8, notice that two pitches are played simultaneously.**

Appendix D

Answers to Ear Training Exercises

Chapter	Page	
2	41	Musicianship 2-1

Patterns of Three Pitches

1. S L S H
2. L H S L
3. S S H L

Patterns of Four Pitches

1. L L H S
2. S H H S
3. H S H L

Patterns of Five Pitches

1. H S L L
2. L S S H
3. S S H H

Various

a. H L S H
b. L S S L
c. L L H L
d. L S S L

Chapter	Page	
3	70	Musicianship 3-2

Predominantly Half Steps

a. H H W H
b. H H H W
c. H H H H
d. H W H W
e. H H W H
f. W H H H

Predominantly Whole Steps

g. W W H W
h. H W W W
i. W W W W
j. H W W W
k. H H W W
l. W W W H

Whole and Half Steps

m. W H H W
n. H H W W
o. H H W H
p. H W W H
q. H W W W
r. W W W H

Directed Listening

Melody A	First Interval H	Last Interval H
Melody B	First Interval W	Last Interval H
Melody C	First Interval H	Last Interval W
Melody D	First Interval H	Last Interval H
Melody E	First Interval W	Last Interval H

4 99

Musicianship 4-2

A.

a. triple **e.** triple
b. duple **f.** duple
c. duple **g.** triple
d. triple **h.** duple

B.

Melodies

Anacrusis Meter

Anacrusis Meter

1. yes triple **5.** yes duple
2. no duple **6.** no triple
3. yes triple **7.** yes triple
4. no duple **8.** no duple

5 114

Musicianship 5-1

Ascending Patterns

1. M O M O M M
2. O M O M O M

Descending Patterns

1. M M O M O O
2. O M M M M O

Ascending and Descending Patterns

1. M O O M M O
2. O O M O O M

6 153

Musicianship 6-2

Perfect Intervals

1. P8 P5 P5 P8 P5 P8
2. P5 P4 P1 P5 P8 P5
3. P1 P4 P5 P4 P8 P5
4. P4 P5 P5 P4 P4 P5
5. P5 P8 P5 P4 P5 P1
6. P4 P8 P5 P5 P4 P8

Musicianship 6-3

Major and Minor Seconds

a. M2 m2 M2 m2 m2 M2
b. M2 m2 M2 M2 M2 m2
c. m2 M2 M2 m2 m2 M2

Major and Minor Thirds

d. M3 m3 m3 m3 M3 M3
e. m3 M3 m3 m3 M3 M3
f. m3 m3 M3 m3 M3 M3
g. M3 m3 m3 M3 M3 m3

Major and Minor Seconds and Thirds

h. M2 M3 m3 M3 M2 M2
i. m2 m3 M3 M2 M2 M3
j. m3 m2 M2 M3 m3 M2
k. m3 M2 M2 M3 M3 m2

Perfect Intervals, Seconds, and Thirds

a. P5 M2 P4 m3 M3 P8
b. M3 M2 m3 P5 m2 P4
c. M3 m2 P8 P5 P4 M3
d. m3 P5 P4 M2 m3 P8

7 197 Musicianship 7-2

Duple Meters

a. simple **e.** compound
b. simple **f.** compound
c. compound **g.** simple
d. simple **h.** compound

Triple Meters

a. compound **e.** simple
b. simple **f.** compound
c. simple **g.** simple
d. compound **h.** simple

8 229 Musicianship 8-2

A.

Ascending

1. M m M m M M
2. m M m M m M

Descending

3. M M m M m m
4. m m M M M m

Various

a. m m M M m M
b. m M M m m M

B.

Scale Degrees 1-5 in Major and Minor

a. M m m M m M
b. m m M M m m
c. M M m m m M

C.

Listening for Leading Tone and Subtonic

a. LT LT ST LT ST ST
b. LT ST LT LT LT ST
c. ST ST LT ST LT ST

10 284 Musicianship 10-1

a. M m m M M m
b. M m m M M M
c. M m m M m m
d. M m m M m m

Musicianship 10-2

Triads: All Qualities, Part I

1. M m M m M M
2. m d d m M m
3. M A M A M m

Triads: All Qualities, Part II

1. m d d M m M
2. m M A m m d
3. A M m d m m

Musicianship 10-3

1. m M M m d m
2. A M M d d M
3. d m A m M m
4. m m A m m d

11	316	Musicianship 11-1 **1.** m m M m d M **2.** M A M A m m **3.** M m d m d M **4.** A m d M M m
12	357	Musicianship 12-2 **1.** T T S T S S **2.** S T S T T T **3.** T T S S S S **4.** S S T S T T

Appendix E
Modes and Other Scales

Essential Terms

Aeolian mode
blues scale
chromatic scale
church modes
Dorian mode
Ionian mode
Locrian mode
Lydian mode
minor pentatonic scale
Mixolydian mode
modal scale
mode
pentatonic scale
Phrygian mode
whole-tone scale

When we talk about the music of the great "classical" composers, the term "mode" refers to the choice between major or minor. In this same context, the terms "mode" and "scale" are virtually synonymous. Although major and minor scales were employed exclusively by composers for a time, many other possibilities exist. Another series of scales, called the *church modes,* was central to Western music for hundreds of years before major and minor scales evolved. Since the late nineteenth century, and especially in jazz and popular music, the intimate colorations of these older melodic materials have been rewarding for many composers. In a modern context, the term **mode** or **modal scale** usually refers to melodic patterns *other* than major and minor scales (the fact that major and minor were added to the modal system in the sixteenth century notwithstanding).

The Modes

The **church modes** date from ancient times and consist of patterns of five whole and two half steps. Eight church modes existed in the medieval system; for our purposes, however, only four of these are relevant. Church modes are named for ancient Greek tribes: *Dorian, Phrygian, Lydian,* and *Mixolydian.* Because modes predate modern scales, scholars use a different vocabulary to discuss them. Without historical context, however, we can disregard both this complex terminology and four of the original eight modes.[1]

Major and Minor Modes

The modes are series of basic pitches beginning on D, E, F, and G, respectively. In modern use, modal scales have an octave range.

[1] In early Western sacred music, modes were known by number: Mode I, Mode II, Mode III, and so on. The odd-numbered modes are those that continue to be used today; even-numbered modes were alternate arrangements of the same patterns, but with significant differences. Note: a modern system of understanding modes as the "second mode of major" (for example) has nothing to do with Mode II of the medieval system.

The **Dorian** and **Phrygian modes** are classified as *minor* because they have a minor third between the first and third pitches. Play the ascending and descending Dorian and Phrygian modes.

Dorian Mode

m3

Lydian and **Mixolydian modes** are *major* since the first three pitches span a major third.

The **Ionian** and **Aeolian modes** were the forerunners of our major and natural minor scales. Unless we are discussing music before about 1675, however, there is no value in using the modal names.

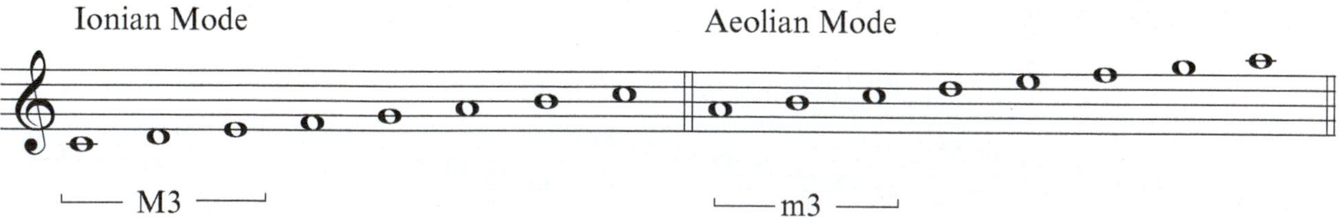

In Chapter 8, you heard the carol "The First Noel" played in major and the three forms of minor page 227. Play the same melody set in major, natural minor, and in each of the four modes. The original version in major is heard first, followed by Lydian and Mixolydian modes.

Mixolydian

In this example, play "The First Noel" in natural minor followed by versions in Dorian and Phrygian modes.

Dorian

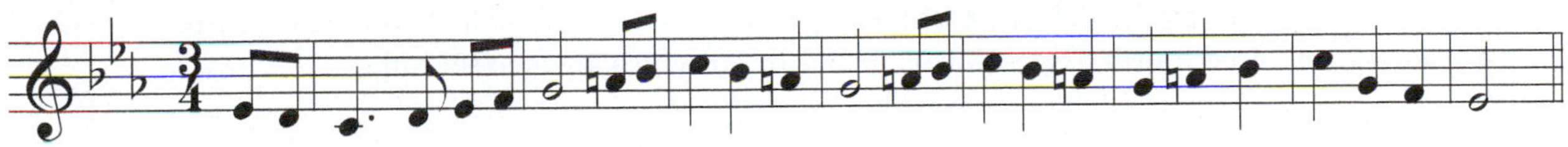

Phrygian

Transposing Modes

For practical purposes, we can view modal scales as variations of either major or natural minor. Beginning with the minor modes, notice that Dorian is a natural minor scale with a raised sixth degree.

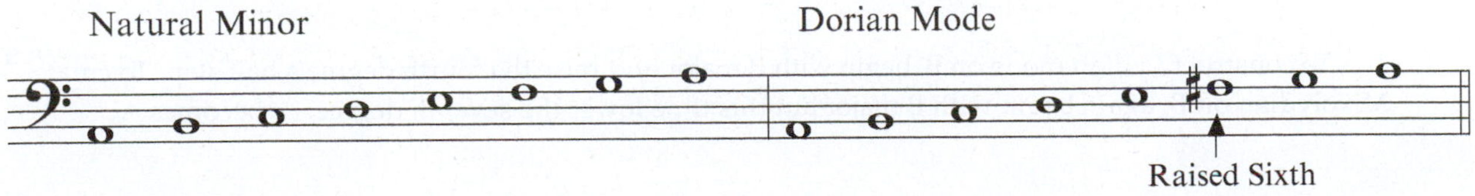

To construct Dorian mode beginning on the pitch A, construct a natural minor scale on A, then raise the sixth degree F to F♯.

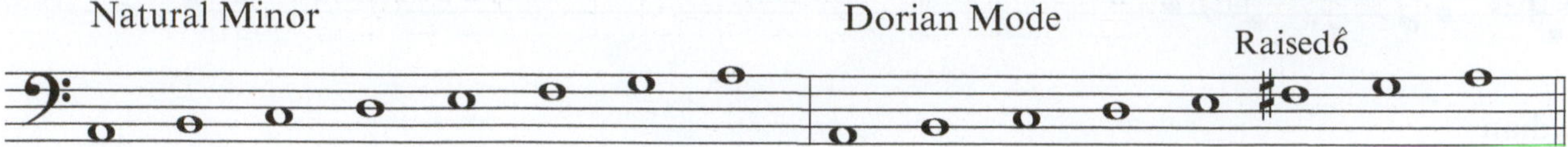

Phrygian mode is natural minor with a lowered second degree.

To construct Phrygian mode on F♯, begin with F♯ natural minor. Next, lower the second scale degree. In this case, the G♯ becomes G♮.

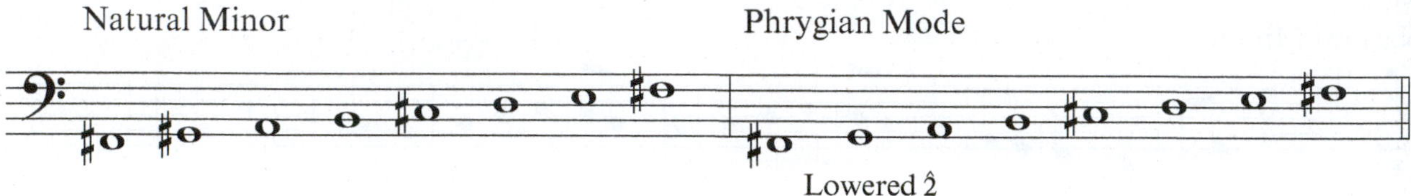

The two major modes can be transposed by making one alteration in a major scale. Lydian mode is major with a raised fourth degree. Mixolydian is major with a lowered seventh.

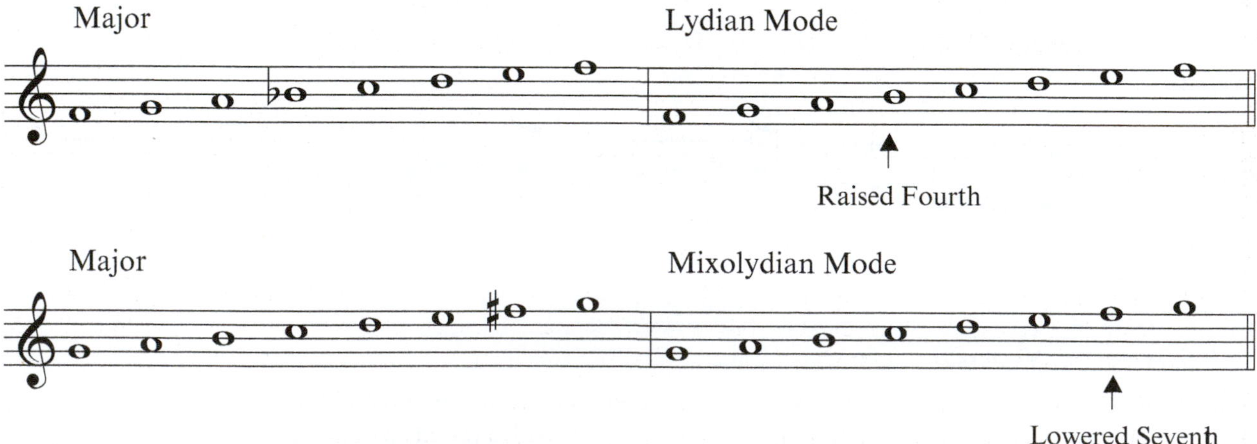

To construct Lydian mode on B, begin with B major and raise the fourth degree a half step. To create Mixolydian on B, again begin with B major but this time lower the seventh degree: A♯ becomes A♮.

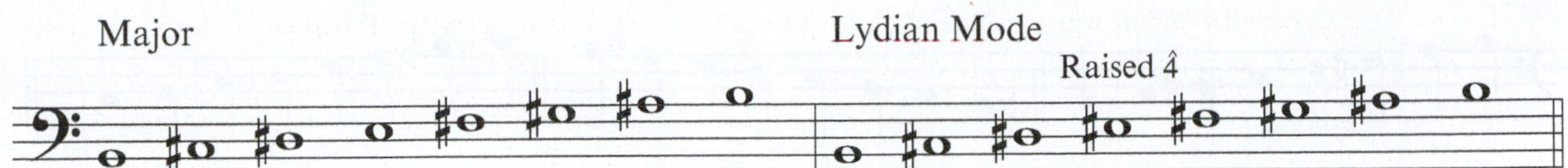

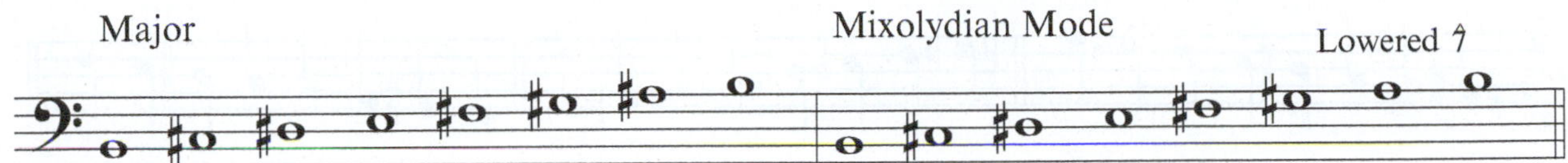

For class discussion or assignment: please do not remove these pages

REVIEW SET: MODES

A. Begin by drafting a major or minor scale (as appropriate), then revise the notation by adding or deleting an accidental.

Phrygian Mode **Lydian Mode**

1.

Dorian Mode **Mixolydian Mode**

2.

Lydian Mode **Phrygian Mode**

3.

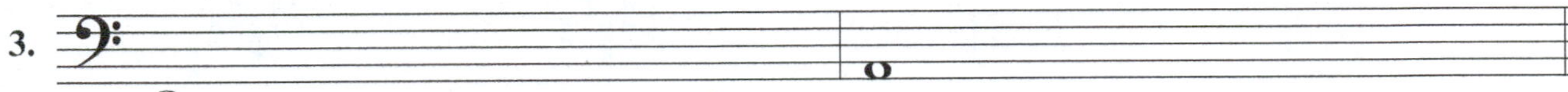

B. These patterns are major, natural minor, or one of the modal scales. Begin by identifying the type as major or minor (look at the last three pitches if the pattern descends). Next, compare the given scale to major or natural minor (as appropriate) and note any differences.

1.

Transposition and Recognition Through Key Signature

The fastest and most accurate method of building and recognizing modal scales is by key signature. The modes have key signatures that differ by one flat or sharp from the corresponding major or minor key.

MAJOR MODES. For Lydian or Mixolydian scales, begin with the corresponding major key. The key signature of G major, for example, is one sharp. When the fourth degree is raised to create Lydian, the basic pitch C becomes C♯. The key signature for G Lydian, therefore, is two sharps.

To determine the key signature of Lydian mode on any pitch, simply add one sharp to the corresponding major key signature. If the major key has flats, the added sharp negates the *last* flat.

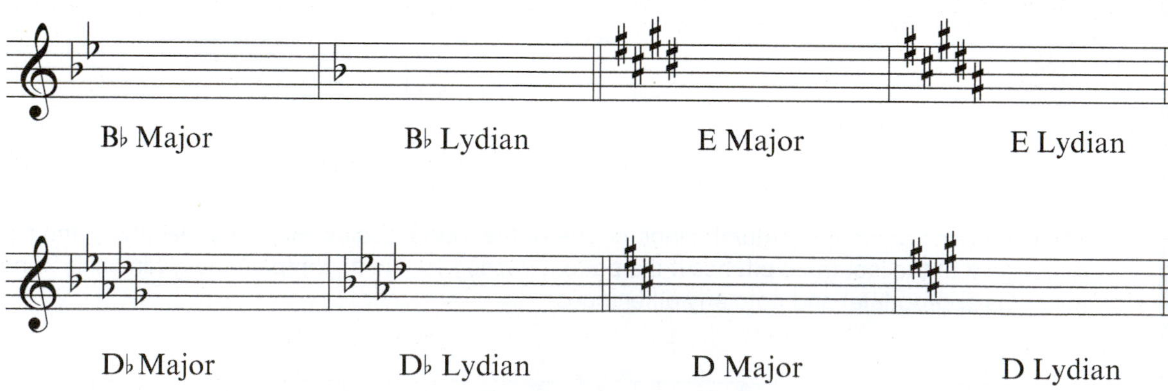

Mixolydian key signatures can also be created through the corresponding major key. The lowered seventh degree of Mixolydian adds a flat to the key signature. If we want Mixolydian on A♭, for example, begin with the key signature for A♭ major, then add a flat. The new flat is always the last flat and provides the lowered seventh.

Add a flat to any major key to create Mixolydian mode. If there are sharps in the signature of the major key, the added flat cancels the last sharp.

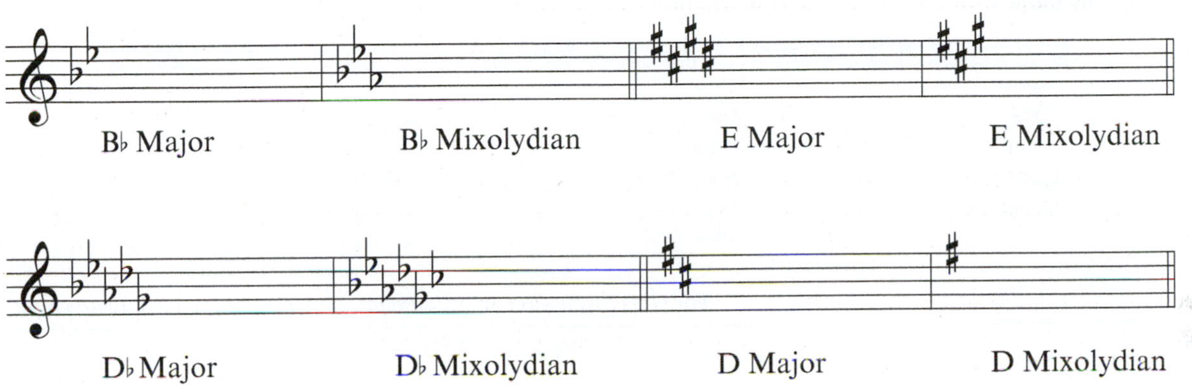

MINOR MODES. Key signatures for Dorian and Phrygian modes are adapted from the corresponding minor key. If we want a Dorian scale on B, for example, begin with B minor (two sharps), then add a sharp. The added sharp creates the characteristic raised sixth. When the minor key has flats, the last flat is canceled by the added sharp. Likewise, add a flat to the minor key signature to determine the accidentals in Phrygian mode. The added flat creates the lowered second scale degree.

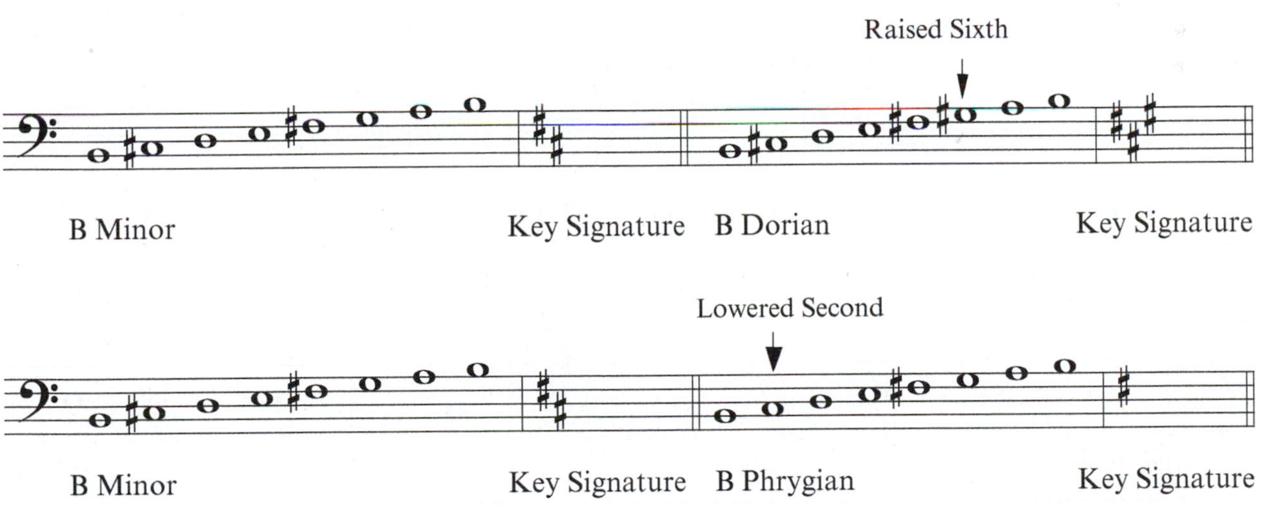

To create a key signature for Dorian mode on any given pitch, begin with the corresponding minor and add a sharp; for Phrygian, add a flat.[2]

[2] Terms like "tonic" and "key" are less often used in discussing modal materials. In traditional tonal music, the tonic is a goal that is emphasized by the leading tone. This and other approaches create a feeling for key. Most modes lack a leading tone and terms like "pitch center" are more appropriate than "tonic."

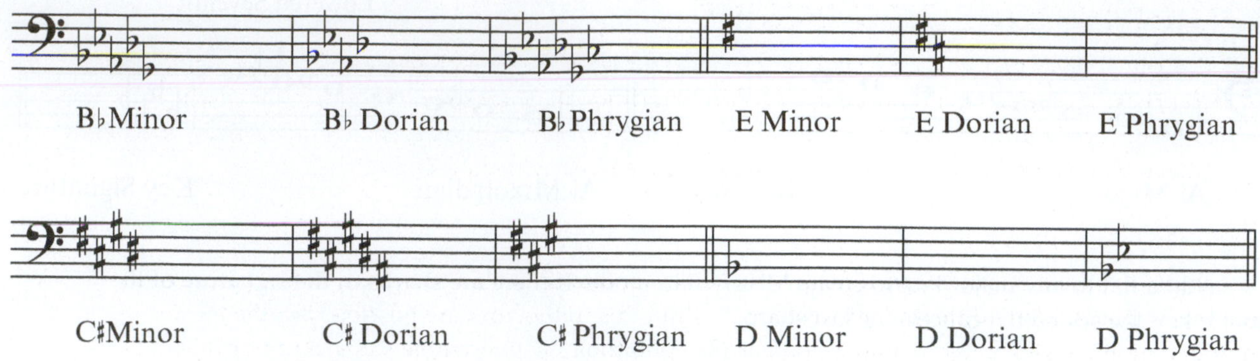

This table summarizes mode construction through key signature.

Mode	Basic Scale	Alteration
Aeolian	Minor	None
Dorian	Minor	Add Sharp
Ionian	Major	None
Lydian	Major	Add Sharp
Mixolydian	Major	Add Flat
Phrygian	Minor	Add Flat

For class discussion or assignment: please do not remove these pages

REVIEW SET: NOTE VALUES

A. Provide key signatures for these major, minor, and modal keys.

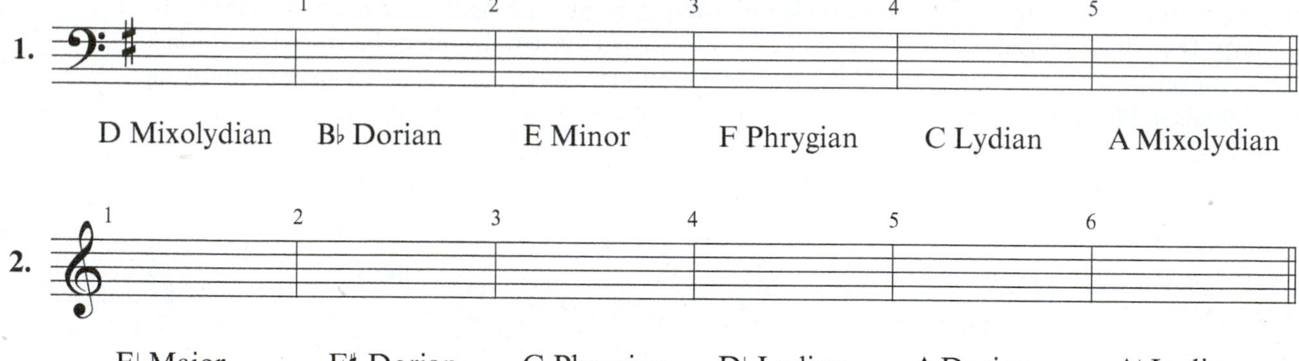

B. For the given key signature and pitch center, identify the scale or mode. Consider major, natural minor, Dorian, Phrygian, Lydian, and Mixolydian modes.

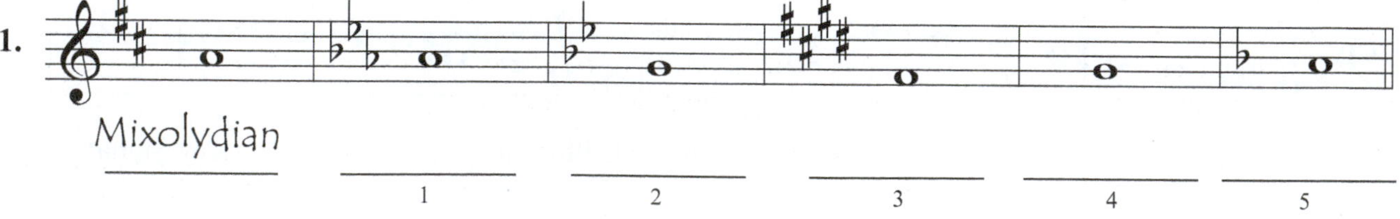

Complete Building Skills E-1 on page 439

Other Modes and Scales

Claude Debussy was one of several composers who returned to the church modes in the late nineteenth century. These patterns remain popular with many traditional composers even today; they have been especially attractive in jazz and pop styles since the late 1950s. In addition to the modes, however, several other scales exerted influence in the late nineteenth and early twentieth centuries.

Pentatonic Scale

So named because it has only five different pitches, a **pentatonic scale** is constructed of major seconds and minor thirds. Many different arrangements within this framework are possible, but the most common pentatonic series (the one understood as *the* pentatonic) is two whole steps, a minor third gap, then another whole step. The octave duplication of the first pitch provides a second minor third. Notice that there are no half steps in this ancient scale.

Pentatonic Scale

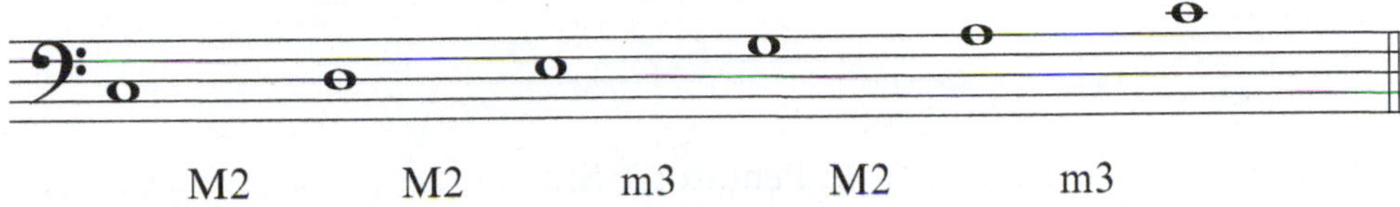

The pentatonic scale is found in the folk music of many different cultures. The American folk song "She's Gone Away" is based on the pentatonic scale shown in the previous example.

American Folk Song, "She's Gone Away"

A Korean folk song, "Arilang," is often heard in the West. Compare this pentatonic melody with "She's Gone Away."

Korean Folk Song, "Arilang"

Finally, the Kenyan lullaby "Yoo, Yoo" has the universal pentatonic structure. Unlike the American and Korean songs, however, the African melody has no tendency to end with the tonic pitch. If we consider the pitch center to be C, notice that there are two occurrences of the fourth scale degree—a pitch outside the pentatonic series. While we might not describe this melody as purely pentatonic (like "She's Gone Away" and "Arilang"), the pentatonic influences are clear nonetheless.

Kenyan Folk Song, "Yoo, Yoo"

CONSTRUCTING PENTATONIC SCALES. The pentatonic scale predates the major scale by centuries, but you may find it helpful to think of pentatonic as major with the fourth and seventh degrees removed.

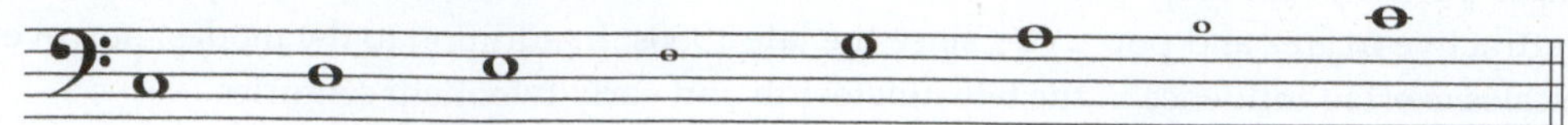

If you want a pentatonic scale on E♭, use degrees $\hat{1}$, $\hat{2}$, $\hat{3}$, $\hat{5}$, $\hat{6}$, and $\hat{8}$ of the E♭ major scale.

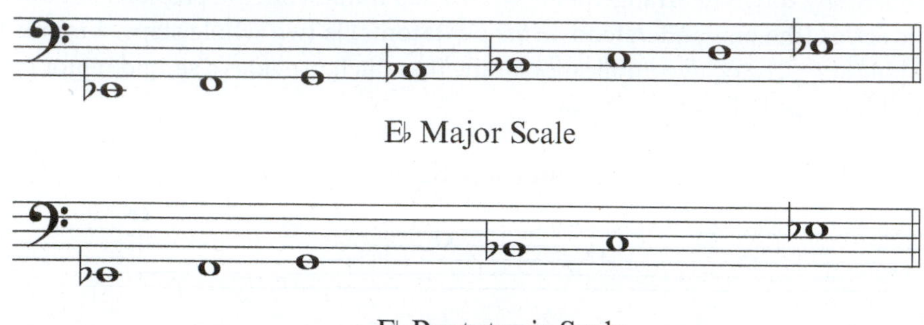

E♭ Major Scale

E♭ Pentatonic Scale

Minor Pentatonic and Blues Scales

If the pentatonic scale begins with a minor third, the effect is minor and the resulting scale is known as **minor pentatonic**.

Minor Pentatonic

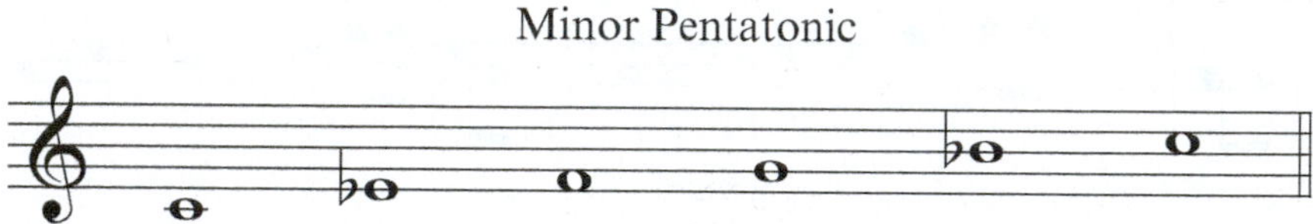

BLUES SCALE. A different form of the minor pentatonic scale, with both a natural and a lowered fifth, is known as the **blues scale**. Play the scale, and notice how the accidentals change the effect to minor.

Blues Scale

Whole-Tone Scale

In the late nineteenth century, some composers began using a scale with only one type of interval: the whole step. The **whole-tone scale** consists of six whole steps. The seventh pitch is the enharmonic octave duplication of the first.

Whole-Tone Scale

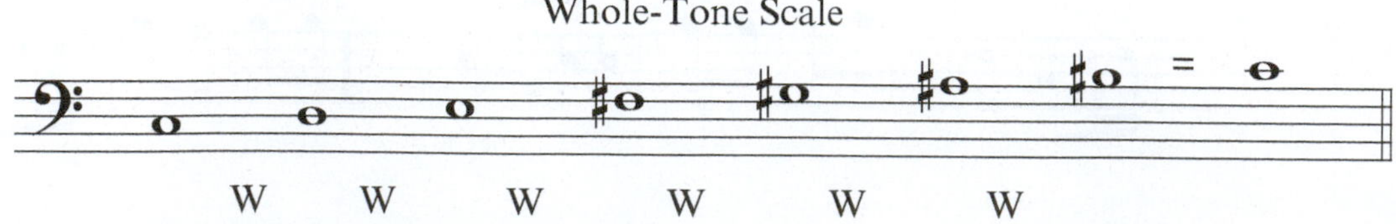

Unlike diatonic scales, enharmonic equivalents are not only acceptable in writing whole-tone scales, but preferable to double sharps or double flats. Each of the following notations is correct for a whole-tone scale beginning on the pitch C.

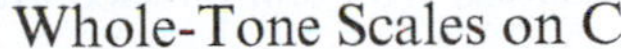
Whole-Tone Scales on C

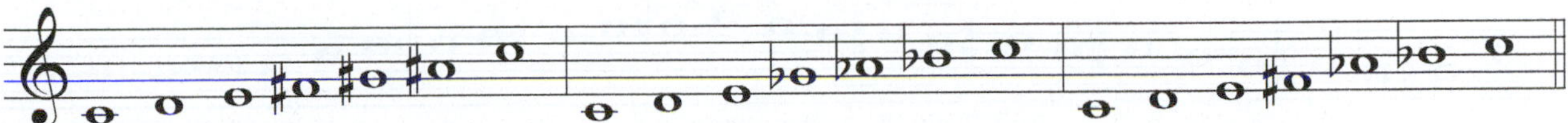

The French composer Claude Debussy is particularly associated with the whole-tone scale. Play the scale and a whole-tone melody. The complete descending scale appears over measures 2 and 3 of the melody.[3]

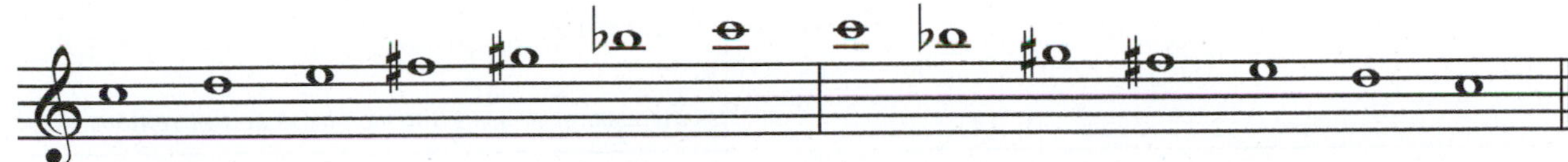

Whole-Tone Scale on C

Claude Debussy, Prelude for Piano

Locrian Mode

The medieval church modes are white-note patterns beginning on D, E, F, and G, respectively. In the sixteenth century, modes beginning on C and A were added. Not until the early twentieth century, however, did composers experiment with **Locrian mode**—the series beginning on B. In addition to the minor second between the first and second pitches, Locrian has a tritone between the first and fifth scale degrees (as does the blues scale).

Locrian Mode

To transpose Locrian mode, begin with a natural minor scale or minor key signature, then add *two* flats. If we need a Locrian scale on F♯, for example, begin with F♯ minor (three sharps), then negate two of those sharps with the added flats. The result is a key signature of one sharp for F♯ Locrian.

Locrian Mode on F♯

[3] Notice that Debussy uses double-dotted notes in this passage. Whether notes or rests, the dot principle never changes. The dot receives half of the value that precedes it.

Chromatic Scale

A scale consisting entirely of half steps is the **chromatic scale**. Strict chromatic passages appear in melodies, but the scale itself is theoretical, representing all twelve half steps spanning an octave. Traditionally, chromatic scales are written with sharps ascending and flats descending.

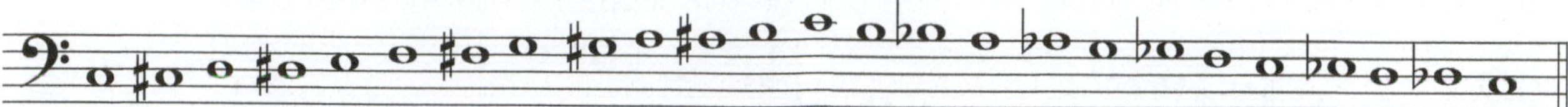

Chromatic Scale on C

Chromatic Scale on A♭

For class discussion or assignment: please do not remove these pages

REVIEW SET: CONSTRUCTING MODES AND SCALES

A. Construct ascending scales as directed. Use accidentals rather than key signatures (although for a number of scales, you might draft a key signature and write in the appropriate accidentals).

Blues Scale   Whole-Tone Scale   Mixolydian Mode

1.
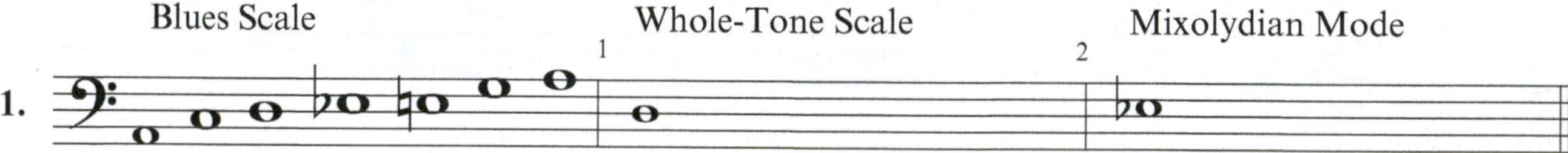

Minor Pentatonic Scale   Lydian Mode   Pentatonic Scale

2.
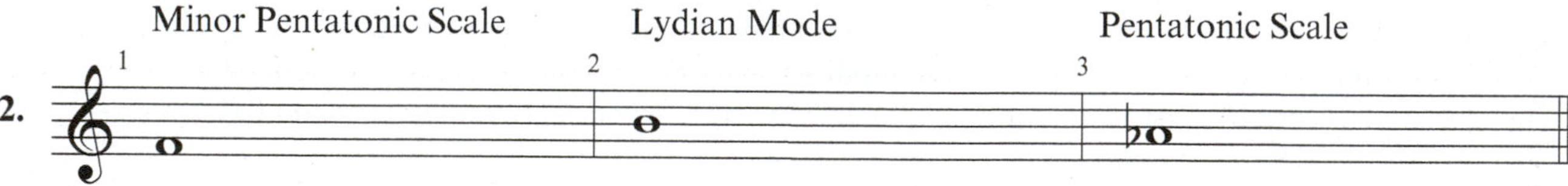

Whole-Tone Scale   Pentatonic Scale   Blues Scale

3.
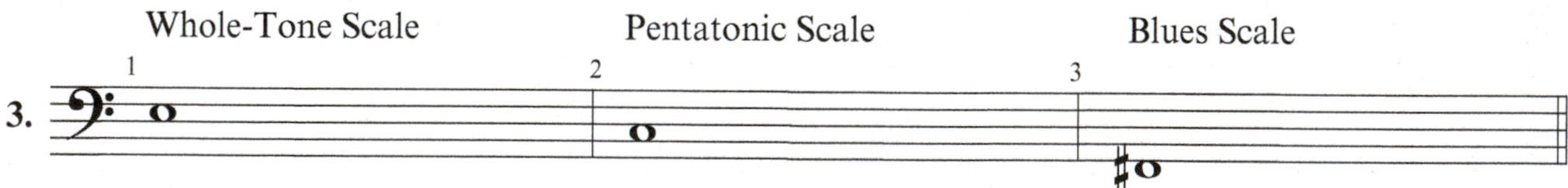

B. Write ascending and descending chromatic scales starting on the pitches indicated.

Ascending   Descending

1.
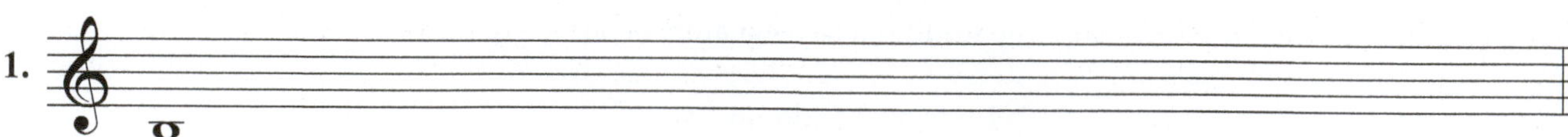

Ascending   Descending

2.

Complete Building Skills E-2 on page 441

MUSICIANSHIP E-1

Keyboard: Group II Major Scales

In Chapter 5 you learned how to play the five major scales in Group I (C, G, D, A, and E). All of these scales begin with the thumb in the right hand and the fifth finger in the left. Group II scales involve more black keys and each fingering is different. Learn to play these scales one octave with right and left hands separately. Practice at a tempo that allows you to play evenly. Observe that there are only three scales in Group II, but due to enharmonics, they represent six different tonics.

Group II Major Scales

D♭ Major (C♯ Major)

B Major (C♭ Major)

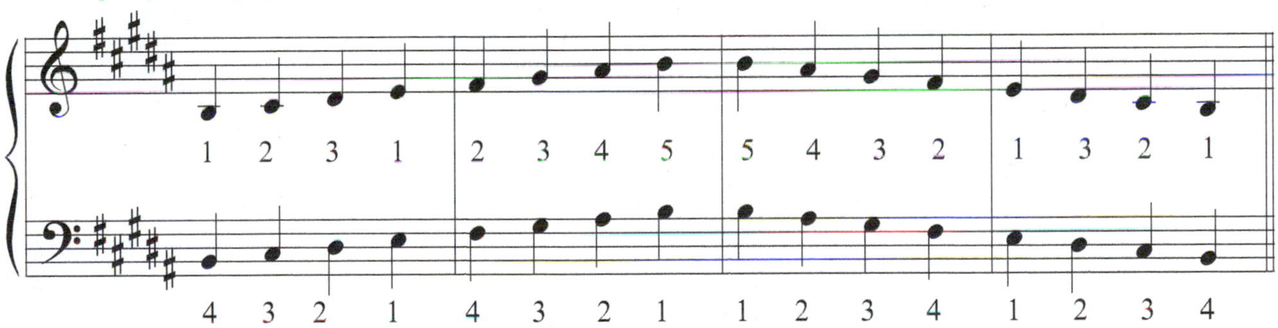

G♭ Major (F♯ Major)

Name ______________________

Page may be removed

Building Skills • E-1

Church Modes

A. **Construct ascending modal and other scales as specified on each given pitch. Use key signatures and add any necessary accidentals.**

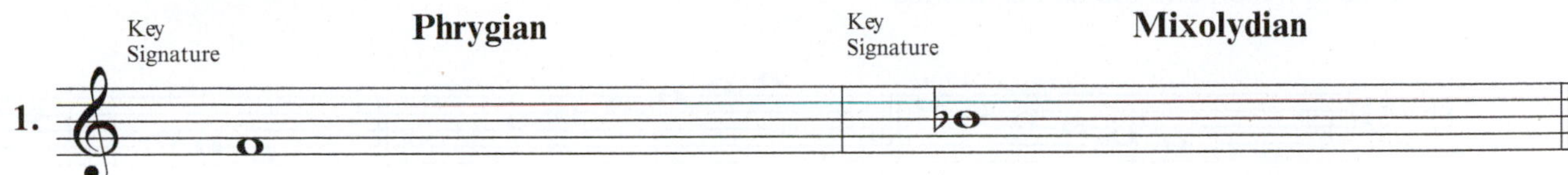

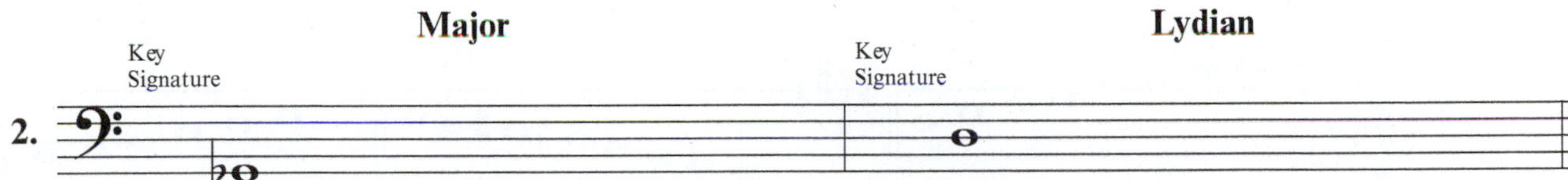

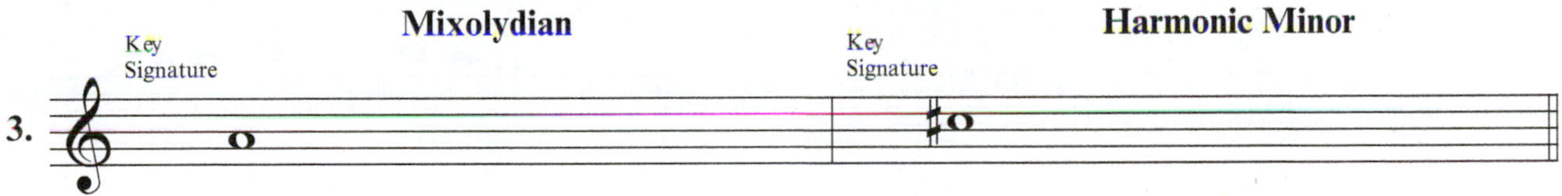

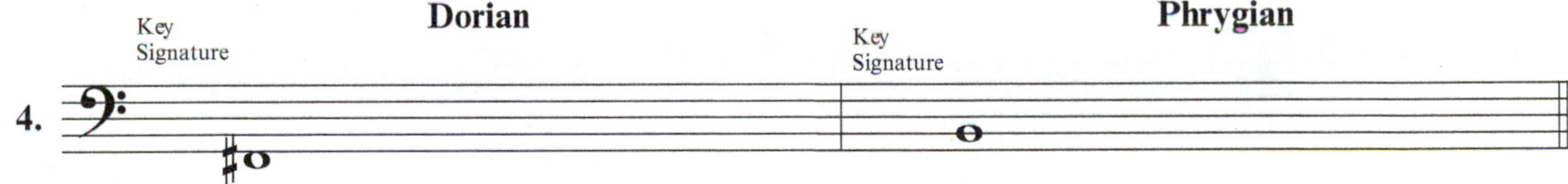

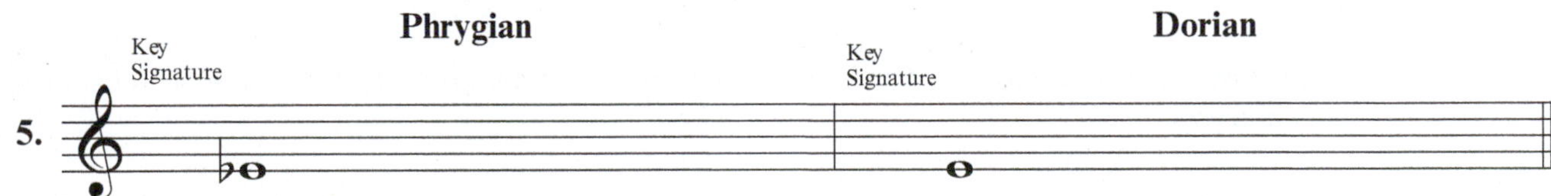

B. Name the resulting scale or mode based on the given key signature and first degree.

C. Based on the given first degree and key signature, determine the scale (and form, if appropriate). Consider major, all forms of minor, and the church modes.

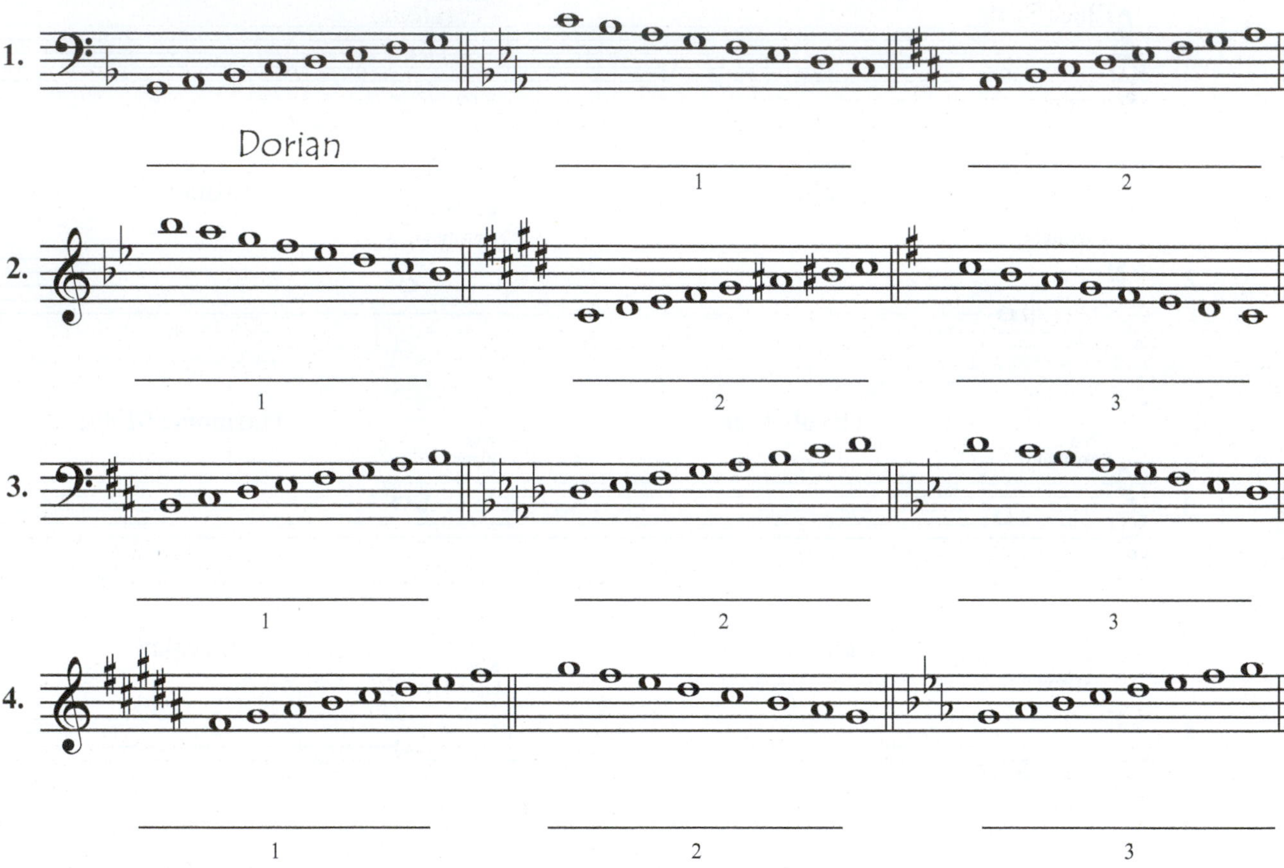

D. Determine the mode of this passage. Which pitch seems to be most important? This is the pitch center and the key to your analysis.

Name ____________________

Page may be removed

Building Skills • E-2

Other Scales

A. The scales and modes in this exercise are incomplete. Add one accidental to some and two accidentals to others as necessary to create the specified type. Do not employ a key signature in this exercise. Likewise, do not alter the first pitch or its octave duplication.

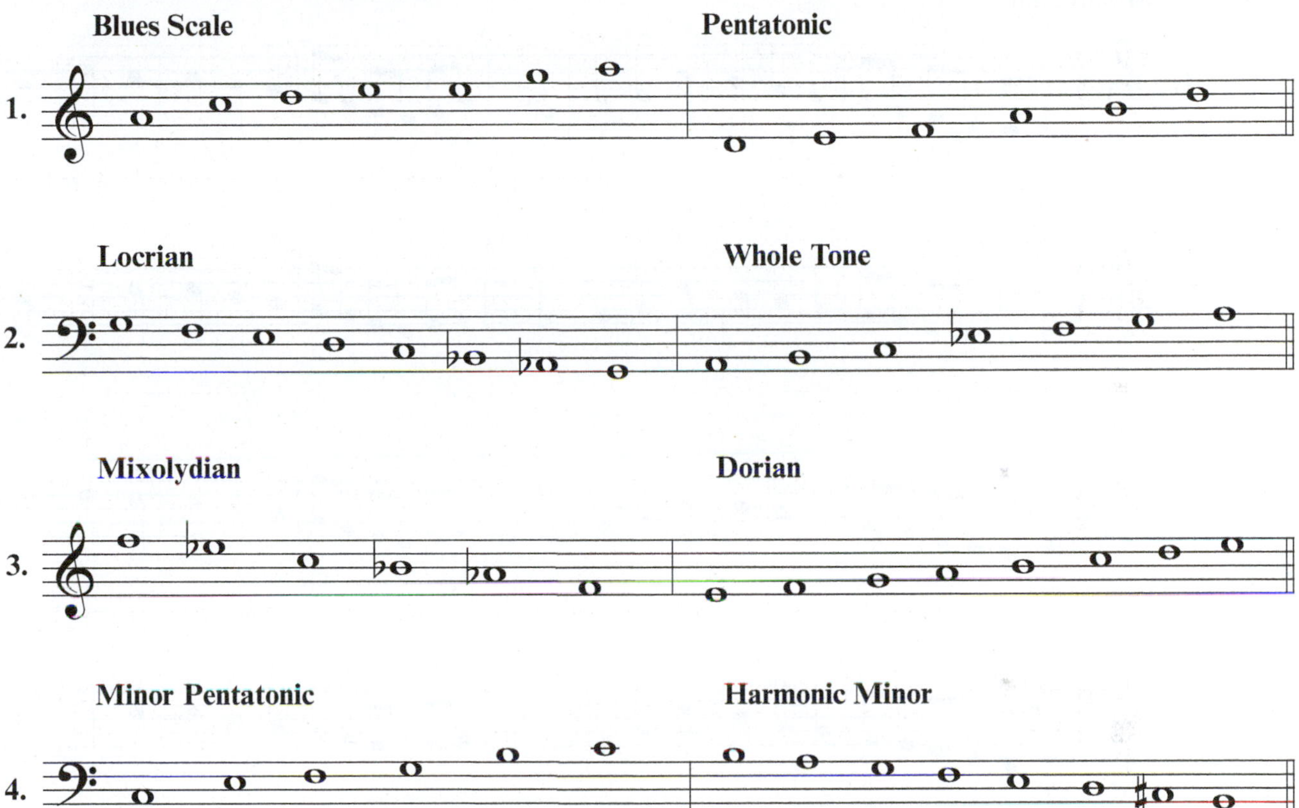

B. Construct a whole-tone scale on G. Next, write an eight-measure melody using this scale. Remember that enharmonic spellings are appropriate and that a key signature is not necessary.

Whole-Tone Scale

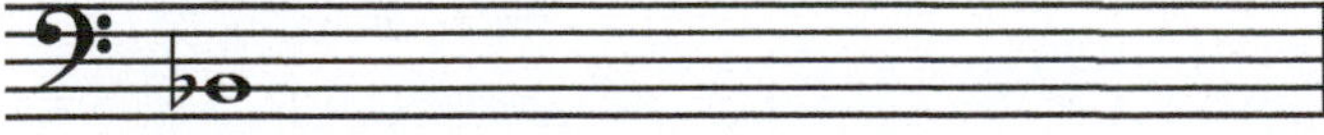

Whole-Tone Melody

C. Study the given melody in C major. In the next four lines, add accidentals to modify the melody using the modes specified.

Major (No Changes)

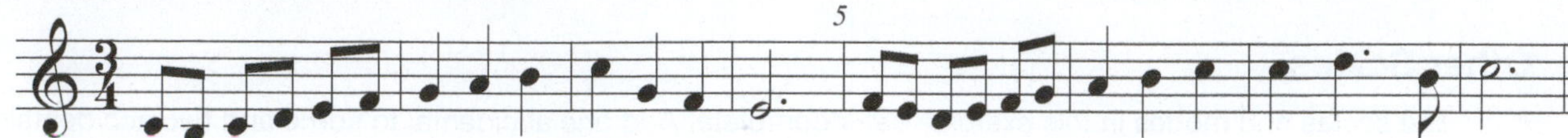

Mixolydian

1. 

Locrian

2. 

Lydian

3. 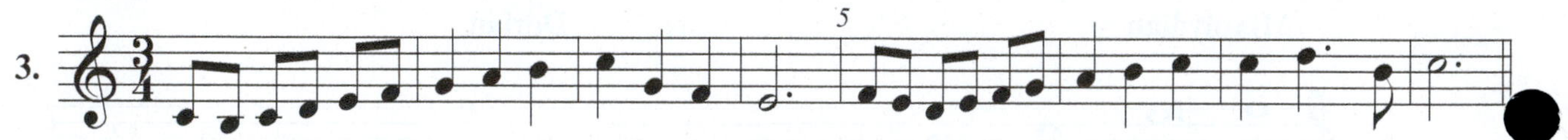

Phrygian

4. 

Name ______________________

Page may be removed

D. Construct forms of pentatonic and blues scales on the given pitches as directed. Use accidentals as necessary.

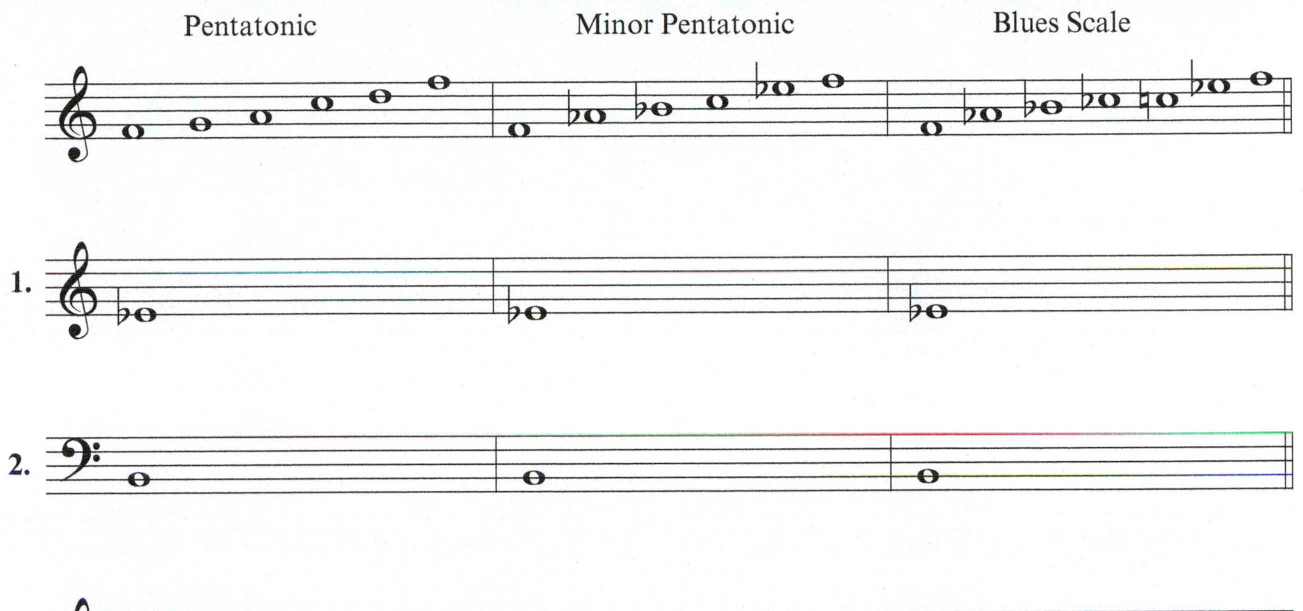

Name ______________________________

Page may be removed

Creative Projects • Appendix E

Complete these melodies using various scales and modes. First, construct the specified scale. If the scale is diatonic (an arrangement of the basic pitches), use a key signature; if the scale is whole tone or pentatonic, a key signature is not necessary. Several lines include melodic fragments and concluding pitches. In the last problem, only the time signature is given. In composing new material, emphasize the characteristic pitches of the specified mode or scale. Likewise, plan your pitch and rhythm content to provide a smooth arrival at the final pitch of each phrase.

E Dorian

Key Signature

1.

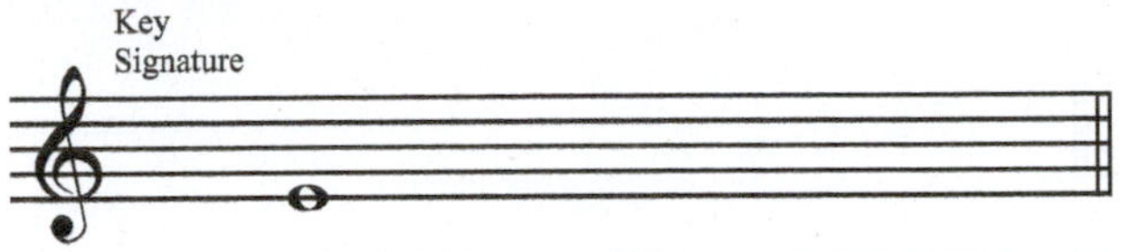

Key Signature

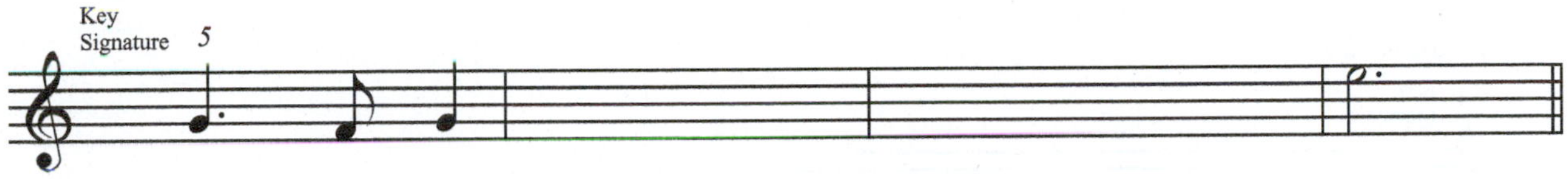

Key Signature *5*

A Locrian

Key Signature

2.

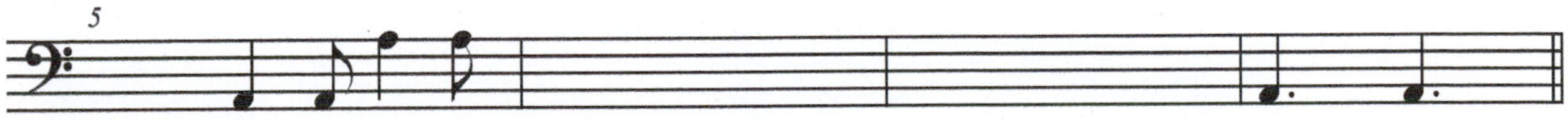

Key Signature

5

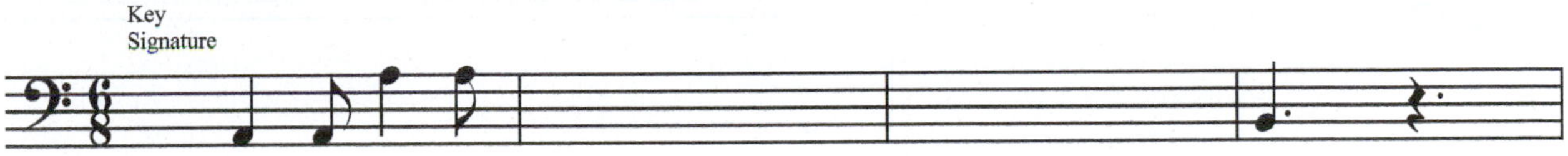

Whole-Tone Scale on A♭ (no key signature necessary)

3.

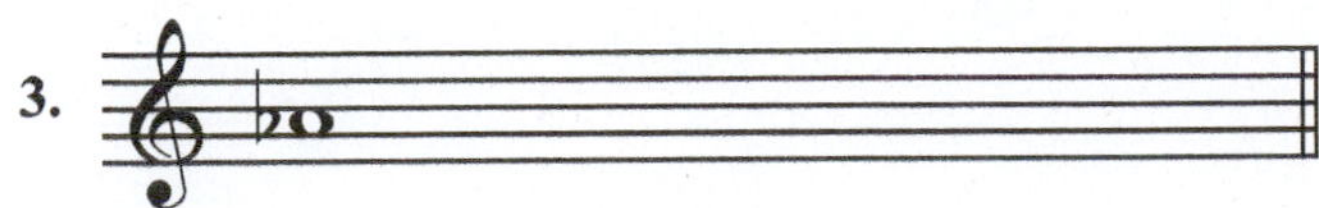

5
Pentatonic on B (no key signature necessary)
4.
5
Lydian on E♭
Key
Signature
5.
Key
Signature
5

Glossary of Terms and Symbols

Terms in *italics* are defined elsewhere in the glossary.

Symbols and Abbreviations

Symbol	Definition
|	A *barline* that separates *measures.*
||	The *double barline* marks the end of a section or composition.
{	The *brace* connects two or more staves.
.	A *dot* adds one-half the value of the *note* or *rest* that precedes it.
‿ ⁀	*Ties* combine the values of two *notes* of the same *pitch.*
>	The *dynamic accent* indicates louder or more marked performance of a *pitch* or pitches.
-	A semi-strong *accent*, lengthening, or emphasis.
^	The *caret* symbol that stands for, or emphasizes, the term *scale degree* ($\hat{2}$, $\hat{6}$, or $\hat{7}$, for example).
𝄐	The *fermata* indicates a lengthening of a note so that the metric accents are disrupted.
𝄆 𝄇	*Repeat sign* indicating that material between the lines is to be repeated.
1 :|	*First ending* symbol that indicates to repeat, taking the *second ending* the second time.
2	With *first* and *second endings*, the material played on the repeat.
𝄋	"The sign" that marks the point for return as used with a *dal segno* indication.
8vb	A symbol that indicates *pitches* sounding an *octave* lower than written.
8va	The *octave sign* that indicates that *pitches* sound an *octave* higher than written.
	A *hook* is attached to the *stem* of a *rest* to indicate lesser value.
♭	A flat is an *accidental* symbol that indicates a *basic pitch* lowered by one *half step* (G♭, for example).
♯	A *sharp* is an *accidental symbol*, such as F♯ or C♯, that indicates a *basic pitch* raised by one *half step.*
♮	An *accidental* symbol called a *natural* that indicates a return to *basic pitch* after the effect of an *accidental* (for example, A♯ and A♮).
𝄪	The *double sharp*, D𝄪 for example, is an *accidental* that raises a *basic pitch* by two *half steps*.
𝄫	The *double flat* symbol specifies that a pitch is to be lowered two *half steps* from the basic pitch (B𝄫, for example).
𝅝	A *whole note*, the largest common value and the one to which other values are related.
𝅗𝅥	The *half note* includes a *stem* and receives one-half the value of the *whole note*.
♩	*Quarter notes* have both a *stem* and a solid *notehead;* they receive one-quarter the value of the *whole note.*
♪	An *eighth note,* with a *flag* or *beam,* has one-eighth the value of the *whole note.*
𝅘𝅥𝅯	With two flags, the *sixteenth note* receives one-sixteenth the value of the *whole note.*
𝄵	A symbol for $\frac{2}{2}$ *meter*. Also known as "cut time."
𝄴	An alternate symbol for $\frac{4}{4}$ meter known as "common time."
𝄞	The *treble clef* identifies the second *staff* line as the position of the *pitch*.
𝄡	The *movable-C clef* identifies the position of the *pitch* C on the *staff.*
𝄢	The *bass clef* identifies the fourth *staff* line as the position of the *pitch* F.
°	An analytical symbol for a diminished triad.
+	A symbol used in analysis for augmented triads.

Abbreviations

al fine Italian term meaning "to the end" (or the point in the music marked "*fine*").

D.C. Italian for *da capo* meaning "the beginning."

D.S. Italian for *dal segno* meaning "return to the sign."

Hz *Hertz*

Terms

accent A stress or emphasis given to a *note*, such as a *metric accent* or *dynamic accent*.

accent pattern The number of beats in a metric group. See also *duple*, *triple*, and *quadruple*.

accidental A symbol, such as the *sharp*, *flat*, or *natural sign* that raises or lowers a *basic pitch* one or more *half steps*.

acoustics The branch of science that deals with the physical (measurable) properties of sound.

active pitch In tonal music, a scale degree other than $\hat{1}$ and $\hat{3}$.

active triad In tonal music, a *triad* that has a tendency to move or *resolve*.

Aeolian mode The octave series of *basic pitches* beginning on A: A B C D E F G and A.

Alberti bass A broken chord accompaniment that generates momentum through rhythmic figures.

alla breve An older term for $\substack{2\\2}$ *meter* still used today and indicated by the symbol 𝄵. Also known as "cut time."

alto The second-highest voice category in traditional four-part writing.

alto clef (𝄡) A *movable C-clef* that identifies the third *staff* line as the position of the *pitch* C.

amplitude The degree of molecular disturbance caused by a sound source that produces the psychological sensation of loudness.

anacrusis An incomplete *measure* that begins a composition or section.

analysis The systematic study of one or more aspects of a musical composition.

antecedent phrase In a *period*, the first of the two phrases. See also *consequent phrase*.

anticipation A type of *nonchord tone* that arrives at a new *harmony* slightly early as a *dissonance*, but is heard as *consonant* when the harmony changes.

Arabic-numeral label The use of Arabic numerals to represent *intervals* sounding above a given *bass*.

arpeggiation The sounding of *chord* tones sequentially in the manner of a harp.

arrangement The revision of a composition with substantial changes (medium, *meter*, *form*, *mode*, and so on).

augmented interval A *major interval* or a *perfect interval* that has been increased in size by one *half step*.

augmented second An interval formed by a *whole step* plus a *chromatic half step*.

augmented triad A type of *triad* that is constructed of a *major third* and an *augmented fifth* above the *root*.

authentic cadence A concluding harmonic formula consisting of *dominant* and *tonic functions*, such as V–I or vii°–I.

bar See *measure*.

barline A vertical line (|) used to separate *measures*.

basic pitch A pitch without an *accidental*, such as A B C D E F or G.

bass (1) The lowest-sounding pitch in a *triad* or *chord*. (2) The lowest voice in traditional four-part composition.

bass clef (𝄢) A symbol that identifies the fourth line on the *staff* as the position of the *pitch* F.

bassa A term used with the *octave sign* to indicate that notes are to be performed an *octave* lower than written.

beam A thick horizontal or slanted line that connects two or more *stemmed* notes and indicates lesser rhythmic value. Beams are equivalent to (and replace) *flags*.

beat A steady and regular pulse that underlies the rhythmic structure of most traditional compositions.

beat division The use of rhythmic values smaller than one beat in duration. Beat division is either *simple* or *compound.*

beat subdivision The further breaking of notes that constitute the *beat division* into two smaller parts.

blues scale A *minor pentatonic* scale with both a lowered and natural fifth degree.

borrowed division A division of the *beat* into two parts in *simple meter* (a *triplet*) or a division of the beat into two parts in *compound meter* (a *duplet*).

brace ({) A symbol that connects two or more *staves.*

cadence A temporary or permanent pause or emphasis in the musical line. See *melodic cadence* and *harmonic cadence.*

calligraphy The process of notating music by hand. More recently, the process of notating music through computer software.

caret (^) A symbol that stands for *scale degree.*

chord A group of three or more different *pitches.* See also *triad, tertian triad,* and *seventh chord.*

chord symbols A system of representing chords with symbols. Unlike *Roman numerals,* chord symbols are the same regardless of key. See also *Roman numeral identification.*

chorus See *refrain.*

chromatic (1) A term associated with music that moves primarily by *half steps.* (2) Pitches other than those designated as *basic.*

chromatic half step A *half step* formed between pitches with the same letter name such as F and F♯ or G and G♭.

chromatic scale An *octave* series of *half steps* usually written with *sharps* ascending and *flats* descending.

church modes Patterns of *whole* and *half steps* through which early Western music was organized. The predecessors of our *major* and *minor scales.* See also *Aeolian, Dorian, Ionian, Lydian, Mixolydian,* and *Phrygian.*

circle of fifths A sequence of *keys* that moves clockwise around an imaginary circle in successive *perfect fifths* and adding a *sharp* to the *key signature* at each point. Counterclockwise movement around the circle adds one *flat* at each step. Adjacent keys on the circle of fifths have all but one *pitch* in common.

clef A symbol that designates the location of one pitch on the *staff.* See also *alto clef, bass clef, mezzo-soprano clef, movable C-clef, soprano clef, treble clef,* and *tenor clef.*

closed position The spatial arrangement of a *triad* where the three pitches are as close together as possible. See also *open position.*

common time (𝄴) An alternate symbol for $\frac{4}{4}$ *meter.*

compound beat division A division of the *beat* into three smaller parts. See also *compound meter.*

compound interval Two *pitches* that are separated by more than an *octave.*

compound meter A meter with a *dotted note* as the *beat* and with a three-part *beat division.*

conductor The leader of a musical ensemble.

consequent phrase In form, the second *phrase* of *period* structure. See also *antecedent phrase.*

consonance A *pitch, interval, triad,* or *chord* that is relatively stable.

contrapuntal A work that is based on *counterpoint.*

copyright In music, the exclusive legal right given to the composer as ownership of their work.

counterpoint A musical *texture* that centers on two or more equal parts or voices.

cut time See *alla breve.*

da capo An Italian term ("to the head") instructing the performer to return to the beginning. Abbreviated D.C.

dal segno An Italian indication ("to the sign") of a repeat to the sign (𝄋).

deceptive cadence A harmonic *cadence* formula limited to *dominant* to *submediant* (V–vi).

diatonic A *pitch, interval,* or *triad* that is limited to *basic pitches* or a *transposition* of the basic pitches.

diatonic half step A *half step* formed between two *pitches* that have different letter names (such as F♯ and G♮ or B♭ and A). See also *chromatic half step.*

diatonic triad *Triads* with no pitches outside the *key.*

diminished interval A *perfect interval* or a *minor interval* that has been narrowed by one *half step.*

diminished triad A *triad* that has as its component intervals a *minor third* above the *root* and a *diminished fifth* above the root.

dissonance (1) A *pitch*, an *interval*, or a *triad* that is relatively unstable. (2) A traditional category of *intervals* that includes *seconds*, *sevenths*, and the *tritone*.

division See *beat division*.

dominant function In tonal composition, a *chord* that has a strong tendency to progress to the *tonic*.

dominant pitch The fifth degree of a *diatonic scale*. See also *scale degree*.

dominant seventh chord A *seventh chord* that consists of a *major triad* and a *minor seventh* above the *root*.

dominant triad The *major triad* built on the *fifth degree* of a *diatonic scale*.

Dorian mode One of the *church modes* and a series that is a literal or *transposed* version of *basic pitches* D E F G A B C and D.

dot (·) A symbol added to a *note* or *rest* to increase its *duration* by one half.

dotted note A note that includes a *dot*.

double barline (||) Two vertical lines that indicate the end of a composition or section.

double flat (𝄫) An *accidental* symbol used to indicate a lowering by two *half steps* of a *basic pitch* (G, G♭, and G𝄫, for example, is a *basic pitch* that is lowered by one and then two *half steps*, respectively). See also *enharmonic*.

double period An arrangement of four phrases, most typically with weak–weak–weak–strong structure.

double sharp (𝄪) An *accidental* symbol that raises a basic pitch by two *half steps*.

doubling In *triads* and *chords*, the use of one pitch in two different voices.

duple meter A recurring strong–weak metric pattern.

duplet A type of *borrowed division* where the beat is broken into two equal parts in a *compound meter*.

duration The length of a sound.

dynamic accent (>) A symbol that indicates louder or more marked performance of a *pitch* or pitches.

ear training The process of learning to hear and duplicate musical patterns.

eighth note (♪) A relative rhythmic symbol that is one-eighth the value of the *whole note*.

enharmonic A *pitch* or *interval* that sounds the same as one given, but is notated differently (the interval F–C♭, for example, is *enharmonic* with the interval F–B).

F clef See *bass clef*.

fermata (𝄐) A symbol indicating a lengthening of a note so that the metric accents are disrupted.

fifth (1) A type of *interval* with five steps between pitches. (2) The element of a *triad* that lies a *fifth* above the *root*.

figured bass A seventeenth- and early eighteenth-century method of shorthand notation involving the use of numbers to represent intervals sounding above the bass. See also *Arabic-numeral labels*.

fine An Italian term meaning "the end."

first ending (⌐1 :‖) A type of repeat sign in which the performer plays through the *first ending*, repeats back to the beginning (or the double bar), then skips to the *second ending* the second time.

first inversion The arrangement of a *triad* with the *third* as the *bass*.

flag j (𝅮) A curved line added to the *stem* of a *note* to indicate lesser value. Flags are equivalent to *beams*.

flat (♭) An *accidental* symbol that lowers basic *pitch* one *half step*.

form The term for the organized development of music over a given time span.

fourth A type of *interval* that includes *pitches* four steps apart (usually with five or six *half steps* between *pitches*).

frequency The number of molecular vibrations per second produced by a sound source. Higher frequency produces the psychological sensation of relatively higher pitch; lower frequency results in our hearing lower sounds.

function In a tonal context, the process of establishing a *key* through an orderly progression of pitches and chords toward *tonic*.

fundamental The lowest *frequency* normally produced by any one *pitch* on an instrument.

G clef See *treble clef*.

grand staff A combination of one *treble* and one *bass staff* used for the notation of *keyboard* instruments.

great staff See *grand staff.*

half cadence A concluding harmonic formula that consists of *tonic* and *dominant* (I–V), or *predominant* and *dominant* functions (ii–V or IV–V).

half note (𝅗𝅥) A relative rhythmic value that is one-half the duration of the *whole note.*

half step The smallest *interval* in Western music. On the *keyboard*, a half step is found between any two adjacent keys. Also termed *semitone*. See also *diatonic half step* and *chromatic half step.*

harmonic cadence The final two (different) chords in a *phrase.*

harmonic dissonance A *chord* that includes a relatively unstable element such as a *seventh* above the *root.*

harmonic function The tendency in Western *tonal* music for *chords* to move in an orderly way through the three *functions* (*tonic, predominant*, and *dominant*).

harmonic interval Two pitches heard simultaneously. See also *melodic interval.*

harmonic minor scale A form of *minor scale* in which the seventh *degree* has been raised a half step to provide a *leading tone.*

harmonic rhythm The rate of *chord* change defined in *beats* or *measures* (one chord change per measure, one chord change every beat, and so on).

harmonic series An acoustical phenomenon by which any one *frequency* is colored by the presence, in varying degrees, of many higher frequencies.

harmonic tendencies See *function.*

harmony The vertical arrangement of *pitches* and their relationships that form *intervals, triads,* and *chords.*

hertz A measurement of *frequency* (abbreviated Hz) equivalent to the number of molecular vibrations as measured by a scientific instrument.

homophony A musical *texture* that involves a melody with accompaniment.

hook (˺) A symbol attached to the *stem* of a *rest* to indicate lesser value. Each hook has the same effect as a *flag.*

imitation The successive entry of voices with the same or nearly the same material and in a *contrapuntal texture.* Rounds like "Row, Row, Row Your Boat" are examples of imitation.

implied triad A *triad* or *chord* with the *fifth* omitted. Abbreviated "IMP" in analysis.

improvisation Composing in *tempo*; that is, creating a new version of a *melody* or *harmonic* pattern spontaneously.

interval The distance between two *pitches.*

interval quality A measurement of *interval* size in the number of *half steps* between the two *pitches.*

interval size A general measurement of *interval* size depending on the number of steps between *pitches* (without regard to the number of *half steps* involved).

inverted interval A corresponding version of an *interval* with the *spatial positions* reversed. The lower *pitch* of the original interval becomes the higher with inversion; alternately, the higher of the two pitches can be inverted to become the lower.

Ionian mode One of the *church modes* added in the sixteenth century. The diatonic series is equivalent to the modern major scale: C D E F G A and B.

key An effect produced when the *tonic* of a given *scale* is heard as the most important *pitch.*

key signature The listing of *accidentals* necessary to produce the effect of a given *key.*

keyboard Instruments like the piano and organ on which the performer has no direct contact with the vibrating string.

lead sheet A modern musical score for popular music that includes full notation for melody and lyrics, but using letter symbols to represent the harmony.

leading tone (1) The *pitch* that lies a *diatonic half step* below the *tonic.* (2) The *triad* or *chord* built on the *leading tone pitch.* See also *subtonic.*

ledger line A temporary extension of the *staff* above or below the customary five lines and four spaces.

line (1) One of the *lines* of the *staff.* (2) The movement of several measures of music toward a goal (*cadence*).

loco An Italian term ("in place") that specifies a return to notated *pitch* following a passage in which the *octave sign* has been used.

Locrian mode A theoretical scale on the pitches B C D E F G A and B (or a *transposition*).

Lydian mode One of the original *church modes*, an arrangement of the *basic pitches* F G A B C D E and F, or a *transposition* of this series.

major interval A category of *interval* consisting of *seconds, thirds, sixths,* and *sevenths*.

major mode Any *scale* series in which the distance between first and third pitches is a *major third* (two *whole steps*).

major scale A literal ordering of basic pitches C D E F G A B and C or any *transposition* of those pitches. Major scales have the *whole-* and *half-step* pattern W W H W W W H.

major-scale comparison A method of relying on the *key signature* to reckon *intervals, triads,* and *chords*.

major triad A type of *triad* consisting of a *major third* above the *root* and a *perfect fifth* above the *root*.

measure One complete *metric* pattern (also called a *bar*). In traditional music, measures are segmented by *barlines*.

mediant (1) The third degree of a *diatonic scale*. (2) The *diatonic triad* built on the third *degree* of a *scale*.

melisma A series of several *notes* on the same syllable of text.

melodic interval Two *pitches* heard consecutively.

melodic minor scale A *minor scale* in which both the *sixth* and the *seventh* degrees are raised a *half step* in the ascending form. Descending melodic minor is identical to *natural minor*.

melodic tendencies In tonal composition, the gravitation of *active pitches* (especially $\hat{4}$ and $\hat{7}$) toward stable ones like $\hat{1}$ and $\hat{3}$.

melody An organized group of pitches and rhythms that is heard as complete.

meter A recurring pattern of strong and weak *beats*. See also *duple meter* and *triple meter*.

meter signature Two numbers that appear at the beginning of a composition to identify the *metric* structure. These numbers indicate the value designated as one *beat*, the manner of *beat division*, and the *accent pattern* (the number of beats in a *measure*).

metric accent The regular strong and weak patterns of *beats* that create *meter*.

metronome A device for producing a steady pulse with a given number of *beats* per minute.

minor interval A category of *intervals* that includes *seconds, thirds, sixths,* and *sevenths*.

minor mode The effect produced when a *scale* is *minor*, that is, when the first and third *degrees* are separated by a *minor third*.

minor pentatonic scale An arrangement of the *pentatonic scale* to begin with a *minor third*.

minor scale A type of scale in which the first and third degrees are separated by a *minor third* (a *whole step* plus a *diatonic half step*).

minor triad A *triad* in which the lower *third* (between *root* and *third*) is *minor* with a *perfect fifth* between *root* and *fifth*.

Mixolydian mode One of the original *church modes*, conforming to the series G A B C D E F and G (or a *transposition* of this series).

modal (1) Describing the choice between the *major* or *minor mode*. (2) Music that is based on scales other than *major* or *minor scales*.

modal scale A modern term for any of the *church modes*.

mode (1) The establishment of either the *major* or *minor* effect within a given *key*. (2) One of eight specific arrangements of the seven *basic pitches*. See also *church modes*.

motive The smallest element of musical *form* (usually only a few *pitches*).

movable C-clef (𝄡) A symbol that identifies the *pitch* C on the *staff*. See also *alto clef* and *tenor clef*.

music Organized sound and silence in time.

music theory A branch of music study that centers on understanding the way a work is constructed and explaining, through *analysis*, why it sounds as it does.

natural division The division of the *beat* according to the metric plan: a two-part division in a *simple meter* or a three-part division in *compound meter*. See also *borrowed division*.

natural half step Points on the *keyboard* where two white keys are adjacent; that is, between E and F and between B and C.

natural minor scale A *minor scale* that conforms to the *whole-* and *half-step* pattern W H W W H W W. See also *harmonic minor* and *melodic minor*.

natural sign (♮) An *accidental* symbol that cancels the effect of a *flat* or *sharp*.

neighboring tone A type of *nonchord tone* where one pitch is embellished by step above or below.

noise Sound produced by uncontrolled or irregular *sound waves*.

nonchord tone A *pitch* that lies outside the *harmony*, but when used in a stereotypical formula, creates interest and momentum.

nondiatonic *Pitches* that lie outside a given *scale*. In the C major scale, the pitches C D E F G A and B are *diatonic*; other pitches are *nondiatonic*.

notation The representation of sounds and silences through symbols.

note The basic symbol for *pitch*.

notehead The oval part of a *note* that locates a pitch on the *staff*.

octave The purest and most stable *interval* that forms the basis of practically all world musical systems. Pitches that appear in different places on the *staff* but have exactly the same letter name (including any *accidental*), are one or more octaves apart.

octave designation A system of identifying *pitches* within a specific *octave range*.

octave sign (8*va*) A symbol that indicates that the *pitches* sound an *octave* higher than notated.

open position The *spacing* of a *triad* so that highest and lowest *pitches* are an *octave* or more apart.

ottava A passage that employs the *octave sign*.

overtone *Frequencies* sounding above a given *fundamental* pitch.

parallel relationship When *major* and *minor keys* have the same *tonic pitch* the relationship is parallel.

partial All *frequencies* associated with a given *fundamental pitch*, including the fundamental itself. See also *overtone*.

pentatonic scale An ancient *scale* built from *whole steps* and *minor thirds* and no half steps. Looking at the piano keyboard, the black keys form a pentatonic scale beginning on C♯ or D♭.

perfect fifth An *interval* that is a *fifth* in type and comprising seven *half steps* between pitches.

perfect interval An *interval* category consisting of *octaves, unisons, fourths,* and *fifths*.

period In musical form, the combination of two phrases in a weak–strong arrangement. See also *antecedent phrase* and *consequent phrase*.

phrase A complete musical thought; the achievement of a musical goal.

phrase group A combination of two or three phrases that *do not* have a weak–strong cadential arrangement. See also *period*.

Phrygian mode One of the original *church modes* that conforms to the pattern E F G A B C D E (or a *transposition*).

pickup See *anacrusis*.

pitch The psychological sensation of hearing a *note* as relatively higher or lower.

plagal cadence A concluding harmonic formula of the *subdominant* to *tonic* (IV–I).

predominant function A midpoint in a *progression* between the stability of the *tonic function* and the momentum of *dominant function*. The *subdominant* and *supertonic triads* are examples of predominant function.

prime See *unison*.

progression A series of *chords* that moves toward a goal or *resolution*.

progressive cadence (1) In a *melody*, a *phrase* ending on an active scale degree, principally $\hat{2}$, $\hat{5}$, or $\hat{7}$. (2) In a harmonic sense, a *cadence* to the *dominant triad* (ii–V, IV–V, or I–V).

psychoacoustics A study of the psychological responses to sound.

pure minor See *natural minor scale*.

quadruple meter A *meter* that has a strong–weak, semi-strong–weak pattern of *accents*.

quarter note (♩) A relative rhythmic value that is one-quarter the value of the *whole note*.

refrain The contrasting section of a short form or song; material that always recurs with the same text.

register The general low, middle, or high range of a set of *pitches*.

relative relationship When *major* and *minor keys* have the same *key signature* (and different *tonics*), the relationship between them is relative.

repeat sign (𝄆 𝄇) A symbol indicating that material between the lines is to be repeated.

resolution The movement of an active *pitch* or *triad* to one that is stable.

rests The symbols employed to notate periods of silence.

rhythm The element of time in music.

Roman-numeral identification A system of musical *analysis* in which roman numerals and other symbols stand for *triads* and other *chords*.

root The lowest element of a *triad* or *chord* when the pitches are arranged over consecutive lines or spaces. See also *root position*.

root position The arrangement of a *tertian triad* with the *root* in the *bass*.

rudiments An alternate term for the fundamentals of music.

scale A series of *pitches* in a fixed order.

scale degree A number assigned to each *pitch* of a *diatonic scale* to define its relationship with the *tonic*. See *caret*.

score The *notation* of a musical work.

scoring The process of assigning *pitches* of a *triad* or *chord* to various instruments or voice categories.

second A type of *interval* where two *pitches* occupy adjacent lines and spaces.

second ending (2 **)** Used with a *first ending*, it is the *measure* or measures played the second time through the repeated material.

second inversion The arrangement of a *triad* or *seventh chord* with the *fifth* in the *bass*.

semitone See *half step*.

sequence The recurrence of a melodic and rhythmic *motive* at consistently higher or lower *pitch* levels (sequence by ascending second or descending third, for example).

seventh (1) A type of *interval* in which the *pitches* are seven lines and spaces apart. (2) The *pitch* that is a seventh above the *root* in a *seventh chord*.

seventh chord A *chord* that is constructed of four different pitches: the *root* plus a *third*, a *fifth*, and a *seventh* above the root. See also *dominant seventh chord*.

sharp (♯) An *accidental* symbol that raises the basic *pitch* a *half step*.

simple beat division A division of the *beat* (a *simple note*) into two parts.

simple meter A *meter* in which the *beat* is a *simple* (undotted) note and divides into two parts.

sixteenth note (𝅘𝅥𝅯) A rhythmic symbol that receives one-sixteenth the value of the *whole note*.

sixth A type of interval in which the two pitches are six lines and spaces apart.

slur (⌣⌢) A symbol indicating that pitches are played on the same breath or bow.

solfège A system of teaching sight singing through syllables.

soprano The highest of the four traditional voice categories.

sound waves Regular patterns of molecular motion created by a sound source.

spacing In *triad* and *chord* construction, the closeness of the arrangement of *pitches*.

spatial position The scoring of a *triad* or *chord* according to *open* or *closed position*.

stable pitch In tonal composition, the *first* and *third scale degrees* are stable.

stable triad In tonal music, a *triad* that has no tendency to move or *resolve*.

staff A grid of five lines and four spaces used for the precise *notation* of music.

staves Plural of *staff*.

stem A vertical line attached to a *notehead* to indicate durational value.

subdivision See *beat subdivision*.

subdominant The fourth *scale degree* or the *triad* with the fourth scale degree as its *root*.

submediant The sixth *scale degree* or the *triad* with the sixth scale degree as its *root*.

subtonic The seventh *scale degree* that lies a *whole step* below the *tonic* or the *triad* with this pitch as its *root*.

supertonic The second *scale degree* or the *triad* with the second scale degree as its *root*.

swing A method of performance in jazz and popular music in which music notated as two equal *beat divisions* is performed instead as an unequal (long–short) *triplet* figure.

syncopation The intentional realignment of natural *metric accents*.

system A set of two or more *staves.*

tempo The speed of the *beat.*

tenor The next-to-lowest voice in traditional four-part writing.

tenor clef (𝄡) A *movable-C clef* that identifies the position of the *pitch* C as the fourth line on the *staff.*

terminal cadence (1) A *phrase* ending with a stronger melodic effect (scale degrees $\hat{1}$ or $\hat{3}$). (2) A *harmonic cadence* that involves *dominant* and *tonic functions.*

tertian triad A group of three pitches that can be arranged to fall over consecutive lines or spaces.

texture The musical "weave" that is relatively thicker or less dense as a result of the way sounds are layered. *Homophony* and *counterpoint* are two musical textures.

third (1) A type of *interval* in which pitches are three lines or spaces apart. (2) A *triad* element that lies a *third* above the *root.*

tie (⌣ ⌢) A symbol that combines the rhythmic values of two or more *notes* of the same *pitch.*

timbre The term used to describe the quality of a musical sound.

time signature See *meter signature.*

tonality A term more or less synonymous with *key*. The establishment of *key* and *mode* (the key of E♭ major, for example).

tonic The first *pitch* of a *scale* or the *triad* built on this *pitch.*

tonic function A goal or point of stability in a *chord progression* (represented chiefly by the *tonic triad*).

traditional music A term used in this text to mean "classical" music between about 1675–1875 and also music composed in later times using those same principles.

transcription (1) The process of revising the notation of music so that although the sound is the same, the visual appearance is changed. (2) Music originally composed for one medium (a piano, for example) that is rewritten for another (such as a choir).

transposition A process that moves music from one key into a different key, but without other changes. The transcription duplicates the original pitches either higher or lower.

treble clef (𝄞) The symbol that identifies the second line on the *staff* as the position of the *pitch* G.

triad A group of three *pitches.* See also *tertian triad.*

triad inversion A *tertian triad* arranged so that the *root* is above the *bass.* See also *root position* and *second inversion.*

triple meter A recurring *accent* pattern that is strong–weak–weak.

triplet A *borrowed division* in a *simple meter* where the *beat* is divided into three equal parts.

tritone In modern terminology, an *augmented* fourth or a *diminished* fifth.

unison The *interval* between two notes that have the same *frequency.*

verse Groups of lines in a song that are repeated, but with different text. See also *refrain.*

vocable A word or syllable that has no meaning ("woo-oh," for example) but is used for emphasis or rhythmic continuity.

voicing See *scoring.*

whole note (𝅝) The longest rhythmic value consistently employed in *traditional music.*

whole step An interval comprised of two *half steps.*

whole-tone scale A series of six consecutive *whole steps* and ending with an *enharmonic octave* duplication of the first *pitch.*

Index

S

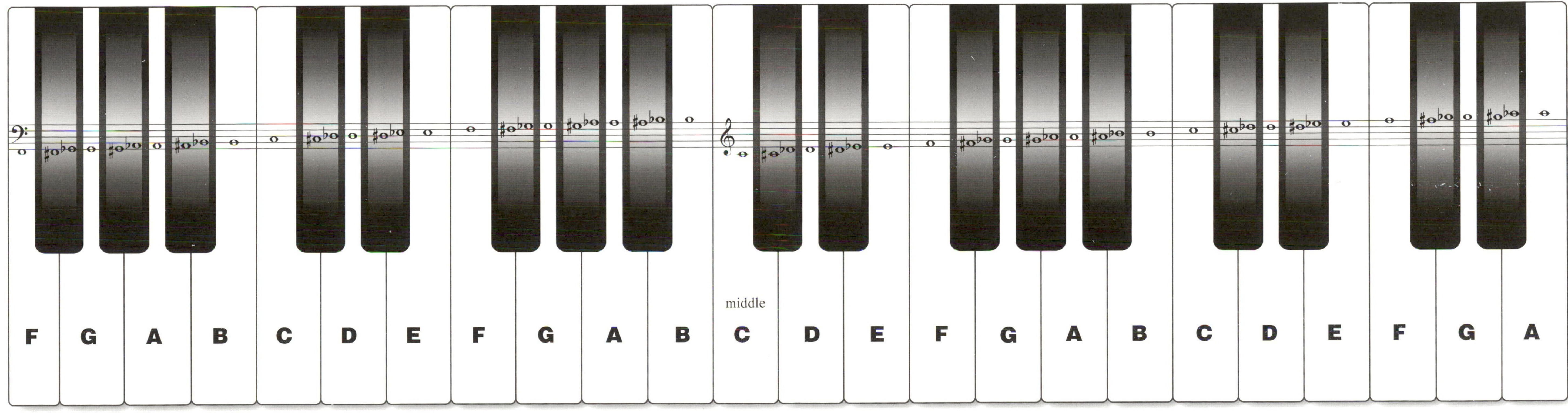
F G A B C D E F G A B
middle
C D E F G A B C D E F G A